THE NEW YORK THEATRICAL SOURCEBOOK

1995 EDITION

Authored and edited
by the
**Association of Theatrical
Artists and Craftspeople**

Sourcebook Press, Inc.
163 Amsterdam Avenue #131
New York, NY 10023
Phone: 212-496-1310
Fax: 212-496-7549

THE NEW YORK THEATRICAL SOURCEBOOK
is published annually in November

THE NEW YORK THEATRICAL SOURCEBOOK
1994 EDITION

ISBN 0-9642679-7-7

Every effort has been made to make sure that the information presented in this book is accurate. However, the publisher cannot accept responsibility for errors of commission or omission.

First printing: November 1994
Manufactured in the United States of America

Table of Contents

A.T.A.C
EDITORIAL STAFF FOR THE 1995 EDITION

editors	Dave Bradley, Leslie Rollins
costumes	Sandra Golbert, Adele Recklies
set design & props	Eileen Connor, Mark McAniff
crafts	Arley Berryhill
lighting design	Nadine Charlsen, Matthew Gilmore
leftovers	Matthew Gilmore
consultants	Mary Mulder, C.J. Simpson

SOURCEBOOK PRESS, INC.
PRODUCTION STAFF FOR THE 1995 EDITION

publishers	John Keck, Jerry Marshall
production manager	Nadine Charlsen
advertising manager	Kevin S. Kuney
proofing	Jim King, Julie Maines
production assts.	Kevin Bohl, Randi Klein
cover design	Victor Weaver
graphics	West Group Communications
legal counsel	Ostrager, Chong & Flaherty
accountant	The John Yavroyan Company

Sourcebook Press would like to thank Mike Huffman, Richard Lerner, and Peter Samelson for guiding us into the wonderful world of computers. Their patience and expertise have been invaluable. Thanks also to Nina Sheffy and Peter Carzasty for their advice and insights.

A special thanks to our advertisers for their continued support of this directory.

ABOUT THE NEW YORK THEATRICAL SOURCEBOOK

The book you are now holding represents the contents of over 500 craftspeople's Rolodexes, Filofaxes, Post-its, index cards and "scribbled-on-bits-of-kraft-paper" collected over an 11 year period. From the very first book compiled entirely by hand and published by the members of A.T.A.C. in 1982 to the modern, computerized edition you are now reading and using, The New York Theatrical Sourcebook has always been a growing and changing creation. New sources are continually being found, verified, and included; old entries updated; and obsolete information deleted. Every year there is something new to be discovered within these pages. This year alone 6 new categories and over 300 new sources have been added. Virtually every listing has been updated and amended in some way.

While the information inside is always changing, one thing about the Sourcebook has remained constant: it has been and always will be written by the people who use it. From the very beginning A.T.A.C.'s goal has been to write a useful and easy to use book containing as much information as practicable without undue regard to advertising revenues. Every source receives an unpaid-for annotation written by A.T.A.C. -- a feature that distinguishes the New York Theatrical Sourcebook from every other directory. Our aim has been to make it possible for craftspeople, decorators, designers, stylists, puppeteers, and other craft professionals, to find what they need quickly so they may get on with their work. In other words, we write the book for ourselves.

Many craftspeople have had a hand in bringing the book to this point: Josie Caruso, who's original concept led to the first Sourcebook, Chris Gardyaz, Karen McDuffee, Mary Mulder, C.J. Simpson and the many theatre professionals who put in countless hours on subsequent editions as well as Cathy B. Blaser, Deborah Hazlett and David Rodger of Broadway Press. To all the past editors and contributors we owe a debt of gratitude for keeping the spirit of the Sourcebook alive during the first 10 years of its growth. In addition, we would like to thank the editorial and production staff for this edition for their hard work.

Today a new team of craftspeople have undertaken the publication of this book. Jerry Marshall and John Keck of Sourcebook Press, Inc. are both working professional craftspeople. Their vision, commitment to the integrity of this project, and willingness to take risks will bring to the publication of the Sourcebook a fresh perspective that in this and future editions will make the book an even more useful tool for its many devoted users.

Finally, it should be pointed out that, no matter how comprehensive and useful the Sourcebook may be, it is the entire community of craftspeople and production professionals who make it a success. Buy it, use it, contribute to it, because it is only through your participation that the Sourcebook will continue to be the valuable and essential tool you have made it.

Thank you,

Leslie Rollins and Dave Bradley
editors
August, 1994

Formed in 1980, **The Association of Theatrical Artists and Craftspeople**, **(A.T.A.C.)**, is America's trade association for professional craftspeople in the performance and presentational media industries. Besides being the authors of **The New York Theatrical Sourcebook,** A.T.A.C. also publishes a quarterly newsletter, organizes seminars and workshops, advocates safety in the arts and rpovides a means of contact and focus for crafts professionals and novices in New York and across the country.

Not long ago A.T.A.C was uncertain about the future of the Sourcebook. We were unhappy about our ability to maintain it's integrity, and had reached a point where it seemed financially impractical to continue. With many questions and no money we contacted a publishing lawyer, Jeffrey Kehl. What a find! Jeffrey took on this mournful lot, guiding us through months of tedious negotiations severing our relationship from one publishing company and starting a new partnership with Sourcebook Press. It was with grace, integrity and much good humor that he kept us from shooting ourselves in the foot, calmed our fears and gave us hope that there should and could be a future for the book. He understood A.T.A.C.'s and the Sourcebook's ideals. Not bad for someone who has never been elbow deep in acetone and Celastic. It seems Jeffrey thinks it is important for people to make beautiful things. So we do. And we did. Thank you, Jeffrey.

C.J. Simpson, Committee Chairperson
and the
Members of A.T.A.C.

Association of Theatrical Artists and Craftspeople
604 Riverside Dr. #6E
New York, NY 10031
212-234-9001

Company Index

- C -

"I found it in the N.Y. Theatrical Sourcebook."

"I found it in the N.Y. Theatrical Sourcebook."

"I found it in the N.Y. Theatrical Sourcebook."

"I found it in the N.Y. Theatrical Sourcebook."

Koppel Pleating Inc. 143
Kordol Fabrics 156
Koto 148
Kraft Hardware Inc. 221
Kraus & Sons Inc. 143, 180, 462
Kravet Fabrics 162, 461
Kreinik Mfg. Co. Inc. 299
Krieger Top Hats 223
Kroll Stationers 426
Ktenas, Pete 401
Kulyk Theatrical Footwear 403
Kushnick, Beth 353
KUTTNER PROP RENTALS, INC.
   212-242-7969 ....15, 367

- L -

L & E Rentals 190, 253
L. Laufer & Co. Inc. 156, 171, 301
L.P. Thur 159
La Belle Epoch 232
La Delice Bakery 45
La Lame.Inc. 157, 306, 455
La Terrine 75, 260
Lab Safety Supply Co. 323
Labovsky,Meyer 78
Lace Collages 15
Lacey Costume Wig 218
Lady Madonna Maternity Boutique 93
Lafitte Inc. 172
Laminex-Craft 244
Laminology 245
Larry & Jeff's Bicycles Plus 51
Larry Vrba.Inc. 233
Larue 110
Laub, A. Glass 214, 385
Laura Ashley Inc. 161, 153, 471
Laura Fisher/ Antique Quilts & Americana 381
LAURA LOPEZ/THE GATE HOUSE
   914-359-8853 ....111, 354, 378
Lauren Bogen Lingerie 89
Law Book Exchange Ltd. 59
Law Enforcement Associates Inc. 139, 140
Lawrence Textiles Inc. 157, 169
Lawrence Wittman & Co. Inc. 67
Laytner's Linen Shop 50, 260
Leathercraft Process Corp. 137
Leathers & Jocobs Corp. 247
Leathersales/Minerva Leather 247
Lechter's Housewares and Gifts 236
Lee, Ralph 110
Lee Spring Co. 425
Lee's Art Shop 33, 192, 309
Lee's Mardi Gras Enterprises Inc. ...93, 218, 404
Lee's Studio Inc. 198, 256
Leekam Design 148
Leesam Kitchen & Bath 338
Lending Trimming Co. Inc. 458

LeNoble Lumber Co. Inc. 245, 265, 319
LEONARD SHILLER/ANTIQUE AUTOS
   718-788-3400 ....40, 369
Let There Be Neon.Inc. 409, 295
Letter Craft Inc. 409
Levitt Industrial Textile Inc. 299
Levy's Sport Center 98, 423
Lew Novik Inc. 157, 168, 460
Lexington Equipment Co. 50
Lexington Luggage Ltd. 262, 263
Liberty House 144
Liberty of London Shops Inc. 162
Librairie de France 59
License Plates/Andy Bernstein 40
Life-Like Products Inc. 225
Light In Form 374
Light Inc. 3, 257
Lighting Associates 33
Lighting by Gregory 257
Liliana's International Boutique 145
LIMELIGHT PRODUCTIONS, INC.
   800-243-4950 441
Lincoln Piano Service 291
LINCOLN SCENIC STUDIOS, INC.
   212-244-2700 394
LINCOLN SCENIC TRANSPORT, INC.
   212-244-2700 289
Lincoln Terrace Cleaners 137
Linda's Ceramics 343
Linden, Lisa J. 353
LINVILLE, JANET
   212-254-8294 110
Lismore Hosiery Company 90
Listokin & Sons Fabrics Inc. 157, 459
Little Folks Shop 84
Livingston, Celeste 110
Loctite Corp. 1
Lolita Corp. 90
Lord John Bootery 404
Lord & Taylor 130
Lorell Games 22
Loria, V. and Sons 423, 462
Lost City Arts ....16, 24 , 257, 280
Louis Chock Inc. 89
Louis Kipnis & Sons Inc. 232
Louis Price Paper Co. Inc. 122
Lovelia Enterprises Inc. 9, 326
Love Saves the Day 81
Lowengard, Sarah 385
Lubanko Tool Co. 448
Lucy Anna 381
Lumber Boys 265
Lumberland 265
Luna Tech Inc. 418
LYNX PRODUCTIONS
   718-784-1414 394

"I found it in the N.Y. Theatrical Sourcebook."

"I found it in the N.Y. Theatrical Sourcebook."

"I found it in the N.Y. Theatrical Sourcebook."

"I found it in the N.Y. Theatrical Sourcebook."

Products & Services

ADHESIVES & GLUES

For millinery glues, see **MILLINERY SUPPLIES**
For leather glues, see **LEATHERCRAFTERS, FURRIERS SUPPLIES**

3M COMPANY
(product info) 612-737-6501
(operator) 612-733-1110
3M Center, St. Paul, MN 55144
• Some minimums required. Distributors of 3M glues and respirators •

AD-TECH., DIV.. OF ADHESIVES TECH., INC.
(Orders) 800-GLUE-GUN
603-926-1616
FAX 603-926-1780
3 Merrill Industrial Drive, Hampton, NH 03842
Hours: 8-4:30 Mon-Fri
• Glitter glues, glue gun with interchangeable tips; flat wide to small round; glue pads. Literature package available. MC/VISA •

BASIC ADHESIVES, INC.
718-497-5200
FAX 718-366-1425
25 Knickerbocker Ave., Brooklyn, NY 11237
Hours: 9-5 Mon-Fri
• Gripstix and other one way water based adhesives. Alplex polyester, the best clear casting polyester on the market. •

CAMIE-CAMPBELL, INC.
314-968-0741
FAX 314-968-0741
9229 Watson, Inc. Park, St. Louis, MO 63126
Hours: 8-4:30 Mon-Fri
• Carry a good styrofoam spray adhesive-#373. A spray with no carboflurocarbons. •

COMMERCIAL PLASTICS
718-849-8100
98-31 Jamaica Ave., (101st St.) Richmond Hill, NY 11418
Hours: 8:30-4 Mon-Fri
• Comstik cement, mylar, acetate and lexan. •

DUO-FAST CORPORATION
201-768-3322
20 Corporate Dr., (off Blaisdell Rd.) Orangeburg, NY 10962
Hours: 8-5 Mon-Fri (phone orders) • 8:30-4 Mon-Fri (repairs)
• Complete line of Jet-Melt adhesives, Polygun applicators, and 3M aerosols. Phone orders, catalog available, no minimum. •

GOTHIC LTD./LONG ISLAND PAINT
516-676-6600
PO Box 189, 1 Continental Hill, Glen Cove, NY 11542
Hours: 7:30-5 Mon-Fri
• Gelatin, flexible and polyvinyl glues; scenic pigments, brushes. Contact Wendy Stern. •
(See display ad under PAINTS & DYES: SCENIC)

LOCTITE CORP.
203-278-1280
800-323-5106
705 N. Mountain Rd., Newington, CT 06111
Hours: 8-5 Mon-Fri (office)
• Distributors of industrial glues. Catalog available; customer and technical assistance. Some minimums required. •

MODERN MILTEX CORP.
718-525-6000
130-25 180th St., (Farmers Blvd.-Springfield) Springfield Gardens, NY 11434
Hours: 7:30-5 Mon-Fri
FAX 718-276-4595
• "Gooloo" for STYROFOAM, low melt hot glue and guns. $100 minimum order. Catalog. •

A-B

H.G. PASTERNACK INC   212-691-9555
    151 West 19th St., (7th Ave.) NYC, NY 10011   800-433-3330
    Hours: 9-5:30 Mon-Fri   FAX   212-924-0024
    • Also authorized distributor of complete line of 3M tapes, spray adhesives, hot melt glue, res-
    pirators, etc. $25 minimum for phone orders. Brochures available. •

PLASTIC TOOLING SUPPLY   800-327-8787
    303 Commerce Drive, Exton, PA 19341   215-363-5440
    Hours 8:30-4:30 Mon-Fri   FAX   215-524-1004
    • Silicones (GI 1000, DOW), epoxy, urethane, adhesive, fiberglass cloth, kevlar, carbon fiber,
    US Gypsum products, Renshape 450 (solid surface material), supplies. Catalog. Casting &
    modeling supplies •

SCENIC SPECIALTIES   718-788-5379
    232 7th Street, (3-4th Ave.) Brooklyn, NY 11215
    Hours: 8:30-5 Mon-Fri by appt.   FAX   718-768-9173
    • Fast and friendly service. Good technical support. Contact Lou. •
    (See display ads in this section.)

SLOMON'S DELTA TECHNICAL COATINGS, INC.   800-423-4135
    2550 Pellissier Pl., Whittier, CA 90601
    Hours: 8-5 Mon-Fri
    • Sobo, Velverette, Quik Glue in quantity; phone for info. Distributors-Tax ID or resale num-
    ber required. $100 minimum order. Ships COD. •

A–B

SMOOTH-ON, INC.   (ext. 72) 908-647-5800
100 Valley Rd., Gillette, NJ 07933   FAX 908-604-2224
Hours: 8:45-5:15 Mon-Fri
• Industrial strength epoxies for set construction; all applications; free samples, literature and technical help available. $20.00 minimum order. •

SPECTRA DYNAMICS   506-843-7202
415 Marble NW, Albuquerque, NM 87102
Hours: 7-7 Mon-Sat
• Manufacture and wholesale Phlexglu and Phlexglu Plasticizer; instructive brochure available; speak to Ford Davis. •

SPROTZER TOOLS & HARDWARE CO., INC.   718-349-2580
36 Eagle St., (Franklin-West) Brooklyn, NY 11222
Hours: 8-5 Mon-Fri
• Hot glue guns and medium quantity cartons of pellets. Wholesale hand tools and cutting tools. Phone orders. •

SUPER GLUE CORP.   718-454-4747
184-08 Jamaica Ave, (184th St.) Hollis, NY 11423
Hours: 9-5:30 Mon-Fri
• Cyanoacrylates; catalog available. $250 minimum order. •

SWIFT ADHESIVES   919-990-7500
2400 Ellis Rd., (P.O. Box 13582 Research Triangle Park) NC 27709
Hours 8-5 Mon-Fri
• Industrial adhesives; hot melt, resin, animal; phone orders. $200 minimum. •

TECHNICAL LIBRARY SERVICES, INC./TALAS 212-736-7744
213 West 35th St. 9th Fl., (7-8th Ave.) NYC, NY 10001
Hours: 9-4:30 Mon-Fri (closed for lunch 11:30-1)
• Acid-free adhesives and glues, conservation supplies and bookbinding supplies. •

UNITED RESIN PRODUCTS, INC. 908-424-1900
239 Route 22, Green Brook, NJ 08812
Hours: 8-5 Mon-Fri
• Resins, hot melts, pastes, animal glue. Brochure available, no minimum. •

VIKING-CRITERION PAPER CO. 718-392-7400
55-30 46th St., (55th Ave.) Maspeth, NY 11378
Hours: 9-5 Mon-Fri
• Hot glue by 25 lb. carton or more; phone orders delivered. •

AMUSEMENT PARK & CIRCUS EQUIPMENT

See also **ARCADE & AMUSEMENT DEVICES**
See also **TOYS & GAMES**

BRIAN DUBE, INC. 212-941-0060
520 Broadway, 3rd Fl., (Spring-Broome) NYC, NY 10012
9-6 Mon-Fri • 12-6 Sat FAX 212-941-0793
• Manufacturer of juggling and circus equipment. •

JUKEBOX CLASSICS & VINTAGE SLOT MACHS., INC. 718-833-8455
6742 Fifth Ave., (67-68th St.) Brooklyn, NY 11220
Hours: by appt. FAX 718-833-0560
• Coin operated antiques, arcade games, slot machines, carousel animals; will help locate unusual items. CREDIT CARDS •

MAPLE AMUSEMENT CORP. 201-933-5247
86 Maple St., Rutherford, NJ 07070
Hours: 9-5 Everyday FAX 201-933-5247
• Various amusement rides, Ferris wheels, game trailers, etc. RENTALS •

SPOTFIELD PRODUCTIONS 908-232-8588
626 South Ave., Garwood, NJ 07027
Hours: 9-5 Mon-Fri FAX 908-232-4668
• Antique circus banners, arcade games carousel horses, and production services; also have portable luxury bathrooms for rental. Contact Rick Shapiro or Tony Sepe. •

ANIMAL RENTAL

For stuffed animal rental, see **TAXIDERMISTS & TAXIDERMY SUPPLIES**

ANIMAL ACTORS 908-537-7800
RD 3 Box 496A, Glen Gardner, NJ 08826
Hours: 24-hour phone service FAX 908-537-7801
• Speak to Steve or Carol. •

ANIMALS FOR ADVERTISING   212-245-2590
310 West 55th St., (8-9th Ave) NYC, NY 10019
Hours: call for appt
• All types; speak to Linda Hanrahan. •

WILLIAM BERLONI THEATRICAL ANIMALS   203-345-8734
18 Old County Rd., Higganum, CT 06411
Hours: by appt.
• Animal rental. Contact William Berloni. •

BLUE RIBBON THROUGHBRED BREEDING FARMS, INC.   516-979-9082
6 Tide Mill Rd., (River Rd) Nissequoque, NY 11780
Hours: by appt.
• Horses, Grand prix jumpers and jumping ponies for action and still work. Contact Martin
Abbene. Rental of riding equipment. •

CAPTAIN HAGGERTY'S THEATRICAL DOGS   201-664-1354
527 Monroe Ave., Westwood, NJ 07675
Hours: by appt.
• Dogs and cats, all types. •

CHATEAU THEATRICAL ANIMALS & CHATEAU STABLE   718-828-4636
608 West 48th St., (11-12th Ave.) NYC, NY 10036
Hours: 9-5 Mon-Fri (office) stables always open
• Horses and horse-drawn vehicles carriages, wagons, carts. AMEX •

CINEMATES   800-455-4495
Hours: On call 24 hours every day.   717-992-0141
• Horses, dogs, barnyard animals. Contact Pete Corby or Jan Thomas. •

CLAREMONT RIDING ACADEMY   212-799-3568
175 West 89th St., (Columbus-Amsterdam Ave.) NYC, NY 10024
6:30am-10pm Mon-Fri • 8-5 Sat, Sun
• Hay. Horse and riding equipment rental. •

DAWN ANIMAL AGENCY   212-575-9396
750 Eighth Ave., (46th St.) NYC, NY 10036
Hours: 10-6 Mon-Fri • on call 24 hours   FAX 212-575-9726
• Rental of exotic and domestic animals, with handlers; also carriages, wagons. •

EXOTICS UNLIMITED   718-816-6537
728 Castleton Ave., Staten Island, NY 10301   718-729-4677
Hours: 8-7 every day
• Animal talent agency; mostly exotics; snakes, birds, large cats. Will train. •

MR. LUCKY'S PERFORMING DOGS AND STANLEY THE WORLD'S SMARTEST PIG
28 Stratford Ave., Dix Hills, NY 11746   516-242-3647
Hours: anytime   800-564-8873
• Dog stunts; brochure available. •

ANTIQUE MALLS

See also **MEMORABILIA**

THE ANTIQUE CENTER OF RED BANK   908-741-5331
   195 W. Front St., Red Bank, NJ 07701
   Hours: 11-5 Mon-Sat •12-5 Sun
      • 150 dealers in 4 buildings, exit 109 off the Garden State Parkway. •

GLENWOOD MANOR ANTIQUES   518 798-4747
   Quaker & Glenwood Road, Glens Falls, NY 12804
   Hours: 10-5 Mon-Sat • 12-5 Sun
      • 35 dealers; will locate specific items. Rt. 87 Exit 19E, one mile on Hwy 254. •

HADLEY ANTIQUE CENTER   413-586-4093
   Rt. 9, Hadley, MA 01035
   Hours:10-5 Thurs-Tues • closed Wed.
      • 70 dealers; excellent small stuff. •

HUDSON ANTIQUE CENTER   518-828-9920
   536 Warren St., (Rts. 82,9,23) Hudson, NY 12534
   Hours: 11-5 Thurs-Tues • closed Wednesday
      • 20 dealers; early American to Modern. CREDIT CARDS •

THE MILLBROOK ANTIQUES CENTER   914-677-3921
   PO Box 789, Rt. 44, Millbrook, NY 12545
   Hours: 11-5 Mon-Sat • 1-5 Sun
      • Owner; Malcom Mokotoff. 44 antique dealers under one roof; the large blue building in the
   center of town. •

NORTHHAMPTON ANTIQUES CENTER   413-584-3600
   912 Market St., (Bridge St.) Northampton, MA 01060
   Hours: 10-5 Mon, Tues, Thurs-Sat• 12-5 Sun Closed Wed.
      • 60 dealers; strong on 20th century design, mission, art deco. MC/VISA •

POMFRET ANTIQUE WORLD   203-928-5006
   Rt 101 & 44, Pomfret, CT 06128
   Hours: 10-5 everyday.• closed Wednesday
      • 90 dealers; immense; have almost everything. MC/VISA. •

REGENT ST. ANTIQUES CENTER   518-584-0107
   153 Regent St., Saratoga Springs, NY 12866
   Hours: 10-5 every day.
      • 25 dealers; wide and varied selection. MC/VISA. •

ANTIQUES: EUROPEAN & AMERICAN

ABC CARPET CO., INC.   212-473-3000
   888 Broadway, (19th St.) NYC, NY 10003
   Hours: 10-8 Mon, Thurs • 10-7 Tues, Wed, Sat • 11-6:30 Sun
      • Sales and rental. Large stock of antiques and reproductions. Also rugs and carpets. CREDIT
   CARDS •

ANTIQUES MARKET 203-389-5440
881 Whalley Ave., (Central-Blake) Westville, CT 06515
Hours:10:30-5 everyday
• All kinds of antiques, especially Old English. Speak to Aaron or Miriam Levine. RENTALS
CREDIT CARDS •

ROGER APPLEYARD 212-529-9505
67 E. 11th St., NYC, NY 10003
Hours: 9-6 Mon-Fri
• Reproduction furniture and mirrors; antique books. Wholesale and rentals. •

BETTER TIMES ANTIQUES 212-496-9001
500 Amsterdam Ave., (84th St.) NYC, NY 10024
Hours: 12-6 Thurs-Tues
• American Pine, English and country items. RENTALS MC/VISA •

BIJAN ROYAL, INC. 212-228-3757
60 East 11th St., (Broadway-University Place) NYC, NY 10003   212-533-6390
Hours: 9-5 Mon-Fri   FAX 212-982-5022
• French and English antique furniture and bronzes; expensive. See Debbie. RENTALS •

E. BUK, ANTIQUES & ART 212-226-6891
151 Spring St. 2nd Floor., (W. Broadway-Wooster) NYC, NY 10012
Hours: Every day by appt.   (toll call) 700-science)

A fine and extensive collection of antiques and Victorian objects. Specializing in mechanics, science, and early technologies from late 18th to early 20th Century. Cast iron objects, sewing machines, irons, fans, appliances, electricals, lighting fixtures, miniatures and scale model objects, clocks, printing and bookbinding equipment, microscopes and telescopes, cameras, globes, office equipment, scales, laboratory apparatus. Also related furniture and accessories. Many rare and hard-to-find objects.

• Specializing in mechanics, science & early technologies from late 18th to early 20th Century. •
(See display ad in this section.)

COBWEB 212-505-1558
116 West Houston St., (Thompson-Sullivan) NYC, NY 10012
Hours: 12-7 Mon-Fri • 12-5 Sat
• Spanish antiques; beds, country furniture, doors, pottery, wrought iron. Sales and rentals,
contact Catherine. •

CONSIGN MART 203-226-0841
877 Post Road East, Westport, CT 06880
Hours: 10-5 Mon-Sat 12-5 Sun.
• Estate jewelry, silver, fine furniture. MC/VISA •

EAGLES ANTIQUES 212-772-3266
1097 Madison Ave., (83-83rd St.) NYC, NY 10028
Hours: 9:30-5:30 Mon-Fri • 10-5 Sat.
• 18th & early 19th century English formal furniture. •

EAST SIDE ANTIQUES•WILLIAM ALBINO ANTIQUES 212-677-8820
55 East 11th St., (Broadway-University Place) NYC, NY 10003
Hours: 9-4:30 Mon-Fri
• Exotica, unusual pieces. •

A-B

ECLECTIC•ENCORE PROPERTIES, INC.
620 West 26th St. 4th Floor, (11-12th Ave.) NYC, NY 10001
Hours: 9-5 Mon-Fri or by appt.

212-645-8880

FAX   212-243-6508

Extensive collection of antiques and furnishings for rental only. Diverse and in depth 75,000 sq. ft. warehouse. 18th century through the 1970's.

Eclectic
Encore
Properties Inc.
620 W. 26th St.
New York, N.Y. 10001
Tel. 212-645-8880
Fax 212-243-6508

• Prop rental house with antique and reproduction furniture and furnishings. RENTALS •
(See display ad under PROP RENTAL HOUSES.)

EVERGREEN ANTIQUES
1249 Third Avenue, (72nd St.) NYC, NY 10021
Hours: 11-7 Mon-Fri • 11-6 Sat
• Country pine furniture, Biedermeier; RENTALS CREDIT CARDS •

212-744-5664

FAX   212-774-5666

FAR EASTERN ANTIQUES & ARTS
799 Broadway, (11th St.) NYC, NY 10003
Hours: 10-6 Mon-Fri • 11-6 Sat   (call before sending) FAX
• Oriental antique furniture and accessories to the trade. RENTALS •

212-460-5030

212-460-5031

FROG ALLEY ANTIQUES
265 East 78th St., (2-3rd Avenue) NYC, NY 10021
Hours: 12-7:30 Tues, Wed • 12-5 Thurs-Sat
• Wicker and country furniture, glassware, costume jewelry. CREDIT CARDS •

212-734-7388

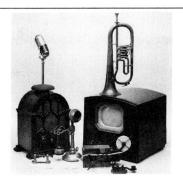

SCIENTIFIC INSTRUMENTS.
MEDICAL, MECHANICAL, INDUSTRIAL AND ELECTRICAL DEVICES.

A fine and extensive collection of period and historical objects, including cameras, radios, televisions, telescopes, sextants, scales, microscopes, globes, furniture, desk accessories, lab apparatus, clocks, typewriters, telephones, tools, machines, microphones, meters, etc.

MANY RARE AND HARD TO FIND OBJECTS.
COMPLETE PERIOD SETTINGS AND CUSTOM WORK.

E. BUK, Antiques and Art
151 Spring St., N.Y.C. 10012 (212) 226-6891
Appointment Advisable

GLOBAL FINE REPRODUCTIONS 212-533-5810
801 Broadway, (11th St.) NYC, NY 10003
Hours: 9-5 Mon-Fri
• 18th & 19th Century French and English reproduction furniture. RENTALS CREDIT CARDS •

GOLDEN OLDIES 718-445-4400
132-29 33rd. Ave., (College Point) Flushing, NY 11354
Hours: 9-5 Mon-Sat • Friday till 8 • 11-5 Sun   FAX 718-445-4986
• European Antiques. Speak to Peter or Sue. MC/VISA •

GOLDEN TREASURY 212-787-1411
550 Columbus Ave., (86-87th St.) NYC, NY 10024
Hours: 12-6:30 Mon-Fri • 1-6:30 Sat, Sun.
• Small antiques and collectibles, some furniture. RENTALS CREDIT CARDS •

GOTHAM GALLERIES 212-677-3303
80th Fourth Ave., (10-11th St.) NYC, NY 10003
Hours: 8:30-6 Mon-Sat
• Furniture, Oriental rugs, bronzes; rental or purchase; custom refinishing. •

GRANNY'S ATTIC ANTIQUES 201-529-5516
142 Franklin Turnpike, Mahwah, NJ 07430
Hours: 10-6 every day   FAX 201-529-5516
• Everything old in a diverse selection of periods and styles. MC/VISA •

JOHNSON & JOHNSON 518-789-3848
Route 22 North, Millerton, NY 12546   203-435-0476
Hours: 10-5 Fri-Sun
• Large selection of antiques and used furniture; inexpensive. See Russ or Gary Johnson. •

HOWARD KAPLAN ANTIQUES 212-674-1000
827 Broadway, (12-13th St.) NYC, NY 10003
Hours: 9-5 Mon-Fri
• French Country antiques for the bedroom, kitchen, living room, dining room and bathroom;
also lighting fixtures. CREDIT CARDS •

KENSINGTON PLACE ANTIQUES 212-533-6378
80 East 11th St., NYC, NY 10003
Hours: 9:30-5 Mon-Fri
• English furniture. Sales only •

THE LITTLE ANTIQUE SHOP 212-673-5173
44 East 11th St., (Broadway-University Place) NYC, NY 10003
Hours: 9-5 Mon-Fri
• 18th - 19th century furniture and objects. RENTALS •

LOVELIA ENTERPRISES, INC. 212-490-0930
356 East 41st St., (Tudor City Place) NYC, NY 10017
Hours: by appt.   FAX 212-69-8550
• Antique pewter, large selection of reproduction Gobelin and wool Aubusson tapestries.
RENTALS •

NANCY MARSHALL SECOND EDITION, LTD. 212-221-4547
37 West 39th St. Suite 705, (6th St.) NYC, NY 10018
Hours: 9:30-5:30 Mon-Fri   FAX 212-221-4550
• Antique vanity and boudoir accessories. RENTALS •

MARTELL ANTIQUES
212-777-4360
53 East 10th St., (Broadway-University Place) NYC, NY 10003
Hours: 10-5:30 Mon-Fri • 11-5 Sat (closed Sat. July, Aug.)
• 18th & 19th century French country antiques; armoires, tables, desks, buffets; ask for William Rodek or Pat Mangan. RENTALS •

MIDTOWN ANTIQUES
800-626-7726
212-529-1880
814 Broadway, (11-12th St.) NYC, NY 10003
Hours: 12-6 Mon-Fri or by appt.
• 17-19th Century English and Continental Furniture, objects d'art; museum-quality restorations done on premises; sales and rentals. AMEX •

ANN MORRIS ANTIQUES
212-755-3308
239 East 60th St., (2-3rd Ave.) NYC, NY 10022
Hours: 9-6 Mon-Fri   FAX   212-838-4955
• English and French Country; Eclectic selection; open to the trade only. RENTALS •

NEWEL ART GALLERY
212-758-1970
425 East 53rd St., (Sutton-1st) NYC, NY 10022
Hours: 9-5 Mon-Fri
• Extraordinary selection of antique furniture, art, architectural pieces and lamps; all periods; rentals or purchase; expensive. No credit cards. •

PIERRE DEUX
212-243-7740
369 Bleecker St., (Charles) NYC, NY 10014
Hours: 10-6 Mon-Sat (Closed Sat, July, Aug.)
• French country antiques. RENTALS •

THE PROP COMPANY KAPLAN & ASSOCIATES
212-691-7767
212-691-PROP
111 West 19th St., 8th Floor, (6-7th Ave.) NYC, NY 10011
Hours: 9-5:30 Mon-Fri   FAX   212-727-3055

Wonderful and carefully chosen selection of china, glass, pottery, kitchenware, decorative accessories, sporting baskets, memorabilia of all kinds, paintings, prints, copper, brass, pewter, linens, textiles, nautical, folk art, mantles, architectural elements, luggage, tables, chairs, scales, vanity sets, perfumes.

THE PROP COMPANY
K A P L A N & A S S O C I A T E S

• Prop rental house with antique and reproduction furnishings and accessories of all kinds. See Maxine Kaplan. RENTALS •
(See display ad under PROP RENTAL HOUSES.)

PROPS FROM YESTERDAY
212-206-0330
121 West 19th St., Reception 3rd Fl., (6-7th Ave.) NYC, NY 10011
Hours: 8:30-5 Mon-Fri   FAX   212-924-0450

Come to us first and we'll work with your budget!
• Acquired from Nostalgia Alley, huge selection of antiques and collectibles.
• Acquired memorabilia and paper collection from The Prop House.
• Acquired New York Shakespeare Festival props.
• Art Deco, 30's, 40's, 50's, 60's etc., folk art, country furniture, Victorian, boudoir, lamps, sofas, memorabilia.
NOW ON 3 FLOORS! ONE STOP PROPPING!

Props from Yesterday

• A full service rental house. •
(See display ad under PROP RENTAL HOUSES.)

ELUX C. PUTTING ANTIQUES 212-838-3850
226 East 51st St., (2-3rd Ave.) NYC, NY 10022
Hours: 10-5 Mon-Fri
• Country furniture, sales and rentals. •

ROLAND'S ANTIQUES 212-260-2000
99 University Place, (11-12th St.) NYC, NY 10003
Hours: 9-6 Mon-Fri FAX 212-260-2778
• Formerly The Great Gatsbys. 18-19th and early 20th Century furniture, paintings, bric-a-brac; wholesaler. RENTALS •

JOHN ROSSELLI INTERNATIONAL 212-772-2137
255 East 72nd St., (2nd Ave.) NYC, NY 10021
523 East 73rd St., (York and the River) NYC, NY 10021
Hours: 10-6 Mon-Fri FAX 212-535-2989
• Beautiful selection of antique decorative items, Chinese vases, crystal, silver, wood. RENTALS •

SPENCERTOWN ARTS & ANTIQUES CO. 518-392-4445
Rt. 203, Spencertown, NY 12165
Hours: 11-5:30 Sat & Sun or by appt.
• Unusual American colonial items; 19th & 20th century American paintings; contact Martin Parker. AMEX •

TIME TRADER ANTIQUES 718-852-3301
368 Atlantic Ave., (Hoyt-Bond) Brooklyn, NY 11217
Hours: 11-7 Mon-Fri • 12-6 Sat & Sun.
• Large selection of English and American furniture. RENTALS CREDIT CARDS •

T & K FRENCH ANTIQUES 212-219-2472
120 Wooster St., (Prince-Spring) NYC, NY 10012
Hours: 11-6:30 Tues-Fri • 12-6 Sat, Sun. FAX 212-925-4876
• 18th & 19th century furniture and unusual decorative accessories from France. RENTALS CREDIT CARDS •

UPSTAIRS DOWNTOWN ANTIQUES 212-989-8715
12 West 19th St., (5-6th Ave.) NYC, NY 10011
Hours: 11-5 Mon, Wed, Fri, Sat • 12-5 Sun. FAX 914-236-3378
• Fine antiques and collectibles. •

VIVE LA FRANCE 212-225-8018
104 West 14th St., (6-7th Ave.) NYC, NY 10011
Hours: by appt. FAX 212-627-1416
• Furniture and accessories from France. 18th century to WWII. RENTALS •

CHRISTINE YOUNG ANTIQUES, INC. 518-766-3445
Rt. 20, (near Rt. 203) Nassau, NY 12123
Hours: 9-5:30 every day. FAX 518-766-9826
• Full line of formal and country antiques. RENTALS CREDIT CARDS •

A - B

ANTIQUES: VICTORIAN & 20TH CENTURY

A REPEAT PERFORMANCE   212-529-0832
    156 1st Ave, (10th St.) NYC, NY 10009
    Hours: 12-8 Mon-Sat • 2-8 Sun
    • Wide assortment of European lamp shades, brocade curtains, furniture, hats, shoes, bric-a-
brac from the 30's - 60's. RENTALS CREDIT CARDS •

AARON AARDVARK & SON   908-246-1720
    119 French St., New Brunswick, NJ 08901
    Hours: 11-6 Tues-Sat
    • Quality used furniture and antiques; see Arthur. CREDIT CARDS •

ABE'S ANTIQUES, INC.   212-260-6424
    815 Broadway, (11-12th St.) NYC, NY 10003
    Hours: 9:30-5:30 Mon-Fri   FAX   212-529-9085
    • 19th Century furniture, chandeliers, objects d'art, and accessories. RENTALS •

ALICE'S ANTIQUES   212-874-3400
    505 Columbus Ave., (84-85th St.) NYC, NY 10024
    Hours: 12-8 Tues-Sun   FAX   212-874-3421
    • Large selection of antique beds as well as furniture. RENTALS CREDIT CARDS •

AMERICA HURRAH ANTIQUES   212-535-1930
    766 Madison Ave., (66th St.) NYC, NY 10021
    Hours: 11-6 Tues-Sat   FAX   212-249-9718
    • Noted for quilts; Americana, American Indian. RENTALS •

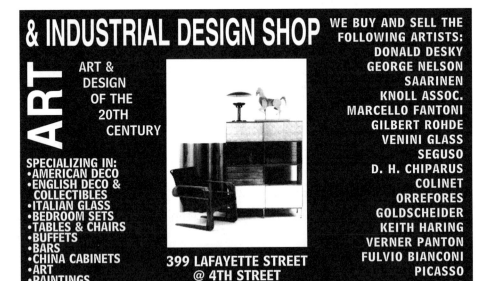
"I found it in the N.Y. Theatrical Sourcebook."

ANTIQUES PLUS   718-941-8805
744 Coney Island Ave., (Ave. C) Brooklyn, NY 11218
Hours: 10-6 Mon-Sat
• Rugs, tapestries, glassware, china, silver, furniture. RENTALS •

ART & INDUSTRIAL DESIGN SHOP   212-477-0116
399 Lafayette, (4th St.) NYC, NY 10003
Hours: 12-7 Mon-Sat
• 20th Century and Art Deco furniture, furnishings, art and objects. Many original works for sale or rent. Also collectibles, clocks and lighting fixtures. RENTALS CREDIT CARDS •
(See display ad in this section.)

ARTISAN ANTIQUES   212-751-5214
81 University Place, (11th St.) NYC, NY 10003   212-353-3970
Hours: 10-6 Mon-Fri   FAX   212-353-3970
• Beautiful collection of French Art Deco furniture, lighting, and decorative accessories. RENTALS AMEX. •

ASSAF ANTIQUES   718-643-0234
400 Atlantic Ave., (Bond) Brooklyn, NY 11217
Hours: 12:30-6 every day
• Nice selection of antique soft goods, small electrical appliances, and decorative accessories. •

BARTER SHOP   203-846-1241
140 Main St., (I-95, Exit 15) Norwalk, CT 06851
Hours: 11-6 every day
• Antiques, collectibles, used furniture and junk in three buildings. One hour from NYC. MC/VISA •

BERTHA BLACK ANTIQUES   212-966-7116
80 Thompson St. (Spring-Broome) NYC, NY 10012
Hours: 2-7 Wed-Sat
• Folk art, painted furniture, religious art, fine retablos, American glass, English ceramics, and antique textiles. RENTALS AMEX •

BYGONE DAYS   413-528-1870
969 Main St., (On Rt. 7, 2 mi. south of Rt. 23) Great Barrington, MA 01230
Hours: 10-5 every day, call first for odd hours.
• Lots of misc. stuff, good prices. Mostly furniture, especially oak and pine tables, chairs,bedroom furniture. RENTALS MC/VISA •

CENTRAL PROPERTIES OF 49TH ST.   212-265-7767
514 West 49th St., (10th Ave.) NYC, NY 10019
Hours: 8-5 Mon-Fri   FAX   212-582-3746

Furniture, accessories and reproductions from every period.
PLUS...Character pieces and much, much more!

Central Props

CENTRAL PROPERTIES

• Prop rental whose with mostly reproduction furniture & accessories. RENTALS •
(See display ad under PROP RENTAL HOUSES.)

CHATSWORTH AUCTION ROOM & FURNITURE STUDIOS   914-698-1001
151 Mamaroneck Ave., (near Boston Post Rd.) Mamaroneck, NY 10543
Hours: 8-6 Tues-Sat • (Thurs till 7)
• Owner: Sam Lightbody. Three floors of antique and used furniture. •

W. Chorney Antiques
203-387-9707
827 Whalley Ave. (Westville Section) New Haven, CT. 06515
Hours: 11:30-5 Tues-Sat • call for Sun hours
• Antique jukeboxes, including diner remotes; period cigarette, gumball, vending and soda machines; radios, kitchen equipment, bicycles. Will search for items. Speak to Wayne. RENTAL AMEX •

Circa Antiques
718-596-1866
377 Atlantic Ave., (Hoyt-Bond) Brooklyn, NY 11217
Hours: 11:30-5:30 Mon-Fri • 11-6 Sat • 12-6 Sun.
• Mostly 19th century American furniture, paintings, lighting, accessories. See Rachel or David. RENTALS •

Cobweb
212-505-1558
116 West Houston St., (Thompson-Sullivan) NYC, NY 10012
Hours: 12-7 Mon-Fri • 12-5 Sat
• Spanish antiques; beds, country furniture, doors, pottery, wrought iron. Contact Catherine. RENTALS •

Corner House Antiques
413-229-6627
N. Main St. (Rt. 7) Sheffield, MA 01257
Hours: open most days, call first.
• Antique wicker furniture. Also general selection of antiques and country accessories. See Kathleen or Thomas Tetro. •

Dale Antiques
718-941-7059
685 Coney Island Ave., (Cortelyou-Ave. C.) Brooklyn, NY 11218
Hours: 9:30-6 Mon-Sat • 12:30-4:30 Sun • call first
• Antique lighting and lamps, period radios. •

Dullsville
212-505-2505
143 East 13th St., (3rd -4th Ave.) NYC, NY 10003
Hours: 11:30-7 Mon-Sat • Sunday hours during Christmas Season.
• Collectibles from 1900-1960 including china, glass, folk art and jewelry-especially bakelite jewelry. RENTALS CREDIT CARDS •

Eclectic/Encore Properties
212-645-8880
620 West 26th St. 4th Fl. NYC. NY 10001
Hours: 9-5 Mon-Fri or by appt.
FAX   212-243-6508

Extensive collection of antiques and furnishings for rental only. Diverse and in depth 75,000 sq. ft. warehouse. 18th century through the 1970's.

• Prop rental house with antique and reproduction furniture and furnishings. RENTALS •
(See display ad under PROP RENTAL HOUSES.)

Elan Antiques
212-529-2724
345 Lafayette St., (Bleecker-Bond) NYC, NY 10012
Hours: 1-7 Mon-Sat • Sunday by chance.
• Art Deco, 50's furniture, lighting accessories. CREDIT CARDS •

Farm River Antiques
203-239-2434
26 Broadway, North Haven, CT 06472
Hours: 9-5:30 Tues-Sat, by appt.
FAX   203-239-6691
• Large selection of original American high style Victorian furniture. See George. •

A-B

FIFTY-50
212-777-3208
793 Broadway, (10-11th St.) NYC, NY 10003
Hours: 11-6 Mon-Fri • 12-5 Sat
• 50's furniture and accessories. RENTALS •

GROVE DECOYS, INC.
212-391-0688
36 West 44th St., (5-6th Ave) NYC, NY 10036
Hours: 10-5:30 Mon-Fri
• Wide selection of rare and not-so-rare decoys, bird carvings and fish lures. RENTALS CREDIT CARDS •

HAY DAY
212-780-9720
84 E. 7th St. (1-2nd Ave.) NYC, NY 10003
Hours: Wed-Mon 1-8 • Sun close at 7
• A small east village shop with American rustic. Items sometimes difficult to find in an urban world. "Peel paint" country chairs, trunks and tables. Mirrors, prints, books and small decorative items. No credit cards. RENTALS •

J.T. HICKS
203-438-9833
423 Main St., Ridgefield, CT 06877
Hours: 10-5 Tues-Sun
• Always interesting selection of antiques and contemporary decorative objects; sales and rentals. AMEX. •

HORSEMAN ANTIQUES
718-596-1048
351 Atlantic Ave. Brooklyn, NY 11217
Hours 10-6 Mon-Fri • 11-6 Sat • 12-6 Sun.
• Oak, repro and antique brass beds and items; rents by the day. •

JOIA INTERIORS, INC.
212-759-1224
149 East 60th St., (Lexington-3rd) NYC, NY 10022
Hours: 10-6 Mon-Thurs.
• Deco furniture, rental and purchase. CREDIT CARDS •

KUTTNER PROP RENTALS, INC.
212-242-7969
56 West 22nd St. 5th Fl. (5-6th Ave.) NYC, NY 10010
Hours: 10-5:30 Mon-Fri
FAX 212-242-1293

Antique tables, chairs, hutches, china, lamps, paintings, pewter, brass & copper items. Linens, folk art, luggage, baskets, & garden related items. Sporting & nautical accessories. Kitchenware.

• Prop rental company with American & English furniture, paintings, accessories, china, glassware, silver, linens, kitchenware. RENTALS •
(See display ad under PROP RENTAL HOUSES)

LACE COLLAGES
212-689-1268
88 Lexington Ave. #12C, (26-27th St.) NYC, NY 10016
Hours: By appt.
• Pillows, Victorian evening purses, scarves and decorative items made from antique laces. Rentals and sales; custom work. •

EILEEN LANE ANTIQUES
212-475-2988
150 Thompson St., (Houston-Prince) NYC, NY 10012
Hours: 11-7 every day
• Art Deco, Swedish and Viennese, Biedemeier, country furniture. RENTALS CREDIT CARDS •

JUDITH & JAMES MILNE, INC.

AMERICANA • QUILTS • FURNITURE • FOLK ART

HOURS:
9:30-5:30
MON-FRI
OTHER TIMES
BY APPOINTMENT

506 E. 74th ST.
NEW YORK, NY 10021
(212) 472-0107

BUY - SELL - RENT

LOST CITY ARTS   212-941-8025
 275 Lafayette St., (Houston-Prince) NYC, NY 10012
 Hours: 10-6 Mon-Fri •12-6 Sat   FAX   212-219-2570
 • Architectural antiques, antique advertising, Art Deco furniture and lighting; 19th century-
 50's. RENTALS CREDIT CARDS •

MAN-TIQUES LTD   212-759-1805
 1050 2nd Ave., (55-56th St.s) NYC, NY 10021
 Hours: 11-5:30 Mon-Sat
 • Fine antiques, canes, and accessories for men; also smoking accessories and desk dressings. RENTALS •

MERRITTS ANTIQUES   800-345-4101
 P.O. Box 277, RD 2, Douglassville, PA 19518   215-689-9541
 Hours: 7:30-5 Mon-Fri • 7:30-12:30 Sat (call first)
 • General antiques, country, 19th, 20th Century. Call for directions. See Rick Merritt, Mgr. •

JUDITH & JAMES MILNE, INC.   212-472-0107
 506 East 74th St. 2nd Fl., (York Ave) NYC, NY 10021
 Hours: 9:30-5:30 Mon-Fri • or by appt.
 • Specializing in American country antiques; sales and rental. MC/VISA •
 (See display ad in this section.)

MONMOUTH ANTIQUE SHOPPES   908-842-7377
 217 West Front St., Red Bank, NJ 07701
 Hours: 11-5 every day
 • Enormous selection of American antiques and collectibles; see John. MC/VISA •

A-B

TERRY L. MORTON • ANTIQUE TEXTILE CUSHIONS 212-472-1446
146 East 84th St., (Lexington-3rd Ave) NYC, NY 10028
Hours: by appt.
• Hundreds of pillows made from antique needlepoint, tapestry, silks. •

ALAN MOSS STUDIOS 212-473-1310
436 Lafayette, (Astor Place) NYC, NY 10012
Hours: 11-6 Mon-Fri • 12-6 Sat • 2-6 Sun 212-473-1310
• 20th century decorative arts. RENTALS •

NICCOLINI ANTIQUES–PROP RENTAL 212-243-2010
19 West 21st St., (5-6th Ave) NYC, NY 10010
Hours: 10-5 Mon-Fri • or by appt. 212-366-6779
• Prop rental house with 19th & 20th century furniture and accessories for home & office.
RENTALS •

1950 212-995-1950
440 Lafayette St., (Astor Place) NYC, NY 10003
Hours: 11-6 Mon-Fri • 12-6 Sat. 212-614-0610
• Unique collection of 50's French furniture. RENTALS •

OAKSMITH & JONES ANTIQUES 212-535-1451
1321 Second Ave., (69-70th St.) NYC, NY 10021
Hours: 11-8 every day
• Eclectic selection; 2 floors; see Stuart. RENTALS CREDIT CARDS •

OLDIES, GOLDIES & MOLDIES LTD. 212-737-3935
1609 Second Ave., (83-84th St.) NYC, NY 10028
Hours: 12-7 Tues-Fri • 11-6 Sat • 11-5 Sun
• 3 levels of furniture, fixtures, clocks, jewelry, clothing, turn of the century to 1950's.
RENTALS •

SUSAN PARRISH 212-645-5020
390 Bleecker St. , (Perry-11th St.) NYC, NY 10014
Hours: 12-6 Tues-Sat • or by appt.
• Large selection of quilts, Navajo rugs, and folk art antiques. RENTALS CREDIT CARDS •

PETER–ROBERTS ANTIQUES 212-226-4777
134 Spring St., (Wooster-Greene St.) NYC, NY 10012
Hours: 11-7 Mon-Sat • 12-6 Sun FAX 212-431-6417
• Mission oak, American Arts & Crafts furnishings. RENTALS •

PROPS FOR TODAY 212-206-0330
121 West 19th St. Reception: 3rd Fl., (6-7th Ave) NYC, NY 10011
Hours: 8:30-5 Mon-Fri FAX 212-924-0450

Come to us first and we'll work with your budget!
• Acquired from Nostalgia Alley huge selection of antiques and collectibles.
• Acquired memorabilia and paper collection from The Prop House.
• Acquired New York Shakespeare Festival props.
• Art Deco, 30's, 40's, 50's, 60's etc., folkart, country furniture, Victorian, boudoir, lamps, sofas, memorabilia.
NOW ON 3 FLOORS! ONE STOP PROPPING!

• Prop rental house with antique and reproduction furniture & accessories. 19th & 20th century. RENTALS •
(See display ad under PROP RENTAL HOUSES.)

A-B

RENEE ANTIQUES, INC.
212-929-6870

8 East 12th St., (Univ. Pl. - 5th Ave) NYC, NY 10003
Hours: 8:30-6 Mon-Fri • 8:30-3 Sat
212-924-8243

Great selection of furniture and decorative items from
1850-1950, including styles from Louis XV, XVI, Empire,
Victorian, Art Nouveaux, Art Deco and Modern. We carry
furniture, paintings, bronzes, lamps, lighting, fixtures,
porcelains, crystal, pedestals, picture frames, miniatures,
perfume bottles, pottery, and Tiffany vases and lamps.

RENEE ANTIQUES, INC.
THE LEADING IMPORTERS OF EUROPEAN
ANTIQUES IN THE U.S.A.

8 EAST 12TH STREET
NEW YORK, N.Y. 10003

• Large selection of antique & reproduction 18th, 19th & 20th century furniture, furnishings
and art works. See Joyce or George Holmes. •

RENT-A-THING
914-628-9298

Rt. 6, Baldwin Place, NY 10505
800-287-9298
Hours: 24 hrs., leave message, will return call
• Good selection of antiques; over 5000 unusual items for rent. Also many sites for location
filming. Will help locate items. •

RICHMAN & ASSOC.
201-772-9827

509 Westminster, Lodi, NJ 07644
Hours: 9-5 Wed -Sat
• Used furniture and estate sale items. Some antiques. Eager to work with film and theatre.
Sales only. •
(See display ad under FURNITURE: RENTAL & PURCHASE-GENERAL)

PAULA RUBENSTEIN, LTD.
212-966-8954

65 Prince St., (B'way-Lafayette St.) NYC, NY 10012
Hours: 12-6 Mon-Sat

Mostly American and boldly graphic textiles, furniture, paintings,
pottery, and oddities from the first half of the 20th Century.
Furnishings for a country cabin (Beacon blankets, rustic
furniture, Navaho rugs); a seashore cottage (rattan, floral
comforters, porch seating); a stylish city apartment (gilt
mirrors, paisleys and lamps).

Paula Rubenstein, Ltd.

65 PRINCE STREET   212-966-8954   MON - SAT 12-6

• Mostly American country textiles and furnishings. Retail, rental and to the trade. CREDIT
CARDS •

SCOTTIE'S GALLERY & ANTIQUES
718-851-8325

624 Coney Island Ave., (Beverly-Avenue C) Brooklyn, NY 11218
Hours: 11-7 Mon-Fri • 12-5 Sat
• Oak and Victorian furniture; Tiffany lamps. •

THE SECOND COMING, LTD
212-431-4424

72 Greene St., (Spring-Broome St.) NYC, NY 10012
Hours: 12-7 Mon-Sat • 1-6 Sun
FAX   212-431-4734
• Art Deco to 50's furniture and accessories, wallpaper. RENTALS CREDIT CARDS •

SECONDHAND ROSE
212-431-7673

270 Lafayette St., (Prince St.) NYC, NY 10012
212-431-ROSE
Hours: 10-6 Mon-Fri • 12-6 Sat
• 20th century furniture and accessories, period wall paper and linoleum. 1850-1940's, many
unusual pieces. Contact Suzanne Lipschutz. •

A-B

SENTIMENTO, INC.   212-245-3111
   14 West 55th St., (5-6th Ave) NYC, NY 10019
   Hours: 9:30-5 Mon-Fri   FAX   212-246-7415
   • Wholesale decorative accessories, furniture, small items, and jewelry. RENTALS •

FRED SILBERMAN & CO.   212-925-9470
   83 Wooster St., (Spring St.) NYC, NY 10012
   Hours: 11-6:30 Mon-Sat
   • Art Deco furniture and accessories. RENTALS CREDIT CARDS •

SOUTHAMPTON ANTIQUES   413-527-1022
   172 College Hwy., (on Rt. 10) Southampton, MA 01073
   Hours: 10-5 Thurs-Sat
   • Three large barns of antique American oak and Victorian furniture. RENTALS CREDIT
   CARDS •

TIME & AGAIN
   787 Coney Island Ave., (Cortelyou-Dorchester Ave) Brooklyn, NY 11218
                                                       718-856-2135
   Hours: 10-6 Mon-Sat
   • Furniture, paintings, china, bric-a-brac, silver, pianos, jewelry, bronzes, tapestries. •

VILLAGE EAST ANTIQUES   212-533-1510
   159 Second Ave., (on 10th between 1-2nd) NYC, NY 10003
   Hours: 12-7 every day
   • Mostly 20th Century antiques and collectibles. •

WAVES   212-989-9284
   32 East 13th St. (5th Univ. P.) NYC, NY 10003
   Hours: 12-6 Tues-Fri • 12-4 Sat

Best selection of Neat Old Radios, T.V.'s, Victrolas, Microphones,
Telephones, and many other Interesting Things.
Bought • Sold • Repaired.
Serving the industry for slightly over 10 years.

   • Interesting collection. RENTALS •

WELCOME HOME ANTIQUES   212-362-4293
   556 Columbus Ave., (87th St.) NYC, NY 10024
   Hours: 12-8 Mon-Fri • 12-6 Sat, Sun
   • 19th & 20th Century furniture, lamps, and accessories. Rentals. Feature original mohair
   couches and chairs. CREDIT CARDS •

THOS. K. WOODARD: AMERICAN ANTIQUES & QUILTS   212-988-2906
   835 Madison Ave, (67-68th St.) NYC, NY 10021
   Hours: 11-6 Mon-Sat (closed Sat: July, Aug)   FAX   212-734-9665
   • Quilts and rugs for rental, purchase or rental-towards-purchase. Selection of Americana for
   sale or rent. (Fragile items for sale only.) CREDIT CARDS •

WOOSTER GALLERY   212-219-2190
   86 Wooster St., (Spring St.) NYC, NY 10012
   Hours: 10:30-6:30 every day.   FAX   212-941-6678
   • Art Deco. RENTALS •

YELLOW SHED ANTIQUES   914-628-0362
   PO Box 706, Rt. 6, Mahopa, NY 10541
   Hours: 10-5 Tues-Sun (July & August Wed. - Sun.)
     • Large selection of Americana; pine and oak furniture, antiques, jewelry, glass, coins,
   stamps, lighting, paintings. RENTALS CREDIT CARDS •

ZERO TO SIXTIES   212-925-0932
   75 Thompson St., (Broome-Spring St.) NYC, NY 10012
   12-7 Tues-Sat. • Sun. by appt.

Furniture • Folkart • Czech Glass • 50's Italian Glass and Pottery •
Lighting • Jewelry • Watches • Clocks • Compacts • Cookie Jars •
Chrome • Plastic Pocketbooks • Paintings • Children's Chairs •
50's Wire and Wrought Iron • Unusual Objects, etc.

• 1900 Thru 1960 •
• Buy • Sell • Rent •

     • 19th & 20th century furniture, furnishings, art, lighting, and accessories. Unusual items. See
   Robin Loew. RENTALS CREDIT CARDS •

APPLIANCES: ELECTRICAL & GAS

See also **KITCHEN EQUIPMENT: HOUSEHOLD**
See also **KITCHEN EQUIPMENT: INDUSTRIAL**

BERNIE'S DISCOUNT CENTER   212-564-8582
   821 Sixth Ave., (28-29th St.) NYC, NY 10001   212-564-8758
   Hours: 9-5:30 Mon-Fri • 11-3:30 Sat   FAX   212-564-3894
     • Small electrical appliances; good prices. •

BLOOM & KRUP   212-673-2760
   206 First Ave., (12-13th St.) NYC, NY 10009   212-529-9787
   Hours: 9-6 Mon-Sat (Thurs till 7:30) • 1-4 Sun
     • Kitchen and bathroom appliances and fixtures, small electrical appliances. Display models
   for photography. RENTALS •

**ELECTRIC APPLIANCE RENTAL & SALES CO.•AC•DC APPLIANCE•AAA APPLIANCE RENTALS &
   SALES CO.**   212-686-8884
   40 West 29th St. 2nd Fl., (B'way-6th Ave.) NYC, NY 10001
   Hours: 8:30-5:30 Mon-Fri
     • Refrigerators, freezers, microwaves, portable ovens, massage tables. RENTALS •

GRINGER & SONS   212-475-0600
   29 First Ave, (1st-2nd Ave.) NYC, NY 10003
   Hours: 8:30-5:30 Mon-Fri • 8:30-4:30 Sat   FAX   212-982-1935
    • Large appliances and microwaves. RENTALS •

ISABELLA   718-278-7272
   24-24 Steinway St., (Astoria Blvd.) Astoria, NY 11103
   9:30-7 M,T,Th,Fri • 9:30-6 Wed • 9:30-5 Sat   FAX   718-545-4324
    • Large electrical & gas appliances; also kitchen and bathroom sinks. RENTALS •

J. EIS & SONS APPLIANCES   212-475-2325
   107 First Ave., (6-7th St.) NYC, NY 10003
   Hours: 9-5:30 Mon-Thurs • 9-3 Fri, Sun (closed Sat.)
   • Ranges, refrigerators, washers, dryers, air conditioners. •

J & R TELEVISION & AIR CONDITIONING   718-638-3040
   108 Seventh Ave., (President-Union St.) Brooklyn, NY 11215
   Hours: 10:30-7:30 Mon-Fri • 10-6 Sat
   • Large and small appliances & new and used televisions; great prices. •

PROPS FOR TODAY   212-206-0330
   121 West 19th St. Reception: 3rd Fl., (6-7th Ave.) NYC, NY 10011
   Hours: 8:30-5 Mon-Fri   FAX   212-924-0450
   • Prop rental house with good selection of modern & period small electrical appliances •
   (See display ad under PROP RENTAL HOUSES.)

ARCADE & AMUSEMENT DEVICES

See also **VENDING MACHINES**
See also **AMUSEMENT PARK & CIRCUS EQUIPMENT**

BACK PAGES ANTIQUES   212-460-5998
   125 Greene St., (Prince-Houston) NYC, NY 10012
   Hours: 9-6 Mon-Fri • 10-6 Sat • 12-6 Sun
   • Jukeboxes, purchase or rental. •

JUKEBOX CLASSICS & VINTAGE SLOT MACHINES., INC.　　718-833-8455
　　6742 Fifth Ave., (68th St.) Brooklyn, NY 11220
　　Hours: 11-5 Sat (call first) or by appt.　　　　　FAX　718-833-0560
　　• Arcade games, slot machines, nickelodeons, carousel animals, neon lights; will help locate
　　unusual items; buy, sell, repair. RENTALS CREDIT CARDS •

LORELL GAMES　　516-931-4486
　　37 Jefry Lane, Hicksville, NY 11801
　　Hours: 9-5 Mon-Fri　　　　　　　　　　　　　FAX　516-931-4487
　　• Jukeboxes, pinball machines, video games, slot machines; new, used and antique, sales, and
　　service. RENTALS •

NOVEL AMUSEMENT CO., DIV.. A-PARAMOUNT VEND.　　212-279-1095
　　587 Tenth Ave., (42-43rd St.) NYC, NY 10036
　　Hours: 9-6 Mon-Fri　　　　　　　　　　　　　FAX　212-279-1298
　　• Jukeboxes, vending machines, video games of all kinds. RENTALS •
　　(See display ad in this section.)

UNIVERSAL GAMES　　201-345-5653
　　69 Grove St., Paterson, NJ 07503
　　Hours: 8:30-5 Mon-Fri　　　　　　　　　　　　FAX　201-345-7358
　　• Casino, bingo, carnival game equipment. See Walter. "Casino Gaming Guide" available.
　　RENTALS •

ARCHITECTURAL ELEMENTS

See also **FIREPLACES & EQUIPMENT**
See also **VACUUMFORMING AND VACUUMFORMED PANELS**
See also **DISPLAY HOUSES & MATERIALS**

AA ABBINGDON AFFILIATES, INC.　　718-258-8333
　　2149 Utica Ave., (Aves. M-N) Brooklyn, NY 11234
　　Hours: 8-4 Mon-Fri (Call ahead)　　　　　　　FAX　718-338-2739
　　• Tin ceilings. Catalog available. CREDIT CARDS •

AMERICAN WOOD COLUMN CORP.　　718-782-3163
　　913 Grand St., (Bushwick-Morgan) Brooklyn, NY 11211
　　Hours: 8-4:30 Mon-Fri　　　　　　　　　　　　FAX　718-387-9099
　　• Columns, pedestals and moldings. Will ship worldwide. •

AMERLITE ALUMINUM CO.　　212-986-9559
　　122 West 25th St. (showroom), (6-7th Ave.) NYC, NY 10001
　　Hours: 9-5 Mon-Fri　　　　　　　　　　　　　FAX　212-645-6885
　　• Anodized aluminum storefront doors and facades; doors. Shipping available . RENTALS •

ARCHITECTURAL ANTIQUE EXCHANGE　　215-922-3669
　　715 N. Second St., (Brown-Fairmont) Philadelphia, PA 19123
　　Hours: 10-5 every day　　　　　　　　　　　　FAX　215-922-3680
　　• Architectural artifacts: 1700's-1940's, mostly Victorian; also plumbing fixtures. RENTALS
　　CREDIT CARDS •

ARCHITECTURAL SCULPTURE LTD.　　212-431-5873
　　242 Lafayette St., (Prince-Spring St.) NYC, NY 10012
　　Hours: 10-6 Tues-Fri • 12-5 Sat　　　　　　　FAX　212-431-7161
　　• Plaster architectural detail; all pieces made to order. Shipping available. •

ART & INDUSTRIAL DESIGN SHOP
212-477-0116
399 Lafayette St., (4th St.) NYC, NY 10003
Hours: 12-7 Mon-Sat
• 20th century and art Deco furniture, furnishings, art and objects. Many original works for sale. Also collectibles, clocks and lighting fixtures. RENTALS CREDIT CARDS •
(See display ad under ANTIQUES: VICTORIAN & 20TH CENTURY)

JULIUS BLUM & CO., INC.
201-438-4600
PO Box 816, Carlstadt, NJ 07072
800-526-6293
Hours: 9-5 Mon-Fri   FAX   201-438-6003
• Ornamental metalwork in a variety of metals. Catalog. Shipping Available •

BRASSCRAFTERS
800-645-1101
4791 N.W. 157th St., Miami, FL 33014
Hours: 9-5 Mon-Fri   FAX   305-685-7667
• Unique selection of pedestals, sconces, wall shelves and valance replicas. Color catalogs available. •

CHELSEA DECORATIVE METAL CO.
713-721-9200
9603 Moonlight Dr., Dept. T, Houston, TX 77096
Hours: 9-5 Mon-Fri   FAX   713-776-8661
• Tin ceilings, catalog available at no charge. Will ship anywhere. •

CO-GNO-SCEN-TI LTD.
718-277-4525
242 Chestnut St., (Atlantic-Fulton) Brooklyn, NY 11208
Hours: 8-4:30 Mon-Fri
• Fiberglass pedestals, columns, jars, urns, animals, Statue of Liberty. Catalog. Minimum order $150. See Libby. •

THE DECORATORS SUPPLY CO.
312-847-6300
3610-12 S. Morgan St., Chicago, IL 60609
Hours: 8-4 Mon-Fri   FAX   312-847-6357
• Over 16,000 repro ornaments for exteriors, interiors and furniture. Capitals and brackets in catalog 127 ($3); complete set of 5 catalogs, $25. No credit cards. •

ERCOLE, INC.
212-941-6098
116 Franklin St., (W. B'way) NYC, NY 10013
Hours: 9-5 Mon-Fri   FAX   212-941-6720
• Plaster columns, pedestals, architectural details; faux finishes and fresco work. Shipping available. •

ELIZABETH ST., INC.
212-941-4800
210 Elizabeth St., (Spring-Prince) NYC, NY 10012
Hours: 9:00-6:00 Mon-Fri • 12:00-5:00 Sat.   FAX   212-274-0057
• French, English, and American stone and marble fireplaces, 17th-19th cent. Garden statuary and furniture, columns, pilasters and keystones. RENTALS •

FABULOUS FORGERIES LTD.
212-840-2248
119 W. 40th St. (6-B'wy) NYC, NY 10018.
Hours: 9-6:30 Mon-Fri.
• Inexpensive frames and framing. •

IRREPLACEABLE ARTIFACTS
212-777-2900
14 Second Ave., (Houston) NYC, NY 10003
Hours: 10-6 Mon-Fri • 11-5 Sat, Sun   FAX   212-780-0642
• Architectural ornamentation from demolished buildings; fireplaces, paneled rooms, bars, urns, garden furniture, etc. Will ship worldwide. RENTALS MC/VISA •

A-B

LOST CITY ARTS
212-941-8025
275 Lafayette St., (Houston-Prince St.) NYC, NY 10012
Hours: 10-6 Mon-Fri • 12-6 Sat, Sun   FAX   212-219-2570
• Interesting and eclectic collection of fixtures, architectural items & urban antiques.
RENTALS •

NEW YORK BARS & BACKBARS
212-431-0600
49 East Houston St., (Mott-Mulberry St.) NYC, NY 10012
Hours: 10-6 Mon-Sat
• Bar room architectural pieces and accessories. RENTALS •

NEWEL ART GALLERY
212-758-1970
425 East 53rd St., (Sutton-1st Ave.) NYC, NY 10022
Hours: 9-5 Mon-Fri
• Columns, doors, mantels and other interesting interior fittings in addition to their incredible collection of exotica. RENTALS •

W.F. NORMAN CORP.
417-667-5552
PO Box 323, 214-32 N. Cedar St., Nevada, MO 64772   800-641-4038
Hours: 8-5 Mon-Fri   FAX   417-667-2708
• Molded zinc architectural detail; statuary in metal; tin ceilings; catalog available. Will ship CREDIT CARDS •

PLASTER GALLERY
718-769-8500
2827 Coney Island Ave, (Ave. Z) Brooklyn, NY 11235
Hours: 11-6 every day   FAX   718-891-2879
• Stock and custom columns, pedestals, etc. in plaster; also plaster statuary and figurines. •

PROPS FOR TODAY
212-206-0330
121 West 19th St., (6th-7th) NYC, NY 10011
Hours: 8:30-5 Mon-Fri   FAX   212-924-0450

Come to us first and we'll work with your budget!
• Acquired from Nostalgia Alley huge selection of antiques and collectibles.
• A good selection of shutters, windows, barn board and other patina surfaces.
• Acquired New York Shakespeare Festival props.
• A collection acquired from Unique Surfaces.
NOW ON 3 FLOORS! ONE STOP PROPPING!

PROPS FOR TODAY

• A full service prop rental house. Phone orders accepted. RENTALS •

SAVE
718-388-4527
337 Berry Street (S. 4th-S. 5th St) Brooklyn, NY 11211
Hours: by appt.
• Warehouse of salvaged architectural elements large & small. Doors, banisters, mantles, windows, all from NYC homes, office buildings, and warehouses. Payment by a NYC bank check only. •

STAMFORD WRECKING CO.
203-324-9537
1 Barry Place, Stamford, CT 06902
Hours: 8:30-4:30 Mon-Fri • 9-3:30 Sat   FAX   203-978-0144
• Toilets, sinks, radiators, bricks & bathtubs. •

STEPTOE & WIFE ANTIQUES, LTD.   416-530-4200
322 Geary Ave., Toronto, Ontario, CAN M6H 2C7
Hours: 9-5 Mon-Fri • Sat by appt.   FAX   416-530-4666
• Victorian cast iron spiral staircases. Catalog #3. •

UNITED HOUSE WRECKING   203-348-5371
535 Hope St., Stamford, CT 06906
Hours: 9:30-5:30 Mon-Sat • 12-5 Sun   FAX   203-961-9472
• Antique and repro doors, mantels, beveled and stained glass, Victorian gingerbread and more. CREDIT CARDS •

URBAN ARCHEOLOGY   212-431-6969
285 Lafayette St., (Houston-Prince St.) NYC, NY 10012
Hours: 8-6 Mon-Fri • 10-4 Sat   FAX   212-941-1918
• Nice interior and exterior architectural pieces; quality reproductions; also does restoration. CREDIT CARDS •

VINTAGE WOOD WORKS   903-356-2158
Highway 34 South, #2682, Quinlan, TX 75474
Hours: 8-54 Mon-Fri   FAX   903-356-3023
• Victorian gingerbread, large finials, newel posts, balusters; catalog $2. Will ship. CREDIT CARDS •

ZAFERO BY LESLIE JOHN KOESER ASSOCIATES   215-763-7054
1530 Parrish St., Philadelphia, PA 19130
Hours: 9-5 Mon-Fri
• Stock or custom fiberglass column, urns, statuary. Catalog, rush orders. RENTALS •

ART RENTAL

See also **ANTIQUES: ALL HEADINGS**
See also **STATUARY**
See also **POSTERS & PRINTS**

ART & INDUSTRIAL DESIGN SHOP   212-477-0116
399 Lafayette St., (4th St.) NYC, NY 10003
Hours: 12-7 Mon-Sat

Specializing in 20th Century Decorative Art, Art Furniture, American Deco., Italian Glass, Italian Furniture, Art, Antiques, Paintings & Sculpture. Industrial design.

• 20th Century and art deco furniture, furnishings art and objects. Many original works for sale or rent. Also collectibles, clocks and lighting fixtures. RENTALS CREDIT CARDS •
(See display ad under ANTIQUES: VICTORIAN & 20TH CENTURY)

CORPORATE ART ASSOCIATES LTD.   212-941-9685
270 Lafayette St. Rm. 402, (Prince St.) NYC, NY 10012
Hours: 9-5 Mon-Fri • or by appt.   FAX   212-941-4780
• Provide contemporary, impressionist and modern art for film and theatre. Contact James Cavello for leasing. RENTALS •

ECLECTIC•ENCORE PROPERTIES, INC. 212-645-8880
(620 West 26th St. 4th Floor, (11-12th Ave.) NYC, NY 10001
Hours: 9-5 Mon-Fri or by appt. FAX 212-243-6508
• Prop rental house with 18th., 19th., and 20th Century furniture, accessories and art. •
(See display ad under PROP RENTAL HOUSES)

ANDREW KOLB & SON, LTD. 212-684-2980
112 Madison Ave., (30th St.) NYC, NY 10016
Hours: 8-4:30 Mon-Fri
• Original and reproduction art. RENTALS •

NEWEL ART GALLERY 212-758-1970
425 E. 53rd St. (Sutton-1st) NYC, NY
• Extraordinary selection of antique furniture, art, architectural pieces, lamps; all periods; expensive. No credit cards. RENTALS •

THE PROP COMPANY KAPLAN & ASSOCIATES 212-691-7767
111 West 19th St. 8nd Fl., (6-7th Ave.) NYC, NY 10011 212-727-3055
Hours: 9-5:30 Mon-Fri
• Prop rental house with paintings, prints, posters, photographs; antique and contemporary. Contact Maxine Kaplan. •
(See display ad under PROP RENTAL HOUSES)

PROPS FOR TODAY 212-206-0330
121 West 19th St. Reception: 3rd Fl., (6-7th Ave.) NYC, NY 10011
Hours: 8:30-5 Mon-Fri FAX 924-0450

Come to us first and we"ll work with your budget!
• Paintings, prints and posters (B'Way, film, rock 'n roll), photographs, samplers, mirrors, kitchen decor, florals, Mexican, Oriental, portraits, equestrian, abstract art, modern, landscapes, memorabilia.
• Recently acquired huge inventory of art from Nostalgia Alley.
NOW ON 3 FLOORS! ONE STOP PROPPING!

PROPS FOR TODAY

• Full service prop rental house. Phone orders accepted. •
(See display ad under PROP RENTAL HOUSES.)

RAYDON GALLERY 212-288-3555
1091 madison Ave., (82nd St.) NYC, NY 10028
Hours: 10-6 Mon-Sat or by appt.
• Many movie and commercial credits, use to working in the industry. Very helpful. Rental of framed pictures; paintings, prints, artwork and posters. •

SAVACOU GALLERY 212-473-6904
240 East 13th St., (2-3rd Ave.) NYC, NY 10003
Hours: 11-7 Tues-Sat
• Original African and Caribbean artwork and batiks. Also custom framing. Sales and rentals. •

ARTIFICIAL FLOWERS, PLANTS, & FOOD

See also **TRIMMINGS: FEATHERS & FLOWERS**
See also **DISPLAY HOUSES & MATERIALS**

BABA'S MARKETPLACE, A Division of Brasscrafters   800-645-1101
    4791 N.W. 157th St. Miami, FL 33014 (mail order)   FAX   305-621-1900
    Hours: 9-5 Mon-Fri

    225 5th Ave. Rm 801 (26-27th St.) NYC, NY (showroom)   212-481-9040
    Hours: 9-5 Mon-Fri
    • Complete line of realistic artifical foods. Color catalog available. $75 minimum. Account required or cash with first order. •

S. BERGER IMPORTS   201-653-6000
    142 2nd St., (off Lewis Marin Blvd.) Jersey City, NJ 07302
    Hours: 8-4 Mon-Fri   FAX   201-653-6000
    • Wholesale artificial flowers and plants; contact Helen Skurzewski •

CULTURED DESIGN LTD.   212-597-2870
    517 W. 46th, (10-11th Ave.) NYC, NY 10036   212-594-8690
    Hours: 9-5 Mon-Fri   FAX   212-597-2858
    • Complete indoor and outdoor greenery services; full range of live & artificial flower services. RENTALS •

FLOWER GALLERY   914-358-2102
    Bradley Parkway, Blauvelt, NY 10913
    Hours: 10-5 Mon-Fri • 1-4 Sat
    • Inexpensive silk flowers, plants, vines, Christmas greenery; catalog available. MC/VISA at retail location. •

SCOTT GRESSEN   215-483-2324
    123 Leverington Ave., Philadelphia, PA 19127
    Hours: 8:30-5 Mon-Fri (Wed till 9) • 10-3 Sat   FAX   215-483-2324
    • Silk and cloth flowers, foliage; floral accessories. Phone orders. •

IMT SERVICES   914-691-3665
    5 Pine Terrace, Highland, NY 12528
    Hours: by appt.   FAX   914-691-3684

Custom fabricates three dimensional representations
of ideas and objects; in plastic, wood, rubber and metal...

I make things!

    • Modelmaking, sculpture, flexibles, fake food for ECU, casting miniatures to oversize. Electromechanical effects. ATAC member. •

JOSLINE DISPLAY   617-396-4700
    327 Mystic Ave., Medford, MA 02155
    Hours: 9-5 Mon-Fri (Thurs till 7)   FAX   617-391-0280
    • Seasonal and decorative dried flowers, grass mats and natural funeral grass. Phone orders. CREDIT CARDS •

A-B

COMPLETE EXTERIORS

ALL SEASONS • TREES • HEDGES • ROCKS • FENCE
• BUSHES • GRASS • PINES • BENCHES • COLUMNS •
FLOWERS • PLANTS • *AND TROPICALS!*

The Uptown Alternative! We Care.

INNOVATIVE FOLIAGE

TROPICAL *Fantasies*

RENTALS

**621 WEST 130th STREET
NEW YORK, NY 10027
212-234-1526**

K & D EXPORT-IMPORT
25 Graphic Place, (Moonachie Rd.) Moonachie, NJ 07074
Hours: 8:45-5 Mon-Fri
• Silk flowers, vegetables and fruits. Limited selection of beautiful baskets. CREDIT CARDS •

201-641-8300
800-543-6969
FAX 201-641-0277

KERVAR, INC.
119 West 28th St., (6-7th Ave.) NYC, NY 10001
Hours: 6:30-3 Mon-Fri
• Silk and plastic foliage and flowers. Fruits, vegetables and floral supplies; wholesale only. •

212-564-2525
FAX 212-594-0030

CHARLES LUBIN CO.
131 Saw Mill River Rd., Yonkers, NY 10701
Hours: 7:30-4:30 Mon-Fri
• Silk flowers, floral supplies. •

914-968-5700
FAX 914-968-5723

MODERN ARTIFICIAL FLOWERS & DISPLAYS LTD.
517 West 46th St., (10-11th Ave.) NYC, NY 10036
Hours: 8:30-5 Mon-Fri
• Complete exterior settings; custom and stock items; live & artifical flowers and plants; statuary; rocks. Phone orders. RENTAL. •

212-265-0414
FAX 212-265-6841

NASCO LIFE FORM MODELS
901 Janesville Ave., (Hwy. 26) Fort Atkinson, WI 53538
Hours: 7:30-4:30 Mon-Fri • 8-12 Sat
• Artificial food, scientific & medical models; catalog available. Phone orders. CREDIT CARDS •

414-563-2556
FAX 414-563-8296

PEOPLE'S FLOWERS CORP.
786 Sixth Ave., (26-27th St.) NYC, NY 10001
Hours: 8:30-5:30 Mon-Sat
• Artificial flowers, foliage, fruits, fish and vegetables; floral supplies, good selection. Phone Orders. CREDIT CARDS •

212-686-6291
FAX 212-696-0620

PETALS
300 Central Ave., White Plains, NY 10606
Hours: 9-6 Mon-Wed • 9-8 Th, F • 10-6 Sat • 12-5 Sun
• Artificial flowers. Catalogue $5. Phone orders. CREDIT CARDS •

914-946-7373
FAX 914-946-7375

SCAFATI & CO.
225 Fifth Ave. #825, (27-28th St.) NYC, NY 10010
Hours: 9-5 Mon-Fri (call if it's before 10am)
• Realistic looking artificial food. Iwasaki Rep. Catalog. See Virginia or Tom. •

212-686-8784
908-291-9325
FAX 908-291-2099

SIGNIFICANT DETAILS
161 West Central Ave., Pearl River, NY 10965
Hours: 8:30-5:30 Mon-Fri • Sat by appt.

914-735-2090
FAX 914-735-1643

• Casting • Sculpture • Food Sculpture •
• Custom Artificial Food and Products • Miniatures •
• Hand Painting • Airbrush • Product Refinement •

Significant Details

• Contact Ann Cimmelli. •

- 1530

SUPERIOR SPECIALTIES, INC.   718-543-1767
    5925 Broadway, (Van Cortland Pk.) Bronx, NY 10463   FAX 718-796-7362
    1040 N. Halsted St. Chicago, IL 60622   312-337-5131
                                  FAX 312-337-5480
    3013 Gilroy St. Los Angeles, CA 90039   213-662-3031
                                  FAX 213-662-0004
    Hours: 7:30-4:30 Mon-Fri
    • Artificial food, seasonal props, small and large pieces. Brochure available. No rentals. $25.
minimum order. MC/VISA •

268 0020

TRENGOVE STUDIOS, INC.   212-~~255-2857~~
    60 West 22nd St., (5-6th Ave.) NYC, NY 10010   800-366-2857
    Hours: 9-5 Mon-Fri   FAX 212-633-8982
    • Realistic looking artificial foods, ice cubes & crushed ice, acrylic props. Brochure available.
MC/VISA •   *175,*

TROPICAL FANTASIES   212-234-1526
    621 West 130th St., (B'way-12th Ave.) NYC, NY 10027
    Hours: 8-4:30 Mon-Fri   FAX 212-234-9251
    • Artificial trees, foliage and floral arrangements; custom props; complete exteriors, planters,
trellis, urns; Christmas trees year-round; contact Kathy Starr-Gerard or Larry Gerard.
RENTALS •
    (See display ad in this section.)

ARTISTS MATERIALS

See also **PAINTS & DYES**

ARTISTS MEDIUM SUPPLY   802-879-1236
    PO Box 756, Williston, VT 05495
    Hours: 8:30-6 Mon-Thurs • 8:30-7 Fri • 10-5 Sat
    • Airbrush parts and supplies. Pasche & Holbein brands. Phone orders, $25 minimum. •

BASICS CRAFT COMPANY   212-679-3516
    1201 Broadway 3rd fl., (28-29th St.) NYC, NY 10001
    Hours: 9-5 Mon-Fri •10-3 Sat   FAX 212-679-3519
    • Supplies for papermaking, bookmaking, weaving & knitting. Retail and wholesale •

DICK BLICK COMPANY   800-447-8192
    P.O. Box 1267, Galesburg, IL 61401
    Hours: 7-7 Mon-Fri   FAX 309-343-5785
    • Good art supply company. Catalog available. CREDIT CARDS •

ARTHUR BROWN & BROTHERS, INC.   212-575-5555
    2 West 46th St., (5th Ave.) NYC, NY 10036
    Hours: 9-6 Mon-Sat   212-575-5825
    • Artists, drafting, photo, framing supplies; some casting supplies. CREDIT CARDS •

CHARRETTE DRAFTING SUPPLY CORP.   212-683-8822
    215 Lexington Ave., (33rd St.) NYC, NY 10016   FAX 212-683-9890
    Hours: 8:30-7 M-F • 10-5 Sat • 12-5 Sun (closed Sun: June, July, Aug)
    • Art, drafting, graphics, model building supplies; catalog; will deliver in Manhattan, ship any-
where. CREDIT CARDS •

CHASELLE, INC.   410-381-9611
   9645 Gerwig Lane, Columbia, MD 21046
   Hours: 9-9 Tues. Wed. Thur. • 9-5:30 Mon Fri Sat   FAX   410-381-3005
   • Complete art supply company. Wonderful catalog. CREDIT CARDS •

CHAVANT, INC.   908-842-6272
   42 West St., Red Bank, NJ 07701   800-CHA-VANT
   Hours: 8-3:30 Mon-Fri for shipping orders
   • Manufacturer and distributor of industrial modeling clays, will ship small quantities; contact Jack North. •

CHEAP PAINT   212-219-3674
   7 Prince St. (Bowery-Elizabeth) NYC, NY 10012
   Hours: 12-7 Tues-Sat.
   • A small source for discount art supplies. Carries mostly paint, some brushes, some canvas. •

CHEAP JOE'S ART STUFF   800-227-2788
   300 A Industrial Park Road, Boone, NC 28607
   Hours: 9-5 Mon-Fri   FAX   800-257-0874
   • Good cheap art supply company. Many students from the Art Student's League in NYC use this company. Catalog available. CREDIT CARDS •

MICHELLE COLE   816-331-3419
   14922 Fuller Ave., Grandview, MO 64030
   Hours: 8:30-5:00 Mon-Fri
   • Representative for: Wally R's acrylic paints, fabric dyes & wood stains. Enhancement: glitter film. Technicraft glue guns and glue sticks, glitter and glow-in-the-dark hot melt glue. 1881: Crackle medium. Very accommodating. •

CREATEX COLORS   203-653-0643
   14 Airport Park Road, East Granby, CT 06026
   Hours: 8:30-5:30 Mon-Fri   FAX   203-653-0643
   • Water-based, non-toxic pigments that work in all kinds of paints. MC/VISA •

CRYSTAL PRODUCTIONS   800-255-8629
   P.O. Box 2159, Glenview, IL 60025   708-657-8144
   Hours: 9-5 Mon-Fri   FAX   708-657-8149
   • Good art supply company. Catalog available. CREDIT CARDS •

DAVID DAVIS   212-982-7100
   148 Mercer St (Prince-Houston) NYC, NY 10012
   Hours: 9:30-6 Mon-Fri • 11-6 sat (closed Sat: July, Aug)
   • Easels, custom brushes, fabric dye, lecturer's chalk, paints; all types of artists materials. •

DIEU DONNE PAPERMILL   212-226-0573
   3 Crosby St., (Howard-Grand) NYC, NY10013
   Hours: 10-6 Mon-Fri (make appt. if possible)   FAX   212-226-6088
   • Papermaking supplies, handmade papers. Workshops and classes on papermaking. Specialty theatre backdrops catalogue available. Contact Mina Takanasi. •

EAGLE SUPPLY CO.   212-246-6180
   327 West 42nd St., (8-9th Ave.) NYC, NY 10036
   Hours: 8-4:30 Mon-Fri
   • Artists, sign painters, and silkscreening supplies; large stock of poster board. Phone orders, no minimum. •

ECO DESIGN CO.–THE NATURAL CHOICE   505-438-3448
1365 Rufina Circle, Santa Fe, NM 87501
Hours: 8-6 Mon-Fri • 10-3 Sat   FAX   505-438-0199
• Personal protective equipment and supplies. Carry environmentally friendly paints, pigments, hand cleaners. Some stains contain toxins, but they are working on developing environmentally friendly products. Catalog available. MC/VISA •

EMPIRE ARTISTS MATERIALS   212-737-5002
851 Lexington Ave., (64-65th St.) NYC, NY 10021   212-737-5003
Hours: 8:30-6 Mon-Fri • 10-6 Sat • 12-6 Sun (closed Sun--July, Aug)
• Artists, drafting supplies, picture framing; will deliver. CREDIT CARDS •

EMPIRE BEROL, CONSUMER AFFAIRS   800-538-4265
PO Box 2248 105 Westpark Drive, Brentwood, TN 37024   615-371-1194
Hours: 8-5 Mon-Fri
• Source of prismacolor pencils. Very nice people. Ask for Joan Floyd. •

SAM FLAX ART SUPPLIES   212-620-3038
12 W. 20th St., (5-6th Ave.) NYC, NY 10011
Hours: 9-6:30 Mon-Fri •10-5:30 Sat   FAX   212-929-3837
• Artists, drafting, graphics, and photo materials. Drafting tables, presentation portfolios; casting rubber and moulage. CREDIT CARDS •

A. I. FRIEDMAN, INC.   212-243-9000
44 West 18th St., (5-6th Ave.) NYC, NY 10011
Hours: 9-6:30 Mon-Fri • 12-5 Sat   FAX   212-929-7320
25 West 45th St. (5th Ave.) NYC, NY 10036   212-243-9000
Hours: 9-6:30 Mon-Fri
• 20% discount card for professionals; monthly sales with low prices. CREDIT CARDS •

GOLDEN TYPEWRITER & STATIONERY CORP.   212-749-3100
2512 Broadway, (94th St.) NYC, NY 10025
Hours: 9:30-6:45 Mon-Sat
• Artists supplies, office supplies & stationery. MC/VISA •

N. GLANTZ & SON   718-439-7707
218 57th St., (2-3rd Ave.) Brooklyn, NY 11220
Hours: 8:30-5 Mon-Fri
• Paints, boards, neon; everything for signmaking; wholesale Cutall sales. Phone orders & deliveries. •

M. GRUMBACHER, INC.   609-655-8282
30 Englehard Dr., Cranberry NJ 08512
Hours: 8-4:30 Mon-Fri
• Artists brushes and paint; wholesale only. •

GUERRA PAINT & PIGMENT   212-529-0628
510 East 13th St., (Aves. A-B) NYC, NY 10009
Hours: 10-6 Mon-Sat • 12-6 Sun
• Fine art paints and pigments; hard-to-find colors; expensive. •

HUNT BIENFANG PRODUCTIONS   800-873-4868
P.O. Box 5819, Statesville, NC 28687   704-873-9511
Hours: 8-7:30 Mon-Fri   FAX   704-872-1766
• Foam board in colors. Also Exacto tools. Catalog. •

A–B

JIFFY FOAM, INC.
401-846-7870
221 Third St., P.O. Box 3609, Newport, RI 02840
Hours: 8-5 Mon-Fri   FAX   401-847-7870
• Sells Balsa-Foam; a plastic product that carves like butter and paints like wood. Comes in variety of sizes. •

KATE'S PARSONS ART SUPPLY
212-675-6406
2 West 13th St., (5-6th Ave.) NYC, NY 10011
Hours 8:30-7:30 Mon-Thurs • 8:30-6 Fri Sat   FAX   212-366-6532
• Good general selection of artists materials. CREDIT CARDS •

LEE'S ART SHOP
212-247-0110
220 West 57th St., (7th-B'way) NYC, NY 10019
Hours: 9-6:30 Mon-Fri • 9:30-6:30 Sat • 12-5:30 Sun   FAX   212-247-0507
• Large stock artists materials, seamless paper, drafting furniture, framing; catalog. No phone orders. CREDIT CARDS •

LIGHTING ASSOCIATES
203-526-9315
PO Box 299, Chester, CT 06412
Hours: 9-6 Mon-Fri
• Lighting, scenic design and furniture templates for theatrical and TV designers; metric templates. Catalogue available, phone orders. •

MENASH, INC.
212-695-8888
462 Seventh Ave., (35th St.) NYC, NY 10018
Hours: 8:30-5:30 Mon-Fri • 9-5 Sat

2307 Broadway (83-84th St.) NYC, NY 10024   212-877-2060
Hours 9-6:30 Mon-Sat   FAX   212-877-8657
• Artists, drafting, graphics, office supplies, stationery; professional discount. CREDIT CARDS •

MULTIMEDIA ARTBOARD
609-953-7282
306 Gettisburg Ct., Medford, NJ 08055
Hours: 9-5 Mon-Fri or by appt.   FAX   609-654-7282
• A wonderful new artboard that comes in black and white and accepts oil or watercolor. The white is translucent for tracing. Product is moldable when wet. Available in NYC at Lee's Art Shop. Brochure available. MC/VISA •

NATIONAL ARTISTS MATERIALS CO., INC.
212-675-0100
4 West 20th St., (5-6th Ave.) NYC, NY 10011
Hours: 8:30-6 Mon-Fri • 10-4 sat   FAX   212-691-0474
• Seamless paper, mat board, transparent slide, negative and photo pages. •

NEW YORK CENTRAL ART SUPPLY, INC.
212-473-7706
62 Third Ave., (11th St.) NYC, NY 10003
Hours: 8:30-6:15 Mon-Sat   FAX   212-475-2513
• Large, well stocked general art papers and art supplies. Always crowded! catalog. Accepts phone orders. CREDIT CARDS •

P.K. SUPPLY CO., INC.
718-377-6444
2291 Nostrand Ave, (Aves. I-J) Brooklyn, NY 11210
Hours: 9:15-5:30 Mon-Fri • 9:30-5 Sat   FAX   718-377-7519
• Art supplies, picture frame molding, silkscreen and commercial sign supplies. •

PEARL ART & CRAFT SUPPLY, INC.   908-634-9400
6000 Rt. 1 & Gills Ln., (opp. Woodbridge Center) Woodbridge, NJ 07095
Hours: 10-9 Mon-Sat • 12-5 Sun

776 Rt. 17 N, Paramus, NJ 07652   201-447-0300
Hours: 9:30-8:45 Mon-Sat   FAX 201-447-4102
• Artists materials and supplies, large crafts section; easily accessible from central New Jersey and Staten Island. Phone orders over $50. CREDIT CARDS •

PEARL PAINT CO., INC.   212-431-7932
308 Canal St., (B'way-Church) NYC, NY 10013
Hours: 9-5:30 Mon-Sat (Thurs till 7) • 11-4:45 Sun   FAX 212-431-6798
2411 Hempstead Turnpike, East Meadow, NY 11554   516-713-3700
Hours: 9:30-5:45 Mon-Sat (Wed, Fri till 8:45) Sun 12-4:45   FAX 516-731-3721
• Large art supply stores, well stocked; competitive prices; catalog. CREDIT CARDS •
                                               (mail order) 800-221-6845.

PEARL SHOWROOM   212-226-3717
42 Lispenard, (Church-B'way) NYC, NY 10013
Hours: 9-6 Mon-Sat (Thurs till 7) • 10-5:30 Sun
• Easels, drafting machines, flat files, airbrushes, light boxes & office furniture. CREDIT CARDS •

SAX ARTS & CRAFTS   800-558-6696
2405 S. Calhoun Road, New Berlin, WI 53131   414-784-6880
Hours: Order line functional 24 hours every day   FAX 414-784-1176
• Art supply company. Catalog available 530 pages-$5.00 refundable with first order. CREDIT CARDS •

SYMPHONY ARTS, INC.   800-654-6279
130 Beckwith Ave., Paterson, NJ 07502   201-278-7200
Hours: 8:30-5 Mon-Fri   FAX 201-278-6789
• Good line of scenic brushes. Good prices. Catalog. Ask for Carlton Bruin. MC/VISA •

UTRECHT ART & DRAFTING SUPPLIES   212-777-5353
111 Fourth Ave., (11-12th St.) NYC, NY10003
Hours: 9-6 Mon-Sat   FAX 212-420-9632
• Specializes in house brand paints and canvas, as well as other art supplies; catalog. Accepts phone orders. CREDIT CARDS •

AUDIO & VIDEO EQUIPMENT

See also **AUDIO & VIDEO EQUIPMENT: ANTIQUE & DUMMY**
See also **LIGHTING & PROJECTION EQUIPMENT RECORDS, TAPES & CDS**

ACE AUDIO VISUAL • T.V. RENTAL CO.   718-458-3800
33-49 55th St., Woodside , NY 11377   718-458-2211
Hours: 8:30-5:30 Mon-Fri   FAX 718-889-1995
• VCRs, stereo equipment rental, speak to Artie. For televisions, call Ted Pappas. CREDIT CARDS •

ACE PROPS
1 West 19th St. Ground Fl., (5th Ave.) NYC, NY 10011   212-206-1475
Hours: 8-5 Mon-Fri • 9-4 Sat or by appt.   212-580-9551
FAX   212-929-9082
• Wide variety of sound, A • V, and video equipment for rent - consumer and professional, period and contemporary. Installation and technical support available. CREDIT CARDS •
(See display ad in this section.)

AUDIO VISUAL WORKSHOP
333 West 52nd St., (8-9th Ave.) NYC, NY 10019   212-397-5020
Hours: 9-5 Mon-Fri   FAX   212-582-6409
• Rentals and sales of audio and video equipment. CREDIT CARDS •

COLEMAN AUDIO
81 Pilgrim Lane, Westbury, NY 11590   516-334-7109
Hours: 9-5 Mon-Fri   FAX   212-541-9128
• Formally Martin Audio Video Corp. Repairs and installs audio/video equipment. •

THE COUNTER SPY SHOP
444 Madison Ave. , (49th-50th St.) NYC, NY 10022   212-688-8500
Hours: 9-6 Mon-Fri • 10-2 Sat or by appt Sat & Sun.   800-722-4490
212-888-6460
• Spy and security equipment and clothing. Security equipment for rental. See Tom Felice.
CREDIT CARDS •

FEDERAL RENT−A−TV CORP.
1588 York Ave., (83-84th St.) NYC, NY 10028   212-734-5777
Hours: 9-6 Mon-Fri • 9-2 Sat   FAX   212-861-6770
• TVs, VCRs, air conditioners, cameras, projection TVs; make rental reservation before 6pm.
CREDIT CARDS •

HARVEY ELECTRONICS
28 West 8th St., (5-6th Ave.) NYC, NY 10011   212-982-7191
Hours: 11-7 Mon-Fri • 10:30-6 Sat • (12-5 Sun during special sales)   FAX   212-777-0590

2 West 45th St. (5th Ave.) NYC, NY 10036   212-575-5000
Hours: 9:30-6 Mon-Fri • 10:30-6 Sat   FAX   212-768-8114
• Rental of stereo equipment. CREDIT CARDS •

J & R MUSIC WORLD
15 Park Row, (Beekman-Ann St.) NYC, NY 10038   212-349-4727
Hours: 9-6:30 Mon-Sat • 10-5 Sun
• Computers and home office outlet. •

23 Park Row, (Beekman-Ann St.) NYC, NY 10038   212-732-8600
Hours: 9-6:30 Mon-Sat • 10-5 Sun   FAX   212-406-4442
• Main store; popular records, CDs, tapes; stereo, TV, VCR equipment. •

27 Park Row, (Beekman-Ann St.) NYC, NY 10038   212-227-4777
Hours: 9-6:30 Mon-Sat • 10-5 Sun
• Portable and car stereos. •

33 Park Row, (Beekman-Ann St.) NYC, NY 10038   (Jazz) 212-349-8400
Hours: 9-6:30 Mon-Sat • 10-5 Sun   (Classical) 212-233-0667
• Classical and jazz records, CDs, tapes; good selection & prices. •

METRO TV RENTALS
179 Lincoln Ave., Orange, NJ 07050   212-308-0900
Hours: 9-5:30 Mon-Sat   201-672-1500
FAX   516-756-9678
• TV & VCR rental. CREDIT CARDS •

MSI SECURITY SYSTEMS, INC. 201-955-1200
62-70 2nd Ave., Kearny, NJ 07032 800-333-1013
Hours: 9-5 Mon-Fri FAX 201-955-1759
• Design & installation of CCTV and access control security systems. Sales and rental of audio intercom systems. •

PARK AVE. AUDIO 212-685-8101
425 Park Ave. South, (29th St.) NYC, NY 10016
Hours: 10-6 Mon-Sat (Thurs till 7) FAX 212-689-0468
• Audio and video equipment; custom installations. CREDIT CARDS •

QUARK ELECTRONIC, INC. 212-889-1808
537 Third Ave., (35th St.) NYC, NY 10016 800-343-6443
Hours: 10-6:30 Mon-Fri By Appt. • 11-4 Sat • 12-6:30 Sun FAX 212-447-5510
• Collection of gadgetry including video camera tie clips, voice scramblers, deep-space telescopes, translators, currency converters, umbrella microphones, night vision monoculars, etc. RENTALS CREDIT CARDS •

R.C.I. RADIO CLINIC, INC. 212-864-6000
2599 Broadway, (98th St.) NYC, NY 10036 (service) 212-663-7700
Hours: 9-7 Mon-Fri • 9-6 Sat • 12-5 Sun FAX 212-663-6933
• Televisions, stereo equipment, electronics, refrigerators, washers & dryers. RENTALS •

S & S SOUND CITY 212-575-0210
58 West 45th St., (5-6th Ave.) NYC, NY 10036
Hours: 9-7 Mon-Fri• 9-6 Sat FAX 212-221-7907
• TV, video, camcorders, radios, stereo equipment & closed circuit security systems. Rents anything in the store! Speak to Mel Tillman. •

"I found it in the N.Y. Theatrical Sourcebook."

UNCLE STEVE'S   212-226-4010
> 343 Canal St., (Wooster-Greene St.) NYC, NY 10013
> Hours: 10-7:30 everyday
> • Large selection, cash only; a real NYC experience. •

AUDIO & VIDEO EQUIPMENT: ANTIQUE & DUMMY

See also **PROP RENTAL HOUSES**

ACE PROPS   212-206-1475
> 1 West 19th St. Ground Floor, (5th Ave.) NYC, NY 10011   212-580-9551
> Hours: 8-5 Mon-Fri • 9-4 Sat or by appt.   FAX   212-929-9082
> • Working and non-working electronic equipment for rent. Specializing in contemporary and
> period consumer and professional AV equipment. CREDIT CARDS •
> (See display ad under AUDIO & VIDEO EQUIPMENT.)

E. BUK, ANTIQUES & ART   212-226-6891
> 151 Spring St. 2nd floor, (W. Broadway Wooster) NYC, NY 10012
> Hours: Every day by appt.   (toll call) 700-SCIENCE)

ANTIQUE AND PERIOD cameras, projectors, radios,
televisions, microphones, phonographs, Victrolas, intercoms;
classic and vintage broadcast equipment; 100's of historical
items; 19th and 20th century.

E.BUK
Antiques and Art

> • Antique and period cameras, projectors, radios, televisions, microphones, phonography,
> Victrolas, intercoms; classic and vintage broadcast equipment; 100's of historical items; 19th
> and 20th century. RENTALS •
> (See display ad under ANTIQUES: EUROPEAN & AMERICAN.)

HARRY POSTER-VINTAGE TV'S   201-794-9606
> P.O. Box 1883, Hackensack, NJ 07606
> Hours: by appt.
> • Vintage TV's and radios for rent and sale. One tube to a full store. •

PROPTRONICS   800-362-8118
> 1175 McCabe, Elk Grove Village, IL 60007   708-952-1851
> Hours: 8-4 Mon-Fri   FAX   708-952-8098
> • Realistic and durable simulated electronic equipment; many items available. Good prices,
> sales only; brochure and price list available. •
> (See display ad under PROP RENTAL HOUSE.)

SOUND OF MUSIC   201-383-7267
> P.O. Box 221, Stillwater, NJ 07875
> Hours: by appt.
> • Vintage radios 1927-1942; will help you locate almost anything; rentals or sales; see
> Howard. •

WAVES   212-989-9284
> 32 East 13th St., (5th-Univ. Pl.) NYC, NY 10003
> Hours: 12-6 Tues-Fri• 12-4 Sat
> • 78's, Victrolas, radios, telephones. RENTALS •

AUTOMOBILE & MOTORCYCLE RENTAL

See also **AUTOMOBILE & TAXICAB ACCESSORIES & SUPPLIES**

AUTO PROPS
201-470-9354
8 Lexington Ave., Wallington, NJ 07057
Hours: by appt.
· Automobiles and trucks of all types and periods including Harley Davidson motorcycles; Stunt rigging, scuba, garage facilities. See Ken Maletsky. ·
(See display ad in this section.)

CARS OF YESTERDAY RENTALS
201-784-0030
PO Box 43, State Hwy. 9W, Alpine, NJ 07620
Hours: 9-5 Mon-Fri by appt.
· Antique to present autos, police cars and taxi cabs including Checkers. ·

COOPER FILM CARS, LTD.
212-929-3909
132 Perry St., (Washington-Greenwich St.) NYC, NY 10014
Hours: 8-6 Mon-Fri · 10-6 Sat   FAX   212-633-6952
· Any car, any period. Studio available for car shoots. ·

CUSTOM TRIM OF KATONAH
914-232-9433
18 Woodsbridge Road, Katonah, NY 10536   (evenings) 914-855-3966
Hours: 9-6 Mon-Fri
· Antique and Muscle cars--hot rods, Corvettes, GTO's Thunderbirds, etc. for rent with owner. Contact Ron Jack. ·

CYCLE TENDERS • NY MOTORCYCLES
718-479-2929
222-02 Jamaica Ave., Queens Village, NY 11428   718-479-7777
Hours: 9-6 Mon-Sat   FAX   718-740-7887
· Motorcycles and film cars; 24 hr. pickup and delivery. ·

DONNA MOTOR SALES
201-759-7838
15 Roosevelt Ave., Belleville, NJ 07109
Hours: 8-5 Mon-Fri
· Antique and modern cars, trucks, taxis, ambulances; rentals only; see Jerry. ·

MOTORCYCLES FOR FILM
212-861-1356
4 Prince St., NYC, NY 10012
Hours: by appt.
· Antique to present cycles and riders; contact Jim Babchack. ·

MOVIE TIME CARS, INC.
201-492-1711
457 Hamburg Trnpk., West Milford, NJ 07480
Hours: 8-6 every day   FAX   201-492-1969
· Good selection of picture cars in stock; vintage, limousines, exotic, motorcycles, police cars and ambulances with NJ and NY markings. Contact Tom Scorsone. ·
(See display ad in this section.)

OBSOLETE FLEET
212-255-6068
45 Christopher St., (7th Ave. S.) NYC, NY 10014
Hours: by appt.
· Antique and classic vehicles; see Daniel List. ·

PICTURE CARS EAST, INC.
718-852-2300
72 Huntington St, (9th St.-Hicks) Brooklyn, NY 11231
Hours: 9-5 Mon-Fri   FAX   718-858-1583
· Prop cars, wagons, cabs, rigging for stunts; see Gino Lucci. ·

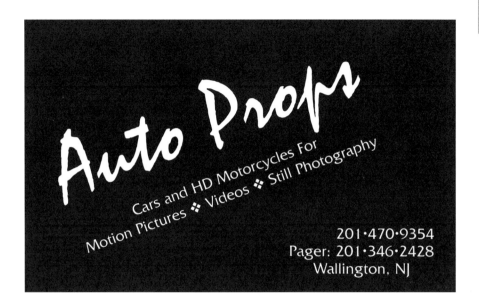

"I found it in the N.Y. Theatrical Sourcebook."

LEONARD SCHILLER ANTIQUE AUTOS 718-788-3400
811 Union St., (6-7th Ave.) Brooklyn, NY 11215
Hours: 24-hour phone

Providing any motor vehicle with the owner as driver -
antique, classic or contemporary. E.G. 1926 Taxi, 1938 Milk
Truck, 1942 Fire Truck, 1947 Seltzer Truck, 1950 Pickup,
1953 Jaguar Roadster, 1958 Motor Scooter and a 1965
Good Humor Truck.

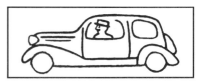

• Old bicycles and automotive related props. •

SPEED AUTO SALES 718-377-5110
2025 Flatbush Ave., Brooklyn, NY 11234
Hours: 8-7 Mon-Fri • 9-4 Sat   FAX   718-692-3778
• Authorized Jeep dealer. Reliable service; see Joseph Vincent. RENTALS •

VOGEL'S EUROCARS, INC. 914-968-8200
385 McLean Ave., Yonkers, NY 10705
Hours: 8-8 Mon-Fri   FAX   914-968-5506
• Daily rental of Mercedes Benz automobiles; front door delivery and pickup available. •

AUTOMOBILE & TAXICAB ACCESSORIES & SUPPLIES

AID AUTO STORES 212-757-6969
645 Eleventh Ave., (47th St.) NYC, NY 10036
Hours: 8:30-6 Mon-Fri • 9-4 Sat
• Complete inventory of parts, accessories, chemicals, and tools for cars. •

AMERICAN TAXIMETER 718-937-4600
21-46 44th Dr., (Ely-21 St.) L.I.C., NY 11101
Hours: 8-4:30 Mon-Fri
• Taxi stickers, license holders, Motorola radios, old taxi meters and accessories. RENTALS •

CUSTOM TRIM OF KATONAH 914-232-9433
18 Woodsbridge Road, Katonah, NY 10536   (evenings) 914-855-3966
Hours: 9-6 Mon-Fri
• Antique and Muscle cars--hot rods, Corvettes, GTO's Thunderbirds, etc. for rentals with
owner. Contact Ron Jack. •

CYBERT TIRE CORP. 212-265-1177
726 Eleventh Ave., (51-52nd St.) NYC, NY 10019
Hours: 8-4 Mon-Fri (closed for lunch 12-1)
• Tire rental and sales; also batteries. •

FRENCH LAKE AUTO PARTS 612-274-8497
3531 Cord 3 NW, (7 miles SW of town) Annandale, MN 55302   612-286-2560
Hours: 8-5 Mon-Fri • 8-3 Sat
• Incredible number of junked autos; they ship parts all over the world. •

LICENSE PLATES • ANDY BERNSTEIN 718-279-1890
43-60 Douglaston Parkway, Douglaston, NY 11363
Hours: by appt.
• Also will buy original plates. •

A-B

MANHATTAN FOREIGN CAR PARTS
212-279-1300

297 Tenth Ave., (27th St.) NYC, NY 10001
Hours: 8:30-5:30 Mon-Fri
• Sale or rental of automotive products and accessories such as steering wheels, road lights, road wheels, logos, badges, driving gloves, etc. •

WORTH AUTO SUPPLY
212-777-5920

31 Cooper Square, (5-6th St.) NYC, NY 10003
Hours: 8:30-6 Mon-Fri • 8:30-5 Sat
212-979-2860
• Older period parts and supplies. No Rentals •

NOTES

NOTES

BACKDROPS

See also **SCENIC SHOPS**
For soft goods, see **CURTAINS & DRAPERIES, THEATRICAL**

ATMOSPHERICS   201-659-8537
113 Willow Ave., Hoboken, NJ 07030
Hours: by appt.   FAX 201-659-8087
• Custom murals, floor cloths and drops. Rental drops for photographic shoots, Speak to Gillian Bradshaw-Smith •

BERKEY K. & L. CUSTOM SERVICES   212-661-5600
222 E. 44th St. 3rd Fl., (2-3rd Ave.) NYC, NY 10017
Hours: 9-5 Mon-Fri   FAX 212-286-1773
• Scanamural: photo-realistic computerized scene painting. See Jim Vazoulas. •

CHARLES BRODERSON, INC.   212-925-9392
873 Broadway #612, (18-19th St.) NYC, NY 10003
Hours: 9-5 Mon-Fri   FAX 212-982-8446
• Backdrop rental; will deliver, ship nationwide •

BETSY DAVIS BACKDROPS   212-645-4197
397 West 12th St. 2nd Fl., (Washington-West) NYC, NY 10014
Hours: by appt.
• Custom-made props and backdrops. RENTALS. •

DIEU BONNE PAPERMILL   212-226-0573
3 Crosby St., (Howard & Grand) NYC, NY 10013
Hours: 10-6 Mon-Fri (make appt. if possible)   FAX 212-226-6088
• Specialty theatre backdrops. •

EASTERN SCENIC BACKDROPS, INC.   212-265-7767
514 West 49th St., (10-11th Ave.) NYC, NY 10019
Hours: 8-5 Mon-Fri   FAX 212-582-3746

Over 200 color scenic backdrops for rental.
Now also featuring MOTTLED backdrops.
Catalog available.

• Large selection of backdrops for rental. Will deliver/ship. Call for catalog. •

IMERO FIORENTINO ASSOC.   212-246-0600
33 West 60th St., (B'way-Columbus) NYC, NY 10023
Hours: 9-5 Mon-Fri   FAX 212-246-6408
• Distributors of Scanamurals; custom canvas backdrops with your artwork (photo or rendering); two week delivery or one week rush service; speak to Angela Linsell. •

JOE GINSBERG CUSTOM BACKDROPS, SURFACES & SETS   718-398-2530
580 Bergen St., Brooklyn, NY 11238
Hours: by appt.   FAX   718-398-2530

- Commission painting for private/corporate interiors.
- Custom sets for television and film.
- Rentals available.
- Full range of styles and finishes.

  - Custom or rental drops and sets.

J.C. BACKINGS CORP.   310-280-5830
10202 W. Washington Blvd., (Overland Ave.) Culver City, CA 90232
Hours: 8-4:30 Mon-Fri   FAX   310-280-7949
  - Over 3500 scenic backdrops for rental, primarily for film and TV; fully equipped union scene shop for custom work. Will ship. Catalog. •

JERMANN STUDIO   914-359-7535
2 Union Avenue, PO Box 245 Sparkill, NY 10976
Hours: by appt.
  - Murals and faux finishes. Will customize everything. Contact David Jermann to see portfolio and examples.

OLIPHANT BACKDROPS   212-741-1233
20 West 20th St. 6th Fl., (5-6th Ave.) NYC, NY 10011
Hours: 9-5 Mon-Fri   212-366-6772

- Over 1,000 backdrops in stock.
- 40 Page catalog.
- Commission painting for private/corporate interiors.

Oliphant Backdrops

  - Rental and custom work. Will deliver/ship. Large stock of rental drops. •

PACIFIC STUDIOS, INC.   718-361-9077
34-40 31st St., (34th St) Long Island City, NY 11106   (LA office)   213-653-3093
Hours: 9-12, 1-6 Mon-Fri   213-653-9509
  - Photographic backgrounds; rental office in Long Island City, main office in LA. Shipping out of LA. Translites and duratrans. Catalog. •

RAVEN BACKDROPS   212-925-0359
425 Broome St., (Crosby-Lafayette St.) NYC, NY 10013
Hours: 9-5 Mon-Fri   FAX   212-925-0359
  - Stock or custom painted backdrops; textures, scenes, skies, interiors, etc.; rental or purchase. Will ship. •

ROSCO LABORATORIES, INC.   914-937-1300
36 Bush Ave., Port Chester, NY 10573   800-ROSCONY
Hours: 9-5 Mon-Fri   FAX   914-937-5954
  - Process converts transparencies or opaque art to large textile drops. Beautiful results. Shipping available. •

VARIETY SCENIC STUDIOS   718-392-4747
25-19 Borden Ave., (25-27th St.) Long Island City, NY 11101
Hours: 7-5 Mon-Fri (office)   FAX   718-784-2919
  - Backdrops; custom. RENTALS. •

"I found it in the N.Y. Theatrical Sourcebook."

BAKERIES

CAKE MASTERS
212-749-3340
2631 Broadway, (99th St.) NYC, NY 10025
Hours: 7am-8pm Mon-Sat • 8am-7pm Sun   FAX   212-666-3183
• Will make special prop cakes to order. Will deliver MC/VISA •

CONNECTICUT MUFFIN CO.
212-925-9773
10 Prince St., (Bowery-Elizabeth St.) NYC, NY 10012
Hours: 7-2:30 every day   FAX   212-925-0183
• Wonderful muffins, scones, pound cakes. Will deliver. •

CREATIVE CAKES
212-794-9811
400 East 74th St., (1st Ave.) NYC, NY 10021
Hours: 8-4:30 Tues-Fri • 9-11am Sat
• Cakes made to order; very helpful. •

D & B COOKIE
212-233-1900
106 Reade St., (Church & West Broadway) NYC, NY 10013
Hours: 24 hours every day   212-233-1998
• Fortune cookies with personalized messages. Phone is answered "Jewelite". •

DIMAS BAKE SHOP
212-924-1818
236 Ninth Ave., (24-25th St.) NYC, NY 10001
Hours: 7-7 Mon-Sat • 7-2 Sun
• European pastries, custom cakes. Will deliver. MC/VISA •

THE EROTIC BAKER, INC.
212-721-3217
582 Amsterdam Ave., (88-89th St.) NYC, NY 10024
Hours: 10-6 Tues-Thurs • 11-8 Fri-Sat
• Breads and pastries, some with an erotic twist; also custom work.Cake tops (erotic or non-erotic) Erotic chocolates; telephone orders only. Delivery in Manhattan shipping nationwide CREDIT CARDS •

LA DELICE BAKERY
212-532-4409
372 Third Ave., (27th St.) NYC, NY 10016
Hours: 7:30-9 Mon-Sat • 7:30-8 Sun
• Will make cakes to order in one day; very helpful. •

MAZUR'S BAKERY
201-438-8500
323 Ridge Rd., Lyndhurst, NJ 07071
Hours: 6am-9pm every day   FAX   201-438-0048
• Custom cakes for all occasions including film needs and weddings. Also breads, pastries, rolls, cookies. •

ORWASHER'S
212-288-6569
308 East 78th St., (1-2nd Ave.) NYC, NY 10021
Hours: 7-7 Mon-Sat
• Fabulous breads of all kinds. •

POSEIDON BAKERY
212-757-6173
629 Ninth Ave., (44-45th St.) NYC, NY 10036
Hours: 9-7 Tues-Sat • 10-4 Sun
• Greek pastries. Strudel, spinach pies, meat pies. •

BALLOONS & HELIUM

A–B

BALLOON CITY USA   800-243-5486
    PO Box 1445, Harrisburg, PA 17105-0397
    Hours: 8-6:30 Mon-Fri   FAX   717-558-4175
    • Mylar balloons, mylar ribbon; wholesale. CREDIT CARDS •

BALOOMS   212-673-4007
    147 Sullivan St., (Prince-W. Houston St.) NYC, NY 10012   212-473-3523
    Hours: 10-6 Mon-Fri • 12-6 Sat
    • Custom balloons, see Marlyne. CREDIT CARDS •

MCKINNEY WELDING SUPPLY   212-246-4305
    535 West 52nd St., (10-11th Ave.) NYC, NY 10019
    Hours: 7-4:30 Mon-Fri   FAX   212-582-3105
    • Helium; industrial, medical and specialty gases; welding equipment. •

PARTY BAZAAR   212-695-6820
    390 Fifth Ave., (36th St.) NYC, NY 10018   FAX   212-643-9462
    Hours: 8-6:30 Mon-Wed • 8-8 Thurs • 8-7 Fri • 9:30-6 Sat • 12-5 Sun
    • Good selection of balloons, will inflate; carries disposable helium tanks. CREDIT CARDS. •

T.W. SMITH WELDING SUPPLY   212-247-6323
    545 West 59th St., (10-11th Ave.) NYC, NY 10019
    Hours: 7:30-4 Mon-Fri

    885 Meeker Avenue (Bridgewater-Varick) Brooklyn, NY 11222   718-388-7417
    Hours: 7:30-4:30 Mon-Fri • 8-12 Sat except holiday weekends.
    • Helium, balloon attachments; deposit required. •

TOY BALLOON CORP.   212-682-3803
    204 East 38th St., (2-3rd Ave.) NYC, NY 10016
    Hours: 9-5 Mon-Fri
    • Novelty, plain or printed balloons to order; helium. •

TOY–TEX NOVELTY CO.   708-673-6600
    7315 N. Linder, Skokie, IL 60077
    Hours: 9-5 Mon-Fri   FAX   708-676-5298
    • Large multi-colored latex balloons; speak to Stefany Gregory. •

U.S. BALLOON MFG. CO.   718-492-9700
    140 58th St., (Brooklyn Army Terminal) Brooklyn, NY 11220
    Hours: 9-6 Mon-Fri   FAX   718-492-8711
    • Large selection of mylar and latex balloons and balloon accessories; carries animal shapes;
    wholesale. CREDIT CARDS. •

BARRELS

ADELPHIA CONTAINER CORP.   718-388-5202
    28 North 3rd St., (Kent St.) Brooklyn, NY 11211
    Hours: 7-3:30 Mon-Fri   FAX   718-388-0967
    • Cardboard barrels and nail kegs; small and large orders. •

"I found it in the N.Y. Theatrical Sourcebook."

BRADBURY BARREL CO.   207-429-8141
PO Box A, Bridgwater, ME 04735
Hours: 8-5 Mon-Fri   207-429-8188
• Handmade cedar barrels and tubs. Display units, barrel liners. Catalog. MC/VISA •

A–B

GREIF BROTHERS   908-381-0200
170 Northfield Ave., Edison, NJ 08018
Hours: 7-4 Mon-Fri   908-381-0207
• Good source for cardboard barrels, shipping containers, large 35 gal. + plastic containers. •

BASKETS & WICKER ITEMS

See also **ETHNIC GOODS**
For supplies see **RATTAN, REED, RAFFIA & WILLOW**

A SUMMER PLACE   203-453-5153
37 Boston St., (on the Green, off Rt. 95) Guildford, CT 06437
Hours: by appt.
• Antique wicker, some quilts, see Mary Jean McLaughlin. •

AZUMA   212-673-2900
25 East 8th St., (Univ. Pl.- 5th Ave.) NYC, NY 10003
Hours: 10-9 Mon-Sat • 12-8:30 Sun
• Importers of baskets, wicker items, bamboo, bamboo shades, mats, furniture, housewares, clothing, gift items. •

BASKETVILLE   802-387-4351
PO Box 710, Main St., Putney, VT 05346   802-387-5509
Hours: 8-6 every day
• Wide selection of oak and ash weave baskets, wooden buckets; wholesale catalog. •

BE SEATED   212-924-8444
66 Greenwich Ave., (6-7th Ave.) NYC, NY 10011
Hours: 11-7 Mon-Fri • 11-6 Sat
• Baskets, small rugs, decorative accessories, vintage fabrics, ikats, block print Indian fabrics. CREDIT CARDS. •

NANCY MOORE BESS, BASKETRY   212-691-2821
5 East 17th St. 6th Fl., (5th Ave.) NYC, NY 10003
Hours: by appt.
• Custom basketry and wicker constructions for props, display and theatrical events. •

CONNECTICUT ANTIQUE WICKER   203-666-3729
1052 Main St., Rear, (Cedar St.) Newington, CT 06111
Hours: 8-5 Mon-Sat call first
• Antique wicker from Victorian to Bar Harbour. See Henry or Maxine Spieske. •

CORNER HOUSE ANTIQUES   413-229-6627
N. Main St. (Rt. 7), (Old Mill Pond Rd.) Sheffield, MA 01257
Hours: open most days (call first)
• Antique wicker furniture. Also general selection of antiques and country accessories. See Kathleen or Thomas Tetro. •

A–B

DEUTSCH, INC. 212-683-8746
31 East 32nd St., (Madison-Park) NYC, NY 10016   (outside NY) 800-223-4550
Hours: 9-6 Mon-Fri • Sat by appt.   FAX 212-545-9877
• Over 800 items of wicker furniture and trunks; good prices; catalog. •

FRAN'S BASKET HOUSE 201-584-2230
295 Rt. 10, Succasunna, NJ 07876
Hours: 9-5:30 Mon-Fri (Thurs till 8:30) • 9:30-6 Sat • 12-5 Sun   201-584-7446
• Large selection wicker baskets, rattan and wicker furniture. •

THE GAZEBO 212-832-7077
127 East 57th St., (Park-Lexington Ave.) NYC, NY 10022
Hours: 10-7 Mon-Sat • 12-6 Sun   212-754-0571
• Quilts, wicker furniture, rag rugs, pillows and country home furnishings. RENTALS.
Expensive. •

K & D EXPORT–IMPORT 201-641-8300
25 Graphic Place, (Moonachie Rd.) Moonachie, NJ 07074   800-543-6969
Hours: 8:45-5:00 Mon-Fri   FAX 201-641-0277
• Limited selection of beautiful baskets; silk flowers and vegetables. Phone orders, catalog
available. CREDIT CARDS •

NATURAL FURNITURE WAREHOUSE 718-857-5967
604 Pacific St., (Flatbush Ave.) Brooklyn, NY 11217   718-857-5959
Hours: 10-7:30 Mon-Sat • 12-6 Sun
• Baskets, importer of wicker furniture and wicker items; cheap. •

PIER 1 IMPORTS 212-447-1610
461 Fifth Ave., (40th St.) NYC, NY 10016
Hours: 10-9 Mon-Fri • 10-6 Sat • 11-5 Sun
• Popular chain of stores carries baskets; wicker furniture and decorative items for the home.
Some lighting, clothing, frames. CREDIT CARDS •

PROPS FOR TODAY 212-206-0330
121-West 19th St. Reception: 3rd Fl., (6-7th Ave.) NYC, NY 10011
Hours: 8:30-5 Mon-Fri   FAX 212-924-0450
• Full service prop rental house. Collection of baskets, outdoor, garden & wicker furniture--
all periods. •
(See display ad under PROP RENTAL HOUSES.)

TODBURN ANTIQUES 203-226-3859
243 Post Road West, Westport, CT 06880
Hours: 10-5 Mon-Sat (call first)
• Antique wicker, country furniture, custom restoration. Speak to Donald Jobe or George
Anderson. •

WALTER'S WICKER, INC. 212-758-0472
979 Third Ave., (58-59th St.) NYC, NY 10022
Hours: 9-5 Mon-Fri   212-826-6775
• Wicker furniture and furnishings; RENTALS. •

WICKER GARDEN 212-410-7000
1318 Madison Ave., (93-94th St.) NYC, NY 10128
Hours: 10-5:30 Mon-Sat   FAX 212-348-0279
• Antique hand-painted furniture, old fashioned baby furniture, children's wear. •

"I found it in the N.Y. Theatrical Sourcebook."

WICKER OUTLET
201-731-1440

173 Main St., Orange, NJ 07052
Hours: 10-5 Mon-Sat (Thurs till 8)
• Wicker & rattan furniture and accessories. Discounts to the trade; delivery available. •

WICKER WAREHOUSE, INC.
201-342-6709

195 South River, Hackensack, NJ 07601
Hours: 10-6 Mon-Sat (Wed, Thurs till 9, April-June)

FAX   201-342-1495

• Wicker and rattan furniture, accessories, baskets. •

THE WICKERY
212-889-3669

342 Third Ave., (25th St.) NYC, NY 10010
Hours: 10:30-6:30 Mon-Fri • 10:30-6 Sat • 11-4 Sun
• Wicker baskets, hampers, trunks, shelf units, screens, furniture. •

BATHROOM ACCESSORIES

See also **HARDWARE, DECORATIVE**
See also **LINENS**
For fixtures, see **PLUMBING SUPPLIES & FIXTURES**

ELEGANT JOHN OF LEX
212-935-5800

812 Lexington Ave., (62-63rd) NYC, NY 10021
Hours: 10-6 Mon-Fri (Thurs till 7) • 10-6 Sat
• Bathroom hardware and accessories, towels, shower curtains, toilet seats, etc; expensive.
RENTALS •

GRACIOUS HOME
212-988-8990

1217 Third Ave., (70-71st St.) NYC, NY 10021
Hours: 9-7 Mon-Sat • 10:30-5:30 Sun   FAX   212-249-1534
• Good selection of bath accessories, faucets, hampers, towel bars, decorative hardware, bed linens, frames,and decorative items. CREDIT CARDS. •

JANOVIC PLAZA
212-627-1100
212-645-5454

161 Sixth Ave., (Spring St.) NYC, NY 10014
Hours: 9:30-6:30 Mon-Fri • 9-6 Sat • 11-5 Sun   FAX   212-691-1504

215 Seventh Ave. (22-23rd St.) NYC, NY 10011   212-645-5454
Hours: 7:30-6:30 Mon-Fri • 9-6 Sat • 11-5 Sun

1150 Third Ave. (67th St.) NYC, NY 10021   212-772-1400
Hours: 7:30-6:30 Mon-Fri • 8:5:45 Sat • 11-5 Sun

159 West 72nd St. (B'way-Columbus) NYC, NY 10023   212-595-2500
Hours: 7:30-6:15 Mon-Fri (Thurs till 7:45) • 9-4:45 Sat • 11-4:45 Sun
• Toilet seats, shower curtains, wallpaper, towels, towel bars, and other accessories. •

HOWARD KAPLAN ANTIQUES
212-674-1000

827-831 Broadway , (12-13th St.) NYC, NY 10003
Hours: 9-5 Mon-Fri   FAX: 212-228-7204
• Antique bathroom accessories and fixtures; French country furniture; expensive; RENTALS
CREDIT CARDS. •

LAYTNER'S LINEN SHOP   212-724-0180
   2270 Broadway, (82nd St.) NYC, NY 10024
   237 E. 86th St. (2-3rd Ave.) NYC, NY 10028
   Hours: 10-7:30 Mon-Fri • 10-6:30 Sat • 12-5 Sun
   • Towels, shower curtains, bath rugs, accessories. •

PROPS FOR TODAY   212-206-0330
   121 West 19th St. Reception: 3rd Fl., (6-7th Ave.) NYC, NY 10011
   Hours: 8:30-5 Mon-Fri   FAX   212-924-0450

Come to us first and we'll work with your budget!
• Vanity items, perfume bottles, shells, comb and brush sets, towels, candles, candlesticks, artificial flowers, vases, clocks, linens, towel bars, boudoir items, fans, figurines, hat boxes, luggage, cheval mirrors, dressing tables, and other bathroom accessories from Country/Antique to Modern/High Tech.
• Recently acquired collection from New York Shakespeare Festival and Nostalgia Alley - antiques and collectibles galore.
NOW ON 3 FLOORS! ONE STOP PROPPING.

   • Prop rental house with wide selection of bath accessories & dressing all styles and periods. •
   (See display ad under PROP RENTAL HOUSES.)

DECORATORS WHOLESALE HARDWARE/LEGS, LEGS, LEGS/M. WOLCHENK & SON, INC.
   16 East 30th St., NYC, NY 10016   212-696-1650
   Hours: 9-6 Mon-Fri • 9-4:30 Sat.   FAX   212-696-1664
   • Furniture legs, many shapes and sizes. Decorative hardware. Bathroom accessories.
   CREDIT CARDS •

BEAUTY SALON EQUIPMENT

For beauty supplies, see **HAIR SUPPLIES & WIGS**
                 see **MAKE-UP SUPPLIES**

JIQU TRADING COMPANY,, INC.   212-689-9738
   42 West 28th St., (5th-6th Ave.) NYC, NY 10001
   Hours: 9-5 Mon-Fri   FAX   212-684-0584
   • Asian import, human and artificial hair and wigs, also "fun" colored hair and wigs; beauty and nail supplies. •

LEXINGTON EQUIPMENT CO.   (office) 718-639-3420
   35-35 75th St., Jackson Heights, NY 11372
   Hours: 8:30-5 Mon-Fri call first
   • Sales and rental of beauty salon equipment. No credit cards. •

PRESTIGE BEAUTY SUPPLY   914-623-8079
   191 W. Rt. 59, Nanuet, NY 10954
   Hours: 9-6 Mon & Sat • 9-9 Tues & Fri • 11-5 Sun   FAX   914-623-5978
   • Beauty salon supply house, some equipment. MC/VISA •

RAY BEAUTY SUPPLY CO., INC.   212-757-0175
   721 Eighth Ave., (45th-46th St.) NYC, NY 10036   800-253-0993
   Hours: 9:30-6 Mon-Fri • 10:30-5 Sat   FAX   212-459-8918
   • Scissors, T-pins, hair dyes, top-stick, etc. Phone orders and shipping. See Bobby RENTALS
   CREDIT CARDS •

SALON INTERIORS 201-488-7888
151 Hudson St., Hackensack, NJ 07601 800-642-4205
Hours: 9-5 Mon-Fri (Mon till 8)
 • Beauty/barber salon furniture and equipment new and used; sinks, hair dryers, reception desks, seating. Purchase or rentals. Not far from the G.W. Bridge. •

TAKARA BELMONT 212-541-6660
17 West 56th St., (5th-6th Ave.) NYC, NY 10019
Hours: 9-5 Mon-Fri by appt. FAX 212-315-4598
 • Manufacturer of salon equipment; for salesmen, call in advance. No credit cards. •

UNITED BEAUTY SUPPLY 212-719-2324
49 West 46th St., (5th-6th Ave.) NYC, NY 10036
Hours: 9:30-5:45 Mon-Fri • 9:30-6:15 Thurs FAX 212-719-3894
 • Beauty salon supplies. Will sell small quantities. Phone orders. Will ship RENTALS
. CREDIT CARDS •

BICYCLES & ACCESSORIES

ANTIQUE RIDEABLE BICYCLE REPLICAS, INC. 510-769-0980
2329 Eagle Ave., Almeda, CA 94501
Hours: 8:30-5 Mon-Fri (PCT) FAX 510-521-7145
 • Rideable full size replicas of bicycles from 1800 - 1950; hi-wheels, 2, 3, and 4 wheel in wood or steel. Rental and sales; catalog and price list available. Contact Mel Barron. Ship worldwide. MC/VISA AMEX •

DIXON'S BICYCLE SHOP 718-636-0067
792 Union St., (7th Ave.) Brooklyn, NY 11215
Hours: 10-8 Mon-Sat • 11-6 Sun (Winter hours: 11-6 Mon-Sat)
 • Sales of new and used bikes. •

FRANK'S BIKE SHOP 212-533-6332
553 Grand St., (Jackson) NYC, NY 10002
Hours: 9-7 Mon-Sat • 10-6 Sun FAX 212-475-1584
 • Sales, repairs and rentals; also has exercise bikes. CREDIT CARDS •

GENE'S 79TH ST. DISCOUNT BICYCLES 212-249-9344
242 East 79th St., (2nd-3rd Ave.) NYC, NY 10021 (machine) 212-288-0739
Hours: 9:30-8 Mon-Fri • 9-7 Sat, Sun
 • Rental and sales of bikes, exercise equipment, skates. MC/VISA •

LARRY & JEFF'S BICYCLES PLUS 212-794-2929
1400 Third Ave., (79th-80th St.) NYC, NY 10021
Hours: 10-7 every day FAX 212-794-2978
 • Sales, service, repair, rentals of bicycles; fitness equipment. CREDIT CARDS •

METRO BICYCLE STORE   212-228-4344
    332 East 14th St., (1st Ave.) NYC, NY 10003
    1690 2nd Ave. (8th St.) NYC, NY 10128   212-722-2201
    546 Sixth Ave. (15th St.) NYC, NY 10011   212-255-5100
    360 W. 47th St. (9th Ave.) NYC, NY 10036   212-581-4500
    1311 Lexington Ave. (88th St.) NYC, NY 10028   212-427-4450
    231 W. 96th St. (B'way-Amsterdam) NYC, NY 10025 212-663-7531
    417 Canal St. NYC, NY 10013   212-334-8000
    Hours: 9:30-6 every day   FAX 212-581-4503
    • Very helpful with bike accessories. RENTALS CREDIT CARDS. •

STUYVESANT BICYCLE   212-254-5200
    349 West 14th St., (8th-9th Ave.) NYC, NY 10014   212-675-2160
    Hours: 9:30-6 Mon-Sat   FAX 212-645-7845
    • Rents to the trade. CREDIT CARDS •

BLACKBOARDS & BULLETIN BOARDS

See also **STATIONERY & OFFICE SUPPLIES**

AYWON CHALKBOARD, INC.   718-853-2300
    22 Canton Place, (Ocean Pkwy-Coney Island Ave.) Brooklyn, NY 11218
    Hours: 8-4:30 Mon-Fri   FAX 718-853-2303

Custom and volume manufacturers.

Chalkboards, Dry Marker Boards, Projection Screens,
Natural Slate, Portables, Tack Boards.

> **AYWON CHALKBOARD INC.**
> *Custom & Volume Mfrs.*

Servicing Architects and Designers.

    • Custom work. Also rolls of cork and cork tiles. •

BULLETIN BOARDS & DIRECTORY PRODUCTS, INC.   914-248-8008
    2986 Navajo St., Yorktown Heights, NY 10598
    Hours: 8-5 Mon-Fri   FAX 914-248-5150
    • All kinds of display boards; bulletin, chalk, directory, and menu. Catalog available; contact Jerry Martin. •

NEW YORK BLACKBOARD OF NEW JERSEY, INC.   201-926-1600
    83 Rt. 22, Hillside, NJ 07205
    Hours: 8:30-4 Mon-Fri
    • Chalkboards, marker boards, corkboards, directory boards. Also custom work. RENTALS. •

STATE SUPPLY   212-645-1430
    210 11th Ave., (24-25th St.) NYC, NY 10001
    Hours: 8:30-5 Mon-Fri
    • Prop rental house with selection of hanging & free standing blackboard and bulletin boards. See Jeff. RENTALS. •

BLACKSMITHING

RALPH CAUSARANO   718-726-2116
    31-57 Vernon Blvd., (31st Ave.) NYC, NY 11106
    Hours: 8-3 Mon-Fri
    • Good blacksmith; will fabricate to your designs; allow time. •

BLADE SHARPENING

EDGE GRINDING SHOP   201-943-4109
    388 Fairview Ave., (entrance on Lincoln St. at back of bldg.) Fairview, NJ 07022
    Hours: 6-2 Mon • 7-3 Tues • 7-5 Wed-Fri
    • Scissors and knives sharpened. Rents knives to butchers and restaurants. •

GRACIOUS HOME   212-517-6300
    1220 Third Ave., (70th-71st St.) NYC, NY 10021
    Hours: 9-7 Mon-Sat • 10:30-5:30 Sun
    • Knife and scissor sharpening while you wait, daily except Tues. and Wed. . CREDIT CARDS •

HENRY WESTPFAL & CO.   212-563-5990
    105 West 30th St., (6th-7th Ave.) NYC, NY 10001
    Hours: 9-6 Mon-Fri
    • Scissors, cutlery and blades sharpened; also leather working tools and sewing supplies.
    Distributors of swiss army knives. Sells scissors, knives. •

BLEACHERS, GRANDSTANDS & TENTS

CHAIR HIRE CO. OF PATERSON   201-772-4737
    381 E. First St., (Lee Place) Clifton, NJ 07011
    Hours: 8-4 Mon-Fri   FAX   201-777-6882
    • Bleachers, grandstands, platforms, staging, tables, chairs, podiums; rental only. Delivery
    available. •

FOUR SEASONS TENTMASTERS   (Days) 517-436-6246
    4221 Livesay Rd., Sand Creek, MI 49279   (Eve.) 517-436-6245
    Hours: 8-5 Mon-Fri
    • Canvas tipis, wall tents, marquees, lean-tos, and wedge tents. 20 years in the business. •

HOFFMAN CHAIR & TENT CO.   201-869-1700
    2111 83rd St., North Bergen, NJ 07047
    Hours: 10-4 Mon-Fri
    • Tents, bleachers, grandstands, tables, chairs; rental or purchase. Delivery available. •

P.J. MCBRIDE, INC..
                                                                           516-694-TENT
    410 Eastern Parkway, (Denton) Farmingdale, NY 11735   516-694-1939
    Hours: 8-5 Mon-Fri   FAX   516-694-1603
    • Long and short term rental for functional and scenic use. Delivery available. Contact Kevin
    McBride. •

A-B

NOMADIC STRUCTURES　　　　　　　　　　　201-589-7334
　　12 Chapel St. Newark, NJ 07105
　　Hours: 8-6 Mon-Fri　　　　　　　　　　FAX　201-589-7272

"fabric and architecture"
Architectural fabric structures
Custom fabric design & manufacturing

nomadic
structures

　　• Carry their own line of tents, cabanas, canopies, bags, covers, and tarps. Specialize in making custom fabric products; fabric ceilings, false walls, scrims •

SAFWAY STEEL PRODUCTS　　　　　　　　　　718-383-8400
　　370 Greenpoint Ave., (N. Henry-Russell) Brooklyn, NY 11222
　　Hours: 8:30-4:30 Mon-Fri　　　　　　　　FAX　718-383-8778
　　• Bleachers ladders, lifts and scaffolding; sales and rentals. Delivery available. MC/VISA •

BLUEPRINTING MACHINERY & SUPPLIES

For blue printers, see **PRINTING AND COPYING**

CHARRETTE DRAFTING SUPPLY CORP.　　　　　212-683-8822
　　215 Lexington Ave., (33rd St.) NYC, NY 10016　　FAX　212-683-9890
　　Hours: 8:30-7 Mon-Fri • 10-5 Sat • 12-5 Sun (closed Sun: June, July, Aug)
　　• Sell print machines and supplies; artists materials; catalog. Phone orders. Will deliver in Manhattan. Ship anywhere. •

GENERAL REPRODUCTION PRODUCTS　　　　　201-434-8368
　　118 Rt. 17 North, Upper Saddle River, NJ 07458
　　Hours: 9-5 Mon-Fri
　　• Lease and sell Diazo machines; provide maintenance and supplies. •

BOOKBINDING SERVICES & SUPPLIES

ALPHA-PAVIA BOOKBINDING CO., INC.　　　　　212-929-5430
　　601 West 26th St. 2nd Mezz., (11th Ave.) NYC, NY 10001
　　Hours: 9-5:30 Mon-Fri
　　• Bookbinders; also sell and rent fake bookbacks. •

BASICS CRAFT COMPANY　　　　　　　　　　212-679-3516
　　1201 Broadway 3rd Fl., (27th-28th St.) NYC, NY 10001
　　Hours: 9-5 Mon-Fri • 10-3 Sat　　　　　　FAX　212-679-3519
　　• Bookbinding and papermaking supplies. Also weaving and knitting supplies. Wholesale, retail. Catalog. •

JOHN GAILOR　　　　　　　　　　　　　　　212-243-5662
　　150 Varick St. 5th Fl., (Spring St.) NYC, NY 10013
　　Hours: 8:30-5 Mon-Fri
　　• Gold-leaf stamping of books, portfolios; die cutting, special orders. •

ANGELA SCOTT
212-431-5148
596 Broadway, (Houston-Prince St.) NYC, NY 10012
Hours: by appt.
• Custom bookbinding, portfolios, restorations, new bindings, cases, gold stamping. Will design for customers. •

TECHNICAL LIBRARY SERVICES, INC./TALAS
212-736-7744
213 West 35th St., 9th Fl., (7th-8th Ave.) NYC, NY 10001
Hours: 9-4:30 Mon-Fri (closed for lunch 11:30-1)
• Bookbinding and conservation supplies; acid-free papers and adhesives. •

BOOKS, FAKE

ALPHA-PAVIA BOOKBINDING CO., INC.
212-929-5430
601 West 26th St. 2nd Mezz., (11th St.) NYC, NY 10001
Hours: 9-5:30 Mon-Fri
• Fake bookbacks by the foot; sale or rentals. •

BOOKSTORES

ACANTHUS BOOKS
212-463-0750
54 W. 21st St. Room 908, (5th-6th Ave.) NYC, NY 10010
Hours: by appt.
FAX 212-463-0752
• Rare and out-of-print books, book rental for displays; posters and decorative prints. •

AMAZON VINEGAR & PICKLING WORKS DRYGOODS, LTD.
319-322-6800
2218 E. 11th St., Davenport, IA 52803
800-798-7979
Hours: 9-5 Mon-Fri
FAX 319-322-4003
• 19th century costume sources; catalog $2.00. Shoe & Boot catalog $5.00 first class mail. CREDIT CARDS •

APPLAUSE THEATRE & CINEMA BOOKS
212-496-7511
211 West 71st St., (B'way-West End Ave.) NYC, NY 10023
Hours: 10-8 Mon-Sat/12-6 Sun
• Theatre and film books, plays, with emphasis on British drama. International mail service. Publisher, out of print screen plays. •

ARGOSY BOOK STORES, INC.
212-753-4455
116 East 59th St., (Park-Lexington Ave.) NYC, NY 10022
Hours: 9-6 Mon-Fri • 10-5 Sat (Oct-April)
• Out-of-print books, maps, prints. •

ARTE PRIMITIVO, INC.
212-570-0393
3 East 65th St., (5th-Madison Ave.) NYC, NY 10021
Hours: 11-5 Mon-Fri • 11-3 Sat
• Books on Pre-Columbian cultures; new, rare, and out-of-print. •

BACKSTAGE, INC.
202-775-1488
2101 P. St. NW, (21st St.) Washington, DC 20037
Hours: 10-6 Mon-Wed • 10-7 Thurs • 10-6 Fri, Sat
• Large selection theatre books and scripts; quarterly newsletter on new releases; mail orders. •

BARNES & NOBLE BOOKSTORES, INC.   212-608-1023
199 Chambers St., (West Side Hwy.) NYC, NY 10007
Hours: 9-8 Mon-Thurs/9-4 Fri
• Bargain priced hardcover and paperbacks, art books, textbooks. Located in Manhattan Community College. CREDIT CARDS. •

105 Fifth Ave. (18th St.) NYC, NY 10003   212-807-0099
9:30-8 Mon-Fri • 9:30-6:30 Sat • 11-6 Sun
• Great prices on remainders, used textbooks, games, and auction catalogs. Also check sales annex across the street. CREDIT CARDS.

600 Fifth Ave. (48th St.) NYC, NY 10020   212-765-0590
Hours: 8:30-6:45 Mon-Fri • 9:45-6 Sat • 12-6 Sun
• Bargain prices hard cover and paperbacks, art books, located in Rockefeller Ctr. CREDIT CARDS.

BOOKS NIPPON   310-604-9701
1123 Dominquez St. Suite K, Carson, CA 90746
Hours: 9-6 Mon-Fri   FAX   310-604-1134
• Japanese and Oriental books, gifts; calligraphy, painting supplies. Catalog available. CREDIT CARDS •

BOOKS OF WONDER   212-989-3270
132 Seventh Ave., (18th) NYC, NY 10011
Hours: 11-7 Mon-Sat • 12-6 Sun
• Wonderful collection of new and antique children's books; no rental. Next door to children's clothing and toy boutique, City Kids. CREDIT CARDS •

CHOICES   212-794-3858
220 East 78th St., (2nd-3rd Ave.) NYC, NY 10021
Hours: 11-7 Tues-Fri • 11-6 Sat • 12-4 Sun (closed Sun,Mon in August.)
• Bookstore specializing in "12-step programs"(Alcoholics Anonymous, Overeaters Anonymous, etc.). Literature, gifts, posters, tapes. •

CITY BOOKS   212-669-8245
1 Centre St. #2223, (Chambers St.) NYC, NY 10007
Hours: 9-5 Mon-Fri
• The NYC government bookstore; NYC forms, maps, souvenirs. •

COLISEUM BOOKS, INC.   212-757-8381
1771 Broadway, (57th St.) NYC, NY 10019
Hours: 8-10 M • 8-11 Tu-Th • 8-11:30 F • 10-11:30 Sat • 12-8 Sun
• Current books of all description, large selection, remainders and sale books, cheap picture books. Magazines. CREDIT CARDS •

COMPLETE TRAVELLER BOOKSTORE   212-685-9007
199 Madison Ave., (35th St.) NYC, NY 10016
Hours: 9-7 Mon-Fri • 10-6 Sat • 12-5 Sun   FAX   212-982-7628
• Wide selection of travel books, maps and accessories. CREDIT CARDS •

B. DALTON, BOOKSELLERS   212-674-8780
396 Sixth Ave., (8th St.) NYC, NY 10011
Hours: 9:30-11 Mon-Sat • 12-8 Sun
666 Fifth Ave. (52nd St.) NYC, NY 10103   212-247-1740
Hours: 8:30-7 Mon-Fri • 9:30-6:30 Sat •12-6 Sun
• Current books. CREDIT CARDS •

DOUBLEDAY BOOK SHOP   212-223-3301
  Citicorp Center, (53rd-Lexington) NYC, NY 10022
  Hours: 8-7 Mon-Fri • 11-6 Sat
  724 Fifth Ave. (56-57th St) NYC, NY 10019   212-397-0550
  Hours: 9-10 Mon-Sat • 12-7 Sun
  • Good selection; very helpful locating books. •

DOVER PUBLICATIONS, INC..   212-255-3755
  180 Varick St., (King-Charlton) NYC, NY 10014
  Hours: 9-4:30 Mon-Fri
  11 East 2nd St., Mineola, NY 11501   516-294-7000
  Hours: 9-3 Mon-Fri
  • Retail store; catalogs; also has selection of damaged books for half-price. •

DRAMA BOOKS   415-255-0604
  134 9th St., San Francisco, CA 94103
  Hours: 10-5 Mon-Sat
  • Theatre books current and out-of-print; catalog. CREDIT CARDS •

DRAMA BOOK SHOP
                                                                    212-944-0595
  723 Seventh Ave. 2nd Fl., (48th-49th St.) NYC, NY 10019   800-322-0595
  Hours: 9:30-7 Mon-Fri (Wed till 8) • 10:30-5:30 Sat/12-5 Sun   FAX   212-921-2013
  • Huge selection of books on every aspect of the performing arts. CREDIT CARDS •
  (See display ad in this section.)

DRAMA BOOK PUBLISHERS   212-725-5377
  260 Fifth Ave., (28th-29th St.) NYC, NY 10001
  Hours: by appt.   FAX   212-725-8506
  • Publishers of theatrical books, British publications; good costume and make-up books; catalog. (Not a retail store.) •

FIRESIDE THEATRE BOOK CLUB   no phone
  401 Franklin Ave., Garden City, NY 11530
  Hours: mail order only
  • Book club featuring play scripts and selected theatrical books. •

FORBIDDEN PLANET   212-473-1576
  821 Broadway, (12th St.) NYC, NY 10003
  Hours: 10-7 Mon-Sat • (Thurs, Fri till 7:30) • 12-7 Sun
  • Science fiction, fantasy, comic books, magazines on special effects. •

SAMUEL FRENCH,, INC.   212-206-8990
  45 West 25th St., 2nd Fl., (B'way-6th Ave.) NYC, NY 10010-2751
  Hours: 9-5 Mon-Fri

  7623 Sunset Blvd., Hollywood, CA 90046   213-876-0570
  Hours: 10-6 Mon-Fri • 10-5 Sat
  • Comprehensive theatrical & film bookstore. Mostly scripts, catalog available. CREDIT
  CARDS •

FRENCH & EUROPEAN PUBLICATIONS, INC.   212-581-8810
  610 5th Ave., (49-50th St.) NYC, NY 10020
  Hours: 9:30-6:15 Mon-Sat
  • French and Spanish books; dictionaries and language learning aids for over 100 foreign languages; mail and phone orders taken. •

"I found it in the N.Y. Theatrical Sourcebook."

GOTHAM BOOK MART
41 West 47th St., (5th-6th Ave.) NYC, NY 10036   212-719-4448
Hours: 9:30-6:30 Mon-Fri • 9:30-6 Sat
• New and used books; 20th century literature, film, drama; helpful on the phone. CREDIT CARDS •

HACKER ART BOOKS
45 West 57th St., (5th-6th Ave.) NYC, NY 10019   212-688-7600
Hours: 9-6 Mon-Sat (closed Sat: June, July, Aug)   FAX 212-754-2554
• Current and out-of-print books. Very helpful staff. •

VICTOR KAMKIN, INC.
925 Broadway, (21st St.) NYC, NY 10010   212-673-0776
Hours: 9:30-5:30 Mon-Fri • 10-5 Sat
• Russian magazines and newspaper, Russian books in English, Russian gifts. •

KINOKUNIYA BOOKSTORE
10 West 49th St., (Rockefeller Plaza) NYC, NY 10020   212-765-1461
Hours: 10-7 :30 every day
• Books from and about Japan. •

LAW BOOK EXCHANGE, LTD.
135 West 29th St. 3rd Fl., (6th-7th Ave.) NYC, NY 10001   212-594-4341
Hours: 9-5 Mon-Fri (call first)
• Law books by the foot for sale. •

LIBRAIRIE DE FRANCE
610 Fifth Ave., (49th-50th St., Rockefeller Ctr.) NYC, NY 10020   212-581-8810
Hours: 9:30-6:15 Mon-Sat
• French books, magazines, newspapers, technical dictionaries, audio and video tapes, foreign language learning materials. •

McGRAW–HILL BOOKSTORE
1221 Sixth Ave., (48th-49th St.) NYC, NY 10020   212-512-4100
Hours: 10-5:45 Mon-Sat
• Mostly technical/science books, computer, business and engineering books. •

MORTON INTERIOR DESIGN BOOKSHOP
989 Third Ave., (59th St.) NYC, NY 10022   212-421-9025
Hours: 11-7 Mon-Sat
• Current books and magazines on interior design. •

NEW YORK BOUND BOOKSHOP / URBAN GRAPHICS
50 Rockefeller Plaza, (50th-51st St.) NYC, NY 10020   212-245-8503
Hours: 10-6 Mon-Fri • 12-4 Sat (closed Sat May-Aug.)
• Old maps of NYC, prints and photos relating to New York. •

NYNEX DIRECTORY CENTER
800-476-7337
216-394-3171
• Domestic and international phone books. Fedex overnight on U.S. books only. Ten day regular mail delivery on all other instock books. Business to Business, Street Address, Fax, 800 numbers, and national directory of addresses. •

"I found it in the N.Y. Theatrical Sourcebook."   **59**

PAGEANT BOOK & PRINT SHOP
212-674-5296
114 W. Houston (Sullivan-Thompson) NYC, NY 10012
Hours: Call for new hours

NO RENTAL TOO LARGE OR SMALL
ANY CENTURY AVAILABLE
NOTICE NEW LOCATION

> # PAGEANT
> BOOK and PRINT SHOP

• Rents books by subject area, by the foot; see Shirley Solomon. •

PAYSON HALL BOOKSHOP
617-484-2020
80 Trapelo Rd., Belmont, MA 02178
Hours: 12-5 Wed-Fri • 10-4 Sat
• Used and rare books and prints. •

PRINCETON ANTIQUE BOOKSERVICE
609-344-1943
29-17 Atlantic Ave., Atlantic City, NJ 08401
Hours: 9-5 Mon-Fri
• Book search service; will find out-of-print books. •

REFERENCE BOOK CENTER, INC.
212-677-2160
175 Fifth Ave., (23rd St.) NYC, NY 10010
Hours: 10-4 Mon-Fri
• Very helpful; good drama selection; catalog $2.00. •

RIZZOLI INTERNATIONAL BOOKSTORE
212-759-2424
31 West 57th St., (5th-6th Ave.) NYC, NY 10019
Hours: 9-8 Mon-Sat • 10:30-7:30 Sun
454 W. Broadway (Houston-Prince) NYC, NY 10012
212-674-1616
Hours: 11-11 Mon-Thurs • 11-Midnight Fri-Sat • 12-8 Sun
• Art, architecture, photography books; magazines. CREDIT CARDS •

RUBY'S BOOK SALE
212-732-8676
119 Chambers St., (Church-W. B'way) NYC, NY 10007
Hours: 10-6 Mon-Fri • 10-5:30 Sat
• Paperbacks, discounted coffee table books, secondhand magazines, discounted computer
books. •

SHAKESPEARE & CO. BOOKSELLERS
212-529-1330
716 Broadway, (Washington Pl.-W. 4th St.) NYC, NY 10003
Hours: 10am-11pm Sun-Thurs • 10am-midnight Fri, Sat
2259 Broadway (81st St) NYC, NY 10024
212-580-7800
Hours: 10-11:30 Sun-Thurs • 10-12:30 Fri-Sat
• Well stocked "general" bookstore; carries some books for all the performing arts. CREDIT
CARDS •

R.L. SHEP
707-937-1436
PO Box 668, Mendocino, CA 95460
Hours: 9-5 Mon-Fri • 9-1 Sat
FAX 707-937-3059
• Publisher of costume and tailoring books, also reprints of old books. Mail order only, free
brochure on request. •

SKY BOOKS INTERNATIONAL
212-688-5086
48 East 50th St. 2nd Fl., (Park-Madison Ave.) NYC, NY 10022
Hours: 10-7 Mon-Sat
• Large selection of aviation, military, naval and uniform books. •

STAR MAGIC   212-228-7770
  745 Broadway, (8th-Waverly Pl.) NYC, NY 10003
  Hours: 10-10 Mon-Sat • 11-9 Sun

  275 Amsterdam Ave., (73rd St) NYC, NY 10023   212-769-2020
  Hours: 10-10 Mon-Sat • 11-9 Sun

  1256 Lexington Ave,. (84-85th St.) NYC, NY 10028   212-988-0300
  Hours: 10-9 Mon-Sat • 11-7:30 Sun
    • Spaceflight books; star maps and finders, space related posters and materials. CREDIT
  CARDS •

RICHARD STODDARD PERFORMING ARTS   212-645-9576
  18 East 16th St. #305, (5th-Union Sq.) NYC, NY 10003
  Hours: 11-6 Mon, Tues, Thurs-Sat
    • Playbills; specializes in out-of-print theatre books, with special interest in scenic and cos-
  tume design. CREDIT CARDS •

STRAND BOOK STORE, INC.   212-473-1452
  828 Broadway, (12th St.) NYC, NY 10003
  Hours: 9:30-9:20 Mon-Sat • 11-9:30 Sun

  159 John St. (South St.-Front St.) NYC, NY 10038   212-809-0875
  Hours: 10-9 Mon-Sat • 11-88 Sun
    • Main store. Used books and remainders; cheap; will help find out-of-print art books CREDIT
  CARDS. •

THEATREBOOKS, LTD.   416-922-7175
  11 Saint Thomas St., Toronto, Ontario, CAN M5S2B7   800-361-3414
  Hours: 10-7 Mon-Fri • 10-6 Sat • 12-5 Sun   FAX 416-922-0739
    • The theatre, film and performing arts bookstore of Canada. Most British publications avail-
  able here earlier than in U.S. Catalog available will ship worldwide. •

THREE LIVES & COMPANY, LTD.   212-741-2069
  154 West 10th St., (Waverly Pl.) NYC, NY 10014
  Hours: 11-8 Mon-Sat • 1-7 Sun
    • Interesting art, architecture, garden/landscape, travel, and photography sections; will spe-
  cial order. •

TOKYO BOOKSTORE   212-697-0840
  521 Fifth Ave., (43rd-44th St.) NYC, NY 10175
  Hours: 10-7 Mon-Fri • 11-7 Sat • 1-5 Sun   FAX 212-983-1765
    • Japanese and Oriental books, gifts; calligraphy, painting supplies. CREDIT CARDS •

SAMUEL WEISER, INC.   212-777-6363
  132 East 24th St., (Park Ave. S.-Lexington Ave.) NYC, NY 10010
  Hours: 9-6 Mon-Wed • 10-7 Thurs-Fri • 9:30-5:30 Sat
    • Huge selection of books on religion and the occult, occult paraphernalia. •

WOODEN PORCH BOOKS   304-386-4434
  Rt. 1 Box 262SB, Middlebourne, WV 26149
  Hours: Phone orders 9-5 every day.   FAX 304-386-4868
    • Out-of-print and one of a kind books on fiber arts, costume, fashion, millinery, and kindred
  subjects; catalog. •

BRASS ITEMS

See also **ANTIQUES**
For Brass Hardware, see **HARDWARE: DECORATIVE**

ANNAPURNA FINE ARTS   212-696-4929
    120 Lexington Ave., (28th St.) NYC, NY 10016
    Hours: 10-7:30 Mon-Sat   FAX   212-696-0229
    • Brass statues, vases, trays, tables, boxes, pots, urns, giftware; imported from India.
    Catalog available. CREDIT CARDS •

BRASSCRAFTERS   800-645-1101
    4791 N.W. 157 St., Miami, FL 33014
    Hours: 9-5 Mon-Fri   FAX   305-685-7667
    • .Large selection of brass and silver items; candlesticks, candelabra, sconces, planters, arch
    pieces, pottery & greenware, silver items, accessories, and decorative hardware. Color catalog
    available. •

E BUK, ANTIQUES & ART   212-226-6891
    151 Spring St. 2nd Fl., (W. B'way-Wooster St.) NYC, NY 10012
    Hours: every day by appt.   **(toll call) 700-SCIENCE**
    • Many unusual antique brass objects and devices, drafting tools, microscopes, old locks and
    keys, scientific and nautical instruments, etc. •
    (See display ads under ANTIQUES: EUROPEAN & AMERICAN and under PROP RENTAL HOUSES.)

DECORATIVE CRAFTS, INC.   203-531-1500
    PO Box 4308, 50 Chestnut St., Greenwich, CT 06830   914-939-3403
    Hours: 9-5 Mon-Fri   800-431-4455
    • Imported brassware, Oriental screens, and furniture; catalog sales to the trade only. •

MAJESTIC REPRODUCTIONS CO., INC.   212-753-1883
    979 Third Ave., (58th-59th St.) NYC, NY 10022   212-753-1850
    Hours: 9-5 Mon-Fri
    • Repro brass and steel items.•

HYMAN E. PISTON ANTIQUES   212-753-8322
    1050 Second Ave., (55th-56th St.) NYC, NY 10022
    Hours: 10-4 Mon-Fri • 10-2 Sat (call first on Sat)
    • Tie backs, andirons; antique copper, brass, pewter items. •

BREAKAWAYS

JAUCHEM & MEEH, INC..   718-875-0140
    43 Bridge St., (Plymouth-Water) Brooklyn, NY 11201
    Hours: 9-5 Mon-Fri or by appt.   FAX   718-596-8329

Standard and custom breakaway glassware,
Sheet glass and specialty items.

> ## JAUCHEM & MEEH, INC.
>
> SPECIAL EFFECTS-SALES, RENTAL, DESIGN

(See display ad under SPECIAL EFFECTS SERVICES.)

"I found it in the N.Y. Theatrical Sourcebook."

— Wash —

A–B

SCENIC SPECIALTIES, INC.
232 7th St., (3rd-4th) Brooklyn, NY 11215   718-788-5379
Hours: 8:30-5 Mon-Fri by appt.   FAX   718-768-9173
• Breakaway furniture, frames and aluminum fabrication; custom props designed and built.
See Lou. •
(See display ad under ADHESIVES & GLUE)

SPECIAL EFFECTS UNLIMITED
PO Box 222, 18 Euclid Ave., Yonkers, NY 10705   914-965-5625
Hours: by appt.
• See Mrs. Drohan; custom orders. •

THEATRE MAGIC
6099 Godown Rd., Columbus, OH 43220   614-459-3222
Hours: 7:30-4:30 Mon-Fri
• Breakaway resin to mold your own bottles, glass, panes, etc. •

TRENGROVE STUDIOS, INC.   *247 W 30*
60 West 22nd St., (5th-6th Ave.) NYC, NY 10010   212-~~255-2857~~
Hours: 9-5 Mon-Fri   800-366-2857
• Breakaway bottles and glasses in stock. MC/VISA •   FAX   212-633-8982

12 —

BURLAP BAGS

AMERICAN NATIONAL BAG & BURLAP CO.
528 Bergen St., (Carlton-6th Ave.) NYC, NY 11217   718-857-8050
Hours: 8-5 Mon-Fri   FAX   718-789-3599
• Large or small orders. •

RACHMAN BAG CO.
7040 W. Palmetto Park Rd., Boca Raton, FL 33433   407-338-6255
Hours: 9-5 Mon-Fri   FAX   407-338-9994
• Burlap, canvas & poly bags made to order. Large or small orders. •

STATE SUPPLY EQUIPMENT & PROP, INC.
210 Eleventh Ave., (24th-25th St.) NYC, NY 10001   212-645-1430
Hours: 8:30-5 Mon-Fri   FAX   212-675-3131
• Various sizes, large or small orders. •

NOTES

Jim Jockle
485-9852

Scenic Specialties —
Co.—
718 788 5379
— 768-9173.

NOTES

"I found it in the N.Y. Theatrical Sourcebook."

CANDLES

CANDLE SHOP 212-989-0148
118 Christopher St., (Bleecker-Hudson St.) NYC, NY 10014
Hours: 12-8 Mon-Thurs • 12-9 Fri-Sat • 1-7 Sun
• Small store, good selection. CREDIT CARDS •

FAROY, INC. 212-679-1573
225 Fifth Ave., (26th-27th St.) NYC, NY 10010
Hours: 9-5 Mon-Fri   FAX 212-689-9755
• All types of candles including votive, wholesale only. •

HOUSE OF TALISMANS 212-281-8070
545 West 145th St., (B'way-Amsterdam Ave.) NYC, NY 10031
Hours: 10-7 Mon-Sat
• Many varieties of candles; wholesale, $10 minimum. MC/VISA •

KERVAR, INC. 212-564-2525
119 West 28th St., (6th-7th Ave.) NYC, NY 10001
Hours: 6:30-3 Mon-Fri   FAX 212-594-0030
• Tapered candles by the dozen, silk flowers, floral supplies. •

PARAMOLD 516-589-5454
90 Bourne Blvd., (Smithtown Ave.) Sayville, NY 11782
Hours: 9-5 Mon-Fri   FAX 516-589-1232
• Variety of candles, sold by the case. Manufacturer. •

PARTY BAZAAR 212-695-6820
390 Fifth Ave., (36th St.) NYC, NY 10018
Hours: 8-6 Mon-Wed • 8-8 Thurs • 8-7 Fri • 9:30-6 Sat • 12-5 Sun   FAX 212-643-9462
• Candles; good selection of party goods. CREDIT CARDS •

CANDY

BIG APPLE ICE CREAM 212-777-6309
81 East 3rd St., (1st-2nd Ave.) NYC, NY 10003
Hours: 8-5 every day   FAX 718-273-8861
• Carries 3 gallon tubs of ice cream; also a Schraffts distributor. •

ECONOMY CANDY CORP. 212-254-1531
108 Rivington, (Essex-Ludlow St.) NYC, NY 10002   800-352-4544
Hours: 8-6 Sun-Fri • 10-5 Sat
• All types of candy, chocolate, nuts, dried fruit, wholesale or retail free catalog, $25 minimum for shipping. CREDIT CARDS •

THE SWEET LIFE 212-598-0092
63 Hester St., (Ludlow St.) NYC, NY 10002
Hours: 9-6 Sun-Fri   FAX 212-598-0092
• Candies, dried fruits, nuts, coffees; sells large lollipops, holiday items; old fashioned, hard to find items. Will ship or use local courier. •

J. WOLSK
212-475-7946
8 Ludlow St., (Broome-Delancey) NYC, NY 10002
212-475-0704
Hours: 9-4:45 Sun-Thurs • 9-2 Fri
• Specialty gifts and gift baskets, wholesale and retail candy, nuts, dried fruits, chocolates. Price list on request. CREDIT CARDS •

CASKETS

R. CONTE
212-534-1416
16 Harrison Ave, Yonkers, NY 10705
Hours: 8-5 Mon-Sat
FAX 914-376-3734
• Pine boxes to the most elaborate. RENTALS •

CASTING, CUSTOM

See also **PROP & SCENIC CRAFTS PEOPLE**
See also **SPECIAL EFFECTS SERVICES**

ALLIED INSULATION CORP.
908-390-8200
20 George St., South River, NJ 08882
Hours: 8-5 Mon-Fri
• Portable spray foam equipment for on-site work; see George Reha. •

AMERICAN ALUMINUM & BRONZE FOUNDRY
718-392-2340
51-25 35th St., (Greenpoint Ave.-VanDam) L.I.C., NY 11101
Hours: 7-3 Mon-Fri
• Castings in aluminum and bronze. •

ARGOS ART CASTING FOUNDRY
914-278-2454
Rt. 312, RD 2, Brewster, NY 10509
Hours: 8-4:30 Mon-Fri
FAX 914-278-6769
• Fine quality art casting in bronze aluminum, silver, pewter, stainless and regular steel. •

AMTEC INTERNATIONAL
516-821-2022
PO Box 527, E. Setauket, NY 11733
Hours: 9-5 Mon-Fri
• Professional polyurethane foam spraying; uniform carvable foam; contact Al. •

DURA-FOAM PRODUCTS, INC.
718-894-2488
63-02 59th Ave., Maspeth, NY 11378
Hours: 8-4:30 Mon-Fri
FAX 718-894-2493
• Fabrication of original designs, laminations and metallic finishes. Price quotes on request. No minimum. No catalog. •
(See display ad under FOAM SHEETING & SHAPES.)

A. HAUSSMANN INTERNATIONAL CORP.
415-431-1336
132 Ninth St, San Francisco, CA 94103
Hours: 8-4 Mon-Fri
• Full line of high quality scenic paints, dyes, and brushes; also casting materials and weave fillers. •

GABRIEL PETRELLA 718-852-1656
196 Fourth Ave. 2nd Fl., (Sackett-DeGraw) Brooklyn, NY 11217
Hours: 8-4:30 Mon-Fri
• Casting, mold making, fiberglass and plaster. •

ROCCA NOTO 718-937-1977
10-06 38th Ave., (10-11th) L.I.C., NY 11101
Hours: 9-5 Mon-Fri FAX 718-937-7237
• Sculpture casting, mold making (large), bronze casting, also fairly large acrylic casting. •

SEAL REINFORCED FIBERGLASS 516-842-2230
23 Bethpage Rd., Copiague, NY 11726
Hours: 8:30-5 Mon-Fri FAX 516-842-2276
• Custom fiberglass casting; speak to Tom Kales. •

WESTCHESTER FIBERGLASS 914-939-5543
55 Purdy Ave., Port Chester, NY 10573
Hours: 9-6 Mon-Sat
• Fiberglass ornament, custom casting; ask for Don. •

M.B. WINSTON 718-388-1500
300 RICHARDSON ST., (KINGSLAND-DEBEVOISE) BROOKLYN, NY 11222
Hours: 8-5 Mon-Fri FAX 718-388-1968
• Custom fiberglass & casting, also models & molds. •

LAWRENCE WITTMAN & CO., INC. 516-842-4770
1395 Marconi Blvd., Copiague, NY 11726 800-439-2000
Hours: 8:30-5:30 Mon-Fri FAX 516-842-4790
• Fiberglass custom molded scenery, props, special and stock shapes; architectural reproductions. Contact Charles Wittman. •

CASTING & MODELING SUPPLIES

See also **MAKE-UP SUPPLIES**
For alginate & plaster bandages **MEDICAL & SCIENTIFIC EQUIPMENT & SUPPLIES: DENTAL**

ALCONE CO., INC. 718-361-8373
5-49 49th Ave., (56th-Vernon) L.I.C., NY 11101
Hours: 9:30-4 Mon-Fri FAX 718-729-8296
• Celastic, foam latex. Theatrical supply house; catalog, $5. (Subway #7 to L.I.C. Vernon/Jackson stop.) •

BJB ENTERPRISES 714-554-4640
13912 Nautilus Dr., Garden Grove, CA 92643
Hours: 8-4 Mon-Fri
• Flexible, castable plastics; flexible urethane foams; various colors and clear; Skin-Flex (for artificial skin and foods). Catalog and phone orders. •

BURMAN INDUSTRIES 818-782-9833
14141 Covello St. Suite G-A, Van Nuys, CA 91405
Hours: 8:30-5 Mon-Fri • 10-3 Sat. FAX 818-782-2863
• Complete line of casting and moldmaking supplies specifically geared to SPFX industries; distributor of BJB products, latex, foam latex, flexible paint, gypsum products, adhesives for latex. Catalog available. •

CEMENTEX LATEX CORP.
480 Canal St., (Hudson) NYC, NY 10013
Hours: 9-5 Mon-Fri

212-226-5832
800-782-9056
FAX 212-334-8349

• Molding and casting compounds.
• Latex for coating polystyrene and casting flexible props.
• Polysul Fixes.
• Polyurethane and Silicon Rubber.

• Good selection of coating, casting, and molding supplies, 88 page catalog, phone orders •

CERAMIC SUPPLY OF NY & NJ, INC.
534 La Guardia Pl, (Bleeker-3rd) NYC, NY 10012
Hours: 9-6 Mon-Fri • 10-5 Sat

212-475-7236

7 Rt 46 West, Lodi, NJ 07644
Hours: 9-5 Mon-Fri

201-340-3005
800-723-7262

• Casting plaster, potter's plaster, ceramic materials and supplies. Use the 800 number for deliveries. •

CHAVANT, INC.
42 West Street, Red Bank, NJ 07701
Hours: 8-3:30 Mon-Fri for shipping orders

908-842-6272
800-cha-vant
FAX 908-842-3621

• Manufacturer and distributor of industrial modeling clay. Will ship small quantities. Contact Jack North. MC/VISA •

CHICAGO LATEX PRODUCTS
1030 Morse Ave., Shaumburg, IL 60193
Hours: 9-5 Mon-Fri

708-893-2880

Chicago Latex is a leading manufacturer of latex casting and molding latex. We have heavy duty high density mold rubber and a variety of portable slip casting latexes to suit any purpose. All compounds are one-part, no-mixing, non-toxic, and they're safe and simple to use. For over 45 years, we have provided latex compounding to doll makers, set & prop makers, figurine & statuary designers and museum reproduction artists.
Casting and modeling compounds; including rigid casting latex #501.

• Casting and molding supplies; including rigid casting latex #501. Catalog and brochures, phone orders. •

CITY CHEMICAL
132 West 22nd St., (6th-7th Ave.) NYC, NY 10011
Hours: 9-4:30 Mon-Fri (closed for lunch 12-1)

212-730-8011

• Stearic acid. •

DEFENDER INDUSTRIES
255 Main St., New Rochelle, NY 10801
Hours: 9-5:45 Mon-Fri • 9-2:45 Sat

914-632-3001
FAX 914-632-6544

• Fiberglass cloth, mat, polyester & epoxy resins; marine supplies. $25 minimum. Phone orders accepted. CREDIT CARDS. •

C–D

DOUGLAS & STURGES   415-421-4456
730 Bryant St., San Francisco, CA 94107
Hours: 8:30-5 Mon-Fri (closed for lunch 12:30-1:30)
• Large selection of pigments, colorants, resin, glass products, mold materials; contact Arty. Catalog, phone orders. •

DURA–FOAM PRODUCTS, INC.   718-894-2488
63-02 59th Ave., Maspeth, NY 11378
Hours: 8-4:30 Mon-Fri   FAX   718-894-2493
• Large selection of flexible and rigid urethane foam in a variety of sizes, shapes, and colors, also foam rubber and adhesives. No minimum. No catalog •
(See display ad under FOAM SHEETING & SHAPES.)

ETI / ENVIRONMENTAL TECHNOLOGIES, INC.   707-443-9323
PO Box 365, Fields Landing, CA 95537
Hours: 8-4:30 Mon-Fri
• Manufacturer of natural latex, polyester casting resin, epoxy finishes, adhesives, pigments and dyes. Brochures, call for local distributors. •

SAM FLAX ART SUPPLIES   212-620-3038
12 W. 20th St., (5th-6th Ave.) NYC, NY 10011
Hours: 9-6:30 Mon-Fri • 10-5 Sat • 12-5 Sun   FAX   212-929-3837
425 Park Ave., (55th St) NYC, NY 10022   212-620-3060
Hours: 9-6 Mon-Fri • 10-5 Sat
• Casting rubber, moulage, art supplies. •

FRP SUPPLY, DIV. ASHLAND CHEMICAL, INC.   201-288-7900
120 North St., Teterboro, NJ 07608   212-695-8135
Hours: 9 -5 Mon-Fri
• Distributors of fiberglass mat and cloth, polyester resin, gel coats, dyes, releases, and catalyst. No catalogs. •

GOUGEON BROS., INC.   517-684-7286
100 Paterson St., Bay City, MI 48706
Hours: 8-5 Mon-Fri
• Boat epoxy and dispensers; manufacturer. •

DAVID HAMBURGER, INC.   718-852-7101
410 Hicks St., (Baltic-Warren) Brooklyn, NY 11201
Hours: 9-5 Mon-Fri   FAX   718-797-4575
• Supplier of celastic. Manufacturer and distributor of theatrical, display materials, and animated figures. Catalog. Phone orders welcome. •

HAPCO, INC.   617-826-8801
353 Circuit Street, Hanover, MA 02339
Hours: 8:30-5:00 Mon-Thur • 8:30-3 Fri.   FAX   617-826-9544
• Casting materials, broad selection, primarily urethane, also synwood (stable solid surface material). Catalog available. •

HEVEATEX   508-675-0181
PO Box 2573, 106 Ferry St., Fall River, MA 02722
Hours: 8:30-4:30 Mon-Fri
• Manufacturer of latex for molds, masks, balloons, shipping takes a week; flier; contact Bruce Hoitt. •

INDUSTRIAL ARTS SUPPLY CO.   612-920-7393
 5724 West 36th St., (near Hwy. 100) Minneapolis, MN 55416
 Hours: 8:30-5 Mon-Fri
  • Distributor of Water-extended polyester: fires with hydrogen peroxide, briefly flexible.
 Brochures, phone orders •

INDUSTRIAL PLASTICS   212-226-2010
 309 Canal St., (B'way-Mercer St.) NYC, NY 10013
 Hours: 9:00-5:30 Mon-Fri • 9:00-4 Sat
  • Two-part rigid urethane, RTV, resins, dyes, fiberglass. •

KINOT COLLINS CO.   800-321-3170
 2651 Elmwood Ave., Cleveland, OH 44111   216-252-4122
                                                                    FAX   216-252-5639
 PO Box 43 Highland Sta., Springfield, Ma 01109   800-628-8967
 Hours: 8-5 Mon-Fri   413-739-9666
  • Pattern & foundry supplies, rubber, silicone, adhesives, woods for carving. catalog. •

MILLENIUM RUBBER COMPANY,, INC.   603-883-6738
 Webb Dr., Merrimack, NH 03054
 Hours: 9-5 Mon-Fri
  • Manufacturer of silicone rubber mold materials including MRC 250, which has superior tear
 resistance; also RTV rubber. Flier. No minimum •

MILLIKEN CHEMICAL CO.   803-573-1587
 P.O. Box 1927, Spartanburg, SC
 Hours: 8-5 Mon-Fri   FAX   803-573-2430
  • Dispersion dyes for polyurethane casting material. 5 gallon minimum. •

MONSANTO, PLASTICS AND RESINS DIV.   800-325-4330
 800 North Lindberg Blvd., St. Louis, MO 63167
 Hours: 7:30-5:15 Mon-Fri
  • Manufacturer of raw materials. Call for product information. •

MUTUAL HARDWARE CORP.   718-361-2480
 5-45 49th Ave., (Vernon) L.I.C., NY 11101
 Hours: 8:30-5 Mon-Fri   FAX   718-729-8296
  • Celastic, also scenic supplies. •

MYDRIN,, INC.   213-724-6161
 5901 Telegraph Rd., Commerce, CA 90040
 Hours: 8-5 Mon-Fri
  • Foam latex, some coloring for latex; RDL (foam). No catalog, custom orders only. •

NORTHWEST FIBRE-GLASS,, INC.   612-781-3494
 3055 Colombia Ave. NE, Minneapolis, MN 55418
 Hours: 8:30-5 Mon-Fri
  • Flexible and rigid urethane foam, fiberglass, casting resins, color pastes; catalog. No minimum •

PERMAGILE INDUSTRIES   516-349-1100
 101 Commercial Street, Plainview, NY 11803
 Hours: 9-5 Mon-Fri   FAX   516-349-1156
  • Silicones, urethanes, epoxies (including water clear, will adjust properties to suit needs).
 MRTV 10 and MRTV 1; very flexible, available as thixotropic paste for large glove type molds.
 Catalog available. •

PHX,, INC.   414-383-8351
6161 N. 64th Street, Milwaukee, WI 53218
Hours: 7-5 Mon-Fri
• Molding latex, specialty latex and adhesive compounding; Phone orders. Formerly Wisconsin Latex and Adhesives. •

PINK HOUSE STUDIOS   802-524-7191
35 Bank Street, St. Albans, VT 05478
Hours: 9-5 Mon-Fri
• Supplies for mold making, catalog and instructional video available. •

PLASTIC ADHESION TECHNOLOGY,, INC.   800-678-9190
PO Box 1366, Eatontown, NJ 07724   (technical assistance) 908-542-2320
Hours: 8:30-5:30 Mon-Fri
• Contact Tom Peterson. Brochure and sample kits available. •

PLASTIC TOOLING SUPPLY   800-327-8787
303 Commerce Drive, Exton, PA 19341   215-363-5440
Hours: 8:30-4:30 Mon-Fri   FAX   215-524-1004
• Silicones (GI 1000, Dow), epoxy, urethane, adhesive, fiberglass cloth, kevlar, carbon fiber, US gypsum products, Renshape 450 (solid surface materials), supplies. Catalog available. •

POLYCOAT SYSTEMS,, INC.   518-747-0654
5 Depot St., Hudson Falls, NY 12839
Hours: 8-5 Mon-Fri
• Rigid polyurethane spray foam systems. Coatings and equipment. Catalog available. •

POLYTEK DEVELOPMENT CORP.   908-534-5990
PO Box 384, Lebanon, NJ 08833
Hours: 8:30-4:30 Mon-Fri
• Manufacturer of rubber mold products, plastic tooling compounds; contact Robert LeCompte. Brochure available, no minimum. •

RAILROAD WAREHOUSE   908-531-1880
75 Monmouth Rd., Oakhurst, NJ (Showroom)
Hours: by appt.   FAX   908-493-2089
• Casting and modeling supplies; catalog available. Also custom train makers, contact Barry. Minimum $100. •

ROSE BRAND TEXTILE FABRICS   212-494-7424
517 West 35th St., (10-11th Ave.) NYC, NY 10001   800-223-1624
Hours: 8:30-5 Mon-Fri   212-629-4826
• Specialty coatings and adhesives including Phlexglu, Sculpt-or-Coat and Plastic Varnish. New: Foamcoat. Also available: paint test kits. CREDIT CARDS •
(See display ad under CURTAINS & DRAPERIES: THEATRICAL)

RUDOLPH BROTHERS & CO.   614-833-0707
PO Box 425 Canal Winchester, OH 43110
Hours: 7:30-5:30 Mon-Fri   FAX   614-833-0456
• Distributor of specialty formulated chemical resins and adhesives for casting & moldmaking. •

SCULPTOR'S SUPPLIES CO.   212-673-3500
222 East 6th St., (2nd-3rd Ave.) NYC, NY 10003
Hours: 9-6 Mon-Fri • 10-3 Sat
• Tools, materials, bases; will mount sculpture. •

SCULPTURAL ARTS COATING,, INC.
PO Box 13113, Greensboro, NC 27415
Hours: 9-5 Mon-Fri

919-621-7379
800-743-0379
FAX   919-621-7379

Distributor of SCULPT OR COAT®, a non-toxic plastic cream:
• Plastic coating for polystyrene scenery & foam rubber.
• Transparent weave filler.
• Toughening coat for breakables.
• Binder for textural materials.
• Dries clear.
• Accepts colorants readily.

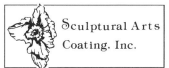

  • Call for more information or product brochure. •

SCULPTURE HOUSE CASTING
155 West 26th St., (6th-7th Ave.) NYC, NY 10001
Hours: 8-6 Mon-Fri • 10-4 Sat

212-645-9430

  • Plaster and metal statuary, busts, casting and sculpting tools and supplies. •

SCULPTURE HOUSE,, INC.
30 East 30th St., (Park-Madison Ave.) NYC, NY 10016
Hours: 10-4 Mon-Fri

212-679-7474

  • Sculpture tools, clay, moulage, plaster, molding and casting supplies. •

SEAL REINFORCED FIBERGLASS
23 Bethpage Rd., Copiague, NY 11726
Hours: 8:30-5 Mon-Fri

516-842-2230

FAX   516-842-2276

  • Hand-held polyester spray and pour equipment; speak to Tom Kaler. •

SEALOFLEX,, INC.   803-552-8352
  2516 Oscar Johnson Dr., Charleston, SC 29405
  Hours: 8-5 Mon-Fri
  • Manufacturer and distributor of water-base products that are hard and paintable; contact Richard Daniel. No minimum, brochure available. •

SILICONES, INC.   800-533-8709
  P.O. Box 363, High Point, NC 27261   910-886-5018
  Hours: 8:30-5 Mon-Fri   FAX 910-886-7122
  • Manufacturer of GI 1000 and other silicone. Catalog available. •

SLIDE PRODUCTS   708-541-7220
  PO Box 156, 430 S. Wheeling Rd., Wheeling, IL 60090   800-323-6433
  Hours: 8:30-5 Mon-Fri
  • Many types of mold releases; even one for foods. Minimum order: 12 can box. •

SMOOTH-ON   (ext. 72) 908-647-5800
  1000 Valley Rd., Gillette, NJ 07933
  Hours: 8:45-5:15 Mon-Fri   FAX 908-604-2224

Flexible mold compounds for pourable and brush-on applications.

Flexible and rigid casting compounds for special effects and prop making.

  • Free samples, literature and technical help available. $20. minimum order. •

STEPAN CHEMICAL CO., URETHANE DEPT.   708-446-7500
  22 West Frontage Rd., Northfield, IL 60093
  Hours: 8:30-5 Mon-Fri
  • Manufacturer of rigid and flexible urethane foam; 55 gal. drums. •

UNNATURAL RESOURCES,, INC.   201-891-4230
  14 Forest Ave., Caldwell, NJ 07006   (orders) 800-992-5540
  Hours: 9-6 Mon-Fri by appt.   FAX   201-226-8106
  • Thermoplastics in mesh, solid, perforated sheets, skin-like and textured fabrics, even a putty material you can mold, in white and colors. Also coatings for foam and latexes. Two part urethane foam systems; hand mixable, flexible, rigid, self skinning; castable latex; coatings for foams. Speak to Loretta. •
  (See display ad in this section.)

ZELLER INTERNATIONAL LTD.   800-722-USFX
  Main St., Box Z, Downsville, NY 13755 (factory)   212-627-7676
  Hours: 9-5 Mon-Fri   FAX   607-363-2071

Renowned for non-toxic, 1:1 moldmaking & casting systems EZ PLASTIC® and FLESHTEX®. Flexible paints and coatings, adhesives & glues, foams, Zello®, Thermogel®, Zelthane®. Major supplier for film FX. Mail order catalog.

ACADEMY AWARD WINNER
zeller
State - of - the - Art
Products & technology

  • Special effects consultation and services. RENTALS •

CHINA, CRYSTAL & GLASSWARE

See also **ANTIQUES; ALL HEADINGS**
See also **DEPARTMENT STORES**
See also **KITCHEN EQUIPMENT: HOUSEHOLD**
See also **KITCHEN EQUIPMENT: INDUSTRIAL**
See also **PARTY GOODS**

ACE IN THE HOLE   212-769-8711
    520 Amsterdam Ave., (85th St.) NYC, NY 10024
    Hours: 11-8 Mon-Fri • ll-7 Sat • 12-6 Sun
     • Good selection of old glassware and silverware; sets and singles; reasonable. •

BACCARAT,, INC.   212-826-4100
    625 Madison Ave., (58th-59th St.) NYC, NY 10022
    Hours: 10-6 Mon-Sat
     • Crystal, china. Expensive. CREDIT CARDS •

BROADWAY BAZAAR   212-873-9153
    2025 Broadway, (69th St.) NYC, NY 10023

    Second Ave. Bazaar   212-683-2293
    501 Second Ave. (28th St.) NYC, NY 10016

    Third Ave. Bazaar   212-861-5999
    1362 Third Ave. (77th St.) NYC, NY 10021

    West 3rd St. Bazaar   212-673-4138
    125 W. 3rd St. (6th Ave.) NYC, NY 10012
    Hours: 10-6:30 Mon-Sat • 11-5:45 Sun
     • Modern glassware, kitchenware, furniture, lamps, picture frames, accessories. CREDIT
    CARDS •

CARDEL LTD.   212-753-8880
    621 Madison Ave., (58th-59th St.) NYC, NY 10022
    Hours: 9:30-6 Mon-Sat
     • Large selection of fine crystal, china, silverware, porcelain collectibles, and pewter; Nice
    people. RENTALS CREDIT CARDS •

CENTRAL PROPERTIES OF 49TH STREET
514 West 49th St., (10th Ave.) NYC, NY 10019   212-265-7767
Hours: 8-5 Mon-Fri   212-582-3746

Fine china, crystal and tableware from such names as Lenox, Mikasa, Spode, Fitz and Floyd and many more! Theme decor and accessories for complete restaurant and banquet settings.

     • Prop rental house with selection of china & glassware. RENTALS •
    (See display ad under PROP RENTAL HOUSES.)

CERAMICA GIFT GALLERY   212-354-9216
    1009 Sixth Ave., (37th-38th St.) NYC, NY 10018
    Hours: 9:30-5:30 Mon-Fri (Thur until 7) • 12-5 Sat
     • Fine china, crystal, porcelain, collectibles; see Shlomo; will ship anywhere. •

FISHS EDDY　　　　　　　　　　　　　　　　　　212-420-9020
　889 Broadway, (19th St.) NYC, NY 10003
　Hours: 10-8 Mon-Fri • 11-7 Sun

　551 Hudson St., (Perry) NYC, NY 10014　　　　212-627-3956
　2176 Broadway (77th St.) NYC, NY 10024　　　212-873-8819
　Hours: 11-10 Mon-Thurs • 11-11 Fri-Sat • 12-10 Sun
　• Interesting selection of china and glassware including restaurant dishes. •

GEORG JENSEN SILVERSMITHS　　　　　　　　212-759-6457
　683 Madison Ave., (61st-62nd St.) NYC, NY 10021
　Hours: 9:30-5:30 Mon-Sat
　• China, crystal, glassware of Scandinavian design. CREDIT CARDS •

LA TERRINE　　　　　　　　　　　　　　　　　212-988-3366
　1024 Lexington Ave., (73rd St.) NYC, NY 10021
　Hours: 10:30-6 Mon-Sat
　• Tabletop ceramics, linens, glassware; RENTALS CREDIT CARDS •

MAYHEW　　　　　　　　　　　　　　　　　　212-759-8120
　507 Park Ave., (59th-60th St.) NYC, NY 10022
　Hours: 9:30-5:30 Mon-Fri • 10-5:30 Sat
　• China, crystal, ceramic and porcelain statues; also outdoor furniture. RENTALS •

ARIS MIXON & CO.　　　　　　　　　　　　　212-724-6904
　381 Amsterdam Ave., (78th-79th St.) NYC, NY 10024
　Hours: 12-7 Mon-Fri • 11-6 Sat • 1-5:30 Sun (closed Sun in Aug.)
　• Some antique glassware and silverware; sets and singles; decorative accessories and
　gifts. •

PLATYPUS　　　　　　　　　　　　　　　　　212-219-3919
　126 Spring St., (Wooster St.) NYC, NY 10012
　Hours: 11-6 Mon-Sat
　• Unique china selection as well as coffee and tea related items. •

POTTERY BARN　　　　　　　　　　　　　　　212-206-8118
　231 Tenth Ave., (24th St.) NYC, NY 10011 (main store)
　Hours: 11-6 Mon-Fri • 11-5 Sat

　700 B'way, (4th St.) NYC, NY 10003　　　　　212-505-6377
　Hours: 11-9 Mon-Sat • 12-7 Sun

　51 Greenwich Ave., (6-7 Ave.) NYC, NY 10014　212-807-6321
　Hours: 11-8 Mon-Sat • 12-6 Sun

　100 Seventh Ave., (16th St.) NYC, NY　　　　212-633-8405
　Hours: 10-8 Mon-Fri • 10-7 Sat • 12-6 Sun

　250 W. 57th St., (8th Ave.) NYC, NY 10019　　212-315-1855
　Hours: 10-8 Mon-Fri • 10-7 Sat • 12-6 Sun

　117 E. 59th St., (Lex.-Park) NYC, NY 10022　　212-753-5424
　Hours: 10-6:30 Mon-Sat (Thurs to 8) • 12-5 Sun

　2109 B'way, (73-74th St.) NYC, NY 10023　　　212-595-5573
　Hours: 10-8 Mon-Fri • 10-7 Sat • 12-6 Sun
　• Good selection of contemporary china, glassware, decorative accessories, and cookware;
　also some housewares, frames and furnishings. •

THE PROP COMPANY KAPLAN & ASSOCIATES
212-691-7767
111 West 19th St. 8th Fl., (6th-7th Ave.) NYC, NY 10011   **212-691-PROP**
Hours: 9-5:30 Mon-Fri   FAX **212-727-3055**
• Fine china, crystal, candlesticks, tableware, decorative accessories. Antique, contemporary, ethnic. Nice collection of antique kitchenware. Very good for styling and table top. Contact Maxine Kaplan. RENTALS •
(See display ad under PROPS RENTAL HOUSE)

PROPS FOR TODAY
212-206-0330
121 West 19th St.: Reception 3rd Fl., (6th-7th Ave.) NYC, NY 10011
Hours: 8:30-5 Mon-Fri   FAX **212-924-0450**

Come to us first and we"ll work with your budget!
• Dishes and tabletop accessories from Country/Antiques to Modern/High Tech.
• Recently acquired collection of china and glass from Nostalgia Alley.
• Great selection of restaurant china and glass.
• The latest high tech, craft and modern patterns - formal and informal.
• Porcelain, period sets, apothecary bottles, banquet settings.
• Ethnic, Mexican, Chinese, Indian, Western, African and Japanese.
NOW ON 3 FLOORS. ONE STOP PROPPING!

• Large selection of china and glassware. Full service prop rental house. Phone orders accepted •
(See display ad under PROP RENTAL HOUSES.)

CAROLE STUPELL LTD.
212-260-3100
29 East 22nd St., (Park- B'way) NYC, NY 10010
Hours: 10-6 Mon-Sat
• Fine china and crystal; decorative accessories; great service: see Keith. RENTALS •

TERRACOTTA
212-243-1952
259 West 4th St., (Perry-Charles St.) NYC, NY 10014
Hours: 12-7 Tues-Sat • 12-6 Sun
• American crafts; handmade pottery, glassware, table top and personal accessories including textiles and jewelry. •

TIFFANY & CO.
212-755-8000
727 Fifth Ave., (57th St.) NYC, NY 10022
Hours: 10-6 Mon-Sat (Thur until 7)
• Fine china, crystal, silver, clocks, watches, jewelry; the very best. CREDIT CARDS •

WILLIAMS-SONOMA
212-633-2203
110 Seventh Ave., (16th-17th St.) NYC, NY 10011
Hours: 10-7 Mon-Fri • 10-6 Sat • 12-5 Sun
• Kitchenware store; china, glassware, cookware, utensils, etc. Catalog. RENTALS (with credit card deposit.) CREDIT CARDS •

CLEANERS: CARPET, DRAPERY & UPHOLSTERY

ACME CARPET CLEANING
201-675-8313
532 N. Grove St, East Orange, NJ 07017   **800-448-7930**
Hours: 8:30-5 Mon-Fri   FAX **201-675-3523**
• Expert repair of special rugs. •

ALDER RUG CLEANING   718-328-4433
644 Whittier St., (off Randel) Bronx, NY 10474
Hours: 9-5 Mon-Fri • 9-1 Sat   FAX 718-328-4434
• Carpet cleaning, repair, refringing and binding. •

CENTRAL WILSON CARPET CLEANING   212-567-9200
301 Norman Ave., (Morgan-Norman) Brooklyn, NY 11222
Hours: 9-5 Mon-Fri
• Cleaners of carpet, area rugs, draperies, upholstery; pick-up and delivery. •

HAKIM RUG GALLERY   212-750-0606
208 East 51st St., (2nd-3rd Ave.) NYC, NY 10022
Hours: 9:30-5:30 Mon-Fri • Sun by appt.   FAX 212-826-6395
• Carpet hand-cleaning, repair and restoration; speak to Mr. Hakim. •

D. KALFAIAN & SON, INC.   718-875-2222
475 Atlantic Ave., (Nevins-3rd. Ave.) Brooklyn, NY 11217
Hours: 9-7 Mon, Thurs, Fri • 9-5 Tues, Wed, Sat • Sun 10-5   FAX 718-855-2213
• Carpet cleaning. See George Kalfaian. RENTALS CREDIT CARDS •

JOHN'S VALET   212-489-0100
734 10th Ave., (50th St) NYC, NY 10019
Hours: 7-6:30 Mon-Fri
• Willing to clean painted fabric, very helpful. •

PARVIZ NEMATI   212-486-6900
510 Madison Ave. 2nd Fl., (53rd St.) NYC, NY 10022
Hours: 9-6 Mon-Fri • 10-4 Sat   FAX 212-755-8428
• Antique carpets and tapestries. All weaving and cleaning done by hand. RENTALS •

REYNOLDS DRAPERY   315-845-8632
7440 Main St., Newport, NY 13416
Hours: 8-4 Mon-Fri   FAX 315-845-8645
• Cleans, repairs and flameproofs theatrical drapery. •

CLOCKS

E BUK ANTIQUES AND ART   212-226-6891
151 Spring St. 2nd Fl., (W. B'way-Wooster St.) NYC, NY 10012
Hours: Every day by appt.   (toll call) 700-SCIENCE
• Antique clocks and watches, antique clock and watchmakers tools and equipment.
RENTALS •
(See display ads under ANTIQUES: EUROPEAN & AMERICAN and under PROP RENTAL HOUSES.)

CENTURYHURST BERKSHIRE ANTIQUES GALLERY   413-229-8131
Rt. #7, (center of town) Sheffield, MA 01257
Hours: 9 -5 Mon-Sat
• Specialize in antique clocks. Also English china, Wedgewood and country furniture. Large
warehouse of antiques. See Ron or Judith Timm. •

CLOCK HUTT   212-759-2395
1050 Second Ave., (55th-56th St.) NYC, NY 10022
Hours: 11-5 Mon-Sat
• Antique clocks; will repair. RENTALS •

CUCKOO CLOCK MFG. CO.   212-255-5133
   31 E. 28th Street 7th Fl., (B'way-6th Ave.) NYC, NY 10016
   Hours: 9-5 Mon-Fri
   • Low cost cuckoo clocks to the trade; repairs. •

ECLECTIC/ENCORE PROPERTIES,, INC.   212-645-8880
   620 West 26th St. 4th Fl., (11th-12th St.) NYC, NY 10001
   Hours: 9-5 Mon-Fri or by appt.   FAX   212-243-6508
   • Extensive collection of antique and period clocks, watchmakers tools, equipment and cabi-
   netry. RENTALS •
   (See display ad under PROP RENTAL HOUSES.)

FANELLI ANTIQUE TIMEPIECES LTD.   212-517-2300
   1131 Madison Ave., (84th-85th St.) NYC, NY 10028
   Hours: 10-6 Mon-Fri • 11-5 Sat (closed Sat: July, Aug)
   • Antique clocks, wristwatches, pocket watches, jewelry, Russian art work. Sales, repairs; ask
   for Cindy. RENTALS •

KLOCKIT   800-556-2458
   P.O. Box 636, Lake Geneva, WI 53147
   Hours: 7-8 Mon-Fri • 8-4 Sat   FAX   414-248-9899
   • Clock parts, movements, kits. Free catalog available. CREDIT CARDS •

LABOVSKY MEYER   212-777-1465
   873 Broadway 7th Floor, (18-19th Street) NYC, NY 10003
   Hours: by appointment
   • Rents clocks from hokey to fine antiques. Rustic surfaces for tabletop backgrounds and
   Boy's Toys. •

NICCOLINI ANTIQUES PROP RENTAL   212-243-2010
   19 West 21st St., (5th-6th Ave.) NYC, NY 10010   212-254-2900
   Hours: 10-5 Mon-Fri • or by appt.   FAX   213-366-6779
   • Large selection of antique clocks of all kinds. RENTALS •

RENT–A–THING   914-628-9298
   Rt. 6, Baldwin Place, NY 10505   800-287-9298
   Hours: 24 hrs.; leave message, will return call
   • Good selection of antique clocks; RENTALS only. •

1750 HOUSE ANTIQUES   413-229-6635
   Rt. 7, South Main St., Sheffield, MA 01257
   Hours: 10-4 Mon-Fri (call first) • 10-5 Sat-Sun
   • Specializes in antique clocks. also service of grandfather clocks. Also general antiques.
   Speak to Bill Leibowitz. •

SUTTON CLOCK SHOP   212-758-2260
   139 East 61st St. 2nd Fl., (Lexington Ave.) NYC, NY 10021
   Hours: 11-4:30 by appt.
   • Antique clocks. RENTALS •

TIC TOCK CLOCK CO.   212-247-1470
   763 Ninth Ave., (51st-52nd St.) NYC, NY 10019
   Hours: 10-6 Tues-Fri • 12-4 Sat
   • New and used, antique and modern clocks and watches. Good collection of cuckoos. Howard
   Miller, dealer. No rentals. •

"I found it in the N.Y. Theatrical Sourcebook."

CLOTHING ACCESSORIES: BELTS, SUSPENDERS, COLLARS, CUFFS, NECKWEAR

See also **EYEGLASSES**
See also **GLOVES**
See also **HATS**
See also **JEWELRY**
See also **LUGGAGE & HANDBAGS**
See also **SHOES & BOOTS**
See also **UMBRELLAS & CANES**

ABRAHAM BOXER   718-972-0144
    6002 Ft. Hamilton Pkwy, Brooklyn, NY 11219
    Hours: 9-5 Mon-Thurs • 8:30-2 Fri   FAX   718-436-0422
    • Suspenders, made to order; stock of clip and button suspenders; also gaiters, armbands, and garters. •

GIBSON LEE,, INC.   617-662-6025
    78 Stone Place, Melrose, MA 02176
    Hours: 8-5 Mon-Fri
    • Cloth and disposable collars, detachable collars, neckband shirts, collar buttons, spats, accessories, shirt fronts. Very helpful. •

TIECRAFTERS,, INC.   212-629-5800
    252 W. 29th (7-8 Avenue) NYC, NY 10001
    Hours: 8:30-5:30 Mon-Thurs • 8:30-5 Fri • 10-2 Sat   FAX   212-967-2240
    • Custom neckware, tie cleaning service available. Contact Andrew Tarshis. Accepts personal checks. No credit cards. •

F.R. TRIPLER & CO.   212-922-1090
    366 Madison Avenue (46th St.) NYC, NY 10017
    Hours: 9-5:45 Mon-Fri (Thurs till 6:30) • 9-5:30 Sat   FAX   212-867-7867
    • Excellent quality menswear, collarless 100% cotton shirts, formal shirts. Will take phone orders. Will ship. CREDIT CARDS •

CLOTHING RENTAL & PURCHASE: ANTIQUE & VINTAGE

See also **THRIFTS SHOPS**
For military surplus, see **CLOTHING RENTAL & PURCHASE: UNIFORMS**

ALICE'S UNDERGROUND   212-724-6682
    380 Columbus Ave., (78th St.) NYC, NY 10024
    Hours: 11-7 Mon-Fri • 11-8 Sat

    431 Broadway, (Grand-Broome) NYC, NY 10013   212-431-9067
    Hours: 11-7:30 every day
    • Vintage clothing, accessories and linens; retail, reasonably priced, good condition. Rentals at 1/3 cost. CREDIT CARDS •

AMAZON VINEGAR & PICKLING WORKS DRYGOODS LTD.   319-322-6800
    2218 E. 11th St., Davenport, IA 52803   800-798-7979
    Hours: 9-5 Mon-Fri (CST)   FAX   319-322-4003
    • Corsets, Victorian shoes, lingerie; catalog $2.00. Shoe & boot catalog $5.00, 1st class mail. CREDIT CARDS •

AMBASSADOR SPAT CO.
215-739-3134
2400 Jasper St., Philadelphia, PA 19125
Hours: 8-3 Mon-Fri
• Spats in many styles. •

ANDY'S CHEE-PEES
212-460-8488
16 West 8th St., (5th-6th Ave.) NYC, NY 10011

691 Broadway, (3-4th St.) NYC, NY 10003   212-420-4980
Hours: 11-8 Mon-Thurs • 11-8:30 Fri-Sat • 12-7 Sun   FAX 212-254-3610
• Wholesale, retail antique clothing and jeans, army surplus. No shipping. CREDIT CARDS •

THE ANTIQUE BOUTIQUE
212-460-8830
712-714 Broadway, (Washington-Waverly St.) NYC, NY 10003
Hours: 10-9 Mon-Thurs • 10-10 Fri-Sat • 11-8 Sun   FAX 212-598-9024

227 E. 59th St. (2-3 Ave.) NYC, NY 10022   212-752-1680
Hours: 11-10:30 Mon-Sat • 12-8 Sun
•Also great selection jewelry and accessories. Phone orders. Will ship. RENTALS CREDIT CARDS $15 minimum•

ANTIQUE CITY
212-219-2069
51 East Houston St., (Mulberry-Mott St.) NYC, NY 10012
Hours: 11-8 Mon-Sat • 12-6 Sun
• Leather jackets and vintage clothing. AMEX •

CHEAP JACK'S VINTAGE CLOTHING
212-777-9564
841 Broadway, (13th-14th St.) NYC, NY 10003   212-995-0403
Hours: 11-8 Mon-Sat/12-7 Sun   FAX 914-238-5733
• Good selection of vintage clothing 1920-1970. Phone orders. RENTALS CREDIT CARDS •

D.L. CERNEY
212-673-7033
13 East 7th St., (2nd-3rd St.) NYC, NY 10003
Hours: 12-8 every day
• Never-worn vintage clothing; also custom work. Antique shoes, accessories. Original designs. Phone orders. CREDIT CARDS •

DEBORAH'S ATTIC
513-322-8842
719 S. Limestone ST., Springfield, OH 45505
Hours: 11-5 Mon-Sat
• Reasonable prices. Victorian- 1960's clothing and accessories; also vintage quilts, linens, trims, notions, fabrics. Will work from photographs to pull. No credit cards. RENTALS •

EARLY HALLOWEEN
212-691-2933
130 West 25th St. 11th Fl., (6th-7th Ave.) NYC, NY 10001   212-243-1499
Hours: by appt only

Vintage men's, women's and children's clothing, shoes, hats, accessories, costume jewelry.

EARLY HALLOWEEN

• Also vintage luggage and memorabilia. •

    "I found it in the N.Y. Theatrical Sourcebook."

THE FAMILY JEWELS VINTAGE CLOTHING   212-679-5023
832 Sixth Ave. 2nd Fl., (29th St.) NYC, NY 10001
Hours: 11-7 Mon-Sat • 11-6 Sun
 • Mostly sales. Victorian-1970's clothing; also textile design research. CREDIT CARDS •

GOHN BROS.   219-825-2400
PO Box 111, Middlebury, IN 46540
Hours: 8-5 Mon-Fri
 • Amish and plain clothing, etc.; catalog. •

GENE LONDON   212-533-4105
10 Gramercy Park South , (Park & 20th St.) NYC, NY 10003
Hours: by appt.   FAX   212-533-4105
 • Rents men's and women's clothing:from Victorian to today's. Huge annual charity sale,
1000's of wearables. Call for dates. •

HARRIET LOVE   212-966-2280
126 Prince, (Wooster-Greene) NYC, NY 10012
Hours: 11:30-7 Tue-Sun
 • Antique clothing, jewelry and accessories. CREDIT CARDS •

HEY VIV – VINTAGE CLOTHING   718-981-3575
125 Port Richmond Ave., (Bennett-Vreeland) Staten Island, NY 10302
Hours: 11-6 Wed-Sat • or by appt.
 • Sale of women's clothing 1930-1960, some men's clothing; excellent condition, reasonable
prices, see Vivian Vassar. Phone orders OK. MC/VISA AMEX •

IAN'S BOUTIQUE,, INC.   212-420-1857
5 St. Mark's Place, (2nd-3rd Ave.) NYC, NY 10003
Hours: 11:30-8 Mon-Sat
 • Men's and women's elegant evening wear, separates, specialty, musicians and dancers.
Phone orders. CREDIT CARDS •

KASBAH   212-982-8077
83 Second Ave. 2nd Fl., (5th St.) NYC, NY 10003
Hours: 12-7:30 Daily
 • Good selection of men's and women's clothing, hats, shoes, formalwear & lingerie; 1920's-
1980's. No credit cards. •

LOVES SAVES THE DAY   212-228-3802
119 Second Ave., (7th St.) NYC, NY 10003
Hours: 12-10 Mon-Thurs • 12-12 Fri-Sat • 1-9 Sun
 • Vintage clothing, toys, props; phone orders; sales. RENTALS CREDIT CARDS •

MY OLD LADY   212-924-7879
205 Seventh Ave., (22nd St.) NYC, NY 10011
Hours: 11-7 Mon-Sat
 • Large selection of 40's and 50's clothing; men's jackets, tuxedo pants; some ladies clothing;
original jewelry good prices. CREDIT CARDS •

C-D

ODDS COSTUME RENTAL
212-268-6227

231 West 29th St. Rm. 304, (7th-8th Ave.) NYC, NY 10001
Hours: 9:30-5 Mon-Fri • Sat by appt.   FAX   212-629-3032

PRINT - FILM - COMMERCIAL - THEATRE
• SPECIALIZING IN QUALITY PERIOD CLOTHES -
VICTORIAN THROUGH MODERN.
• HAND PICKED UNIQUE SELECTION OF ODD PIECES
FOR PERIOD, CHARACTER, AND NOVELTY TYPES.

ODDS

ABET
CHARACTER
PERIOD
CONTEMPORARY
UNIQUE

COSTUME AND FUR RENTAL

• Rental only. $250 minimum for shipping. CREDIT CARDS •
(See display ad under COSTUME RENTAL & CONSTRUCTION.)

PANACHE ANTIQUE CLOTHING
212-242-5115

525 Hudson St., (10th-Charles St.) NYC, NY 10014
Hours: 12-7 Mon-Sat • 1-6 Sun
• Good quality men's and ladies wear, 20's to 60's; see Annie or Barbara. Phone orders.
RENTALS CREDIT CARDS •

ROBERT PUSILO STUDIO
212-675-2179

255 West 18th St., (7th-8th Ave.) NYC, NY 10011
Hours: by appt.
• 1880-1970 clothing for film and commercials only. RENTALS CREDIT CARDS •

REMINISCENCE,, INC.
212-243-2292

74 Fifth Ave., (13th St.) NYC, NY 10011   (wholesale) 212-807-0300
Hours: 11-8 Mon-Sat • 1-6 Sun   FAX   212-807-0321
• 50's and later clothing and jewelry. Phone orders. CREDIT CARDS •

RICK'S FASHION AMERICAIN
919-341-7522

641 North 4th St., Wilmington, NC 28401
Hours: 11-6 Mon-Fri • 12-5 Sat
• Men's suits, ties and accessories from the 30's-60's. RENTALS •

SCREAMING MIMI
212-677-6464

382 Lafayette, (4th & Great Jones) NYC, NY 10003
Hours: 11-8 Mon-Fri • 12-8 Sat •1-7 Sun
• All New: 50's, 60's and 70's and punk. Phone orders. CREDIT CARDS RENTALS •

JACK SILVER
212-582-3298
212-582-3389

1780 Broadway #303, (57th-58th St.) NYC, NY 10019
Hours: 9-6 Mon-Fri • 10-4 Sat   FAX   212-765-6933
• Some period attire; all formal attire , women's & children's tuxedos. Will ship. CREDIT
CARDS •

JANA STARR / JEAN HOFFMAN
212-861-8256

236 East 80th St., (2nd-3rd Ave.) NYC, NY 10021
Hours: 12-6 Mon-Sat
• 1890-1950's clothing, lace, jewelry, collectibles, textiles. CREDIT CARDS •

SOURCE III
212-243-2164

49 West 24th St. 7th Fl., (5th-6th Ave.) NYC, NY 10010
Hours: 9:30-6 Mon-Fri (call first)
• Vintage and character clothing for men, women and children; see Dorothy. RENTALS •

C-D

STAR STRUCK
212-691-5357

47 Greenwich Ave., (Charles- Perry St.) NYC, NY 10014
Hours: 11-8 Mon-Sat • 12-7 Sun

270 Bleeker St., (Morton St.) NYC, NY 10011
212-366-9826
Hours: 12-8 Mon-Sat • 12-7 Sun
• Large selection of 30's-60's clothing. Phone orders. CREDIT CARDS RENTALS •

THE SECOND COMING LTD.
212-431-4424
72 Greene St., (Spring-Broome St.) NYC, NY 10012
Hours: 12-7 Mon-Sat • 1-6 Sun
FAX 212-431-4734
• Vintage department store with furniture and housewares. Good quality men's and women's clothing and never-worn shoes; 30's, 40's & 50's. Phone orders. CREDIT CARDS RENTALS •

TRASH & VAUDEVILLE,, INC.
212-982-3590
4 Saint Marks Place, (2nd-3rd Ave.) NYC, NY 10003
Hours: 12-8 Mon-Thurs • 11:30-8 Fri • 1:30-9 Sat • 1-7:30 Sun
• Punk and rock and roll; wholesale or retail. CREDIT CARDS •

TROUVAILLE FRANCAISE
212-737-6015
Hours: by appt.
FAX 212-737-9530
• Antique clothing and linens; French, Belgian, English and American, mostly whites; speak to Muriel Clarke or Bert Clarke. Personal checks accepted. No credit cards. RENTALS. •

HELEN UFFNER VINTAGE CLOTHING
212-570-0019
Hours: by appt.
• Men's, women's, children's vintage clothing and accessories 1860's-1930; rental or purchase; also period fabric, lace and trim. No credit cards •

RICHARD UTILLA
718-834-8761
359 Dean St., (4th Ave.) Brooklyn, NY 11217
Hours: by appt.
• Men's and women's clothing and accessories; 30's and onwards. CREDIT CARDS RENTALS •

WEST MURRAY
212-334-9851
149 Franklin St., (Varick-Hudson St.) NYC, NY 10013
Hours: by appt.
• 1920's-1960's vintage clothing for rent; infant to size 16; also toys and props. Will ship. No credit cards. •

OPAL WHITE
212-677-8215
131 Thompson St., (Prince-Houston St.) NYC, NY 10012
Hours: 12-6 Wed-Sun/call for appt.
•Victorian wedding dresses and clothes from 1890-1960's. AMEX•

CLOTHING RENTAL & PURCHASE: CHILDREN'S

See also **CLOTHING RENTAL & PURCHASE: ANTIQUE & VINTAGE**

C–D

CITYKIDS   212-620-0906
> 130 Seventh Ave., (17th-18th St.) NYC, NY 10011
> Hours: 10-6 Mon-Sat
> • Children's clothing boutique, toys, books, shoes,unusual imported items. Next door to Books of Wonder, a great childrens bookstore. No phone orders. CREDIT CARDS. •

CONWAY STORES   212-967-3460
> 1333 Broadway, (35th-36th St.) NYC, NY 10018
>
> 450 Seventh Ave., (34-35th St.) NYC, NY 10001   212-967-1371
>
> 11 W. 34th St., (B'way-7th St.) NYC, NY 10001   212-967-5300
> Hours: 9:30-7 Mon-Sat • 11:30-6 Sun
> • Reasonably priced children's clothing, footwear and accessories. CREDIT CARDS •

CRAFT CLOTHES   212-764-6122
> 247 West 37th St., (7th-8th Ave.) NYC, NY 10018
> Hours: 9:30-6 Mon-Fri • 9:30-3 Sat   FAX   212-997-7318
> • School uniforms, caps and gowns, cheerleading uniforms; also clerical apparel. Phone orders. Will ship. CREDIT CARDS •

GAP KIDS   212-730-1087
> 1212 Sixth Ave., (48th St.) NYC, NY 10036   212-704-0285
> Hours: By appt. only Studio services   FAX   818-762-9194
> • Studio Services program available at this location, or by calling Jordan Salim at 818-762-9192. Check your telephone directory for locations of regular retail stores in your area. No cash accepted for studio services. CREDIT CARDS •

IDEAL   718-252-5090
> 1814-16 Flatbush Ave., (Ave. K) Brooklyn, NY 11210
> Hours: 10-5:45 Mon-Sat(Thurs till 6:45) • (Thurs till 8:45 Aug-Sept)   FAX   718-692-0492
> • School uniforms, camp uniforms and Scout uniforms, cheerleading, caps and gowns, teen's clothing. Will ship. No rentals. CREDIT CARDS •

LITTLE FOLKS SHOP   212-982-9669
> 123 East 23rd St., (Park-Lexington Ave.) NYC, NY 10010
> Hours: 9:30-7 Mon-Sat • 12-5 Sun   FAX   212-228-7889
> • Clothing from newborn to 14 yrs; toys, books, baby furniture. Phone orders. RENTALS CREDIT CARDS •

SECOND ACT CHILDREN'S WEAR,, INC.   212-988-2440
> 1046 Madison Ave., (79th-80th St.) NYC, NY 10021
> Hours: 8:45-4:45 Tues-Sat
> • Consignment store for children's clothes, sports equipment, books and toys. Specializing in last minute orders. No credit cards. RENTALS •

CLOTHING RENTAL & PURCHASE: DANCEWEAR

See also **SHOES & BOOTS**
See also **COSTUME RENTAL & CONSTRUCTION**

A & R ENTERPRISES 212-567-7289
　PO Box 47 Ft George Sta., NYC, NY 10040 (mailing address)
　Hours: 9:30-6 Mon-Sat
　• Imported dance shoes for jazz, ballroom, and ballet. •

BACKSTAGE 503-686-2671
　62 West Broadway, Eugene, OR 97401 800-882-4888
　Hours: 9-5:30 Mon-Sat • 12-4 Sun
　• Large selection; catalog; also theatrical supplies. Phone orders. CREDIT CARDS •

B.T. INDUSTRIES 201-866-0201
　2900-06 Kennedy Blvd., Union City, NJ 07087 800-992-6629
　Hours: 9-4:30 Mon-Fri FAX 201-866-9433
　• Formerly Bal-Toggery Knits,, Inc. Leotards, unitards, tights, Lycra, cotton Lycra; manufacturer. $250 minimum order $100. minimum on orders thereafter. No rentals. No credit cards. •

CAPEZIO DANCE THEATRE SHOP 212-245-2130
　1650 Broadway 2nd Fl., (entrance on 51st St.) NYC, NY 10019
　　(David Shaffer) 212-765-1613
　Hours: 9:30-6:30 Mon-Fri (Thurs till 7) • 9:30-6 Sat FAX 212-757-7635
　• Dancewear, shoes, lingerie, large selection; call ahead for large orders. Pete Ktenas now on premises. Account service available to designers and stylists. Helpful, ask for David. Phone orders. Will ship. No rentals. CREDIT CARDS •
　(See display ad in this section.)

CAPEZIO'S EAST 212-758-8833
　136 East 61st St., (Lexington Ave.) NYC, NY 10021
　Hours: 10-6:30 Mon-Fri (Thurs till 7) • 11-6:30 Sat • 12-5 Sun
　• Dancewear; large selection for students. No rentals. No credit cards •

CAPEZIO IN THE VILLAGE 212-477-5634
　177 MacDougal St., (8th St.) NYC, NY 10011
　Hours: 12-8 Mon-Fri • 11:30-8 Sat • 1-6 Sun
　• Dancewear, shoes, casual streetwear. Phone orders. Will ship. CREDIT CARDS •

THE COTTON COLLECTION 216-659-3190
　PO Box 343, Richfield, OH 44286
　Hours: 9-5 Mon-Fri

"Dancewear with Extra - texture"
Customized dancewear made of Springweave cotton fabric.

　• Custom Danceware. Speak to Janet. No rentals. No credit cards. •

DANSKIN,, INC. 212-764-4630
　111 West 40th St., 18th Fl., (B'way-6th Ave.) NYC, NY 10018
　Hours: 9-5 Mon-Fri FAX 800-288-6749
　• Showroom for buyers; new styles of dancewear and activewear. Wholesale. •

ON STAGE
212-725-1174

197 Madison Ave., (34th-35th St.) NYC, NY 10016
Hours: 9-7 Mon-Fri • 11-6 Sat

THE ULTIMATE SOURCE
Dancewear, Bodywear, Swimwear, Shoes, Lingerie, Hosiery and Accessories.
Very large selection and special orders available.
Complete shows and school orders are our specialty.
Specializing in last minute orders.

On Stage
THE ULTIMATE BODY SHOP
Dance Wear • Dance Shoes • Swimwear
Hosiery • Lingerie • Activewear

• Large selection of leotards, tights, unitards and accessories; will special order. Catalog available; will do mail order. Phone orders. CREDIT CARDS •

REPETTO
212-582-3900

30 Lincoln Plaza, (62nd-63rd St. on Broadway) NYC, NY 10023
Hours: 12-6 Mon-Thurs • 11-7 Fri & Sat (Office 9-6 Mon-Fri)   FAX   212-582-5545
• French dance products for children and adults. Account service available to designers and stylists. Phone orders. CREDIT CARDS •

S & S HOSIERY
212-586-3288

135 West 50th St., (6th-7th Ave.) NYC, NY 10020
Hours: 8:30-6:30 Mon-Fri • 11:30-5:30 Sat
• Stockings, black and white tights, corsets, leotards, tights and men's and ladies' undergarments. Phone Orders. Personal checks. CREDIT CARDS •

CLOTHING RENTAL & PURCHASE: ECCLESIASTICAL

See also **COSTUME RENTAL & CONSTRUCTION**

C.M. ALMY & SON,, INC.   203-531-8484
PO Box 2644, 10 Glenville St., Greenwich, CT 06836
Hours: 9-6 Mon-Fri • Sat by appt.   FAX   203-531-9048
• Vestments, sacred vessels, choir robes, clerical clothing.; catalog; MC/VISA •

BENTLEY & SIMON   201-489-7686
204 Mohawk Dr., River Edge, NJ 07661
Hours: 8:30-4 Mon, Wed, Fri
• Custom ecclesiastical clothing and choir robes. •

CRAFT CLOTHES   212-764-6122
247 West 37th St. 17th Fl., (7th-8th Ave.) NYC, NY 10018
Hours: 9:30-6 Mon-Fri • 9:30-3 Sat   FAX   212-997-7318
• Sales and rentals; religious apparel, religious goods, pulpit robes, choir robes, judicial robes; also school uniforms. Phone orders. CREDIT CARDS •

DUFFY & QUINN,, INC.   212-725-0213
307 Fifth Ave. 15th Fl., (31st-32nd St.) NYC, NY 10016
Hours: 9-5:30 Mon-Fri • 9:30-2 Sat
• Bishop's robes and furnishings, pulpit robes, choir robes, judicial robes. Also graduation caps and gowns. RENTALS CREDIT CARDS •

HOLY LAND ART CO.,, INC.   800-962-4659
160 Chambers St., (Greenwich St.) NYC, NY 10007

12 Sullivan St., Westwood, NJ 07675   800-334-3621

300 Prosperity Farms Rd., N. Palm Beach, FL 33408   800-526-1294
Hours: 9-5 Mon-Thurs • 9-4 Fri   FAX   212-962-5740
• Clerical clothing, vestment materials, etc. Will ship. RENTALS CREDIT CARDS •

J. LEVINE CO.   212-695-6888
5 West 30th St., (5th-B'way) NYC, NY 10001
Hours: 9-6 Mon-Wed • 9-7 Thurs • 9-2 Fri • 10-5 Sun   FAX   212-643-1044
• Prayer shawls, great selection of yarmulkes, lots of books and other religious items. Phone orders. CREDIT CARDS •

CLOTHING RENTAL & PURCHASE: FORMAL WEAR

See also **COSTUME RENTAL & CONSTRUCTION**

ACADEMY CLOTHES,, INC.   212-765-1440
1703 Broadway, (54th St.) NYC, NY 10019
Hours: 9:30-6:30 Mon-Sat
• Tuxes for men and women, fancy waiters outfits; vintage clothing available. Leatherwear. Reasonable. RENTALS CREDIT CARDS •

DAVID'S OUTFITTERS,, INC.
212-691-7388
36 West 20th St., (5th-6th Ave.) NYC, NY 10011
Hours: 9-5 Mon-Fri
• Formal wear and all types of uniforms. No phone orders. Will ship. RENTALS only. CREDIT CARDS •

A. T. HARRIS
212-682-6325
11 East 44th St., (Madison-5th Ave.) NYC, NY 10017
Hours: 9-6 Mon, Wed, Fri • 9-7 Thurs • 10-4 Sat by appt. **FAX 212-682-6148**
• Considered by many to be the place for tuxedos. Phone orders. RENTALS CREDIT CARDS •

HERMAN'S FORMAL WEAR
212-719-2278
28 West 48th St, (5th-6th Ave.) NYC, NY 10036
Hours: 9-7 Mon, Thurs, Fri • 9-6 Tues, Wed
• Free delivery. Sales. See Sid Tishman. RENTALS CREDIT CARDS •

JACK & CO.
212-722-4455
212-722-4609
128 East 86th St., (Lexington-Park Ave.) NYC, NY 10028
Hours: 10-7 Mon-Fri • 10-4 Sat
• Complete line of formal wear and accessories. Same day service. Phone orders OK. RENTALS. CREDIT CARDS •

MEL'S LEXINGTON FORMAL WEAR
212-867-4420
12 East 46th St., 2nd Fl., (Madison-5th Ave.) NYC, NY 10017
Hours: 9-7 Mon, Thurs, Fri • 9-5:30 Tues, Wed • 10-4 Sat **FAX 212-867-1368**
• Large selection of formal clothing and accessories, men's, women's and boy's. RENTALS CREDIT CARDS •

OFF-BROADWAY BOUTIQUE
212-724-6713
139 West 72nd St., (B'way-Columbus) NYC, NY 10023
Hours: 11-7 every day **FAX 212-595-4901**
• Women's tuxedos, collapsible top hats, gowns, accessories. Gently worn star's clothes available. Phone orders. Will ship. RENTALS CREDIT CARDS •

O. K. UNIFORM CO.
212-966-1984
212-966-4733
507 Broadway, (Spring-Broome St.) NYC, NY 10012
Hours: 9:30-5:30 Mon-Thurs • 9:30-call Fri • 11:30-4:30 Sun **FAX 212-226-6668**
• Sales only. Men's and women's tuxedos, vests, skirts, shirts, bowties and accessories including top hats and derbies. CREDIT CARDS •
(See display ad under CLOTHING RENTAL & PURCHASE: UNIFORMS.)

JACK SILVER
212-582-3298
212-582-3389
1780 Broadway #303, (57th-58th St.) NYC, NY 10019
Hours: 9-6 Mon-Fri • 10-4 Sat **FAX 212-765-6933**
• Men's and women's tuxes and tails, children's tuxedos. RENTALS CREDIT CARDS •

TED'S FINE CLOTHING
212-966-2029
83 Orchard St., (Grand-Broome St.) NYC, NY 10002
Hours: 10-6 Sun-Thurs • 10-4 Fri
• Reasonable prices. Shipping. Phone orders. RENTALS MC/VISA •

THE TUXEDO WHOLESALER
602-951-1606
800-828-2802
7750 East Redfield Rd. # 101, Scottsdale, AZ 85260
Hours: 9-5 Mon-Fri • 10-4 Sat **FAX 602-951-1760**
• New and used formal wear, standard and period, catalog.Phone orders, RENTALS CREDIT CARDS •

"I found it in the N.Y. Theatrical Sourcebook."

CLOTHING RENTAL & PURCHASE: FURS

See also **CLOTHING RENTAL & PURCHASE: ANTIQUE & VINTAGE**

JOSEPH CORN & SON,, INC.   212-695-1635
    145 West 28th St., (6th-7th Ave.) NYC, NY 10001
    Hours: 10-6 Mon-Fri • 10-5 Sat, Sun
    • New and secondhand furs; sales. CREDIT CARDS •

FABULOUS-FURS   800-848-4650
    700 Madison Ave., Covington, KY 41011
    Hours: 9-5 Mon-Fri   FAX   606-291-9687
    • Luxury man-made furs; volume discount; immediate shipment. Phone orders. CREDIT
    CARDS •

ODDS COSTUME RENTAL   212-268-6267
    231 West 29th St. #304, NYC, NY 10001
    Hours: 9:30-5 Mon-Fri • Sat by appt   FAX   212-268-3032
    • Sales RENTALS CREDIT CARDS •
    (see display ad under COSTUME RENTAL & CONSTRUCTION)

CLOTHING RENTAL & PURCHASE: LINGERIE

BAB'S SPORTSWEAR,, INC.   212-923-8004
    4001 Broadway, (168th St.) NYC, NY 10032
    Hours: 9-7 Mon-Fri • 10-7 Sat   FAX   212-923-8133
    • Women's lingerie; heavily padded bras, 1940's era. CREDIT CARDS •

LAUREN BOGEN LINGERIE   212-570-9529
    1044 Lexington Ave., (74th-75th St.) NYC, NY 10021   (outside NY) 800-944-2643
    Hours: 10-6:30 Mon-Sat 9 (Thurs until 7)   FAX   212-570-9534
    • Ladies' lingerie, men's and children's undergarments & sleepwear. Phone orders. CREDIT
    CARDS •

BRIEF ESSENTIALS   212-921-8344
    1407 Broadway, (38th-39th St.) NYC, NY 10018
    Hours: 8:30-5:30 Mon-Fri
    • All types of ladies lingerie. No phone orders. CREDIT CARDS •

COSMO HOSIERY SHOPS   212-532-3111
    425 Fifth Ave., (38th St.) NYC, NY 10016
    Hours: 9-6:30 Mon-Fri • 10-6 Sat • 12-4:30 Sun
    • All types of ladies lingerie. Phone orders. CREDIT CARDS •

LOUIS CHOCK, INC.   212-473-1929
    74 Orchard St., (Grand-Broome St.) NYC, NY 10002   800-222-0020
    Hours: 9-5 Sun-Thurs • 9-1 Fri   FAX   212-473-6273
    • Hosiery, underwear and sleepwear for the whole family. Catalog available. Phone orders.
    MC/VISA •

ENELRA   212-473-2454
   48 1/2 East 7th St., (1st-2nd Ave.) NYC, NY 10003
   Hours: 12-8 Sun-Wed • 12-10 Thurs-Sat
   • Great selection of lingerie and exotic dancewear. CREDIT CARDS •

FREDERICK'S OF HOLLYWOOD   310-637-7770
   6608 Hollywood Blvd., Hollywood, CA 90028   (express orders) 800-278-7874
   Hours: 6:30-5 Mon-Fri   800-323-9525
   • Sexy lingerie for women and men; bathing suits, hooker shoes, casualwear. Catalog. Phone
   orders. CREDIT CARDS •

GOLDMAN & COHEN BRAS & GIRDLES   212-966-0737
   55 Orchard St., (Hester-Grand St.) NYC, NY 10002
   Hours: 9-5 Mon-Thurs • 9-3 Fri • 9-5:30 Sun
   • Inexpensive, good quality. Experienced accommodating and helpful sales people. Phone
   orders. CREDIT CARDS •

ISAAC SULTAN & SONS   212-979-1645
   332 Grand St., (Ludlow-Orchard St.) NYC, NY 10002
   Hours: 9-5 Sun-Thurs • 9-3 Fri   (outside NY State.) 800-999-1645
   • Discount lingerie and girdles. Phone orders CREDIT CARDS •

LISMORE HOSIERY COMPANY   212-674-3440
   334 Grand St., (Orchard-Ludlow) NYC, NY 10002
   Hours: 9:45-5:45 Sun-Thurs • 9:45-2:45 Fri   FAX   212-674-3974
   • Complete line of hosiery for men, women, children; including tights, leotards, seamed stockings and pantyhose in all sizes. Will ship. MC/VISA •

LOLITA CORP.   212-982-9560
   70 Orchard St., (Grand-Broome St.) NYC, NY 10002
   Hours: 12-5:30 Sun-Thurs
   • Old-fashioned bras and corsets. No credit cards •

S & S HOSIERY   212-582-3288
   135 W. 50th St., (6-7th Ave.) NYC, NY 10020
   Hours: 8:30-6:30 Mon-Fri • 11:30-5:30 Sat
   • Undergarments, leotards, tights, men's undergarments, phone orders, personal checks.
   CREDIT CARDS •

ISAAC SULTAN & SONS   212-979-1645
   332 Grand St., (Ludlow-Orchard St.) NYC, NY 10002
   Hours: 9-5 Sun-Thurs • 9-3 Fri   (outside NY State.) 800-999-1645
   • Discount lingerie and girdles. Phone orders CREDIT CARDS •

THE VILLAGE CORSET SHOP   212-463-0365
   113 W. 10 St., (6th Ave.) NYC, NY 10011
   Hours: 10:30-6:30 Mon-Fri • Thur 11-7 • 12-6 Sat
   • Women's lingerie; merry widows. Very helpful will find what you need. CREDIT CARDS •

CLOTHING RENTAL & PURCHASE: MEN'S & WOMEN'S

See also **COSTUME RENTAL & CONSTRUCTION**
See also **DEPARTMENT STORES**
See also **ETHNIC GOODS**
See also **FENCING EQUIPMENT**
See also **RIDING EQUIPMENT**
See also **SPORTING GOODS**
See also **THRIFT SHOPS**
See also other headings in **CLOTHING RENTAL & PURCHASE**

BANANA REPUBLIC   212-730-1087
  1212 Sixth Ave., (48th St.) NYC, NY 10036   212-764-0285
  Hours: By Appt. only- studio services
   • Contact Jordan Salim at 818-762-9192 , (FAX 818-762-9194) for information regarding obtaining clothes through the Studio Services program. Check your telephone directory for locations of regular retail stores in your area. No cash accepted for studio services. CREDIT CARDS. •

BARNEY'S NEW YORK   212-929-9000
  106 Seventh Ave. Ave., (16-17th St.) NYC, NY 10021
  660 Madison Ave., (61-62nd St.) NYC, NY 10021
  Hours: 10-9 Mon-Thurs • 10-8 Fri • 10-7 Sat • 12-6 Sun
   • Quality contemporary men's clothing and accessories; also women's wear. Expensive. CREDIT CARDS •

BFO PLUS,, INC.   212-673-9026
  149 Fifth Ave. 2nd Fl., (21st St.) NYC, NY 10010
  Hours: 10-5:45 every day (Mon, Thurs Till 6:45)
   • Two floors of reasonably priced contemporary menswear. CREDIT CARDS •

BROOKS BROTHERS   212-682-8800
  346 Madison Ave., (44th St.) NYC, NY 10017   (Customer Service) 800-274-1886
  Hours: 8:30-6 Mon-Fri (Thurs till 7) • 9-6 Sat
   • The best in Ivy League menswear. Catalog available. Phone orders. CREDIT CARDS •

CANAL JEAN CO.,, INC.   212-226-0737
  504 Broadway, (Broome-Spring St.) NYC, NY 10012   212-226-1130
  Hours: 11-7 Sun-Thurs • 10-8 Fri, Sat   FAX   212-226-8084
   • Large vintage collection, casual clothing; good prices. Phone orders. RENTALS CREDIT CARDS •

CHIPP II   212-687-0850
  11 East 44th, (Madison-5th Ave.) NYC, NY 10017
  Hours: 9-5:30 Mon-Fri • 10-3:45 Sat   FAX   212-687-5048
   • Men's suits, ties, pants, shirts, jackets; see Paul. RENTALS. •

EISNER BROTHERS   212-475-6868
  75 Essex., (Delancey-Broome) NYC, NY 10002   800-426-7700
  Hours: 8:30-6 Mon-Thurs • 8:30-12:30 Fri • 9-5 Sun   FAX   212-475-6824
   • Caps, t-shirts, sweatshirts, jackets for football, baseball teams, etc.; catalog. No rentals. No credit cards. •

C–D

Unless you're planning on doing
"Oh, Calcutta!" this season,
you'll need...

The one-stop resource
for **clothing** the entire cast—
men, women, and children.
Call for a personal tour—
the whole store is yours
for the asking!

STUDIO SERVICES AT SAKS FIFTH AVENUE/NEW YORK
611 Fifth Avenue, New York, New York 10022 • (212) 940-4234/4560 • Store: (212) 753-4000

STUDIO SERVICES AT SAKS FIFTH AVENUE/LOS ANGELES
9600 Wilshire Boulevard, Beverly Hills, California 90212 • (310) 271-6726 • Store: (310) 275-4211 ext. 267.

SAKS FIFTH AVENUE

"I found it in the N.Y. Theatrical Sourcebook."

Eleganza Italiana
212-944-5880
1375 Broadway, 7th Fl., (37th St.) NYC, NY 10018
Hours: 9-4:30 Mon-Fri   FAX   212-768-9131
  • Couture fantasy theme wedding & ball gowns. Custom work. See Toni. RENTALS No credit cards. •

Forman's
212-228-2500
82 Orchard St., (Grand-Broome St.) NYC, NY 10002
Hours: 9-6 Sun-Wed • 9-8 Thurs • 9-2 Fri
  • Jones NY and classic styles at discounts. Phone orders. No rentals. MC/VISA •

The Gap Stores
1212 Sixth Ave., (48th St.) NYC, NY 10036
Hours: 9-5:30 Mon-Fri
  • Please contact Jordan Salim at 818-762-9192 , (FAX 818-762-9194) for information regarding obtaining clothes through the Studio Services program. Check your telephone directory for locations of regular retail stores in your area. Cash not accepted for studio services. CREDIT CARDS •

H Bar C California
310-532-8980
14600 S. Main St., Gardenia, CA 90248
Hours: 9-5 Mon-Fri   FAX   310-327-0342
  • Western clothing, sports clothes, manufacturer. Wholesale. Formerly H Bar C Ranchwear •

Imperial Wear Men's Clothing
212-719-2590
48 West 48th St., (5th-6th Ave.) NYC, NY 10036   800-344-6132
Hours: 9-6 Mon-Sat (Thurs till 8)   FAX   212-719-2596
  • Big and tall sizes. Phone orders. No rentals. CREDIT CARDS •

Lady Madonna Maternity Boutique
212-988-7173
793 Madison Ave., (67th St.) NYC, NY 10021
Hours: 10-6 Mon-Sat (Thurs till 7) • 12-5 Sun   FAX   212-988-7190
  • Fashionable maternity clothes. Phone orders. CREDIT CARDS •

Lee's Mardi Gras Enterprises,, Inc.
212-645-1888
400 West 14th St., 3rd Fl., (9th Ave.) NYC, NY 10014
Hours: 11:30-6:30 Mon-Sat
  • Complete line of ladies clothing for men, including shoes and wigs. CREDIT CARDS •

Mark Jeffries
212-752-7903
140 East 55th St., (Lexington-3rd Ave.) NYC, NY 10022
Hours: 10:30-6 Mon-Sat (Thurs till 7) • 12-5 Sun   FAX   212-752-7903
  • Men's clothing, purchase only; see Richard. •

Moe Ginsburg
212-242-3482
162 Fifth Ave., (21st St.) NYC, NY 10010
Hours: 9:30-7 Mon-Fri (Thurs till 8) • 9:30-6 Sat, Sun   FAX   212-727-2561
  • Discount men's clothing. CREDIT CARDS •

NBO Menswear
212-595-1550
1965 Broadway, (66th St.) NYC, NY 10023
Hours: 10-9 Mon-Sat • 12-6 Sun
  • Wide variety of men's clothes and accessories. Leather outerwear. Very reasonable. CREDIT CARDS •

Paul Stuart, Inc.
212-682-0320
Madison Ave & 45th St., NYC, NY 10017
Hours: 8-6 Mon-Fri (Thurs till 7) • 9-6 Sat
  • Fashionable menswear. Phone orders. RENTALS CREDIT CARDS •

SAINT LAURIE LTD.
895 Broadway 3rd Fl., (19th-20th St.) NYC, NY 10003   212-473-0100   FAX   212-473-2092
Hours: 10:30-6 Mon-Fri (Thurs till 8) • 9:30-6 Sat • 12-5 Sun (closed Sun: July, Aug)

Largest selection of quality, hand-tailored clothing for men and women in NYC. Every suit, sport coat, trouser, skirt, tuxedo, overcoat made on premises. Off season suits always available. Custom-made suits and shirts also available. Savings are 33% off typical retail.

• Excellent prices; sales only. Phone orders. CREDIT CARDS •

SAKS FIFTH AVE.
(direct line) 212-940-4321
611 Fifth Ave., (49th-50th St.) NYC, NY 10022
Hours: 10-6 Mon-Fri (studio services)   FAX   212-940-4803
• Fashionable clothing and accessories for men, women, children. Great memo service for stylists and costume designers. CREDIT CARDS •
(See display ad in this section.)

SECOND AVE. ARMY & NAVY WEAR,, INC.
212-737-4661
1598 Second Ave., (83rd St.) NYC, NY 10028
Hours: 10-8 Mon-Sat • 12-6 Sun
• Men's, women's and children's sport clothes. CREDIT CARDS •

THE SHIRT STORE
212-557-8040
51 East 44th St., (Corner of Madison Ave.) NYC, NY 10017
Hours: 8-6:30 Mon-Fri • 10-5 Sat   FAX   212-599-6220
• Stock and Custom men's shirts. Contact Carol. Phone orders. CREDIT CARDS •

SHOWROOM SEVEN
212-840-7277
241 West 37th St., (7th-8th Ave.) NYC, NY 10018
Hours: 9-6 Mon-Fri   FAX   212-768-2224
• Extensive selection of designer fashions; shoes, handbags, hats, gloves, belts and scarves. List of designers they carry available upon request. No credit cards. •

A. SULKA & CO.,, INC.
212-980-5226
301 Park Ave., (50th St.) NYC, NY 10022   212-980-5200
Hours: 9-6 Mon-Fri • 10-5 Sat
• Exquisite, expensive dressing gowns and smoking jackets, fine men's wear. Phone orders. CREDIT CARDS •

SYMS CLOTHING
212-797-1199
42 Trinity Pl., (Wall St.) NYC, NY 10004   800-444-SYMS
Hours: 9-6:30 Mon-Wed • 9-8 Thurs, Fri • 10-6:30 Sat • 12-5:30 Sun
• Great selection of men's and women's name-brand clothing; great prices. CREDIT CARDS •

TEPEE TOWN,, INC.
212-563-6430
Port Authority Bus Terminal, (40th-41st St. on 8th Ave.) NYC, NY 10036
Hours: 9-6:30 Mon-Fri • 9:30-6:30 Sat
• Indian goods and western wear. No phone orders. CREDIT CARDS •

F. R. TRIPLER & CO.
212-922-1090
366 Madison Ave. (46th St.) NYC, NY 10017
Hours: 9-5:45 Mon-Fri (Thurs till 6:30) • 9-5:30 Sat   FAX   212-867-7867
• Excellent quality men's wear, 100% cotton collarless shirts with separate collars available. CREDIT CARDS •

CLOTHING RENTAL & PURCHASE: UNIFORMS

See also **COSTUME RENTAL & CONSTRUCTION**
See also **POLICE EQUIPMENT**

ACADEMY CLOTHES,, INC.   212-765-1440
    1703 Broadway, (54th St.) NYC, NY 10019
    Hours: 9:30-6:30 Mon-Sat
    • Half-price tuxedos, waiters, police, chauffeur, hotel uniforms; RENTALS CREDIT CARDS. •

ALLAN UNIFORM RENTAL   212-529-4655
    121 East 24th., (Lexington-Park Ave.) NYC, NY 10010
    Hours: 9-5 Mon-Fri   FAX   212-505-7781
    • . Police and doorman uniforms. RENTALS CREDIT CARDS •

ARMY & NAVY SURPLUS STORES   212-534-1600
    1938 Third Ave., (107th St.) NYC, NY 10029
    Hours: 9:30-7 Mon-Sat
    • Military clothing and surplus. CREDIT CARDS •

BATTLEZONE EXCHANGE   203-795-8387
    371 Boston Post Road, Orange, CT 06477
    Hours: 10-6 Mon-Sat • 10-2 Sun
    • Military dress uniforms, battle fatigues, boots, medals, ribbons, military surplus and accessories; mostly Vietnam items, some WW II items also. Phone orders. RENTALS CREDIT CARDS •

BENNER MEDICAL PROPS,, INC.   212-727-9815
    601 West 26th St. 16th Fl., (11th-12th Ave.) NYC, NY 10001
    Hours: 9-4:30 Mon-Fri   FAX   212-727-9824
    • Complete line of medical uniforms and accessories; RENTALS. Cash or check only •

BRIGADE QUARTERMASTERS, LTD.   404-428-1234
    1025 Cobb International Blvd., Kennesaw, GA 30144   800-241-3125
    Hours: 8:30-8 Mon-Fri (store) • 10-4 Sat (phone orders)   FAX   800-892-2999
    • Combat, SWAT uniforms and accessories; survival, camping, climbing, hunting and expedition gear, outdoor action gear. Catalog. No rentals. CREDIT CARDS •

BUFFALO ENTERPRISES   (Info) 717-259-0991
    PO Box 183, 308 West King St., East Berlin, PA 17316   (Orders) 717-259-9081
    Hours: 10-5 Tues-Sat (Fri till 9) • 1-5 Sun (by appt. only week-ends May-Sept)
                                          FAX   717-292-3535
    • 18th and 19th century historical clothing and accouterments; military and civilian. MC/VISA •

FRANK BEE STORES, INC.   718-823-9475
    3439 East Tremont Ave., (off I-95/Bruckner) Bronx, NY 10465
    Hours: 9-6 Mon-Sat • 9-2 Sun   FAX   718-823-9812
    • School, cheerleading and Scout uniforms and accessories. Caps and gowns, choir robes, judicial robes and clerical vestments. RENTALS •

CHURCH ST. SURPLUS   212-226-5280
    327 Church St., (Canal St.) NYC, NY 10013
    Hours: 10:30-5:30 Mon-Sat (closed Sat: July-Aug)
    • A good supply of Army/Navy surplus, antique military. RENTALS CREDIT CARDS •

ATAC

THE COCKPIT 212-925-5456
   595 Broadway, (Prince-Houston St.) NYC, NY 10012
   Hours: 11-7 Mon-Sat • 12:30-6 Sun
   • A selection of WW II to current aviation gear; catalog. CREDIT CARDS •

GERRY COSBY & CO.,, INC. 212-563-6464
   3 Penn Plaza, (Madison Sq. Garden) NYC, NY 10001
   Hours: 9:30-6:30 Mon-Fri • 9:30-6 Sat • 12-5 Sun
   (Open till game time - Knicks & Rangers night games.) FAX 212-967-0876
   •Athletic outfitters for official sports uniforms. Sell and apply iron on numbers and letters.
   Some vintage uniform pieces. Clothing: sales only. See Patty or Herb. Phone orders. CREDIT
   CARDS•

CRAFT CLOTHES 212-764-6122
   247 West 37th St., (7th-8th Ave.) NYC, NY 10018
   Hours: 9:30-6 Mon-Fri • 9:30-3 Sat FAX 212-997-7318
   • School uniforms, caps and gowns, clerical apparel, judicial robes and accessories, jewelry,
   cheerleading uniforms; can order letter sweaters. Will ship. RENTALS CREDIT CARDS •

DAVID'S OUTFITTERS,, INC. 212-691-7388
   36 West 20th St., (7th-8th Ave.) NYC, NY 10011
   Hours: 9-5 Mon-Fri
   • Formal wear and all types of uniforms. Will ship. CREDIT CARDS •

DORNAN UNIFORMS 212-247-0937
   653 Eleventh Ave. 2nd. Fl., (47th-48th St.) NYC, NY 10036 800-223-0363
   Hours: 8:30-4 Mon-Fri (Thurs till 6) FAX 212-956-7672
   • Complete line of uniforms and accessories - in stock and custom; chauffeur, butler, maid,
   doormen, janitorial, police, security, fire, medical, etc. Will ship. No rentals. CREDIT CARDS
   with phone orders. •

"I found it in the N.Y. Theatrical Sourcebook."

EAVES–BROOKS COSTUME CO.,, INC.
718-729-1010
21-07 41st Ave., (21st-22nd St.) L.I.C., NY 11101
Hours: 9-5 Mon-Fri   FAX   **718-729-5118**
• Large selection of military, service, restaurant and industrial uniforms; will also build to order. In house assistance available. Full service costume shop; construction, alterations located in own 100,000 sq. ft. bldg. Large costume research library. RENTALS CREDIT CARDS •
(See display ad under COSTUME RENTAL & CONSTRUCTION.)

EMPIRE SPORTING GOODS MFG.
800-221-3455
212-966-0880
443 Broadway, (Grand-Howard) NYC, NY 10013
Hours: 9-4 Mon-Fri by appt.   FAX   **212-941-7113**
• Manufacturer of all sports uniforms, team jackets, custom chenille emblems and lettering, silkscreen printing. Mainly wholesale; will service the industry by appt.; Call Richard Chwang. Catalog available. MC/VISA •

FRANK'S SPORT SHOP
718-299-9628
430 East Tremont Ave., (Park) Bronx, NY 10457
Hours: 9-8 Mon-Fri • 9-7 Sat   FAX   **718-583-1652**
• Military uniforms and insignia; postal, sanitation, parks dept., traffic, corrections , baseball, football uniforms and equipment; sporting goods, hunting and archery equipment. Catalog available. CREDIT CARDS •

G. GEDNEY GODWIN,, INC.
215-783-0670
PO Box 100, Valley Forge, PA 19481
Hours: 9:30-4:30 Mon-Fri   FAX   **215-783-6083**
• 18th century military gear and accessories; catalog. See Tina Perkins or G. Gedney Godwin. MC/VISA •

GOVERNMENT SURPLUS SALES,, INC.
203-247-7787
30 Atlantic St., Hartford, CT 06103
Hours: 10-6 Mon-Fri • Sat by appt.
FAX   203-548-9905
• New and used government issue (pre-WWII through present), military uniforms (WWI through present), military surplus, flight equipment, helmets, etc. See David Schweitzer. CREDIT CARDS •

H. KNOBEL UNIFORM CORP.
718-853-1200
3903 Ft. Hamilton Pkwy., (39th St.) Brooklyn, NY 11218
Hours: 9-5 Mon-Thurs • 9-2 Fri • 12-5 Sun
FAX   718-853-1617
• Men's and women's industrial uniforms, white ducks, lab coats; embroidery and printing, large sizes. MC/VISA •

ICEBERG OF SOHO ARMY-NAVY
212-226-8485
455 Broadway, (Grand-Canal St.) NYC, NY 10013
Hours: 10-6 Mon-Fri • 11-6 Sat-Sun
FAX   212-274-1816
• Good selection of Army-Navy surplus clothes, boots, etc. RENTALS CREDIT CARDS. •

IDEAL
212-252-5090
1814-16 Flatbush Ave., (Ave. K) Brooklyn, NY 11210
Hours: 10-5:45 Mon-Sat
FAX   718-692-0492
• School uniforms, letter sweaters, monograms, camp and Scout uniforms, cheerleading, caps & gowns, teens. Will ship. CREDIT CARDS •

KATZIN'S UNIFORMS
201-623-3457
201-623-3522
228 Market St., Newark, NJ 07102
Hours: 9-5:30 Mon-Sat (Fri till 6)
• Police uniforms, equipment and accessories; work clothes. Phone orders. No rentals. MC/VISA •

KAUFMAN'S ARMY & NAVY
212-757-5670
319 West 42nd St., (8th-9th Ave.) NYC, NY 10036
Hours: 10-6 Mon-Sat (Thurs till 7)
• Rentals and sales of military uniforms and equipment. Also related props, work clothes, Levi's and boots. Popular among costumers and stylists. •
(See display ad in this section.)

LEVY'S SPORTS CENTER
201-861-7100
Bergenline Ave. and 62nd St., West New York, NJ 07093
Hours: 9-6 Mon-Thurs • 9-8 Fri • 9-6 Sat • 10-4 Sun
FAX   201-861-8836
• Sports uniforms, t-shirts, jackets, etc. - retail and custom. Also custom pads and matting. Will ship. CREDIT CARDS •

MADISON MEN'S SHOP
212-741-9777
212-463-0610
26 Eleventh Ave., (Corner W. 15th St.) NYC, NY 10011
Hours: 8-4:30 Mon-Fri • 9-3:30 Sat
• Great selection of "blue-collar" clothing. Workclothes, boots, arctics, etc.. CREDIT CARDS •

NATIONAL MOUNTED TRAINING GROUP
914-359-3854
800-638-2080
PO Box 358, Main St., Sparkill, NY 10976
Hours: 9-5 Mon-Fri
• Mounted police uniforms and boots; riding and horse equipment; catalog. MC/VISA •

"I found it in the N.Y. Theatrical Sourcebook."

O. K. UNIFORM CO.
212-966-1984
212-966-4733
507 Broadway, (Spring-Broome St.) NYC, NY 10012
Hours: 9:30-5:30 Mon-Thurs • 9:30-call Fri • 11:30-4:30 Sun   FAX   212-226-6668
• Complete selection of uniforms and accessories for all service industries; kitchen uniforms, work clothes, formal uniforms, protective clothing, disposables, footwear, name and logo emblems, hats and gloves, Sales only. •
(See display ad in this section.)

THE QUEENSBORO SHIRT CO.
718-782-0200
800-847-4478
80 North 5th St., Williamsburg, NY 11211
Hours: 9-5 Mon-Fri
• Quantity purchases of cotton polo shirts, many colors and sizes; with or without your embroidered logo; catalog. •

RELIABLE AND FRANKS NAVAL UNIFORMS
718-858-6033
106 Flushing Ave., (Adelphi St.-Carlton Ave.) Brooklyn, NY 11205
Hours: 9-5 Mon-Fri • 9-2 Sat (closed Sat: July-Labor Day)
•Good selection of real uniforms; New and used military clothing, insignias and equipment. Sales only. No credit cards•

SCAFATI UNIFORMS,, INC.
212-695-4944
405 West 42nd St., (9-10th Ave.) NYC, NY 10036
Hours: 9-6 Mon-Fri
• Doorman, bellboy, waiter outfits to purchase; also custom orders; top quality, pleasant service, reasonable rates. CREDIT CARDS •

B. SCHLESINGER & SONS,, INC.
212-206-8022
249 West 18th St., (7th-8th Ave.) NYC, NY 10011
Hours: 9-6 Mon-Fri • 10-4 Sat
•Police, security guard, emergency medical service and postal uniforms; workclothes; accessories. Phone orders. No rentals. CREDIT CARDS•

SOME'S UNIFORMS
201-843-1199
212-564-6274
65 Rt. 17, Paramus, NJ 07652
Hours: 9-6 Mon-Sat (Thurs till 8) • 9-5 Sat   FAX   201-842-3014
• Uniforms, accessories and related items for the military, law enforcement, firemen and service industries. Catalog. Phone orders. CREDIT CARDS •

SUPPLY STORE NYFD
718-694-2544
250 Livingston, (near Fulton St.) Brooklyn, NY 11201
Hours: 9-1 Mon-Fri
• Firemen's uniforms. Cash only. No credit cards •

JAMES TOWNSEND & SON
800-338-1665
PO Box 415, 133 North 1st St., Pierceton, IN 46562
Hours: 10-5 Mon-Sat   FAX   219-594-5580
• 18th and 19th century military uniforms, clothing, hats, patterns, guns, pistols, knives, axes, barrels, kegs, baskets, blankets, lanterns; repro colonial household goods; catalog. CREDIT CARDS •

THE TRADER
212-925-6610
212-925-6634
385 Canal St., (Thompson-W. B'way) NYC, NY 10013
Hours: 10-7 every day   FAX   212-966-4535
• New and used uniforms, military clothing and surplus. RENTALS CREDIT CARDS •

UNIFORMS BY PARK COATS,, INC.   718-499-1182
790 Third Ave., (27th St.) Brooklyn, NY 11232
Hours: 9-6 Mon-Fri • 9-3 Sat   FAX 718-499-1646
• Manufacturer of police, fire and law enforcement uniforms-all styles-shoes and accessories. No rentals. CREDIT CARDS •

WEISS & MAHONEY   212-675-1915
142 Fifth Ave., (corner 19th St.) NYC, NY 10011   212-675-1367
Hours: 9-7 Mon-Fri • 10-6 Sat • 11-5 Sun   FAX 212-633-8573
• Inexpensive military clothing and surplus goods; shoes, medals, camping attire and equipment. No rentals. CREDIT CARDS •

COINS & CURRENCY

BRIGANDI COIN CO.   212-869-5350
60 West 44th St., (5th-6th Ave.) NYC, NY 10036
Hours: 9-5 Mon-Fri   FAX 212-869-5359
• Coin and paper money, including foreign; also baseball cards. VISA AMEX •

DORY DUPLICATES   518-854-7613
PO Box 546, Salem, NY 12865
Hours: 9-5 Mon-Thurs   FAX 518-854-7613
• Coin reproductions; including US, foreign, biblical, pirate. Large scale coins for props; many finishes available. •

HARMER ROOKE   212-751-1900
32 East 57th St., (Park-Madison Ave.) NYC, NY 10022
Hours: 10-5 Mon-Fri • Sat by appt.   FAX 212-758-1713
• Rare coins, currency, ancient art, americana. CREDIT CARDS •

JULES J. KARP   212-279-1024
372 Seventh Ave., (30th-31st St.) NYC, NY 10001
Hours: 9-5:15 Mon-Fri • 10:15-3 Sat   FAX 212-268-4932
• Rare coins, currency and jewelry. AMEX •

STACK'S   212-582-2580
123 West 57th St., (6th-7th Ave.) NYC, NY 10019
Hours: 10-5 Mon-Fri   FAX 212-245-5018
• Foreign and U.S. coins and currency. Also books and some publications. •

COMPUTERS & BUSINESS MACHINES

47TH ST. PHOTO,, INC.   212-921-1287
115 West 45th St., (6th-B'way) NYC, NY 10036
Hours: 9:30-7 Mon-Thurs • 9:30-2 Fri • 10-5 Sun

67 West 47th Street, (5-6th Avenue) NYC, NY 10036
Hours: 9-6:30 Mon-Thurs • 9-2 Fri • 10-5 Sun
• Computers, copiers, typewriters, etc.; cameras and photo equipment. Watch for frequent sales. •

"I found it in the N.Y. Theatrical Sourcebook."

A & B BEACON BUSINESS MACHINES   718-786-0400
   43-09 Vernon Blvd., (43rd) L.I.C., NY 11101
   Hours: 8:30-5 Mon-Fri   FAX 718-786-0652
   • New and used. RENTALS CREDIT CARDS •

ACE PROPS
212-206-1475
   1 West 19th St. Ground Fl., (5th Ave.) NYC, NY 10011   212-580-9551
   Hours: 8-5 Mon-Fri • 9-4 Sat or by appt.   FAX 212-929-9082
   • Prop rental house with old and new electronics, computers, sound equipment. CREDIT CARDS •
   (See display ad under PROP RENTAL HOUSES.)

AJAX TYPEWRITER CORP.   212-832-9650
   230 East 59th St., (2nd-3rd Ave.) NYC, NY 10022   800-898-AJAX
   Hours: 8:30-5:30 Mon-Fri   FAX 212-371-6466
   • New and used typewriters. RENTALS MC/AMEX •

ALL SERVICE COMPUTER RENTAL
212-524-0003
   Hours: 9-6 Mon-Fri • deliveries available on weekends   FAX 212-732-2369
   • Desktop computers, monitors, printers, notebook computers, facsimiles, desktop copiers and other business equipment on a rental basis. •

ALPHA BUSINESS MACHINES   212-643-5555
   151 West 30th St., (6th-7th Ave.) NYC, NY 10001
   Hours: 8:30-5 Mon-Fri
   • Typewriters, cash registers, copiers. RENTALS CREDIT CARDS •

COMPUTRS   212-254-9000
   7 Great Jones St., (Broadway-Lafayette) NYC, NY 10012   212-254-9191
   Hours: 10-6:30 Mon-Fri (Thurs till 7) • 11-6 Sat
   • Formerly Village Computers,, Inc. Sales of computer equipment and supplies; also working and non-working computer equipment for props. Complete line of software for scriptwriting, script breakdown, production scheduling and budgeting. RENTALS CREDIT CARDS •

J & R MUSIC WORLD   212-349-4727
   15 Park Row, (Beekman-Ann St.) NYC, NY 10038   212-238-9070
   Hours: 9-6:30 Mon-Sat • 10-5 Sun
   • Computers and home office outlet. CREDIT CARDS •

MIDTOWN TYPEWRITER   212-255-4752
   134 West 26th St, (6th-7th Ave.) NYC, NY 10011
   Hours: 9 to 5 Mon-Fri
   • New and used typewriters. MC/VISA •

P C COMPUTER RENTAL   212-594-2222
   360 West 31st St. 9th Fl., (8th-9th Ave.) NYC, NY 10001
   Hours: 9-5 Mon-Fri   FAX 212-594-1312
   • Rents Compaqs, IBM PC's and Macintoshes; will pickup and deliver. AMEX •

C-D

PCR Personal Computer Rentals
437 West 16th St. (9th-10th) NYC, NY 10011
Hours: 8:30-6 Mon-Fri (24-hour on call service)

212-645-2800

FAX   212-645-4478

Nationwide computer rental company specializing in service
and reliability. IBM, Apple Compaq, Hewlett-Packard. Large
monitors, printers, modems and peripherals.
Experts in AV/Computer Interfacing.
Same day delivery and installation on most items in stock.
Daily, weekly, monthly rentals. Technical service and support.

• Large selection. CREDIT CARDS •

Personal Computer Service / P.C. Services,, Inc.
26 West 23rd St., (5th-6th Ave.) NYC, NY 10010
Hours: 9-5:30 Mon-Fri
• RENTALS; needs 2-3 days notice. CREDIT CARDS •

212-255-7600

FAX   212-255-9257

William Steinberg
266 Bowery, (Prince-Houston St.) NYC, NY 10012
Hours: 8:30-5 Mon-Fri
• Large selection of cash registers- from antique to new; also scales, mixers and grinders.
RENTALS •
(See display ad under KITCHEN EQUIPMENT: INDUSTRIAL.)

212-473-7670
718-657-5177

Sussman Brothers Cash Register Corp.
2010 Coney Island Ave., (Quentin Rd.) Brooklyn, NY 11223
Hours: 8-5 Mon-Fri/8-1 Sat
• Antique and new cash registers, scales; RENTALS •

212-226-0290

FAX   718-998-8012

Tytell Typewriter Co.
116 Fulton St., (William-Nassau St.) NYC, NY 10038
Hours: 10-3 Mon-Fri (or by appt.)
• The expert source for typewriters and business machines; Yiddish to Russian, 145 languages; antique to modern; Teleprompter, typewriters. Restoration. RENTALS •

212-233-5333

FAX   212-233-5336

Union Cash Register
184 Bowery, (Spring-Delancy St.) NYC, NY 10012
Hours: 6:30-5 Mon-Fri • 8-1 Sat
• New and used cash registers. MC/VISA •

212-431-3200

CORK

AMERICAN STAR CORK CO.,, INC. 718-335-3000
33-53 62nd St., (34th Ave.) Woodside, NY 11377
Hours: 8-4:45 Mon-Fri
• Cork and metal stampings. Cork $50 minimum •

AYWON CHALKBOARD,, INC. D/B/A THE CORK STORE 718-853-2300
22 Caton Place, (Ocean Pkwy-Coney Island Ave.) Brooklyn, NY 11218
Hours: 8-4:30 Mon-Fri FAX 718-853-2303

We offer imported and domestic decorative floor, wall and ceiling cork tile. All at *warehouse prices!*
One of the largest inventories of:
• Vinyl impregnated roll cork
  for wall covering & Bulletin boards
• Composition (natural) cork
  for underlayment & economy bulletin boards

AYWON CHALKBOARD INC.
Custom & Volume Mfrs.

• Also custom chalkboards. •

WOLF-GORDON WALLCOVERING,, INC. 212-319-6800
997 Third Ave. Rm. 1518, (58th-59th St.) NYC, NY 10022 (Showroom)
33-00 47th Avenue (33-34th) L.I.C., NY 11101 (Offices) 718-361-6611
Hours: 9-5 Mon-Fri
• Wallcoverings: vinyl, cork; showroom. •

SOMMER CORK COMPANY 800-242-0808
6342 W. Irving Park Road, Chicago, IL 60634 312-283-5340
Hours: 9-4:30 Mon-Fri FAX 312-283-4822
• Cork Stoppers and bulletin board cork. •

COSTUME CRAFTSPEOPLE, MASKS & MILLINERY₁

A **BOLD LISTING** indicates the person or company is a member of ATAC, Association of Theatrical Artists and Craftspeople, a professional trade association for craftspeople working in the entertainment, performance and presentational media industries. See display ad in this section.

DEBORAH ANDERKO   212-289-2988
   161 E. 89th Street, (3rd-Lexington) NYC, NY 10128
   Hours: by appt.
      • Dressmaking, alterations, custom bridal and formal wear; stylist. •

AUSTIN & COMPANY   718-636-9110
   198 Prospect Place, Brooklyn, NY 11238
   Hours; by appt.   FAX   212-206-8922
      • Costume design and fabrication, wardrobe, styling, crafts and make-up expertise. Research & shopping services available. Contact Karen Hart or Ribin McGee. •

ROBERT W. BAKER   212-740-4915
   801 West 181st St. #69, (Ft. Washington) NYC, NY 10033
   Hours: by appt.
      • Headdresses, millinery, jewelry, decapitated heads, all types of masks, make-up and prosthetics; for any medium. •

KATHLEEN BARTLETT   212-772-1214
   334 East 77th St. #5, NYC, NY 10021
   Hours: by appt.
      • Costume design, construction and crafts. Also period research, styling, shopping. All areas; theatre, film, dance, industrials, display. •

ANDREW BENEPE STUDIO   718-488-0001
   43 Bridge St., Brooklyn, NY 11121
   Hours: by appt.
      • Monster and animal costumes, sculpture, special effect rigging, costume crafts, props, puppets. •

ARLEY BERRYHILL   718-204-4913
   21-05 33rd St. #5B, (21st Ave.), Astoria, NY 11105
   Hours: by appt.
      • Costume crafts, foam sculpture, millinery, puppets, masks, mold making. •

MARCY BETHEL   415-282-7660
   668 62nd Street, Oakland, CA 94609
   Hours: by appt.
      • Milliner, costume craftsperson, costume technician. •

JANET BLOOR / EURO CO.   212-629-9665
   247 West 30th St. 8th Fl., NYC, NY 10001
   Hours: 9-6 Mon-Fri
      • Special fabric effects. •

FABRIC EFFECTS INCORPORATED

DYEING

SILKSCREENING

HAND PAINTING

SAMPLING

PROTOTYPES

DESIGN DEVELOPMENT

FABRIC DESIGN

Proprietors:
Gene Mignola Joni Johns Richard S. Lerner

20 West 20th Street, 5th Floor
New York City 10011
fax 212.255.3077

We specialize in custom orders
& small production.

We have extensive
experience in
THEATER,
FILM,
FASHION &
ENTERTAINMENT.

Our clients include:
Polo/Ralph Lauren
Nike
Calvin Klein
Donna Karan/DKNY
Isaac Mizrahi
Reebok
J. Crew
Peter Marino
Naomi Leff
Walt Disney
Ringling Bros. Barnum & Bailey
Cats
Tommy
Beauty & the Beast
Guys & Dolls
Phantom of the Opera
Will Rogers Follies
Sunset Boulevard
Dracula
Bronx Tale
Forrest Gump
Lincoln Center Theater
City Opera
Houston Opera
Joffrey Ballet
Alvin Ailey
American Ballet Theater
Ballet Met
Dance Theater of Harlem
San Francisco Ballet

☎ 212.255.5225

CHRIS BOBIN
212-255-5225
212-475-7268

20 West 20th St. c/o Fabric Effects (5th-6th Ave.) NYC, NY 10011
Hours: by appt.

Sewn solutions for props, costumes and illustrations.
Unique works created to your specifications in any
sizes - miniature to oversize - using quilting, applique
and/or embroidery techniques.

• Call for free color flyer; beautiful stuff. •

OLIVIA BOOTH
212-279-3054

484 West 43rd St. #5F, (9th-10th Ave.) NYC, NY 10036
Hours: by appt.
• Fabric and costume painting, millinery, prop and costume crafts, sculpture for stage, film,
TV. •

GARY BROUWER (C/O EAVES BROOKS COSTUME CO.)
718-729-1010

21-07 41st Ave., (21st-22nd St.) L.I.C., NY 11101
Hours: by appt.
• Experienced milliner; fashion to theatre. •

RANDY CARFAGNO
212-947-0302

347 West 39th St. #7E, (8th-9th Ave.) NYC, NY 10018
Hours: by appt.
• Professional puppeteer for TV, film, stage; puppet mascot building- all types. Masks, sculpt-
ing, latex shoes, mold making, foam and wood carving. •

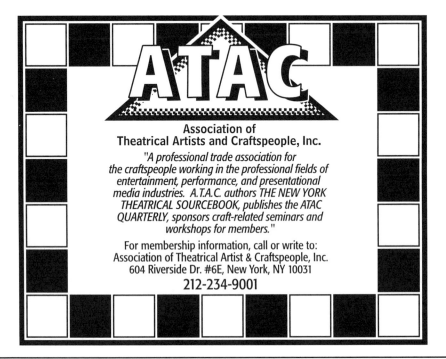

Association of
Theatrical Artists and Craftspeople, Inc.

*"A professional trade association for
the craftspeople working in the professional fields of
entertainment, performance, and presentational
media industries. A.T.A.C. authors THE NEW YORK
THEATRICAL SOURCEBOOK, publishes the ATAC
QUARTERLY, sponsors craft-related seminars and
workshops for members."*

For membership information, call or write to:
Association of Theatrical Artist & Craftspeople, Inc.
604 Riverside Dr. #6E, New York, NY 10031
212-234-9001

"I found it in the N.Y. Theatrical Sourcebook."

CHAPEAUX CARINE
47 Irving Pl., (17th St.) NYC, NY 10003
212-777-8393
Hours: by appt.
• Custom-made hats: bridal, felt, straw, fur, fabric; for theatre and film; period or contemporary. Contact Carine Fraley. •

BRENDA COLLING
592 Manhattan Ave. #3L, (Nassau-Driggs) Brooklyn, NY 11222
718-383-3839
Hours: by appt.
• Costume designer, costume crafts, millinery. •

DIANA COLLINS
866 Carroll St., (Prospect Pk. W-8th) Brooklyn, NY 11215
718-398-2414
Hours: by appt.
• Costume design and assistance, shopping; costume crafts including fabric painting, dyeing, distressing, foam, feathers, leather; wardrobe and shop management. •

EILEEN CONNOR
PO Box 154, Radio City Station, NYC, NY 10101
212-246-6346
Hours: by appt.
• Scenic painting and faux finishes, fabric painting, prop and costume crafts. •

MILDRED DEL RIO
324 West 17th St. #2W, (8th-9th Ave.) NYC, NY 10011
212-741-0670
Hours: by appt.
• Dressmaking, alterations, custom bridal, christening, formal wear; millinery; dresser and stylist. •

DYE-NAMIX
16 Mercer St. 3rd Fl, (Howard) NYC, NY 10013
212-941-6642
Hours: 10-6 Mon-Fri or by appt.
FAX   212-941-7407

Dyeing, Hand Painting, and Silk Screening

Recognized in Broadway theatre, feature films and the fashion industry.

Competitive rates and fast service.
Pickup and delivery service.

DYE·NAMIX

• Creative dyeing, painting, and silkscreening of samples, yardages, and garments for the fashion, theatre, and film industries. Contract Raylene Marasco for project estimates. •

OLIVIA EATON
P.O. Box 40-0161, Brooklyn, NY 11240
718-875-4592
Hours: by appt.
• Sculpture, metal fabrication, costume construction, knitting, and sewing. •

HENRI EWASKIO
3 Vine St., Staten Island, NY 10301
718-727-0899
Hours: by appt.
• Puppets, millinery, display miniatures, costume props, masks, costume construction. •

FABRIC EFFECTS
20 West 20th St. 5th Fl., (5th-6th Ave.) NYC, NY 10011
212-255-5225
Hours: 9-5 Mon- Fri (or by appt.)
FAX   212-255-3077
• Dyeing, silkscreening, hand painting - all kinds of fabric coloring - done by three of NY's top textile artisans. •
(See display ad in this section.)

C-D

MARIA FICALORA KNITWEAR, LTD.
212-645-6905
136 West 21st St., 6th Fl., (6th-7th Ave.) NYC, NY 10011
Hours: 9-5 Mon-Fri
• Custom knitwear for stage and screen. •

JOAN FEDYSZYN
212-769-0895
341 West 71st St., (West End Ave.) NYC, NY 10023
Hours: by appt.
• Costume designer, construction, stylist, shopper; specializing in characters for film, commercials and music videos. •

DIANE ROSETTI FINN
212-719-5604
233 West 42nd St., (7th-8th Ave.) NYC, NY 10036
Hours: by appt.
• Costume designer; period and fantasy costumes; scenic painter. •

B. E. FLESCH-ARTISAN
406-685-3420
208 Broadway, Pony, MT 59747
Hours: 10-7 Tues-Fri/10-5 Sat
• Leather accessories for theatrical purposes; repairs and alterations; specialize in application of taps; also makes boot and shoe lasts. •

GEPPETO SOFT SCULPTURE & DISPLAY
718-398-9792
107 Lexington Ave., (Franklin-Classon) Brooklyn, NY 11238
Hours: 10-6 Mon-Fri
• Custom construction of soft sculpture animal & body puppet costumes and props, foam rubber masks, oversized foam props, and 3-D illustrations. Contact Scott, brochure available. •
(See display ad under PROP SHOPS.)

C–D

PAMELA B. GOLDMAN
212-459-4217
914-636-7624
PO Box 636, New Rochelle, NY 10802
Hours: by appt. (24-hour ans. svc.)
• Specialty costumes, special effects painting and backdrops. Shopping, props, costume collection rental. Available for print, theatre, TV, film. Member Local 829. •

JANE GOOTNICK
212-724-2056
204 West 88th St., (B'way) NYC, NY 10024
Hours: by appt.
• Props, masks, creatures. •

RODNEY GORDON
212-779-0160
132 East 28th St., (Lexington-3rd Ave.) NYC, NY 10016
Hours: 10-6 Mon-Fri
• Costume crafts: specializing in millinery and masks. •

YVETTE HELIN
718-782-3513
85 North 3rd St. 4th Fl., (Wythe-Berry) Brooklyn, NY 11211
Hours: by appt.
• Costume design and construction; theatrical, promotional and special events. •

ANNIE HICKMAN
914-359-4019
300 Ferdon Ave., Piermont, NY 10968
Hours: by appt.
• Sculptural fantasy costumes of the creature kind. •

MILENDA HODGES FINE MILLINERY
212-925-0699
122 Hudson St. 5th Fl., (N. Moore-Varick) NYC, NY 10013
Hours: 9:30-5 Mon-Fri by appt.
• Sales and repairs of custom or stock hats. RENTALS No credit cards •

YASUO IHARA
185 Sterling Pl., (Flatbush Ave.) Brooklyn, NY 11238
718-622-3584
Hours: 9-5 Mon-Fri
• Armor, animal heads, headpieces, foam bodies, masks in Celastic, latex and foam. •

MARTIN IZQUIERDO STUDIO
118 West 22nd St. 9th Fl., (6th-7th Ave.) NYC, NY 10011
212-807-9757
Hours: 9-6 Mon-Fri weekends by appt.
FAX 212-366-5249
• Costume crafts; fabric painting, soft sculpture, dyeing, aging, fantasy costumes, mold making for theatre, film, commercials and video. No rentals •
(See display ad under COSTUME RENTAL & CONSTRUCTION.)

ROBERT W. JONES
97 Arden St. #3C, (1st-2nd Ave.) NYC, NY 10040
212-569-8532
Hours: by appt.
• Props for theatre and commercials; masks, Celastic fabricator. •

JAN KASTENDIECK
40 Harrison St. #14B, (West-Greenwich St.) NYC, NY 10013
212-962-1042
Hours: by appt.
• Draper, patternmaker, cutter, dyer, shop foreman. •

BRYAN KOLLMAN
594 Ninth Ave. 2nd Fl., (2nd-3rd Ave.) NYC, NY 10036
212-765-6280
Hours: by appt.
• Theatrical fabric painter. Affiliated with Carelli Costumes. •

LARUE
222 West 23rd St. Rm. 1005, (7th-8th Ave.) NYC, NY 10011
212-645-9513
Hours: 10-6 Mon-Fri
• Costume design and production; promotional, theatrical; craft work. •

CATHY LAZAR COSTUMES & SOFT PROPS
212-473-0363
Hours: by appt.
• Specialty costumes and soft props for TV, film, print, performance, promotion. •

RALPH LEE
463 West St. #D405, (12th St.) NYC, NY 10014
212-929-4777
Hours: by appt.
• Masks, larger-than-life puppets and costumes; wide range of materials. •

JANET LINVILLE
72 E. 7th St. #3B, NYC, NY 10003
212-254-8294
212-807-9757
Hours: by appt.

Millinery, masks and other costume crafts for theatre and fashion; pattern making for fabric hats a specialty.

• Millinery, masks and other crafts for theatre and fashion; •

CELESTE LIVINGSTON
26 Thompson St. #4A, (Grand) NYC, NY 10013
212-226-4182
Hours: by appt.
• Costumer. •

LAURA LOPEZ/GATE HOUSE
914-359-8853
P.O. Box 495, Piermont, NY 10968
Hours: by appt.   FAX   914-398-2821
• Network of suburban craftspeople; specialty costumes, masks and fabric works
(See display ad in this section.)

LYNNE MACKEY
212-927-1868
570 Ft. Washington Ave. #35B, NYC, NY 10033
Hours: by appt.
• Custom millinery. •

JENNIE MARINO / MOONBOOTS PRODUCTIONS
914-358-0199
6 Washington St., Nyack, NY 10960
Hours: by appt.
• Fantasy costumes, masks, make-up, props, puppets. Design and decoration for social, corporate and civic events; performing variety artist. •

MCL DESIGNS,, INC.
212-587-1511
47 Ann St., NYC, NY 10010
Hours: by appt.
• Customized costumes, full-figure puppets, hand puppets, masks, props. Contact Susan McClain-Moore. •

MARY MEYERS
718-956-1466
128 Amity St. Brooklyn, NY 11201
Hours: by appt.
• Prop and costume crafts, scenic painting and decorative finishes, costume display work. •

STACY MORSE
718-783-4375
802-257-5660
42 Berkeley Pl., (5th-6th) Brooklyn, NY 11217
Hours: by appt.
• Promotional body puppets, animal and fantasy costumes designed and built, realistic, oversized portrait heads and masks, animal heads in Celastic, latex, vacuumformed. •

ZOË MORSETTE
718-784-8894
11-14 46th Ave. #2-I, (11th) L.I.C., NY 11101
Hours: by appt.
• Theatrical and display props, specialty costumes, full-head masks, millinery, sculpture, soft goods. •

GREGORY JAMES MOWRY
213-665-4830
1836 N. New Hampshire Ave. #311, Los Angeles, CA 90027
Hours: by appt.
• Pattern maker/tailor, custom made-to-order garments; male and female, period and haute couture. •

MULDER/MARTIN INC
212-234-0889
604 Riverside Dr. #6E, (137th-138th St.) NYC, NY 10031
Hours: 9-5 Mon-Fri   FAX   212-234-0885
• Full body character costumes, costume props and puppets for theatre, film, television and promotional events. •
(See display ad in this section.)

FREDERICK NIHDA
718-834-1276
374 Union St., (Smith-Hoyt) Brooklyn, NY 11231
Hours: 10-6 Mon-Fri by appt.
• Custom props and costumes for theatre, film, promotions and TV; available for freelance work or staff position. •

SHELLEY NORTON　　　　　　　　　　　　　　　　718-636-5730
　　260 Fifth Ave. #2, (Garfield) Brooklyn, NY 11215
　　Hours: by appt.
　　• Costume painting, costume crafts, costume design. •

DENNIS PAVER / ECCENTRICITIES　　　　　　　　212-924-9411
　　41 Union Square West #1027, (B'way-17th St.) NYC, NY 10003
　　Hours: 10-6 Mon-Fri
　　• Costume design, construction, illustration; costumes, props for theatre, display. •

ROSEMARY PONZO　　　　　　　　　　　　　　　212-463-7971
　　181 Seventh Ave. #3B, (21st-22nd St.) NYC, NY 10011
　　Hours: by appt.
　　• Costume designer, fashion coordinator, fashion designer and stylist. •

VALERIE PORR　　　　　　　　　　　　　　　　212-966-6514
　　23 Greene St., (Canal-Grand Ave.) NYC, NY 10013
　　Hours: 8:30-6 or by appt.
　　• Dress, suit and formal wear design and construction; children and large sizes. Also works in
　　feathers. RENTALS •

JULIE PRINCE　　　　　　　　　　　　　　　　212-486-9249
　　141 East 56th St. #9G, (Lexington-3rd Ave.) NYC, NY 10022
　　Hours: by appt.
　　• Life-casting; masks, sculptures and fragments; also props. •

KATHERINE RADCLIFFE-HAND MARBLED PAPERS & FABRICS　212-691-4697
　　7 Jane St., NYC, NY 10014 (mailing address)
　　Hours: 11-7 Mon-Fri by appt.
　　• Hand marbled paper and fabric. Yardage for costumes and soft goods. Brochure and samples available. •

ADELE RECKLIES　　　　　　　　　　　　　　718-768-9036
　　420 Fourth Ave. #1, (7th-8th) Brooklyn, NY 11215
　　Hours: by appt.
　　• Custom knitwear for theatre and film, crocheting, beading, embroidery. •

Custom knitting and crochet for theatre, films, and dance.
Specializing in period costumes and knitted chainmail.
Research service for your convenience.

RHIAN STUDIOS　　　　　　　　　　　　　　　212-679-4512
　　1265 Broadway #811, (31st-32nd St.) NYC, NY 10001
　　Hours: by appt.
　　• Design and construction of costumes and crafts, specializing in character costumes; fabric
　　painting. Contact Geff Rhian. •

ELLEN RIXFORD STUDIO　　　　　　　　　　　212-865-5686
　　308 W. 97th St. #71, (WEA-Riverside) NYC, NY 10025
　　Hours: 9-6 Mon-Fri by appt.
　　• Foam & Soft Sculptures, costumes, body parts, and mechanisms. •

SUE SCHMIDT　　　　　　　　　　　　　　　212-932-3577
　　69 West 105th St., (Columbus-Manhattan Ave.) NYC, NY 10025　　212-724-2800
　　Hours: by appt.
　　• Textile painting, masks, model making, puppets and puppet mechanics. •

"I found it in the N.Y. Theatrical Sourcebook."

C–D

JODY SCHOFFNER
818-992-6574
41118 Philiprimm, Woodland Hills, CA 91367
Hours: by appt.
• Draper for stage or specialty costumes, puppet maker. •

LINDA C. SCHULTZ
212-222-0477
125 West 96th St. #6J, (Columbus-Amsterdam Ave.) NYC, NY 10025
Hours: by appt.
• Costumer, stylist, wardrobe, draper, soft goods (props). •

SUSAN KAY SCHUSTER
201-569-9287
166 Grand Ave. #13-C, Englewood, NJ 07631
Hours: by appt.
• Millinery and costume crafts; experienced in theatre and opera. •

JAMIE PAUL SEGUIN
212-580-8275
355 West 85th St. #8, (Riverside Dr.) NYC, NY 10024
Hours: by appt.
• Costume design: dance, theatre; shopper, wardrobe, make-up teacher. •

LISA SHAFTEL
206-706-0868
206-361-0733
333 N. 79th St., Seattle, WA 98103
Hours: by appt.
• Scenic/lighting design, scene painting, puppets, animal figures, masks, property crafts, soft goods. •

STANLEY ALLAN SHERMAN /MASK ARTS COMPANY
212-243-4039
203 West 14th St. #57, (7th Ave.) NYC, NY 10011
Hours: by appt.
• Handcrafted molded leather masks and simple leather masks for theatre, opera, dance, commedia, parties, etc. Specialty in molding leather. Repairs, odd projects, custom hats. RENTALS •

KATHERINE SILVERII / ECCENTRICITIES
212-924-9411
41 Union Square West #1027, (B'way-17th St.) NYC, NY 10003
Hours: 10-6 Mon-Fri
• Designer and constructor of custom display and costume pieces. •

DAPHNE STEVENS-PASCUCCI
212-724-9898
146 West 73rd St. #2B, (Columbus Ave.) NYC, NY 10023
Hours: by appt.
•Costume designer, design assistant, costume painting, distressing, dyeing.•

RICHARD TAUTKUS
212-691-8253
718-729-1010
21-07 41st Ave., (21st-22nd) L.I.C., NY 11101
Hours: by appt.
•Masks, millinery, etc,; specialty and unusual costumes and props.•

BARB TAYLORR
614-862-3215
11726 Woodbridge Lane, Baltimore, OH 43105
Hours: by appt.
• Custom millinery, theatrical headgear, costume accessories, custom bridal headpieces. •

ANNE-MARIE WRIGHT *Acw FesT..*
212-226-8357
248 Elizabeth St. #4, (Houston-Prince St.) NYC, NY 10012
Hours: by appt.
• Costume design and construction for theatre, TV and film. Member United Scenic Artist #829. Have sewing machine--will travel •

COSTUME PATTERNS

AMAZON VINEGAR & PICKLING WORKS DRYGOODS LTD.　　　319-322-6800
2218 E. 11th St., Davenport, IA 52803　　　800-798-7979
Hours: 9-5 Mon-Fri　　　FAX　319-322-4003
　• A large selection of patterns; catalog $7.00. First class mail. CREDIT CARDS •

COSTUME CONNECTION,, INC.　　　703-237-1373
PO Box 4518, Falls Church, VA 22044
Hours: by appt.　　　FAX　703-237-1374
　• Formerly Medieval Miscellanae. Patterns, chain-mail t-shirts, fabrics, jewelry, books and pavilions. MC/VISA •

KIEFFER'S　　　201-798-2266
P.O. Box 7500, Jersey City, NJ 07307
Hours: 9-5 Mon-Fri　　　FAX　201-798-5107
　• Lingerie patterns, assorted stretch dance fabrics, supplies; catalog available. •

PAST PATTERN REPLICAS　　　616-245-9456
PO Box 7587-NY, Grand Rapids, MI 49517
Hours: 9-5 Mon-Fri　　　FAX　616-245-3584
　• Authentic patterns of women's fashions 1830-1949; catalog $4.00. CREDIT CARDS •

PATTERNS OF HISTORY　　　608-2646551
816 State St., Madison, WI 53706
Hours: 9-5 Mon-Fri　　　FAX　608-264-6571
　• Authentic patterns from 1835-1896, good directions, clear patterns, brochure available. MC/VISA •

PEGEE OF WILLIAMSBURG　　　804-220-2722
PO Box 127, , Williamsburg, VA
Hours: 9-9 Mon-Sat
　• Series 1776 patterns for men, women and children, all classes; Gone With The Wind Scarlett dresses; contact Pegee Miller. •

RICHARD THE THREAD / ROY COOPER　　　213-852-4997
8320 Melrose Ave., Los Angeles, CA 90069　　　800-473-4997
Hours: 9-5 Mon-Fri
　• Elizabethan, Victorian, Edwardian, Etc., men's and women's; free catalog. UPS-COD •

THE TAUNTON PRESS　　　800-477-8727
PO Box 5506, 63 S. Main St. , Newtown, CT 06470-5506
Hours: 9-5 • 24 hr. phone orders　　　FAX　203-426-3434
　• Patterns of folkwear garments. Catalog available. •

JAMES TOWNSEND & SON　　　800-338-1665
PO Box 415, 133 North First St., Pierceton, IN 46562
Hours: 10-5 Mon-Sat　　　FAX　219-594-5580
　• 18th and 19th century costume patterns, clothing and hats; repro colonial household goods; catalog. •

WOODEN PORCH BOOKS　　　304-386-4434
Route 1, PO Box 262, Middlebourne, WV 26149
Phone orders 9-5 everyday　　　FAX　304-386-4868
　• Out-of-print books on textile, fashion & costumes. Catalog. •

COSTUME RENTAL & CONSTRUCTION

See also **COSTUME CRAFTSPEOPLE, MASKS & MILLINERY**

ABRACADABRA   212-627-5745
10 Christopher St., (near 6th St.) NYC, NY 10014   800-MAGIC-66
Hours: 11-7 Mon-Sat   FAX 212-627-5876
 • Many kinds of Halloween and theatrical costumes for rent; also masks, theatrical make-up and costume accessories. Catalog available. April Fools' Day parade. CREDIT CARDS •

ANIMAL OUTFITS FOR PEOPLE,, INC.   212-877-5085
2255 Broadway 3rd Fl., (81st St.) NYC, NY 10024
Hours: 11-6 by appt
 • Animal, fruit, vegetable, people costumes; ask for Chet or Gloria. •

CARELLI COSTUMES   212-765-6166
588 Ninth Ave. 2nd Fl., (42nd-43rd St.) NYC, NY 10036
Hours: 9-5 Mon-Fri
 • Construction shop: dance, opera, theatre; see Carolyn. •

THE COSTUME COLLECTION   212-989-5855
601 West 26th St., (11th-12th Ave.) NYC, NY 10001
Hours: 10-5 Mon-Fri by appt.
 •Rental for non-profit organizations only; some construction. •

M·A·R·T·I·N
IZQUIERDO
S·T·U·D·I·O

118 West 22 New York. (212) 807-9757

COSTUME SHOP,, INC.   919-343-0044
PO Box 570, Wilmington, NC 28402
Hours: by appt.
• Full service rental house; garments, accessories, uniforms, and wardrobe supplies. •

COSTUMES AND CREATURES   612-333-2223
420 N. 5th St. #350, Minneapolis, MN 55401
Hours: 8-6 Mon-Thurs
• A division of VEE Corp., producer of Sesame Street Live tours; specializing in full body character and animal costumes; period garments, accessories, soft props. Custom design and construction; contact Janet Delvoye. •

CREATIVE COSTUME CO.   212-564-5552
330 West 38th St., (8th-9th Ave.) NYC, NY 10018
Hours: 9:30-4:30 Mon-Fri
• Large stock of character costumes. RENTALS CREDIT CARDS •

EARLY HALLOWEEN   212-691-2933
130 West 25th St. 11th Fl., (6th-7th Ave.) NYC, NY 10001   212-243-1499
Hours: by appt.

Vintage men's, women's and children's clothing, shoes, hats, accessories, costume jewelry.

EARLY
HALLOWEEN

• Also vintage luggage, and memorabilia. •

"I found it in the N.Y. Theatrical Sourcebook."

C-D

EAVES-BROOKS COSTUME CO., INC.   718-729-1010
21-07 41st Ave., (21st-22nd St.) L.I.C., NY 11101
Hours: 9-5 Mon-Fri   FAX 718-729-5118
• Full service costume shop; construction, alterations located in own 100,000 sq. ft. bldg. Large costume research library. Brochure, measurement blanks and illustrated costume plots available. RENTALS CREDIT CARDS •
(See display ad in this section.)

ECCENTRICITIES   212-924-9411
41 Union Square West #1027, (B'way-17th St.) NYC, NY 10003
Hours: 10-6 Mon-Fri
• See Dennis Paver or Katherine Silverii. •

Custom design and fabrication of costumes, millinery, masks, soft props; styling and shopping service.

EURO CO.   212-629-9665
247 West 30th St. 8th Fl., (7th-8th Ave.) NYC, NY 10001
Hours: 9-6 Mon-Fri   FAX 212-629-9608
• Costume construction for film, theatre and TV. No rentals •

FARRELL COSTUMES LTD.   919-343-0044
1525 S. Front St., Wilmington , NC 28401
Hours: 9-5 Mon-Fri   FAX 9109-343-1777
• To the theater & movie industry. Contact Peggy Farrell •

GRACE COSTUMES
212-586-0260
244-250 West 54th St. #502, (B'way-8th Ave.) NYC, NY 10019
Hours: 9-5 Mon-Fri • by appt.   FAX   212-586-0256

Construction and alterations for Broadway, opera, dance,
television and film.

GRACE COSTUMES, INC.

• Construction only: Broadway, opera, dance, television, film. Alterations. Office space. •

JODI HEAD DESIGNS
212-353-2348
67 Pitt St. #1A, (Delancy-Rivington St.) NYC, NY 10002
Hours: by appt.
• Custom hand beading. Bead bustier and dress design. •

HOOKER-HOWE COSTUME COMPANY
508-373-3731
46-52 South Main St., Bradford, MA 01835
800-848-6795
Hours: 9-6 Mon-Fri • 10-4 Sat   FAX   508-373-6818
• All period costumes available. CREDIT CARDS •

IN COSTUME,, INC.
212-255-5502
37 West 20th St. Room #706, (5th-6th Ave.) NYC, NY 10011
Hours: by appt.   FAX   212-255-3788
• Rentals for print ads, commercials, industrials, etc.; contemporary and theatrical items;
speak to David Toser. •

MARTIN IZQUIERDO STUDIOS
212-807-9757
118 West 22nd St. 9th Fl., (6th-7th Ave.) NYC, NY 10011
Hours: 9-6 Mon-Fri • Weekends by appt.   FAX   212-366-5249
• Costume crafts and props for theatre, film, commercials, display and video; full service shop.
Shop and dye facilities for long or short term rental. •
(See display ad in this section.)

DONNA LANGMAN
212-382-2558
39 West 38th St. 4th Fl., (5th-6th Ave.) NYC, NY 10018
Hours: 9-5 Mon-Fri • by appt.

• Costume construction for theatre, dance,
opera, film and television.

> *Donna Langman*
> *costumes*
> *couture*

• A full service costume shop; exquisite work. •

MALABAR LTD.
416-598-2581
14 McCaul St., Toronto, Ontario, CAN M5T 1V6   FAX   416-598-3296
Hours: 10-6 Tue-Fri • 10-3 Sat
• Large costume rental house. MC/VISA •

BARBARA MATERA
212-475-5006
890 Broadway 5th Fl., (19th-20th St.) NYC, NY 10003
Hours: 9-5:30   FAX   212-254-4550
• Construction, all areas: Broadway, film, opera, ballet, and dance; see Barbara Matera. •

MICHAEL-JON COSTUMES,, INC.   212-741-3440
411 W. 14th St. 3rd Fl., (9-10 Ave.) NYC, NY 10014
Hours: 9-4:45 Mon-Fri
  • Construction only: B'way, film, TV, variety; see Michael Stanton or Tom Slack •

MULDER/MARTIN,, INC.   212-234-0889
604 Riverside Dr. #6E, (137th-138th St.) NYC, NY 10036
Hours: 9-5 Mon-Fri   FAX   212-234-0885
  • Character costumes and puppets for television, theatre, film, and special events. •
(See display ad under COSTUME CRAFTSPEOPLE & MILLINERY.)

NORCOSTCO   201-575-3503
373 Rt. 46 West, Fairfield, NJ 07004   212-690-5567
Hours: 9:30-6 Mon-Fri • 10-5 Sat   FAX   201-575-2563
  • Theatrical costume rentals, catalog •

ODDS COSTUME RENTAL   212-268-6227
231 West 29th St. Rm. 304, (7th-8th Ave.) NYC, NY 10001
Hours: 9:30-5 Mon-Fri • Sat by appt.
  • Quality clothes - Victorian through modern - RENTALS. •
(See display ad in this section.)

PARSONS-MEARES LTD.·   212-242-3378
142 West 14th St. 5th Fl., (6th-7th Ave.) NYC, NY 10011
Hours: by appt.   FAX   212-741-1869
  • Custom draping, tailoring, dyeing and painting services available. •

PIERRE OF PARIS LTD.   212-947-0316
450 7th Ave., Suite 2105 NYC, NY 10123   212-947-0322
Hours: 9-8 Mon-Fri

• Custom tailoring for Gents and Ladies
• Alterations for both Gents and Ladies
• Design first-class quality suits
• Thirty-five years experience as custom tailor and ten years
  experience in New York working on movie and theatrical projects.
• Worked with Peggy Farrell Costume Shop and others.

    • Custom tailor with film experience •

PRODUCTION VALUES,, INC.   404-874-8431
588 Armour Circle, (North Highland Ave.) Atlanta, GA 30324
Hours: 9-5 Mon-Fri • 10-2 Sat
  • Costume design, construction and rental for not-for-profit groups. •

ADELE RECKLIES CO.   718-768-9036
420 Fourth Ave. #1, Brooklyn, NY 11215
Hours: by appt.
  • Custom knitwear for theatre and, crocheting, beading, and embroidery •

C-D

FRANKIE STEINZ
212-925-1373

24 Harrison 2nd fl., (Hudson-Greenwich) NYC, NY 10013
Hours: by appt.

Extensive, unusual and interesting collection of high quality costumes for rental only. Also available vintage clothing for men and women from 1900's thru 1960's and a huge selection of great hats of every kind.

Costume design, wardrobe styling and shopping services performed with expertise and flair.

• Costume rentals, design services, styling. Contact Frankie. •

STUDIO
212-967-4736

322 Seventh Ave., (28th St.) NYC, NY 10001
Hours: 9-5 Mon-Fri • by appt.
• Construction for B'way, Off-B'way, dance, commercials, industrials, etc. •

STUDIO ROUGE
212-989-8363

100 West 25th, 3rd Fl., (near 6th Ave.) NYC, NY 10001
Hours: 9-6 Mon-Fri • Weekends by appt.   FAX   212-989-8363

Costume design, construction and alterations for film, theatre and television. Wardrobe, styling and shopping services available.

studio · rouge

• Costume design, construction and alterations. Wardrobe and shopping services available. Contact Rosi Zingales. •

KAY STUNTZ
212-274-9011

561 Broadway Rm 4D, (Prince-Spring) NYC, NY 10012
Hours: 9:30-6 Mon-Fri   FAX   212-274-9011
• High quality costumes of all types, made-to-order; focus on women's wear. Table space to rent. •

VINCENT'S
212-741-3423

136 West 21st St. 6th Fl., (6th-7th Ave.) NYC, NY 10011
Hours: 8:30-5:30 Mon-Fri
• Men's tailoring for NY costume shops and free-lance designers; construction and tailoring. •

WESTERN COSTUME CO.
818-760-0900

11041 Van Owen Ave., North Hollywood, CA 91605
Hours: 8-5:30 Mon-Fri   FAX   818-508-2182
• Large costume rental house on the West Coast; film stock. •

COSTUME SHOP & WARDROBE SUPPLIES

See also **LABELS, WOVEN & PRINTED**
See also **SEWING MACHINES & DRESS FORMS**
See also **IRONS & STEAMERS**
See also **SHELVING & LOCKERS**
See also **NOTIONS: GENERAL & TAILORS**

AMERICAN HANGER AND FIXTURE,, INC.
520 West 27th St., (10th-11th Ave.) NYC, NY 10001
Hours: 9-5 Mon-Fri
• The place for coathangers. CREDIT CARDS. •

212-279-5280
800-221-2790
FAX 212-594-6872

BAER FABRICS
515 East Market, Louisville, KY 40202
Hours: 9-5:30 Mon-Sat
• All workroom and drycleaning supplies and equipment; prompt shipment. CREDIT CARDS •

(costumes) 800-769-7778
(fashion) 800-769-7776
FAX 502-582-2331

BACIG MFG. CO.
3611 14th Ave., (36th-37th St.) Brooklyn, NY 11218
Hours: 9-5 Mon-Thurs • 9-1 Fri
• Wholesale garment bags, large orders only. •

718-871-6106
800-421-6106
FAX 718-871-0162

CHERISH
PO Box 941, NYC, NY 10024
Hours: by appt.
• Items for conservation-minded costume storage; padded hangers, fabric dust covers, acid-free costume storage boxes and tissue, cleaning products. Museum quality to preserve valuable costumes. •

212-724-1748

COAT CONFORMERS,, INC.
155 West 29th St. 3rd Fl., (6th-7th Ave.) NYC, NY 10001
Hours: 9-5 Mon-Fri
• All types of garment hangers in various finishes; fast and helpful service. •

212-695-5167
FAX 212-695-5168

C–THRU RULER CO.
PO Box 356, 6 Britton Drive, Bloomfield, CT 06002
Hours: 8:30-4:30 Mon-Fri
• C-Thru plastic rulers. •

203-243-0303
800-243-8419
FAX 203-243-1856

JAF INDUSTRIES
248 West 35th St., (7th-8th St.) NYC, NY 10001
Hours: 8-5 Mon-Fri (close early on Fri)
• Plastic drycleaning bags by the roll. •

212-563-3831

MID CITY HARDWARE CORP.
130 West 25th St., (6th-7th Ave.) NYC, NY 10001
Hours: 8:30-4:30 Mon-Fri

212-807-8713
212-807-8714
FAX 212-675-1911

Complete line serving Wardrobe Departments and Theatres. We stock Albatross products, Jiffy steamers, Fresh Again, End Bac, Z'Out, Magic Wand, Bite Lights, Wisk, Tech, Prevail spray guns and power units, spray starch, ironing boards and irons, laundry baskets, Barge cement, janitorial supplies, toilet tissue, paper towels, liquid hand soap, garbage liners, etc. PROMPT DELIVERY.

Mid-City Hardware Corp.

• Contact Helene or Ted Morrell. AMEX •

MINNESOTA CHEMICAL   612-646-7521
    2285 Hampden, St. Paul, MN 55114   800-328-5689
    Hours: 7:30-4:30 Mon-Fri
    • Commercial laundry and drycleaning equipment and supplies; parts and service. •

PINCOVER INDUSTRIAL SUPPLY CO.,, INC.   212-569-1010
    4730 Broadway, (near G.W. Bridge) NYC, NY 10040   800-282-5233
    Hours: 8:30-5 Mon-Fri (call first)   FAX   212-942-8486
    • Razor blades for industrial use. •

LOUIS PRICE PAPER CO.,, INC.   718-728-8993
    34-40 11th St., (34th-35th Ave.) L.I.C., NY 11106
    Hours: 8-5 Mon-Fri   FAX   718-728-8247
    • Pattern and grading paper, packaging, office and janitorial supplies. •

TRAVEL AUTO BAG CO.,, INC.   212-840-0025
    264 West 40th St., (7th-8th Ave.) NYC, NY 10018
    Hours: 9-4:30 Mon-Fri   FAX   212-302-8267
    • All types of garment bags, collapsible rolling racks, steamers, hangers, mannequins and display fixtures. CREDIT CARDS •

CURTAIN & DRAPERIES: THEATRICAL

For rigging, see also **THEATRICAL HARDWARE & RIGGING EQUIPMENT**

ALCONE INC   718-361-8373
    5-49th Ave., (5th St.-Vernon) L.I.C., NY 11101
    Hours: 9:30-4 Mon-Fri   FAX   718-729-8296
    • Fabrics, draperies, track. Theatrical supply house; catalog, $5. (Subway #7 to L.I.C., Vernon Jackson stop.) •

ASSOCIATED DRAPERY & EQUIPMENT CO.   516-671-5245
    40 Sea Cliff Ave., Glen Cove, NY 11542
    Hours: 8-5 Mon-Fri   FAX   516-674-2213
    • Custom-made curtains and draperies; also scenic fabrics; contact Howard Kessler. •

BMI SUPPLY   518-793-6706
    28 Logan Ave., Glens Falls, NY 12801   800-836-0524
        FAX   518-793-6181
    60 Airview Drive, Greenville, SC 29607   803-288-8983
    Hours: 8-5 Mon-Fri   FAX   803-281-0841

Theatrical Draperies, Scrims and Drops -
Custom made. Hampers in stock.
Theatrical Fabrics and Touring Bags
Also General Theatrical Supplies
JUST A PHONE CALL AWAY

BMI SUPPLY
Serving the Entertainment Industry

    • Good selection, good service. MC/VISA •

SAYZIE CARR   212-529-3669
    96 East 7th St. Rm. 5, (1st-Ave. A) NYC, NY 10009
    Hours: by appt.
    • Formerly Proscenium Seven. Custom (only) draperies, sewing, tablecloths, wall treatment, banners, soft sculpture, Also painted backdrops. •

COMMERCIAL DRAPES CO., INC.
718-649-8080
9209 Flatlands Ave., (E. 92nd-93rd. St.) Brooklyn, NY 11236
Hours: 9-4:30 Mon-Fri   FAX   718-272-2295
• Fabricator of stage curtains, window shades, verticals, scrims, drops, cycloramas and projection screens. Also flameproofing. •

CONSOLIDATED DISPLAY CO., INC.
708-851-8666
31 W 630 Schoger Dr., Naperville, IL 60564
Hours: 8-4:30 Mon-Fri   FAX   708-851-8756

Scatter Flakes® Snow, snow blankets, confetti, glitters, foils, mylar, foliage and fabrics.

Consolidated Display Co., Inc.

• Custom mylar fringe draperies at stock prices. •

GENERAL DRAPERY SERVICE
718-665-9200
135 East 144th St., Bronx, NY 10451
Hours: 9-5 Mon-Fri   FAX   718-665-9672
• Theatrical draperies and hardware; flameproofing and consulting service available. •

GERRIETS INTERNATIONAL
609-758-9121
RR #1, 950 Hutchinson Rd., Allentown, NJ 08501
Hours: 8:30-5 Mon-Fri   FAX   609-758-9596
• Materials in stock and to order, finished draperies, projection screens, wide muslin and drops. Catalog, shipping. •

JOSEPH C. HANSEN   212-246-8055
  423 West 43rd St., (9th-10th Ave.) NYC, NY 10036
  Hours: 9-5 Mon-Fri   FAX   212-246-8189
    • Theatrical curtain rental: cycs, scrims, velours, painted drops,star drops, curtain track and
    stands. Brochure available. RENTALS •

REYNOLDS DRAPERY SERVICE,, INC.   315-845-8632
  7440 Main St., Newport, NY 13416
  Hours: 8-4 Mon-Fri   FAX   315-845-8645
    • Manufacture, cleaning, and repair of theatrical draperies. •

ROSE BRAND TEXTILE FABRICS   212-594-7424
  517 West 35th St., (10th-11th Ave.) NYC, NY 10001   800-223-1624
  Hours: 8:30-5 Mon-Fri   FAX   212-629-4826

Draperies, cycs, drops, scrims, borders, legs, rain curtains, etc. sewn
to your specifications. Professional staff available for technical
assistance and estimates. Largest stock and selection of theatrical
fabrics nationwide. Flame retardant, extra-wide seamless goods,
velour (24 colors), scrim, muslin, canvas, duvetyn, commando,
metallics, specialty and hard-to-find fabrics. New: Inherently FR
sharkstooth scrim, imported square gauze. Call us for fast service
and immediate delivery.

THEATRICAL SUPPLIES, FABRICS & FABRICATION

ROSE ⚜ BRAND

517 WEST 35th STREET, NEW YORK, NY 10001

    • Wide selection flame retardant fabrics, by the yard or bolt. Also carry scenic paint and
    accessories. Catalog available. •
    (See display ad in this section.)

I.WEISS & SONS INC

Stage Draperies & Masking Curtains
Curtain Tracks & Theatrical Hardware
Canvas Hampers - Standard & Custom Sizes

CONSULTATIONS & ESTIMATES

718-706-8139 / Fax: 718-482-9410

2-07 Borden Avenue, Long Island City, NY 11101

C-D

STAGEDROPS
718-358-0834
65-12 169th St., Flushing, NY 11365
Hours: 9-5 Mon-Sat by appt.

• Curtains and drops fabricated in all theatrical fabrics.
• No job too small!
• We guarantee quality workmanship at low cost.

• Curtain and drops fabricated in all theatrical fabrics. Contact Bill Ruffini. •

TWENTIETH CENTURY DRAPERIES
212-925-7707
72 Wooster St., NYC, NY 10012
Hours: 9-5 Mon-Fri   **FAX:**   **212-274-0134**
• Tablecloths and upholstery; your fabric or theirs •

VARIETY SCENIC STUDIOS
718-392-4747
25-19 Borden Ave., (25th-27th) L.I.C., NY 11101
Hours: 7-5 Mon-Fri   **FAX**   **718-784-2919**
• Custom and rentals. •

I WEISS & CO.
718-706-8139
2-07 Borden Ave., (Vernon-Jackson Ave.) L.I.C., NY 11101
Hours: 8:30-5 Mon-Fri   **FAX**   **718-482-9410**
• Cycs, scrims, raincurtains & hardware. •
(See display ad in this section.)

CURTAINS, SHADES & BLINDS

MARTIN ALBERT INTERIORS
212-673-8000
9 E. 19th St., (Broadway) NYC, NY 10003   **800-525-4637**
Hours: 9:30-5 Sun-Fri   **FAX**   **212-673-8006**
• Custom windows treatments, upholstery & silpcovers. Fabric by the yard; drapery hardware.
Fabric library of 100,000 samples. Showroom representing all major manufacturers. •

ALLSTATE GLASS CORP.
212-226-2517
85 Kenmare St., (Lafayette-Mulberry St.) NYC, NY 10012
Hours: 8-4 Mon-Fri • 9-4 Sat   **FAX**   **212-966-7904**
• Good selection shades and blinds; also glass and mirrors. CREDIT CARDS •

BZI DISTRIBUTORS
212-966-6690
105 Eldridge St., (Grand-Broome St.) NYC, NY 10002
Hours: 9-5:30 Sun-Fri   **FAX**   **212-219-3666**
• Vertical and mini blinds, many styles of curtain rods and hardware. Trimmings, upholstery
supplies, foam rubber. $25 minimum on credit cards CREDIT CARDS •

DECOR COUTURE DESIGN
212-727-0123
25-37 37th St. 3rd Floor, Astoria, NY 11103   **212-627-3495**
Hours: 10-5 Mon-Fri by appt.
• Design and fabrication of custom soft goods & costume crafts for theatre, film, video, display
and residential. Contact Cory Mansueto or Lisa Linden. •

C–D

ECLECTIC/ENCORE PROPERTIES,, INC.   212-645-8880
620 West 26th St., 4th Fl., (11th-12th Ave.) NYC, NY 10001
Hours: 9-5 Mon-Fri or by appt.   FAX   212-243-6508
• Large collection of draperies and curtains (all manner of textiles); antique, period, traditional
and theatrical. A full service prop rental company. •
(See display ad under PROP RENTAL HOUSES.)

M. EPSTEINS SON,, INC.   212-265-3960
809 Ninth Ave., (53rd-54th St.) NYC, NY 10019
Hours: 8-5:15 Mon-Fri • 8:30-3 Sat (closed Sat in summer)   FAX   212-765-8841

We do window shades. We do vertical blinds.
We do horizontal blinds. We do custom orders.

M. EPSTEIN'S SON, INC.

• Large stock floorcoverings, paints & dyes, bronzing powders & leafing supplies; household,
scenic, wallcoverings. Custom service within 24 hrs. See Marty. CREDIT CARDS •
(See display ad under PAINTS & DYES: SCENIC.)

GIRARD DESIGNS/JANET GIRARD   718-782-6430
300 Morgan Ave., (Metropolitan-Grand) Brooklyn, NY 11211
Hours: by appt.   FAX   718-782-3805
• Custom draperies, window treatments, upholstery, fabric tension structures; quilting, soft
sculpture, leather sculpture, fabric painting. •

JANOVIC PLAZA   212-627-1100
161 Sixth Ave, (Spring St.) NYC, NY 10014
Hours: 7:30-6:30 Mon-Fri • 9-6 Sat • 11-5 Sun
• Window shades, vertical blinds in stock or custom work. (Paint dept. opens at 7:30, all other
depts. open at 9:30.) CREDIT CARDS •

PATERSON SILKS   212-929-7861
39 East 14th St., (Univ. Pl.) NYC, NY 10003
Hours: 9-7 Mon-Sat (Mon & Thurs till 8) • 10-5 Sun

151 West 72nd St. (Amsterdam-Columbus) NYC, NY 10023   212-874-9510
Hours: 9-7:45 Mon, Thurs, Fri • 9-6:45 Tues, Wed, Sat
• Remnants, discount fabrics, draperies; foam for cushions. •

PINTCHIK PAINTS   718-783-3333
478 Bergen St., (Flatbush Ave.) Brooklyn, NY 11217
278 3rd Ave. (22nd St.) NYC, NY 10010   212-982-6600
1555 3rd Ave. (87th St.) NYC, NY 10028   212-289-6300
2475 Broadway (92nd St.) NYC, NY 10025   212-769-1444
Hours: 8-6:50 Mon-Fri • 8:30-5:50 Sat • 10-4:50 Sun
• Shades and blinds of all types. •

ROY RUDIN DECORATORS,, INC.   212-265-4716
545 8th Ave. 7th Floor, (37-38th St.) NYC, NY 10036   212-967-2611
Hours: 9-5 Mon-Fri
• Custom work. Formerly Harold Rudin Decorators, Inc. •

"I found it in the N.Y. Theatrical Sourcebook."

TWENTIETH CENTURY DRAPERY,, INC.   212-925-7707
70 Wooster St., (Spring-Broome St.) NYC, NY 10012
Hours: 9-5 Mon-Fri   FAX   212-274-0134
• Custom draperies in their workshop. Blinds & shades to order. Many film credits. See Bob. •

HARRY ZARIN CO.   212-925-6112
292 Grand St., (Allen-Eldridge) NYC, NY 10002
Hours: 9-5 Sun-Fri
• Vertical and mini blinds, draperies, bedcoverings, drapery rods. CREDIT CARDS •

C–D

NOTES

NOTES

"I found it in the N.Y. Theatrical Sourcebook."

DANCE & STAGE FLOORING

AMERICAN HARLEQUIN CORP.
3111 West Burbank Blvd., Burbank, CA 91505
Hours: 7-5 Mon-Fri (calls accepted 24 hrs.)

800-642-6440
818-846-5555
FAX 818-846-8888

C–D

Producers of Harlequin Floorings; leading international range of
quality dance, stage, studio, exhibition and television floorings
for portable, semi-permanent and permanent applications.
Specialist advisers to designers, architects and contractors.

• Inventory on East and West Coasts to service entire country ; dance, stage, and exhibit flooring. •

H. BARNETTE ASSOCIATES, INC.
202 Highpoint Ave., Weehawken, NJ 07087
Hours: 8-6 Mon-Fri

201-392-0478

FAX 201-392-1910

RENTAL AND SALES OF PORTABLE VINYL DANCE FLOORS.
DELIVERY AND INSTALLATION SERVICES AVAILABLE.
DANCE FLOOR IS WAREHOUSED IN MID-TOWN MANHATTAN.

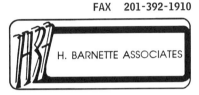

• Can provide theatrical design, technical consultation, moving and assembly crews and supplies. Call for an appointment. RENTALS •

BYRKE DECKS
71 Redmond St., New Brunswick, NJ 08901
Hours: 9-5 Mon-Fri
• Dance sub-flooring. RENTALS •

609-924-7446

GERRIETS INTERNATIONAL
29 Hutchinson Rd., Allentown, NJ 08501
Hours: 8:30-5 Mon-Fri
• Vario portable dance floor 63" wide in 8 colors. Also a complete line of scenic fabrics and materials in stock. •

609-758-9121

FAX 609-758-9596

OASIS / STAGE WERKS
249 Rio Grande, Salt Lake City, UT 84101
Hours: 9-6 Mon-Fri • 10-2 Sat
• D'anser floor, resilient sub-floor, 30'x40' rentable dance floor. •

801-363-0364

FAX 801-575-7121

ROSCO LABORATORIES, INC.
36 Bush Ave., Port Chester, NY 10573
Hours: 9-5 Mon-Fri
• Roscofloor: durable, non-skid, non-reflective, matte vinyl; also portable 4'x8' interlocking dance flooring. Shipping available. •

914-937-1300
800-ROSCONY
FAX 914-937-5984

ROSE BRAND TEXTILE FABRICS
517 West 35th St., (10-11th Ave.) NYC, NY 10001
Hours: 8:30-5 Mon-Fri
• Complete line of Rosco floors; dance, studio, show floor and Roscotiles for portable or permanent installations. Supermatte to high gloss; wide range of colors. Durable & easy to maintain. Call for product specifications. •
(See display ad under CURTAINS & DRAPERIES: THEATRICAL)

212-494-7424
800-223-1624
FAX 212-629-4826

STAGESTEP   215-829-9800
    PO Box 328, Philadelphia, PA 19105   800-523-0961
                                             800-877-3342
    Hours: 9-5 Mon-Fri   FAX 215-829-9800
    • Full line of dance floors. Also Mirrorlite®, books, records, CD's videos. Catalog. CREDIT CARDS •

DEPARTMENT STORES

See also **VARIETY STORES**

ABRAHAM & STRAUSS (A & S)   212-594-8500
    899 Sixth Ave., (33rd St.) NYC, NY 10001
    Hours: 9:45-8:30 Mon, Thurs, Fri • 8-9:30 Tues • 8-11 Wed • 8-9 Sat • 11-6 Sun
    • Good quality and selection. CREDIT CARDS •

BERGDORF GOODMAN   212-753-7300
    754 Fifth Ave., (57th-58th St.) NYC, NY 10019 (Men's store)
    Hours: 10-6 Mon-Sat (Thurs till 8)
    • High fashion clothing department store. Men's store across the street. CREDIT CARDS •

BLOOMINGDALES   212-355-5900
    1000 Third Ave., (59th-60th) NYC, NY 10022
    Hours: 10-7 Mon, Tues, Wed, Fri • 10-9 Thur • 10-6:30 Sat • 11-6:30 Sun
    • Designer clothing, housewares, linens, draperies; very stylish. CREDIT CARDS •

HAMMACHER-SCHLEMMER   212-421-9000
    147 East 57th St., (Lexington-3rd Ave.) NYC, NY 10022
    Hours: 10-6 Mon-Sat
    • Unusual gifts items and gadgets. CREDIT CARDS •

IKEA, ELIZABETH   908-289-4488
    1000 Center Dr., Elizabeth, NJ 07201
    Hours: 10-9 Mon-Sat • 10-6 Sun

IKEA, HICKSVILLE   516-681-4532
    1000 Broadway Mall, Hicksville, NY 11801 (LIE Exit 415 or NSP Exit 355)
    Hours: 10-9:30 Mon-Sat • 10-6 Sun
    • International Swedish department store for the home; specializing in furniture and home furnishings; catalog; inexpensive. CREDIT CARDS •

LORD & TAYLOR   212-391-3344
    424 Fifth Ave., (38th-39th St.) NYC, NY 10018
    Hours: 10-7 Mon, Tues • 10-8:30 W-F • 10-7 Sat • 12-6 Sun
    • Stylish women's clothing; good kitchenware department. CREDIT CARDS •

MACY'S DEPARTMENT STORE   212-736-5151
    151 West 34th St., (B'way) NYC, NY 10001
    Hours: 10-8:30 Mon, Thurs, Fri • 10-7:30 Tues, Wed, Sat • 11-6 Sun
    • The world's largest department store; great kitchenware, housewares, gifts. CREDIT CARDS •

C–D

SAKS FIFTH AVE.   212-753-4000
611 Fifth Ave., (49th-50th ST.) NYC, NY 10022
Hours: 10-6 Mon-Fri (studio services)
Hours: 10-6:30 Mon-Sat (Thurs till 8:30) (store)   FAX 212-940-4803
• Fashionable clothing and accessories for men, women, children. Great memo service for stylists and costume designers. Also linens and home furnishings. Connie Buck's office for studio services is on the 6th floor. Call 212-940-4321 for appointment. CREDIT CARDS •
(See display ad under CLOTHING RENTAL & PURCHASE: MEN'S & WOMEN'S)

TERA VERDE TRADING COMPANY   212-925-4533
120 Wooster St., (Prince St.) NYC, NY 10012
Hours: 11-7 Mon-Sat • 12-6 Sun
• The "ecological department store". Stocks environmentally safe products such as furniture, appliances, bedding, kitchenware, books, stationary, paint, furniture polish; much more. •

DISPLAY HOUSES & MATERIALS

See also **MANNEQUINS**
For specific materials, see index

KURT S. ADLER   212-924-0900
1107 Broadway, (24th-25th St.) NYC, NY 10010
Hours: 9-5:30 Mon-Fri
• Christmas: lights, decorations, ornaments, nativity scenes, "Santa's World"; wholesale, $300 minimum. Catalog •

BLAINE KERN ARTISTS, INC.   504-362-8211
PO Box 6307, (233 Newton St.) New Orleans, LA 70114
Hours: 8-5 Mon-Fri   FAX 504-361-3164
• Custom and stock. Extensive inventory from 47 years of Mardi Gras Parade floats; papier maché, fiberglass props, figures, statuary, masks. Brochure available. RENTALS •

BOND PARADE FLOAT, INC.   201-778-3333
111 Clifton Blvd., Clifton, NJ 07011
Hours: 8:30-4:30 Mon-Sat   FAX 201-778-6950
• Parade floats and float ornaments. RENTALS •

CO-GNO-SCEN-TI LTD.   718-277-4525
242 Chestnut St., (Atlantic-Fulton St.) NYC, NY 11208
Hours: 8-4:30 Mon-Fri
• Fiberglass pedestals, columns, jars, urns, animals, Statue of Liberty; see Libby; catalog. •

JAMES A. COLE CO.   212-741-1500
41 West 25th St., (B'way-6th Ave.) NYC, NY 10010
Hours: 9-5 Mon-Fri
• Wholesale Christmas items: lights, decorations, garlands, trees, etc.; open for retail sales Nov - Christmas at 50% off. •

COLONIAL DECORATIVE DISPLAYS   212-255-9620
160 Eleventh Ave., (22nd St.) NYC, NY 10011
Hours: 10-4 Mon-Fri   FAX 212-255-9627
• Primarily a floral house; Spring, Fall & Christmas items; see Irving. No catalog. •

CONSOLIDATED DISPLAY CO. INC.
708-851-8666
31 W 630 Schoger Dr., Naperville, IL 60564
Hours: 8-4:30 Mon-Fri
FAX 708-851-8756

Scatter Flakes® Snow, snow blankets, confetti, glitters, foils, mylar, foliage and fabrics.

• Custom mylar fringe draperies at stock prices. •

SUSAN CRANE, INC.
214-631-6490
8107 Chancellor Row, Dallas, TX 75247
800-527-2439
Hours: 8-5 Mon-Fri
FAX 214-631-8149
• Seasonal display items, furniture, sculpture, vases, giftwrap; highly recommended. •

CULTURED DESIGN LTD.
212-957-2870
517 West 46th St., (10th-11th Ave.) NYC, NY 10036
212-594-8690
Hours: 9-5 Mon-Fri
FAX 212-957-2858
• Snow, Christmas and seasonal items: artificial flowers and foliage; custom fabrication. •

ELECTRA DISPLAYS
516-585-5659
90 Remington Blvd., Ronkonkoma, NY 11779
212-420-1188
Hours: 9-5 Mon-Fri
• Electric signs, letters, architectural and vacuumformed pieces, props; see Art Ruderman. •

F.A.S.T CORP.
608-269-7110
PO Box 258, Sparta, WI 54656
Hours: 8-5 Mon-Fri
FAX 608-269-7514
• Large scale fiberglass animals, amusement slides, fountains and trademarks. Catalog available. •

GEPPETTO SOFT SCULPTURE & DISPLAY
718-398-9792
107 Lexington Ave., (Franklin-Classon) Brooklyn, NY 11238
Hours: 10-6 Mon-Fri
• Custom construction of soft sculpture promotion and display props, character costumes, foam rubber masks, oversized foam props and 3-D illustrations. Contact Scott, brochure available. •
(See display ad under PROP SHOPS.)

DAVID HAMBERGER, INC.
718-852-7101
410 Hicks St., (Baltic-Warren) Brooklyn, NY 11201
Hours: 9-5 Mon-Fri
FAX 718-797-4575
• Manufacturer and distributor of theatrical, display materials and animated figures Carries Celastic®. Phone orders. Catalog. •

M. LEVIN, INC.
212-674-3579
269 Bowery, (Houston St.) NYC, NY 10002
Hours: 9-5 Mon-Fri
• Store fixtures, display cases, gondolas. •

MECHANICAL DISPLAYS, INC.
718-258-5588
4420 Farragut Rd. (East 45th St.) Brooklyn, NY 11203
Hours: 8-4:30 Mon-Fri
FAX 718-258-6202
• Stock and custom animated figures with simple or pneumatic mechanisms; also turntables. See Lou Nasti for photos and price list •

"I found it in the N.Y. Theatrical Sourcebook."

C–D

MODERN ARTIFICIAL FLOWERS & DISPLAYS, LTD 212-265-0414
517 West 46th St., (10th-11th Ave.) NYC, NY 10036
Hours: 8:30-5 Mon-Fri   FAX 212-265-6841
• Complete exterior settings and stock items; snow, Christmas trees and decor year round.
Phone orders. RENTALS •

NIEDERMAIER 212-645-0171
135 W. 25th Street, NYC, NY 10014 (studio)
Hours: 9-5 Mon-Fri

120 Wooster Street (Spring) NYC, NY 10012 (Display Store)
• Chic display items; pottery, columns, sculpture, oversized items. •

ORCHIDS OF HAWAII 718-654-7630
3703 Provost Ave., (E. 223rd-Conners) Bronx, NY 10466
Hours: 9-5 Mon-Fri
• Chinese, Polynesian and tropical restaurant decor; bamboo. Great catalog. •

PROVOST DISPLAYS 212-719-2803
505 Eighth Ave. #1110, (35th St.) NYC, NY 11101
Hours: 9-5 Mon-Fri   FAX 212-869-1463
• Vacuumformed plastic decorative panels up to 4' x 12'. Catalog of stock designs available;
also custom work. •

RAINTREE DESIGNS, LTD. 516-242-7246
44C Jefryn Blvd. West, Deer Park, NY 11729
Hours: 8:30-5:30 Mon-Fri • Sat by appt.   FAX 516-242-7259
• Scenery, display props, gardenscapes, wholesale to the trade. •

ELLEN RIXFORD STUDIO 212-865-5686
308 W. 97th St. #71, (WEA-Riverside) NYC, NY 10025
Hours: 9-6 Mon-Fri (by appt.)
• Intricately made wall hangings, paper sculptures, soft sculpture and puppets; 3D illustrations of existing buildings and people; advertising, display, print, theatre. Custom work, very
beautiful. •

ROBELAN DISPLAYS, INC. 516-564-8600
395 Westbury Blvd., Hempstead, NY 11550
Hours: 7:30-5 Mon-Fri
• Animation, display props and fabrication, foliage, artificial snow, snow blankets. Phone
orders. Catalog. •

ROBERT ROGERS CO.   (Outside CT) 800-457-0785
20-4 East Pembroke Road, Danbury, CT. 06811   (Within CT) 203-791-1907
Hours: 9-5 Mon-Fri
• Stock and custom display figures in various sizes and prices. See Robert Rogers for custom
quotes, designs and brochures of available stock. •

ROTOCAST DISPLAY PRODUCTS 305-693-4680
3645 N.W. 67th St. Miami, Fl 33147 800-327-5062
Hours: 8-5 Mon-Fri
• Polyethylene urns and planters in many shapes, sizes, colors; polyethylene rocks, pedestals,
globes, bird baths, garden benches. Catalog. •

SPAETH DESIGN 212-489-0770
423 West 55th St. (9th-10th Ave.) NYC, NY 10019
Hours: 9-5 Mon-Fri   FAX 212-265-6261
• Custom animated displays, animatronic characters, props, and seasonal decor; contact David Spaeth. •

"I found it in the N.Y. Theatrical Sourcebook." **133**

C–D

SOUTHERN FLORALS   502-584-0412
705 East Market St., Louisville, KY 40202
Hours: 9-5 Mon-Fri   FAX   502-584-0412
• Plaster composition urns, corbels, brackets and garden figures at reasonable prices; finishing available. Some stock, shipping, minimum order. See Garwood Linton for catalog and ordering information. Showrooms around the country. CREDIT CARDS •

SYLVOR CO., INC.   212-929-2728
126 Eleventh Ave., (20th-21st St.) NYC, NY 10011
Hours: 9-5 Mon-Fri   FAX   212-691-2319
• Designers and manufacturers of decorative displays, silkscreen graphics, dimensional wood props, backgrounds, hand-painted props; contact Bonnie Sylvor. •

TOLIN'S   718-232-0724
1849 86th St., (Ulricht-86th) Brooklyn, NY 11214
Hours: 10-6 Mon-Fri • 10-5 Sat • 11-4 Sun   FAX   718-259-6039
• All Christmas merchandise - all year round; also housewares. •

TRIM CORPORATION OF AMERICA   212-989-1616
133 West 25th St., (6th-7th Ave.) NYC, NY 10001 (showroom)
459 W. 15th St. (9-10th Ave.) NYC, NY 10011 (Corp. Office)
Hours: 9-5 Mon-Fri
• Seasonal displays, props, fixtures, custom designs. •

TROPICAL FANTASIES   212-234-1526
621 West 130th St., (B'way-12th Ave.) NYC, NY 10027
Hours: 8-4:30 Mon-Fri   FAX   212-234-9251
• Artificial foliage and floral arrangements; artificial snow; fiberglass statuary, rocks, urns, etc. •
(See display ad under ARTIFICIAL FLOWERS, PLANTS & FOOD.)

WITKIN DESIGN GROUP   212-691-1286
459 West 15th St., (10th-11th Ave.) NYC, NY 10011
Hours: 8-6 Mon-Fri   FAX   212-366-1660
• Custom displays and props for commercial and special promotions. •

ZAFERO BY LESLIE JOHN KOESER, ASSOCIATES   215-763-7054
1530 Parrish St., Philadelphia, PA 19130
Hours: 9-5 Mon-Fri
• Stock or custom fiberglass column, urns, statuary. Catalog; rush orders. RENTALS •

DOLL PARTS

AMERICAN OPTICAL CO.   (ext. 2115) 508-765-9711
14 Mechanic St., Southbridge, MA 01550
Hours: 8-5 Mon-Fri
• Doll and mannequin eyes, custom-made eyes, sclera cover shells. •

S. AXELROD CO., INC.   212-594-3022
7 West 30th St., (5th-B'way) NYC, NY 10001
Hours: 9-5 Mon-Fri
• Moving eyes, decorative trims, rhinestones, metal findings. •

DOLLSPART SUPPLY CO. INC. 718-361-0888
8000 Cooper Ave., Glendale, NY 11385
Hours: 8-5 Mon-Fri
• All parts for dolls; collector dolls; catalog. •

DOLLS & DOLLHOUSES

See also **TOYS & GAMES**
For additional basswood mouldings, see **HOBBY SHOPS & SUPPLIES**

IRIS BROWN 212-593-2882
253 East 57th St., (2nd Ave.) NYC, NY 10022
Hours: 11-5:30 Mon-Fri • 12:30-5 Sat
• Antique dolls and dollhouses; dollhouse furnishings; miniatures and furniture; also Christmas ornaments. RENTALS •

CREATIVE TOYMAKER 203-773-3522
934 State St., New Haven, CT 06511
Hours: 10-6 Mon-Sat • 11:30-4 Sun
• Dolls and doll furniture; also general toys. •

DOLLSPART SUPPLY CO., INC. 718-361-0888
800 Cooper Ave., Glendale, NY 11385
Hours: 8-5 Mon-Fri
• Collector's dolls; doll eyes, parts and stringing hooks; catalog available. •

EUGENE DOLL & NOVELTY CO. 718-366-5840
47 Stewart Ave., (Meserole-Scholes) Brooklyn, NY 11237
Hours: 9-5 Mon-Fri
• Doll factory; catalog. •

EUGENE WORLD 212-675-8020
1107 Broadway, Rm. 411, (25th St.) NYC, NY 10010
Hours: 9-5 Mon-Fri by appt.
• Doll showroom; catalog. •

MANHATTAN DOLL HOSPITAL 212-989-5220
176 Ninth Ave., (21st St.) NYC, NY 10011
Hours: 11-6 Mon-Fri • 11-5 Sat
• Doll house kits, furniture, dolls, miniatures. Repair service. RENTALS •

NEW YORK DOLL HOSPITAL 212-838-7527
787 Lexington Ave., 2nd Fl. (61st-62nd St.) NYC, NY 10021
Hours: 10-6 Mon-Sat
• Antique dolls and teddy bears. Repairs all types of dolls and stuffed toys; also will make new clothes for your doll. RENTALS •

PALO IMPORTS 203-792-2411
184 Greenwood Ave., Bethel, CT 06801
Hours: 9:30-6 Mon-Sat (Thurs till 8) • 11:30-4 Sun
• Retail toy store. Novelties. Dollhouse supplies. •

PAUL'S SPECIALTIES   407-676-2570
   527 Lee Ct., West Melbourne, FL 32904
   Hours: leave message on machine
   • 1/4", 1/2" and 1" scale model lighting fixtures, all periods; 12 volt electrifying systems. •

B. SHACKMAN & CO., INC.   212-989-5162
   85 Fifth Ave., (16th St.) NYC, NY 10003
   Hours: 9-5 Mon-Fri • 10-4 Sat
   • Dollhouse furniture, props; mostly 1" scale; toy and doll antique reproductions; wholesale
   and retail. Wholesale catalog. •

TINY DOLL HOUSE   212-744-3719
   1146 Lexington Ave., (79th-80th St.) NYC, NY 10021
   Hours: 11-5:30 Mon-Fri • 11-5 Sat
   • Dollhouse moldings, turnings, decorative castings, lighting systems and parts. •

DOWN, BATTING & FIBERFILL

See also **UPHOLSTERY TOOLS & SUPPLIES**

BUFFALO BATT & FELT CORP.   716-683-4100
   3307 Walden Ave., Depew, NY 14043
   Hours: 8:30-4:45 Mon-Fri
   • Polyester batting by the roll; mail order. •

CANAL RUBBER SUPPLY CO.   212-226-7339
   329 Canal St., (Greene St.) NYC, NY 10013
   Hours: 9-5 Mon-Fri • 9-4:30 Sat   FAX 212-219-3754
   • Fluffy Dacron batting by the yard or roll. No credit cards. •

COMFORT INDUSTRIES   718-392-5300
   36-46 33rd St., (36th Ave.) L.I.C., NY 11106
   Hours: 8:30-4:30 Mon-Fri   FAX 718-392-7501
   • Fire retardant Dacron fluff, down feathers. Aerated Scotfoam, foam rubber, fibre foam, pillows & cushions; foam cut to size, mattresses. No minimum. •

DOWN EAST ENTERPRISES, INC.   212-925-2632
   73 Spring St. #503, (Lafayette St.) NYC, NY 10012
   Hours: 11-6 Mon-Fri
   • Down, nylon fabric, Fastex buckles, zippers, snaps. CREDIT CARDS •

FOAM-TEX CO., INC.   212-727-1780
   150 West 22nd St., (6-7th Ave.) NYC, NY 10011   800-982-3626
   Hours: 8:30-5 Mon-Fri • 12-4 Sat   FAX 212-727-1777

Fibre Fill • bonded and plain
Costume Foam • EFom • Bluefoam • EPS • EVA
Black Ester • HI Density • Med Density • Poly Foam
Cut and Shape to specifications
Samples on request

   • Bonded Dacron, all kinds of foam and pillow forms; cushions and mattresses made to order.
   Samples on request. CREDIT CARDS. •
   (See display ad under FOAM SHEETING & SHAPES.)

"I found it in the N.Y. Theatrical Sourcebook."

PATERSON SILKS   212-929-7861
    36 East 14th St., (Univ. Pl.) NYC, NY 10003   212-874-9510
    Hours: 9-7 Mon-Sat (Mon, Thurs till 8) • 10-5 Sun

    151 W. 72nd St., (Amsterdam-Columbus) NYC, NY 10023   212-874-9510
    Hours: 9-7:45 Mon, Thurs, Fri, • 9-6:45 Tues, Wed, Sat
    • Fiberfill by the bag; also foam cushions, fabrics. •

DRYCLEANERS

LEATHERCRAFT PROCESS CORP.   212-564-8980
    214 West 35th St., (7-8th Ave.) NYC, NY 10001
    Hours: 7:30-6 :30 Mon-Fri
    • Costume services, drycleaners, leather cleaners. •

LINCOLN TERRACE CLEANERS   212-874-3066
    149 Amsterdam Ave., (66th St.) NYC, NY 10023
    Hours: 7:30-7 Mon-Fri • 8-5 Sat
    • Theatrical drycleaning. •

MINERVA CLEANERS   718-726-2336
    29-09 Broadway (29-30 St.) Astoria, NY 11106
    Hours: 7-7 Mon-Fri • 7-5 Sat

• Quality drycleaning of clothes & costumes servicing the
specific needs of the Film, Theatre, & Television industries.
• We specialize in antique and custom costumes.
• Free pick up & delivery.
• Bulk cleaning & laundering.
• Fast friendly service.

    • Reasonable prices and fast service; theatrical drycleaning. Contact Joe. No credit cards. •

NEIGHBORHOOD CLEANERS ASSOCIATION   212-967-3002
    252 W. 29th St., (7-8th Ave.) NYC, NY 10001
    Hours: 9-5 Mon-Fri
    • Theatrical drycleaning; very cooperative; very good. CREDIT CARDS. •

NORTON DRAPERY SERVICES   212-691-3686
    89-01 Astoria Blvd. (89th St.) Jackson Heights, NY 11369
    Hours: 7:30-5 Mon-Fri
    • Drycleaning. •

R & S CLEANERS, INC.   212-475-9412
    176 Second Ave., (11th St.) NYC, NY 10003
    Hours: 7:30-6:30 Mon-Fri • 7:30-4 Sat   FAX   212-475-0336
    • Fast service for theatrical costumes; leather cleaners; reasonable prices; pickup and delivery service. •

ERNEST WINZER   718-294-2400
    1828 Cedar Ave. (179th-Major Deegan) Bronx, NY 10453
    Hours: 6:30-5 Mon-Fri
    • Theatrical drycleaning; pickup and delivery service. •

DYERS

DYE-NAMIX
212-941-6642
16 Mercer St., 3rd Fl., (Howard) NYC, NY 10013
Hours: 9:30-6 Mon-Fri (or by appt.)
FAX   212-941-7407
* Dyeing, Hand Painting and Silk Screening.
* Recognized in Broadway theatre, feature films
and the fashion industry.
* Competitive rates and fast service.
* Pickup and delivery service.

• Creative dyeing, painting, and silkscreening of samples, yardages, and garments for the fashion, theatre, and film industries. Contact Raylene Marasco for project estimates. No credit cards. •

ELISSA TATIGIKIS IBERTI
718-852-4262
223 Water St., (Bridge) Brooklyn, NY 11201
Hours: 9-6 Mon-Fri
• Hand painted fabric, costumes; will pickup and deliver; prefers natural fibers. •

FABRIC EFFECTS
212-255-5225
20 West 20th St., 5th Fl., (5th-6th Ave.) NYC, NY 10011
Hours: 9-5 Mon-Fri (or by appt.)
FAX   212-255-3077

Specializing in dyeing, silkscreening and hand painting.
Custom orders and small production.
Extensive experience in Theatre, Film, and Fashion.

FABRIC EFFECTS INCORPORATED

• Dyeing, silkscreening, hand painting - all kinds of fabric coloring - done by three of NY's top textile artisans. •
(See display ad under COSTUME CRAFTSPEOPLE & MILLINERY.)

MASTER DYEING CO.
718-726-1001
24-47 44th St., (Astoria Blvd.-25th Ave.) L.I.C., NY 11103
Hours: 8-4:30 Mon-Fri
• Dyers of garments and linens; large quantities only. •

PRINCE STREET DESIGNS
212-431-6775
242 Lafayette St., (Prince & Spring) NYC, NY 10012
Hours: 9-4 Mon-Sat
FAX   212-431-6775
• Small vat dying of garments and yardage. No minimum. •

ELECTRICAL DEVICES: ANTIQUE & MODERN

ACE PROPS
212-206-1475
212-580-9551
1 West 19th St. Ground Fl., (5th Ave.) NYC, NY 10011
Hours: 8-5 Mon-Fri • 9-4 Sat or by appt.

Wide variety of hard to get props - electronic gear, video cameras, microphones, lighting and projection equipment, prop guns, photographic equipment, good technical support.

• Audio & video equipment: consumer & professional, period & contemporary. RENTALS CREDIT CARDS •
(See display ad under AUDIO & VIDEO EQUIPMENT)

E. BUK, ANTIQUES & ART
212-226-6891
(toll call) 700-SCIENCE
151 Spring St, (W. Broadway-Wooster) NYC, NY 10012
Hours: Every day by appt.

ANTIQUE, PERIOD AND HISTORICAL electric, electronic, electro-mechanical devices, meters, motors, lab and test equipment, radio, television, telephone, telegraph, tools, appliances, fans, light bulbs, quackery, panels, boards, switches, Buck Rodgers gizmos, Frankenstein props; 100's of hard-to-find items.

• Complete period settings and custom work. RENTALS •
(See display ad under ANTIQUES: EUROPEAN & AMERICAN)

LAW ENFORCEMENT ASSOCIATES, INC.
800-426-6240
PO Box 639, 100 Hunter Place, (Highway 96 & 1A) Youngsville, NC 27596
Hours: 8-4:30 Mon-Fri
919-556-6270
• Phone scramblers, baggage x-rays, security equipment. MC/VISA •

HARRY POSTER - VINTAGE TV'S
201-794-9606
PO Box 1883, So. Hackensack, NJ 07606
Hours: by appt.
• Vintage TV's, transistor and tube radios, mics. One tube to a full store. Also signage from the 1930-1960's. •

RADIO SHACK
212-221-7435
1100 Sixth Ave., (42nd St.) NYC, NY 10036
Hours: 9-7 Mon-Fri • 10-6 Sat • 11-5 Sun
• Good supplier of radio, telephone, electronic items and components, other outlets in NYC but best stock here. CREDIT CARDS •

HERMAN STICHT CO.
800-221-3203
718-852-7602
57 Front St., Brooklyn, NY 11201
Hours: 9-5 Mon-Fri
FAX 718-852-7915
• Meters. MC/VISA •

ELECTRICAL & ELECTRONIC SUPPLIES

See also **MOTORS & MECHANICAL COMPONENTS**

A. P. W.   201-627-0643
    72 Main St., Rockaway, NJ 07866
    Hours: 8-4 Mon-Fri   FAX   201-627-6396
    • A.C. or D.C. Electromagnets. Brochure available. •

BARBIZON   212-586-1620
    426 West 55th St., (9-10th) NYC, NY 10019
    Hours: 8:30-5:30 Mon-Fri • 9-1 Sat   FAX   212-247-8818

    3 Draper St., Woburn, MA 01801   617-935-3920
    Hours: 8:30-5:30 Mon-Fri • 9-1 Sat   FAX   617-935-9273

    6437G General Green Way, Alexandria, VA 22312   703-750-3900
    Hours: 8:30-5:30 Mon-Fri • 9-1 Sat   FAX   703-750-1448

    2401 Mercer Avenue, West Palm Beach, FL 33401   407-833-2020
    Hours: 8:30-5:30 Mon-Fri • 9-1 Sat   FAX   407-833-3582

    101 Krog St., Atlanta, GA 30307-2422   404-681-5124
    Hours: 8:30-5:30 Mon-Fri • 9-1 Sat   FAX   404-681-5315
    • Theatrical electrics, fixtures and related products. MC/VISA •

BLAN ELECTRONICS   212-233-6288
    56 Warren St, (W B'way-Church) NYC, NY 10007
    Hours: 9-4 Mon-Fri   FAX   212-233-6091
    • Electronics; special relays, switches, solenoids, etc. •

BROADWAY ELECTRIC   212-673-3906
    862 Broadway, (17th) NYC, NY 10003
    Hours: 8:30-5 Mon-Fri   FAX   212-475-5957
    • General electrical and electronics supplies. Helpful. •

ELECTRIC APPLIANCE RENTAL & SALES CO./ AC/DC APPLIANCE/
AAA APPLIANCE RENTALS & SALES CO.   212-686-8884
    40 West 29th St. 2nd Fl., (B'way-6th) NYC, NY 10001
    Hours: 8:30-5:30 Mon-Fri
    • Electric transformers (220-110) for overseas use; RENTALS •

JENSEN TOOLS INC.   602-968-6231
    7815 S. 46th St., Phoenix, AZ 85044   800-426-1194
    Hours: 6-5:30 Mon-Fri   FAX   800-366-9662
    • Electronic test tools, cases, dental tools. CREDIT CARDS •

LAW ENFORCEMENT ASSOCIATES, INC.   800-426-7072
    PO Box 639, 100 Hunter Place, (Highway 96 & 1A) Youngsville, NC 27596
    Hours: 8-4:30 Mon-Fri   FAX   919-556-6240
    • Phone scramblers, baggage X-rays, security equipment. •

MAGNET WIRE, INC.   516-667-9315
    161 Rodeo Dr., Edgewood, NY 11717
    Hours: 9-5 Mon-Fri   FAX   516-254-2099
    • Carries tungsten wire, piano wire, as well as a large selection of other wire. MC/VISA •

NEWARK ELECTRONICS   908-851-2290
  1435 Morris Ave., Union, NJ 07083-3636
  Hours: 9-5 Mon-Fri/phone orders only
  • Electronic components and equipment; voluminous catalog available to serious users. CRED-
  IT CARDS •

RADIO SHACK   212-221-7435
  1100 Sixth Ave., (42nd St.) NYC, NY 10036
  Hours: 9-7 Mon-Fri • 10-6 Sat • 11-5 Sun
  • Good supplier of radio, telephone, electronic items and components; many other outlets in
  NYC but best stock here. CREDIT CARDS •

CLARK REISS DISTRIBUTORS INC.   212-226-6400
  51-53 Leonard St., (Church-W. B'way) NYC, NY 10013
  Hours: 9-5 Mon-Fri
  • Resistors, potentiometers, relays, switches, pilot lights, bulbs, fuses. •

ROSETTA ELECTRICAL CO. INC.   212-233-9088
  73 Murray St., (Greenwich St.-W B'way) NYC, NY 10013
  Hours: 8:30-5:30 Mon-Fri • 9:30-4:30 Sat   FAX 212-385-4151
  • Large selection lamps, fixtures. CREDIT CARDS

  21 West 46th St., (5-6th Avenue) NYC, NY 10036   212-719-4381
  Hours: 9-6 Mon-Fri • 9:30-5:45 Sat   FAX 212-768-3120
  • Good selection fixtures, conduit, miscellaneous supplies. CREDIT CARDS

S & L JACK ELECTRONICS   718-545-8843
  28-14 Steinway St., (28-30th Ave.) Astoria, NY 11103
  Hours: 9:30-7 Mon-Fri • 9:30-6 Sat   FAX 718-545-8919
  • Miniature lamps, other electronic supplies. MC/VISA •

SILVER & SONS HARDWARE   212-247-6969
  711 Eighth Ave., (44-45th) NYC, NY 10036   212-247-6978
  Hours: 9-5:30 Mon-Fri • 10-3 Sat
  • Complete selection of electrical and lighting supplies; delivery available, UPS COD orders OK,
  FAX available; ask for Steve or Jay. CREDIT CARDS •

HERMAN STICHT CO.   718-852-7602
  334 Furman St., (Joralemon) Brooklyn, NY 11201
  Hours: 9-5 Mon-Fri
  • Meters. •

SWITCHES UNLIMITED   718-478-5000
  34-11 56th St., (B'way-Northern Blvd.) Woodside, NY 11377   800-221-0487
  Hours: 8:30-5 Mon-Fri (closed 12-1)   FAX 718-672-6370
  • Switches, indicator lights, panel lights. MC/VISA •

TECHNI-TOOL   215-825-4990
  Apollo Road, Plymouth Meeting, PA 19462
  Hours: 8:30-5 Mon-Fri
  • Specializes in electronic tools and testing tools; catalog. •

TUDOR ELECTRICAL SUPPLY CO. INC.   212-867-7550
  226 East 46th St., (2-3rd) NYC, NY 10017
  Hours: 9-5 Mon-Thurs • 9-4:30 Fri   FAX 212-867-7569
  • Electrical supplies. •

UNION CONNECTOR   516-623-7461
   300 Babylon Turnpike, Roosevelt, NY 11575
   Hours: 9-5 Mon-Fri   FAX   516-623-7475
   • Lighting panels and boxes, patch panels, plugs connectors, adapters, wiring. •

ELEVATORS

ABLE ELEVATOR & DOOR REPAIR CO. INC.   212-674-7607
   37-02 27th. St., (37th) L.I.C., NY 11101
   Hours: 8:30-4:30 Mon-Fri   FAX   718-706-0618
   • Very helpful; has elevator door track. •

CENTURY ELEVATOR   718-937-6200
   37-39 9th St, (37th Ave.) L.I.C., NY 11101
   Hours: 8:30-4:30 Mon-Fri   FAX   718-361-5731
   • Installations, repair and maintenance. •

EMBROIDERY, PLEATING & BUTTONHOLES

See also **PROMOTIONAL MATERIALS**

ACME EMBLEM   212-255-7880
   150 Coolidge Ave., Englewood, NJ 07631
   Hours: 9-4 Mon-Fri   FAX   800-221-8612
   • Custom work, 100 pc. min., 3-4 wk. delivery; see Ms. Marks. •

BARBER & BROMBERG EMBROIDERY & STITCHING   212-719-0800
   247 West 38th St. 3rd Fl., (7-8th) NYC, NY 10018
   Hours: 8:30-4 Mon-Fri
   • Beading, pearls, applique stitching, large orders only. •

CHRIS BOBIN   212-255-5225
   20 West 20th St. c/o Fabric Effects, (5-6th) NYC, NY 10011   212-475-7268
   Hours: By appt.
   • Sewn solutions for props, costumes, and illustrations. Unique works created to your specifications. Beautiful stuff. Call for free color flyer. •

BUTTONHOLE FASHIONS   212-354-1420
   580 Eighth Ave., (38-39th) NYC, NY 10018
   Hours: 8-5 Mon-Fri
   • Leather, piped and bound, machine buttonholes and eyelets. •

CITY EMBLEM MFG. CO   718-366-2040
   6031 Myrtle Ave., (Sommerfield) Ridgewood, NY 11385
   Hours: 10-6 Mon-Sat (Fri till 7)
   • Chenille, embroidered and felt lettering; one week service. CREDIT CARDS •

DE' COR EMBROIDERIES CO. INC.   212-354-8668
   250 West 40th St., (7-8th) NYC, NY 10018
   Hours: 8-4 Mon-Fri
   • Applique, rhinestones, nailheads, bonnaz, crochet beading, hand embroidery. •

D & R EMBROIDERY CO.   212-686-6920
　　29 East 31st St., (5th-Madison) NYC, NY 10010
　　Hours: 9-5 Mon-Fri
　　• Embroidery in bulk; no one-of-a-kind. •

KOPPEL PLEATING INC.   718-893-1500
　　890 Garrison Ave. 3rd Fl., (Tiffany-Lafayette) Bronx, NY 10474
　　Hours: 7:30-5 Mon-Fri
　　• Custom pleating service. •

KRAUS & SONS INC.   212-620-0408
　　158 West 27th St., (6-7th) NYC, NY 10001
　　Hours: 9-5 Mon-Fri
　　• Embroidered, silkscreened, or appliqued banners and flags; custom trophies and ribbons;
　　established 1886. No credit cards. •

METROPOLITAN–KELLER CO.   212-391-0990
　　270 West 38th St. 10th Fl., (7-8th) NYC, NY 10018
　　Hours: 8:30-4:30 Mon-Thurs • 8:30-3 Fri   FAX 212-391-1395
　　• Beading in bulk for shows and film; will do small embroidery orders fast. No credit cards. •

PENN AND FLETCHER   212-239-6868
　　242 West 30th St. 2nd Floor, (7-8th) NYC, NY 10001   FAX 212-239-6914
　　Hours: 9-5 Mon-Fri

Fine Embroidery by hand and machine.
Beading • Bonnaz • Computerized • Schiffli

Domestic & Imported Laces & Trims.
Single pieces and production.

> ### *Penn & Fletcher, Inc.*
> Custom Embroidery, Laces and Trimmings
> Custom Design Services

　　• Custom embroidery, hand beading specialists; also high quality laces and trims. MC/VISA •

PROFESSIONAL PROMOTION SERVICES   212-239-7211
　　270 W. 38th St., Rm. 2001, NYC, NY 10018
　　Hours: 8-6 Mon-Fri   FAX 212-239-7318
　　• Computer embroidery and silkscreening on satin, denim, cotton, canvas, wool and leather;
　　varsity jackets, baseball caps, and other premium items; specialize in B'way show and crew
　　jackets. •

REGAL ORIGINALS   212-921-0270
　　247 West 37th St., (7-8th) NYC, NY 10018
　　Hours: 7-6:30 Mon-Fri
　　• Pleating, shirring, smocking, piping, applique, embroidery; good and fast; speak to Rodger
　　Cohen. •

STITCH WORKS   212-255-2573
　　27 West 24th St., Suite 9D, (5-6th Ave.) NYC, NY 10011
　　Hours: 10-6 Mon-Fri   FAX 212-366-5085
　　• Video-Computerized operation; custom work and rush orders welcome; small & one-of-a-
　　kind orders; large stock of rayon and metallic threads; you supply the items to be embroi-
　　dered. •

YOUNG EMBROIDERY CO.   212-989-3243
　　1133 Broadway, (26th St.) NYC, NY 10010
　　Hours: 6:30-3:30 Mon-Fri
　　• Custom embroidery to your design. •

EROTIC GOODS

PINK PUSSYCAT BOUTIQUE   212-243-0077
   167 West 4th St., (6th Ave.) NYC, NY 10014
   Hours: 10am-2am Sun-Thurs • 10am-3am Fri,Sat
   • Leather, studs, lingerie, inflatable dolls, handcuffs, sex toys. Mail orders. Catalog. CREDIT
   CARDS •

PLEASURE CHEST   212-242-2158
   156 Seventh Ave. South, (Charles-Perry) NYC, NY 10014
   Hours: 12-9:30 Mon, Tues, Wed • 12-11 Thur, Fri, Sat • 12-10 Sun   FAX 212-242-4185
   • Erotic postcards, leather goods, lingerie, S & M items, sex toys. Shipping. CREDIT CARDS •

ETHNIC GOODS: AFRICAN & WEST INDIAN

AFRICAN TRADER ART GALLERY   607-746-2384
   RFD #1, Box 528, Delhi, NY 13752
   Hours: by appt.
   • African goods, masks, statues. Phone orders. Will ship. •

BACK FROM GUATEMALA   212-260-7010
   306 East 6th St., (1-2) NYC, NY 10003
   Hours: 12-11 Mon-Sat • 2-10 Sun
   • Clothing, jewelry, and artifacts from over 20 countries; Andes to the Himalayas. CREDIT
   CARDS •

CRAFT CARAVAN INC.   212-431-6669
   63 Green St., (Spring-Broome) NYC, NY 10012
   Hours: 10-6 Tues-Fri • 11-6 Sat,Sun
   • African imports; clothing, hats, jewelry, furniture, baskets, toys, traditional African handicrafts. Retail and Wholesale. RENTALS CREDIT CARDS. •

THE HEMINGWAY AFRICAN GALLERY   212-838-3650
   1050 Second Ave. #95, (55-56th) NYC, NY 10022   212-752-5867
   Hours: 10:30-6 Mon-Sat • 11-5 Sun   FAX 212-838-3650
   • Interesting selection of masks, skins, animal trophies, horns, etc. See Brian Gaisford.
   RENTALS •

LIBERTY HOUSE   212-799-7640
   2389 Broadway, (87-88th) NYC, NY 10024
   Hours: 10-6:45 Tues, Wed, Fri, Sat • 10-7:45 Mon, Thurs • 1-5:45 Sun FAX 212-875-1710
   • Clothing and jewelry for women. Accessories, Kilim rugs. Objects from everywhere. CREDIT
   CARDS. •

MIDTOWN INTERNATIONAL   212-725-9840
   246 Fifth Ave., (28th) NYC, NY 10001
   Hours: 9-6 Mon-Fri • 10-5 Sat,Sun   FAX 212-725-9868
   • African baskets, textiles, beads, etc. Sales only. •

ETHNIC GOODS: EAST INDIAN

ANAND INDIA SHOP   212-247-2054
30 Rockefeller Plaza, Concourse Shop 11, (50th St-6th Ave.) NYC, NY 10020
Hours: 9-6 Mon-Fri • 10-6 Sat
• Indian and international jewelry, gifts, brass. Phone orders. Will ship. CREDIT CARDS •

ANNAPURNA FINE ARTS   212-696-4929
120 Lexington Ave., (28th Street) NYC, NY 10016
Hours: 10-7:30 Mon-Sat   FAX   212-696-0229
• Brass sculpture and art ware, wooden carved figures, silk paintings, hand embroidered wall hangings, handicrafts from India. Catalog available. CREDIT CARDS •

BE SEATED INC.   212-924-8444
66 Greenwich Ave., (6-7th) NYC, NY 10011
Hours: 11-7 Mon-Fri • 11-6 Sat
• Ikats, block print Indian fabrics; baskets, small rugs, decorative accessories. CREDIT CARDS. •

CHANDS ENTERPRISES   718-639-0606
37-52 74th Street, (37th Ave.) Jackson Heights, NY 11372
Hours: 10 :30-7:30 Mon-Sat.
• Indian fabrics and jewelry. •

FINAL CAUSE   212-475-8760
42 1/2 St. Marks Pl., (1-2nd) NYC, NY 10003
Hours: 2-6 Wed-Sun or by appt
• Clothing, jewelry, bags, scarves, and crafts from India, Asia, South America, and American Indian. No Rentals. CREDIT CARDS. •

LILIANA'S INTERNATIONAL BOUTIQUE   212-691-5703
48 1/2 Greenwich Ave., (6-7th) NYC, NY 10011
Hours: 2-7 every day
• Men's and women's clothing and accessories. Jewelry. South American also. RENTALS CREDIT CARDS •

PARACELSO   212-966-4232
414 West Broadway, (Prince-Spring) NYC, NY 10012
Hours: 1-7 every day.
• Women's clothing and jewelry. CREDIT CARDS •

POPULAR SARI HOUSE   718-507-8588
37-20 74th Street, (37th Avenue) Jackson Heights, NY 11372
Hours: 10:30-7:30 Mon-Sat
• Indian silks, fabrics, and saris. •

TAJ SARI PALACE, LTD.   718 -639-4444
37-44 74th St., (37th Ave.) Jackson Heights, NY 11372
Hours: 10:30-7:30 Mon-Sun
• Indian fabrics, jewelry, and saris. •

USHA SAREE CENTER   212-532-9399
128 East 28th Street, (Lexington & Park) NYC, NY 10016
Hours: 10-7:30 every day
• Indian silks and saris. •

ETHNIC GOODS: MEXICAN, SOUTH AMERICAN, AMERICAN INDIAN

ABRACADABRA   800-Magic-66
  10 Christopher St., (near 6th) NYC, NY 10014   212-627-5745
  Hours: 11-7 Mon-Sat (also open Sun in Oct., Dec)   **FAX**   212-627-5876
    • Indian costumes, headdresses, necklaces, spears, peace pipes, bells, etc. Also 6 ft. cigar
    store Indians. Catalog available. April Fool's Day Parade. CREDIT CARDS •

ARTE PRIMITIVO INC.   212-570-0393
  3 East 65th St., (5th Ave. & Madison) NYC, NY 10021
  Hours: 11-5 Mon-Fri • 1-3 Sat
    • Books on Pre-Columbian cultures; new, rare, out-of-print. •

BAZAAR SABADO   212-941-6152
  54 Greene St., (Broome-Grand) NYC, NY 10013
  Hours: 11:30-6:30 Mon-Sat • 12-5:30 Sun
    • Good variety of Mexican and Central American furniture, accessories, and folk art.
    Reasonable. Phone orders. RENTALS CREDIT CARDS •

CLAIBORNE GALLERY   212-475-3072
  452 West Broadway, (Prince-Houston) NYC, NY 10012
  Hours: 11-7 Mon-Fri • 11-6 Sat • 12-6 Sun   **FAX**   212-475-3072
    • Large selection Mexican furniture and furnishings; chairs, cupboards, armoires, stools,
    tables, wooden crosses, candlesticks, ceramics, contemporary iron furniture; RENTALS CRED-
    IT CARDS •

THE COMMON GROUND INC.   212-645-0577
  19 Greenwich Ave., (6th) NYC, NY 10014   **FAX**   212-989-0573
  Hours: 11:30-7:30 Mon, Tues, Thurs, Fri • 11:30-6:30 Wed • 11-7 Sat • 1-7 Sun
    • Antique and contemporary American Indian jewelry, clothing, pottery, furniture. Phone
    orders. RENTALS CREDIT CARDS •

CRAZY CROW TRADING POST   903-463-1366
  PO Box 314, Dennison, TX 75020
  Hours: 8-5 Mon-Fri   **FAX**   903-463-7734
    • Indian craft supply house; mail and phone orders only; catalog $3.00 MC/VISA •

FINAL CAUSE   212-475-8760
  42 1/2 St. Marks Pl., (1-2nd) NYC, NY 10003
  Hours: 2-6 Wed-Sun or by appt.
    • Clothing, jewelry, bags, scarves, and crafts from South America, American Indian, India, and
    Asia. No rentals. CREDIT CARDS. •

GREY OWL INDIAN CRAFTS   718-341-4000
  132-05 Merrick Blvd., (Bel Knap) Jamaica, NY 11434
  Hours: 9-5 Mon-Fri
    • Kits for American Indian headdresses and crafts; catalog. CREDIT CARDS •

MEXICAN FOLK ART   212-673-1910
  66 East 7th St., (1-2nd Ave.) NYC, NY 10003
  Hours: 2-9 daily
    • Native American goods. Mexican and South American clothes and artifacts, sportswear.
    RENTALS CREDIT CARDS. •

ETHNIC GOODS: MIDDLE EASTERN

AEGEAN IMPORTS   415-593-8300
    1200 Industrial Rd. Rm. 5, San Carlos, Ca 94070
    Hours: 8:30-4 Mon-Fri (closed Fri in summer)
    • Greek fishermen's hats; quantity mail order only. •

JACQUES CARCANAGUES INC.   212-431-3116
    21 Green St, (Grand-Canal) NYC, NY 10013 (wholesale showroom)
    Hours: 10:30-6 Tues-Sat by appt.   FAX   212-274-8780

    106 Spring St., (Mercer) NYC, NY 10012 (retail store)
    Hours: 11-7 daily
    • Middle to Far Eastern clothing, jewelry, rugs, textiles, furniture, baskets, wicker items.
    RENTALS CREDIT CARDS. •

POSEIDON BAKERY   212-757-6173
    629 Ninth Ave., (44-45th) NYC, NY 10036
    Hours: 9-7 Tues-Sat • 10-4 Sun
    • Greek pastries. •

RASHID SALES CO.   718-852-3295
    191 Atlantic Ave., (Court-Clinton) Brooklyn, NY 11201
    Hours: 9:30-7 Mon-Sat • 12-7 Sun   FAX   718-643-9522
    • Music, books, periodicals, castanets, giftware, videos. Phone orders. RENTALS MC/VISA •

ETHNIC GOODS: ORIENTAL

See also **ARCADE & AMUSEMENT DEVICES**
See also **TOYS & GAMES**

ASIAN HOUSE   212-581-2294
    888 Seventh Ave., (56th St.) NYC, NY 10019
    Hours: 10-6 Mon-Sat • 12-5 Sun
    • Oriental goods; furniture, lamps, prints, jewelry, etc. Some rentals. CREDIT CARDS •

AZUMA   212-673-2900
    25 East 8th St., (Univ. Pl.-5th) NYC, NY 10003
    Hours: 10-9:45 Mon-Sat • 12-8:15 Sun
    • Reasonably priced housewares, gift items and a good selection of baskets and wicker items.
    Other locations throughout city. CREDIT CARDS •

BOOKS NIPPON   310-604-9701
    1123 Dominguez St. Suite K, Carson, CA 90746
    Hours: 9-6 Mon-Fri   FAX   310-604-1134
    • Japanese and Oriental books; gifts; calligraphy and painting supplies. Catalog available.
    CREDIT CARDS •

CHINA SEAS   212-752-5555
    979 Third Ave., (58-59th St.) NYC, NY 10022
    Hours: 9-5 Mon-Fri
    • Textiles and wallcoverings featuring Indonesian batik, handwoven textures, screen prints,
    sheers and ultra suede. No credit cards. RENTALS •

HANDLOOM BATIK
212-925-9542
214 Mulberry St., (Spring) NYC, NY 10012
Hours: 12-7 Wed-Sat • 1-6 Sun
• Asian imports; beautiful batik and handwoven fabrics; reasonably priced. Paper, soapstone carvings. Accepts personal checks. •

HULA SUPPLY CENTER
808-941-5379
800-237-3347
2346 South King St., Honolulu, HI 96826
Hours: Daily
• Hawaiian, Tahitian, Samoan, Maori costumes and dance instruments; write for catalog. MC/VISA •

KATAGIRI & CO. INC.
212-755-3566
224 East 59th St., (2-3rd Ave.) NYC, NY 10022
Hours: 10-7 Mon-Sat • 11-6 Sun   FAX   212-752 -4197

226 East 59th St., (2-3rd Avenue) NYC, NY 10022   212-838-5453
Hours: 10-7 Mon-Sat • 11-6 Sun
• Japanese groceries, cooking utensils, giftware. Catalog. RENTALS MC/VISA •

KOTO
212-533-8601
71 West Houston St., (W.B'way-Wooster) NYC, NY 10012
Hours: 12-7:30 every day   FAX   212-533-8601
• Japanese products: kimonos, pillows, ceramics, lacquerware, framed art, chopsticks, accessories. CREDIT CARDS. •

LEEKAM DESIGN
212-226-7226
93 Mercer St., (Spring-Broome) NYC, NY 10012
Hours: 11-6 Tues-Fri • 11-7 Sat • 12-6 Sun
• Rental/Purchase of Chinese jewelry; and handicrafts to the trade only; great selection. CREDIT CARDS. •

MIYA SHOJI & INTERIORS INC.
212-243-6774
109 West 17th St., (6-7th Ave.) NYC, NY 10011
Hours: 9-5 Mon-Fri
• Shoji screens, lamps, cabinets; short term rentals. MC/VISA •

NORTHSOUTH TRADING INC.
212-964-4459
28 Elizabeth St., (Canal-Bayard) NYC, NY 10013
Hours: 11-7 every day
• Oriental fabrics and dresses made-to-order, brocades, silks, slippers, shoes. No credit cards. RENTALS •

NUSRATY AFGHAN IMPORTS INC.
212-691-1012
215 West 10th St., (Bleeker) NYC, NY 10014
Hours: 1-9 Sun-Thurs • 1-11 Fri,Sat
• Oriental and tribal rugs; jewelry, dresses, embroidery; unusual antiquities. RENTALS CREDIT CARDS. •

OLD JAPAN, INC.
212-633-0922
382 Bleeker St., (Perry-Charles) NYC, NY 10014
Hours: 12-7 Wed-Sun • Mon, Tues by appt.
• Japanese antique furniture, folk art objects. Kimino sales and rentals. CREDIT CARDS. •

ORCHIDS OF HAWAII   718-654-7630
   3703 Provost Ave., (E. 223rd-Connors) Bronx, NY 10466
   Hours: 9-5 Mon-Fri
   • Chinese, Polynesian, and tropical restaurant decor, bamboo. •

THE ORIENTAL DRESS   212-349-0818
   38 Mott St., (Bayard) NYC, NY 10013
   Hours: 10-5:30 every day
   • Chinese brocade. Silk fabric •

PEARL RIVER CHINESE PRODUCTS EMPORIUM   212-431-4770
   277 Canal St., (B'way) NYC, NY 10013   212-966-1010
   200 Grand St., (Mott) NYC, NY 10013
   Hours: 10-8 every day
   • Chinese groceries, cookware, dishware, clothing, fans, lanterns, tablecloths; a Chinese
   department store. Great selection. CREDIT CARDS. •

RADIO HULA   212-226-4467
   169 Mercer St., (Houston-Prince) NYC, NY 10012
   Hours: 12-7 Tues-Sun
   • Good selection of Hawaiian home accessories, both vintage and contemporary. Also, great
   Hawaiian shirts in silk and rayon as well as other clothing, jewelry, fabric by the yard and food
   products. CREDITS CARDS •

SINO-AMERICAN COMMODITIES CENTER INC.   718-392-5671
   3501 Queens Blvd., Long Island City, NY 11101-1720
   Hours: 9:30-6:30 Mon-Sat • 10-6 Sun   FAX   718-392-5705
   • Chinese department store; furniture, rugs, apparel, shoes, housewares. Phone orders. No
   rentals. CREDIT CARDS •

TIBET WEST   212-255-3416
   19 Christopher St., (6-7th Ave.) NYC, NY 10014
   Hours: 11-8 Mon-Sat • 1-8 Sun   FAX   212-686-7811
   • Exotic jewelry, clothing, rugs, and antiques. RENTALS CREDIT CARDS. •

TOKYO BOOKSTORE   212-697-0840
   521 Fifth Ave., (43-44th St.) NYC, NY 10175
   Hours: 10-7 Mon-Fri • 11-7 Sat • 1-5 Sun   FAX   212-983-1765
   • Japanese and Oriental books, gift section, calligraphy and painting supplies Hand-made
   paper and stationary. Phone orders. RENTALS CREDIT CARDS. •

VISION OF TIBET   212-995-9276
   167 Thompson St., (Houston-Bleeker) NYC, NY 10012
   Hours: 11-7 Tues-Sun
   • Treasures from the Himalayan Kingdom. Jewelry, masks, carpets, furniture. Phone orders.
   RENTALS CREDIT CARDS. •

YOMIURI PRESS/YOMIURI SHIMBUN   212-765-1111
   666 Sixth Ave., (52-53rd. St.) NYC, NY 10103
   Hours: 9:30-5:30 Mon-Fri
   • Current Japanese newspapers. •

YUNG KEE TRADING INC.   212-679-3778
   838 Sixth Ave., (29-30th St.) NYC, NY 10001
   Hours: 8:30-6 Mon-Fri • 8:30-5 Sat • 9:30-4 Sun   FAX   212-532-8651
   • Wholesale oriental goods. No credit cards. •

E-F

ETHNIC GOODS: RUSSIAN & EASTERN EUROPEAN

A LA VIEILLE RUSSIE, INC.   212-752-1727
   781 Fifth Ave., (59th St.) NYC, NY 10022
   Hours: 10-5 Mon-Fri • 10:30-4 Sat (closed Sat; June, July, Aug)
   • Fine Russian antiques. CREDIT CARDS. •

ECLECTIC/ENCORE PROPERTIES   212-645-8880
   620 West 26th St. 4th Fl. (11-12th Ave.) NYC, NY 10001
   Hours: 9-5 Mon-Fri or by appt.   FAX   212-243-6508
   • Czech, Russian, Polish, German paintings, porcelains, glassware & decorative objects.
   Furniture, statuary & religious items. Contact Barry or Regina. • .
   (See display ad under PROP RENTAL HOUSES)

VICTOR KAMKIN INC.   212-673-0776
   925 Broadway, (21st St.) NYC, NY 10010
   Hours: 9:30-5:30 Mon-Fri • 10-5 Sat
   • Current Russian newspapers, periodicals, gifts, books (in English). •

ETHNIC GOODS: SCOTTISH & IRISH

IRISH BOOKSHOP   212-274-1923
   580 Broadway, Rm. 1103, (Prince-Houston) NYC, NY 10012
   Hours: 11-5 Mon-Fri • 1-4 Sat
   • (Formerly Irish Books and Graphics) Irish books, music, tapes and prints. Mail and phone
   orders, MC/VISA •

THE IRISH SECRET   212-334-6711
   155 Spring St., (W. B'way-Wooster) NYC, NY 10012
   Hours: 11-7 everyday
   • Irish clothing for men and women. CREDIT CARDS •

MATTIE HASKINS SHAMROCK IMPORTS   212-564-7474
   A & S Plaza, 901 Sixth Ave., 5th Fl., (32-33rd St.) NYC, NY 10001
   Hours: 9:45-6:45 Mon-Sat (Mon,Thurs, Fri till 8:30)
   • Irish goods, clothing. Mail and phone orders. CREDIT CARDS. •

SCOTTISH PRODUCTS INC.   212-687-2505
   141 East 44th Suite 311, (Lexington-3rd) NYC, NY 10022
   Hours: 11-5:15 Mon, Tues, Thur, Fri • closed Wed. • Sat by Appt.
   • Limited selection of Scottish clothing, clan tartans, books, jewelry, knick-knacks. MC/VISA •

EYEGLASSES

CAPALDO & SMITH, INC.   212-247-3398
   871 Seventh Ave., (55th St.) NYC, NY 10019
   Hours: 9-6 Mon-Fri
   • Pince-nez, monocles, good selection. CREDIT CARDS •

COHEN'S FASHION OPTICAL   212-674-1986
  117 Orchard St., (Delancey) NYC, NY 10002
  Hours: 9-6 daily

  545 Fifth Ave., (44-45th St.) NYC, NY 10017   212-697-0915
  Hours: 9-6 Mon-Fri • 10-6 Sat

  767 Lexington Ave., (60th St.) NYC, NY 10022   212-751-6652
  Hours: 9-8 Mon & Thurs • 9-7 Tues-Sat • 11-5 Sun
  • Low cost frames. CREDIT CARDS •

ECONOMY OPTICAL CO./OPTICAL CITY   212-243-4884
  223 West 14th St., (7-8th Ave.) NYC, NY 10011
  Hours: 10-6 Mon-Sat
  • Modern frames and a few period frames. CREDIT CARDS •

M. EISING & CO.   212-744-1270
  1036 Lexington Ave., (74th St.) NYC, NY 10021
  Hours: 10-6 Mon-Fri • 10-3 Sat
  • Good selection period eyeglasses and pince-nez. CREDIT CARDS •

THE EYE SHOP   212-673-9450
  50 West 8th St., (6th-MacDougal) NYC, NY 10011
  Hours: 10-7 Mon-Fri • 10:30-6:30 Sat • 12-6 Sun
  • Good selection of styles. CREDIT CARDS •

E.B. MEYROWITZ INC.   212-227-0881
  150 Broadway Rm. 1110, (Wall St.) NYC, NY 10038
  Hours: 8-5:15 Mon-Fri

  520 Fifth Ave., (43-44th) NYC, NY 10036   212-840-3881
  Hours: 9:30-6 Mon-Fri

  1171 Madison Ave., (86th St.) NYC, NY 10028   212-744-6565
  Hours: 9-5:30 Mon-Fri • 9-5 Sat
  • Modern eyeglasses and lorgnettes. CREDIT CARDS •

SOL MOSCOT   212-477-3796
  118 Orchard St. 2nd Fl., (Delancey) NYC, NY 10002
  Hours: 9-5:15 every day
  • Large selection; glasses made while-you-wait; good prices. CREDIT CARDS •

ODDS COSTUME RENTAL   212-268-6227
  231 West 29th St. Rm. 304, (7-8th Ave.) NYC, NY 10001
  Hours: 9:30-5 Mon-Fri • Sat by appt.
  • Period through modern eyeglasses including lorgnettes. RENTALS •
  (See display ad under COSTUME RENTAL & CONSTRUCTION.)

HARRIET REDERMAN, PUBLIC RELATIONS   516-484-9245
  44 Harbor Park Dr., Port Washington, NY 11050
  Hours: 9-5 Mon-Fri
  • BerDel International and Avant Garde Optic frames; designer frames-Armani, Valentino, YSL
  and more; contact Judy Saltzman. No credit cards. •

UNIQUE EYEWEAR   212-947-4977
  19 West 34th St. Rm. 1218, (5-6th Ave.) NYC, NY 10001
  Hours: 9-5 Mon-Fri (Thurs till 6) • 10-2:30 Sat
  • Eyeglasses at wholesale prices. No credit cards. •

NOTES

"I found it in the N.Y. Theatrical Sourcebook."

FABRICS: GENERAL

For specific types of fabrics, see also other fabric headings.

A & N FABRICS   212-719-1773
268 West 39th St., (7th-8th Ave.) NYC, NY 10018
Hours: 9-6 Mon-Fri • 9-5 Sat
• Large selection of fabrics at discount prices; large supplier of felts and burlaps.
Wholesale/retail; quick service, see Harry. CREDIT CARDS •

ANDROS IMPORTED SHIRTING, INC.   212-481-4788
12 East 33rd St., (5th-Madison Ave.) NYC, NY 10016
Hours: 9-5 Mon-Fri
• Shirting fabrics; see Angelo or Jim. No credit cards. •

ART-MAX FABRICS, INC.   212-398-0755
250 West 40th St., (7th-8th Ave.) NYC, NY 10018   212-398-0756
Hours: 8:30-6 Mon-Fri • 9-5 Sat
• Silks, jerseys, woolens, organza, dress goods; see Allan or Herman. CREDIT CARDS •

ASSOCIATED FABRICS CORP.   212-689-7186
104 East 25th St., (Lexington-Park Ave.) NYC, NY 10010
Hours: 8:30-4:30 Mon-Fri • closed 12-1 everyday   FAX   212-260-3531
• Full range of theatrical fabrics: metallics, spandex, fluorescents and novelty fabrics.
MC/VISA •

LAURA ASHLEY, INC.   212-735-5022
714 Madison Ave., (63-64th Street) NYC, NY 10021
Hours: 10-6 Mon-Sat (Thurs till 8) 12-6 Sun   **(Interior design service)** 212-735-5010
• Calico, Laura Ashley prints, dress and upholstery fabrics, matching wallpaper. CREDIT CARDS •

B & J FABRICS   212-354-8150
263 West 40th St., (7th-8th Ave.) NYC, NY 10018   212-354-8212
Hours: 8-5:45 Mon-Fri • 9-4:45 Sat
• Designer fabrics and linings, crepes, tricot, polyknits. CREDIT CARDS •

BAER FABRICS   (commercial fabrics) 800-769-7779
515 East Market, Louisville, KY 40202   (fashion) 800-769-7776
Hours: 9-9 Mon • 9-5 Tue-Sat   (costume fabrics) 800-769-7778
   FAX   502-582-2331
• Over 1/2 million yards, imported, domestic, all fibers; prompt shipment. Phone orders.
CREDIT CARDS •

BECKENSTEIN MEN'S FABRIC   212-475-6666
121 Orchard St., (Delancy St.) NYC, NY 10002
Hours: 9-5:30 Mon-Sun • closed Sat   FAX   212-473-1710
• Fine suit woolens to uniform weight wool; good selection. •

JERRY BROWN IMPORTED FABRICS   212-753-3626
37 West 57th St., (5th-6th Ave.) NYC, NY 10019
Hours: 9:30-6 Mon-Fri • 10-5 Sat
• Expensive; silks, woolens, cottons. CREDIT CARDS •

C & B LIBERTY FABRICS   212-354-9360
250 West 39th St., (7th-8th Ave.) NYC, NY 10018
Hours: 9-6 Mon-Fri • 10-6 Sat
• General fabrics, good selection sequined fabrics, brocade, lames; reasonable prices; good
stock. CREDIT CARDS •

Cover Your Stars

in

GLADSTONE FABRICS

Supplying Theatrical,
Display &
Imported
Fabrics
Since
1930

GLADSTONE

F·A·B·R·I·C·S

ORCHARD HILL ROAD   P.O. BOX 566   HARRIMAN, NY 10926

(914) 783-1900   (800) 724-0168   Fax: (914) 78FAX ME

"I found it in the N.Y. Theatrical Sourcebook."

CHARBERT FABRICS CORP.   212-564-4866
485 7th Ave., (36th St.) NYC, NY 10018
Hours: 9:30-5:30 Mon-Fri
• Cotton knits and stretch fabric similar to milliskin; wholesale. No credit cards •

D & C TEXTILE CORP.   212-564-6200
470 Seventh Ave., (35th-36th St.) NYC, NY 10018
Hours: 9-5 Mon-Fri
• Cottons, poplins, jacquards, broadcloth; will order; one week delivery. No credit cards. •

DARMAR ENTERPRISES, INC.   516-586-1660
60-Q South 2nd St., Deer Park, NY 11729   (outside NY) 800-532-7827
Hours: 8:30-4:30 Mon-Fri   FAX 516-586-1772
• Formerly Robbie Robinson Textile Corp.. Nets, tulles, batiste; also linings, interfacings and basics by the bolt. •

DIAMOND FABRICS   212-460-9531
218 East 14th St., (2nd-3rd Ave.) NYC, NY 10003
Hours: 9-7 Mon-Sat • 10-5 Sun
• The two former stores have been combined into one! Batiste, poly, slipcover goods. •

DISCOUNT FABRICS OF BURLINGTON NJ   212-354-9275
202 West 40th St., (7th-8th Ave.) NYC, NY 10018
Hours: 8-6 Mon-Fri • 10-5 Sat
• Mostly poly blends; fashion sample remnants, cut pieces only; inexpensive. CREDIT CARDS •

N. ERLANGER, BLUMGART & CO.   212-221-7100
1040 6th Ave., (39-40th St.) NYC, NY 10018
Hours: 8:45-5:15 Mon-Fri
• Manufacture linings, silks, poly/cottons, poly/linens; retail and wholesale. •

F & R FABRIC SHOP, INC.   212-391-9083
239 West 39th St., (7th-8th Ave.) NYC, NY 10018   212-391-9084
Hours: 8:30-5:45 Mon-Fri • 10-4:30 Sat
• Wools, silks, cottons, tapestries, bridal velvets. CREDIT CARDS •

THE FABRIC COMPANY   212-219-3469
390 Broadway, (White-Walker) NYC, NY 10013
Hours: 9-4:30 Mon-Fri
• Wholesaler: cottons, Lycra, velvets, silks, woolens, seasonal. •

FABRIC, INC.   212-239-4411
212 West 35th St., (7th-8th Ave.) NYC, NY 10001
Hours: 9-5 Mon-Fri
• Silks, polyesters, general dress goods; also glitzy fabrics, lurex; jobber. No credit cards. •

FABRIC WAREHOUSE   212-431-9510
406 Broadway, (Canal-Walker) NYC, NY 10013
Hours: 9-6 Mon-Fri • Thurs till 7:30 • 10-5 Sat & Sun
• Inexpensive, remnants; notions and trims in the basement. MC/VISA •

FELSEN FABRIC CORP.   212-398-9010
264 West 40th St., (7th-8th Ave.) NYC, NY 10018   800-FELSONS
Hours: 8:30-5:45 Mon-Fri • 9-4:45 Sat   FAX 212-840-2268
• Selection of laces, embroideries and bridal fabrics, silks, wools, and cut velvets. CREDIT CARDS •

E
I
F

FIRST AVENUE FABRICS   212-353-1355
    180 First Ave., (11th St.) NYC, NY 10009
    Hours: 10-7 Daily
    • Fabrics from 7th Ave., "downtown", and independent designers. Bizarre collection of fabrics, from fine silks to really cheesy polyester. Quantitiy discounts. CREDIT CARDS •

FISHER & GENTILE, LTD.   212-221-1800
    1412 Broadway, 6th Fl., (39th St.) NYC, NY 10018
    Hours: 9-5 Mon-Fri
    • Prints, 30's fabrics, crepes; cash only. •

FRIEDMAN & DISTILLATOR / OWL MILLS   212-226-6400
    53 Leonard St., (Church-W.B'way) NYC, NY 10013
    Hours: 9-5 Mon-Fri   FAX   212-219-1402
    • Silk organza; speak to Toni; also trimmings, braids, ribbons, linens. No credit cards. •

GLADSTONE FABRICS
       914-783-1900
    PO Box 566, Orchard Hill Rd., Harriman, NY 10926   800-724-0168
    Hours: 9-6 Mon-Fri • Sat by appt.   FAX   914-783-2963
    • Prompt shipment. Swatching service. CREDIT CARDS •
    (See display ad in this section.)

HENRY GLASS & CO.   212-840-8200
    1071 Sixth Ave., (40th-41st St.) NYC, NY 10018
    Hours: 9-5 Mon-Fri
    • Cottons and cotton blends. No credit cards. •

HANDBLOOM BATIK   212-925-9542
    214 Mulberry St., (Spring St.) NYC, NY 10012
    Hours: 12-7 Wed-Sat • 1-6 Sun
    • Good selection of beautiful batik and handwoven fabrics, reasonably priced; Asian gift items. •

HOMESPUN   805-642-8111
    PO Box 3223-NY, Ventura, CA 93006
    Hours: 11-4 Mon-Fri   FAX   805-642-0759
    • Ten foot wide cotton fabric. Catalog. No credit cards. •

JASCO FABRICS, INC.   212-563-2960
    450 Seventh Ave., (34th-35th St.) NYC, NY 10123
    Hours: by appt.
    • Manufacturer of knits; wholesale only. •

KABAT TEXTILE CORP.   212-398-0011
    215 West 40th St., (7th-8th Ave.) NYC, NY 10018
    Hours: 8:30-5 Mon-Fri
    • Light crepe, silk and poly chiffon; wholesale. •

KORDOL FABRICS   212-254-8319
    194 Orchard St., (Houston-Stanton) NYC, NY 10002
    Hours: 9-5 Sun-Fri
    • Woolens, silks, big selection of crepe-de-chine; no swatches, no checks. CREDIT CARDS •

L. LAUFER & CO., INC.   212-242-2345
    115 West 27th St., 12th Fl., (6th-7th Ave.) NYC, NY 10001
    Hours: 9-4 Mon-Fri
    • Corset supplies, Scotch-mate; call first. No credit cards. •

E-F

LA LAME, INC.　　212-921-9770
　250 West 39th St., 4th Fl., (7-8th Ave.) NYC, NY 10018
　Hours: 9-5 Mon-Fri
　• Great for ecclesiastical costumes; metallic and non-metallic brocades and tapestries. No credit cards. •

LAWRENCE TEXTILES, INC.　　212-730-7750
　1412 Broadway, 20th Fl., (39th St.) NYC, NY 10018
　Hours: 9-5 Mon-Fri　　FAX　212-730-7754
　• Complete line of metallic, fur and costume fabrics, brocades, lames, nets and laces. Good about swatching, speak to Philip Lawrence. Converter of exotic fabrics. •

LISTOKIN & SONS FABRICS, INC.　　212-226-6111
　87 Hester St., (Orchard-Allen) NYC, NY 10002
　Hours: 9:30-5:30 Sun-Thur • 9-2 Fri
　• Bridal and formal fabrics; polyester heaven. CREDIT CARDS •

MAXINE FABRICS CO.　　212-674-1196
　357 Grand St., (Essex St.) NYC, NY 10002
　Hours: 9-5 Mon-Fri　　FAX　212-674-1098
　• Many theatrical fabrics; quality dress goods, black and white Milliskin; dancewear patterns; specialize in mail orders for theatre; swatch catalogs available; call first. No credit cards. •

MILLIKEN & CO.　　212-819-4200
　1045 Sixth Ave., (39th-40th St.) NYC, NY 10018
　Hours: 9-5 Mon-Fri
　• Milliskin, nylon, Lycra, activewear; wholesale only. •

A. E. NATHAN CO.　　212-686-5194
　11 East 36th St., (Madison-5th Ave.) NYC, NY 10016
　Hours: 9-5 Mon-Fri
　• Piece goods, shirting. No credit cards. •

NOR-BROOK INDUSTRIES, INC.　　212-889-2708
　152 Madison Ave., (32nd St.) NYC, NY 10016
　Hours: 9-5 Mon-Thurs • 9-4 Fri　　FAX　212-679-0633
　• Nylon, spandex, sheers, laces. Contact Suzanne Brooke. •

LEW NOVIK, INC.　　516-599-8678
　381 Sunrise Highway, Linebrook, NY 11563
　Hours: 9-5 Mon-Fri　　FAX　516-599-8696
　• Lace motifs and yardage; net, tulle, maline, marquisette; wholesale only, must order from sample books. CREDIT CARDS •

OUTDOOR WILDERNESS FABRICS　　208-466-1602
　16195 Latah Drive, Nampa, ID 83651　　800-333-6930
　Hours: 8-5 Mon-Fri
　• Trademark fabrics in poly, nylon, fleece, coated and uncoated, webbing, zippers, plastic buckles. Great prices. Catalog. Swatches avalable.Call before 1pm for same day shipment. CREDIT CARDS •

PARI'S FABRIC MART, INC.　　212-473-6506
　166 First Ave., (10th-11th St.) NYC, NY 10009　　212-979-8281
　Hours: 11-7 Daily
　• Spandex, lycra, silks, velvets, brocades, tapestries, furs, wools, chiffon, knits, polyesters, and more; retail and wholesale. CREDIT CARDS •

PARON FABRICS   212-247-6451
>60 West 57th St., (5-6th Ave.) NYC, NY 10019
>Hours: 9:15-6 Mon-Sat
>• Cottons, silks, woolens, velvets, novelties; quality dress goods. CREDIT CARDS •

PARON FABRICS EAST   212-773-7353
>855 Lexington Ave., (64-65th St.) NYC, NY 10021
>Hours: 9-5:45 Mon-Fri
>• Extension of main store. Quality dress goods. CREDIT CARDS •

PARON FABRICS II   212-247-6451
>56 West 57th St., 2nd Fl., (5-6th Ave.) NYC, NY 10019
>Hours: 9-5:45 Mon-Sat
>• Discounted goods from the main store. CREDIT CARDS •

PARON FABRICS WEST   212-768-3266
>206 West 40th St., (7-8th Ave.) NYC, NY 10018
>Hours: 9-5:45 Mon-Sat   FAX   212-768-3260
>• Cottons, silks, woolens, velvets, novelties; quality dress goods. CREDIT CARDS •

PATERSON SILKS   212-929-7861
>36 East 14th St., (Univ. Pl.) NYC, NY 10003
>Hours: 9-7 Mon-Sat • Mon & Thurs till 8 • 10-5 Sun
>
>151 West 72nd St., (Columbus-Amsterdam) NYC, NY 10023   212-874-9510
>Hours: 9-7:45 Mon, Thurs, Fri • 9-6:45 Tues, Wed. Sat.
>• Remnants, discount fabrics, draperies, foam cushions. CREDIT CARDS •

PIERRE DEUX FABRICS   212-570-9343
>870 Madison Ave., (71st St.) NYC, NY 10021
>Hours: 10-6 Mon-Sat
>• French country prints. Mostly white and off-white. CREDIT CARDS •

POLI FABRICS   212-245-7589
>132 West 57th St., (6-7th Ave.) NYC, NY 10019
>Hours: 9-6 Mon-Sat   FAX   212-245-4359
>• Silk taffeta and satin, woolens, brocades, cottons, imports; good quality, reasonable. CREDIT CARDS •

QUEST OUTFITTERS   800-359-6931
>2590 17th St., Box B, Sarasota, FL 34234
>Hours: 8-4 Mon-Fri
>• Trademark fabrics in poly, nylon. Zippers, plastic buckles. Shipping. CREDIT CARDS •

BEN RAYMOND CO.   212-966-6966
>545 Broadway, (Spring-Prince St.) NYC, NY 10012
>Hours: 8-5:30 Mon-Fri • 9-3 Sat   (call first) FAX   212-966-0130
>• Jobber; laces, embroidered batistes. No credit cards. •

ROSEN & CHADICK   212-869-0136
>246 West 40th St., (7-8th Ave.) NYC, NY 10018
>Hours: 8:45-6 Mon-Fri • 9-5 Sat
>• Quality dress goods, difficult to swatch. CREDIT CARDS •

SEGAL FABRIC CENTER, INC.   212-673-3430
>159 Orchard St., (Rivington-Stanton St.) NYC, NY 10002
>Hours: 9-5:30 Mon-Thur • 9-2 Fri • 9-5 Sun
>• Wholesale, retail; cotton, silk, wool, rayon, novelties. No credit cards. •

SHAMASH & SONS, INC.   212-840-3111
   42 West 39th St., 12th Fl., (5th-6th Ave.) NYC, NY 10018
   Hours: 9-5 Mon-Fri   FAX   212-575-7891
   • Printed wool challis, silks; interior design section; wholesale and retail. AMEX. •

D. SINGER TEXTILE CO.   212-925-4818
   55 Delancy St., (Eldridge St.) NYC, NY 10002   212-925-4109
   Hours: 10-5 Sun-Thurs • 10-1 Fri   FAX   212-228-1369
   • Wool suiting, imported linens, cottons, some silks, cashmeres. No credit cards. •

SPANDEX HOUSE INC.   212-354-6711
   228 West 38th St., (7-8th Ave.) NYC, NY 10018
   Hours: 10-6 Mon-Sat
   • Specializing in spandex and lycra. Theatrical, costume, and display fabrics. •

STERN & STERN INDUSTRIES, INC.   212-972-4040
   708 Third Ave., (44th-45th St.) NYC, NY 10017
   Hours: 9-5 Mon-Fri   FAX   212-818-9230
   • Woven nylon net fabric; swatch cards available. No credit cards. •

STYLECREST FABRICS, LTD.   212-354-0123
   215 West 39th St., (7th-8th Ave.) NYC, NY 10018
   Hours: 8:30-6 Mon-Fri • Sat by appt.
   • Wholesale lames, metals, glitter, sequined velvets, chiffons, satins; better grade theatrical fabrics. •

SUTTER TEXTILE CO.   212-398-0248
   257 West 39th St., (7th-8th Ave.) NYC, NY 10018   212-398-0249
   Hours: 9:30-6 Mon-Fri • 10-5 Sat   FAX   212-398-0250
   • Dress goods, remnants, upholstery and drapery fabrics; inexpensive. MC/VISA •

TESTFABRICS, INC.   908-496-6446
   200 Blackford Ave., Middlesex, NJ 08846
   Hours: 9-5 Mon-Fri
   • Undyed cottons, rayons, silks; order from swatchbook; one week delivery. MC/VISA •

L.P. THUR   212-243-4913
   126 West 23rd St., (6th-7th Ave.) NYC, NY 10011
   Hours: 9:30-5:30 Mon-Fri • 11-5 Sat
   • Velvets, lamé, spandex, cotton lycra, rayons, some upholstery fabrics, blackout fabrics.
   Swatching OK. MC/VISA •

TREBOR TEXTILES, INC.   212-221-1818
   251A West 39th St., (7th-8th Ave.) NYC, NY 10018

   215 W. 40th St. (7-8th Ave.) NYC, NY 10018   212-221-1610
   Hours: 9-6 Mon-Fri • 10:30-4:30 Sat   FAX   212-302-2217
   • Good general assortment. CREDIT CARDS •

VELVETS, INC.   201-379-4272
   PO Box 165, Short Hills, NJ 07078
   Hours: 9-5 Mon-Fri
   • Wholesale by the yard or piece; order from color card; will custom dye large quantities. No
   credit cards. •

WEISS & KATZ FABRIC WAREHOUSE OUTLET   212-477-1130
   187 Orchard St., (Houston St.) NYC, NY 10002
   Hours: 9-5 Sun-Fri
   • General assortment of fabrics. Cash only. •

WELLER FABRICS, INC. 212-247-3790
24 West 57th St., (5th-6th Ave.) NYC, NY 10019
Hours: 9-6:30 Mon-Fri • 9-6 Sat FAX 212-247-8147
• Lots of silk chiffon, brocades. CREDIT CARDS •

A. WIMPFHEIMER 212-563-3400
350 Fifth Ave., Rm. 3101, (34th St.) NYC, NY 10118 800-223-7228
Hours: 8:30-4:30 Mon-Fri FAX 212-629-6431
• Rayon, velvet, velveteen; 18-20 yd. minimum. No credit cards. •

FABRICS: BURLAP, CANVAS, GAUZE, MUSLIN

See also **FABRICS: SCENIC**

ATLAS CLEANING CLOTH CORP. 212-226-1042
10 Greene St., (Canal-Grand St.) NYC, NY 10013 212-966-9833
Hours: 9-4 Mon-Fri (till 6:30 by appt.) FAX 212-966-9570

Bleached and unbleached cheesecloth and muslin - all grades.
Purchase orders accepted for large quantities.
Please call ahead for minimum amounts.

• Cheesecloth and muslin by yd. or box. See Enid or Happy. No credit cards. •

JOHN BOYLE & CO. 800-544-3675
847 Bethel Ave., Pennsauken, NJ 08110
Hours: 8:30-5 Mon-Fri
• Acrylic, vinyl, laminates, cotton duck, awning hardware; wholesale only. •

DAZIAN, INC. 212-307-7800
423 West 55th St., (9th-10th Ave.) NYC, NY 10019
Hours: 9-5 Mon-Fri FAX 212-315-1263
• Canvas, burlap, gauze, muslin, and more; samples on request. No credit cards. •

JENSEN–LEWIS CO., INC. 212-929-4880
89 Seventh Ave., (15th St.) NYC, NY 10011
Hours: 10-7 Mon-Sat • Thurs till 8 • 12-5 Sun

1496 Third Ave., (84th St) NYC, NY 10028 212-439-6440
Hours: 10:30-7 Mon-Sat • 12-5 Sun
• Canvas by the yard, all colors and weights; also furniture & housewares. CREDIT CARDS •

MATERA CANVAS PRODUCTS 212-966-9783
5 Lispenard St., (W. B'way-Church St.) NYC, NY 10013
Hours: 10:30-5:30 Mon-Fri FAX same as above
• Custom manufacturers of canvas. •

PHYLMOR FURRIER SUPPLY, INC. 212-563-5410
149 West 28th St., (6th-7th Ave.) NYC, NY 10001
Hours: 8-5 Mon-Fri FAX 212-268-5753
• Muslin, drill, canvas; wholesale and retail. •

ROSE BRAND TEXTILE FABRICS   212-594-7424
517 West 35th St., 4th Fl., (10-11th Ave.) NYC, NY 10001   800-223-1624
Hours: 8:30-5 Mon-Fri
• Flame retardant and non-flame retardant canvas and muslins in many weights, specializing in wide widths; burlap, scrims, bobbinette, gauzes, etc. Catalog. CREDIT CARDS •
(See display ad under CURTAINS & DRAPERIES, THEATRICAL.)

ZANFINI CANVAS   718-625-6630
189 Conover St., (Redhook Section of) Brooklyn, NY 11231
Hours: 5am-3pm Mon-Fri • or by appt.
• Canvas specialties; canvas items custom-made or fabric by the yard or bolt. No credit cards. •

FABRICS: DRAPERY, SLIPCOVER, UPHOLSTERY

LAURA ASHLEY, INC.   212-735-5022
714 Madison Ave., (63-64th Street) NYC, NY 10021
Hours: 10-6 Mon-Sat (Thurs till 8) 12-6 Sun   (Interior design service) 212-735-5010
• Calico, Laura Ashley prints, dress and upholstery fabrics, matching wallpaper. CREDIT CARDS •

THE BARN   203-334-3396
50 Hurd Ave., (Grand St.) Bridgeport, CT 06604
Hours: 10-5 Mon-Sat • 12-4 Sun
• Great upholstery fabrics; also drapery, slipcover, and general fabrics. Alma Slade, manager. MC/VISA •

BECKENSTEIN'S HOME FABRICS   212-475-4887
130 Orchard St., (Delancey St.) NYC, NY 10002
Hours: 9-5:30 Sun-Fri   FAX   212-673-8809
• Good selection of upholstery and drapery fabrics, lace curtain panels; also some trims. •

CALICO CORNERS   914-698-9141
1040 Mamaroneck Ave., Mamaroneck, NY 10543
Hours: 9:30-5:30 Mon-Sat • 12-5 Sun
• Large selection of discounted drapery and upholstery fabrics. MC/VISA •

CLARENCE HOUSE   212-752-2890
212 East 58th St. , (2-3rd Ave.) NYC, NY 10022
Hours: 9-5 Mon-Fri
• Showroom to the trade. (Account required) Repros of traditional and historical patterns; special order trims. Very expensive. •

DECORATORS WALK   212-319-7100
979 Third Ave., 18th Fl., (58th St.) NYC, NY 10022
Hours: 9-5 Mon-Fri
• To the trade; upholstery, machine quilted bedding fabric, taffetas, drapery fabrics; some wonderful character patterns as well as contemporary and traditionals. Expensive. •

DONGHIA TEXTILES   212-925-2777
979 Third Ave., (58th St.) NYC, NY 10022
Hours: 9-5 Mon-Fri
• Showroom to the trade. (Account required) Contemporary and deco styled patterns of fabrics and wallcoverings. Special order furniture. •

E-F

DuKane Fabrics 212-925-8400
    451 Broadway, (Grand) NYC, NY 10013
    Hours: 9-5 Mon-Fri
    • Wholesale upholstery fabrics. •

Inter-Coastal Textile Corp. 212-925-9235
    480 Broadway, (Broome-Grand Ave.) NYC, NY 10013 212-925-9236
    Hours: 10-6 Mon-Thurs • 10-5 Fri
    • Upholstery, slipcover and drapery fabrics; a large selection of casements and plain sheers;
    inexpensive and nice about swatching. MC/VISA •

Kravet Fabrics 212-421-6363
    979 Third Ave., 3rd Fl., (58th-59th St.) NYC, NY 10022
    Hours: 9-5 Mon-Fri
    • To the trade;(account required) large selection of all kinds of drapery, sheer & upholstery
    fabrics and trims. Large quantities available. Very helpful. •

Liberty of London Shops, Inc. (wholesale) 212-391-2150
    630 Fifth Ave., (51st St.) NYC, NY 10022 (retail) 212-459-0800
    Hours: 9:30-6 Mon-Sat
    • Fine cotton prints and paisleys; English fabrics; special order. CREDIT CARDS •

Marimekko Store 212-838-3842
    698 Madison Ave., 2nd Fl., (62-63rd St.) NYC, NY 10021
    Hours: 10-6 Mon-Sat • Thurs. til 8 FAX 212-838-4472
    • Stylish contemporary fabrics, special orders. •

Paterson Silks 212-929-7861
    36 East 14th St., (Univ. Pl.) NYC, NY 10003
    Hours: 9-7 Mon-Sat • Mon, Thurs till 8 • 10-5 Sun

    151 West 72nd St. (Columbus-Amsterdam) NYC, NY 10023 212-874-9510
    Hours: 9-7:45 Mon, Thurs, Fri • 9-6:45 Tues, Wed, Sat.
    • Discount drapery and upholstery fabric, limited yardage; custom work available, foam and
    batting. •

Rose Brand Textile Fabrics 212-594-7424
    517 West 35th St., (10-11th Ave.) NYC, NY 10001 800-223-1624
    Hours: 8:30-4:45 Mon-Fri FAX 212-629-4826

Draperies, cycs, drops, scrims, borders, legs, rain curtains, etc. sewn
to your specifications. Wide variety of items in stock including
flame retardant, extra-wide seamless goods, velour (24 colors),
scrim, muslin, canvas, duvetyn, commando, metallics, specialty and
hard to find fabrics. Fringe, trim and tassels available, or can be
made to order. Fast, professional service, immediate delivery.

THEATRICAL SUPPLIES, FABRICS & FABRICATION
ROSE ⚹ BRAND
517 WEST 35th STREET, NEW YORK, NY 10001

    • Also theatrical supplies, tape. Custom work. CREDIT CARDS •
    (See display ad in this section.)

D. F. Saunders & Co. 212-879-4998
    952 Madison Ave., (58th St.) NYC, NY 10022
    Hours: 9-5 Mon-Fri FAX 212-794-4998
    • Showroom to the trade only. William Morris and other Arts and Crafts period designs of fab-
    rics and wall coverings. •

"I found it in the N.Y. Theatrical Sourcebook."

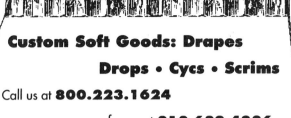

SCALAMANDRE SILKS, INC.   212-980-3888
  950 Third Ave., (57th St.) NYC, NY 10022
  Hours: 9-5 Mon-Fri   FAX   212-688-7531
   • Showroom to the trade. Account required. Wide selection of drapery, upholstery, decorator fabrics and trimmings; very expensive. •

F. SCHUMACHER & CO.   212-753-6511
  235 E. 58th St., (2-3rd Ave.) NYC, NY 10022

  939 Third Ave., (56th St.) NYC, NY 10022 (annex)   212-415-3900
  Hours: 9-5 Mon-Fri   FAX   212-415-3907
   • Showroom to the trade; (account required) collection of historic reproduction wallpapers and matching fabrics. Will occasionally place fabrics in high profile movies & theatres. •

SILK SURPLUS   212-753-6511
  235 East 58th St., (2nd-3rd Ave.) NYC, NY 10022
  Hours: 10-5:30 Mon-Sat
   • Outlet for Scalamandre fabrics; trims and casements; good about swatching. Limited quantities. Selection changes quickly. MC/VISA •

STROHEIM & ROMANN, INC.   212-468-1500
  155 East 56th St., (3rd-Lexington Ave.) NYC, NY 10022
  Hours: 9-5 Mon-Fri   FAX   212-980-1782
   • Showroom to the trade only; upholstery and drapery fabrics; order 24 hrs. before pickup. •

HARRY ZARIN CO. (WAREHOUSE)   212-925-6112
  72 Allen St., 2nd Fl., (Grand Ave.) NYC, NY 10022
  Hours: 9-5:30 Sun-Fri   FAX   212-980-1782
   • Large selection of drapery and upholstery fabrics; limited yardages, fair prices. CREDIT CARDS. •

FABRICS: FELT, VINYL, HOOK & LOOP, LAMINATES

For millinery felt, see **MILLINERY SUPPLIES**

AETNA FELT CORP. 610-791-0900
2401 W. Emaus Ave., Allentown, PA 18103
Hours: 8:30-4:30 Mon-Fri FAX 610-791-5791
• Industrial felt, light felt, novelty felt; swatch catalog. VISA/MC. •

AMERICAN FELT & FILTER CO. 914-561-3560
311 First St., Newburg, NY 12550
Hours: 8-5 Mon-Fri
• Industrial felt, hat felt, light-weight felt; color cards, call for information. •

APEX PLASTIC INDUSTRIES, INC. 516-231-8888
155 Marcus Blvd., PO Box 11008, Hauppauge, NY 11788-0701
(Outside NY) 800-APEX-INC
Hours: 8-5 Mon-Fri FAX 516-231-8890
• Large selection of plastics and vinyls, many felt backed for upholstery. Interesting textures, patterns and colors. See Michael Rosenthal for samples and price lists. •

BARR SPECIALTY CORP. 212-243-4562
236 West 26th St., (7th-8th Ave.) NYC, NY 10001
Hours: 9-3 Mon-Thurs
• Vinyl, web straps, chains, leashes, bells (jingle and cowbells). No credit cards. •

FRANK BELLA & CO., INC. 516-932-3838
485-17 S. Broadway, Hicksville, NY 11801
Hours: 8:30-4:30 Mon-Fri • 8-12 Sat FAX 516-932-7347
• Distributor of U.S. Naugahyde; wholesale; sample book available. •

CENTRAL SHIPPEE 201-838-1100
46 Star Lake Rd., Bloomingdale, NJ 07403
Hours: 9-5 Mon-Fri FAX 201-838-8273
• Catalog; industrial and decorator felt, quick and helpful service. Swatch cards available. •

CIRCLE FABRICS 212-247-2260
263 West 38th St., (7th-8th Ave.) NYC, NY 10018 212-719-5153
Hours: 9-5 Mon-Fri FAX 212-704-0918
• Felt, vinyl, glitzy, novelty and display fabrics. Wholesale and retail. Swatch cards available. •

DESIGN CRAFT FABRIC CORP. 800 755-1010
7227 Oak Park, Niles, IL 60648 708-647-0888
Hours: 8:30-5 Mon-Fri
• Wholesaler of Foam-backed fabric, 60" wide loop weave fabric for hook & loop applications; "attaches like magic". •

ECONOMY FOAM CENTER / AAA FOAM CENTER 212-473-4462
173 East Houston St., (Allen St.) NYC, NY 10002
Hours: 9-5:45 Sun-Fri • 11-6 Sat
• Vinyl fabrics, foam rubber sheets, shapes, batting. CREDIT CARD •

THE FELTERS CO. 803-576-7900
U.S. 221 & I-26, Roebuck, SC 29376
Hours: 8-5 Mon-Fri FAX 803-574-1366
• Wholesale manufacturer of industrial and decorator felt; swatch card available. •

NATIONAL FELT: COMMONWEALTH FELT DIVISION   800-234-1039
P.O. Box 150, 180 Pleasant St., Easthampton, MA 01027   800-333-3469
Hours: 8-5 Mon-Fri
• Manufacturer and die cutter of wool and synthetic felts and non-woven fabrics. •

ROSE BRAND TEXTILE FABRICS   212-594-7424
517 West 35th St., (10-11th Ave.) NYC, NY 10001   800-223-1624
Hours: 8:30-4:45 Mon-Fri   FAX   212-629-4826
• Display and synthetic felt, full line of Velcro products. 54: patent vinyl, 72: soft clear vinyl, and new 336" white table vinyl. Shipping. CREDIT CARDS •
(See display ad under FABRICS: DRAPERY, SLIPCOVER, UPHOLSTERY.)

SUPREME FELT & ABRASIVES CO.   708-344-0134
4425 T-James Place, Melrose Park, IL 60160
Hours: 8-4:30 Mon-Fri   FAX   708-344-0285
• Industrial felt. •

FABRICS: FUR & PILE

BIG FOUR PILE FABRICS   212-374-9534
370 Broadway, (White-Franklin St.) NYC, NY 10013   800-USA-PILE
Hours: 9-4:30 Mon-Thurs • 9-2 Fri
• Outlet for fur fabrics of all kinds. No credit cards •

DYERSBURG & MORGAN, INC.   212-869-6600
1460 Broadway, (41st St.) NYC, NY 10036
Hours: 9-5 Mon-Fri   FAX   212-869-5677
• Wholesale fur and pile fabrics, also sweatshirt, terry velour; large quantities only. •

FABULOUS FURS   800-848-4650
700 Madison Ave., Covington, KY 41011
Hours: 9-5 Mon-Fri   FAX   606-291-9687

...the luxurious alternative to animal fur.
• Specializing in the finest fur-like fabrics
• New Fabu-Leather; washable, breathes,
  has stretch & recovery
• Classic Fur coats, jackets & accessory patterns
• Notions & findings for sewing with man made furs
• Volume discount; immediate shipment

• Full line of fur fabrics, patterns, fur coat kits, sewing notions; also instructional books and videos. Phone orders. CREDIT CARDS •

GLADSTONE FABRICS   914-783-1900
PO Box 566, Orchard Hill Rd., Harriman, NY 10926   800-724-0168
Hours: 9-6 Mon-Fri • Sat by appt.   FAX   914-783-2963
• Fast shipment, swatching service, knowledgeable staff. CREDIT CARDS •
(See display ad under FABRICS: GENERAL.)

HOUSE OF PILE FABRIC, INC.   718-384-0344
115 Lorimer St., (Union) Brooklyn, NY 11206
Hours: 8:30-5 Mon-Thurs • 8:30-2 Fri
• Fake furs, all colors; wholesale. •

NATIONAL HAIR TECHNOLOGIES
300 Canal St., Lawrence, MA 01840
Hours: 8:30-5 Mon-Fri

508-686-2964
800-842-2751
FAX 508-686-1497

The manufacturing specialists in long and short fibre materials. A complete range from dense animal hair to sparse facial hair. Any color, or variegated colors. Short or long runs. Custom-made samples within 48 hours.

N	A	T	I	O	N	A	L			H	A	I	R
T	E	C	H	N	O	L	O	G	I	E	S		

• The world specialists in hair and fur fabrics. Catalog. Minimum 8 sq. feet. •

FABRICS: LINING, INTERFACING, FUSIBLE

See also **NOTIONS: GENERAL & TAILORS**

BECKENSTEINS MEN'S FABRICS
121 Orchard St., (Delancy St.) NYC, NY 10002
Hours: 9-5:30 Mon-Sun • closed Sat

212-475-6666

FAX 212-473-1710
• Complete line of lining fabrics, canvas interfacing; also good selection of quality woolens. •

CROWN TEXTILES
1211 Fort Lashley, Dalladega, AL 35160
Hours: 7:30-4:30 Mon-Fri

800-245-7113

FAX 205-362-1055
• Interfacing; non-woven, fusible, non-fusible; polycrepe lining, polyunderlining. •

DELATEX
210 Delawanna Ave., Clifton, NJ 07014
Hours: 7:30-4:30 Mon-Fri

212-736-0249
201-472-7273

• Custom backings and treatments for fabrics; pressure sensitive backing, Scotchgarding; speak to Jamie. •

GOLD ROSE FABRICS
519 Eighth Ave., 16th Fl., (35th-36th St.) NYC, NY 10018
Hours: 9-5 Mon-Fri

212-563-5799

FAX 212-629-0048
• Swatch card; distributors of lining, underlining, rayon, siri; wholesale and retail. •

HYMO TEXTILE CORP.
444 Broadway, (Grand-Howard St.) NYC, NY 10013
Hours: 7:30-4:30 Mon-Fri

212-226-3583

FAX 212-966-9168
• Jobber for Hymo products; wholesale only. •

PELLON CORP.
1040 6th Ave., 14th Fl., (39-40th St.) NYC, NY 10018
Hours: 9-5 Mon-Fri

212-391-6300

FAX 212-764-0516
• Interfacing; non-woven fusible & non-fusible; catalog; wholesale & retail. •

"I found it in the N.Y. Theatrical Sourcebook."

FABRICS: SCENIC

See also **BURLAP, CANVAS, GAUZE, MUSLIN.**

ALCONE CO., INC.   718-361-8373
5-49 49th Ave., (5th St.-Vernon) L.I.C., NY 11101
Hours: 9:30-4 Mon-Fri   FAX 718-729-8296
• Muslin, scrim, velour, repp. Theatrical supply house; catalog, $5. (Subway #7 to L.I.C., Vernon/Jackson stop.) •

ASSOCIATED DRAPERY & EQUIPMENT CO.   516-671-5245
40 Sea Cliff Ave., Glen Cove, NY 11542
Hours: 8-5 Mon-Fri   FAX 516-674-2213
• Custom-made curtains and drops; also flameproofed scenic fabrics; contact Howard Kessler. •

BAER FABRICS   800-769-7779
515 East Market, Louisville, KY 40202
Hours: 9-9 Mon • 9-5 Tue-Sat   FAX 502-582-2331
• 108" muslin, artists canvas, duvetyne, etc. CREDIT CARDS •

DAZIANS, INC.   212-307-7800
423 West 55th St., (9th-10th Ave.) NYC, NY 10019
Hours: 9-5 Mon-Fri   FAX 212-315-1263
• Scrim, muslin, velour etc.; catalog and/or color cards on request. •

FOX-RICH TEXTILES, INC.   914-533-2445
54 Danbury Rd., Suite 228, Ridgefield, CT 06877
Hours: 9-5 Mon-Fri   FAX 914-533-2943
• Muslin, duvetyne, comando, lining, sharkstooth, lino, nassau, canvas, ranger and netting, some flame retardant, from stock or dyed to order. No credit cards. •

GERRIETS INTERNATIONAL   609-758-9121
29 Hutchinson Rd., Allentown, NJ 08501   FAX 609-758-9596
Hours: 8:30-5 Mon-Fri
• Complete line of scenic fabrics. Call for samples. •

ROSE BRAND TEXTILE FABRICS   212-594-7424
517 West 35th St., (10th-11th Ave.) NYC, NY 10001   800-223-1624
Hours: 8:30-5:00 Mon-Fri   FAX 212-629-4826

Largest stock and selection of theatrical fabrics anywhere. Flame retardant and non-flame retardant muslins, in many weights and widths. We specialize in wide width and difficult to find fabrics. Scrim, canvas, bobbinette, commando, duvetyn, burlap, felt, metallics. 24 colors of flame retardant velour. Custom sewing to your specification. New: 108", 144" & 197" FR muslin. Inherently FR sharkstooth scrim, imported square gauze. Full line of scenic art supplies, paint and tape. Call us for great prices and fast service. Volume discounts available.

• Scrim, bobinette, muslin, velour, etc. by the yard or made up. Also theatrical supplies. Custom work, catalog available. CREDIT CARDS •
(See display ad under CURTAINS & DRAPERIES, THEATRICAL.)

THE SET SHOP   212-979-9790
37 East 18th St., (B'way-Park Ave. S.) NYC, NY 10003
Hours: 8:30-6 Mon-Fri • 10-4 Sat   FAX 212-979-9852
• Muslin in 12 colors or raw. Seamless papers etc. •

STERLING NET 212-783-9800
18 Label St., Montclair, NJ 07042
Hours: 9-5 Mon-Fri
• Theatrical, decorative, agricultural, fishing, cargo nets; bulk and custom. •

VALLEY FORGE FABRICS, INC. 800-223-7979
6881 N.W. 16th Terr., Ft. Lauderdale, FL 33309 305-971-1776
Hours: 8:30-5:30 Mon-Fri FAX 305-968-1775
• Velours, muslin, scrim, cyc, and acoustical fabrics; manufacture flame retardant fabrics; samples available. Speak to Daniel or Milo. •

FABRICS: SHEERS, NETS, LACES

See also **MILLINERY SUPPLIES**

BAER FABRICS (commercial fabrics) 800-769-7779
515 East Market, Louisville, KY 40202 (fashion) 800-769-7776
Hours: 9-9 Mon • 9-5 Tue-Sat (costume fabrics) 800-769-7778
FAX 502-582-2331
• Sheers/taffeta all colors, fibers; laces import/domestic; prompt shipment. Phone orders. CREDIT CARDS •

S. BECKENSTEIN'S, INC. 212-475-6666
121 Orchard St., (Delancy St.) NYC, NY 10002
Hours: 9-5:30 Mon-Sun • closed Sat FAX 212-473-1710
• Huge selection. Phone orders accepted. •

DARMAR ENTERPRISES, INC. 516-586-1660
60-Q South 2nd St., Deer Park, NY 11729 (outside NY) 800-532-7827
Hours: 8:30-4:30 Mon-Fri FAX 516-586-1772
• Formerly Robbie Robinson Textile Corp. Nets, tulles, batiste; also linings, interfacings and basics by the bolt. •

FRIEDMAN & DISTILLATOR / OWL MILLS 212-226-6400
53 Leonard St., (Church-W.B'way) NYC, NY 10013
Hours: 9-5 Mon-Fri FAX 212-219-1402
• Silk organza; speak to Toni; also trimmings, braids, ribbons, linens. No credit cards. •

GLADSTONE FABRICS 914-783-1900
PO Box 566, Orchard Hill Rd., Harriman, NY 10926 800-724-0168
Hours: 9-6 Mon-Fri • Sat by appt. FAX 914-783-2963
• Wide selection of theatrical fabrics including nude souffle. Prompt shipment. Swatching service. CREDIT CARDS •
(See display ad under FABRICS: GENERAL.)

HOWARD KAPLAN FRENCH COUNTRY STORE 212-529-1200
35 East 10th St., (B'way-Univ. Pl.) NYC, NY 10003
Hours: 10-6 Mon-Sat
• French country fabrics and lace fabrics; antiques, accessories; antique bath fixtures. •

LEW NOVIK, INC. 516-599-8678
381 Sunrise Highway, Linebrook, NY 11563
Hours: 9-5 Mon-Fri FAX 516-599-8696
• Lace motifs and yardage; net, tulle, maline, marquisette; wholesale only, must order from sample books. CREDIT CARDS •

BEN RAYMOND CO. 212-966-6966
545 Broadway, (Spring-Prince St.) NYC, NY 10012
Hours: 8-5:30 Mon-Fri • 9-3 Sat (call first) FAX 212-966-0130
• Jobber; laces, embroidered batistes. No credit cards. •

ROSE BRAND TEXTILE FABRICS
212-594-7424
517 West 35th St., (10th-11th Ave.) NYC, NY 10001
800-223-1624
Hours: 8:30-5:00 Mon-Fri FAX 212-629-4826
• They stock imported tutu nets (soft, medium, stiff), 100% dyeable cotton net, tutu soft: power stretch (nylon), chiffons, sheers, and specialty fabrics. Many costume fabrics. CREDIT CARDS •
(See display ad under CURTAINS & DRAPERIES, THEATRICAL.)

STERN & STERN INDUSTRIES, INC. 212-972-4040
708 Third Ave., (44th-45th St.) NYC, NY 10017
Hours: 9-5 Mon-Fri FAX 212-818-9230
• Nylon net. No credit cards •

TINSEL TRADING 212-730-1030
47 West 38th St. (5-6th Ave.) NYC, NY 10018
Hours: 10:30-5 Mon-Fri • 12-5 Sat (Closed Sat--summer)
• Gold mesh fabrics; also metallic and antique trims; see Marsha. •

FABRICS: SILK

See also **ETHNIC GOODS: AFRICAN & WEST INDIAN**
See also **ETHNIC GOODS: EAST INDIAN**
See also **ETHNIC GOODS: ORIENTAL**

CALAMO SILK 212-840-1570
55 West 39th St., 14th Fl., (5th-6th Ave.) NYC, NY 10018
Hours: 9-5 Mon-Fri FAX 212-704-2086
• Silks at good prices. •

GLADSTONE FABRICS
914-783-1900
PO Box 566, Orchard Hill Rd., Harriman, NY 10926
800-724-0168
Hours: 9-6 Mon-Fri • Sat by appt. FAX 914-783-2963

FAMOUS SELECTION OF THEATRICAL FABRICS
Spandex, milliskin, nude souffle, sequin cloth, metallic lame′ and lace, novelty nets and tulle, buckram and fake furs. Also unique antique ribbons, braids, trims, beaded and feathered appliques, as well as the fundamental cottons, linens, woolens and silks.

• Fast shipment, swatching service, knowledgeable staff. CREDIT CARDS •
(See display ad under FABRICS: GENERAL.)

GRAND SILK HOUSE 212-475-0114
357 Grand St., (Essex St.) NYC, NY 10002
212-475-0115
Hours: 9-5:30 Sun-Thurs • 9-5 Fri
• Silk, woolens, cottons, velvets, gauze. CREDIT CARDS •

HORIKOSHI, INC.   212-354-0133
    55 West 39th St., (5th-6th Ave.) NYC, NY 10018
    Hours: 9-5 Mon-Fri   FAX   212-354-2971
    • Real china silk; (color card), crepe-de-chine, charmeuse, silk/rayon china silk. Wholesale. •

LAWRENCE TEXTILES, INC.   212-730-7750
    1412 Broadway, 20th Fl., (39th St.) NYC, NY 10018
    Hours: 9-5 Mon-Fri   FAX   212-730-7754
    • Good selection of costume fabrics; large selection of silks, brocades, lames; easy to swatch, see Philip Lawrence. Converter of exotic fabrics. •

RUPERT, GIBBON, & SPIDER, INC.   800-442-0455
    PO Box 425, Healdsburg, CA 95448   707-433-9577
    Hours: 8-5 Mon-Fri   FAX   707-433-4906
    • Imported silk for costumes (white & natural), economical full sizes, novelty paints, metallics, flourescents, sparkles. Catalog. Will COD. CREDIT CARDS •

SUREWAY TRADING ENTERPRISES   716-282-4887
    826 Pine Ave. Suites 5 & 6, Niagara Falls, NY 14301
    Hours: 9-3:30 Mon-Fri   FAX   716-282-8211
    • All kinds of silk. Very helpful. Ask for Jean. •

STYLEX IMPORT & EXPORT, INC.   212-719-0631
    265 West 40th St., (7th-8th Ave.) NYC, NY 10018
    Hours: 9-5 Mon-Fri • by appt.   FAX   212-719-0642
    • Formarly Amerinco International. Wholesale only; beautiful Indian raw silks by the bolt. •

SUPER TEXTILE CO., INC.   212-643-8700
    134 West 37th St., 4th Fl., (B'way-7th Ave.) NYC, NY 10018   212-354-5725
    Hours: 9-5 Mon-Fri • call for summer hours.
    • Gorgeous silks at reasonable prices; retail or wholesale. •

FABRICS: STRETCH & CORSET

BAER FABRICS   (commercial fabrics) 800-769-7779
    515 East Market, Louisville, KY 40202   (fashion) 800-769-7776
    Hours: 9-9 Mon • 9-5 Tue-Sat   (costume fabrics) 800-769-7778
                                     FAX   502-582-2331
    • Lycra spandex, 2 weights, all colors; girdle fabrics; tricot; prompt shipment. Phone orders. CREDIT CARDS •

S. BECKENSTEIN'S, INC.   212-475-6666
    121 Orchard St., (Delancy St.) NYC, NY 10002
    Hours: 9-5:30 Mon-Sun • closed Sat   FAX   212-473-1710
    • Good selection lycra and stretch fabrics. Phone orders accepted. •

CHARBERT FABRICS CORP.   212-564-4866
    485 7th Ave., (36th St.) NYC, NY 10018
    Hours: 9:30-5:30 Mon-Fri
    • Cotton knits and stretch fabric similar to milliskin; wholesale. Nice people. No credit cards •

GLADSTONE FABRICS
PO Box 566, Orchard Hill Rd., Harriman, NY 10926
Hours: 9-6 Mon-Fri • Sat by appt.

914-783-1900
800-724-0168
FAX   914-783-2963

FAMOUS SELECTION OF THEATRICAL FABRICS
Spandex, milliskin, nude souffle, sequin cloth, metallic lame´ and lace, novelty nets and tulle, buckram and fake furs. Also unique antique ribbons, braids, trims, beaded and feathered appliques, as well as the fundamental cottons, linens, woolens and silks.

• Spandex, milliskin, stretch lames, two way stretch fabrics; wide selection of theatrical fabrics. CREDIT CARDS •
(See display ad under FABRICS: GENERAL.)

L. LAUFER & CO., INC.
115 West 27th St., 12th Fl., (6th-7th Ave.) NYC, NY 10001
Hours: 9-4 Mon-Fri
• Corset supplies, Scotch-mate; call first. No credit cards. •

212-242-2345

MAXINE FABRICS CO.
357 Grand St., (Essex St.) NYC, NY 10002
Hours: 9-5 Mon-Fri
• Black & white milliskin; also quality dress goods; call first. No credit cards. •

212-674-1196
FAX   212-674-1098

MILLIKEN & CO.
1045 Sixth Ave., (39th-40th St.) NYC, NY 10018
Hours: 9-5 Mon-Fri
• Milliskin, nylon, Lycra, activewear; wholesale only. •

212-819-4200

ROSE BRAND TEXTILE FABRICS
517 West 35th St., (10th-11th Ave.) NYC, NY 10001
Hours: 8:30-5:00 Mon-Fri
• Carries stretch sequin cloth, spandex, super stretch, marvel stretch. Also 7, 12, & 18 oz 100% cotton canvas. Many costume fabrics. CREDIT CARDS •
(See display ad under CURTAINS & DRAPERIES, THEATRICAL.)

212-594-7424
800-223-1624
FAX   212-629-4826

SPANDEX HOUSE, INC.
228 West 38th St., (7-8th Ave.) NYC, NY 10018
Hours: 10-6 Mon-Sat
• Specializing in spandex and lycra. Theatrical, costume, and display fabrics. •

212-354-6711

FABRICS: WOOLENS & UNIFORM

BECKENSTEIN MEN'S FABRICS
121 Orchard St., (Delancy St.) NYC, NY 10002
Hours: 9-5:30 Mon-Sun • closed Sat
• Fine suit woolens to uniform weight wool; good selection. •

212-475-6666
FAX   212-473-1710

M. J. CAHN CO., INC.
510 West 27th St., (10th-11th Ave.) NYC, NY 10001
Hours: 8:45-4:45 Mon-Fri
• Woolens for uniforms and menswear; period fabrics. •

212-563-7292
FAX   212-563-7299

ES Woolen, Inc.   718-454-7475
    184-08 Jamaica Ave., (184th St.) Hollis, NY 11423
    Hours: 9-5 Mon-Fri   FAX   718-454-6836
    • Formerly Edward Stein Woolen Co.. Gabardine, fabrics for uniforms. •

European Woolens, Inc.   212-254-1520
    177 Orchard St., (Houston-Stanton St.) NYC, NY 10002
    Hours: 10-5 Mon-Thurs • 10-2 Fri • 9:30-5 Sun
    • Also silks, cottons. No credit cards. •

Hamburger Woolen Co., Inc.   212-505-7500
    440 Lafayette St., (Astor Pl.-8th St.) NYC, NY 10003
    Hours: 9-5 Mon-Fri   FAX   212-979-0671
    • Uniform, tropical weight, gabardines, solid colors. No credit cards. •

Lafitte, Inc.   212-354-6780
    151 West 40th St., 19th Fl., (7th-B'way) NYC, NY 10018
    Hours: 9-5:30 Mon-Fri • or by appt.
    • Fine wools, wool crepe, Italian silks; expensive. No credit cards. •

Modern Woolens   212-473-6780
    129 Orchard St., (Delancy-Rivington St.) NYC, NY 10002
    Hours: 9-6 every day
    • Complete line of English worsteds, mohairs, blends for men and women. CREDIT CARDS •

Padob Fabrics, Inc.   212-221-7808
    251 West 39th St., 3rd Fl., (7th-8th Ave.) NYC, NY 10018   800-273-1808
    Hours: 9-5 Mon-Fri
    • Uniform woolens, gabardine, solids, plaids; tropical weights. •

Scottish Products, Inc.   212-687-2505
    141 East 44th St., Suite 311, (Lexington-3rd Ave) NYC, NY 10022
    Hours: 11-5:15 Mon-Fri (Closed Wed) • Sat by appt.
    • Authentic clan tartans, limited selection. MC/VISA •

FENCING EQUIPMENT

American Fencer's Supply Co., Inc.   415-863-7911
    1180 Folsom St., San Francisco, CA 94103
    Hours: 9-5 Mon-Fri • Wed till 7:30 • 10-2 Sat   FAX   415-431-4931
    • Epees, foils, rapiers, hilts, blades, mats, clothing; catalog: $3. MC/VISA •

Blade   212-620-0114
    212 West 15th St., (7th-8th Ave.) NYC, NY 10011
    Hours: 10-7 Mon-Fri • 11-3 Sat   FAX   212-620-0116
    • Fencing and stage equipment and clothing; catalog. CREDIT CARDS •

George Santelli, Inc.   201-871-3105
    465 S. Dean St., Englewood, NJ 07631
    Hours: 9-5 Mon-Fri • 11-3 Sat • closed Sat: May-Sept   FAX   201-871-8718
    • Modern fencing equipment and swords; catalog. •

"I found it in the N.Y. Theatrical Sourcebook."

FIBRE CASES

BRAGLEY MANUFACTURING CO., INC.   718-622-6474
924 Bergen St., (Classon-Franklin Ave.) Brooklyn, NY 11238
Hours: 8-4 Mon-Fri   FAX   718-857-3557
• Fibre cases made-to-order. •

FIBER BUILT CASES, INC.   212-675-5820
601 West 26th St., (11th-12th Ave.) NYC, NY 10001   (outside NY) 800-847-4176
Hours: 9-4 Mon-Fri   FAX   212-691-5935
• Fibre storage and shipping cases; custom work. CREDIT CARDS •

FIBRE CASE NOVELTY CO., INC.   212-254-6060
708 Broadway,10th Fl., (4th-Waverly) NYC, NY 10003   212-477-2729
Hours: 9-5 Mon-Fri   FAX   212-460-8794

Grip cases, fibre cases, prop cases, display cases, etc.
Any size or design. Immediate delivery.

• Custom work. Contact Elliot. •

OXFORD FIBRE SAMPLE CASE CORP.   718-858-0009
755 Wythe Ave., (Corner of Rutledge) Brooklyn, NY 11211   718-858-0013
Hours: 8-5:30 Mon-Thurs • 8-4:30 Fri
• Stock & custom fibre cases. Catalog. Will ship UPS. •

FIREARMS & ARMOR

See also **FENCING EQUIPMENT**
See also **POLICE EQUIPMENT**

ACE PROPS   212-206-1475
1 West 19th St., Ground Fl., (5th Ave.) NYC, NY 10011   212-580-9551
Hours: 8-5 Mon-Fri • 10-4:45 Sat • or by appt.   FAX   212-929-9082
• Rental of non-working replicas of famous firearms; Uzzis, 357 Magnums, etc.- no license
required. CREDIT CARDS •
(See display ad in this section.)

AMERICAN OUTDOOR SPORTS   516-249-1832
2040 Route 110, Farmingdale, NY 11735
Hours: 9:30-9:30 Mon-Fri • 9:30-6:30 Sat • 11-5 Sun
• Firearms, reproduction guns. •

CENTRE FIREARMS CO., INC.
212-244-4040

10 West 37th St., 7th Fl., (5th-6th Ave.) NYC, NY 10018
Hours: 9-4 Mon-Fri

FAX   212-947-1233

Serving the Motion Picture and Theatrical Industries for 45 years
• Complete Firearms, Period Weaponry and Accessories
• Full Machine Shop and Manufacturing Facilities - Custom Props
• Armorer Service / Weapons Coordinator
• Firearms Training, Seminars and Consultations
• New York City Licensed Gunsmiths

• Complete NYC approved weapons, blanks, props; gunsmithing. Call to verify specific need for permits. Seminars offered on firearm handling, pertinent laws and safety. Needless to say, a knowledgable staff. Catalog available. RENTALS •

COLLECTOR'S ARMOURY
703-684-6111

PO Box 59, 800 Slaters Lane, Alexandria, VA 22313
Hours: 8:30-5 Mon-Fri

FAX   703-683-5486

Full size suits of armour, medieval swords and shields, Japanese Samurai swords. Non-firing replica guns of all eras. Blank-firing modern and Western guns. Civil war sabers, knives, bayonets and uniform items. WW II medals and badges.

• Great prop and costume prop weapons. Color catalog available. •

COLLECTOR'S HERITAGE, INC.   908-953-0938
PO Box 355, Bernardsville, NJ 07924
Hours: 9-5 Mon-Fri (phone orders only)   FAX   908-953-0941
• Sales and some rental. Large inventory; replicas of period, military and ethnic weapons; swords, sabers, bayonets, foils, etc. Also have some period costume accessories. CREDIT CARDS •

CONTINENTAL ARMS CORP.   212-768-8210
16 West 45th St. , (5th-6th Ave.) NYC, NY 10036
Hours: 10-3:30 Mon-Fri
• Firearms, blank ammunition. •

COSTUME ARMOUR INC   914-534-9120
PO Box 85, 2 Mill St., Cornwall, NY 12518
Hours: 9-4 Mon-Fri   FAX   914-534-8602

Sale and rental of stock and costume armor, accessories and replica weapons for stage, film, display and print. for over 20 years. Major credits include *Beauty & the Beast, Sunset Boulevard, Siegried & Roy - Vegas '90, Phantom of the Opera, La Mancha, Camelot, Pippin*, Nintendo, The Met, NYC Opera, ABT-Coppe'lia, NYC Ballet, NY Shakespeare Festival.

> COSTUME ARMOUR, INC.
> & CHRISTO-VAC

• Replica weapons, arms, armor. RENTALS •
(See display ad under PROP SHOPS.)

FRANK'S SPORT SHOP   718-299-9628
430 East Tremont Ave., (Park Ave.) Bronx, NY 10457   718-583-1652
Hours: 9-8 Mon-Fri • 9-7 Sat   FAX   718-583-1652
• Complete line of hunting and archery equipment and clothing. Also sporting goods and career apparel. Catalog available. CREDIT CARDS •

JAUCHEM & MEEH, INC.   718-875-0140
43 Bridge St., (Plymouth-Water) Brooklyn, NY 11201
Hours: 9-5 Mon-Fri • or by appt.   FAX   718-596-8329

Sales and rental of rifles and handguns for theatre and film.

Custom and standard blank ammunition.

Retractable and special effects knives.

> **JAUCHEM & MEEH, INC.**
>
> SPECIAL EFFECTS-SALES, RENTAL, DESIGN

• Rentals and sales of custom and stock, real or replicas. •
(See display ad under SPECIAL EFFECTS SERVICES.)

THE MUSEUM OF HISTORICAL ARMS   305-672-7480
1038 Alton Rd., Miami Beach, FL 33139
Hours: 10-4 Mon-Fri   FAX   305-534-7679
• Antique reproduction arms and armor; mail order 200 page catalog $10.00. CREDIT CARDS •

MUSEUM REPLICAS LTD.   800-241-3664
PO Box 839, 2143 Geesmill Rd., Conyers, GA 30207
Hours: 9-6 Mon-Fri
• Replica swords, daggers, rapiers, battle and pole axes, helmets, etc.; catalog. CREDIT CARDS •

MYCROFT HOLMES   914-265-3756
144 Main St., (off Rt.90 & Rt.9) Cold Spring, NY 10516
Hours: 12-6 Tues-Sun
• Victorian firearms, no rentals; see Burt Murphy. •

PRINCELY CO., INC.   201-867-5971
914 21st St., Union City, NJ 07087
Hours: 9-5 Mon-Fri • 10-4 Sat • call first
• Replica non-firing pistols, muskets, powder horns. •

GEORGE SANTELLI, INC.   201-871-3105
465 S. Dean St., Englewood, NJ 07631
Hours: 9-5 Mon-Fri • 11-3 Sat • closed Sat: May-Sept
• Fencing equipment and swords; catalog. CREDIT CARDS •

SFX DESIGN   614-459-3222
6099 Godown Rd., Columbus, OH 43220
Hours: 7:30-4:30 Mon-Fri
• Formerly Theatre Magic. Decorative and fighting swords, handguns, rifles, machine guns; any period, able to fire blanks. •

U.S. CAVALRY   502-351-1164
2855 Centennial Ave., Radcliff, KY 40160
Hours: 9-6 Mon-Sat
• Military sabers, arms. Catalog $3.00. •

WEAPONS SPECIALISTS   212-941-7696
33 Greene St., #1W, (Grand) NYC, NY 10013   (pager)917-874-7696
Hours: by appt.   FAX   212-941-7654

• Rental, consultation, training and safety supervision; see Rick. •

ZIRMO   212-732-0231
8 Warren St., (B'way-Church St.) NYC, NY 10007
Hours: 9-5:30 Mon-Fri
• Guns, ammo, hunting equipment; no rentals. •

FIREPLACES & EQUIPMENT

See also **ARCHITECTURAL PIECES**
See also **BRASS ITEMS**

DANNY ALESSANDRO LTD.   212-421-1928
307 East 60th St., (1st-2nd Ave.) NYC, NY 10022   212-759-8210
Hours: 10-5 Mon-Fri • closed for lunch 1-2   FAX   212-759-3819
• Rentals available of period reproduction mantels and fireplace accessories. Phone orders and delivery. CREDIT CARDS •

A & R ASTA LTD.
212-750-3364
1152 Second Ave., (60th-61st St.) NYC, NY 10021
Hours: 9:30-5 Mon-Fri • 11-4 Sat
FAX   same

Antique and reproduction English and French mantels,
fireplaces and accessories.

Wood and Marble.

A & R ASTA L.T.D.

• Will rent; for installation, contact Vincent. Phone orders and delivery avilable. •

THE DECORATORS SUPPLY COMPANY
312-847-6300
3610-12 S. Morgan St., Chicago, IL 60609
Hours: 8-3:30 Mon-Fri
FAX   312-847-6357
• Mantels in Catalog 131 ($2) are built to order; allow 4 weeks; can also build to your specifications. Speak to Jack. No credit cards •

ELIZABETH STREET, INC.
212-941-4800
210 Elizabeth St., (Spring-Prince St.) NYC, NY 10012
Hours: 9-6 Mon-Fri • 12-5 Sat
FAX   212-274-0057
• French, English and American stone and marble fireplaces, 17th-19th century. Garden statuary and furniture, and all types of architectural elements. RENTALS •

IRREPLACEABLE ARTIFACTS
212-777-2900
14 Second Ave. (main showroom), (Houston St.) NYC, NY 10003
Hours: 10-6 Mon-Fri •11-5 Sat • or by appt.
FAX   212-780-0642
• Architectural ornamentation from demolished buildings; antique fireplaces; will rent only in "as is" condition. 100,000 sq. ft. warehouse by appt. MC/VISA •

WILLIAM H. JACKSON CO.
212-753-9400
210 East 58th St., (2-3rd Ave.) NYC, NY 10022
Hours: 9:30-5 Mon-Fri
FAX   212-753-7872
• Antique reproduction mantels and fireplace accessories; will rent. Phone orders and delivery available. RENTALS CREDIT CARDS •

JAUCHEM & MEEH, INC.
718-875-0140
43 Bridge St., (Plymouth-Water) Brooklyn, NY 11201
718-596-8329
Hours: 9-5 Mon-Fri • or by appt.

• Sales and rental of propane fireplace rigs, butane torches and simulated fire effects.
• Custom construction of fire rigs.

JAUCHEM & MEEH, INC.

SPECIAL EFFECTS-SALES, RENTAL, DESIGN

• Special effects company. RFents gas fueled fireplace rigs. •
(See display ad under SPECIAL EFFECTS SERVICES.)

FIRERETARDING SERVICES & SUPPLIES

For flameproof/flame retardant fabrics, see also **FABRICS: SCENIC**

E-F

ASSOCIATED DRAPERY & EQUIPMENT CO.   516-671-5245
    40 Sea Cliff Ave., Glen Cove, NY 11542
    Hours: 8-5 Mon-Fri
    • Flameproofing service and compounds; also custom-made curtains and drapes; contact Howard Kessler. Catalog. •

ATLANTIC RESEARCH LABS CORP.   718-784-8825
    20-05 40th Rd., (29th St.) L.I.C., NY 11101
    Hours: 8-5 Mon-Fri
    • Equipment and supplies for flameproofing. Wide variety of materials, sprayers and equipment. •

BONOMO'S GRACE LTD.   410-526-4888
    8 Ivy Bridge, Reisterstown, MC 21136   410-243-4214
    Hours:8-6 Mon-Fri   FAX   410-526-4889

Manufacturers of fire retarding products, product service and fire safety support for Film, Video and Theatre industries.

    • Manufacturers of fire retarding products; service & fire safety support for film, video and theater. See Mick Kipp. •

FLAMEPROOF CHEMICAL CO.   212-242-2265
    345 East Terra Cotta Ave., Crystal Lake, IL 60014   800-435-5700
    Hours: 9-5 Mon-Fri
    • Distributors of DuPont fire retardants. •

GOTHIC LTD./ LONG ISLAND PAINT   516-676-6600
    PO Box 189, 1 Continental Hill, Glen Cove, NY 11542
    Hours: 7:30-5 Mon-Fri
    • Sells flameproofing compounds; catalog. Contact Wendy Stern. •
    (See display ad under PAINTS & DYES: SCENIC.)

NEW YORK FLAMEPROOFING CO., INC.   718-665-9200
    135 East 144th St., Bronx, NY 10451
    Hours: 9-5 Mon-Fri
    • Complete flameproofing service, $75 min.; supply orders $38 min. For information, ask for Carol. •

REYNOLDS DRAPERY SERVICE, INC.   315-845-8632
    7440 Main St., Newport, NY 13416
    Hours: 8-4 Mon-Fri   FAX   315-845-8645
    • Flameproofing service for theatrical draperies & do-it-yourself kits. •

ROSE BRAND TEXTILE FABRICS
517 West 35th St., (10th-11th Ave.) NYC, NY 10001
Hours: 8:30-5:00 Mon-Fri

212-594-7424
800-223-1624
FAX 212-629-4826

Full line of flame retardant compounds: Rosco C26, S33 & W40 .
Also: FR-1 Flame retardant paint additive for water based coatings;
MG 702 multi-purpose spray for wood, synthetics, cottons, paper,
silk and leather (quart and gallon sprayers); X-mas tree spray for
live foliage. Large selection of FR fabrics: muslin, scrim, canvas,
duvety, commando, nets, gauzes, velours & drapery fabrics.

• Theatrical supplies. Custom work catalog available. CREDIT CARDS •
(See display ad under CURTAINS & DRAPERIES, THEATRICAL.)

I WEISS & SONS, INC.
2-07 Borden Ave., (Vernon-Jackson Ave.) L.I.C., NY 11101
Hours: 8:30-5 Mon-Fri

718-706-8139

FAX 718-482-9410
• Flameproofing service. Also carry flame retardant scenic fabrics. •
(See display ad under CURTAINS & DRAPERIES, THEATRICAL.)

WORLD WIDE COATINGS
P.O.Box 27638, Tucson, AZ 85726
Hours: 8-5 Mon-Fri

800-626-7983

FAX 602-885-0906
• Fire retardants to add to paints for spraying on cloth or hard scenery. Brochure available. •

ZELLER INTERNATIONAL LTD.
Main St., Box Z, Downsville, NY 13755 (factory)
Hours: 9-5 Mon-Fri

800-722-USFX

FAX 607-363-2071
• Products for flameproofing of costumes, scenery, paint and objects. RENTALS •

FISHING TACKLE

See also **MARINE EQUIPMENT**
See also **SPORTING GOODS**

CAPITOL FISHING TACKLE
218 West 23rd St., (7th-8th Ave.) NYC, NY 10011
Hours: 8:30-5:30 Mon-Wed till 6:30 Thurs & Fri • 9-5 Sat

212-929-6132

FAX 212-929-0039
• A good selection of fly and line equipment. Tackle, lead wts., monofilament, black nylon fishline, high test squid line; small or large orders. CREDIT CARDS •

GUDEBROD, INC.
PO Box 357, Pottstown, PA 19464
Hours: 8:30-4:30 Mon-Fri

215-327-4050

• Braided fishline, variety of tests on spools; $150 minimum. •

ORVIS
355 Madison Ave., (45th St) NYC, NY 10017
Hours: 9-6 Mon-Fri • 10-5 Sat

212-697-3133

• Fly fishing supplies; gentlemen's equipment and clothing. •

FLAGS & BANNERS

AAA AMERICAN FLAG DECORATING CO., INC.
40 West 37th St., 5rd Fl., (5th-6th Ave.) NYC, NY 10018
Hours: 8:30-4 Mon-Thurs • 8:30-3:30 Fri
• Stock & custom banners, flags, bunting. Contact Ian. •

212-279-4644

FAX 212-695-8392

ABACROME, INC.
151 West 26th St., 6th Fl., (6th-7th Ave.) NYC, NY 10001
Hours: 9-5 Mon-Fri
• Custom flags and banners; heavy-duty nylon fabric by the yard; catalog. •

212-989-1190

FAX 212-645-3809

ACE BANNER & FLAG CO.
107 West 27th St., (6th Ave.) NYC, NY 10001
Hours: 7:30-4 Mon-Fri
• Foreign and domestic flags; custom banners; screen-printing. •
(See display ad in this section.)

212-620-9111

FAX 212-463-9128

ALL SUFFOLK FLAG RENTAL SERVICE
812 Sayville Ave., (13th) Bohemia, NY 11716
Hours: 9-6 Mon-Fri
• Sales and rental of flags, bunting, pennants, windsocks; will ship same day; contact Ray Dougherty. •

516-589-2295
800-734-4144

ARISTA FLAG CORP.
575 Eighth Ave., 5th Fl., (38th St.) NYC, NY 10018
Hours: 8:30-5 Mon-Fri
• Custom orders; heavy duty nylon by the yard; $25 minimum. •

212-947-8887

FAX 212-947-8951

ART FLAG CO., INC.
8 Jay St., (Greenwich St.-Hudson St.) NYC, NY 10013
Hours: 8-5:30 Mon-Fri
• Custom and stock, flags and banners. •

212-334-1890

FAX 212-941-9631

BIG APPLE SIGN CORP.
247 West 35th St., (7th-8th Ave.) NYC, NY 10001
Hours: 8:30-6 Mon-Fri • 10-5 Sat
• Full service sign company; 24 hour service available. •

212-575-0706

FAX 212-629-4954

JEWELITE SIGNS & LETTERS, INC.
106 Reade St., (Hudson-Greenwich St.) NYC, NY 10013
Hours: 24 hours every day
• Flags, banners, custom signs and letters. Reliable service. Contact Bobby or Dana Bank. •
(See display ad under SIGNS & LETTERS.)

212-NY-SIGNS
212-233-1900
FAX 212-233-1998

KRAUS & SONS, INC.
158 West 27th St., (6th-7th Ave.) NYC, NY 10001
Hours: 9-5 Mon-Fri
• Embroidered, silkscreened, or appliqued banners and flags; custom trophies, ribbons. No credit cards. •

212-620-0408

CUSTOM · DISPLAY

Banners

INDOOR · OUTDOOR · ANY SIZE

Ace Banner & Flag Co.
107 W. 27th St., NY, NY 10001
FAX (212)463-9128
(212)620-9111

Large stock of foreign and U.S. flags.
Custom manufactured banners, flags, bunting, pennants, T-shirts, etc.
Wide color range of nylon fabric available.

Serving production companies, ad agencies, stylists, movie companies and theatres since 1916.

NATIONAL FLAG & DISPLAY   212-675-5230
    42 East 20th St., (Park Ave.) NYC, NY 10010
    Hours: 9:30-5 Mon-Fri
    • Stock flags; custom work. •

SPECIALTY SIGNS CO., INC.   212-243-8521
    54 West 21st St., 2nd Fl., (5th-6th Ave.) NYC, NY 10010   800-394-3433
    Hours: 8:30-5 Mon-Fri   FAX   212-243-6457
    • Custom work specializing in rush orders. •
(See display ad under SIGNS & LETTERS)

FLOCKING SERVICES & SUPPLIES

AMERICAN FINISH & CHEMICAL CO.   617-884-6060
    1012 Broadway, Chelsea, MA 02150
    Hours: 8:30-4:30 Mon-Fri
    • Flock glue. $200 min. order. Brochure available. •

AMERICAN FLOCK ASSOCIATION   617-542-8220
    230 Congress St., Boston, MA 02110
    Hours: 9-5 Mon-Fri   FAX   617-542-2199
    • Free directory guide to the Flocking Industry. •

CREATIVE COATING CORP.   800-229-1957
28 Charron Ave., Nashau, NH 03063   603-889-8040
Hours: 8:30-5 Mon-Fri   FAX   603-889-3780
• Supplier of flock, flocking equipment, flocked fabrics and display fabrics. MC/VISA •

DONJER PRODUCTS CO.   908-359-7726
Ilene Court Bldg 8, Belle Mead, NJ 08502   800-336-6537
Hours: 9-4:30 Mon-Fri • or by appt.
• Flock and adhesive, flocking equipment and tools; also custom flocking for 3-D items. No minimum. Brochure. •

FLOCK PROCESS   203-853-4587
PO Box 497, 79 Day St., South Norwalk, CT 06856
Hours: 8-4:30 Mon-Fri
• A flocking service for small or large jobs; speak to Mr. Wilder. •

FLOORCOVERINGS

See also **ANTIQUES**
See also **DANCE & STAGE FLOORING**
See also **TILE, BRICKS & COBBLESTONES**

ABC CARPET CO., INC.   212-473-3000
888 Broadway, (19th St.) NYC, NY 10003
Hours: 10-8 Mon & Thurs • 10-7 Tue, Wed, Fri, Sat • 11-6:30 Sun
• Sales and rental. Rugs, carpets, carpet remnants, and runners. Also linens, furniture, antiques and decorative items. CREDIT CARDS •

1055 Bronx River Ave., (Bruckner Blvd.) Bronx, NY 10473 (warehouse)
Hours: 10-6 every day.
• Closeouts •

AMERICAN HARLEQUIN CORP.   800-642-6440
3111 West Burbank Blvd., Burbank, CA 91505   818-846-5555
Hours: 7-5 Mon-Fri • calls accepted 24 hrs.   FAX   818-846-8888
• Floorings for dance, stage, studio; portable to permanent applications. Inventory on both coasts. •

SAMUEL ARONSON & SON   212-243-4993
135 West 17th St., (6th-7th Ave.) NYC, NY 10011
Hours: 10-7 Mon-Fri • Thurs till 8 • 9-6 Sat • 11-5 Sun
• Moderate to good selection of linoleum; also ceramic tile and carpeting. Phone orders. MC/VISA •

CARPET FASHIONS   212-752-1717
143 East 54th St., (3rd-Lexington Ave.) NYC, NY 10022
Hours: 9-6 Mon-Fri • 10-5 Sat
• Will custom make carpets and rugs. MC/VISA •

CENTRAL CARPET   212-787-8813
426 Columbus Ave., (80th-81st St.) NYC, NY 10024
Hours: 10-7 Mon-Fri • Thurs till 8 • 9-6 Sat • 11-5 Sun
• Large selection of antique, Oriental and Dhurrie rugs; see Ike. Phone orders OK. MC/VISA RENTALS •

CHELSEA FLOOR COVERING ACQUISITION CORP.   212-243-0375
   139 West 19th St., (6th-7th Ave) NYC, NY 10011
   Hours: 9-4:30 Mon-Fri
     • Carpet, all kinds of tile, wood floors; carpet and tile adhesives; will contract installation. •

COLOR TILE   212-979-8788
   903-907 Broadway, (20th St.) NYC, NY 10010
   Hours: 10-7 Mon-Fri • Mon, Thurs till 8 • 10-6 Sat • 11-5 Sun
     • Part of the national chain. Carpet, linoleum, ceramic tile, floor tile. •

DANIELS CARPET SERVICE   718-377-2387
   3322 Ave. K., (E. 34th St-New York Ave.) Brooklyn, NY 11210
   Hours: by appt.
     • Large selection of floorcoverings, to the trade;some retail. See Lou Fanelli. •

M. EPSTEIN'S SON, INC   212-265-3960
   809 Ninth Ave., (53rd-54th St.) NYC, NY 10019
   Hours: 8-5:15 Mon-Fri • 8:30-3 Sat • closed Sat in summer   **FAX**   212-765-8841

If it goes on the floor and you want it today. . .
          . . . we have it!

Linoleum • Floor • Tile • Ceramics • Carpeting

     • Good selection of floor tiles and linoleums. Quick and reliable service. CREDIT CARDS •
   (See display ad under PAINTS & DYES: SCENIC.)

ESSE FLOOR COVERING   212-234-8699
                                                212-862-7000
   3531 Broadway, (145th St.) NYC, NY 10031
   Hours: 9-6 Mon-Fri • 9-5 Sat
     • Cheap linoleum, vinyl floor tile, carpet and rugs. CREDIT CARDS •

HAKIM RUG GALLERY   212-750-0606
   208 East 51st St., (2nd-3rd Ave.) NYC, NY 10022
   Hours: 9:30-5:30 Mon-Fri • Sun by appt.   **FAX**   212-826-6395

Oriental rugs and carpets, floor and wall coverings.

Tapestries-Aubbossons, semi-antique and antiques.

Carpet hand-cleaning, restoration and appraisals.

     • Restoration and cleaning. Speak to Mr. Hakim. RENTALS AMEX •

VICTOR HENSCHEL   212-688-1732
   1061 Second Ave., (56th St.) NYC, NY 10022
   Hours: 9-6 Mon-Fri • 10-4 Sat
     • Carpeting for sale or rent; good source for linoleum, will order. •

D. KALFAIAN & SONS, INC.   718-875-2222
   475 Atlantic Ave., (Nevins-3rd Ave.) Brooklyn, NY 11217
   Hours: 9-5 Mon-Sat • Mon, Thurs, Fri til 7 • Sat 10-5
     • Sales and rentals. See George Kalfaian; also does carpet cleaning. CREDIT CARDS •

E-F

MANJITK CUSTOM RUG COLLECTION   212-371-8833
  789 Lexington Ave., (61st & 62nd St) NYC, NY 10022
  Hours: 10-6 Tue, Wed & Fri • 12-8 Thurs • 12-5 Sat
  • Formerly Kamdin Dhurries. Contemporary and traditional hand woven rugs and pillows. Will ship. RENTALS CREDIT CARDS. •

NUSRATY AFGHAN IMPORTS, INC.   212-691-1012
  215 West 10th St., (Bleecker St.) NYC, NY 10014
  Hours: 1-9 Sun-Thurs • 1-11pm Fri & Sat
  • Oriental and tribal rugs; clothing, jewelry. RENTALS CREDIT CARDS •

PARVIZ NEMATI   212-486-6900
  510 Madison Ave., 2nd Fl., (53rd St) NYC, NY 10022
  Hours: 9-5 Mon-Fri   FAX 212-755-8428
  • Sales & rentals of antique carpets and tapestries. All weaving & cleaning done by hand. •

RUG WAREHOUSE   212-787-6665
  220 West 80th St., (B'way) NYC, NY 10024
  Hours: 10-6 Mon-Sat • Thurs till 8 • 11-5 Sun   FAX 212-787-6628
  • Good selection of Oriental and contemporary area rugs. RENTALS CREDIT CARDS •

FLORAL SUPPLIES

See also **ARTIFICIAL FLOWERS, PLANTS & FOOD**
For containers, see **BASKETS & WICKER ITEMS**
                POTTERY & GREENWARE

A & S RIBBON SUPPLY CO.   212-255-0280
  118 West 28th St., (6th-7th Ave.) NYC, NY 10001
  Hours: 8-5 Mon-Fri
  • Wholesale satin and grosgrain ribbon; especially Christmas ribbons and decorations. •

ASTY, DIV. OF SCHEER INTERNATIONAL LTD.   718-499-0988
  167 41st St., (2nd Ave.) Brooklyn, NY 11232
  Hours: 8-4 Mon-Fri   FAX 718-965-1253
  • Flowers, Christmas and holiday decorations for display. $55 min. •

JOEL HARVEY DISTRIBUTORS, INC.   718-629-2690
  8800 Ditmas Ave., (E. 88th St.) Brooklyn, NY 11236
  Hours: 9-5 Mon-Fri   FAX 718-629-2732
  • Floral supplies; art flowers, wire, paint, tape, etc. MC/VISA •

KERVAR, INC.   212-564-2525
  119 West 28th St., (6th-7th Ave.) NYC, NY 10001
  Hours: 6:30-3 Mon-Fri   FAX 212-594-0030
  • Floral supplies, vases & containers, silk flowers, artificial greenery, fruits, vegetables; wholesale only. •

CHARLES LUBIN CO.   914-968-5700
  131 Saw Mill River Rd., Yonkers, NY 10701
  Hours: 7:30-4:30 Mon-Fri   FAX 914-968-5723
  • Floral supplies, silk flowers. •

PARAMOUNT WIRE CO., INC.   718-232-8866
   1523 63rd St., (15th-16th Ave.) Brooklyn, NY 11219
   Hours: 9-5 Mon-Fri
    • Cotton and rayon covered wire; paper stakes. $100 min. •

PEOPLE'S FLOWERS CORP.   212-686-6291
   786 Sixth Ave., (26th-27th St.) NYC, NY 10001
   Hours: 8:30-5:30 Mon-Sat   FAX 212-696-0620
    • Floral supplies, silk flowers, baskets, greenery, artificial food; retail or wholesale. Phone orders welcome. CREDIT CARDS •

FLOWERS & PLANTS: LIVE

For containers, see **BASKETS & WICKER ITEMS**
                    POTTERY & GREENWARE

BILL'S FLOWER MARKET, INC.   212-889-8154
   816 Sixth Ave., (28th St.) NYC, NY 10001
   Hours: 7:30-6 Mon-Fri
    • Flowers, plants, arrangements, moss, reasonable prices. •

CHELSEA GARDEN CENTER   212-929-2477
   501 West 23rd St., (10th Ave.) NYC, NY 10011
   Hours: 9-5 every day   FAX 212-675-3255

   401 W. 22nd St., (9th Avenue) NYC, NY 10011   212-366-6771
   Hours: 9-5 everyday
    • Plants, trees, shrubs, landscape supplies, flowers, large & small planters and landscaping. CREDIT CARDS •

GUY D. COCKBURN, LTD.   914-424-3574
   Albany Post Road, Garrison, NY 10524
   Hours: by appt.
    • Quality Christmas trees, wreaths, garland year round. Will deliver into NYC. •

DELEA SOD FARMS   516-368-8022
   444 Elwood Rd., (Jericho Tpke-Clay Pitts Rd.) E. Northport, NY 11731
                                800-244-7637
   Hours: 6-5 Mon-Fri • 6-2 Sat   FAX 516-368-8032

Sod allows you to have an "instant lawn" wherever and whenever you need it. We will deliver anywhere in the metropolitan area. Or why not come and use our hundreds of acres of lawn for location shoots. We are only a short drive from New York City, near Huntington.

    • A large sod farm filling large or small orders. Delivery service available on purchases of 600 sq. ft. or more. Contact Joel or Vinnie. MC/VISA •

FARM & GARDEN NURSERY   212-431-3577
   2 Sixth Ave., (White-Walker) NYC, NY 10013
   Hours: 9-6 every day • 10-5 Jan-March   FAX 212-431-4162
    • Good selection trees, plants, seeds, gardening tools. Delivery available in NYC, free over $150. CREDIT CARDS. •

GREENHOUSE GARDEN CENTER 718-636-0020
115 Flatbush Ave., (4th Ave.) Brooklyn, NY 11217
Hours: 9-7 Mon-Sat • 9-5 Sun • shorter hours Jan-Mar, call   **FAX** 718-858-0641
• Gardening supplies, flowers, plants, sod, pots; will deliver. CREDIT CARDS •

NYC DEPT. OF PARKS – FORESTRY DIV. 212-860-1844
16 West 61st St., (B'way) NYC, NY 10023
Hours: 7-4 Mon-Fri
• Arrange to pickup logs and branches from NYC parks; no charge. •

PEOPLE'S FLOWERS CORP. 212-686-6291
786 Sixth Ave., (26th-27th St.) NYC, NY 10001
Hours: 8:30-5:30 Mon-Sat   **FAX** 212-696-0620
• Live plants of all types; artificial plants and food, baskets and floral supplies. Phone orders welcome. CREDIT CARDS •

RAINTREE DESIGNS, LTD. 516-242-7246
44C Jefryn Blvd. West, Deer Park, NY 11729
Hours: 8:30-5:30 Mon-Fri • Sat by appt.   **FAX** 516-242-7259
• Scenery, display props, gardenscapes, wholesale to the trade •

WILKENS FRUIT & FIR FARM 914-245-5111
1313 White Hill Rd., Yorktown Heights, NY 10598
Hours: by appt.
• Christmas trees; available year round, all sizes; 45 min. from Manhattan. •

FLYING

FOY INVENTERPRISES, INC. 702-454-3500
32-75 East Patrick Lane, Las Vegas, NV 89120   702-454-3300
Hours: 8-5 Mon-Fri   **FAX** 702-454-7369
• Custom flying and spectacle effects. Contact Garry Foy. •

FOAM SHEETING & SHAPES

See also **UPHOLSTERY TOOLS & SUPPLIES**

A & S NOVELTY PACKAGING & DISPLAY CORP. 201-865-5300
15 UPS Drive, Seacaucus, NJ 07094
Hours: 8-4:45 Mon-Fri
• Ethafoam rod and sheet, plastic foam; will die cut foam. •

ACME FOAM CORP. 718-622-5600
900 Dean St., (Classon-Grand) Brooklyn, NY 11238
Hours: 8-4:45 Mon-Fri
• Ethafoam plank and roll, foam rubber, polystyrene; excelsior. Catalog. $35 minimum on phone orders. •

CANAL RUBBER SUPPLY CO. 212-226-7339
329 Canal St., (Greene St.) NYC, NY 10013
Hours: 9-5 Mon-Fri • 9-4:30 Sat   **FAX** 212-219-3754
• Good stock of foam rubber, variety of type, size, thickness and density; also latex and rubber tubing. •

E-F

FOAMS:
COSTUME FOAM
BLACK ESTER
HI - DENSITY
MED - DENSITY
POLYFOAM
   (CUT TO ORDER)
EFOM:
   SHEETS
    ROLLS
     RODS
EVA - 2LB , 4LB, 8LB
CUSHIONS &
   MATTRESSES
    MADE TO ORDER
STYROFOAM
BLUE FOAM
BEADED FOAM (EPS)
THROW PILLOWS
SLEEPING PILLOWS
  POLYESTER FIBRE
  FEATHER, & DOWN
POLY FILL
   BONDED & LOOSE
SPRAY GLUES FOR
  FOAM AND
  STYROFOAM

FAST DELIVERY
AND
FRIENDLY SERVICE

**FULL SERVICE
FABRICATIONS TO
MEET ALL YOUR
FOAM PRODUCT
NEEDS**

150 WEST 22 STREET
NEW YORK, NY 10011

TEL: 212-727-1780

FAX: 212-727-1777

ORD: 800-982-3626

ASK FOR ED

E-F

"I found it in the N.Y. Theatrical Sourcebook."

COMFORT INDUSTRIES   718-392-5300
  36-46 33rd St., (36th Ave.) LIC, NY 11106
  Hours: 8:30-4:30 Mon-Fri   FAX 718-392-7501
  • Aerated Scotfoam; foam rubber, fiber foam, cushions and pillows made of foam, fiber, feather and down. Foam cut to size. No minimum. •

DIXIE FOAM CO.   212-645-8999
  104 West 17th St., (6th Ave.) NYC, NY 10011
  Hours: 10-5:30 Mon-Sat
  • Foam rubber, mattress sizes; pricey. Brochures. •

DURA-FOAM PRODUCTS, INC.   718-894-2488
  63-02 59th Ave., Maspeth, NY 11378
  Hours: 9-5:45 Sun-Fri   FAX 718-894-2493
  • Excellent selection. No minimum, no catalog. •
  (See display ad in this section.)

ECONOMY FOAM CENTER / AAA FOAM CENTER   212-473-4462
  173 East Houston, (Allen) NYC, NY 10002
  Hours: 9-5:45 Sun-Fri • 11-6 Sat
  • Foam rubber sheets, shapes, batting by the bag or roll, pillow shapes, vinyl fabrics, futons. •

FOAM-TEX CO., INC.   212-727-1780
  150 West 22nd St., (6th-7th Ave.) NYC, NY 10011 800-982-3626
  Hours: 8:30-5 Mon-Fri • 12-4 Sat   FAX 212-727-1777
  • Samples and brochures on request. CREDIT CARDS •
  (See display ad in this section.)

INDUSTRIAL PLASTICS   212-226-2010
  309 Canal St., (B'way-Mercer St.) NYC, NY 10013
  Hours: 9-5:30 Mon-Fri • 9-4 Sat
  • Plastic foam sheets and shapes; component foams and resins. •

MODERN MILTEX CORP.   718-525-6000
  130-25 180th St., (Farmers Blvd.-Springfield) Springfield Gardens, NY 11434
  Hours: 7:30-5 Mon-Fri   FAX 718-276-4595
  • Fabricators and distributors of styrofoam Brand plastic foam of all types, $100 minimum
  order. Catalog available. •

REMPAC FOAM CORP.   201-881-8880
  61 Kuller Rd., Clifton, NJ 07015
  Hours: 8:30-5 Mon-Fri
  • Ethafoam rod and sheet, beadboard, estafoam; will die cut foam. $35 minimum order.
  Brochure. •

ROGERS FOAM CORP.   617-623-3010
  20 Vernon St., Somersville, MA 02145
  Hours: 8-4 Mon-Fri   FAX 617-629-2585
  • Scotfoam and other foams. $300 minimum. No catalog. •

SNOW CRAFT CO., INC.   516-739-1399
  200 Fulton Ave., Garden City Park, NY 11040
  Hours: 9-5 Mon-Fri
  • Plastic foam, will cut to size; other foams and packing materials; delivery is extra. $150 mini-
  mum. •

E-F

STRUX CORP.   516-957-8000
    100 East Montauk Highway, Lindenhurst, NY 11757
    Hours: 8-4:30 Mon-Fri   FAX   516-957-7203
    • Complete line of urethane foams in assorted densities and thicknesses. Sample kit available.
    MC/VISA •

URETHANE PRODUCTS CO., INC. / LORRAINE TEXTILE SPECIALTIES   718-343-3400
    PO Box 308, 1750 Plaza Ave., New Hyde Park, NY 11040   516-488-3600
    Hours: 7-5 Mon-Fri
    • Great source for polyurethane foam sheeting for animal costumes, kapok stuffing; excellent
    selection and prices, $90 minimum. No catalog. See Harry Stone. •

FOG MACHINES & FOG JUICE

See also **SPECIAL EFFECTS SERVICES**

ABRACADABRA   212-627-5745
    10 Christopher St., (near 6th Ave.) NYC, NY 10014   800-MAGIC-66
    Hours: 11-9 Mon-Sat (also open Sun in Oct, Dec.)   FAX   212-627-5876
    • Fog machines for rental and purchase; also bubble machines and smoke effects. Catalog
    available. CREDIT CARDS. •

BIG APPLE LIGHTS CORP.   212-226-0925
    533 Canal St., (Washington-Greenwich St.) NYC, NY 10013
    Hours: 8:30-4 Mon-Fri • 10-2 Sat   FAX   212-941-9803
    • Manufacturer of Fog-it dry ice machine; rental and sale of smoke machine and juice.
    MC/VISA •

EFEX RENTALS,, INC.   718-937-2417
    43-17 37th St., (43rd Ave.) L.I.C., NY 11101
    Hours: 8:30-5:30 Mon-Fri   FAX   718-937-3920
    • Distributors of many types of fog machines, smoke cookies, fog juice; also special effect
    materials; snow, breakaways, turntables and rigging. Catalog available. •

JAUCHEM & MEEH, INC.   718-875-0140
    43 Bridge St., (Plymouth-Water St.) Brooklyn, NY 11201
    Hours: 9-5 Mon-Fri or by appt.   FAX   718-596-8329
    • Design, rental and sales of all types of fog/smoke systems and supplies. •
    (See display ad under SPECIAL EFFECTS SERVICES.)

L & E RENTALS   914-297-1415
    Market Street Industrial Park, Wappingers Falls, NY 12590
    Hours: 8:30-5 Mon-Fri   FAX   914-297-9270
    • Fog machines; rentals and sales; also lighting equipment. •

MUTUAL HARDWARE CORP.   718-361-2480
    5-45 49th Ave., (Vernon Ave.) L.I.C., NY 11101
    Hours: 8:30-5 Mon-Fri   FAX   718-729-8296
    • Fog machines, fog juice in stock; theatrical hardware. •

"I found it in the N.Y. Theatrical Sourcebook."

PRODUCTION ARTS LIGHTING   212-489-0312
    636 Eleventh Ave., (46th St.) NYC, NY 10036   FAX   212-245-3723

    35 Oxford Dr., Moonachie, NJ 07077   201-440-9224
    Hours: 9-5:30 Mon-Fri   FAX   201-440-9335
    • Fog machines and fog juice, lighting equipment rental. •

ROSCO LABORATORIES, INC.   914-937-1300
    36 Bush Ave., Port Chester, NY 10573   800-ROSCONY
    Hours: 9-5 Mon-Fri   FAX   914-937-5984
    • Fog machines and chemicals for specialized applications. Shipping available. •

THE SET SHOP   212-979-9790
    37 East 18th St., (B'way-Park Ave. S.) NYC, NY 10003
    Hours: 8:30-6 Mon-Fri • 10-4 Sat   FAX   212-979-9852
    • Bee Smokers and juice-style machines. •

SFX DESIGN   614-459-3222
    6099 Godown Rd., Columbus, OH 43235
    Hours: 8:30-5:30 Mon-Fri   FAX   614-459-3222
    • Formerly Theatre Magic. Fog-Master machines and Aquafog component; also cobweb system. •

SLD LIGHTING   212-245-4155
    318 West 47th St., (8th-9th Ave.) NYC, NY 10036
    Hours: 9-5:30 Mon-Fri • 10-2 Sat   FAX   212-956-6537

• Supplier of theatrical and architectural luminaries.
• Rosco, Martin and Jem fog machines.
• Liquid and dry ice fog machines for sale and rental.
• Excellent stock of fog canisters, liquid fog juice
  and lighting equipment.

$ L D
L I G H T I N G

    • Call for 150 page catalog of lighting fixtures and supplies. •

TRENGOVE STUDIOS, INC.   212-255-2857
    60 West 22nd St., (5th-6th Ave.) NYC, NY 10010   800-366-2857
    Hours: 9-5 Mon-Fri   FAX   212-633-8982
    • Sales and rental of fog machines; supply fog juice with rental. MC/VISA •

ZELLER INTERNATIONAL LTD.   800-722-USFX
    Main St., Box Z, Downsville, NY 13755 (factory)
    Hours: 9-5 Mon-Fri   FAX   607-363-2071
    • Smoke/fog/steam products and effects; catalog. CREDIT CARDS RENTALS •

FRAMES & FRAMING

See also **ARTISTS MATERIALS**
For picture glass see **GLASS & MIRRORS**

AMERICAN FRAME & PICTURE CO.   212-233-3205
    45 John St., 11th Fl., (Nassau St.) NYC, NY 10038
    Hours: 8:30-4:30 Mon-Fri   FAX   212-233-4637
    • Framing, lamination; mats cut and glass replaced while-you-wait. Catalog. Ask for Terri.
    RENTALS •

APF Holdings, Inc.
212-988-1090
172 East 75th, (Lexington-3rd Ave.) NYC, NY 10021
Hours: 9:30-5:30 Mon-Fri • 10-5 Sat   FAX   212-794-3254
• Custom framing and restoration. Catalog. CREDIT CARDS •

Bark Frameworks, Inc.
212-431-9080
85 Grand St., (Greene) NYC, NY 10013
Hours: by appt.   FAX   212-219-9387
• Museum quality framing; expensive, but worth it. •

Arthur Brown & Brothers, Inc.
212-575-5555
2 West 46th St., (5th-6th Ave.) NYC, NY 10036
Hours: 9-6:30 Mon-Fri • 10-6 Sat   FAX   212-575-5825
• Framing supplies, custom framing available; art supplies. •

Chelsea Frames by You
212-807-8957
207 Eighth Ave., (20-21st St.) NYC, NY 10011
Hours: 11-8 Mon-Thur   FAX   212-924-3208
• Custom framing. Delivery or shipping available. MC/VISA •

G. Elter – Framed on Madison, Inc.
212-734-4680
740 Madison Ave., (64th-65th St.) NYC, NY 10021
Hours: 10:30-6 Mon-Sat (Thurs till 7)   FAX   212-988-0128
• Victorian and other antique picture frames in a variety of materials. MC/VISA •

Fleischer Frames
212-840-2248
119 West 40th St., (6th-B'way) NYC, NY 10018
Hours: 8-6 Mon-Fri
• Inexpensive frames and framing. Catalog. Drop shipping. CREDIT CARDS. •

Frames By You, Inc.
212-874-2337
136 West 72nd St., (Columbus-B'way) NYC, NY 10023
Hours: 10:30-8:30 Mon-Thurs • 10:30-6:30 Fri • 11-6 Sat • 12-5 Sun FAX   212-874-2529
• Custom frames; quick turn-around. See owner, Bernard. MC/VISA •

Lee's Art Shop
212-247-0110
220 West 57th St., (7th-B'way) NYC, NY 10019
Hours: 9-7 Mon-Fri • 9:30-6:30 Sat • 12-5:30 Sun   FAX   212-247-0507
• Framing supplies, custom framing; art supplies. CREDIT CARDS •

Julius Lowy Frame & Restoring Co., Inc.
212-586-2050
28 West End Ave., (60th-61st St.) NYC, NY 10023
Hours: 9-5:30 Mon-Fri • call first   FAX   212-489-1948

223 East 80th St., (2-3rd Ave.) NYC, NJ 10021   212-861-8585
Hours: 8:30-5 Mon-Fri • 10-4 Sat   FAX   212-988-0443
• Good selection of ornate antique frames; also restoration and reproduction of frames, paintings & furniture. Will ship. MC/VISA •

Manhattan Frame & Art
212-268-5643
259 West 30th St., (7-8th Ave.) NYC, NY 10001
Hours: 9:30-5:30 Mon-Fri   FAX   212-268-5644
• Picture framing at better prices; custom work. Show your NY THEATRICAL SOURCEBOOK, the green one, AND RECEIVE A 20% DISCOUNT! Will ship. CREDIT CARDS. •

    "I found it in the N.Y. Theatrical Sourcebook."

MARCO POLO ANTIQUES   212-734-3775
   1135 Madison Ave., (84th-85th St.) NYC, NY 10028
   Hours: 10:30-5:30 Mon-Fri • 12-4 Sat
   • Small period reproduction picture frames; some small English antiques; modern frames as
   well. Will ship. CREDIT CARDS. •

NEW YORK CENTRAL II – FRAMING & FURNITURE ANNEX   212-420-6060
   102 Third Ave., (13th St.) NYC, NY 10003
   Hours: 9:30-6:15 Mon-Sat
   • Large selection of ready-made frames for rental or purchase; custom framing, glass and mat
   cutting, dry mounting, shrink wrapping; also studio furniture and easels. RENTALS •

ONE HOUR FRAMING SHOP   212-869-5263
   131 West 45th St., (6th-7th Ave.) NYC, NY 10036
   Hours: 9-7 Mon-Thurs • 9-6 Fri   FAX   212-674-8144

   210 East 51st St., (3rd Ave.) NYC, NY 10022   212-888-9130
   Hours: 9-6 Mon-Fri • 10-6 Sat

   1109 Second Ave., (58-59th St.) NYC, NY 10022   212-935-4475
   Hours: 10-7 Mon-Fri • 10-6 Sat
   • Metal, wood frames, custom framing, dry mounting. Offers some discount prices; will cut
   glass and mats while you wait. Will ship. CREDIT CARDS •

PEARL PAINT CO., INC.   212-431-7932
   308 Canal St., (B'way-Church St.) NYC, NY 10013
   Hours: 9-5:30 Mon-Sat (Thurs till 7) • 11-4:45 Sun   FAX   212-431-6798

   2411 Hempstead Turnpike, East Meadow, NY 11554   516-731-3700
   Hours: 9:30-5:45 Mon-Sat (Wed, Fri till 8:45) • Sun 12-4:45   FAX   516-731-3721
   • Large selection of section frames and stock sizes at very good prices; art supplies; catalog.
   Phone orders (800-221-6845) over $50. •

J. POCKER & SON, INC.   212-838-5488
   135 East 63rd St., (Lexington-3rd Ave.) NYC, NY 10021
   Hours: 9-5:30 Mon-Fri • 10-5:30 Sat   FAX   212-752-2172
   • Frames, custom framing, dry mounting; posters and prints. Will ship.   CREDIT CARDS •

YALE PICTURE FRAME CORP.   718-788-6200
   770 Fifth Ave., (27th-28th St.) Brooklyn, NY 11232   (outside NY) 800-331-YALE
   Hours: 8-5 Mon-Thurs • 8-3 Fri • 10-3 Sun   FAX   718-788-5852
   • Custom and ready made frames; also glass, matting, etc. Excellent work. Can handle rush.
   Catalog of available frame moldings. Will ship. MC/VISA •

FURNITURE PARTS

ACKERMAN & WEINBERG   212-334-0409
   407 Broome St., NYC, NY 10013
   Hours: 9-5 Mon-Fri
   • Wood turnings & carvings. Custom work, furniture restoration. Will also work on site. •

AMERICAN WOOD COLUMN CORP.   718-782-3163
   913 Grand St., (Bushwick-Morgan) Brooklyn, NY 11211
   Hours: 8-4:30 Mon-Fri   FAX   718-387-9099
   • Columns, pedestals, and moldings. Will ship world wide! •

ARNOLD WOODTURNING CO.   914-381-0801
    875 Mamaroneck Ave., Mamaroneck, NY 10543
    Hours: 8:30-4:30 Mon-Fri   FAX   914-381-0804
     • Turnings of all types, finials, legs and columns. •

DECORATORS WHOLESALE HARDWARE CO.,/ LEGS, LEGS, LEGS / M. WOLCHONK & SON, INC.
                                                212-696-1650
    16 E. 30th St., (5th-Madison Ave.) NYC, NY 10016
    Hours: 9-6 Mon-Fri • 9-4:30 Sat   FAX   212-696-1664
     • Furniture legs, many shapes and sizes, decorative hardware. Also bath accessories. CREDIT
    CARDS. •

PERRY & GUNDLING   201-854-7036
    52 68th St., Guttenberg, NJ 07093
    Hours: by appt.
     • Custom wood turnings: finials, balusters & furniture components. Fast, reliable, capable
    with an exquisite touch in turnings. Also teaches. •

FURNITURE RENTAL & PURCHASE: GENERAL

See also **ANTIQUES**
See also **DEPARTMENT STORES**
See also **PROP RENTAL HOUSES**
See also **THRIFT SHOPS**

ARENSON OFFICE FURNISHINGS, INC.   212-838-8880
    315 East 62nd St., (1st-2nd Ave.) NYC, NY 10021
    Hours: 9-5 Mon-Fri • or by appt.

A complete selection-from budget to up-scale. Contemporary,
hi-tech, transitional and traditional furniture for commercials, print,
features, industrials and TV. Including: desks, desk top accessories,
partitions, folding chairs and tables, chairs from clerical to CEO,
filing cabinets, credenzas, coat racks, book cases, reception
furniture, computer furniture, board rooms, conference rooms, etc.
We also have complete production office set-ups.

ARENSON *office* FURNISHINGS

     • Long and short term rentals- same day delivery! Contact Richard Slavin. RENTALS •
    (See display ad under FURNITURE RENTAL & PURCHASE: OFFICE and PROP RENTAL HOUSES.)

ART & INDUSTRIAL DESIGN SHOP   212-477-8116
    399 Lafayette, NYC, NY 10003
    Hours: 12-7 Mon-Sat

Specializing in 20th Century Decorative Art, Art Furniture,
American Deco., Italian Glass, Italian Furniture, Art,
Antiques, Paintings & Sculpture. Industrial design.

     • 20th Century and Art Deco furniture, furnishings, art and objects. Many original works for
    sale or rent. Also collectibles, clocks and lighting fixtures. RENTALS CREDIT CARDS •
    (See display ad under ANTIQUES: VICTORIAN & 20TH CENTURY)

E. J. AUDI   212-337-0700
  160 5th Ave. , 3rd Fl., (20-21 St.) NYC, NY 10010
  Hours: 9:30-5:30 Mon-Fri (Thurs till 8) • 9:30-5 Sat   FAX   212-229-2189
  • American traditional furniture, rental or purchase. MC/VISA •

BOMBAY COMPANY   212-420-1315
  900 Broadway, (20th St.) NYC, NY 10003
  Hours: 10-8 Mon & Thurs. • 10-7 Tue, Wed, Fri • 10-6 Sat • 12-6 Sun
    • National chain of 18th and 19th century reproduction home furnishings and accessories; cat-
  alog available. CREDIT CARDS •

BRANCUSI OF N.Y., INC.   212-688-7980
  938 First Ave., (51st-52nd St.) NYC, NY 10022
  Hours: 9:30-6 Mon-Sat (Mon, Thurs till 9:30) • 10-6 Sat   FAX   212-688-7982
  • Glass tables, coffee tables, bed frames, mirrors, rental or purchase. Delivery service available. MC/VISA •

CASTLE ANTIQUE & REPRO   800-345-1667
  515 Welwood Ave., Hawley, PA 18428   717-226-8550
  Hours: 9-5 Mon-Sat • 10-5 Sun   FAX   717-226-0454
  • Repros, almost anything; rental or purchase. Speak to Roy, Ralph or Mary. MC/VISA •

CENTRAL PROPERTIES OF 49TH STREET
514 West 49th St., (10th Ave.) NYC, NY 10019
Hours: 8-5 Mon-Fri

212-265-7767

FAX   212-582-3746

Huge selection of furniture from EVERY PERIOD - Victorian, Georgian, Americana, Chippendale, Queen Anne, Art Deco. Contract furniture, medical furnishings and equipment. Custom refinishing and upholstering.

• A full service prop rental house. Excellent selection of living, dining and bedroom furniture. Also accessories. •
(See display ad under PROP RENTAL HOUSES.)

CLAIBORNE GALLERY
452 West Broadway, (Prince-Houston St.) NYC, NY 10012
Hours: 11-6 Mon-Fri • 12-5 Sat • 12-6 Sun

212-475-3072

FAX   same as above
• Hand-forged iron, benches, chairs and tables; Mexican furnishings; rental or purchase. •

DAKOTA JACKSON, INC.
979 3rd Ave., 5th Fl., (58th-59th St.) NYC, NY 10022
Hours: 9-6 Mon-Fri

212-838-9444

• Contemporary designer furniture; seating, cabinets, desks, tables. •

DECORATIVE CRAFTS, INC.
PO Box 4308, 50 Chestnut St., Greenwich, CT 06830
Hours: 9-5 Mon-Fri

203-531-1500
914-939-3403
800-431-4455

• Furniture, Oriental screens, imported brassware; catalog sales to the trade only. •

DESIGN & COMFORT, INC.
464 Park Ave. South, (31st St.) NYC, NY 10016
Hours: 10-7 Mon-Fri (Thurs till 8) • 10-6 Sat • 12-5 Sun

212-679-9088

• Modern, contemporary furniture; Will deliver. RENTALS MC/VISA •

DINETTE INTERIORS
16 East 30th St., (5th-Madison Ave.) NYC, NY 10016
Hours: 10-6 Mon-Sat

212-447-9111

• Large selection of contemporary dining furniture, including lacquer, glass, formica. RENTALS MC/VISA •

THE DOOR STORE
1 Carlton Ave., (Flushing Ave.) Brooklyn, NY 11205
Hours: 9-4:30 Mon-Sat • 12-4:30 Sun

718-596-1938

134 Washington St., (Cedar) NYC, NY 10006
123 West 17th St., (6-7th St.) NYC, NY 10011
1 Park Ave., (33rd St.) NYC, NY 10022
1201 Third Ave., (69-70th St.) NYC, NY 10021
Hours: 10-6 Mon-Sat (Thurs till 8) • 12-5 Sun

212-267-1250
212-627-1515
212-679-9700
212-772-1110

• Contemporary furniture; showroom, clearance center and warehouse at first address. CREDIT CARDS •

"I found it in the N.Y. Theatrical Sourcebook."

E–F

ECLECTIC / ENCORE PROPERTIES, INC..
620 West 26th St. 4th Fl., (11th-12th Ave.) NYC, NY 10001
Hours: 9-5 Mon-Fri • or by appt.

212-645-8880

FAX 212-243-6508

Extensive collection of antiques and furnishings for rental only. Diverse and in depth 75,000 sq. ft. warehouse. 18th century through the 1970's.

Eclectic *Encore*
Properties Inc.
620 W. 26th St.
New York, N.Y. 10001
Tel. 212-645-8880
Fax 212-243-6508

• History for rent. Great selection of older styles and the unusual. •
(See display ad under PROP RENTAL HOUSES.)

ETHAN ALLEN GALLERIES
192 Lexington Ave., (32nd St.) NYC, NY 10016
Hours: 10-8 Mon-Thurs • 10-6:30 Tues, Wed, Fri •10-6 Sat • 12-5 Sun
• American traditional and several new contemporary lines; rental or purchase. MC/VISA •

212-213-0600
FAX 212-889-8900

EVERYTHING GOES
140 Bay St., Staten Island, NY 10301
Hours: 11-6:30 Tues-Sat (Thurs. until 7:30)
• Convenient to the ferry, this 4 shop business has a constantly changing stock of estate sale furniture; furnishings and some antiques. Call for directions. RENTALS CREDIT CARDS •

718-273-0568

FAX 718-448-6842

FOREMOST FURNITURE
8 West 30th St., (5th-B'way) NYC, NY 10001
Hours: 9-6 Mon-Fri • 9-5 Sat • 11-6 Sun
• Sales of historic & modern, original & reproduction furniture. CREDIT CARDS •

212-889-6347

FAX 212-213-8260

E-F

FULL HOUSE   212-529-2298
   133 Wooster St., (Houston-Prince St.) NYC, NY 10012
   Hours: 12-7 Mon-Sat   FAX   212-529-9546
   • Modern furniture collectibles, 50's classics. RENTALS CREDIT CARDS •

GOTHAM GALLERIES   212-677-3303
   80 Fourth Ave., (10th-11th St.) NYC, NY 10003
   Hours: 8:30-6 Mon-Sat
      • Furniture, Oriental rugs, bronzes; rental or purchase; custom refinishing. •

IKEA, ELIZABETH   908-289-4488
   1000 Center Dr., (Exit 13A off NJ Tpke.) Elizabeth, NJ 07201
   Hours: 10-9 Mon-Sat • 10-6 Sun

IKEA, HICKSVILLE   516-681-4532
   1100 Broadway Mall, (LIE Exit 415, NSP Exit 355) Hicksville, NY 11801
   Hours: 10-9 Mon-Sat • 11-7 Sun
      • International Swedish department store for the home; specializing in furniture and home fur-
   nishings; catalog; inexpensive. CREDIT CARDS •

INTERNATIONAL FURNITURE RENTALS   212-421-0340
   345 Park Ave., (51st St.) NYC, NY 10154
   Hours: 9-6 Mon-Fri • 10-2 Sat   FAX   212-421-0624
   • Modern wooden furniture (hotel like, very generic) some office; short and long term rentals;
   brochure available. CREDIT CARDS •

INTERNATIONAL HOME   212-684-4414
   440 Park Ave. South, (30th St.) NYC, NY 10016
   Hours: 10-5:30 Mon-Sat • 11-5 Sun   FAX   212-447-6409
   • Contemporary furniture; leather, marble, modular units. RENTALS MC/VISA •

JENNIFER CONVERTIBLES   212-677-1539
   750 Broadway, (8th St.) NYC, NY 10003
   Hours: 10-9 Mon-Fri • 10-6 Sat • 12-5 Sun
      • Large selection of sofas and loveseats in both sleeper and regular styles; many items in
   stock for immediate delivery; good prices. Call #516-371-2200 for other locations. CREDIT
   CARDS •

KNOLL INTERNATIONAL   212-207-2200
   655 Madison Ave., (60th St.) NYC, NY 10021
   Hours: 9-5 Mon-Fri

   105 Wooster St., (Prince & Spring) NYC, NY 10012   212-343-4000
   Hours: 9-5 Mon-Fri • 12-6 Sat   FAX   212-343-4174
   • Modern classic and high tech furniture; expensive. •

LEE'S STUDIO, INC.   212-581-4400
   1755 Broadway, (56th St.) NYC, NY 10019
   Hours: 10-7 Mon-Sat   FAX   212-581-7023
   • This West Side showroom has a large selection of modern European furniture, lighting fixtures and fans; expensive. RENTALS CREDIT CARDS •

MANES STREET   212-684-7050
   200 Lexington Ave., (32nd-33rd St.) NYC, NY 10016
   Hours: 9-5 Mon-Fri   FAX   212-684-7170
   • Designer furnishings; desks, seating, storage units and accessories. Also lamps, lighting fix-
   tures, rugs and tapestries. Sales and rentals; highly decorative designer prices. •
   (See display ad in this section.)

MELODROM FURNITURE LTD.   212-219-0013
   60 Greene St., (Spring-Broome St.) NYC, NY 10012
   Hours: 9-6:30 Mon-Fri • 12-6 Sat & Sun   FAX   212-431-3931
   • Bauhaus and modern European classics; upscale. RENTALS CREDIT CARDS •

MIYA SHOJI & INTERIORS, INC.   212-243-6774
   109 West 17th St., (6th-7th Ave.) NYC, NY 10011
   Hours: 9-5 Mon-Fri
   • Shoji screens, lamps, cabinets; short term rentals. MC/VISA •

MODERN AGE GALLERIES LTD.   212-674-5603
   795 Broadway, (10th-11th Ave.) NYC, NY 10003
   Hours: 10-6 Mon-Fri • 12-6 Sat   FAX   212-674-5604
   • Sleek designer pieces or cool modern European furniture. CREDIT CARDS •

PACE COLLECTION   212-838-0331
   31 East 62nd St., (1st-2nd Ave.) NYC, NY 10021
   Hours: 10-6 Mon-Fri   FAX   212-421-8584
   • Modern and stylish furniture; expensive; occasional short term rentals. CREDIT CARDS •

PALAZETTI   212-832-1199
   515 Madison Ave., (53rd St.) NYC, NY 10022
   Hours: 10-5 Mon-Fri • 11-5 Sat

   246 West 80th St., (Broadway) NYC, NY 10024   212-799-8200
   Hours: 11-7 Mon-Fri • 12-6 Sat
   • Modern, classic and Bauhaus furniture, expensive. Carries Isamu Noguchi lamps for sale
   only. RENTALS •

PORTICO   212-941-7800
   379 West Broadway, (Spring-Broome St.) NYC, NY 10012
   Hours: 11-7 Mon-Sat • 12-6:30 Sun   FAX   212-925-4279
   • Handsome selection of Shaker inspired furniture; also decorative items for the home; expensive. RENTALS CREDIT CARDS •

THE PROP COMPANY KAPLAN & ASSOCIATES   212-691-7767
   111 West 19th St., (6th-7th Ave.) NYC, NY 10011   212-691-PROP
   Hours: 9-5:30 Mon-Fri   FAX   212-727-3055
   • Unique collection of contemporary and antique tables, chairs, and surface decoration.
   Contact Maxine Kaplan. •
   (See display ad under PROP RENTAL HOUSES.)

PROPS FOR TODAY   212-206-0330
   121 West 19th St. Reception: 3rd Fl., (6th-7th Ave.) NYC, NY 10011
   Hours: 8:30-5 Mon-Fri   FAX   212-924-0450

Come to us first and we'll work with your budget!
• New huge upholstery and case goods department
• Huge selection of tables, chairs, surfaces, office furniture, vanities,
  garden furniture etc. Traditional, contemporary, & antique
• New High Tech furniture department
• Bar stools, tables, chairs, sofas, desks, bookcases, coffee tables,
  end tables, wall units, consoles, screens
NOW ON 3 FLOORS! ONE STOP PROPPING!

   • Full service prop rental house. Very good selection of head boards and living room furniture.
   Contemporary and antique. Phone orders accepted. •
   (See display ad under PROP RENTAL HOUSES.)

RICHMAN AND ASSOCIATES
201-772-9027
509 Westminster, Lodi, NJ 07644
Hours: 9-5 Wed-Sat
• Used furniture and estate sale items. Some antiques. Eager to work with film & theatre. Sales only. •
(See display ad in this section)

SCOTTY'S NEW & USED FURNITURE
212-865-3500
275 St. Nicholas Ave., (125th St.) NYC, NY 10027
Hours: 10-6 Mon-Sat
• Large collection of new and used household furniture; some antiques; no rental. •

SMITH & WATSON, INC.
212-355-5615
305 East 63rd St., (1st-2nd Ave.) NYC, NY 10021
Hours: 9-5 Mon-Fri   FAX   212-371-5624
• English and American reproductions; catalog available. Also custom furniture. RENTALS •

SPATIAL ENVIRONMENTAL ELEMENTS LTD.
212-228-3600
920 Broadway, (20th-21st St.) NYC, NY 10010
Hours: 10-7 Mon-Sat • 12-6 Sun   FAX   212-228-0558
• Large showroom of modern design furniture; also some lighting, accessories and objects; RENTALS CREDIT CARDS •

VALLEY ANTIQUES
413-584-1956
413-584-3063
15 Bridge St., (Rt.9) Northhampton, MA 01060
Hours: 11-5 Wed-Sat • or by appt.
• Oak reproductions. Also many antiques. CREDIT CARDS •

WEISSMAN-HELLER
212-673-2880
129 Fifth Ave., (20th St.) NYC, NY 10003
Hours: 9-5 Mon-Fri • 10-3:30 Sat   FAX   212-529-7694
• Contemporary furniture for home and office, sofabeds. Also some period styles. RENTALS CREDIT CARDS •

WORKBENCH
212-675-7775
161 Sixth Ave., (Spring St.) NYC, NY 10014
Hours: 9:30-6:30 Mon-Fri (Thurs till 6:30) • 10-6 Sat • 11-5 Sun

470 Park Ave. South, (32nd St.) NYC, NY 10016   212-481-5454
Hours: 10-7 Mon-Fri (Thurs till 8) • 10-6 Sat • 12-5 Sun

2091 Broadwa,y (72-73rd St.) NYC, NY 10023   212-724-3670
Hours: 10-6:30 Mon-Fri (Mon, Thurs till 8) • 10-6 Sat • 12-5 Sun

336 East 86th St., (1-2nd Ave) NYC, NY 10028   212-794-4418
Hours: 10-6 Mon-Sat (Mon, Thurs till 8) • 12-5 Sun

130 Clinton St., (Joralemon) Brooklyn, NY 11201   718-625-1616
Hours: 10-6:30 Mon-Fri (Mon,Thurs till 8) • 10-6 Sat • 12-5 Sun
• Contemporary furniture, clean lines, teak & solid woods. Some upholstery. Stock items. CREDIT CARDS •

"I found it in the N.Y. Theatrical Sourcebook."

FURNITURE RENTAL & PURCHASE: CHILDREN'S

CENTRAL PROPERTIES OF 49TH
212-265-7767
514 West 49th St. (10th Ave.) NYC, NY 10019
Hours: 8-5 Mon-Fri
FAX 212-582-3746

Childrens furniture, accessories, toys and games.

• General selection. Full service prop rental house. •
(See display ad under PROP RENTAL HOUSES.)

PROPS FOR TODAY
212-206-0330
121 West 19th St., Reception 3rd Fl., (6th-7th Ave.) NYC, NY 10011
Hours: 8:30-5 Mon-Fri
FAX 212-924-0450

Come to us first and we'll work with your budget!
• Children's furniture, toys, games and accessories from
Country/Antique to Modern/HighTech.
• Largest children's department in NYC on an additional two floors.
NOW ON 3 FLOORS! ONE STOP PROPPING!

• Full service prop rental house. Phone orders accepted. •
(See display ad under PROP RENTAL HOUSES.)

SCHNEIDER'S
212-228-3540
20 Avenue A, (2nd St.) NYC, NY 10009
Hours: 10-6 Mon-Sat • 10-5 Sun
• Children's furniture, carriages and accessories. See Roy. MC/VISA RENTALS •

FURNITURE RENTAL & PURCHASE: CUSTOM & UNFINISHED

For antique repro frames, see **FURNITURE: FRAMES**

BETA CUSTOM FURNITURE
516-365-3939
1180 Northern Blvd., (Miracle Mile Mall) Manhasset, NY 11030
Hours: 10-5 Mon-Sat (Thurs till 8)
FAX 516-365-3972
• Custom and stock furniture of all styles; will do formica work. •

THE BUILDING BLOCK
212-714-9333
550 West 30th St., (11th Ave.) NYC, NY 10001
Hours: 8-4 Mon-Fri
FAX 212-714-9411
• Custom architectural woodworking: doors, table tops and bases, butcher block, chairs, cabinets, mantels, restaurant booths, stairs and more. Brochure available. Contact Derald Plumer. •

GOTHIC CABINET CRAFT   (factory) 718-626-1480
    27-50 1st St., (27th Ave.) L.I.C., NY 11102
    Hours: 10-7 Mon-Fri • 10-5:30 Sat   FAX 718-626-1489

    360 Sixth Ave., (Washington-Waverly) NYC, NY 10014   212-982-8539
    909 Broadway, (20-21 St) NYC, NY 10003   212-673-2270
    1655 Second Ave., (86th St.) NYC, NY 10028   212-288-2999
    2543 Broadway, (95-96th St.) NYC, NY 10025   212-749-2020
    Hours: 10-7 Mon-Fri • 10-6 Sat • 11-5 Sun
    • Custom and ready-made unfinished utilitarian furniture; formica work; cheap. CREDIT CARDS •

OLYMPIC CUSTOM FURNITURE   718-392-1600
    34-09 Queens Blvd., (34th St.) L.I.C., NY 11101
    Hours: 9-6 Mon-Fri • 9-5 Sat   FAX 718-392-2309
    • Custom and ready-made unfinished furniture. •

UNPAINTED FURNITURE BY KNOSOS   212-242-0966
    538 Sixth Ave., (14th-15th St.) NYC, NY 10011
    Hours: 10-7 Mon-Fri • 10-6 Sat • 11-5 Sun   FAX 212-727-9316
    • Custom and ready-made unfinished furniture. MC/VISA •

FURNITURE RENTAL & PURCHASE: FRAMES

ARTISTIC FRAME CO.   212-289-2100
    390 McGuinness Blvd., (Dupont St.) Brooklyn, NY 11222   718-441-6660
    Hours: 10-5 Mon-Thurs • 10-1 Fri   FAX 718-349-0135
    • Period reproduction furniture frames, raw, ready for finishing; to the trade; see Lois; cata-
    log; reasonable. They will also finish and upholster their frames. •

DEVON SHOPS   212-686-1760
    111 East 27th St., (Lexington-Park Ave. S.) NYC, NY 10016
    Hours: 10-6 Mon-Fri • 11-5 Sat & Sun   FAX 212-686-2970
    • Period reproduction furniture; raw frame or finished with muslin; expensive. Good quality.
    catalog. •

IPF INTERNATIONAL   201-345-7440
    11-13 Maryland Ave., Paterson, NJ 07503
    Hours: 9-5 Mon-Fri   FAX 201-345-7532
    • Period reproduction furniture, raw frame or finished with muslin; catalog and finish samples
    available. High quality, expensive. •

RESSLER IMPORTERS, INC.   212-674-4477
    80 West 3rd St., (Thompson-Sullivan St.) NYC, NY 10012   212-533-5750
    Hours: 8-4:30 Mon-Fri by appt.   FAX 212-353-9446
    • Period and contemporary reproductions, raw furniture frames, or finished with upholstery;
    reasonable prices; catalog. •

"I found it in the N.Y. Theatrical Sourcebook."

FURNITURE RENTAL & PURCHASE: GARDEN

CENTRAL PROPERTIES OF 49TH STREET
514 West 49th St., (10th Ave.) NYC, NY 10019
Hours: 8:30-5 Mon-Fri

212-265-7767

FAX   212-582-3746

BEAUTIFUL GARDEN FURNITURE
Wicker • Contemporary • Wood and more!

• Prop rental house with good selection of furniture. •
(See display ad under PROP RENTAL HOUSES.)

ECLECTIC / ENCORE PROPERTIES, INC.
620 West 26th St., 4th Fl., (11th-12th Ave.) NYC, NY 10001
Hours: 9-5 Mon-Fri • or by appt.
• Wicker, Adirondack, wrought iron, willow, cast iron, redwood, twig, architectural ornamentation, poolside, park, outdoor cafe, etc. •
(See display ad under PROP RENTAL HOUSES.)

212-645-8880

FAX   212-243-6508

ELIZABETH STREET,, INC.
210 Elizabeth St., (Spring-Prince St.) NYC, NY 10012
Hours: 9-6 Mon-Fri • 12-5 Sat
• Benches, tables, chairs, fountains, birdbaths, gazebos, etc. in iron, wood, marble, bronze.
Also fireplaces, statuary, and architectural elements. RENTALS •

212-941-4800

FAX   212-274-0057

FLORENTINE CRAFTSMEN, INC.
46-24 28th St., (Skillman-47th Ave.) L.I.C., NY 11101
Hours: 8-4:30 Mon-Fri
• Cast iron fountains, statues, columns, tables, chairs, benches for outdoor use; expensive.
Catalog. Rentals available. CREDIT CARDS •

718-937-7632
212-532-3926

FAX   718-937-9858

IRREPLACEABLE ARTIFACTS
14 Second Ave., (Houston St.) NYC, NY 10003
Hours: 10-6 Mon-Fri • 11-5 Sat & Sun
• Architectural ornamentation from demolished buildings; will rent only in "as is" condition;
cast iron outdoor furniture and interesting pieces for the garden. •

212-777-2900

FAX   212-780-0642

JENSEN-LEWIS CO., INC.
89 Seventh Ave., (15th St.) NYC, NY 10011
Hours: 10-7 Mon-Sat (Thurs. till 8) • 12-5 Sun

212-929-4880

1496 Third Ave., (84th St.) NYC, NY 10028
Hours: 10:30-7 Mon-Sat • 12-5 Sun
• Casual residential furnishings for the urban garden. CREDIT CARDS •

212-439-6440

MAYHEW
507 Park Ave., (59th-60th St.) NYC, NY 10022
Hours: 9:30-5:30 Mon-Fri • 10-5:30 Sat
• Some formal & stylish garden furniture among the china & crystal. RENTALS •

212-759-8120

FAX   212-753-7355

PROPS FOR TODAY   212-206-0330
121 West 19th St. Reception, 3rd Fl., (6th-7th Ave.) NYC, NY 10011
Hours: 8:30-5 Mon-Fri   FAX   212-924-0450

Come to us first and we'll work with your budget!
• Wicker, Adirondack, wrought iron, retro, contemporary and twig furniture.
• Architectural props: windows, doors, columns, surfaces, barn siding etc.
• Outdoor furniture and pedestals on new floor.
• Now 10,000 feet of upholstery on additional floor.
NOW ON 3 FLOORS! ONE STOP PROPPING!

> • Good selection of wicker and iron. Antique and contemporary. Full service prop rental house. Phone orders accepted. •
> (See display ad under PROP RENTAL HOUSES.)

FURNITURE RENTAL & PURCHASE: OFFICE

ADIRONDACK RENTS   212-682-6484
300 East 44th St. (showroom), (2nd Ave.) NYC, NY 10017
Hours: 8:30-5:30 Mon-Fri
> • Contemporary office furniture for rental, see Perry Marinelli. Also rents for special events. •

ALLEN OFFICE FURNITURE   212-929-8228
165 West 23rd St., (6th-7th Ave.) NYC, NY 10011
Hours: 9-5 Mon-Fri • 9-3:30 Sat
> • Office furniture, new and used. •

ARENSON OFFICE FURNISHINGS, INC.   212-838-8880
315 East 62nd St., (1st-2nd Ave.) NYC, NY 10021
Hours: 9-5 Mon-Fri • or by appt

A complete selection-from budget to up-scale. Contemporary, hi-tech, transitional, and traditional furniture for commercials, print, features, industrials and T.V. Including: desks, desk top accessories, partitions, folding chairs and tables, chairs from clerical to CEO, filing cabinets, credenzas, coat racks, book cases, reception furniture, computer furniture, board rooms, conference rooms, etc. We also have complete production office set-ups.

ARENSON officeFURNISHINGS

> • Long and short term rentals--same day delivery! See Richard Slavin •
> (See display ads in this section and under PROP RENTAL HOUSES.)

BIG APPLE OFFICE FURNITURE   212-695-1211
335 West 35th St., (8th-9th Ave.) NYC, NY 10001
Hours: 9-5 Mon-Fri
> • Good selection of used office furniture. RENTALS •

OFFICE FURNITURE
FOR
PROP RENTAL
AND SALES

**A COMPLETE SELECTION OF CONTEMPORARY • HI-TECH
TRANSITIONAL • TRADITIONAL FURNITURE FOR COMMERCIALS
PRINT • FEATURES • INDUSTRIALS • TV
FROM BUDGET TO UPSCALE**

**Desks
Desk Top Accessories
Partitions
Folding Chairs and Tables
Chairs: From Clerical To CEO
Filing Cabinets
Credenzas
Coat Racks
Book Cases
Reception Furniture
Computer Furniture
Board Rooms
Conference Rooms
Any Office Set.
PRODUCTION OFFICE SET-UPS.**

212-838-8880
FAX 212-758-5001

*Contact Richard Slavin
"King of Props"*

315 East 62nd. St. New York, NY 10021

ARENSON*office* FURNISHINGS

"I found it in the N.Y. Theatrical Sourcebook."

E. BUK, ANTIQUES & ART
212-226-6891
151 Spring St., 2nd Fl., (W. B'way-Wooster St.) NYC, NY 10012
Hours: Every day by appt.
(toll call) 700-SCIENCE

ANTIQUE AND PERIOD office furniture and desktop accessories, files, typewriters, calculators, lamps, telephones, staplers, pencil sharpeners, maps, globes. Many hard-to-find 19th and 20th century props for still photography and film.

• Rentals, complete period settings and custom work. •
(See display ads under ANTIQUES and under PROP RENTAL HOUSES.)

CENTRAL PROPERTIES OF 49TH STREET
212-265-7767
514 West 49th St., (10th Ave.) NYC, NY 10019
Hours: 8-5 Mon-Fri
FAX 212-582-3746

Traditional, modern and contemporary office furniture, as well as desk accessories, lamps, books, etc.

• A full service prop house with a large selection. Helpful people. •
(See display ad under PROP RENTAL HOUSES.)

DALLEK
212-684-4848
269 Madison Ave., (39th-40th St.) NYC, NY 10016
Hours: 8:45-5:45 Mon-Thurs • 8:45-5 Fri
• Office furniture; expensive. •

FURNITURE RENTAL ASSOCIATES
212-868-0300
12 West 32nd St., 7th Fl., (5th-6th Ave.) NYC, NY 10001
800-633-3748
Hours: by appt
• Traditional, contemporary, modern and computer office furniture. RENTALS •

INTERNATIONAL FURNITURE RENTALS
203-348-7585
680 Main St., (Elm St.) Stamford, CT 06901
Hours: 9-6 Mon-Fri (Fri till 5:30) • 10-2 Sat
• Good quality office & residential furniture. Short & long term rentals. See Richard. •

MANES STREET
212-684-7050
200 Lexington, (32-33rd St.) NYC, NY 10016
Hours: 10-6 Mon-Fri
FAX 212-684-7170
• Designer office furnishings; desks, seating, storage units, and accessories. Also lamps, lighting fixtures, rugs and tapestries. Sales and rentals; highly decorative designer pieces. •
(See display ad under FURNITURE RENTAL & PURCHASE: GENERAL.)

NICCOLINI ANTIQUES–PROP RENTALS
212-243-2010
19 West 21st St., (5th-6th Ave.) NYC, NY 10010
212-254-2900
Hours: 10-5 Mon-Fri • or by appt
FAX 212-366-6779
• Antique desks, filing cabinets, chairs and accessories. Mostly American. •

PEARL SHOWROOM
212-226-3717
42 Lispenard, (Church-B'way) NYC, NY 10013
Hours: 9-6 Mon-Sat (Thurs till 7) • 10-5:30 Sun
• Drafting tables, chairs, lamps, easels, flat files, blueprint racks, etc. for sale at very good prices. CREDIT CARDS •

"I found it in the N.Y. Theatrical Sourcebook."

PROPS FOR TODAY
212-206-0330

121 West 19th St. Reception: 3rd Fl., (6th-7th Ave.) NYC, NY 10011
Hours: 8:30-5 Mon-Fri

FAX 212-924-0450

Come to us first and we'll work with your budget!
- Expanded office furniture and accessories from Country/Antique to Modern/High-Tech.
- Desks, bookcases, desk accessories, art, computers, files.
- Great lighting section.
- Rentals & Sales.

NOW ON 3 FLOORS! ONE STOP PROPPING!

• Full service prop rental house with new and antique items. Also accessories. Phone orders accepted. •
(See display ad under PROP RENTAL HOUSES.)

SECURITY OFFICE FURNITURE CO., INC.
212-924-1485

155 West 23rd St., (6th-7th Ave.) NYC, NY 10011
Hours: 8:30-5:30 Mon-Fri • 8:30-4 Sat
• Rentals and sales of new & used standard quality office furniture. See Gail or Kevin. •

STAMFORD WRECKING OFFICE FURNITURE OUTLET
203-967-8367

375 Fairfield Ave., Stamford, CT 06902
Hours: 9-5:30 Mon-Fri • 11-5 Sat
• Part of Stamford Housewrecking. They have new and old office furniture. RENTALS •

FURNITURE RENTAL & PURCHASE: RESTAURANT

See also **KITCHEN EQUIPMENT: INDUSTRIAL**

ALEXANDER BUTCHER BLOCKS & SUPPLY
212-226-4021
212-966-7245

176 Bowery, (Delancey St.) NYC, NY 10012
Hours: 10-5 Mon-Fri • 10-4 Sat
• Tables, chairs, bentwoods, butcher block; commercial & residential. RENTALS •

ARENSON OFFICE FURNISHINGS, INC..
212-838-8880

315 East 62nd St., (1st-2nd Ave.) NYC, NY 10021
Hours: 9-5 Mon-Fri • or by appt
• Pedestal tables, folding and stacking chairs. See Richard Slavin •
(See display ads under FURNITURE RENTAL & PURCHASE: OFFICE and PROP RENTAL HOUSES.)

CENTRAL PROPERTIES OF 49TH STREET
212-265-7767

514 West 49th St., (10th Ave.) NYC, NY 10019
Hours: 8-5 Mon-Fri

FAX 212-582-3746

Theme decor, furniture and accessories for complete restaurant settings including fine china, crystal and tableware.
Tables, chairs, stools, serving pieces and much more!

Central Props
CENTRAL PROPERTIES

• One stop shopping for restaurant furniture & accessories. •
(See display ad under PROP RENTAL HOUSES.)

CHAIRS & STOOLS ETC.   212-925-9191
   222 Bowery, (Prince-Spring St.) NYC, NY 10012
   Hours: 9-5 Mon-Fri • 10-3 Sat • 11-4 Sun
   • Nice selection of commercial chairs, stools, table tops, and bases. See Paul Vetrano.
   RENTALS •

EMPIRE STATE CHAIR DIVISION   914-429-5700
   Liberty St., Haverstraw, NY 10927
   Hours: 8:30-5 Mon-Fri
   • Bentwood chairs, raw or unfinished; must order 6-8 weeks in advance; 12 piece minimum. •

GARGOYLES LTD.   212-255-0135
   138 West 25th St., (6th-7th Ave.) NYC, NY 10001
   Hours: 9-5 Mon-Fri • appt recommended   FAX 212-242-3923

   512 S. Third St., Philadelphia, PA 19197   215-629-1700
   Hours: 9-5:30 Tues-Fri • 11-6 Sat   FAX 215-592-8441
   • Theme decor for restaurants, country and period advertising memorabilia, period advertising
   mirrors, English and American antiques, scale models. Flier. •

KABRAM & SONS, INC.   212-477-1480
   257 Bowery, (Prince-Houston St.) NYC, NY 10002
   Hours: 8:30-5 Mon-Fri • 9-4 Sat
   • Rents and sells tables, chairs, stools, booths, and restaurant appliances. They have been
   renting to the business since the 1950s. An interesting collection of the new and old. Some
   wonderful character pieces •
   (See display ad under KITCHEN EQUIPMENT, INDUSTRIAL.)

WILLIAM KONIAK, INC.   212-475-9877
   191 Bowery, (Spring-Delancey St.) NYC, NY 10002
   Hours: 8:30-5 Mon-Fri • 9-3 Sat
   • Used tables, chairs, and stools. •

NEW YORK BARS & BACKBARS   212-431-0600
   49 East Houston St., (Mott-Mulberry St.) NYC, NY 10012
   Hours: 10-6 Mon-Sat
   • Always changing selection of bars and backbars; 8-30 ft. long; Victorian and Deco; for sale
   and rental. •

PROPS FOR TODAY   212-206-0330
   121 West 19th St.: Reception 3rd Fl., (6th-7th Ave.) NYC, NY 10011
   Hours: 8:30-5 Mon-Fri   FAX 212-924-0450

Come to us first and we'll work with your budget!
• Expanded, full service facility for all party, banquet
  and restaurant needs. Party planning consultants available.
• Theme items, china, crystal, tables, chairs, linens,
  garden furniture, screens, columns and pedestals,
  butcher blocks, stools, etc.
• Rentals & sales.
NOW ON 3 FLOORS! ONE STOP PROPPING!

   • Full service prop rental house. Large selection of china and glassware. Phone orders accepted. •
   (See display ad under PROP RENTAL HOUSES.)

RESNICK-RITE EQUIPMENT, INC.   718-292-1800
   560 Concord Ave., Bronx, NY 10455
   Hours: 9-5 Mon-Fri   FAX   718-292-1874
   • Supermarket and restaurant equipment, refrigerator cases, janitorial supplies and new and
   used diner booths, decor and signage . Rentals and delivery available. MC/VISA •

ROLLHAUS BROS., INC.   212-334-1111
   26 Bleecker St., (Mott St.) NYC, NY 10012
   Hours: 8-4:30 Mon-Thurs • 8-2:30 Fri   FAX   212-941-8193
   • Sells and rents booths, chairs, tables; stock and custom furniture available. •

TIP TOP / LEBENSFELD TOP EQUIPMENT CORP.   212-353-0056
   219 Bowery, (Rivington-Stanton St.) NYC, NY 10002
   Hours: 8:30-4:30 Mon-Fri • 10-2 Sat   FAX   212-353-0202
   • Restaurant and office chairs, tables, stools, cast iron table bases. •

THE WAREHOUSE STORE FIXTURE CO.   203-575-0111
   249 Thompson Ave., Waterbury, CT 06702
   Hours: 8-6 Mon-Fri (Thurs till 9) • 8-5 Sat
   • Restaurant tables, chairs, booths, etc.; store and kitchen fixtures. CREDIT CARDS •

FURNITURE REPAIR & REFINISHING

See also **UPHOLSTERERS**
For supplies, see **FURNITURE PARTS**
                UPHOLSTERY TOOLS & SUPPLIES

ACKERMAN & WEINBERG   212-334-0409
   407 Broome St., NYC, NY 10013
   Hours: 9-5 Mon-Fri
   • Furniture restoration. Architectural and surface treatments. Wood turnings and carvings.
   Will work on sight. •

BAREWOOD ARCHITECTURAL WOODWORK LTD.   718-875-9037
   106 Ferris St., (Van Dyke-Coffey St.) Brooklyn, NY 11231
   Hours: 8-5 Mon-Fri
   • Excellent repair, carving and stripping of wood; also does custom work. •

FINE ART FINISHING   212-831-6128
   315 East 91st St.,6th Fl., (1st-2nd Ave.) NYC, NY 10128
   Hours: 8-4:30 Mon-Fri
   • Stripping and finishing. •

GOTHAM GALLERIES   212-677-3303
   80 Fourth Ave., (10th-11th St.) NYC, NY 10003
   Hours: 8:30-6 Mon-Sat
   • Custom refinishing; estate furniture, Oriental rugs, and bronzes. •

POOR RICHARD'S RESTORATION ATELIER   201-783-5333
   101 Walnut St., (N. Willow) Montclair, NJ 07042
   Hours: by appt.
   • Furniture stripping and refinishing, reupholstery and conservation of fabric and leather,
   reweaving of cane, rush, wicker. •

E–F

PROFESSIONAL FURNITURE REFINISHERS   212-532-0606
200 Lexington Ave., (32nd-33rd St.) NYC, NY 10016
Hours: 8-4 Mon-Fri
• Furniture refinishing. •

VETERAN'S CANING SHOP   212-868-3244
550 West 35th St., (10th-11th Ave.) NYC, NY 10001
Hours: 8-4:30 Mon-Thurs • 8-4 Fri • 9-12 Sat
• Hand and machine caning, rush and splint seating, wicker repairs; pickup and delivery available. Very nice and helpful people. •

WEST SIDE CHAIRS CANED   212-724-4408
371 Amsterdam Ave., 2nd Fl., (77th-78th St.) NYC, NY 10024
Hours: 11-7 Wed-Sat • 1-5 Sun or by appt.
• Furniture repair, hand and machine caning, rush, splint and wicker repair. •

YORK END CANING   212-288-6843
454 East 84th St., (1st Ave-York) NYC, NY 10128
Hours: 9-6 Mon-Fri • 10-2 Sat (closed on Sat in Summer)
• Caning and rushwork; furniture repair and restoration. See Jack Hubsmith. •

YORKVILLE CANING, INC.   212-432-6464
3104 60th St ., Woodside, NY 11377
Hours: 7-4:15 Mon-Thurs • 7-4 Fri
• Repair of rattan, wicker, caning, splint. Also re-glueing and basic upholstery. •

NOTES

GLASS & MIRRORS

AAA GLASS CO.
212-463-8000

152 West 26th St., (6-7th Ave.) NYC, NY 10001
Hours: 8-5 Mon-Fri
• Large selection of clear, tinted, etched and bulletproof glass and mirrors. Can be cut to size while you wait. Also glass blocks, imported glass and mirrors. •
(See display ad in this section.)

ALL STATE GLASS CORP.
212-226-2517

85 Kenmare St., (Lafayette-Mulberry) NYC, NY 10012
Hours: 8-4 Mon-Fri • 9-4 Sat

FAX   212-966-7904

All thicknesses of clear and tinted glass.
Fluted glass, shelves, furniture tops, mirrors,
ground and sandblasted glass.
Fast and helpful service. Skilled installation. Established 1923.

• Also patterned glass. CREDIT CARDS •

ART CUT GLASS STUDIO
908-583-7648

RD#1 Box 10, Fawn Drive, Matawan, NJ 07747
Hours: 9-5 Mon-Thurs • or by appt.
• Cutting, engraving, monogramming; design and repair. •

S. A. BENDHEIM CO., INC.
212-226-6370

122 Hudson St., (North Moore) NYC, NY 10013
Hours: 9:30-5 Tues-Fri • 9-1 Sat
• All types of stained and textured glasses, tools and supplies; carries different "distortion" degrees of Colonial mouth-blown window glass. Also teaches glass leading. •

CAPITOL GLASS & SASH CORP., INC.
212-243-4528

641 Hudson St., (12-13th St.) NYC, NY 10014
Hours: 7-5 Mon-Fri • 8-12 Sat • (closed Sat; June, July, Aug)   FAX   212-924-4216
• Glazing contractors, complete line of glass and mirrors; also full line of millwork and windows. •
(See display ad in this section.)

EAST SIDE GLASS CO.
212-674-8355

201 Chrystie St., (Stanton-Rivington) NYC, NY 10002
Hours: 8:30-4:30 Mon-Fri

FAX   212-475-6210

• All types of glass and mirrors. •

GEM GLASS CO.
212-247-7145

790 Eleventh Ave., (54-55th St.) NYC, NY 10019
Hours: 7:30-4:30 Mon-Fri
• Picture glass and framing. •

GLASS RESTORATIONS
212-517-3287

308 East 78th St., (1-2nd Ave.) NYC, NY 10021
Hours: 9:30-5 Mon-Fri
• Cuts, grinds and repairs chipped or scratched glass; also repairs broken glass and polishes. Speak to Gus. •

G–H

MORRIS GLASSER & SON, INC.   212-831-8750
   234 East 128th St., (2-3rd Ave.) NYC, NY 10035
   Hours: 7:30-5:30 Mon-Fri
      • Glass, mirror; very fast and helpful; worth the trip. •

F. J. GRAY & CO.   718-297-4444
   139-24 Queens Blvd., Jamaica, NY 11435
   Hours: 9-5 Mon-Fri   FAX   718-297-4742
      • All types of glass: sheet, rod, tube, shapes, and pyrex. Glass fabrication in quantity. •

KAMAR PRODUCTS   914-591-8700
   PO Box 227, Irvington-On-Hudson, NY 10533
   Hours: 8:30-4:30 Mon-Fri
      • Manufacturers of Mirrorlite™; lightweight, unbreakable mirrors; custom work. No minimum. •

KNICKERBOCKER PLATE GLASS CORP.   212-247-8500
   439 West 54th St., (9-10th Ave.) NYC, NY 10019
   Hours: 8:30-4:30 Mon-Fri   FAX   212-489-1449

GLASS, MIRRORS AND PLASTIC FOR EVERY PURPOSE

      • 24-hour emergency boarding service. •

"I found it in the N.Y. Theatrical Sourcebook."

THE CLEAR CHOICE

FEATURING :
A COMPLETE LINE OF GLASS AND MIRRORS
AVAILABLE FOR PICK UP OR DELIVERY.

- A leader in Theatrical Services ● Innovative Ideas
- Obsolete Patterned Glass in stock ● Professional Staff
- Prompt Delivery and Installations ● Millwork
- 24 hour service Available ● Picture Framing
- Glass and Mirrors cut while you wait

Capitol Glass & Sash Company, Inc.

(212) 243-4528

641 HUDSON STREET
NEW YORK, NEW YORK 10014

FAX : (212) 924-4216

"I found it in the N.Y. Theatrical Sourcebook."

A. LAUB GLASS 212-734-4270
1873 Second Ave., (96-97th St.) NYC, NY 10029
Hours: 8-5 Mon-Fri • 9-4 Sat
• Stained and leaded glass. Tiffany pieces. •

MANHATTAN SHADE & GLASS CO. 212-288-5616
1299 Third Ave., (74-75th St.) NYC, NY 10029
Hours: 8:30-5:30 Mon-Fri • 10-4 Sat
• Glass and mirror, blinds and shades. •

MIRREX BY APACHE 908-486-1811
2025 East Linden Ave., Linden, NJ 07036
Hours: 7-3:30 Mon-Fri
• Heat shrink mirror and two-way mirror, built to order on metal frames. •

NISA GLASS SYSTEMS, INC. 212-265-0882
667 Tenth Ave., (47th St.) NYC, NY 10036
Hours 9-5 Mon-Fri • 10-3 Sat
• Glass and mirror. •

RAMBUSCH 212-675-0400
40 West 13th St., (5-6th Ave.) NYC, NY 10011
Hours: by appt. FAX 212-620-4687
• Manufacturer of stained glass & church fixtures. •

ROSEN-PARAMOUNT GLASS 212-532-0820
45 East 20th St., (Park Ave. S-B'way) NYC, NY 10003
Hours: 9-5 Mon-Fri • 10-3 Sat
• Glass and mirror. •

SARACO GLASS CORP. 718-438-7757
3710 13th Ave., (37-38th St.) Brooklyn, NY 11218
Hours: 9-5 Mon-Fri • Weekends by appt.
• All types of glass and mirrors. •

GLOVES

ARIS ISOTONER GLOVES 212-532-8627
417 Fifth Ave., 2nd Fl., (37-38th St.) NYC, NY 10016
Hours: 9-5 Mon-Fri
• Manufacturer; will help obtain out-of-season men's and women's gloves, quantity. •

FINALE, INC. 516-371-1313
375 Pearsall Ave., Cedarhurst, NY 11516
Hours: 7:30-3:30 Mon-Fri FAX 516-371-1358
• Vinyl, leather men's gloves; ladies gloves, including long lace, satin, velvet, sheer. •

GLAMOUR GLOVE CORP. 212-447-1002
6 East 32nd St., 6th Fl., (Madison-5th Ave.) NYC, NY 10016
Hours: 9-5 Mon-Fri FAX 212-696-0759
• Wholesale gloves in volume, custom work, full fashion nylon and leather gloves; contact Jay Ruckel. •

G–H

GLOVES BY HAMMER OF HOLLYWOOD   213-938-0268
7210 Melrose Ave., Los Angeles, CA 90046
Hours: 9-5 Mon-Fri
• Large selection, many sizes, styles and materials; catalog available. •

PAUL'S VEIL & NET CORP.   212-391-3822
42 West 38th St., (5-6th Ave.) NYC, NY 10018   212-391-3823
Hours: 8:30-4 Mon-Fri • 8:30-2 Sat   FAX   212-575-5141
• Lace gloves. •

SAND & SIMAN, INC.   212-564-4484
10 West 33rd St., Rm 714, (5-6th Ave.) NYC, NY 10001   800-322-7220
Hours: 9-5 Mon-Fri
• White cotton gloves; satin, nylon, and lace gloves; catalog. •

GRAPHICS & TYPESETTING

See also **PRINTING & COPYING**
See also **NEWSPAPERS**

BAUMWELL GRAPHICS   212-868-3340
450 West 31st. St., (9-10th Avenue) NYC, NY 10001
Hours: 8:30-6:00 Mon-Fri   FAX   212-689-3386
• Typesetting, desktop publishing services, design, layout, photostats. Contact Clyde
Baumwell. Also makes custom transfers. •

B F GRAPHICS   718-339-3800
1960 Coney Island Avenue, (Ave. P-Quentin Rd.) Brooklyn, NY 11223
Hours: 9-5 Mon-Thur • 9-12 Fri   FAX   718-998-5268
• Typesetting, photostats, paste-ups; reliable. •

DEPENDABLE MENU PRINTING   212-929-7121
121 West 19th St., 2nd Floor, (6-7th Avenue) NYC, NY 10011
Hours: 7:30-4 Mon-Fri   FAX   718-317-1719
• Menu printing, covers, lamination, clips, tassels, leatherette menus; ask for Leonard. •

DIGITAL EXCHANGE   212-929-0566
1 West 20th St., (Fifth) NYC, NY 10011
Hours: 24 Hours a day Mon-Fri • 10-4 Sat   FAX   212-929-0043
• Formerly Stat Store. Imaging from discs. Large color prints. Vinyl backdrops. •

ECLECTIC PRESS   212-645-8880
620 West 26th St. 4th Floor, (11-12th Avenue) NYC, NY 10001
Hours: 9-5 Mon-Fri • or by appt.   FAX   212-243-6508
• Graphics design; paste-ups, color copying and reproduction, newspaper offset printing.
Contact Franklyn Robb. •
(See display ad under NEWSPAPERS.)

G.F.I. (GRAPHICS FOR INDUSTRY)   212-889-6202
8 West 30th St., (5th & Broadway) NYC, NY 10001
Hours: 9-5:30 Mon-Fri   FAX   212-545-1276
• Color correct product and packaging for TV & Film, some modelmaking, transfers, high quality full graphic service. •

DAWN GOTTMAN   212-255-0569
111 W. 24th St. #3, 3rd Floor, (6th Ave.) NYC, NY 10011
Hours: 9-5 Mon-Fri • or by appt.   FAX 212-229-2736
• Computer typesetting - fast service. Also layout and design and advertising services. •

THE HAND PROP ROOM, INC.   213-931-1534
5700 Venice Blvd., Los Angeles, CA 90019
Hours: 7-7 Mon-Fri   Fax 213-931-2145
• Full printing and graphics service; newspapers, license plates, IDs, "Greeked" product
labels. CREDIT CARDS •

EARL HAYS PRESS   818-765-0700
10707 Sherman Way, Sun Valley, CA 91352
Hours: 8-5 Mon-Fri   FAX 818-765-5245
• Period repro newspapers books, diplomas, also license plates, "Greeked" product labels, etc. •

IMAGES   212-645-6100
216 West 18th St., (7-8th Ave.) NYC, NY 10011
Hours: 24 Hours Mon-Fri   FAX 212-645-7804
• Full pre-press, MAC department, transfers. Rush service available. •

QUAD RIGHT   212-222-1220
711 Amsterdam Ave., (94th St.) NYC, NY 10025
Hours: 8-8 Mon-Thurs. • 8-5:30 Fri   FAX 212-222-2084
• Typesetting, B & W stats, veloxes, graphic design; will pickup and deliver. •

ROYAL OFF SET COMPANY,, INC.   212-255-3753
27 West 20th, Rm. 702, (5th Ave.) NYC, NY 10011
Hours: 8:30-5 Mon-Fri   FAX 212-206-7065
• Commercial printing, from business cards to 23' x 29' posters. Large and small quantities.
Reasonable rates. Up to 4 colors. •

SMP GRAPHIC SERVICE CENTER, INC./STAT SHOP   212-254-2282
26 East 22nd St., (Broadway - Park Ave. South) NYC, NY 10010
Hours: 8-Midnight Mon-Thur • 8-10 Fri • 11-6 Sat-Sun   FAX 212-979-2934

142 West 26th St., (6-7th Ave.) NYC, NY 10001   212-929-2010
Hours: 9-6 Mon-Fri
• Color and B & W photostats, dry mounting, blow-ups, many other services. CREDIT CARDS •

SWEETBRYAR CALAGRAPHICS   212-233-6682
124 East Broadway, (Pike-Essex) NYC, NY 10002
Hours: 10-7 Mon-Sat by appt.   FAX 212-233-6682

COMPLETE DESIGN STUDIO
Specializing in classic, innovative handlettering for Advertising and
Promotion. SERVING Theatre, Television, Film, Advertising and
Publishing. Posters, Banners, Signage, Identity, Testimonials, logos,
and Illustration including Airbrush. Historically accurate Graphics.
From Mailings to Murals • • • • From Ruffs to Ready
NO TASK TOO TINY, NO DELUGE TOO HUGE

• Calligraphy and sign painting, air brushing,
hand lettering, logos, banners, posters (all custom), menus. On location if necessary. •

SCOTT WILSON GRAPHICS   212-629-3333
201 West 54th St., Apt 3C, NYC, NY 10019
Hours: 9-5 Mon-Fri   FAX 212-757-1726
• Small graphics company, transfers, airbrush, some modelmaking. Very helpful. •

G–H

JOAN WINTERS
236 East 5th St., #D3, (2-3rd Ave.) NYC, NY 10003
Hours: by appt.
• Graphic design and production services for specialty props including magazines, books, newspapers, badges, and letterheads. Logos, posters, computer typesetting. Major film credits. •

212-475-6605

FAX   212-475-6605

HAIR SUPPLIES & WIGS

See also **BEAUTY SALON EQUIPMENT**

ABRACADABRA
10 Christopher St., (near 6th Ave.) NY, NY 10014
Hours: 11-9 Mon-Sat • Also open Sun in Oct, Dec.
• Catalog available. Wigs, mustaches and beards. Crepe hair and human. CREDIT CARDS

212-627-5745
800-MAGIC-66

FAX   212-627-5876

ANIMAL HAIR MFG.
175 Beard St., (Convoel) Brooklyn, NY 11231
Hours: 7-3 Mon-Fri
• Real horses tails, etc.; mfg. brushes, not wigs. No minimum. Sorry, no catalog. •

718-852-3592

CHICAGO HAIR GOODS CO.
428 S. Wabash Ave., 6th fl., Chicago, IL 60605
Hours: 9-5 Mon-Fri • 9-7 Thurs
• Inexpensive wigs; catalog. Phone orders and shipping. CREDIT CARDS •

312-427-8600

FAX   312-427-8605

JAQUES DARCEL, INC.
50 West 57th St., (5-6th Ave.) NYC, NY 10019
Hours: 10-6 Mon-Sat
• Wigs and hairpieces. •

212-753-7576

DEMEO BROTHERS, INC.
129 West 29th St., (6-7th Ave.) NYC, NY 10001
Hours: Mon-Fri by appt.
• Theatrical laces, yak hair, fine European hair, wig-making and hairpiece-making supplies; hair sample matching; order by mail. Price list available. No minimum. •

212-268-1400

ELSEN ASSOCIATES
780 Riverside Drive, (155th St.) NYC, NY 10032
Hours: by appt.
• Custom built wigs for all media; staffed with a network of qualified wig and make-up designers nationwide. •

212-283-7708

GOLDSMITH MANNEQUINS
10-09 43rd Ave., (10-11th St.) L.I.C., NY 11101
Hours: 9-4 Mon-Fri
• Wig heads, new and secondhand mannequins. Free Catalog. Will ship. RENTALS •

718-937-8476

PAUL HUNTLEY LTD.
19 West 21st St., Rm. 1204, (5-6th Ave.) NYC, NY 10010
Hours: by appt.
• Custom made, excellent quality wigs; expensive. One of the best. •

212-787-5200

G-H

IDEAL WIG CO. 718-361-8601
37-11 35th Ave., (37-38th St.) Astoria, NY 11101
Hours: 9-5 Mon-Fri
• Theatrical hair goods, character designed, light weight, adjustable, washable. Wholesale. $750 minimum. •

JIGU TRADING COMPANY, INC. 212-689-9738
42 West 28th St., (5-6th Ave.) NYC, NY 10001
Hours: 9-5 Mon-Fri FAX 212-684-0584
• Asian import, human hair and artificial hair and wigs; also "fun" colored hair and wigs; beauty and nail supplies. •

BOB KELLY WIG CREATIONS, INC. 212-819-0030
151 West 46th St., (6-7th Ave.) NYC, NY 10036
Hours: 9-4:30 Mon-Thurs • 9-3 Fri
• Custom made wigs. Artificial hair, straight or styled; theatrical make-up and cosmetic products; catalog. •

LACEY COSTUME WIG
212-695-1996
505 8th Ave., 11th Fl., (35th St.) NYC, NY 10018 800-562-9911
Hours: 8-5 Mon-Fri FAX 212-695-3860
• Free catalog available. Reasonably priced novelty & period wigs. No minimum. Contact Elliot Brill or Mason Kaplan. •

LEE'S MARDI GRAS ENTERPRISES, INC. 212-645-1888
400 West 14th St., (9th Ave.) NYC, NY 10014
Hours: 12-6 Mon-Sat
• Ladies wigs for men; complete line of ladies apparel for men. CREDIT CARDS •

NATIONAL HAIR TECHNOLOGIES
508-686-2964
300 Canal St., Lawrence, MA 01840
Hours: 8:30-5 Mon-Fri FAX 508-686-1497
• Custom-made specialty wigs; designed by you, made by them in the USA. Catalog. •

PUCCI MANIKINS 212-633-0452
44 West 18th St., (5-6th Ave.) NYC, NY 10011 FAX 212-633-1058
Hours: 9-4:30 Mon-Fri
• Mannequin wigs and mannequins. $20 catalog. •

RAY BEAUTY SUPPLY CO., INC. 212-757-0175
721 Eighth Ave., (45th-46th St.) NYC, NY 10036 800-253-0993
Hours: 9:30-6 Mon-Fri • 10:30-5 Sat FAX 212-459-8918
• Wide variety hair supplies and make-up; beauty salon equipment rental; see Bobby. Phone orders and shipping available. CREDIT CARDS. •

IRA SENZ 212-752-6800
13 East 47th St., (5th-Madison Ave.) NYC, NY 10017
Hours: 8-4:30 Mon-Fri
• Wigs. Expensive. •

WIG CITY 212-421-1618
217 East 60th St., (2nd-3rd Ave.) NYC, NY 10022
Hours: 10-6:30 Mon-Sat
• Inexpensive Wigs. •

ZAUDER BROTHERS   516-379-2600
    10 Henry St., Freeport, NY 11520
    Hours: 8:30-5:30 Mon-Thurs • 8:30-2:45 Fri
    • Custom made wigs. Yak hair, also make-up. $25 minimum. Sorry, no catalog. •

HAMPERS

MUTUAL HARDWARE CORP.   718-361-2480
    5-45 49th Ave., (Vernon) L.I.C., NY 11101
    Hours: 8:30-5 Mon-Fri   FAX 718-729-8296
    • Canvas storage hampers; theatrical hardware. •

SCENIC SPECIALTIES, INC.   718-788-5379
    232 7th St., (3-4th Ave.) Brooklyn, NY 11215
    Hours: 8:30-5 Mon-Fri by appt.   FAX 718-768-9173
    • Heavy duty canvas and molded plastic hampers. Custom sizes available. •
(See ad under ADHESIVES & GLUES)

W.H. SILVER'S HARDWARE   212-247-4406
    832 Eighth Ave., (50th-51st St.) NYC, NY 10019   212-247-4425
    Hours: 8-5:30 Mon-Fri   FAX 212-246-2041
    • Specialty hampers, hand trucks, handling equipment. •

STATE SUPPLY EQUIPMENT & PROPS, INC.   212-645-1430
    210 Eleventh Ave., (24th-25th St.) NYC, NY 10001
    Hours: 8:30-5 Mon-Fri   212-675-3131
    • Canvas hampers; sales and rental; also prop rental. •

I WEISS & SONS, INC.   718-706-8139
    2-07 Borden Ave., (Vernon-Jackson Ave.) L.I.C., NY 11101
    Hours: 8:30-4:30 Mon-Fri   FAX 718-706-8139
    • Canvas storage hampers, standard & custom sizes. Plywood tops, swivel casters. •
(See ad under CURTAINS & DRAPERIES: THEATRICAL)

HANDICRAFTS

See also **ETHNIC GOODS: ALL HEADINGS**
For specific craft materials, see **INDEX**

CAMPBELL CLASSICS   703-582-2212
    6201 Mallard Rd., PO Box 380, Thornburg, VA 22565
    Hours: 9-5 Mon-Fri   FAX 703-582-5319
    • Wholesale mass-produced folk art wood carvings for display and theatre; styles from across
    the US. Minimum order. Call for color catalog and prices. •

THE ELDER CRAFTSMEN   212-861-5260
    846 Lexington Ave., (64th St.) NYC, NY 10021
    Hours: 10-5:30 Mon-Sat • closed Sat in summer
    • Handmade afghans, quilts, baby linens and clothes, toys, gifts. •

G-H

HAND-MADE BY MARY PAT   718-768-3571
  41 Prospect Park SW, (10th) Brooklyn, NY 11215
  Hours: 10-7 Mon-Sat
  • Knitted and crocheted items of all kinds: sweaters, socks, hats, blankets, dresses, jackets, pants, etc. •

NEW YORK EXCHANGE FOR WOMEN'S WORK   212-753-2330
  1095 Third Ave., (64-65th St.) NYC, NY 10021
  Hours: 10-6 Mon-Sat
  • Handmade gifts, toys, quilts, afghans, clothing, linens. •

HARDWARE, DECORATIVE

See also **LUMBER**
See also **TOOLS & HARDWARE**

BALDWIN BRASS CENTER   212-421-0090
  248 E. 58th St., (2-3rd Ave.) NYC, NY 10022
  Hours: 8:30-5:30 Mon-Fri   FAX   212-371-7088
  • Carries the complete line of Baldwin products as well as other major lines. Also bath accessories. Full catalog for $45. CREDIT CARDS •

DECO WARE INC.   718-871-1212
  944 McDonald Ave., (Ave. F -18th Ave.) Brooklyn, NY 11230
  Hours: 9-6 Mon-Wed • 9-7 Thurs • 9-2 Fri • Closed Sat. • 10-5 Sun. FAX 718-972-3277
  • Large selection of decorative hardware and plumbing fixtures. Delivery service available. •

DECORATORS WHOLESALE HARDWARE CO. / LEGS, LEGS, LEGS / M. WOLCHONK & SON, INC.
                                                             212-696-1650
  16 E. 30th St., (5-6th Ave.) NYC, NY 10016
  Hours: 9-6 Mon-Fri • 9-4:30 Sat   FAX   212-696-1664
  • Large assortment of hardware and bath accessories; also metal and wood furniture legs and pedestals. CREDIT CARDS •

CHARLOTTE FORD TRUNK LTD.   806-659-3027
  PO Box 536, Spearman, TX 79081
  Hours: 8:30-4:30 Mon-Fri   FAX   806-659-5614
  • Trunk supplies and parts; locks, draw-bolts, corners, hinges; catalog. CREDIT CARDS •

GRACIOUS HOME   212-988-8990
  1217 Third Ave., (70-71st St.) NYC, NY 10021
  Hours: 9-7 Mon-Sat • 10:30-5:30 Sun   FAX   212-249-1534
  • Decorative hardware, faucets, towel bars, hampers, bath accessories; also bed linens, frames and decorative items. CREDIT CARDS •

P. E. GUERIN   212-243-5270
  23 Jane St., (Greenwich Ave.-8th St.) NYC, NY 10014
  Hours: By appt.   FAX   212- 727-2290
  • Primarily custom, 6-8 week delivery. Excellent selection of all types of hardware for your home or palace!. Catalog; very expensive. •

H. T. SALES / HARDWARE SYSTEMS, INC.   212-265-0747
  726 Tenth Ave., (49th-50th St.) NYC, NY 10019   (billing) FAX 212-262-0150
  Hours: 7:30-4:30 Mon-Fri   (ordering) FAX 212-262-5082
  • Decorative and bath hardware division, same phone number as main store. CREDIT CARDS •

KRAFT HARDWARE, INC.   212-838-2214
306 East 61st St., (1st-2nd Ave.) NYC, NY 10021
Hours: 9-5 Mon-Fri   212-644-9254
• Door, cabinet and bathroom hardware. MC/VISA •

DAVE SANDERS & CO.   212-334-9898
107 Bowery, (Grand-Hester St.) NYC, NY 10002
Hours: 8-4:30 Mon-Fri   FAX   212-966-4185
• Catalog available; large assortment decorative and functional hardware. •

SELBY FURNITURE HARDWARE CO.   718-993-3700
321 Rider Ave., (140th St.) Bronx, NY 10451
Hours: 8:30-5 Mon-Fri   FAX   718-933-3143
• Furniture hardware wholesalers; $15 cash minimum, $25 check minimum. Shipping charge
for orders under $100. Catalog. $100 minimum on VISA/MC •

SIMON'S HARDWARE   212-532-9220
421 Third Ave., (29th-30th St.) NYC, NY 10016
Hours: 8-5:30 Mon-Fri • 8-7 Thurs • 10-5 Sat   FAX   212-725-3609
• Enormous selection decorative and functional hardware; go early in the day. Catalog.
MC/VISA •

TREMONT NAIL CO.   508-295-0038
PO Box 111, Wareham, MA 02571
Hours: 8:30-4 Mon-Fri   FAX   508-295-1365
• 20 varieties of old-fashioned and special patterned cut nails; catalog. $20 minimum.
MC/VISA •

HARDWOODS & VENEERS

See also **LUMBER**

MAURICE L. CONDON CO.   914-946-4111
250 Ferris Ave., White Plains, NY 10603
Hours: 8-4:30 Mon-Fri
• Hardwood lumber, hardwood and marine plywood and moldings; planing and ripping facilities, deliveries. Good prices, no minimum. Good quality. •

ALBERT CONSTANTINE & SONS   718-792-1600
2050 Eastchester Rd., (Seminole-McDonald St.) Bronx, NY 10461
Hours: 8-5 Mon-Fri • Thurs till 8 • 8-3 Sat • (May-Aug: 8-5 Mon-Fri • 8-1 Sat)
• Hardwoods, veneers, exotic woods, molding, hardware and woodworking tools. Good products, good service. •

ROSENZWEIG LUMBER CORP.   718-585-8050
801 East 135th St., (Bruckner Blvd.) Bronx, NY 10454
Hours: 8-5 Mon-Fri
• Good selection hardwoods, veneers, plywood, lumber and moldings; good prices, prompt
next day delivery. •

HATS

For custom millinery see: **COSTUME CRAFTSPEOPLE, MASKS, & MILLINERY**

AEGEAN IMPORTS   415-593-8300
    1200 Industrial Rd., Rm. 6, San Carlos, CA 94070
    Hours: 8:30-4 Mon-Fri (closed Fri in summer)
    • Greek fisherman's hats; quantity mail order only. •

AMERICAN UNIFORM HEADWEAR   201-943-0143
    36 Anderson Ave., Fairview, NJ 07022
    Hours: 9-4:30 Mon-Fri
    • Made to order; stock of police and fireman's hats. •

GEORGE BOLLMAN & CO.   212-564-6480
    350 Fifth Ave., (34th St.) NYC, NY 10118
    Hours: 8:30-5 Mon-Thurs • 8:30-4:30 Fri
    • Manufacturer of period hats. MC/VISA •

BURANELLI HATS, INC.   212-473-1343
    101 Delancey St., (Ludlow St.) NYC, NY 10002
    Hours: 9:30-5:30 Sun-Fri • 9:30-5 Sat
    • Specializing in Stetson hats. Mail and phone orders. CREDIT CARDS •

CARLOS NEW YORK HATS   212-869-2207
    45 West 38th St., (5th-6th Ave.) NYC, NY 10018   800-852-9499
    Hours: 9-5 Mon-Fri   FAX   212-827-0037
    • Design and manufacture of hats for special occasions, weddings, theatre, etc.. Wholesale
    and retail. CREDIT CARDS •

CONCORD MERCHANDISING CORP.   212-840-2720
    1026 6th Ave., (38-39th St.) NYC, NY 10018
    Hours: 9-6 Mon-Sat
    • Hats, veiling, horsehair, colored tubular horsehair, and flowers. •

GERRY COSBY & CO., INC.   212-563-6464
    3 Penn Plaza, (Madison Sq. Garden) NYC, NY 10001
    Hours: 9:30-6:30 Mon-Fri • 9:30-6 Sat • 12-5 Sun
    (Open till game time - Knicks & Rangers night games.)   FAX   212-967-0876
    • Hats and helmets for sports. Athletic outfitters. Sales only. Phone orders. CREDIT CARDS •

ESTEE EINSTEIN   212-677-2350
    184 Second Ave., (11th-12th St.) NYC, NY 10003
    Hours: 9:30-5:30 Mon-Fri • or by appt.   FAX   212-677-2747
    • Custom-made hats in a wide variety of styles and fabrics. AMEX •

FIBRE-METAL PRODUCTS CO.   215-459-5300
    Baltimore Pike, Concordville, PA 19331   800-523-7048
    Hours: 8-4:30 Mon-Fri
    • Hard hats in quantity; manufacturer. Catalog. Will ship. •

GREY OWL INDIAN CRAFTS   718-341-4000
    132-05 Merrick Blvd., (Bel Knap) Jamaica, NY 11434
    Hours: 9-5 Mon-Fri
    • Kits for American Indian headdresses and crafts. Catalog. CREDIT CARDS •

HAT BRANDS, INC.   212-564-5799
350 Fifth Ave., Rm. 1021, (31st St.) NYC, NY 10018
Hours: 9-5 Mon-Fri
• Formerly Dobbs Hats. Wholesale, contemporary men's hats, western and sports hats. •

HAT /CAP EXCHANGE   401-348-2244
PO Box 377, Betterton, MD 21610
Hours: 9-5:30 Mon-Fri
• Wholesale hats, good prices; extra charge for split cartons. MC./VISA •

HATCRAFTERS, INC.   215-623-2620
20 North Springfield Rd., Clifton Heights, PA 19018
Hours: 8:30-4:30 Mon-Fri
• Theatrical hats, stock and custom; military reproductions; catalog $5. MC./VISA •

HATS IN THE BELFRY   212-406-2574
Pier 17 Pavilion 1st Fl., South St. Seaport, NYC, NY 10038
Hours: 10-9 Mon-Sat • 11-7 Sun
• An assortment of theatrical and other unusual headwear. CREDIT CARDS •

MELINDA HODGES FINE MILLINERY   212-925-0699
122 Hudson St., 5th Fl., (N. Moore-Varick St.) NYC, NY 10013
Hours: 9:30-5 Mon-Fri • or by appt.
• Contemporary hats in stock & custom hats for sales and rentals. No credit cards. •

J. J. HAT CENTER   212-239-4368
310 Fifth Ave., (31-32nd St.) NYC, NY 10001
Hours: 8:45-5:45 Mon-Sat • Thurs till 7   FAX   212-971-0406
• All types of hats including Stetsons. •

JACOBSON HAT CO., INC.   717-342-7887
Prescott Ave. and Ridge Row, Scranton, PA 18510   800-233-4690
Hours: 8-5:30 Mon-Fri
• Theatrical hats and hat frames, custom-made; large orders; catalog. MC./VISA •

KEYSTONE UNIFORM CAP   215-922-5493
428 North 13th St., Philadelphia, PA 19123
Hours: 7:30-4 Mon-Fri   FAX   212-922-5161
• Uniform hats. •

KRIEGER TOP HATS   516-599-3188
3 Taft Ave., Lynbrook, NY 11563
Hours: 9-4 Mon-Fri   FAX   516-889-4519
• Satin top hats, collapsible top hats, custom work, affordable. •

O. K. UNIFORM CO.
212-966-1984
507 Broadway, (Spring-Broome St.) NYC, NY 10012   212-966-4733
Hours: 9:30-5:30 Mon-Thurs • 9:30-call Fri • 11:30-4:30 Sun   FAX   212-226-6668
• Sales only. Large assortment of hats & caps for hospital and service uniforms, work and formal attire. •
(See display ad under CLOTHING RENTAL & PURCHASE: UNIFORMS.)

ROTH IMPORT CO.   212-840-1945
13 West 38th St., (5-6th Ave.) NYC, NY 10018
Hours: 9-5:30 Mon-Fri
• Millinery for theatre, streetwear, bridal; costume trimmings; wholesaler, large orders only. •

"I found it in the N.Y. Theatrical Sourcebook."   **223**

SACRED FEATHER   608-255-2071
  417 State St., Madison, WI 53703
  Hours: 10-6 Mon-Sat • 11-5 Sun
  • Derbies, toppers, western, fedoras, some theatrical, etc.; no catalog. Phone and mail orders.
  CREDIT CARDS •

STETSON HATS   816-233-8031
  4500 Stetson Trail, St. Joseph, MO 64502
  Hours: 6-5 Mon-Sat
  • Derbies, toppers, western hats; wholesale only. •

TOP THIS, INC.   314-422-3377
  PO Box 204, Vienna, MO 65582
  Hours: 7-3:30 Mon-Fri   FAX   SAME
  • Contemporary styles, mostly women's. •

TRACEY TOOKER   212-472-9603
  1211 Lexington Ave., (82nd-83rd St.) NYC, NY 10028
  Hours: 11-7 Mon-Sat • 12-6 Sun   FAX   212-966-6695
  • Custom fashion hats, some stock hats. CREDIT CARDS •

VANDYKE HATTERS   212-929-5696
  94 Greenwich Ave., (12th St.) NYC, NY 10011
  Hours: 7:30-6 Mon-Fri • 9-4 Sat
  • Stetson, Borsalino, western and house brand hats; also cleans and blocks hats. No credit
  cards. •

WORTH & WORTH LTD.   212-867-6058
  331 Madison Ave., (43rd St.) NYC, NY 10017   800-428-7467
  Hours: 9-6 Mon-Fri • 10-5 Sat
  • All styles of headwear; quantity. Phone and mail orders accepted. RENTALS CREDIT
  CARDS •

HOBBY SHOPS & SUPPLIERS

See also **DOLLS & DOLLHOUSES**

ACE HOBBIES   212-268-4151
  35 West 31st St., 3rd Fl., (5th-Bway) NYC, NY 10001
  Hours: 10-5:45 Mon-Fri • 10-4:45 Sat.
  • Replica guns, model kits for all kinds of vehicles. •

THE AIRPLANE SHOP   516-742-6949
  PO Box 544, Commack, NY 11725
  Hours: 10-5 Mon-Fri
  • Model airplane supplies; Mail order only. Catalog. •

AMERICA'S HOBBY CENTER / MODAD'S   212-675-8922
  146 West 22nd St., (6th-7th Ave.) NYC, NY 10011
  Hours: 9-5:30 Mon-Fri • 9-3:30 Sat
  • Train and airplane kits, good for model hardware; slow service; catalogs. •

CHARRETTE DRAFTING SUPPLY CORP.   212-683-8822
215 Lexington Ave., (33rd St.) NYC, NY 10016   FAX 212-683-9890
Hours: 8:30-7 Mon-Fri • 10-5 Sat • 12-5 Sun (closed Sun: June, July, Aug)
• Basswood moldings; drafting supplies and equipment. Phone orders will deliver in Manhattan. Will ship anywhere. CREDIT CARDS •

THE COMPLETE STRATEGIST   212-685-3880
11 East 33rd St., (Madison-5th Ave.) NYC, NY 10016
Hours: 10:30-6 Mon-Sat • Thurs till 9

320 West 57th St., (8-9th Ave.) NYC, NY 10019   212-582-1272
Hours: 11-8 Mon-Sat • 12-5 Sun
• Games, miniature figures, soldiers, tanks, military model kits & books on period uniforms. •

DREMEL SERVICE CENTER   414-554-1390
495 21st St., Racine, WI 53401
Hours: 8-4:45 Mon-Fri
• Sales, cleaning and repair of Dremel tools. •

EASTERN MODEL AIRCRAFT   718-768-7960
365 40th St., (3rd-4th Ave.) Brooklyn, NY 11232
Hours: 9-5 Mon-Fri
• Balsa wood and aircraft plywood in 6 sizes, wholesale; flier available. •

ENGINEERING MODEL ASSOCIATES   818-912-7011
1020 S. Wallace Pl., City of Industry, CA 91748
Hours: 7:30-4 Mon-Fri
• Wide selection of plastic industrial model parts for architectural and engineering models. Wholesale and retail. Catalog. $10 minimum. •

HOBBY KING, INC.   718-648-5399
2720 Ave. U, (E.27th) Brooklyn, NY 11229
Hours: 10-9 Mon-Sat • 11-7 Sun
• Trains, cars, dollhouses, arts and crafts. •

JAN'S HOBBY SHOP   212-861-5075
1557 York Ave., (82nd-83rd St.) NYC, NY 10028
Hours: 10-7 Mon-Sat • 12-5 Sun • (closed Sun: July, Aug)
• Good selection of model kits; balsa, some brass. Jan knows what's in stock, is very helpful on the phone. •

K & S ENGINEERING   312-586-8503
6917 W. 59th St., Chicago, IL 60638
Hours: 8:30-5 Mon-Fri
• Brass rod, tubing, angle, channel in 12" lengths; some items in 36" lengths. Tools accessories, catalog; $15 minimum. Phone and mail orders only. •

LIFE-LIKE PRODUCTS, INC.   410-889-1023
1600 Union Ave., Baltimore, MD 21211
Hours: 8:30-5 Mon-Fri
• Lichen, surface texturing materials, trees; various local distributors; catalog. $25 minimum. •

M. H. INDUSTRIES   717-774-7096
PO Box 322, New Cumberland, PA 17070
Hours: 9-5 Tues-Sat
• Basswood stripwood, moldings, dollhouse lumber, model trains and accessories, all gauges. Catalog. Check about minimum. •

G-H

MICROFORM MODELS, INC.   603-883-6673
5 Northern Blvd., #10, Amherst, NH 03031
Hours: 8:30-4:30 Mon-Fri   FAX   603-598-8082
• Cast metal furniture, props, trees, etc., great selection in 1/4", some 1/2" chairs, inexpensive. Phone orders, shipping. Catalog with life-size photos. •

NORTHEASTERN SCALE MODELS, INC.   508-688-6019
PO Box 727, Methuen, MA 01844
Hours: 7:30-4 Mon-Fri
• Precision scale moldings and stripwood in basswood and other hardwoods; samples available. Catalog. •

PEARL PAINT CO., INC.   212-431-7932
308 Canal St., (B'way-Church St.) NYC, NY 10013
Hours: 9-5:30 Mon-Sat • Thurs till 7 • 11-4:45 Sun   FAX   212-431-6798

2411 Hempstesd Tpke., East Meadow, NY 11554   516-731-3700
Hours: 9:30-5:45 Mon-Sat (Wed,Fri till 8:45) • Sun 12-4:45   FAX   516-731-3721
• Basswood, balsa, sculpey, dremel tools, brass: art supplies; Catalog, phone orders over $50;
CREDIT CARDS •   **(mail order)**   800-221-6845

PLASTRUCT   818-912-7036
1020 S. Wallace Place, City of Industry, CA. 91748
Hours: 7:30-4 Mon-Fri   FAX   818-912-7036
• Good selection of model pieces and supplies: 1/2" & 1/4" scale. Catalog. $10 minimum,
$20 minimum on credit cards. 30% professional discount. Same day service on in-stock
items. •

POLYFORM PRODUCTS   708-678-4836
9420 W. Byron St., Schiller Park, IL 60176
Hours: 9-4:30 Mon-Fri
• Sculpey manufacturer. Wholesale and retail. Brochure; $10 minimum. •

THE RED CABOOSE   212-575-0155
16 West 45th St., 4th Fl., (5th-6th Ave.) NYC, NY 10036
Hours: 10-7 Mon-Fri • 10-5:30 Sat
• Brass, simulated surfaces, choppers; train and ship models and accessories. •

RAILROAD WAREHOUSE   908-531-1880
75 Monmouth Rd., Oakhurst, NJ
Hours: By appt.   FAX   908-493-2089
• Custom train makers. •

RUDY'S HOBBY SHOP   718-545-8280
3516 30th Ave., Astoria, NY 11103
Hours: 10:30-6:45 Tues-Fri • 10:30-5:45 Sat
• Great hobby shop. Also carries art supplies. •

SPECIAL SHAPES CO., INC.   312-586-8517
1354 Napierville Dr., PO Box 7487, Romeoville, IL 60441
Hours: 9-4 Mon-Fri
• Brass rod and structural shapes in 3' lengths, brass strips, sheets and miniature screws; 2-3
week delivery. Flier. •

TRAIN WORLD   718-436-7072
751 McDonald Ave., (Ditmas-Cortelyou Rd.) Brooklyn, NY 11218
Hours: 10-6 Mon-Sat
• Large stock of trains and accessories. •

WESTCHESTER HOBBY 914-949-7943
    102 East Post Rd., White Plains, NY 10601
    Hours: 9-5 Mon-Sat • Thurs till 7:45
    • Model trains, cars, ships, airplanes; miniature molding, wallpaper, food, lighting. •

HYDRAULICS & PNEUMATICS

See also **SCENIC SHOPS**
See also **SPECIAL EFFECTS SERVICES**

PAUL HARDMAN MACHINERY CO. 914-664-6220
    621 South Columbus Ave., Mt. Vernon, NY 10550
    Hours: 9-5 Mon-Fri FAX 914-644-6414
    • Suppliers of pneumatic equipment, controls and switches. Very helpful. •

HYDRO/AIR, INC. 201-575-0935
    145 Fairfield Rd., Fairfield, NJ 07004 212-267-4524
    Hours: 8:30-5 Mon-Fri FAX 201-575-0076
    • Wide selection of pneumatic and hydraulic components and systems; technical advice; application assistance. Some switches and controls. $35 minimum. MC/VISA •

NORTHERN HYDRAULICS, INC. 800-533-5545
    PO Box 1499, 801 East Cliff Rd., Burnsville, MN 55337
    Hours: 24 Hours every day (catalog sales) FAX 617-894-0083
    • Pumps, valves, accessories; catalog available. CREDIT CARDS •

G-H

NOTES

G–H

"I found it in the N.Y. Theatrical Sourcebook."

ICE, DRY ICE & FIREWOOD

AA ARMATO & SON   212-737-1742
    1701 Second Ave., (88th St.) NYC, NY 10128
    Hours: 9-6 every day
    • Ice, dry ice, firewood. •

BRUSCA ICE & WOOD   212-744-6986
    2148 Second Ave., (110th St.) NYC, NY 10029
    Hours: 9-5 Mon-Fri
    • Ice, dry ice, firewood. •

CASAMASSIMA & SONS/ DIAMOND ICE CUBE   212-355-3734
    325 West 16th St., (8-9th Ave.) NYC, NY 10011
    Hours: 7-7 Mon-Sat • 8-12 Sun • (8-5 Sun in summer)
    • Ice; block, cube. Call day before for dry ice. Firewood. •

MOUNTAIN ICE CO.   212-397-1500
    443 West 50th St., (9th Ave.) NYC, NY 10019
    234 Coster St., Bronx, NY   718-378-0740
    Hours: day and night deliveries
    • Ice, dry ice, ice sculpture. •

UNITED CITY ICE CUBE CO.   212-563-0819
    503 West 45th St., (10-11th Ave.) NYC, NY 10036
    Hours: 24 hours every day • call first
    • Block, cube, dry ice. •

IRONS & STEAMERS

BERNSTEIN & SONS   212-683-2260
    30 West 29th St., (B'way-6th Ave.) NYC, NY 10001   800-757-7225
    Hours: 9-5:30 Mon-Fri   FAX   212-956-1443
    • Rents and sells Jiffy steamers, hangers, garment bags, rolling racks and display fixtures.
    Free catalog. Will ship. CREDIT CARDS •

HI-STEAM CORP.   201-460-9333
    610 Washington Ave., Carlstadt, NJ 07072
    Hours: 9-5 Mon-Fri   FAX   201-460-3578
    • Dist. for Namoto gravity-feed steam irons; full line of pressing equipment. MC/VISA •

JIFFY STEAMER CO.   901-885-6690
    PO Box 869, 4462 Ken-Tenn Hwy., Union City, TN 38261
    Hours: 8-4 Mon-Fri   FAX   901-885-6692
    • Mfg. garment, hat and wig steamers. MC/VISA •

NEEDLE TRADE SUPPLY / S & K STEAM PRESSING   718-641-6500
    101-10 97th St., Ozone Park, NY 11416
    Hours: 8:30-5 Mon-Fri
    • All types of steam pressing equipment. •

THE SET SHOP　　　　　　　　　　　　　　　　　　　　　212-979-9790
　　37 East 18th St., (Broadway-Park Ave. S.) NYC, NY 10003
　　Hours: 8:30-6 Mon-Fri • 10-4 Sat　　　　　　　　FAX　212-979-9852
　　• Rental and sale of professional-style and compact garment steamers. •

SUSSMAN AUTOMATIC CORP.　　　　　　　　　　　　　　718-937-4500
　　43-20 34th St., (Queens Blvd.-43rd Ave.) L.I.C., NY 11101　800-238-3535
　　Hours: 9-5 Mon-Fri
　　• Formerly Automatic Steam Products Corp.; manufacturer of Sussman irons and steamers;
　　pressing tables. 24 hour delivery service. •

S & G LIMITED　　　　　　　　　　　　　　　　　　　　717-344-4000
　　1321 East Drinker, Dunmore, PA 13512
　　Hours: 8-4:30 Mon-Fri　　　　　　　　　　　　　FAX　717-343-0618
　　• Formerly Supreme Steam Appliance Corp. Sussman products, new and used, some repairs
　　done. MC •

JEWELERS TOOLS & SUPPLIES

See also **METALS & FOILS**
See also **TRIMMINGS: GENERAL**

A.R.E., INC.　　　　　　　　　　　　　　　　　　　　　802-533-7007
　　Box 8, Greensboro Bend, VT 05842
　　Hours: 9-4 Mon-Fri
　　• Jewelers and silversmiths tools; precious metals in sheets, wire and findings. One of the
　　few sources of large metalworking stokes. Catalog $4. No minimum. •

ALBEST STAMPING CORP.　　　　　　　　　　　　　　718-388-6000
　　1 Kent Ave., (N.13-N.14th St.) Brooklyn, NY 11211
　　Hours: 8-5 Mon-Fri
　　• Wholesale metal findings, buckles; minimum order $150. •

ALL CRAFT TOOL & SUPPLY　　　　　　　　　　　　　212-840-1860
　　45 West 46th St., NYC, NY 10036
　　Hours: 8:30-4:30 Mon-Fri
　　• Complete jewelers supply: Tools, metals, wire, wax, findings, buffing supplies, flexible
　　shafts; scales, benders, chemicals, and soldering supplies. $5 catalog, refundable with a $25
　　order. •

E. BUK ANTIQUES & ART　　　　　　　　　　　　　　212-226-6891
　　151 Spring St., 2nd Fl., (W. B'way-Wooster St.) NYC, NY 10012
　　　　　　　　　　　　　　　　　　　　(toll call) 700-SCIENCE
　　Hours: every day by appt.
　　• Antique watchmakers and jewelers tools, equipment and machinery. •
　　(See display ads under PROP RENTAL HOUSES and under ANTIQUES.)

EASTERN FINDINGS CORP.　　　　　　　　　　　　　212-695-6640
　　19 West 34th St., 12th Fl., (5th-6th Ave.) NYC, NY 10001
　　Hours: 9-4 Mon-Fri • (closed for lunch 12:30-1:15)
　　• Jewelry findings, bracelet and necklace chain; check for minimum orders. Catalog. •

EDWIN FREED, INC.   201-420-7800
  150 Bay St., Jersey City, NJ 07302   212-391-2170
  Hours: 9-4 Mon-Fri
  • Jewelers tools and cleaners; jewelry display cases. Catalog. •

GAMPEL SUPPLY CORP.   212-398-9222
  39 West 37th St., (5th-6th Ave.) NYC, NY 10018   212-398-9223
  Hours: 8:30-4 Mon-Fri
  • Pins, clips, beads, wire chenille tools; good assortment. •

GAMZON   212-719-2550
  21 West 46th St., (5th-6th Ave.) NYC, NY 10036
  Hours: 8:30-4:45 Mon-Fri   FAX   212-764-0550
  • Complete jeweler's supply. •

C. R. HILL CO.   313-543-1555
  2734 West 11 Mile Rd., Berkley, MI 48072
  Hours: 9-6 Mon • 9-4 Tues, Thurs, Fri • 9-12 Sat • (closed Sat in summer)
  • Jewelers tools, casting supplies, metal sheet and tubing; catalog. •

HUGO'S JEWELRY SUPPLIES   212-944-8964
  57 West 46th St., 2nd Fl., (5th-6th Ave.) NYC, NY 10036
  Hours: 9-5 Mon-Fri • 10-2 Sat.   FAX   212-768-2189
  • Complete jeweler's supplies. •

ORNAMENTAL RESOURCES, INC.   303-279-2102
  PO Box 3010, 1427 Miner St., Idaho Springs, CO 80452
  Hours: 9-5 Mon-Fri
  • Jewelry findings and supplies, new and antique stones and beads. Costume jewelry. 20
  years in business! Used by many Broadway shows. 350 page catalog: $25; $50 min. order. •

C. S. OSBORNE TOOLS   201-483-3232
  125 Jersey St., Harrison, NJ 07029
  Hours: 8:30-5:30 Mon-Fri
  • Tools for metalwork; catalog. •

T. W. SMITH WELDING SUPPLY   212-247-6323
  545 West 59th St., (10th-11th Ave.) NYC, NY 10019
  Hours: 7:30-4 Mon-Fri • 8-12 Sat (call first)

  885 Meeker Ave., (Bridgewater-Varick) Brooklyn, NY 11222   718-388-7417
  Hours: 7:30-4:30 Mon-Fri • 8-12 Sat (call first)
  • Soldering and welding supplies, propane. •

WELLER SOLDERING EQUIPMENT, DIV. COOPER TOOLS   919-362-7510
  Box 728, Lufkin Rd., Apex, NC 27502
  Hours: 8-4:30 Mon-Fri
  • Soldering tools; catalog. •

JEWELRY

See also **CLOTHING RENTAL & PURCHASE: ANTIQUE & VINTAGE**
See also **ETHNIC GOODS: ALL HEADINGS**
For custom work, see **COSTUME CRAFTSPEOPLE, MASKS, & MILLINERY**

ART & INDUSTRIAL DESIGN SHOP   212-477-8116
399 Lafayette, (4th St.) NYC, NY 10003
Hours: 12-7 Mon-Sat
• 20th Century and Art Deco furniture and furnishings. Collector's jewelry: many pieces by
20th century artists. Also decorative accessories. RENTALS CREDIT CARDS •
(See display ad under antiques: Victorian & 20th Century)

C'EST MAGNIFIQUE   212-475-1613
120 MacDougal St., (3rd-Bleecker St.) NYC, NY 10012
Hours: 10-10 Mon-Fri • 10-midnight Sat
• Gold and diamond jewelry from all over the world; see Alfonso or Alfred. RENTALS
MC/VISA •

EQUIVAQUE   212-302-6490
34 West 38th St., 2nd Fl., (5-6th Ave.) NYC, NY 10018
Hours: 9-6 Mon-Fri
• Modern French and Italian jewelry, wholesale. Call for new address late in 1994. •

THE HAMMER – ROBIN DAVID LUDWIG   212-267-3742
PO Box 651, Knickerbocker Station, NYC, NY 10002 (mailing address)
Hours: 10-7 Mon-Sat. by appt.

Finely detailed hand-wrought jewelry & metal art, from rings to
chalices and coronets. Specializing in highly visible display and
stage wear. Historical accuracy guaranteed. Miniature to full
scale arms and armor. Can create designs or work from yours.
Multiples, rush orders, no problem. Also, miniature scenes and
model railroads.

• Custom jewelry and prop pieces; specializes in historically based art; works with gold, silver,
and brass; also miniature to full scale armor. Portfolio available on request. •

INTERNATIONAL GOLD CORP.   212-688-0005
900 Third Ave., (54th St.) NYC, NY 10022
Hours: 9-5:30 Mon-Fri   FAX   212-371-5466
• Will promote real gold items for film, commercials, and still photography. •

KENJO JEWELERS   212-333-7220
40 West 57th St., (5th-6th Ave.) NYC, NY 10019
Hours: 10-6:15 Mon-Fri • 10-6 Sat
• Rental and sales of jewelry, wedding bands, contemporary watches; pricey; not costume
jewelry. CREDIT CARDS •

LOUIS KIPNIS & SONS, INC.   212-674-7210
252 Broome St., (Ludlow-Orchard St.) NYC, NY 10002   212-674-0397
Hours: 10-4 Sun-Fri   FAX   212-674-0345
• Costume jewelry, hair accessories; also novelties. No credit cards. •

LA BELLE EPOCH   212-489-8683
1515 Broadway, Rm.1011, (51st St.) NYC, NY 10019
Hours: By appt. only.
• Reproduction jewelry. Mail order available. RENTALS •

HARRICE MILLER   212-532-1394
   300 East 33rd St., #11J, (1st-2nd Ave.) NYC, NY 10016
   Hours: by appt.
   • Collection of 1920's-1970's vintage costume jewelry. Consultant/expert in costume
   jewelry. •

ORNAMENTAL RESOURCES,, INC.   303-279-2102
   PO Box 3010, 1427 Miner St., Idaho Springs, Co 80452
   Hours: 9-5 Mon-Fri
   • Jewelry findings and supplies; costume jewelry, new & antique, stones & beads. Broadway
   credits. 350 page catalog $25.00; $50 minimum order. •

RINGS BY MARTY
F.W. WOOLWORTH CO.   212-563-3523
   120 West 34th St., (6-7th Ave.) NYC, NY 10001
   Hours: 10-5:30 every day • Mon, Thurs, Fri till 7:30
   • Located in Woolworth's. A good selection of men's and women's rings. Friendly service and
   good prices. CREDIT CARDS. •

SENTIMENTO, INC.   212-245-3111
   14 West 55th St., (5-6th Ave.) NYC, NY 10019
   Hours: 9:30-6 Mon-Fri   FAX   212-246-7415
   • Rent and sell (wholesale) desk accessories, luggage, and various small decorative items and
   jewelry; some antique and vintage. Sorry, no credit cards. •

SHOP OF BEADS & STONES   212-529-8426
   179 Orchard St., (Houston-Stanton St.) NYC, NY 10002
   Hours: 10-5:30 every day
   • Discount costume jewelry; see Peter Tsao. No credit cards. •

SHOWROOM SEVEN   212-840-7277
   241 West 37th St., (7-8th Ave.) NYC, NY 10018
   Hours: 9-6 Mon-Fri   FAX   212-768-2224
   • Extensive selection of designer jewelry and fashions; shoes, handbags, hats, gloves, belts
   and scarves. List of designers they carry available upon request. No credit cards. •

LARRY VRBA, INC.   212-475-3196
   25 Fifth Ave., Rm. 7G, (9th St.) NYC, NY 10003
   Hours: by appt.
   • Custom made jewelry for the theatre or fashion. No credit cards. •

NOTES

"I found it in the N.Y. Theatrical Sourcebook."

KEYS & LOCKSMITHS

ABBEY LOCKSMITHS   212-535-2289
    1558 Second Ave., (81st St.) NYC, NY 10028
    Hours: 7-6 Mon-Fri • 8-5 Sat
    • Antique keys, locksmiths. •

CHARLES LOCKSMITH, INC.   212-879-2740
    1368 Third Ave., (77-78th St.) NYC, NY 10021
    Hours: 8-6 Mon-Sat • 24 hr. emergency service
    • Large selection of antique keys and locks, rental or purchase. Hard-to-find keys and locks
for antique furniture. •

COHEN COOLING & SECURITY   212-722-7953
    1727 Second Ave., #3RS, (89th St.) NYC, NY 10028   212-410-6107
    Hours: 24 hours every day
    • Locks repaired and installed, security systems, fire alarms. Refrigeration, AC, heating, venti-
lating, air compressors and mechanical systems serviced and maintained. Contact Mitch
Cohen. •

FOX POLICE LOCK CO.   212-924-0211
    46 West 21st St., (5-6th Ave.) NYC, NY 10010
    Hours: 9-12 Mon-Fri
    • Wholesale Fox locks; no installation. •

K-L

KITCHEN EQUIPMENT: HOUSEHOLD

See also **APPLIANCES: ELECTRICAL & GAS**
For oriental cooking supplies, see **ETHNIC GOODS: ORIENTAL**

BOWL & BOARD   212-673-1724
    9 St. Marks Place, (2nd-3rd Ave.) NYC, NY 10003
    Hours: 11-7 every day
    • Wooden items: bowls, boards, furniture, etc. MC/VISA •

BRIDGE KITCHENWARE   212-688-4220
    214 East 52nd St., (2nd-3rd Ave.) NYC, NY 10022
    Hours: 9-5:30 Mon-Fri • 10-4:30 Sat   FAX 212-758-5387
    • Large selection of professional cookware, bakeware, cutlery and utensils. MC/VISA •

BROADWAY BAZAAR   212-873-9153
    2025 Broadway, (69th St.) NYC, NY 10023

    Second Avenue Bazaar   212-683-2293
    501 Second Ave., (28th St.) NYC, NY 10016

    Third Avenue Bazaar   212-861-5999
    125 West 3rd St., (6th Ave.) NYC, NY 10012

    West Third Street Bazaar,   212-673-4138
    125 West 3rd St., (6th Ave.) NYC, NY 10012
    Hours: 10-6:30 Mon-Sat • 11-5:45 Sun
    • Modern kitchenware, furniture, lamps, picture frames, accessories. No rentals. CREDIT
CARDS •

BROADWAY PANHANDLER
212-966-3434
520 Broadway, (Spring St.) NYC, NY 10012
Hours: 10:30-6 Mon-Fri • 11-6 Sat • 12-6 Sun
• Kitchen equipment and utensils, cake decorating supplies, mugs, etc. No rentals. •

CENTRAL PROPS OF 49TH STREET
212-265-7767
514 West 49th St., (10th Ave.) NYC, NY 10019
Hours: 8-5 Mon-Fri
FAX   212-582-3746

Large selection of furniture, accessories and housewares
from every period. Including fine china, crystal, crockery,
tableware, serving pieces and much more!

• Full service prop rental house. •
(See display ad under PROP RENTAL HOUSES.)

THE CHOCOLATE GALLERY
212-675-CAKE
34 West 22nd St., (5-6th Ave) NYC, NY 10010
Hours: 10-6 Mon-Sat • additional class hours
FAX   212-675-2545
• All kinds of cake decorating supplies. Specialty pans, novelty cake decor and items for the
professional. Wilton dealer. Cake decorating classes. CREDIT CARDS. •

DEAN & DELUCA
212-431-1691
560 Broadway, (Spring-Prince St.) NYC, NY 10012
Hours: 8-8 Mon-Sat • 9-7 Sun
FAX   212-334-6183
• Gourmet supermarket with a large kitchenware department; unique selection of tabletop
and cooking items. CREDIT CARDS. •

FORZANO ITALIAN IMPORTS, INC.
212-925-2525
128 Mulberry St., (Hester-Grand St.) NYC, NY 10013
Hours: 10-10 every day
FAX   212-334-6719
• Italian; everything for the kitchen. RENTALS CREDIT CARDS. •

GRACIOUS HOME
212-517-6300
1220 Third Ave., (70th-71st St.) NYC, NY 10021
Hours: 9-7 Mon-Sat • 10:30-5:30 Sun
• Large selection of housewares, hardware and small appliances. CREDIT CARDS. •

LECHTER'S HOUSEWARES AND GIFTS
212-956-7290
57th St. & Broadway, NYC, NY 10107
Hours: 10-9:30 Mon-Fri • 9-7 Sat • 11-7 Sun

10 West 34th St., (Empire St. Bldg.) NYC, NY 10118
212-564-3226
Hours: 8-9 Mon-Fri • 9-9 Sat • 11-6 Sun

1504 Third Ave., (85th St.) NYC, NY 10028
212-988-3730
Hours: 10-9 Mon-Sat • 11-7 Sun

60 East 42nd St., (Grand Central) NYC, NY 10165
212-682-8476
Hours: 8-8 Mon-Fri • 9-7 Sat

18th St., & First Ave., NYC, NY 10009
212-677-6481
Hours: 9-8 Mon-Fri • 10-7 Sat • 11-6 Sun

• Larger versions of the chain of housewares stores; good selection of no-frills items, including kitchenware, storage and bath. CREDIT CARDS •

"I found it in the N.Y. Theatrical Sourcebook."

PLATYPUS   212-219-3919
  126 Spring St., (Wooster St.) NYC, NY   10012
  Hours: 11-6 Mon-Sat • 12-6 Sun
    • Unique china selection as well as coffee and tea related items. RENTALS CREDIT CARDS •

POTTERY BARN   212-206-8118
  231 Tenth Ave., (24th St.) NYC, NY 10011 (main store)
  Hours: 11-6 Mon-Fri • 11-5 Sat • 12-5 Sun

  51 Greenwich Ave., (6-7th St.) NYC, NY 10014   212-807-6321
  Hours: 11-8 Mon-Sat • 12-5 Sun

  250 West 57th St., (8th Ave.) NYC, NY 10019   212-315-1855
  Hours: 10-8 Mon-Fri • 10-7 Sat • 12-6 Sun

  117 East 59th St., (Lexington-Park) NYC, NY 10022   212-753-5424
  Hours: 10-6:30 Mon-Sat (Thurs till 8) • 12-6 Sun

  2109 Broadway, (73-74th St.) NYC, NY 10023   212-595-5573
  Hours: 10-8 Mon-Fri • 10-7 Sat • 12-6 Sun

    • The Tenth Ave. Store is the "outlet" for Pottery Barn, William-Sonoma and Holds Everything.
  Good selection of contemporary china, glassware, decorative accessories and cookware; also
  some housewares, rugs, frames and furnishings. Check other Manhattan locations. Catalog.
  CREDIT CARDS •

PROPS FOR TODAY   212-206-0330
  121 West 19th St. Reception: 3rd Fl., (6th-7th Ave.) NYC, NY 10011
  Hours: 8:30-5 Mon-Fri   FAX 212-924-0450

Come to us first and we'll work with your budget!
• New York's LARGEST selection of kitchen and dining
  furniture, housewares and accessories.
• All periods of china, glass, crockery, kitchen
  appliances, bowls, trays, housewares, tableware,
  furniture, silver, flatware, linens, etc.
NOW ON 3 FLOORS! ONE STOP PROPPING!

    • Full service prop rental house. Some vintage appliances and equipment. Phone orders
  accepted. •
  (See display ad under PROP RENTAL HOUSES.)

RENT-A-THING   914-628-9298
  Rt. 6, Baldwin Place, NY 10505   800-287-9298
  Hours: 24 hrs., leave message, will return call
    • Vintage kitchen & household items. Antique stoves. 24 hour service; pick-up and delivery
  available. RENTALS •

RICK & CO.   212-242-1681
  30 Greenwich Ave., (10th- Charles St.) NYC, NY 10014
  Hours: 10:30-7 Mon-Sat • 12-6 Sun (closes at 5 in summer)
    • Good selection of housewares, some general hardware. Also carries a nice selection of
  vinyl contact papers. CREDIT CARDS. •

RIVERSIDE HOUSEWARES, INC.   212-873-7837
  2315 Broadway, (83rd St.) NYC, NY 10024
  Hours: 9-6:30 Mon-Fri • 9-6 Sat •12-5 Sun   FAX   212-721-7611
    • Great selection of housewares, small appliances; a few antiques. Repair service. RENTALS
  CREDIT CARDS. •

WILLIAMS–SONOMA   212-633-2203
    110 Seventh Ave., (16th-17th St.) NYC, NY 10011
    Hours: 10-7 Mon-Fri • 11-6 Sat • 12-5 Sun
        • Terrific kitchenware store with a large selection of cookware, utensils and unusual items.
    Also some china and glassware. Catalog. RENTALS CREDIT CARDS •

WOLFMAN–GOLD & GOOD   212-431-1888
    116 Greene St., (Spring-Prince St.) NYC, NY 10012
    Hours: 11-6 Mon-Sat • 12-5 Sun   FAX 212-226-4955
        • Stylish & beautiful antique and new linens; also cookie cutters, tureens, birdhouses, lace
    panels, etc. Mostly in white and off white. RENTALS •

ZABAR'S MEZZANINE   212-787-2000
    2245 Broadway, (80th St.) NYC, NY 10024
    Hours: 9-6 every day   FAX 212-580-4477
        • Extensive selection kitchen equipment, pots, pans, utensils, small electrical appliances, etc.;
    very reasonable. Outfitters for the home chef. American & European items. CREDIT CARDS •

KITCHEN EQUIPMENT: INDUSTRIAL

See also **FURNITURE RENTAL & PURCHASE: RESTAURANT**
See also **APPLIANCES: ELECTRICAL & GAS**

BALTER SALES   212-674-2960
    209 Bowery, (Rivington St.) NYC, NY 10002
    Hours: 8:30-4:30 Mon-Fri   FAX 212-460-5269
        • Wholesaler of restaurant china and glassware. •

BARI RESTAURANT EQUIPMENT   212-925-3786
    240 Bowery, (Houston-Prince St.) NYC, NY 10012
    Hours: 9-5 Mon-Fri • 9-3 Sat   FAX 212-941-7054
        • Big selection used and new appliances, furnishings. RENTALS •

BRIDGE KITCHENWARE   212-688-4220
    214 East 52nd St., (2nd-3rd Ave.) NYC, NY 10022
    Hours: 9-5:30 Mon-Fri • 10-4:30 Sat   FAX 212-758-5387
        • Large selection of professional cookware, bakeware, cutlery and utensils. VISA •

CHEF RESTAURANT SUPPLIES   212-254-6644
    294-296 Bowery, (Houston St.) NYC, NY 10012   212-254-6714
    Hours: 9-5:30 Mon-Sat • 11-5 Sun   FAX 212-353-0841
        • Restaurant supplies, glassware and dishes, and woks. MC/VISA •

DAROMA RESTAURANT EQUIPMENT CORP.   212-226-6805
    196 Bowery, (Spring St.) NYC, NY 10012
    Hours: 9-5 Mon-Fri • 9-3 Sat   FAX 212-979-1335
        • Large and small appliances and restaurant supplies including Metro shelving. Rentals avail-
    able, certified check required. Credit card purchases on smaller items. •

KABRAM & SONS,, INC.   212-477-1480
    257 Bowery, (Prince-Houston St.) NYC, NY 10002
    Hours: 8-4:30 Mon-Fri
        • Good selection of large restaurant appliances, furniture and dressing for rental. They have
    been renting to the business since the 1950s. An interesting collection. •
    (See display ad in this section.)

K-L

PARAGON RESTAURANT WORLD   212-226-0954
  250 Bowery, (Prince-Houston St.) NYC, NY 10012
  Hours: 8-4:30 Mon-Fri • 9-3 Sat (closed Sat in summer)   FAX   212-219-8213
  • Restaurant supplies including dishes, utensils, paper goods, dispensers, condiments, signs
  and those great little drink umbrellas. Walk-in retail. •

REGENCY SERVICE CARTS   718-855-8304
  337-361 Carroll St., (Hoyt-Bond St.) Brooklyn, NY 11231
  Hours: 7-5 Mon-Fri   FAX   212-834-8507
  • Silver plated domes and desert carts, room service carts, holloware; catalog. Ask for Jack
  Abbate. RENTALS •

RESNICK–RITE EQUIPMENT, INC.   718-292-1800
  560 Concord Ave., Bronx, NY 10455
  Hours: 7-5 Mon-Fri • 8-12 Sat • 24 hr. phone service   (call first) FAX   718-292-1824

  PO Box Q, Mountaindale, NY 12763   914-434-8200
  Hours: 6-4:30-Mon-Fri • 7-12 Sat • Sun by appt.
  • Supermarket, restaurant, janitorial equipment and supplies, including refrigerated cases.
  Signage and decorations. Delivery available. RENTALS MC/VISA •

SANG KUNG KITCHEN SUPPLIES, DIST.   212-925-3059
  108-110 Bowery, (Grand-Hester St.) NYC, NY 10013   212-226-4527
  Hours: 9-5:30 Mon-Sat
  • Reasonably priced Chinese restaurant supplies. •

K-L

• •

Largest selection of slicing machines and cash registers -- from antique to new.

Also scales, mixers, and grinders.

We specialize in helpful service.

WE LOVE TO RENT
REASONABLE RATES

• •

William Steinberg
266 Bowery, NYC 10012
(212) 473-7670
(718) 657-5177

WILLIAM STEINBERG
212-473-7670
718-657-5177
266 Bowery, (Prince-Houston St.) NYC, NY 10012
Hours: 8:30-5 Mon-Fri
• Large selection of slicing machines and cash registers from antique to new. Also scales, mixers and grinders. •
(See display ad in this section.)

TRIBORO SODA FOUNTAIN & REFRIGERATION SERVICE
718-756-1400
PO Box 112, 431 Lincoln Rd., Brooklyn, NY 11225
Hours: 8-5 Mon-Fri
FAX 718-967-6969
• Carries soda fountain and bar dispensing equipment, portable bar units available; speak to Bob Golden. RENTALS •

SAMUEL UNDERBERG, INC.
718-638-4171
620 Atlantic Ave., (5th Ave.) Brooklyn, NY 11217
Hours: 8-4 Mon-Fri
FAX 718-398-4194
• Complete supplies for food stores. Shopping carts, scales, baskets, platters, utensils and knives, pans and trays, price markers, paper cutters, plastic dividers for deli cases, blackboards and numbered ticket dispensers. RENTALS •

THE WAREHOUSE STORE FIXTURE CO.
203-575-0111
249 Thompson Ave., Waterbury, CT 06702
Hours: 8-6 Mon-Fri • 8-5 Sat
FAX 203-575-9140
• Immense stock of store and kitchen fixtures for rental or purchase. CREDIT CARDS •

K-L

NOTES

NOTES

"I found it in the N.Y. Theatrical Sourcebook."

LABELS, WOVEN & PRINTED

AUBURN LABEL & TAG CO. 212-244-4363
10 West 33rd St., Rm. 1222, (5th Ave-B'way) NYC, NY 10001
Hours: 9-5 Mon-Fri FAX 212-244-4397
• 1000 woven labels per roll, 5000 label minimum. •

PAXAR 717-297-5250
PO Box 279, Troy, PA 16947
Hours: 8-5:30 Mon-Fri FAX 717-297-3447
• Formerly American Silk Label. Woven and printed labels. •

SUPREME LABEL CORP 212-255-2090
109 West 27th St., (6-7th Ave.) NYC, NY 10001 800-233-6411
Hours: 8-4 Mon-Thurs • 7:30-12 Fri FAX 212-675-5241
• Printed and woven labels. •

TREO LABEL CO., INC. 718-384-3300
808 Driggs Ave., (S. 4th St.) Brooklyn, NY 11228
Hours: 9-5 Mon-Fri FAX 718-384-3646
• Woven labels. •

LADDERS, LIFTS & SCAFFOLDING

INDUSTRIAL SUPPLY OF LONG ISLAND, INC. 718-784-1291
47-30 Vernon Blvd., (47-48th Ave.) L.I.C., NY 11101
Hours: 7-5:30 Mon-Fri • FAX 718-482-9353
• Ladders and scaffolding, rigging and welding supplies, tools, hardware, etc. •
(See display ad under THEATRICAL HARDWARE & RIGGING EQUIPMENT.)

MANHATTAN LADDER CO., INC. 718-721-3352
31-15 14th St. , (31st Rd.) L.I.C., NY 11106
Hours: 6:30-3 Mon-Fri FAX 718-278-3017
• Sales and rental of wood and aluminum ladders; delivery. •

PUTNAM ROLLING LADDER, INC. 212-226-5147
32 Howard St., (B'way-Lafayette) NYC, NY 10013
Hours: 8-4:30 Mon-Fri FAX 212-941-1836
• All types of ladders-amazing selection in catalog; custom work. •
(See display ad in the section)

SAFWAY STEEL PRODUCTS 718-383-8400
370 Greenpoint Ave., (N. Henry-Russell) Brooklyn, NY 11222
Hours: 8:30-4:30 Mon-Fri FAX 718-383-8778
• Bleachers and scaffolding; sales and rental. •

YORK LADDER, INC. 718-784-6666
37-20 Twelfth St., (38th Ave.) L.I.C., NY 11101
Hours: 7-4:30 Mon-Fri FAX 718-582-9016
• All types ladders, scaffolding, suspended systems. Catalog. RENTALS MC/VISA •

K-L

PUTNAM LADDERS

Since 1905. All types of ladders.
Famous for custom-made oak ladders
for homes, lofts, stores, home libraries.
wine cellars, etc. Other woods (e.g. ash,
birch, cherry, maple, Honduras
mahogany) and finishes available.
Track and hardware in black, brass
plated or chrome plated. Also available:
step ladders, straight ladders, extension
ladders, steel warehouse ladders,
scaffolding, stools, etc. We well wood,
aluminum and fiberglass ladders. We
have thirteen (13) grades of wooden
stepladders alone.

Putnam Rolling Ladder Co. Inc.
32 Howard St.
New York, NY 10013
212-226-5147
212-941-1836 (FAX)

LAMINATES

See also **LUMBER**

ADMIRAL ENGRAVING & ETCHING, LTD.   212-924-3400
555 West 25th St., (10-11th) NYC, NY 10001
Hours: 9-5 Mon-Fri   FAX   212-924-3589
• Name tags, trophies and awards, silver items; engraving, printing, signs and lamination;
broad spectrum of services •

IDESCO CORP.   212-889-2530
37 West 26th St., (5-6th Ave.) NYC, NY 10010
Hours: 9-5 Mon-Fri
• All kinds of laminating, fast service. $75 min. on shipped items. CREDIT CARDS •

L.I. LAMINATES   516-434-3210
35 Engineers Rd., Happauge, NY 11788   (outside NY) 800-221-5454
Hours: 9-4:45 Mon-Fri   FAX   516-434-3115
• Water based non-toxic finishing products. Pre-curved plywood, Pionate dealer. •

LAMINEX-CRAFT.   212-751-6143
866 U.N. Plaza, 49th St., Lobby, (1st-East River) NYC, NY 10017
Hours: 9-5 Mon-Fri
• Laminating specialists, signs. •

LAMINOLOGY　　　　　　　　　　　　　　　　　　212-505-2280
37 East 18th St., (B'way-Park Ave. S.) NYC, NY 10003
Hours: 9-6 Mon-Fri　　　　　　　　　　　　FAX　212-979-9852
• Portfolio, transparency, photo, menu & I.D. lamination. CREDIT CARDS •

LeNOBLE LUMBER CO., INC.　　　　　　　　　　　212-246-0150
525 West 52nd St., (10-11th Ave.) NYC, NY 10019
Hours: 8-5 Mon-Fri • (closed for lunch 12-1)
• Doors, plywood, formica, moldings, masonite, millwork, windows, sonotube. Cutting 1-3:30 pm. Delivery. Cash, certified check or accounts only. •

MANHATTAN LAMINATES LTD.　　　　　　　　　　212-255-2522
528 West 21st St., (10-11th Ave.) NYC, NY 10011
Hours: 7:30-5:30 Mon-Fri　　　　　　　　　FAX　212-255-4670
• Large selection. Will deliver. Metal laminate: formica, MDF, foamcore, plywood, tools, glue, hardware. •

MIDTOWN LUMBER　　　　　　　　　　　　　　　212-675-2230
276 West 25th St., (7-8th Ave.) NYC, NY 10001
Hours: 8-4:30 Mon-Fri • 9-2 Sat (Sept-May)
• Good selection of formica and other laminates; moldings, hardwood flooring, tileboard, glass block, hardware and lumber cut to size. Contact Mike. •

NEW YORK METAL MOULDING CO., INC.　　　　　718-726-8000
19-22 45th St., (19th) Astoria, NY 11105　　　718-956-5600
Hours: 8-5 Mon-Fri　　　　　　　　　　　FAX　718-956-1009
• Stocks Wilsonart brand decorative laminate and tambours; warehouse and executive office here. $50 minimum delivery. •

PLASTI-CRAFT PRODUCT CORP.　　　　　　　　　914-358-3490
164 West Nyack Rd., Nyack, NY 10994
Hours: 8-5 Mon-Fri　　　　　　　　　　　FAX　914-358-3007
• Plastic sheet, rod & tubes; adhesives; laminates. •

LAMP SHADES & PARTS

See also **LIGHTING FIXTURES**

BRADFORD CONSULTANTS　　　　　　　　　　　510-523-1968
PO Box 4020, Alameda, CA 94501
Hours: 9-5 Mon-Fri
• Reproduction period light bulbs; brochure available. •

CITY KNICKERBOCKER　　　　　　　　　　　　212-586-3939
781 Eights Ave., (47-48th St.) NYC, NY 10036
Hours: 8-4:30 Mon-Fri　　　　　　　　　　FAX　212-262-2889
• Convenient midtown location; the best stop for rental of antique and some contemporary lighting fixtures and shades. Nice people, see Ken or Scott •

CLASSIC ACCENTS　　　　　　　　　　　　　　313-282-5525
PO Box 1181, Southgate, MI 48195
Hours: 9-5 Mon-Sat
• Picture lights, pushbutton light switches, cover plates, molding hooks. Catalog. •

K-L

GRAND BRASS LAMP PARTS 212-226-2567
221 Grand St., (Elizabeth) NYC, NY 10013
Hours: 8-5 Tues-Sat • Thurs till 8
• Lamp bases, globes, chimneys, metal shades, lamp hardware. •

JUST BULBS 212-228-7820
938 Broadway, (22nd St) NYC, NY 10010
Hours: 9-6 Mon-Fri
• Any light bulb available, including novelty string lights; expect to pay full retail. •

JUST SHADES 212-966-2757
21 Spring St., (Elizabeth) NYC, NY 10012
Hours: 9:30-4 Thurs-Tues
• Fabric lampshades in silk and parchment; stock and custom. Remember, not open Wednesday! •

LOUIS MATTIA 212-753-2176
980 Second Ave., (52nd Street) NYC, NY 10022
Hours: 9-6 Mon-Fri
• Antique lamps, lighting fixtures and shades; some custom work; RENTALS •

NOWELL'S VICTORIAN LIGHTING 415-332-4933
PO Box 295, 490 Gate Five Rd., Sausalito, CA 94966
Hours: 9:30-6 Mon-Sat
• Repro and antique Victorian and Edwardian fixtures and shades; custom work; catalog $5. •

ORIENTAL LAMP SHADE CO., INC. 212-832-8190
816 Lexington Ave., (62-63rd Street) NYC, NY 10021 212-873-0812
Hours: 10-6 Mon-Sat
• Good selection of stock shades; custom work available. •

ROSETTA ELECTRICAL CO., INC. 212-233-9088
73 Murray St., (Greenwich St.-W.B'way) NYC, NY 10007   FAX   212-385-4151

21 West 46th St., (5-6th Ave.) NYC, NY 10036   212-719-4381
Hours: 8:30-5:30 • 9:30-4:30 Sat   FAX   212-768-3120
• Contemporary fixtures, lamps, electrical supplies, lamp parts. MC/VISA •

ROY ELECTRIC CO., INC. -718-434-7002
1054 Coney Island Ave., (Foster) Brooklyn, NY 11230   800-366-3347
Hours: 10-5 Mon-Sat   FAX   718-421-4678
• Stock and custom lighting fixtures; antique and reproduction chandeliers, sconces, pendants; replacement glass shades and globes. Repairs made; lighting catalog $5. •

SANELLE WOOD PRODUCTS CORP. 201-863-8002
315 East 86th St., (1-2nd Ave.) NYC, NY 10028
Hours: 8-4:15 Mon-Fri
• Lamp bases and parts custom made; wholesale only; salesman will visit you. •

WEISS & BIHELLER 212-979-6990
116 East 16th St., (Park-Irving Pl.) NYC, NY 10003
Hours: 9-5 Mon-Fri
• Large stock of chandeliers, sconces, lamp parts; also crystal trimmings. •

K-L

LEATHER & FUR

For fake fur, see **FABRICS: FUR & PILE**

ATLAS LEATHER CO　212-736-7044
　352 7th Ave., 4th Fl., (29-30th St.) NYC, NY 10001
　Hours: 9-5 Mon-Fri　FAX　212-736-7045
　• Leather; surplus and job lots. •

DIAMOND KAMVAKIS　212-736-1924
　165 West 29th St., (6-7th Ave.) NYC, NY 10001
　Hours: 9-5 Mon-Fri　FAX　212-967-8554
　• Furs and skins. •

FABULOUS FURS　800-848-4650
　700 Madison Ave., Covington, KY 41011
　...the luxurious alternative to animal fur.
• Specializing in the finest fur-like fabrics
• New Fabu-Leather - washable, breathes, has stretch & recovery
• Classic Fur coats, jackets & accessory patterns
• Notions & findings for sewing with man made furs
• Volume discount; immediate shipment

　Hours: 9-5 Mon-Fri　FAX　606-291-9687
　• Full line of fur fabrics, patterns, fur coat kits, sewing notions; also instructional books and videos. Phone orders. CREDIT CARDS •

LEATHERS & JOCOBS CORP.　212-683-7460
　10 East 33rd St., 9th Fl., (5th-Madison) NYC, NY 10001
　Hours: 9-5 Mon-Fri　FAX　212-683-7462
　• Suede, cabretta, cowhide, pigskin; dyed: catalog. •

LEATHERSALES/MINERVA LEATHER　212-925-6270
　78 Spring St., (Lafayette-B'way) NYC, NY 10012　212-925-6271
　Hours: 9:30-4:30 Mon-Wed • 9-5 Thurs • 9-2 Fri
　• Garment and upholstery leather, suede, and cowhide

·RENAR LEATHER CO.　212-349-2075
　68 Spring St., (Lafayette) NYC, NY 10012
　Hours: 8:30-5 Mon-Fri • call for summer hours
　• Chamois, shoe, garment, novelty leathers. •

SIGMA-STEINBERG　203-775-8500
　50 Pocono Rd., Brookfield, CT 06804
　Hours: 8:30-5 Mon-Fri
　• Leather; wholesale only. •

SEYMOUR WINIK, INC.　914-764-4246
　96 Horseshoe Hill Rd., Pound Ridge, NY 10576
　Hours: 9:30-4 Mon-Fri　FAX　914-764-0355
　• Good furs, Icelandic sheepskins, beaver skins. •

LEATHERCRAFTERS & FURRIERS TOOLS & SUPPLIES

See also **NOTIONS: BUCKLES, BUTTONS, GROMMETS, ETC.**

A & B LEATHER & FINDINGS CO.   212-265-8124
769 Tenth Ave., (52nd St.) NYC, NY 10019
Hours: 6-2 :30 Mon-Fri
• Barge, Magix, Fiebings, shoe rubber, rawhide lacing, glovers and lacing needles. •

ALBEST STAMPING CORP.   718-388-6000
1 Kent Ave., (N.13-N.14th St.) Brooklyn, NY 11211
Hours: 8-5 Mon-Fri
• Wholesale metal buckles, hardware for leather work; minimum order $150. •

AMITY FINDINGS   718-335-1222
5905 39th Ave., Woodside, NY 11377
Hours: 9-4:30 Mon-Fri • call first
• Leather supplies, Magix, etc. Wholesale only, will ship. Some catalogs available. •

SAMUEL BAUER & SONS, INC.   212-868-4190
135 West 29th St., (6-7th Ave.) NYC, NY 10001
Hours: 9-5 Mon-Fri
• Furriers supplies; dyes for fur. •

FIEBING COMPANY, INC.   414-271-5011
PO Box 04125, Milwaukee, WI 53204
Hours: 7:30-4:15 Mon-Fri
• Manufacturer of the popular leather dyes; chart of products available. •

FURS AND MORE   517-835-8415
3815 Greenbrier, Midland, MI 48642
Hours: By appt.
• Computer designed fur patterns. Book available. Furriers tools and supplies on a limited basis. Will assist in locating sources. •

JOSEPH M. HART & SONS   516-567-7722
365 Central Ave., Bohemia, NY 11716
Hours: 9-5 Mon-Fri   FAX   516-567-7809
• Grommets, studs, and boot hooks. •

KAUFMAN   212-777-1700
346 Lafayette St., (Houston-Bleeker) NYC, NY 10012
Hours: 6:30-2 Mon-Fri
• Barge, Magix, dyes, skins, shoe rubber and lacing. •

NATIONAL LEATHER & SHOE FINDINGS CO.   718-797-3434
617 Sackett St., (3-4th Ave.) Brooklyn, NY 11271
Hours: 7-4 Mon-Fri
• Good stock Magix, leather dyes, shoe rubber and lacing; phone in orders and pickup. •

OHIO TRAVEL BAG   216-621-5963
811 Prospect Ave., Cleveland, OH 44113
Hours: 8-5:30 Mon-Fri
• Wholesale buckles and hardware for leatherwork; catalog. •

C.S. OSBORNE TOOLS   718-768-0300
   125 Jersey St., Harrison, NJ 07029
   Hours: 8:30-5 Mon-Fri
   • Leather dyes, leather needles, etc. •

VETERAN LEATHER CO.   718-768-0300
   204 25th St., (4th Ave.) Brooklyn, NY 11232
   Hours: 8-4:30 Mon-Fri
   • Skins, tools, leather dyes and needles. Catalog available. •

LIGHTING & PROJECTION EQUIPMENT

ACE PROPS   212-206-1475
   1 West 19th St., Ground Fl., (5th) NYC, NY 10011   212-580-9551
   Hours: 8-5 Mon-Fri • 9-4 Sat • or by appt.   FAX 212-929-9082
   • Battery belts and lights, all types of film and TV lighting equipment; also film, slide and video projection equipment. Dealer for Anton Bauer, Perrott & Cine 60 batteries; Lowell, LTM, Cool-Lux & Desisti lighting, etc. Also produces industrials and special events. MC/VISA •
   (See display ad in this section.)

ALTMAN STAGE LIGHTING, INC.   914-476-7987
   57 Alexander St., Yonkers, NY 10701   212-569-7777
   Hours: 8:30-5 Mon-Fri   FAX 914-963-7304
   • Mfg. of theatre, film and TV luminaires; sales and rentals. Catalog. •

ASSOCIATES & FERREN   516-537-7800
   Wainscott NW Rd., Wainscott, NY 11975
   Hours: 8-6 Mon-Fri   FAX 516-537-4343
   • Standard front and rear process projection equipment. Also design atmospherics, pyrotechnics, motion control, projection and video effects for stage and screen. •

AUDIO VISUAL PROMOTION AIDS, INC.   212-477-5540
   611 Broadway, #618, (Houston-B'way) NYC, NY 10012
   Hours: 10-6 Mon-Fri   FAX 212-460-9947
   • Sales of AV equipment: screens, projectors, equipment and supplies; Chaos Audio Intercom Systems, (headsets). RENTALS •

BARBIZON   212-586-1620
   426 West 55th St., (9-10th) NYC, NY 10019
   Hours: 8:30-5:30 Mon-Fri • 9-1 Sat   FAX 212-247-8818

   3 Draper St, Woburn, MA 01801   617-935-3920
   Hours: 8:30-5:30 Mon-Fri • 9-2 Sat   FAX 617-935-9273

   6437G General Green Way, Alexandria, VA 22312   703-750-3900
   Hours: 8:30-5:30 Mon-Fri • 9-1 Sat   FAX 703-750-1448

   2401 Mercer Ave., W. Palm Beach, Fl 33401   407-833-2020
   Hours: 8:30-5:30 Mon-Fri • 9-1 Sat   FAX 407-833-3582

   101 Krog St., Atlanta, GA 30307   404-681-5124
   Hours: 8:30-5:30 Mon-Fri • 9-1 Sat   FAX 404-681-5315
   • Theatrical lighting supplier; GE, Sylvania, HMI lamps, etc. MC/VISA •

K-L

K–L

BASH THEATRICAL LIGHTING, INC.
3401 Dell Ave., North Bergen, NJ 07047

212-279-9265
201-863-3300
FAX   201-863-6364

4215 Southwest 34th St., Orlando, Fl. 32811

407-246-7071
FAX   407-246-8077

5277 Cameron #160, Las Vegas, NV 89118

702-367-2274

Sales, Rentals, Consultations, Installations, and Service.
Suppliers for Broadway, Touring, Industrials, Ballets,
Operas, Television, and Film.

National Coverage
•
Regional Service

Hours: 9-5 Mon-Fri • 10-1 Sat (closed Sat: June, July & Aug)   FAX   702-367-0115
• A large company now inclusive of American Theatrical. Rentals, sales, and service of lighting equipment and controls. Comprehensive catalog of theatrical lighting and supplies is available. CREDIT CARDS. •

BESTEK LIGHTING AND STAGING
218 W. Hoffman Ave., Lindenhurst, NY 11757
Hours: 9-5 Mon-Fri
• Equipment sales and rentals, design and installation. MC/VISA •

516-225-0707
516-225-0106
FAX   516-225-0787

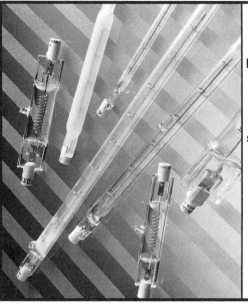

K–L

BIG APPLE LIGHTS CORP.   212-226-0925
533 Canal St, (Washington-Greenwich St) NYC, NY 10013

Sales & Rentals - theatrical lighting and dimming equipment.
Perishables - color, patterns, drafting templates, lamps, etc.
Manufacturer - Fog-It Dry Ice fog machine.
Friendly, helpful staff with years of design & electrical
experience at your service.
We're...BOUND TO SERVE YOU BETTER.

Hours: 8:30-4 Mon-Fri • 10-2 Sat   FAX   212-941-9803
• Sales, consulting. Also fog machines. RENTALS MC/VISA •

BMI SUPPLY   518-793-6709
28 Logan Ave., Glens Falls, NY 12801   800-836-0524
                                             FAX   518-793-6181

60 Airview Drive Greenville, SC 29607   803-288-8933

• Lighting and Dimming Equipment
• Lamps, Cable and Accessories.
• General Theatrical Supplies
• Sales only
JUST A PHONE CALL AWAY

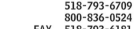
Serving the Entertainment Industry

Hours: 8-5 Mon-Fri   FAX 803-281-0841
• Good selection, good service. MC/VISA •

BULBTRONICS
45 Banfi Plaza, Farmingdale, NY 11735
Hours: 9-5 Mon-Fri

800-654-8542
516-249-2272
FAX   516-249-6066

1054 N. Cahuenga Blvd., Hollywood, CA 90038
Hours: 9-5 Mon-Fri

800-227-2852
213-461-6262
FAX   213-461-7307

• Full service lamp and bulb distributor. Also supplies, gaffer tape, blackwrap, color media, patterns, sockets and fixtures; ask for stage and studio dept. Brochure and price list available. CREDIT CARDS •
(See display ad in this section.)

CINE 60
630 Ninth Ave., (44-45th) NYC, NY 10036
Hours: 8:30-4:45 Mon-Fri

212-586-8782

FAX   212-259-9556

• Film and video equipment for sale or rent; source for battery belts and packs. CREDIT CARDS •

CINECRAFT, INC.
215B Central Ave., Farmingdale, NY 11735
Hours: 8:30-5 Mon-Fri

516-752-0700
800-752-3608
FAX   516-752-3607

• Audio visual services; duplicating, editing, and staging. Also projection equipment; reasonable prices. RENTALS CREDIT CARDS •

ELECTRA DISPLAYS
90 Remington Blvd., Ronkonkoma, NY 11779
Hours: 9-5 Mon-Fri

516-585-5689
212-420-1188

• Mirror balls, sheets and projecting kaleidoscopes. •

14TH ST. STAGE LIGHTING, INC.
869 Washington St., (13-14th St.) NYC, NY 10014

212-645-5491

Lighting equipment, controlling and dimming equipment, cable, complete line of stage and studio lamps, color, patterns and tape. Serving the downtown dance and theatre community has been our specialty for years. Our knowledgeable and helpful staff will work with you - if you need it, we can get it!

Hours: 9-5 Mon-Fri • Sat 11-3

FAX   212-924-7669

• Full sales and rentals of equipment and perishables. Reasonable rates, contact Mary Hayes or Joe Birchak. AMEX •

FOUR STAR STAGE LIGHTING
30 Warren Pl., Mt. Vernon, NY 10550
Hours: 8-5 Mon-Fri

914-667-9200

FAX   914-667-6271

• Lighting equipment: boards, cable, instruments; major supplier of packages for Broadway. •

GERRIETS INTERNATIONAL
29 Hurthinson Rd., Allentown, NJ 08501
Hours: 8:30-5 Mon-Fri

609-758-9121

FAX   609-758-9596

• Manufacturer of projection cycloramas and screens made of six different, inherently flame-retardant, front/rear projection materials, ultrasonically welded to sizes up to 100' high. •

K-L

The Great American Market
826 N. Cole Ave., Hollywood, CA 90028
213-461-0200
Hours: 8-5 Mon-Fri • Sat by appt.
• Sells steel projection patterns (gobos), scenic projectors, color filters; special effects, lighting and controls. Catalog. •

Jauchem and Meeh, Inc.
43 Bridge St., (Plymouth-Water St.) Brooklyn, NY 11201
718-875-0140

• Specialty lighting sources: 350W-2° xenon, Xenon Flash, laser and laser imitations, stars.
• Projection equipment, projection periscopes, keystone correction service.
• Flicker candles: battery operated and custom installations.

> ### JAUCHEM & MEEH, INC.
> SPECIAL EFFECTS-SALES, RENTAL, DESIGN

Hours: 9-5 Mon-Fri • or by appt.
FAX 718-596-8329
• Speak to Greg Meeh. •
(See display ad under SPECIAL EFFECTS SERVICES.)

Kliegl Bros. Lighting, Inc.
5 Aeriel Way, Syossett, NY 11797
516-937-3900
Hours: 8:30-5 Mon-Fri
• Manufacturer of lighting equipment. Sales and consultation. •

L & E Rentals
Market Street Industrial Park, Wappingers Falls, NY 12590
914-297-1415
Hours: 8:30-5 Mon-Fri
FAX 914-297-9270
• Rental of stage lighting equipment; filters, mirror balls; also fog machines. •

MLS Lighting Ltd.
27 West 24th St., #1105, (5-6th Ave.) NYC, NY 10010
212-691-1910
Hours: 9-5 Mon-Fri
• Formerly Star Lighting. Grip and lighting equipment, rental and sales. •

O'Ryan Industries
12711 NE 95th St., Vancouver, WA 98662
206-892-0447
800-426-4311
Hours: 8-5 Mon-Fri
FAX 206-892-6742
• Laser light systems, audio driven or manual. CREDIT CARDS •

Precision Projection Systems, Inc.
17508 Studebaker, Cerritos, CA 90701
310-865-8552
Hours: 9-6 Mon-Fri
• Sales of laser and fiber optic systems; also repairs. Contact Carl Hannigan. •

The Production Advantage
17 Pine Haven Shore, Sheburne, VT 05482
800-424-9991
802-985-3956
Hours: 8-5 Mon-Fri
FAX 802-985-1028
• Complete line of lamps, filters, color, patterns, connectors, cable, instruments, and accessories. Price list available, contact John. CREDIT CARDS •

K-L

PRODUCTION ARTS LIGHTING
636 11th Ave., (46th St.) NYC, NY 10036
Hours: 9-5:30 Mon-Fri

35 Oxford Dr., Moonachie, NJ 07074

212-489-0312

FAX   212-245-3723

201-440-9224

Rental and sales of lighting equipment for theatre, television and film. Specialists in electronic dimming and control systems. Exclusive distributors of Ludwig Pani scenic projectors and followspots in the United States and Canada.

Hours: 9-5:30 Mon-Fri
• Also fog machines and juice. •

FAX   201-440-9335

RAVEN SCREEN
80 Eighth Ave., (11th St.) NYC, NY 10014
Hours: 9-5 Mon-Fri

112 Spring St, Monroe, NY 10950
Hours: 9-5 Mon-Fri
• Carries all types of projection screening: glass, fabrics, etc. Chalk and tack boards, lectern units, and other AV furniture. •

212-534-8408

914-782-1844

ROSCO LABORATORIES, INC.
36 Bush Ave., Port Chester, NY 10573
Hours: 9-5 Mon-Fri
• Stainless steel gobos; also complete line of projection screens and color media. Shipping available. •

914-937-1300
800-ROSCONY
FAX   914-937-5984

SCIENCE FACTION
333 West 52nd St., 9th Fl., (8-9th) NYC, NY 10019
Hours: 9:30-6 Mon-Fri
• Laser special effects, including ability to digitize and "animate" from flat line art. •

212-586-1911

FAX   212-265-9786

SEE FACTOR INDUSTRY, INC.
37-11 30th St., (30th St-37th Ave.) L.I.C., NY 11101
Hours: 9-7 Mon-Fri
• Supplying equipment and services to local, national and international shows, concert tours and industrials. •

718-784-4200

FAX   718-784-0617

SFX DESIGN
6099 Godown Rd., Columbus, OH 43235
Hours: 7:30-4:30 Mon-Fri
• Formerly Theatre Magic. Stock and custom gobos. Catalog. •

614-459-3222

SLD LIGHTING
318 West 47th St., (8-9th) NYC, NY 10036

212-245-4155

Supplier of theatrical and architectural luminaries. Sales and rentals including fixtures, dimmer boards, fog machines, specialty lighting effects, lasers, color media and lamps. Knowledgeable sales staff and tremendous stock is our specialty.

Hours: 9-5:30 Mon-Fri • 10-2 Sat
• Call for 150 page catalog of lighting fixtures and supplies. Also fog machines. •

FAX   212-956-6537

"I found it in the N.Y. Theatrical Sourcebook."

STAGING TECHNIQUES   212-736-5727
   342 West 40th St., (8-9th) NYC, NY 10018
   Hours: 9-5 Mon-Fri
   • Audio visual house; programming facilities, screening room; equipment rental and sales.
   AMEX. •

STRAND LIGHTING   201-791-7000
   20 Bushes Lane, Elmwood Park, NJ 07407
   Hours: 9-5 Mon-Fri

   18111 S. Santa Fe Ave, Rancho Dominguez, CA 90221   310-637-7500
   Hours: 7-3:30 Mon-Fri
   • Provides much of the lighting equipment, controls and fixtures used in Broadway shows. •

TIMES SQUARE LIGHTING   914-947-3034
   Route 9W, Hold Drive Industrial Park, Stony Point, NY 10980
   Hours: 9-5 Mon-Fri   FAX   914-947-3047
   • Manufacturer of lighting instruments and fog machines. •

UNIVERSE STAGE LIGHTING, INC.   212-246-0597
   308 West 47th St., (8-9th Ave.) NYC, NY 10036
   Hours: 9:30-6 Mon-Fri   FAX   212-315-0300
   • Lighting equipment and supplies. RENTALS •

VANCO LIGHTING SERVICES, INC.   914-942-0075
   380 Route 210, Stony Point, NY 10980
   Hours: 8:30-4:30 Mon-Fri   914-942-0099
   • Large union shop; rental, sales; B'way, tours, TV; specialize in custom packages. •

K-L

LIGHTING FIXTURES

See also **LAMP SHADES & PARTS**

ANTAN   203-661-4769
   38 West Putnam Ave., Greenwich, CT 06830
   Hours: 10-5 Mon-Sat   FAX   203-661-0657
   • Lamps, both antique and modern, lamp shades, antiques, French trims and tassels; good
   prices. •

AURORA LAMPWORKS   203-787-1535
   597 East St., (State St.) New Haven, CT 06511
   Hours: 10-5 Tues, Thurs. & Fri • 10-4:30 Wed • 10-1 Sat
   • Antique lighting fixtures, track lighting. Speak to Dawn. •

BARRY OF CHELSEA ANTIQUES   212-242-2666
   154 Ninth Ave., (20th St.) NYC, NY 10011
   Hours: 12-7 Tues-Fri • 12-6 Sat & Sun
   • Victorian to Art Deco lighting fixtures. Sales only. •

BOWERY LIGHTING CORP   212-941-8244
   132 Bowery, (Grand) NYC, NY 10013
   Hours: 9-5:30 Mon-Fri • 9-6 Sat & Sun
   • General range of lighting fixtures at good prices. •

CITY KNICKERBOCKER
781 Eights Ave., (47-48th St.) NYC, NY 10036

212-586-3939

Large selection of chandeliers, wall sconces, floor
and table lamps and Tiffany reproductions available
for rental or purchase. Replacement globes for period fixtures.
80 Years of Serving the Theatrical Community.

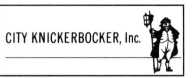

Hours: 8-4:30 Mon-Fri   FAX   212-262-2889
* Convenient midtown location; the best stop for rental of antique and some contemporary
lighting fixtures and shades. Nice people, see Ken or Scott. *

CREST HILL INDUSTRIES/ ROTH & STEINER
519 8th Ave., NYC, NY 10018
Hours: 8:30-5 Mon-Fri
* Large selection of lighting fixtures made from sea shells. Wholesale. *

212-947-1960

ECLECTIC/ENCORE PROPERTIES, INC.
620 West 26th St., 4th Fl., (11-12th Ave.) NYC, NY 10001
Hours: 9-5 Mon-Fri • or by appt.   FAX   212-243-6508
* Large collection of period and antique lighting fixtures, antique chandeliers, table lamps,
wall sconces, standing lamps including many classics from the 50's, 60's and 70's. A full service prop rental company. *
(See display ad under PROP RENTAL HOUSES.)

212-645-8880

GEM MONOGRAM & CUT GLASS CORP.
40 Withers St., Brooklyn, NY 11211
Hours: 9-4:30 Mon-Fri
* Cut glass chandeliers, sconces & fixtures. Very knowledgeable. Custom work. RENTALS *

718-599-7300

HAREM LITES
139 Bowery, (Broome-Grand) NYC, NY 10002
Hours: 9-5:30 every day   FAX   212-334-3973
* Nice selection of high-tech fixtures, track and recessed lighting. *

212-226-3042

KARL
396 Atlantic Ave., (Hoyt-Bond) Brooklyn, NY 11217
Hours: 12-5 Sat, Sun • or by appt.
* Arts & Crafts style lighting fixtures, beautiful stuff. *

718-596-1419

GEORGE KOVACS LIGHTING, INC.
330 East 59th St., (1-2nd Ave.) NYC, NY 10022
Hours: 10-6 Mon-Fri • 10-5 Sat
* High tech lamps and lighting fixtures. RENTALS *

212- 838-3400

LEE'S STUDIO, INC.
1755 Broadway, (56th St.) NYC, NY 10019
Hours: 10-7 Mon-Sat   FAX   212-581-7023

212-581-4400

1069 Third Ave., (63rd. St.) NYC, NY 10021
Hours: 10-7 Mon-Sat • 12-5 Sun.
* Contemporary, up-scale and avant garde mostly halogen lighting for the home or studio.
Fans; repairs & rental available at West Side store. Expensive. CREDIT CARDS *

212-371-1122

LIGHT, INC. 3   212-838-1130
    223 East 58th St., (2-3rd Ave.) NYC, NY 10021
    Hours: 10-6 Mon-Fri • 11-5 Sat
    • Great modern fixtures. RENTALS •

LIGHTING BY GREGORY   212-226-1276
    158 Bowery, (Delancey-Broome) NYC, NY 10012
    Hours: 8:30-5:30 Mon-Fri • 9-5:30 Sat & Sun
    • Good selection of track lighting, contemporary and high tech lamps. RENTALS •

LIGHTING BY GREGORY EAST   212-941-8278
    171 Bowery, (Delancey-Broome) NYC, NY 10002
    Hours: 8:30-5:30 every day
    • Great source for Tiffany's, Deco; Ceiling fans. Some neon. RENTALS •

LOST CITY ARTS   212-941-8025
    275 Lafayette St., (Houston-Prince) NYC, NY 10012
    Hours: 10-6 Mon-Fri • 12-6 Sat & Sun   FAX 212-219-2570
    • Unusual antique & vintage lighting fixtures, lamps, illuminated clocks, etc. RENTALS •

MANES STREET   212-684-7050
    200 Lexington Ave., (32-33rd St.) NYC, NY 10016
    Hours: 9-5 Mon-Fri   FAX 212-684-7170
    • Unique designer lamps and lighting fixtures by Missoni and Mila Schon. Also tapestries by
    Missoni and unique office furnishings. Highly decorative designer pieces. RENTALS •
    (See display ad under FURNITURE RENTAL & PURCHASE; GENERAL)

MARVIN ALEXANDER, INC.   212-838-2320
    315 East 62nd St., (1-2nd Ave.) NYC, NY 10021
    Hours: 9-5 Mon-Fri
    • Antique lamps, chandeliers, sconces; decorative accessories. RENTALS •

LOUIS MATTIA   212-753-2176
    980 Second Ave., (52nd Street) NYC, NY 10022
    Hours: 9-6 Mon-Fri
    • Antique lamps, lighting fixtures and shades; some custom work. RENTALS •

NOWELL'S VICTORIAN LIGHTING   415-332-4933
    PO Box 295, 490 Gate Five Rd., Sausalito, CA 94966
    Hours: -9:30-6 Mon-Sat
    • Repro and antique Victorian and Edwardian fixtures and shades; custom work; catalog $5. •

THE PROP COMPANY KAPLAN & ASSOCIATES   212-753-2176
    111 West 19th St., 8th Fl., (6-7th Ave.) NYC, NY 10011   212-691-PROP
    Hours: 9-5:30 Mon-Fri   FAX 212-727-3055
    • Some contemporary, antique and designer fixtures and lamps for the home and office.
    Contact Maxine Kaplan. •
    (See display ad under PROP RENTAL HOUSES.)

K-L

PROPS FOR TODAY   212-206-0330
121 West 19th St. Reception; 3rd Fl., (6-7th Ave.) NYC, NY 10011

Come to us first and we'll work with your budget!
• Huge selection of lamps and lighting fixtures from
  Country/Antique to Modern/High Tech.
• Neon, Victorian, Arts & Crafts, Modern, Office, Deco,
  Noguchi, etc.
NOW ON 3 FLOORS! ONE STOP PROPPING!

PROPS
FOR
TODAY

Hours: 8:30-5 Mon-Fri   FAX   212-924-0450
• Full service prop rental house. Mostly contemporary, but a good general selection. Phone
orders accepted. •
(See display ad under PROP RENTAL HOUSES.)

RED BARN ANTIQUES   413-528-3230
PO Box 25, Rt. 23, South Egremont, MA 01258
Hours: 10-5 every day
• Antique lighting fixtures, some furniture and accessories. Speak to John or Mary Walther. •

ROSETTA ELECTRICAL CO., INC.   212-233-9088
73 Murray St., (Greenwich St.-W.B'way) NYC, NY 10007   FAX   212-385-4151

21 West 46th St., (5-6th Ave.) NYC, NY 10036   212-719-4381
Hours: 8:30-5:30 • 9:30-4:30 Sat   FAX   212-768-3120
• Contemporary fixtures, lamps, electrical supplies, lamp parts. MC/VISA •

ROY ELECTRIC CO., INC.   718-434-7002
1054 Coney Island Ave., (Foster) Brooklyn, NY 11230   800-366-3347
Hours: 10-5 Mon-Sat   FAX   718-421-4678
• Stock and custom lighting fixtures; antique and reproduction chandeliers, sconces, pendants;
replacement glass shades and globes. Repairs made; lighting catalog $5. •

SARSAPARILLA–DECO DESIGNS   201-863-8002
5711 Washington St., West New York, NJ 07093   800-234-1008
Hours: 8-4:15 Mon-Fri
• Art Deco reproduction lamps, tin signs; wholesale; catalog $5. MC/VISA •

SUPERIOR LAMP & ELECTRICAL SUPPLY CO., INC.   212-677-9191
938 Broadway, (22nd Street) NYC, NY 10010
Hours: 8-5 Mon-Fri
• Track lighting, industrial & institutional fluorescent fixtures; discounts on large purchases. •

U.S. BALLOON MFG. CO.   718-492-9700
140 58th St., (Brooklyn Army Terminal) Brooklyn, NY 11220
Hours: 9-6 Mon-Fri   FAX   718-492-8711
• Lighted balloon fixtures, 3 sizes; rental or purchase. CREDIT CARDS •

UPLIFT, INC.   212-929-3632
506 Hudson St., (Christopher-10th St.) NYC, NY 10014
Hours: 1-8 every day
• Great selection of Art Deco, antique, reproduction sconces, lamps and floor lamps. CREDIT
CARDS •

WEISS & BIHELLER   212-979-6990
116 East 16th St., (Park-Irving Pl.) NYC, NY 10003
Hours: 9-5 Mon-Fri
• Large stock of chandeliers, sconces, lamp parts; also crystal trimmings. •

LINENS

ABC CARPET
212-743-3000
888 Broadway, (19th Street) NYC, NY 10003
Hours: 10-8 Mon & Thurs • 10-7 Tues, Wed, Fri & Sat • 11-6:30 Sun
• Large selection of sheets, towels, spreads, pillows, tablecloths and accessories. Sales and rentals. Pricey. CREDIT CARDS. •

AD HOC SOFTWARES
212-925-2652
410 West Broadway, (Spring) NYC, NY 10012
Hours: 11-7 Mon-Sat •11:30-6 Sun   FAX   212-941-6910
• Great looking stylish towels, bedding, tablecloths, shower curtains and a select collection of housewares. Will ship. CREDIT CARDS •

ANICHINI/THE COLLECTION
212-752-2130
745 Fifth Ave., (57-58th St.) NYC, NY 10151
Hours: by appt.   FAX   212-752-2817
• Period linens and lace. CREDIT CARDS •

BED, BATH AND BEYOND
212-255-3550
620 Avenue of the Americas, (18th St.) NYC, NY
Hours: 9:30-9 Mon-Fri •9:30-8 Sat • 10-6 Sun
• A bit of suburbia in Manhattan. A department store for the bedroom and bathroom with picture frames, kitchen utensils, seasonal gift items and furnishings. CREDIT CARDS •

BOUTROSS IMPORTS
718-965-0070
209 25th St., (4th Ave.) Brooklyn, NY 11232
Hours: 9-5 Mon-Fri
• Damask linen tablecloths; catalog, will ship. See Mike. AMEX •

ELDRIDGE TEXTILE CO.
212-925-1523
277 Grand St., (Eldridge) NYC, NY 10002
Hours: 9-5:30 Sun-Fri • 10-4 Sat   FAX   212-219-9542
• Sheets, bedding, towels, tablecloths and custom window treatments. $3 refundable charge for catalog. Will ship. MC/VISA •

ELGRIDGE JOBBING HOUSE CORP.
212-226-5136
88-90 Eldridge St., (Hester-Grand) NYC, NY 10002
Hours: 9-5 Sun-Fri • closed Sat   FAX   212-966-8929
• Bed linens. Catalog. Will ship. $25 minimum. CREDIT CARDS •

F & F TERGAL IMPORTERS
212-354-5166
265 West 40th St., 2nd Fl., (7-8th Avenue) NYC, NY 10018   212-840-7444
Hours: 9-6 Mon-Thurs • 9-2 Fri • by appt. Sun
• Wide selection of drapery and tablecloth laces; reasonable. Will ship. CREDIT CARDS •

GUILD NEEDLECRAFTS, INC.
212-268-7768
134 West 29th St., 8th Fl., (6-7th Ave.) NYC, NY 10001
Hours: 8-4:15 Mon-Fri
• Custom quilting and manufacturing of bedspreads and draperies. Large orders or small, one-of-a-kind work is charged by the piece. Will ship. Speak to Jack Kaufman. •

HAND BLOCK
212-799-4342
487 Columbus Ave., (83-84th Street) NYC, NY 10024
Hours: 10-8 Mon-Fri • 10-7 Sat • 11-7 Sun
• Interesting selection of pillows, bedspreads, window treatments, throw rugs, etc. RENTALS CREDIT CARDS •

K-L

WILLIAM ITZKOWITZ   212-477-1788
174 Ludlow St., (Houston-Stanton) NYC, NY 10002
Hours: 9:30-4 Sun-Fri • call first
• Sells and reconditions down comforters and pillows, custom chair cushions. •

K. KATEN & CO., INC.   908-381-0220
65 East Cherry St., Rahway, NJ 07065
Hours: 9:30-3 Mon-Fri   FAX   908-381-0221
• Table linens, beautiful damask, cut work and hemstitch linens. Will ship; see Alfred Katen. •

LA TERRINE   212-988-3366
1024 Lexington Ave., (73rd Street) NYC, NY 10021
Hours: 10:30-6: Mon-Sat
• Tabletop ceramics, linens, glassware; will ship. CREDIT CARDS •

LAYTNER'S LINEN SHOP   212-724-0180
2270 Broadway, (82nd Street) NYC, NY 10024
237 East 86th St., (2-3rd Ave) NYC, NY 10028   212-996-4439
Hours: 10-7:30 Mon-Fri •10-6:30 Sat • 12-6 Sun
• Nice selection of bedding, towels, bath rugs, shower curtains; will ship. CREDIT CARDS •

MABEL'S   212-734-3263
849 Madison Ave., (70-71st Street) NYC, NY 10021
Hours: 10-6 Mon-Sat   FAX   212-734-7914
• Cushions and decorative items with an animal theme. Will ship. CREDIT CARDS •

MADISON QUILT SHOP   718-733-2100
2307Grand Concourse, (183rd Street) NYC, NY 10468
Hours: 10-6 Mon-Sat • call first   FAX   718-733-9373
• Reconditions down comforters and pillows; custom pillows and comforters. Will ship. CREDIT CARDS •

MARVCO CORP.   516-621-0654
P.O. Box 1302, Roslyn Heights, NY 11577
Hours: 9-5 Mon-Fri   FAX   516-621-2650
• Exceptional value on name brand sheets, towels and bathroom accessories. Catalog available. MC/VISA •

TERRY L. MORTON • ANTIQUE TEXTILE CUSHIONS   212-472-1446
146 East 84th St., (Lexington-3rd Ave) NY, NY 10028
Hours: by appt.
• Hundreds of pillows made from antique needlepoint, tapestry, silks. •

NECESSITIES   (factory) 718-797-0530
329 Atlantic Ave., (Smith-Hoyt) Brooklyn, NY 11201 (office) 718-834-0678
Hours: 10-4 Sat, call first   FAX   718-797-0360
• Wholesale only. Tablecloths and napkins, fabrics; contact Bruce Andreozzi. $100 minimum, will ship. •

THE PROP COMPANY KAPLAN & ASSOCIATES   212-691-7767
111 West 19th St., (6-7th Ave.) NYC, NY 10011   212-691-PROP
Hours: 9-5:30 Mon-Fri   FAX   212-727-3055
• Beautiful selection of contemporary and antique table linens, tapestries, quilts, blankets, pillows, lace panels, fabrics, pure white to vibrant colors. Contact Maxine Kaplan. RENTALS •
(See display ad under PROP RENTAL HOUSES.)

K-L

PROPS FOR TODAY
212-206-0330
121 West 19th St. Reception; 3rd Fl., (6-7th Ave.) NYC, NY 10011
Hours: 8:30-5 Mon-Fri   FAX   212-924-0450
• Full service prop rental house. Good selection of tapestries, samplers, throws, afghans, chenilles, Pendletons, etc. New comforter and bed linen department from all periods. Also good selection of head boards •
(See display ad under PROP RENTAL HOUSES.)

J. SCHACTER CORP
718-384-2732
5 Cook St., Brooklyn, NY 11206
Hours: 9-5 Mon-Thurs • 9-2 Fri • 10-4:30 Sun   FAX   718-384-7634
• Comforters, pillows, sheets, blankets, pillow shams, towels, and dust ruffles. Reconditions down comforters and pillows. Catalog. Will ship. CREDIT CARDS •

SUNHAM & CO. (USA), INC.
212-695-1218
308 Fifth Ave., (31-32nd St.) NYC, NY 10001
Hours: 9-5:30 Mon-Fri
• Embroidered tablecloths and handkerchiefs, lace tablecloths. •

SUPERIOR LINEN
201-343-3300
80 Atlantic St., Hackensack, NJ 07601
Hours: 8:30-5 Mon-Fri
• Custom tablecloths and napkins in stock colors, rush orders, good prices; see Norman. •

TROUVAILLE FRANCAISE
212-737-6015
Hours: by appt.   FAX   212-737-9530
• Antique American country linens to the fancy French, Belgian and English linens and laces for bed and table. No credit cards, however personal checks OK. •

WOLFMAN-GOLD & GOOD
212-431-1888
116 Greene St., (Spring- Prince) NYC, NY 10012
Hours: 11-6 Mon-Sat •12-5 Sun   FAX   212-226-4955
• Beautiful antique and new linens; also cookie cutters, tureens, birdcages, lace panels, etc. •

LUGGAGE, HANDBAG & LEATHER REPAIR

ANTIQUE TRUNK SUPPLY CO.
216-941-8618
3706 West 169th St., Cleveland, OH 44111
Hours: 9-5 Mon-Fri • (mail order only)
• Trunk repair parts; catalog available ($1.00); also repair manuals ($5) and identification guides ($5.00). •

ROBERT FALOTICO STUDIOS
212-369-1217
315 East 91st St., 6th Fl., (1-2nd Ave.) NYC, NY 10128
Hours: 8:30-3 Mon-Fri
• Repairs on leather furniture; including couches, folding screens, desks; repair of leather accessories; no clothing, handbags, or luggage. •

JOHN R. GERARDO, INC.
212-695-6955
30 West 31st St., (B'way-5th Ave.) NYC, NY 10001
Hours: 9:30-5:30 Mon-Fri • 10-2 Sat
• Good work done on repairs; also sells luggage. CREDIT CARDS •

K-L

K-L

KAY LEATHER GOODS REPAIR SERVICE   212-481-5579
333 Fifth Ave., (corner of 33rd St.) NYC, NY 10016
Hours: 9-5 Mon-Fri
• Luggage and handbag repair; leather handles. •

THE LEATHER SOLUTION   516-667-0600
20 B East Industry Court, Deer Park, NY 11729
Hours: 8-4 Mon-Fri • Sat by appt.
• Formerly Total Leather Care. Repair and restoration of leather furniture. •

LEXINGTON LUGGAGE LTD.   212-223-0698
793 Lexington Ave., (61-62nd Street) NYC, NY 10021
Hours: 9-6 Mon-Sat   FAX 212-759-5238
• Repairs done on premises; luggage, trunks, leather gifts for sale; pricey. CREDIT CARDS •

MODERN LEATHER GOODS & ZIPPER SERVICE   212-947-7770
2 West 32nd St., (5th Ave.) NYC, NY 10001
Hours: 8:30-5:15 Mon-Thurs • 8:30-5 Fri • 9-2 Sat
• Repairs of luggage, briefcases; zipper repair for bags and luggage. MC/VISA •

SUPERIOR LEATHER RESTORERS   212-889-7211
133 Lexington Ave., (29th Street) NYC, NY 10016
Hours: 10-7 Mon-Wed • 10-8 Thurs •10-6 Fri • 10-3 Sat   FAX 212-532-8437
• Repairs of leather clothing, luggage, etc. CREDIT CARDS •

LUGGAGE & HANDBAGS

See also **LUGGAGE, HANDBAG & LEATHER REPAIR**

A TO Z LUGGAGE   212-686-6905
425 Fifth Ave., (38-39th St) NYC, NY 10016
Hours: 9-6:30 Mon-Thurs • 9-5 Fri
• Modern, good looking luggage. RENTALS CREDIT CARDS •

ALTMAN LUGGAGE   212-254-7275
135 Orchard St., (Delancey-Rivington) NYC, NY 10002   800-372-3377
Hours: 9-6 Sun-Fri   212-254-7663
• Rentals & sales of luggage and trunks. CREDIT CARDS •

T. ANTHONY LTD.   212-750-9797
445 Park Ave., (56th St.) NYC, NY 10022   800-722-2406
Hours: 9:30-6 Mon-Fri • 10-6 Sat   212-486-1184
• Luggage; rental and purchase. CREDIT CARDS •

BER–SEL HANDBAGS   212-966-5517
79 Orchard St., (Grand-Broome) NYC, NY 10002   212-226-6036
Hours: 9:30-6 Sun-Thurs • 9:30-4 Fri
• Large selection ladies handbags. CREDIT CARDS •

BETTINGER'S LUGGAGE   212-674-9411
80 Rivington St., (Orchard-Allen) NYC, NY 10002   212-475-1690
Hours: 9:30-6 Sun-Fri   212-475-1750
• Luggage, Trunks, leather goods; also repairs. RENTALS CREDIT CARDS •

"I found it in the N.Y. Theatrical Sourcebook."

CROUCH & FITZGERALD
212-755-5888
400 Madison Ave., (48th St.) NYC, NY 10017
800-627-6824
Hours: 9-6 Mon-Sat   FAX 212-832-6461
• Luggage, expensive. CREDIT CARDS •

JOHN R. GERARDO, INC.
212-695-6955
30 West 31st St., (B'way-5th) NYC, NY 10001
Hours: 9:30-5:30- Mon-Fri • 10-2 Sat   FAX 212-759-5238
• Luggage, briefcases & leather goods; also does repairs. CREDIT CARDS •

LEXINGTON LUGGAGE, LTD.
212-223-0698
793 Lexington Ave., (61-62nd St.) NYC, NY 10021
Hours: 9-6 Mon-Sat
• Luggage, small leather goods, personal gifts. CREDIT CARDS •

MOORMEND LUGGAGE SHOP
212-289-2978
1228 Madison Ave., (88-89th St.) NYC, NY 10128
Hours: 9-6 Mon-Fri • 9-5 Sat
• Luggage, trunks, leather goods, prices; repairs done on premises. CREDIT CARDS •

ODDS COSTUME RENTAL
212-268-6227
231 West 29th St., Rm. 304, (7-8th Ave.) NYC, NY 10001
Hours: 9:30-5 Mon-Fri • Sat by appt.
• Vintage through modern handbags. RENTALS •
(See display ad under COSTUME RENTALS & CONSTRUCTION)

E. VINCENT LUGGAGE
212-752-8251
1420 Sixth Ave., (58th St.) NYC, NY 10019
Hours: 9-6:30 Mon-Thurs • 9-6 Fri, Sat • 12-5 Sun
• Diverse selection luggage, small leather goods. CREDIT CARDS •

LUMBER

See also **HARDWOODS & VENEERS**

AASBO LUMBER & CABINET MAKERS
212-222-6200
1834 Second Ave., (95th Street) NYC, NY 10128
Hours: 9-7 Mon-Sat
• Will deliver, small orders ok; pleasant; expensive but good quality. •

BAY RIDGE LUMBER
718-492-3300
6330 Fifth Ave., (63-64th Street) Brooklyn, NY 11220

East Second St. and Lexington Ave., Bayonne, NJ 07002   201-437-9200
777 New Durham Rd., Edison, NJ 08817   908-906-8334
Hours: 7:30-4 Mon-Fri
• Fire retardant and pressure treated plywood, Homopol, Mevamar laminates, moldings; good prices, will deliver. CREDIT CARDS •

BLUE BELL LUMBER & MOULDING CO., INC.   718-665-7799
501 East 164th St., (Washington-3rd) Bronx, NY 10456

2360 Amsterdam Ave. (177-178th) NYC, NY 10033   212-923-0200
Hours: 9-5 Mon-Fri • 8-12 Sat
• Treated fir plywood, hardwoods, veneers, millwork, doors and moldings. CREDIT CARDS •

BROADWAY LUMBER CO   212-226-0768
557 Broadway, (Spring-Prince St.) NYC, NY 10017
Hours: 8-4:30 Mon-Fri • 8-4 Sat

501 West 19th St., (10-11th Ave.) NYC, NY 10011   212-924-6222
Hours: 6-4 Mon-Fri

517 West 42nd St., (10-11th Ave.) NYC, NY 10036   212-695-0380
Hours: 7-4:30 Mon-Fri • 8-1 Sat
• Lumber and building materials, including fire-retardant lumber. CREDIT CARDS •

BUTLER LUMBER   212-369-9012
2311 Third Ave., (125-126th St.) NYC, NY 10035
Hours: 8-4:30 Mon-Fri • 8-3 Sat

W. Fordham Rd. & Harlem River, Bronx, NY 10468   718-365-1000
Hours: 7:30-4:30 Mon-Fri • 7:30-3 Sat
• Formica, wall paneling, moldings, millwork and hardware. CREDIT CARDS •

CANAL LUMBER   212-226-5987
18 Wooster St., (Canal-Grand) NYC, NY 10013
Hours: 8-5 Mon-Fri • 8-1 Sat
• Power tools, formica, millwork, fireproof lumber, plywood. No credit cards. •

DYKES LUMBER   212-246-6480
248 West 44th St., (8-9th Ave.) NYC, NY 10036   212-582-1930
Hours: 7:30-5 Mon-Fri • 7:30-1 Sat
• Excellent for midtown; moldings and millwork . Wood or styro beams. Delivery. CREDIT
CARDS •

167 6th St., (2-3rd Ave.) Brooklyn, NY 11215   718-624-3350
Hours: 7:30-5 Mon-Fri • 8-1 Sat

26-16 Jackson Ave., (near Queens Plaza) L.I.C., NY 11101   718-784-3920
Hours: 7:30-4:30 Mon-Fri • 8-12:30 Sat
• Lumber, plywood, moldings, millwork, beams. CREDIT CARDS •

FELDMAN LUMBER   718-417-7777
101 Varick Ave., (Woodward) Brooklyn, NY 11237
Hours: 7-5 Mon-Fri • pickup by 2pm

692 Thomas Boyland St., (Bumont) Brooklyn, NY 11212   718-498-6600
Hours: 8-5 Mon-Fri • pickup by 2pm
• Large orders at good prices; see Walter or Brian; will deliver. CREDIT CARDS •

MURRY M. FINE LUMBER   718-381-5200
175 Varick Ave., (Metropolitan-Grand) Brooklyn, NY 11237
Hours: 8-5 Mon-Fri • pickup by 4 pm
• Used large beams and timber. •

FOREMOST LUMBER 718-388-7777
60 North 1st St., (Kent-Wythe) Brooklyn, NY 11211
Hours: 8-4:30 Mon-Fri
• Lumber, moldings, some cabinet plywood, micas, special millwork; good prices. No credit cards. •

GRILLON CORP. 718-875-8545
189-193 First Street, (3-4th Ave.) Brooklyn, NY 11215
Hours: 9-4:30 Mon-Thurs • 9-4 Fri • 10-2 Sat by appt.
• Decorative wooden panels and grillwork; Stock & custom work. Domestic and international shipping. Brochure available. •

LENOBLE LUMBER CO., INC. 212-246-0150
525 West 52nd St., (10-11th Ave.) NYC, NY 10019
Hours: 8-5 Mon-Fri • (closed for lunch 12-1)
• Doors, plywood, formica, moldings, masonite, millwork, windows, sonotube; Cutting 1-3:30 pm. Delivery. Cash, certified check or accounts only. •

LUMBER BOYS 212-683-0410
689 Second Ave., (38th Street) NYC, NY 10016
Hours: 7:30-4:30 Mon-Fri • 7:30-2 Sat
• Lumber cut to size. CREDIT CARDS •

LUMBERLAND 212-696-0022
409 Third Ave., (29th Street) NYC, NY 10016
Hours: 9-7 Mon-Sat • 12-5 Sun
• Wooden spindles, hardwood, some decorative hardware, mouldings, and power tools; same day delivery for orders received by 1 pm. •

MAXWELL LUMBER 212-337-3121
211 West 18th St., (7-8 Ave.) NYC, NY 10011
25-30 Borden Ave. (25-27th St.) L.I.C. NY 212-929-6088
Hours: 7:30-4:30 Mon-Fri
• Lumber, catalog of moldings, doors, spindles and newel posts. No credit cards. •

METROPOLITAN LUMBER & HARDWARE 212-966-3466
175 Spring St., (W B'way-Thompson) NYC, NY 10012
Hours: 8-6 Mon-Fri • 9-6 Sat • 9-4 Sun

617 Eleventh Ave., (46-47th St.) NYC, NY 10036 212-246-9090
Hours: 7-6:300 Mon-Fri • 8-6 Sat • 10-4 Sun

108-56 Roosevelt Ave., (108-111th St.) Corona, NY 11368 718-898-2100
Hours: 7-7 Mon-Fri • 8-6 Sat • 9-4 Sun
• Hardwoods, plywood, hand and power tools, doors, windows, formica, moldings; complete building center. Free delivery on orders over $100. Lumber yards closes one hour before showroom. CREDIT CARDS •

MIDTOWN LUMBER 212-675-2230
276 West 25th St., (7-8th Ave.) NYC, NY 10001
Hours: 8-4:30 Mon-Fri • 9-2 Sat (Sept-May)
• Prop kit supplies, moldings, hardwood flooring, tileboard, glass block, doors, hardware, lumber cut to size and formica. Contact Mike. CREDIT CARDS •

MIKE'S LUMBER STORE, INC. 212-595-8884
254 West 88th St., (B'way-West End Ave.) NYC, NY 10024
Hours: 9-6 Mon-Fri • 9-5 Sat
• Formicas, some hardware, unfinished furniture, doors, stain, moldings. •

K-L

"I found it in the N.Y. Theatrical Sourcebook."

MIKE'S LUMBER STORE, INC. 212-595-8884
254 West 88th St., (B'way-West End Ave.) NYC, NY 10024
Hours: 9-6 Mon-Fri • 9-5 Sat
• Formicas, some hardware, unfinished furniture, doors, stain, moldings. •

MIRON LUMBER CO. 718-497-1111
268 Johnson Ave., (near Bushwick) Brooklyn, NY 11206
Hours: 7-5 Mon-Fri • (closed for lunch 11:30-1)
• Hardwood, moldings, good prices, will deliver to Manhattan; pickups till 2:30. No credit cards. •

PRINCE LUMBER CO., INC. 212-777-1150
404 West 15th St., (9-10th Ave.) NYC, NYC 10011
Hours: 7-4:30 Mon-Fri • 7:30-1:30 Sat
• Pleasant, good service; formica, plywood, moldings, doors, windows. CREDIT CARDS •

ROSENZWEIG LUMBER CORP. 718-585-8050
801 East 135th St., (near Bruckner Blvd.) Bronx, NY 10454
Hours: 7:30-4 Mon-Fri
• Hardwoods, veneers, plywood, lumber and moldings; good prices, prompt next day delivery or pickup 10:30-3:30. •

NOTES

"I found it in the N.Y. Theatrical Sourcebook."

MACHINISTS & MACHINISTS TOOLS

MANHATTAN SUPPLY CO.   800-645-7270
 151 Sunnyside Blvd., Plainview, NY 11803
 Hours: 8am-9pm Mon-Fri • 8-1 Sat
  • Mail order machine tools; drill, reamers, cutters, etc.; great catalog, $25 minimum. •

MATHIESON   212-675-5081
 153 West 27th St., #803, (6-7th Ave.) NYC, NY 10001
 Hours: 8:30-4:30 Mon-Fri
  • Complete machine shop; reliable service. •

MCMASTER-CARR SUPPLY CO.   908-329-3200
 P.O.Box 440, Monmouth Junction Rd., New Brunswick, NJ 08903-0440
 Hours: 7-4 Mon-Fri   FAX   908-329-3772
  • Top quality items, esp. hardware. A vast selection of even hard to find stuff. Great catalog. •

S. POMPONIO   212-925-9453
 315 Church St., (Lispenard-Walker St.) NYC, NY 10013
 Hours: 9-5:30 Mon-Fri
  • Cuts stencils, models, jigs, lighting templates, trophy bases out of any material. •

TRAVERS TOOL CO.   718-886-7200
 P.O.Box 1550, 128-15 26th Ave., Flushing, NY 11354
 Hours: 8:30-4:30 Mon-Fri
  • Drill bits, chuck keys, clamps, sanding belts, more. CREDIT CARDS •

VICTOR MACHINERY EXCHANGE   212-226-3494
 251 Centre St., (Grand-Broome St.) NYC, NY 10013
 Hours: 8:15-4 Mon-Fri   FAX   212-941-8465
  • Tool room equipment, vises, micrometers, etc.. •

MAGAZINES & COMIC BOOKS

See also **BOOKSTORES**

A & S BOOK CO.   212-714-2712
 308 West 40th St., (8-9th Ave.) NYC, NY 10018
 Hours: 10:30-6:30 Mon-Fri • 10:30-5 Sat
  • Back-date magazines and comic books. Will ship. •

ABRAHAM'S MAGAZINE SERVICE   212-777-4700
 56 East 13th St., (B'way-Univ. Pl.) NYC, NY 10003
 Hours: 9-5 Mon-Fri
  • 18th-20th century literature, medical science; magazines and published materials. •

COLLECTOR'S STADIUM   212-353-1531
 214 Sullivan St., (Bleecker-W.3rd St.) NYC, NY 10012
 Hours: 11-7 every day   FAX   212-353-1571
  • Extensive collection of sports publications, lithographs, photos; also autographed sports
  items and a huge collection of baseball cards. Helpful sports enthusiasts. Shipping. RENTALS
  CREDIT CARDS •

M-N

"I found it in the N.Y. Theatrical Sourcebook."   **267**

FORBIDDEN PLANET   212-473-1576
    821 Broadway, (12th St.) NYC, NY 10003
    Hours: 10-7 Mon, Tue, Sat • 10-7:30 Wed, Thurs, Fri • 12-7 Sun
        • Current and back issue special effects magazines, fantasy comic books. •

FUNNY BUSINESS COMICS   212-799-9477
    660 B Amsterdam Ave., (92nd St.) NYC, NY 10025
    Hours: 1-4:30 Tues-Fri • Wed, Fri till 6 • 12-5 Sat, Sun • (longer hrs. in summer)
        • Great selection of current and back-date comic books. MC/VISA. •

HOTALING NEWS AGENCY   212-840-1868
    142 West 42nd St., (B'way-6th Ave.) NYC, NY 10036
    Hours: 7:30-9 Mon-Fri • 7:30-8 Sat, Sun   FAX   212-944-8857
        • In business since 1905! Good selection of current out-of-town and foreign magazines and
    newspapers. Will ship. CREDIT CARDS •

HOLMES AND MEIER   212-374-0100
    160 Broadway, (Maiden Lane) NYC, NY 10038
    Hours: 9-5 Mon-Fri   FAX   212-374-1313
        • Formerly International University Booksellers. Books & periodicals of scholarly interest,
    including costume design. •

JAY BEE MAGAZINE STORES INC.   212-675-1600
    134 West 26th St., Basement, (6-7th Ave.) NYC, NY 10001
    Hours: 10-4 Mon-Fri • 12-3 Sat
        • A basement full of back-date magazines piled high; list of titles carried available. Will ship.
    Catalog $2. MC/VISA •

MANHATTAN COMICS & CARDS   212-243-9349
    228 West 23rd St., (7-8th Ave.) NYC, NY 10011
    Hours: 10-6 Mon-Wed • 10-7 Thurs • 10-9:30 Fri • 10-8 Sat • 12-5:30 Sun
        • Back-date magazines, primarily comics, some science fiction, lots of baseball cards.
    MC/VISA •

CARMEN D. VALENTINO RARE BOOKS   215-739-6056
    2956 Richmond St., (Ann-Indiana) Philadelphia, PA 19134
    Hours: by appt. only, leave message on machine
        • Specializes in American printed matter, mostly pre-1920. Periodicals, newspapers, calendar
    art, prints, books, etc. •

MAGIC SUPPLIES & NOVELTIES

ABRACADABRA   212-627-5745
    10 Christopher St., (near 6th Ave.) NYC, NY 10014   800-MAGIC 66
    Hours: 11-7 Mon-Sat • also open Sun in Oct, Dec   FAX   212-627-5876
        • Magic tricks & illusions: gags & novelties. CREDIT CARDS •

FRANK BEE COSTUMES CENTER   718-823-9792
    3435 East Tremont Ave., (Bruckner Blvd.) Bronx, NY 10465
    Hours: 9-6 Mon-Sat • till 7 Fri • 9-3 Sun   FAX   718-824-2979
        • Wide selection of Halloween and mascot costumes, make-up, wigs, magic supplies. Volume
    discount. Also carries Rit and Tintex dyes. RENTALS CREDIT CARDS •

FUNNY STORE INC.   212-704-0032
1481 Broadway, (42nd St.) NYC, NY 10036
Hours: 9-8 every day   FAX   212-704-0046
• Gags, magic tricks. Will ship. CREDIT CARDS •

GORDON NOVELTY CO. INC   212-254-8616
933 Broadway, (21st-22nd St.) NYC, NY 10010
Hours: 9-4:30 Mon-Fri
• Wholesale and retail; good prices. Will ship. •

FLOSSO HORNMANN MAGIC CO.   212-279-6079
45 West 34th St., Rm. 607, (5th-6th Ave.) NYC, NY 10001
Hours: 10-5:30 Mon-Fri • 10-3:30 Sat
• Carries items for both beginners and professionals. Catalog $1. RENTALS MC/VISA •

JIMSONS NOVELTIES INC.   212-477-3386
28 East 18th St., (Park Ave. S.-B'way) NYC, NY 10003
Hours: 9-5:30 Mon-Fri • 10-3 Sat   FAX   212-228-3394
• Every imaginable kind of gag joke and novelty item, especially ones in bad taste. Catalog.
MC/VISA •

PARTY PROFESSIONALS   800-874-4087
8610 Milliken Ave., Rancho Cucamonga, CA 91730   909-944-3559
Hours: 8-5 Mon-Fri   FAX   800-648-7772
• Rubber latex masks; inexpensive. Catalog available. •

D. ROBBINS & CO. INC.   718-625-1804
70 Washington St., (York-Front St.) Brooklyn, NY 11201
Hours: 8-4:30 Mon-Fri   FAX   718-858-2351
• Wholesale magic supplies; quantity sales only; catalog. Will ship. •

TANNEN'S MAGIC   212-239-8383
6 West 32nd St., 4th Fl., (5th-B'way) NYC, NY 10001
Hours: 9-5:30 Mon-Fri • 9-4 Sat   FAX   212-643-0199
• Flash powder, flash paper; will assist with complicated tricks; consulting service available.
Catalog $15. CREDIT CARDS •

THINK BIG   212-925-7300
390 West Broadway, (Spring-Broome St.) NYC, NY 10012
Hours: 11-7 Mon-Sat • 12-6 Sun
• Giant crayons, pencils, toothbrushes, paint brushes, tennis balls, etc.; catalog available.
$300 minimum on rentals. Will ship. CREDIT CARDS •

MAKE-UP SUPPLIES

See also **HAIR SUPPLIES & WIGS**
For artificial eyes, see **TAXIDERMISTS & TAXIDERMY SUPPLIES**
For additional latex supplies, see **CASTING & MODELING SUPPLIES**

ABRACADABRA   212-627-5745
10 Christopher St., (near 6th Ave.) NYC, NY 10014   800-MAGIC-66
Hours: 11-7 Mon-Sat • also open Sun in Oct & Dec   FAX   212-627-5876
• Full line of theatrical make-up. Professional equipment. Catalog available. CREDIT CARDS •

ADM TRONICS UNLIMITED INC. 201-767-6040
224 S. Pegasus Ave., Northvale, NJ 07647
Hours: 9-5 Mon-Fri   FAX   201-784-0620

Pros-Aide, a non-toxic adhesive used by hundreds of makeup pro's. Excellent for bonding makeup appliances to the skin. Also useful as a bonding agent blended with makeup colors and paints. For applications requiring an "easier-to-remove" adhesive, try new *Pros-Aide II.*
Also try *Aquacream Lotion,* a great companion product to use before and after applying *Pros-Aide.*

• Specializes in non-toxic water based adhesives, coatings and additives. •

ALCONE CO. INC. *Mary —* 718-361-8373
5-49 49th Ave., (5th St.-Vernon Ave.) L.I.C., NY 11101
Hours: 9:30-4 Mon-Fri   FAX   718-729-8296
• Theatrical make-up, stage blood, latex, foam latex. Theatrical supply house; catalog, $5. (Subway #7 to L.I.C., Vernon/Jackson stop.) •

HOSMER DORRANCE CORP. 408-379-5151
PO Box 37, Campbell, CA 95009
Hours: 7:30-4 Mon-Fri
• Prosthetic making supplies; latex and pigments; catalog. •

BOB KELLY WIG CREATIONS INC. 212-819-0030
151 West 46th St., 9th Fl., (6th-7th Ave.) NYC, NY 10036
Hours: 9-4:30 Mon-Thurs • 9-3 Fri
• Theatrical make-up; also custom wigs; catalog. •

THE LASHETTE CO. INC. 508-653-1420
PO Box 205, 308 N. Main St., Natick, MA 01760
Hours: 7-3:30 Mon-Fri
• Mfg. of false eyelashes; price list available. •

THE MAKE-UP CENTER LTD. 212-977-9494
150 West 55th St., (6th-7th Ave.) NYC, NY 10019
Hours: 10-6 • Thurs till 8 • 10-5 Sat
• Make-up and supplies, many brands; stage blood. •

MEHRON INC. 914-268-4106
45E Rt. 303, Valley Cottage, NY 10989
Hours: 9-5 Mon-Fri
• Theatrical make-up, kits; catalog and color chart. •

BEN NYE MAKE-UP INC. 310-839-1984
5935 Bowcroft St., Los Angeles, CA 90016
Hours: 8-4:30 Mon-Fri   310-839-2640
• Theatrical make-up kits; catalog. •

PLAYBILL COSMETICS / IDEAL WIG CO. 718-361-8601
37-11 35th Ave., (37th-38th St.) Astoria, NY 11101
Hours: 9-5 Mon-Fri
• Make-up in pencil form (55 shades) and make-up remover pads. Wholesale only. $750 min. •

ALAN STUART INC. 212-719-5511
49 West 38th St. 5th Fl., (5th-6th Ave.) NYC, NY 10018
Hours: 9-5:30 Mon-Fri
• Make-up and hair brushes and combs; wholesale. •

TEMPTU MARKETING, INC.
212-675-4000
26 West 17th St., #503, (5th-6th Ave.) NYC, NY 10011
Hours: 9-5 Mon-Fri   FAX   212-941-1972
• Make-up & novelties, tattoos, stage blood. •

TRI-ESS SCIENCES INC.
213-245-7685
1020 West Chestnut St., Burbank, CA 91506
800-274-6910
Hours: 8:30-5 Mon-Fri • 8-12 Sat   FAX   818-848-3521
• Special effects make-up products and supplies; also special effects materials and equipment. Catalog available. •

ZAUDER BROTHERS / M. STEIN THEATRICAL COSMETICS
516-379-2600
10 Henry St., Freeport, NY 11520
Hours: 8:30-5:30 Mon-Thurs • 8:30-2:45 Fri
• Full line of make-up, cream, cake and greasepaint; custom wigs. Catalog. $25 minimum. •

ZELLER INTERNATIONAL LTD.
800-722-USFX
Main St., Box Z, Downsville, NY 13755 (factory)
212-627-7676
Hours: 9-5 Mon-Fri   FAX   607-363-2071
• Safe, specialty chemicals used by make-up and FX people. •

MANNEQUINS

BERNSTEIN & SONS
212-683-2260
30 West 29th St., (B'way-6th Ave.) NYC, NY 10001
800-757-7225
Hours: 9-5:30 Mon-Fri   FAX   718-956-1443
• Mannequins, great selection of display fixtures, rolling racks, hangers, garment bags, 3-fold mirrors and clothes steamers; catalog. Will ship. RENTALS CREDIT CARDS •

E.T. CRANSTON
212-206-5046
133 West 25th St., (6-7th Ave.) NYC, NY 10001
Hours: 9-5 Mon-Fri   FAX   212-645-5046
• Mannequins and forms-realistic or abstract. Store and jewelry fixtures. Ask for Flora Saitta. •

GOLDSMITH MANNEQUINS
718-937-8476
10-09 43rd Ave., (10th-11th Ave.) L.I.C., NY 11101
Hours: 9-4 Mon-Fri
• New and secondhand mannequins; wig heads. Catalog. Will ship. RENTALS •

PUCCI MANIKINS
212-633-0452
44 West 18th St., (5-6th Ave.) NYC, NY 10011
Hours: 10-5 Mon-Fri   FAX   212-633-1058
• Mannequins and mannequin wigs. $20 catalog. •

STUDIO E 15
718-797-4561
79 Washington St., (York-Front St.) Brooklyn, NY 11201
Hours: 9-6 Mon-Fri   FAX   718-797-4562
• Custom lifecast figures for museums and display. •

TOBART MANNEQUINS
212-279-0137
520 West 27th St., (10th-11th Ave.) NYC, NY 10001
800-221-2790
Hours: 9-5 Mon-Fri   FAX   212-594-6872
• Good selection of all types, free catalog. Contact Phil Steinhardt. CREDIT CARDS •

M-N

MAPS

ARGOSY BOOK STORES INC.   212-753-4455
116 East 59th St., (Lexington-Park Ave.) NYC, NY 10022
Hours: 9-6 Mon-Fri • 10-5 Sat (Oct-April)   FAX   212-593-4784
• Maps, prints, some out-of print books. Phone orders welcome. CREDIT CARDS •

THE COMPLETE TRAVELLER BOOKSTORE   212-679-4339
199 Madison Ave., (35th St.) NYC, NY 10016   212-685-9007
Hours: 9-7 Mon-Fri • 10-6 Sat • 12-5 Sun   FAX   212-982-7628
• Wide selection of maps and travel books. CREDIT CARDS •

HAGSTROM TRAVEL CENTER   212-398-1222
57 West 43rd St., (5th-6th Ave.) NYC, NY 10036
Hours: 9:30-5:30 Mon-Fri   FAX   212-398-9856
• Wide selection of national and foreign maps, globes, travel books. CREDIT CARDS •

NEW YORK BOUND BOOKSHOP / URBAN GRAPHICS   212-245-8503
50 Rockefeller Plaza, (50-51st St.) NYC, NY 10020
Hours: 10-6 Mon-Fri • 12-4 Sat • Closed Sat May- Aug
• Old maps, prints, books and unique gifts of NYC; phone orders welcome. CREDIT CARDS •

NEW YORK NAUTICAL INSTRUMENT & SERVICE CORP.   212-962-4522
140 West Broadway, (Thomas-Duane St.) NYC, NY 10013
Hours: 9-5 Mon-Fri • 9-12 Sat   FAX   212-406-8420
• Star and nautical maps of the world; nautical instruments. Phone orders welcome. CREDIT CARDS •

POWERS ELEVATION   800-824-2550
P.O. Box 440-889, Aurora, CO 82601
Hours: 6am-8pm Mon-Fri   FAX   303-321-2218
• USGS and topographical maps, satellite maps. Very helpful. Will ship. CREDIT CARDS •

RAND MCNALLY & CO.   212-758-7488
150 East 52nd St., (3rd.-Lexington Ave.) NYC, NY 10022
Hours: 9-6 Mon-Fri • Thurs till 7 • 11-5 Sat
• Up-to-date Rand McNally maps, topographical maps, guide books and travel accessories. Largest selection of globes in NYC. Phone orders welcome. CREDIT CARDS •

RAVEN MAPS & IMAGES   800-237-0798
24 North Central Ave., Medford, OR 97501
Hours: 8-5 Mon-Fri   FAX   503-773-6834
• Topographic maps as an art form. CREDIT CARDS •

SOUTH STREET SEAPORT MUSEUM   212-669-9499
207 Front St., (Fulton-Beckman St.) NYC, NY 10038
Hours: 9-5:30 Mon-Fri   FAX   212-406-0457
• Maritime maps and books. Contact Robert Astorita. CREDIT CARDS •

MARBLE

A & R ASTRA LTD.   212-750-3364
1152 Second Ave., (60th-61st St.) NYC, NY 10021
Hours: 9-5 Mon-Fri • 11-4 Sat
• Custom cutting; tables, sinks, fireplaces, etc. RENTALS •

ACME MARBLE WORKS INC.   718-788-0527
160 17th St., (3rd-4th Ave.) Brooklyn, NY 11215   718-965-3560
Hours: 8-4 Mon-Fri
• Large selection of marble, custom work and cutting. •

ALCAMO MARBLE WORKS INC.   212-255-5224
541 West 22nd St., (10-11th Ave.) NYC, NY 10011
Hours: 8-4:30 Mon-Fri
• Marble and granite for rental or purchase; see Francesca. •

BERGEN BLUESTONE CO. INC.   201-261-1903
404 Rt. 17N, Paramus, NJ 07652   800-955-7625
Hours: 7:30-4:30 Mon-Fri • 8-1Sat   FAX 201-261-8865
• Natural stone suppliers and contractors. Carries marble, granite, limestone, slate, sandstone, quartzite, landscaping stones, boulders, petrified wood. •

DESIGN LOGISTICS MARBLE & STONE   718-326-4400
61-35 98th St., #15G, Rego Park, NY 11374
Hours: 8-5 Mon-Fri
• Sells, fabricates, installs and repairs marble; stocks about 20 varieties of marble. •

EMPIRE STATE MARBLE MFG. CORP.   212-534-2307
207 East 110th St., (2nd-3rd Ave.) NYC, NY 10029
Hours: 8-4 Mon-Fri
• Will cut to size; also sells tile. RENTALS •

MANHATTAN MARBLE   212-226-4881
267 Elizabeth St., (Houston-Prince St.) NYC, NY 10012
Hours: 8-4:30 Mon-Fri
• Rental of stock marble pieces. •

MARBLE MODES   718-539-1334
115-25 130th St., (20th Ave.) College Point, NY 11356
Hours: 7:30-5 Mon-Fri
• Marble fabrication and repair; sells about 130 varieties of marble. •

NEW YORK MARBLE WORKS INC.   212-929-1817
430 West 14th St., (9-10th Ave.) NYC, NY 10014
Hours: 9-6 Mon-Fri
• Sells marble cut to size. •

NORTH SHORE MASONRY   516-482-6200
96 Cutter Mill Rd., Great Neck, NY 11022
Hours: 7-4 Mon-Fri • 7-1 Sat   FAX 516-482-5039
• Sand, lava rock, marble and granite. •

MARINE EQUIPMENT

See also **FISHING TACKLE**

ARRANGEMENTS, INC. MARINE DIVISION   914-238-1300
301 Roaring Brook Rd., (Saw Mill River Pkwy) Chappaqua, NY 10514
Hours: 9-5 Mon-Fri • or by appt.
• 100's of ship models, ranging in size from 1' to 7', all types of vessels, cased or uncased, will ship or deliver. Contact Gabriel Rosenfeld or Katherine Savarin. RENTALS •

E. BUK ANTIQUES AND ART   212-226-6891
151 Spring St., 2nd Fl., (W.B'way-Wooster St.) NYC, NY 10012
Hours: every day by appt.   (toll call) 700-SCIENCE

ANTIQUE marine and nautical instruments and objects; mapping and navigational tools and devices, sextants, compasses, binoculars, telescopes, ship models, brass items, block and tackle.

• Complete period settings and custom work. •
(See display ads under ANTIQUES and under PROP RENTAL HOUSES.)

CAPT. HOOK MARINE ANTIQUES & SHELLS   212-344-2262
South Street Seaport, (Fulton St.) NYC, NY 10038
Hours: 10-7 Mon-Sat •11-6 Sun • Longer hours in summer
• Mostly tourist seaside novelties, some marine antiques and seashells. Phone orders welcome. CREDIT CARDS •

J. COWHEY & SONS INC. MARINE EQUIPMENT   718-625-5587
440 Van Brunt St., (Beard-Van Dyke St.) Brooklyn, NY 11231
Hours: 8-4:30 Mon-Fri   FAX   718-625-5772
• Good prices on marine equipment, aircraft cable, rigging. Catalog. Phone orders welcome. •

DEFENDER INDUSTRIES   914-632-3001
255 Main St., New Rochelle, NY 10801
Hours: 9-5:45 Mon-Fri • 9-2:45 Sat   FAX   914-632-6544
• Extensive stock of marine supplies: boat hardware, sailcloth, epoxies, polyester gel coat, release, fiberglass supplies and more. Catalog. $25 minimum. Phone orders. CREDIT CARDS •

GOLDBERG'S MARINE   212-594-6065
12 West 37th St., (5th-6th Ave.) NYC, NY 10018
Hours: 9:30-5:30 Mon-Fri • 9:30-2:30 Sat   FAX   212-594-0721
• Everything for the sail and power boat; scuba and marine equipment. Catalog available. RENTALS CREDIT CARDS •

NEW YORK NAUTICAL INSTRUMENT & SERVICE CORP.   212-962-4522
140 West Broadway, (Thomas-Duane St.) NYC, NY 10013
Hours: 9-5 Mon-Fri • 9-12 Sat   FAX   212-406-8420
• Nautical instruments, star and nautical maps of the world. Phone orders.CREDIT CARDS •

MEDICAL & SCIENTIFIC EQUIPMENT & SUPPLIES: DENTAL

ARISTA SURGICAL SUPPLY CO. 212-679-3694
67 Lexington Ave., (25th St.) NYC, NY 10010
Hours: 8:30-4:45 Mon-Fri • 9-12 Sat
• Surgical and dental tools, doctors bags, stethoscopes, limited selection of lab glass. •

BENNER MEDICAL PROPS INC. 212-727-9815
601 West 26th St., 16th Fl., (11th-12th Ave.) NYC, NY 10001
Hours: 9-4:30 Mon-Fri FAX 212-727-9824
• A selection of new and antique medical equipment, examining room furnishings, utensils, research, medical staff uniforms and accessories; also medical consulting and coordinating services. •

B. L. DENTAL CO. INC. 718-658-5440
135-24 Hillside Ave., (136th) Richmond Hills, NY 11418
Hours: 9-4 Mon-Fri
• Bio-fast in clear, white and pink; dental supplies. Catalog. Shipping. MC/VISA •

E. BUK, ANTIQUES & ART 212-226-6891
151 Spring St., 2nd Fl., (W.B'way-Wooster St.) NYC, NY 10012
Hours: every day by appt. (toll call) 700-SCIENCE
• Extensive collection of antique dental tools and equipment, chairs, x-ray equipment, cabinets, lamps, etc. •
(See display ads under ANTIQUES and under PROP RENTAL HOUSES.)

ETHICAL DENTAL SUPPLIES 718-376-2025
3104 Quentin Rd., (Nostrand Ave.) Brooklyn, NY 11234
Hours: by appt. only 8:30-5 Mon-Fri
• Equipment, supplies, and teeth. Will ship. MC/VISA •

GEMCO DENTAL LAB INC. 718-438-3270
1010 McDonald Ave., (Foster-Parkville Ave.) Brooklyn, NY 11230 718-871-3900
Hours: 8-6 Mon-Fri
• Dental tools, teeth, lab equipment; see Leo Weiss. CREDIT CARDS •

HUNTINGTON DENTAL SUPPLY / RUBENSTEIN DENTAL EQUIPMENT CORP. 212-563-0818
29 West 35th St., 3rd Fl., (5th-6th Ave.) NYC, NY 10001
Hours: 8:30-5 Mon-Fri • Tues, Wed till 7 • 8:30-3 Sat
• Dental tools, equipment and supplies, alginate. Catalog. CREDIT CARDS •

MEDICAL & SCIENTIFIC EQUIPMENT & SUPPLIES: HOSPITAL & SICKROOM

ABBEY HEARING AID CENTER INC. 212-697-5190
505 Fifth Ave., (42nd St.) NYC, NY 10017
Hours: 8-4 Mon-Fri
• Full line of modern and antique hearing aids; repair and service of all major brands; Ear molds for rock musicians, consulting. Contact Saul Kaplan. •

ADVANCE HOME MEDICAL SUPPLIES, INC. 203-523-1076
509 Farmington Ave., (Sisson Ave.) Hartford, CT 06105
Hours: 8:30-5 Mon-Fri
• Phone orders and rentals welcome. See Sandy Cohen, owner. Free delivery in CT. •

M-N

AIMES INC.   201-279-7200
   119 Dale Ave., Patterson, NJ 07509
   Hours: 8-4:30 Mon-Fri
      • Formerly American International Medical Equipment Sales. Lab and hospital equipment,
   wheelchairs. RENTALS •

ARCHFRAME INC.   212-831-3600
   125 East 87th St., (Lexington-Park Ave.) NYC, NY 10128
   Hours: 9:30-6 Mon-Fri
      • Surgical supports, braces, back supports, pillows, wheelchairs, walkers. MC/VISA •

ARISTA SURGICAL SUPPLY CO.   212-679-3694
   67 Lexington Ave., (25th St.) NYC, NY 10010
   Hours: 8:30-4:45 Mon-Fri • 9-12 Sat
      • Surgical and dental tools, doctor's bags, stethoscopes; limited selection of lab glass. •

BELL MEDICAL SUPPLY   212-744-4059
   165 East 35th St., (Lexington-3rd Ave.) NYC, NY 10021
   Hours: 9-5 Mon-Fri
      • Phone orders only, no showroom; wheelchairs, sickroom supplies and compressed gasses.
   CREDIT CARDS •

BENNER MEDICAL PROPS INC.   212-727-9815
   601 West 26th St.,16th Fl., (11th-12th Ave.) NYC, NY 10001
   Hours: 9-4:30 Mon-Fri   FAX   212-727-9824
      • Good selection of new and antique medical equipment; examining room furnishings, utensils,
   research, medical staff uniforms and accessories. •

E. BUK, ANTIQUES & ART   212-226-6891
   151 Spring St., 2nd Fl., (W.B'way-Wooster St.) NYC, NY 10012
   Hours: every day by appt.   (toll call) 700-SCIENCE
      • Specializing in antique medical and surgical supplies, unusual wheelchairs, crutches, sickbed
   equipment, etc. •
   (See display ads under ANTIQUES and under PROP RENTAL HOUSES.)

CINEMA WORLD PRODUCTS INC.   718-389-9800
   220 DuPont St., (Provost St.) L.I.C., NY 11222
   Hours: 9-7 Mon-Fri • or by appt.   FAX   718-389-9897
      • Complete medical equipment rental and consultation; contact Mark Oppenheimer or Maurice
   Keshner. •
   (See display ad in this section.)

FALK SURGICAL CORP.   212-744-8082
   259 East 72nd St., (2nd Ave.) NYC, NY 10021
   Hours: 9-7:30 Mon-Fri • 9:30-6 • 10-6 Sun
      • Orthopedic and sickroom equipment; RENTALS CREDIT CARDS •

GEM SERVICE   718-463-3800
   144-67 Northern Blvd., (146th) Flushing, NY 11354
   Hours: 9-5 Mon-Sat   FAX   718-461-2621
      • Wheelchair retreading and repair; some vintage models. Helpful. RENTALS CREDIT
   CARDS •

KEEFCARE LTD.   212-988-8800
   40-18 Berrian Blvd., Astoria, NY 11105   800-479-1600
   Hours: 9-5 Mon-Fri
      • Motorized wheelchairs, canes, crutches, walking accessories, hospital beds; Catalog.
   RENTALS CREDIT CARDS •

M-N

CINEMA WORLD STUDIOS

THE CLOSEST SOUND STAGE TO MANHATTAN

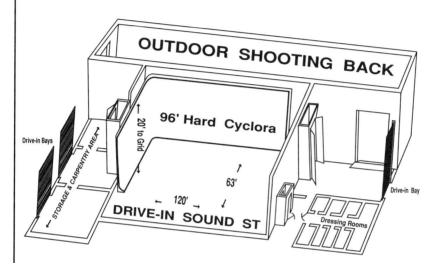

We won't be upstaged! Cinema World offers a contemporary "State of The Art" 27,000 square foot production facility for $850.00 per day, a dramatic savings over other sound stages in the metropolitan area. Cinema World, the closest sound stage to Manhattan offers:

- 7500 square foot sound stage with a twenty foot height to grid including a five ton capacity skycam remote crane with 360 degree rotation.
- 6000 feet of enclosed outdoor backlot with overhead structural lighting grid.
- Street level drive-in.
- 6000 AMP/3 phase electrical capacity.
- Two massive 2400 square foot tractor trailer drive-in storage/prep areas on either end of the sound stage.
- Ample set storage with three drive-in bays.
- Hard cyclorama on premises .
- Complete carpentry shop.
- Ten production offices and suites.
- Multiple dressing rooms, shower, make-up, wardrobe and green room.
- A well designed hi-tech working kitchen with full catering capabilities.
- Ample parking for your vehicles.
- We are the closest sound stage to Manhattan. Shuttle service available.

EAST COAST EXCLUSIVE

"THE FISHER LIGHT™"

Fully set up on stage and pre-rigged on a motorized overhead tracking system.

CINEMA WORLD STUDIOS
220 DUPONT STREET
L.I. CITY/ GREENPOINT,N.Y.11222

Tel. 718-389-9800
Fax 718-389-9897

M-N

MARBURGER SURGICAL   212-420-1166
   34 Irving Place, (16th St. between 3rd & 4th Ave.) NYC, NY 10003
   Hours: 8:30-5 Mon-Thurs • 8:30-3 Fri   FAX   212-420-1167
   • Surgical and physicians equipment; some rentals. MC/VISA •

NATIONAL MEDICAL HOME CARE   800-926-5125
   60-71 Metropolitan Ave., (Fresh Pond Rd.) Ridgewood, NY 11385
   Hours: 9-5 Mon-Fri • 9-3 Sat
   • Will rent or sell; new and used equipment. Pick-up & delivery. •

SHOP RITE INSTITUTIONAL SUPPLY INC.   718-733-3823
   243 East 204th St., (Grand Concourse-Valentine Ave.) Bronx, NY 10458
   Hours: 8:30-5:30 Mon-Fri
   • Medical and hospital equipment and supplies; sales or rental; will deliver. Catalog.
   MC/VISA •

MEDICAL & SCIENTIFIC EQUIPMENT & SUPPLIES: LAB & SCIENTIFIC

ANATOMICAL CHART CO.   708-679-4700
   8221 N. Kimbal, Skokie, IL 60076   800-621-7500
   Hours: 7:30-6 Mon-Fri
   • Biological and scientific products; skeletons, skulls, anatomical charts; catalog. •

E BUK, ANTIQUES & ART   212-226-6891
   151 Spring St., 2nd Fl., (W.B'way-Wooster St.) NYC, NY 10012
   Hours: every day by appt.   (toll call) 700-SCIENCE
   • Complete period settings and custom work. RENTALS •
   (See display ads under PROP RENTAL HOUSES and under ANTIQUES.)

CAROLINA BIOLOGICAL SUPPLY   800-584-0381
   2700 York Rd., Burlington, NC 27215   910-584-0381
   Hours: 8-5 Mon-Fri • (closed for lunch 12-1)   FAX   800-222-7112
   • Lab equipment and supplies. Human & animal anatomical parts; charts, skulls, bones, skeletons; great catalog; good prices and helpful service. Phone orders. CREDIT CARDS •

CASWELL-MASSEY CO. LTD.   212-755-2254
   518 Lexington Ave., (48th St.) NYC, NY 10017
   Hours: 9-7 Mon-Fri • 10-6 Sat   FAX   212-888-4915
   • Antique apothecary bottles. For catalog call 800-326-0500. CREDIT CARDS •

CLEAN ROOM PRODUCTS   516-588-7000
   1800 Ocean Ave., Ronkonkoma, NY 11779
   Hours: 8:30-5 Mon-Fri
   • Formerly Colonial Gloves & Garments. Industrial gloves for laboratories or "clean rooms". •

COLE PARMER INSTRUMENT CO.   800-323-4340
   7425 N. Oak Park Ave., Chicago, IL 60648
   Hours: 7-7 Mon-Fri
   • Supply house for lab and scientific equipment; catalog, rush orders. •

EDMUND SCIENTIFIC CO.   609-547-3488
   101 East Gloucester Pike, Barrington, NJ 08007
   Hours: 9-8 Mon-Sat
   • Lab equipment, optics, microscopes, pumps, scientific toys and more; catalog. CREDIT CARDS •

FISHER SCIENTIFIC CO.   201-467-6400
  52 Fadem Rd., Springfield, NJ 07081
  Hours: 8:30-5 Mon-Fri   FAX   800-926-1166
   • All sorts of tubing and lab equipment. Free catalog. $100 minimum. MC/VISA •

MAXILLA AND MANDIBLE LTD.   212-724-6173
  451 Columbus Ave., (81st-82nd St.) NYC, NY 10024
  Hours: 11-7 Mon-Sat • 1-5 Sun   FAX   212-721-1073
   • Human and animal skulls, bones, skins, horns, fossils and seashells; catalog $7.95. Phone
  orders welcome. RENTALS CREDIT CARDS •

NASCO LIFE FORM MODELS   414-563-2446
  901 Janesville Ave., (Hwy 26) Fort Atkinson,, WI 53528
  Hours:7:30-4:30 Mon-Fri • 8-12 Sat   FAX   414-563-8296
   • Scientific models, artificial food; catalog available. Phone orders welcome. CREDIT CARDS •

OMAHA VACCINE CO.   800-367-4444
  PO Box 7228, 3030 L St., Omaha, NE 68107
  Hours: 7-9 Mon-Fri • 8-5 Sat • 11-5 Sun FAX   402-731-9829
   • Oversized medical equipment, giant syringes, etc.; catalog. Also veterinary and animal care
  supplies. CREDIT CARDS •

P.C.I. SCIENTIFIC   201-244-9002
  41 Plymouth St., Fairfield, NJ 07004
  Hours: 8:30-5 Mon-Fri   FAX   201-244-9448
   • Lab and scientific supplies. Very helpful. Also carry vacuum chambers. MC/VISA •

M-N

MEMORABILIA

AS TIME GOES BY / EPHEMERA AND ANTIQUES   413-528-3002
  PO Box 73, Jct. Rt. 7 and Rt. 23N, Great Barrington, MA 01230
  Hours: Open most days 11-4 • call first
   • Antique paper goods; see A. David Rutstein. •

COCA-COLA BOTTLING CO.   718-292-2424
  977 East 149th St., (Bruckner Blvd.) Bronx, NY 10455
  Hours: 9-5 Mon-Fri
   • Helpful with hard-to-find items. •

COLLECTOR'S STADIUM   212-353-1531
  214 Sullivan St., (Bleecker-W.3rd St.) NYC, NY 10012
  Hours: 11-7 every day   FAX   212-353-1571
   • Sports collectibles & cards; Knowledgeable sports enthusiasts to assist; will ship. Contact
  Bob or Arthur. RENTALS CREDIT CARDS •

ECLECTIC PRESS
212-645-8880
620 West 26th St., 4th Fl., (11th-12th Ave.) NYC, NY 10001
Hours: 9-5 Mon-Fri • or by appt.   FAX   212-243-6508

Extensive and important collection of ephemera, advertising, greeting cards, photographs, documents, brochures, maps, signage, passports, ID's, WW I ephemera, WW II ephemera, 1960's to 70's ephemera Very extensive collection of non-important papers and documents; large collection of product and household collectibles, i.e. food and cleaning supplies as well as newspapers, magazines, diaries, telephone books, letters, etc.

The Eclectic Press
620 W. 26th St. 4th Floor
New York, N.Y. 10001

• A full service prop rental house with many older items. •
(See display ad under NEWSPAPERS.)

GARGOYLES LTD.
212-255-0135
138 West 25th St., (6th-7th Ave.) NYC, NY 10001   212-242-3923
Hours: 9:30-5 Mon-Fri • appt. recommended

512 S. Third St. Philadelphia, PA 19147   215-629-1700
Hours: 9-5:30 Tue-Fri • 11-6 Sat   FAX   215-592-8441
• Theme decor for restaurants, country and period advertising memorabilia, period advertising mirrors, English and American antiques, scale models. Flier. •

KATONAH IMAGE, INC.
914-232-0961
10 Woods Bridge Road, Katonah, NY 10536
Hours: 9-5 Mon-Sat   FAX   914-232-3944

Memorabilia • Antiques • Collectibles
Juke box, slot machines, fortune tellers, carousel horses & figures, coke signs & machines, advertising signs, gas pumps & globes, mannequins, life like figures of Marilyn, Lucy, James Dean, Art Deco collectibles, housewares, furniture, vintage clothes, textiles & country farm collectibles.
If you can't find it we can.

KATONAH IMAGE INC.

• Props, rentals & sales. MC/VISA •

LOST CITY ARTS
212-941-8025
275 Lafayette St., (Houston-Prince St.) NYC, NY 10012
Hours: 10-6 Mon-Fri • 12-6 Sat & Sun   FAX   212-219-2570
• Good collection of memorabilia, advertising clocks, antique toys and collectibles. RENTALS •

NICCOLINI ANTIQUES-PROP RENTALS
212-243-2010
19 West 21st St., (5th-6th Ave.) NYC, NY 10010   212-254-2900
Hours: 10-5 Mon-Fri • or by appt.   FAX   212-366-6779
• Photographs, toys, tins, snapshots, greeting cards, signs. •

NOSTALGIA DECORATING CO.
717-472-3764
PO Box 1312, Kingston, PA 18704
Hours: 9-5 Mon-Fri • call first
• Repro prints, turn-of-the-century ads and magazine covers; also enameled metal ad signs; brochure. •

OFFSTAGE DESIGN
914-762-4658
63 Central Ave. Ossining, NY 10562
Hours: by appt.

Collection of period household labels & containers, miscellaneous paper goods, photos, documents, certificates, and postal.

Available to search for your specific needs.

• Contact Denise Grillo or Denny Clark. •

THE PROP COMPANY KAPLAN & ASSOCIATES
212-691-7767
111 West 19th St., 8th Fl., (6th-7th Ave.) NYC, NY 10011   212-691-PROP
Hours: 9-5:30 Mon-Fri   FAX   212-727-3055
    • Postcards, pens, books, sheet music, prints, photographs, tins, maps, advertising, letters, memorabilia from the 18th to the 20th Century. Contact Maxine Kaplan. •
(See display ad under PROP RENTAL HOUSES.)

PROPS FOR TODAY
212-206-0330
121 West 19th St. 3rd Fl., (6-7th Ave.) NYC, NY 10011
Hours: 8:30-5 Mon-Fri   FAX 212-924-0450

Come to us first and we'll work with your budget!
• Recently acquired memorabilia from NY Shakespeare Festival & Nostalgia Alley - antiques & collectibles.
• An unique collection of period items; photographs, playbills, valentines, menus, telephones, eyeglasses, vintage radios, wristwatches and more.
NOW ON 3 FLOORS! ONE STOP PROPPING!

    • A full service prop rental house. Ask for Laura Sheets.
(See display ad under PROP RENTAL HOUSES.)

RENT-A-THING
914-628-9298
800-287-9298
Rt. 6, Baldwin Place, NY 10505
Hours: 24 hrs., leave message, will return call
    • Antiques & collectibles for rent. •

SARSAPARILLA – DECO DESIGNS
800-234-1008
201-863-8002
5711 Washington St., West New York, NJ 07093
Hours: 8-4:15 Mon-Fri
    • Tin signs, Art Deco reproduction lamps; wholesale; catalog. MC/VISA •

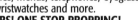

MEMORABILIA: THEATRE & FILM

ACTORS' HERITAGE
212-944-7490
262 West 44th St., (B'way-8th Ave.) NYC, NY 10036
Hours: 9:30 am-11:30 pm Mon-Sat • 11-7 Sun   FAX   212-944-2896
    • B'way t-shirts, sweatshirts, records, cassettes, posters, scripts, books, programs, film stills. CREDIT CARDS •

M-N

PAPER COLLECTABLES   212-473-2404
    126 East 12th St., basement, (3rd-4th Ave.) NYC, NY 10003
    Hours: 10-6 Mon-Sat   FAX   212-473-0840
    • Formerly Memory Shop. Out-of-print 20th century art, toys, back dated magazines, film photos and posters, pre-1970's stills. •

MOVIE STAR NEWS   212-620-8160
    134 West 18th St., (6th-7th Ave.) NYC, NY 10011
    Hours: 10-6 Mon-Sat   FAX   212-727-0634
    • Movie posters and stills; color and B&W portraits, scenes from movies. Catalog $1.
    RENTALS CREDIT CARDS •

NOSTALGIA & ALL THAT JAZZ   212-420-1940
    217 Thompson St., (3rd-Bleecker St.) NYC, NY 10012
    Hours: 1:30-9 every day
    • Film posters, prints, books, records, memorabilia. •

JERRY OHLINGER'S MOVIE MATERIAL STORE INC.   212-989-0869
    242 West 14th St., (7th-8th Ave.) NYC, NY 10011
    Hours: 1-7:45 every day   FAX   212-989-1660
    • Can be difficult but he really knows his business. 8x10's, film stills, movie posters. CREDIT CARDS •

ONE SHUBERT ALLEY   212-944-4133
    1 Shubert Alley, (44th-45th St. between B'way-8th Ave.) NYC, NY 10036 Hours:
    9:30am-11:30pm Mon- Sat •12-5 Sun   (mail order) 212-586-7610
    • Broadway show t-shirts, posters; New York souvenirs. •

SILVER SCREEN   212-967-2419
    35 East 28th St., (Park-Madison Ave.) NYC, NY 10016
    Hours: 10-4:30 Mon-Sat
    • Stock photo agency featuring motion picture and entertainment personalities, vintage movie stills, posters, etc. •

TRITON GALLERIES INC.   212-765-2472
    323 West 45th St., (8th-9th Ave.) NYC, NY 10036
    Hours: 10-6 Mon-Sat   FAX   212-956-6179
    • Good collection of Broadway posters, some foreign theatre and film posters; picture and poster framing. CREDIT CARDS •

MERCHANDISING & PROMOTION

AT&T PRODUCT PLACEMENT
ROGERS & COWAN, INC.   818-954-6944
    3701 W. Oak St. Bldg. 3, Burbank, CA 91505
    Hours: 9-5 Mon-Fri   FAX   818-954-4991
    • Placement of AT&T products for plays, film, TV. See Kip Bickel. •

GEORGE FENMORE ASSOCIATES INC.   212-977-4140
    250 West 54th St., (7-8th Ave.) NYC, NY 10019
    Hours: 9-5:30 Mon-Fri
    • Prop promotion for plays, TV and video. •

M-N

RUTH SUSSMAN   212-757-8968
    340 West 57th St., (8th-Columbus Ave.) NYC, NY 10019
    Hours: by appt.
     • Prop promotion for plays. •

METALS & FOILS

See also **JEWELER'S TOOLS & SUPPLIES**
For model brass, see **HOBBY SHOPS & SUPPLIES**
For gold leaf, see **PAINTS & DYES: BRONZING POWDERS & LEAFING SUPPLIES**

ADMIRAL METALS, CONKLIN DIVISION   718-643-6360
    270 Nevins St., (Sackett-Union St.) Brooklyn, NY 11217
    Hours: 8:30-5 Mon-Fri
     • Brass and copper sheets, rods; minimum requirements, will cut; catalog. •

ALUFOIL PRODUCTS CO. INC.   516-231-4141
    PO Box 11023, 135 Oser Ave., Hauppauge, NY 11788
    Hours: 8-5 Mon-Fri
     • Manufacturer of plain and color foils; foil papers and boards; catalog. Check about mini-mums. •

AMERICAN MODERN   201-623-3335
    25 Belgrove Drive, Kearny, NJ 07032
    Hours: 8-5 Mon-Fri   FAX 201-891-6981
     • Aluminum extruder and drawn product fabricator. •

CANAL SURPLUS   212-966-3275
    363 Canal St., (Wooster St.) NYC, NY 10013
    Hours: 10-5 Mon-Sat • 10-4 Sun
     • Good source sheet metal, pierced metal, wire, chain, "junk". •

DAVIDSON ALUMINUM   800-883-6057
    100 West Industry Court, Deer Park, NY 11729
    Hours: 8:30-5 Mon-Fri   FAX 516-586-8154
     • All types of aluminum. MC/VISA •

GRAND BRASS LAMP PARTS   212-226-2567
    221 Grand St., (Elizabeth St.) NYC, NY 10013
    Hours: 8-5 Tues-Sat • Thurs till 8
     • Decorative brass trims; also shades, lamp bases, globes, chimneys. •

HADCO ALUMINUM & METAL CORP.   718-291-8060
    104-20 Merrick Blvd., (Liberty-104th Ave.) Jamaica, NY 11433
    Hours: 8:30-5 Mon-Fri
     • Aluminum plate, rod, tubes, sheets, etc. Catalog. No minimum. •

RAPID STEEL SUPPLY CORP.   516-354-3800
    27 Denton Ave., (1 1/2 block N. of Jericho Tpke.) New Hyde Park, NY 11040
    Hours: 7-5 Mon-Fri • 7-12 Sat   FAX 516-354-0585
     • Will deliver small quantities of steel. MC/VISA •

SPACE SURPLUS METALS INC.   212-966-4358
    325 Church St., (Canal-Lispenard St.) NYC, NY 10013
    Hours: 8:30-5:30 Mon-Fri • 8:30-4:30 Sat
     • Aluminum rods, etc. Inexpensive; reasonably complete stock. •

M-N

TRIBORO IRON WORKS   718-361-9600
  38-30 31st. Street, (39th Ave.) LIC, NY 11101   718-361-9611
  Hours: 8-5 Mon-Fri   FAX 718-361-5422
  • Steel and iron in small quantities. •

WHITING & DAVIS   212-736-5810
  10 West 33rd Street. (5th Ave.) NYC, NY 10001
  Hours: 9-5 Mon-Fri
  • Metal chain, metal mesh, aluminum or brass, catalog. •

MILLINERY SUPPLIES

See also **FABRIC, ALL HEADINGS**
See also **SPRINGS, SPRING STEEL & WIRE**
See also **TRIMMINGS**

BEACON CHEMICAL   914-699-3400
  125 MacQuesten Parkway South, Mt. Vernon, NY 10550
  Hours: 8:30-4:30 Mon-Fri
  • Manufacturers of millinery adhesives and lacquers. Catalog. $50 minimum. •

CALIFORNIA MILLINERY   213-622-8746
  721 South Spring St., Los Angeles, CA 90014
  Hours: 9-5:30Mon-Fri • 10-3 Sat
  • Millinery supplies, buckram forms, flowers, feathers, and felt. Price list available. •

CONCORD MERCHANDISING CORP.   212-840-2720
  1026 6th Ave., (38-39th St.) NYC, NY 10018
  Hours: 9-6 Mon-Sat
  • Straw & wool felt hat shapes; trims, flowers, ribbon; all stock is visible in store. •

EAGLE BUCKRAM CO., INC.   212-477-5529
  951 West 2nd St., Hazelton, PA 18201
  Hours: 7:30-4:15 Mon-Fri
  • Buckram sold by the roll. •

FRIEDMAN & DISTILLATOR / OWL MILLS   212-226-6400
  53 Leonard St., (Church-W.B'way) NYC, NY 10013
  Hours: 9-5 Mon-Fri   FAX 212-219-1402
  • French belting, ribbon, wire, custom bindings; will ship; see Toni. No credit cards •

GLADSTONE FABRICS   914-783-1900
  PO Box 566, Orchard Hill Rd., Harriman, NY 10926 800-724-0168
  Hours: 9-6 Mon-Fri • Sat by appt.   FAX 914-783-2963

FAMOUS SELECTION OF THEATRICAL FABRICS
Spandex, milliskin, nude souffle, sequin cloth, metallic lame' and
lace, novelty nets and tulle, buckram and fake furs. Also unique
antique ribbons, braids, trims, beaded and feathered appliques,
as well as the fundamental cottons, linens, woolens and silks.

  • Fast shipment, swatching service, knowledgeable staff. CREDIT CARDS •
  (See display ad under FABRICS: GENERAL.)

MANNY'S MILLINERY SUPPLY CO.   212-840-2235
　　26 West 38th St., (5th-6th Ave.) NYC, NY 10018
　　Hours: 9:30-5:30 Mon-Fri • 9:30-4 Sat　　　　　FAX　212-944-0178
　　• Sizing, Sobo, 2-ply buckrum, millinery wire, felt bodies, trimmings; catalog. •

NATIONAL BEATTY-PAGE INC.   718-330-1280
　　Brooklyn Navy Yard, Bldg. #5, 6th Fl., (Clinton Ave.) Brooklyn, NY 11205
　　Hours: 9-4 Mon-Fri, • call first
　　• Manufacturer of hatbands. Catalog. $50 minimum. •

VOGUE HAT BLOCK & DIE CORP.
　　252 Norman Ave., (Monitor-Kingsland Ave.) Brooklyn, NY 11222　718-383-5800
　　Hours: by appt.
　　• Hat blocks custom made. No stock. •

WASHINGTON MILLINERY SUPPLY   301-963-4444
　　18810 Woodfield Rd., Gaithersburg, MD 20879
　　Hours: 9-5 Mon-Fri • 10-2 Sat
　　• Millinery supplies, cape net; wholesale. •

ZEEMAN CORP.   212-302-2822
　　270 West 38th St., (7th-8th Ave.) NYC, NY 10018
　　Hours: 9-4 Mon-Fri
　　• Buckram, adhesives, sizing, ribbons, wire, cape net. Catalog. No minimum. •

MOLDINGS

See also **LUMBER**

BENDIX MOLDINGS   800-526-0240
　　37 Ramland Rd. S., Orangeburg, NY 10962   914-365-1111
　　Hours: 9-5 Mon-Fri • pickup 9-11 & 1-3　　　　　FAX　914-365-1218
　　• Moldings and ornaments; catalog available. MC/VISA •

ALBERT CONSTANTINE & SONS   718-792-1600
　　2050 Eastchester Road, (Seminole-McDonald St.) Bronx, NY 10461
　　Hours: 8-6 Mon-Fri • Thurs till 8 • 8-3 Sat • (May-Aug: 8-5 Mon-Fri • 8-1 Sat)
　　• Wood moldings; woodworking tools; exotic woods. Good products, good service. MC/VISA •

THE DECORATORS SUPPLY COMPANY   312-847-6300
　　3610-12 S. Morgan St., Chicago, IL 60609
　　Hours: 8-3:30 Mon-Fri　　　　　　　　　　　FAX　312-847-6357
　　• Repro ornaments and moldings; can be steamed to take a curve; catalog #214 ($15) con-
　　tains over 16,000 items; speak to Jack. No CREDIT CARDS •

DYKES LUMBER   212-246-6480
　　348 West 44th St., (8-9th Ave.) NYC, NY 10036   212-582-1930
　　Hours: 7:30-5 Mon-Fri • 7:30-1 Sat

　　167 6th St., (2-3rd Ave.) Brooklyn, NY 11215   718-624-3350
　　Hours: 7:30-5 Mon-Fri• 8-1 Sat

　　26-16 Jackson Ave., (near Queens Plaza) L.I.C., NY 11101   718-784-3920
　　Hours: 7:30-4:30 Mon-Fri • 8-12:30 Sat
　　• Lumber, styro and wood beams; large molding catalog. •

"I found it in the N.Y. Theatrical Sourcebook."　　　　　　　**285**

FLEX MOLDING 201-487-8080
16 East Lafayette St., Hackensack, NJ 07601
Hours: 8-4:30 Mon-Fri FAX 201-487-6637
• Flexible and rigid moldings; selection of decorative ornaments; catalog. •

MAXWELL LUMBER 212-337-3121
211 West 18th St., (7th-8th Ave.) NYC, NY 10011
Hours: 7:30-4:30 Mon-Fri

25-30 Borden Ave. (25-27th St..) L.I.C. NY 11101 212-929-6088
Hours: 7-4 Mon-Fri
• Lumber, large molding catalog. •

NEW YORK METAL MOULDING CO., INC. 718-726-8000
19-22 45th St., (19th) Astoria, NY 11105 718-956-5600
Hours: 8-5 Mon-Fri FAX 718-956-1009
• Stocks a large variety of aluminum and stainless steel moldings, including counter edging, price tag, angles, nosing, bars, channels; Wilsonart Laminate. $50 minimum on deliveries; catalog. •

YALE PICTURE FRAME CORP. 718-788-6200
770 Fifth Ave., (27th-28th) Brooklyn, NY 11232 (outside NY) 800-331-YALE
Hours: 8-4:30 Mon-Thurs • 11-3 Sun FAX 718-788-5852
• Wide selection of picture frame moldings, all styles & widths. Catalog. Will ship. MC/VISA •

MOTORS & MECHANICAL COMPONENTS

AMERICAN SCIENCE AND SURPLUS 708-475-8440
3605 Howard St. (warehouse), Skokie, IL 60076 312-763-0313
Hours: 8-4 Mon-Fri FAX 800-934-0722
• Sail on surplus. Catalog of gadgets and weird items from industrial and military surplus. •

B & B ELECTRIC MOTOR & CONTROL CORP. 718-784-1313
39-40 Crescent, (39th Ave.) L.I.C., NY 11101
Hours: 9-5 Mon-Fri
• Speed controls, servo systems, clutches, brakes, design and modification. •

BEARDSLEE TRANSMISSION EQUIP. CO. 718-784-4100
27-22 Jackson Ave., (Dutchkills-Queens St.) L.I.C., NY 11101
Hours: 7:30-5 Mon-Fri
• Gear boxes, belts, ball bearings, maintenance items. •

WINFRED M. BERG 516-599-5010
499 Ocean Ave., East Rockaway, NY 11518
Hours: 8:30-5 Mon-Fri FAX 516-599-3274
• Suppliers of precision mechanical components from stock; catalog. •

EDMUND SCIENTIFIC CO. 609-547-3488
101 East Gloucester Pike, Barrington, NJ 08007
Hours: 9-8 Mon-Sat
• Fine catalog; hobby motors, magnets lasers, kaleidoscopes, mirrors, strobes, etc. CREDIT CARDS •

GRAINGER, DIV. OF W.W. GRAINGER INC.   212-629-5660
527 West 34th St., (10-11th) NYC, NY 10001

150 Varick St. (Spring) NYC, NY 10013   212-463-9566
Hours: 8-5 Mon-Fri
• Dayton motors, bearings; also electrical, shop, maintenance & storage equipment & supplies; national chain; huge catalog. MC/VISA •

HERBACH & RADEMAN CO. CORPORATION   215-788-5583
18 Canal St., (Beaver-Canal) Bristol, PA 19007   (orders only) 800-848-8001
Hours: 8-5 Mon-Fri • 1-4 Sat (pick up hours only)   FAX   215-788-9577
• Surplus motors, fans, electrics, lenses, etc. Minimums: $25 cash, C.O.D.; $50 open account; $500 international. CREDIT CARDS •

MCMASTER-CARR SUPPLY CO   908-329-3200
PO Box 440, Monmouth Junction Rd., New Brunswick, NJ 08903-0440
Hours: 7-4 Mon-Fri   FAX   908-329-3772
• Top quality items; motors, components; a vast selection of even hard to find stuff. Great catalog. •

MICRO-MO ELECTRONICS INC.   813-822-2529
742 Second Ave. A, St. Petersburg, FL 33701
Hours: 8:30-5 Mon-Fri
• Services PM motors and gearheads; encoders, tachs at list prices. •

NORTHERN HYDRAULICS INC.   800-533-5545
PO Box 1499, 801 East Cliff Rd., Burnsville, MN 55337
Hours: 24 hours every day (catalog sales)   FAX   612-894-0083
• Generators, compressors, air tools, winches, accessories; catalog. CREDIT CARDS •

PATRON TRANSMISSION CO. INC.   212-226-1140
PO Box 284, 497 Washington Ave., Carlstadt, NJ 07072   201-933-7400
Hours: 8-5 Mon-Fri   FAX   201-933-7409
• Power transmission equipment, conveyers, gears, chains, sprockets, etc; catalog. •

PIC DESIGNS   800-243-6125
PO Box 1004, Benson Rd., Middlebury, CT 06762   203-758-8272
Hours: 8-5 Mon-Fri
• Stock mail order mechanical components; ask for catalog #40. •

SAVA INDUSTRIES INC.   201-835-0882
PO Box 30, 4 N. Corporate Dr., Riverdale, NJ 07457
Hours: 8-5 Mon-Fri
• Aircraft cable, fittings, small ball bearing pulleys; minimum order applies; ask for catalog #14. •

SEGAL BROTHERS   718-383-2995
205 Nassau Ave., (Russell) Brooklyn, NY 11222
Hours: 8-5 Mon-Fri
• Large selection of motors. CREDIT CARDS •

SMALL PARTS INC.   305-751-0856
PO Box 4650, 13980 NW 58th Court, Miami Lakes, FL 33014-0650
Hours: 8-6:30 Mon-Fri   FAX   800-423-9009
• Great selection of parts, mechanical components, tools; catalog #11. •

STOCK DRIVE PRODUCTS   516-328-0200
2101 Jericho Turnpike, New Hyde Park, NY 11042   (sales) 516-328-3300
Hours: 8:30-5 Mon-Fri   FAX   516-326-8827
• Invaluable catalog of mechanical components, gears, rack and pinions, timing belts, etc. •

M-N

FRANK TRACY-BEARING INDUSTRY CORP.   212-226-3500
    14 Wooster St., (Grand-Canal) NYC, NY 10013
    Hours: 7:30-4:30 Mon-Fri   FAX   212-226-3505
    • Gears, bearings, transmissions, small mechanicals. •

MOVING, TRANSPORT & STORAGE

See also **SHIPPING**
For packing materials & containers see **FIBRE CASES**
                    see **PACKING MATERIALS**

ANTHONY AUGLIERA   203-937-9080
    34 Hamilton St., West Haven, CT 06516
    Hours: 9-4:30 Mon-Fri   FAX   201-937-0140
    • Interstate theatrical haulers. •

ATLANTIC STUDIO INC.   201-481-9242
    661 N. 4th St., Newark, NJ 07107   212-594-8649
    Hours: 8-5 Mon-Fri   FAX   201-481-9159
    • Large warehouse space available for storage; some moving and storage services available.
    Ask for John. •
    (See display ad under SCENIC SHOPS.)

CENTRAL MOVERS   718-622-2660
    358 Classon Ave., (Clifton Pl.-Lafayette) Brooklyn, NY 11238   800-777-6060
    Hours: 9-5 Mon-Fri • 9-1 Sat   FAX   718-622-2715
    • Interstate, local and international; storage, fully licensed & insured. •

CLARK TRANSFER   212-580-4075
    800-A Paxton St., Harrisburg, PA 17104   800-488-7585
    Hours: 8-5 Mon-Fri

OVER 40 YEARS OF COMPETITIVE PRICING AND RELIABLE SERVICE.

SINCE 1948
LET'S GET THE SHOW ON THE ROAD.

    • Interstate theatrical hauling. •

VALENTIN COTTO   212-663-0334
    117 West 96th St., (Columbus-Amsterdam Ave.) NYC, NY 10025
    Hours: by appt.
    • Van with driver. •

CROZIER FINE ARTS   212-741-2024
    525 West 20th St., (10th-11th Ave.) NYC, NY 10011   800-822-2787
    Hours: 9-5 Mon-Fri   FAX   212-243-5209
    • Fine art movers; custom crates. •

EGOTRIPS INC.   215-732-4974
    2022 Spruce St., Philadelphia, PA 19103
    Hours: 10-6 Mon-Fri   FAX   215-732-0700
    • Theatrical hauling throughout the U.S.; contact Jim Bodenhiemer. •

ERIE TRANSFER CO.
212-242-3366
Pier 62, West 23rd St., (11th-12th Ave.) NYC, NY 10011   212-245-0890
Hours: 4:30 am-4 pm Mon-Fri
• New York City theatrical and film haulers. •

HAPPY HOOSIER TRUCKING CO.
212-765-7868
342 West 56th St., (B'way) NYC, NY 10019
Hours: leave message on machine
• Local moving man with van, reliable. •

INS & OUTS TRANSPORT
212-568-9133
720 Ft. Washington Ave., #1E, (190th St.) NYC, NY 10040   (pager) 212-389-9853
Hours: by appt.

Production transport for theatrical, industrial and special events.
Rates commensurate with your budget and storage is available.

INS & OUTS

• Theatrical shipping and receiving in the metropolitan area; reasonable rates. Ask for Ray; they will take calls anytime. •

INTERSTATE CONSOLIDATION
(ext. 203) 213-720-1771
5800 E. Sheila St., Los Angeles, CA 90040   800-824-4316
Hours: 8-5 Mon-Fri   FAX 213-726-8334
• Interstate theatrical hauling. •

LINCOLN SCENIC TRANSPORT INC.
212-244-2700
560 West 34th St., (10th-11th Ave.) NYC, NY 10001
Hours: 8-5 Mon-Fri   FAX 212-643-0467

Specializing in the transportation and storage of

scenery and props for the entertainment industry.

• Scenery transport and storage. Access to full service scenic shop. Reliable professionals. •

NETWORK TRANSPORTATION SYSTEMS, INC.
908-689-4000
35 Brown St., (Rt. 31 and Rt. 57) Washington, NJ 07882
Hours: 8-5 Mon-Fri   FAX 908-689-4516
• Trucking & warehousing for scenery, lighting & trade shows. •

THE PADDED WAGON
212-222-4880
120 West 107th St., (Amsterdam-Columbus Ave.) NYC, NY 10025
Hours: 9-5 Mon-Fri   FAX 212-222-8564
• Furniture and art movers. •

PROP SERVICES
212-465-2300
552 West 43rd St., (10th-11th Ave.) NYC, NY 10036
Hours: 8-6 Mon-Fri • or by appt.
• Local trucking service geared to the film industry; reliable. Storage space available. •

RAPID MESSENGER SERVICE
212-620-7130
154 West 27th St., (6th-7th Ave.) NYC, NY 10010
Hours: 8:30-5:30 Mon-Fri
• NYC area trucking; reasonable rates, by the trip or by the hour. •

M-N

"I found it in the N.Y. Theatrical Sourcebook."   **289**

SCENIC CENTRAL　　　　　　　　　　　　　　　718-797-1196
　　196 Van Dyke St., (Ferris-Conover St.) Brooklyn, NY 11231
　　Hours: 8:30-5:30 Mon-Fri　　　　　　　　FAX　718-643-1685
　　• Low cost trucking & storage for scenery & props. •

SHOWMAN FABRICATORS, INC　　　　　　　　718-935-9899
　　29 Imlay, (Hamilton-Bowne St.) Brooklyn, NY 11231
　　Hours: 8-5:30 Mon-Fri　　　　　　　　　FAX　718-855-9823
　　• Storage space rental for sets and props; contact Mark Viola, Robert Usdin or Michael Cioffi. •

STEIGELBAUER ASSOC. INC.　　　　　　　　　718-624-0835
　　Bldg. 20, Brooklyn Navy Yard, (Cumberland-Flushing Ave.) Brooklyn, NY 11205
　　Hours: 7-2:30 Mon-Fri　　　　　　　　　FAX　718-624-0844
　　• Union scenic shop; storage rental available; contact Mike. •

U-HAUL MOVING & STORAGE　　　　　　　　212-620-4177
　　562 West 23rd St., (10th-11th Ave.) NYC, NY 10011
　　Hours: 7am-8pm Mon-Sat • 9-5 Sun
　　• Truck rental; packing blankets, dollies, boxes. •

VAN GOGH MOVERS　　　　　　　　　　　　212-226-0500
　　43 Renwick, (Spring-Canal St.) NYC, NY 10013
　　Hours: 7-5 Mon-Fri　　　　　　　　　　FAX　212-226-6671
　　• Interstate and international moving; commercial or residential; also fine art crating. •

WALTON HAULING & WAREHOUSE CORP.　　　212-246-8685
　　609 West 46th St., (11th-12th Ave.) NYC, NY 10036
　　Hours: 7-5 Mon-Fri　　　　　　　　　　FAX　212-586-4628
　　• 115 plus year-old theatrical hauling company; local, some storage. •

MUSICAL INSTRUMENTS & SHEET MUSIC

ACCORDION-O-RAMA　　　　　　　　　　　212-675-9089
　　307 7th Ave., 20th Fl., (27-28th St.) NYC, NY 10001
　　Hours: 9-4 Tues-Fri • 11-3 Sat • or by appt.
　　• Sale, rental and repair of new and reconditioned accordions and concertinas. MC/VISA •

SAM ASH MUSIC STORES　　　　　　　　　212-719-2299
　　160 West 48th St., (6th-7th Ave.) NYC, NY 10036
　　Hours: 10-6 Mon-Sat
　　• Guitars, amps, wind and string instruments; rental, repair, purchase; sheet music. •

AYERS PERCUSSION　　　　　　　　　　　212-582-8410
　　410 West 47th St., (9th-10th Ave.) NYC, NY 10036
　　Hours: 10-6 Mon-Fri • or by appt.　　　　FAX　212-586-0862
　　• Rental and repairs of acoustic percussion; will custom build; very helpful. Will ship. MC/VISA •

ROD BALTIMORE MUSIC CO. LTD./INT'L WOODWIND & BRASS CENTER, INC.　212-575-1508
　　174 W. 48th St., 3rd Fl., (6th-7th Ave.) NYC, NY 10036　　　　　212-840-7165
　　Hours: 9-6 Mon-Fri • 10-5 Sat　　　　　FAX　212-575-7835
　　• Rentals and purchases, see Hartley. CREDIT CARDS •

BARGAIN SPOT   212-674-1188 / 212-674-1189
64 Third Ave., (11th Ave.) NYC, NY 10003
Hours: 9-4:45 Mon-Sat
• A large pawn shop. Rental or purchase of old and new musical instruments, cameras, binoculars, power tools and more. CREDIT CARDS •

BEETHOVEN PIANOS   212-765-7300
232 West 58th St., (7th- Bway.) NYC, NY 10019
Hours: 8:30-7:30 Mon-Sat • 12-4 Sun
• Piano rentals, sales, restoring, tuning, rebuilding, refinishing, storage and moving. Nice selection. CREDIT CARDS •

BROWN'S MUSIC   212-541-6236
61 West 62nd St., (B'way-Columbus) NYC, NY 10023
Hours: 10-7 Mon-Sat • 12-6 Sun
• Sheet music, libretti, books, scores, etc. Will ship. CREDIT CARDS •

CARROLL MUSICAL INSTRUMENT RENTAL   212-868-4120
351 West 41st St., (8th-9th Ave.) NYC, NY 10036
Hours: 7-9 Mon-Fri • 8-4 Sat & Sun   FAX 212-868-4126
• Large stock instruments, stands, etc. Rental only; see Dennis. CREDIT CARDS •

CENTER FOR MUSICAL ANTIQUITIES   212-744-8168
544 East 86th St., (York-East End Ave.) NYC, NY 10028
Hours: by appt.
• Antique and foreign musical instruments; see Lillian or Stuart Caplin. RENTALS •

COLONY RECORDS   212-265-2050
1619 Broadway, (49th St.) NYC, NY 10019
Hours: 9:30am-midnight Sun-Thurs • 10am-2am Fri, Sat   FAX 212-956-6009
• Large selection of sheet music, records, tapes, CD's; will ship anywhere. CREDIT CARDS •

K. DETRICH   212-245-1234
211 West 58th St., (7th-B'way) NYC, NY 10019
Hours: 10-6 Mon-Fri • 10-4 Sat   FAX 212-541-5521
• Unusual pianos. RENTALS •

DRUMMERS WORLD INC.   212-840-3057
147 West 46th St., (B'way-6th Ave.) NYC, NY 10036
Hours: 10-6 Mon-Fri • 10-4 Sat   FAX 212-391-1185
• Anything dealing with percussion and/or sound effects; the familiar and the unusual. Very helpful, will order; see Barry. Catalog. CREDIT CARDS •

FORD PIANO SUPPLY   212-569-9200
4898 Broadway, (204th-207th St.) NYC, NY 10034
Hours: 8-5:30 Mon-Fri • call for Sat hours   FAX 212-567-5408
• Custom gutted pianos for theatrical needs; piano rentals and piano wire. CREDIT CARDS •

KEYNOTE PIANO RENTALS   212-777-1388
77 Bleecker St., (B'way-Mercer St.) NYC, NY 10012
Hours: by appt.
• Rents Yamaha pianos; speak to Sylvia Calabrese. •

LINCOLN PIANO SERVICE   212-734-6385
1459 Third Ave., (82nd-83rd St.) NYC, NY 10028
Hours: 10-5 Mon-Sat
• Rental or purchase; some older period-type upright pianos. •

M-N

MANNY'S MUSICAL INSTRUMENTS & ACCESSORIES INC. 212-819-0576
156 West 48th St., (6th-7th Ave.) NYC, NY 10036   800-448-8478
Hours: 10-6 Mon-Sat   FAX   212-391-9250
• Large stock of instruments, amps, music stands and lights; sales only. Catalog. CREDIT CARDS •

MUSIC EXCHANGE 212-354-5858
151 West 46th St., 10th Fl., (6th-7th Ave.) NYC, NY 10036
Hours: 10-5 Mon-Fri
• Sheet music, records, tapes, CD's; for a fee, will track down anything. Ask for Lillian. •

MUSIC INN 212-243-5715
169 West 4th St., (6th-7th Ave.) NYC, NY 10014
Hours: 1-7 Tues-Sat
• Sales and rental; antique, ethnic, standard musical instruments. Also ethnic artifacts and jewelry. Will ship. CREDIT CARDS •

MUSIC STORE AT CARL FISHER 212-677-0821
62 Cooper Square, (4th Ave. & 7th St.) NYC, NY 10003   212-777-0900
Hours: 10-5:45 Mon-Sat
• Excellent source for sheet music and books. MC/VISA •

MUSIC THEATRE INTERNATIONAL 212-868-6668
545 Eighth Ave., (37th-38th St.) NYC, NY 10018
Hours: 9-6 Mon-Fri
• Mail order catalog of musical scores. •

JOSEPH PATELSON MUSIC HOUSE 212-582-5840
160 West 56th St., (6th-7th Ave.) NYC, NY 10019
Hours: 9-6 Mon-Sat   FAX   212-246-5633
• Large selection of sheet music, scores, opera libretti, books. CREDIT CARDS •

PIONEER PIANO CORP. 212-586-3718
934 Eighth Ave., (55th St.) NYC, NY 10019
Hours: 10-6 Mon-Fri • 11-5 Sat • 12-5 Sun
• Pianos, rental or purchase. •

PRO PIANO 212-206-8794
85 Jane St., (Washington-Greenwich Ave.) NYC, NY 10014
Hours: 9-5 Mon-Fri • 10-4 Sat
• Pianos, rental or purchase. CREDIT CARDS •

ROGERS & HAMMERSTEIN THEATRE LIBRARY 212-541-6900
1633 Broadway, Rm. 3801, (50th St.) NYC, NY 10019
Hours: 9:30-5:30 Mon-Fri
• Mail order catalog of musicals. •

STEINWAY & SONS 212-246-1100
109 West 57th St., (6-7th Ave.) NYC, NY 10019   (factory) 718-721-2600
Hours: 9-6 Mon-Fri • Thurs till 7:30 • 9-5 Sat • 12-5 Sun
• The legend continues; sales, tuning, restoration; will buy used Steinways. •

STUDIO INSTRUMENT RENTALS 212-627-4900
520 West 25th St., (10-11th Ave.) NYC, NY 10001
310 West 52nd St. (8-9th Ave.) NYC, NY 10019
Hours: 8-midnight every day   FAX   212-627-7079
• Large selection of instruments for rent. Rehearsal studios. CREDIT CARDS •

TOTAL PIANO AND ORGAN RENTAL　　　　　　　　　212-868-4125
　351 West 41st St., (8th-9th Ave.) NYC, NY 10036
　Hours: 8-7 Mon-Fri • 9-5 Sat • call for Sun hours　　FAX　212-868-4126
　　• All types of pianos and organs for rental or sale. CREDIT CARDS •

MATT UMANOV GUITARS　　　　　　　　　　　　212-675-2157
　273 Bleecker St., (6-7th Ave.) NYC, NY 10014
　Hours: 11-7 Mon-Sat • 12-6 Sun　　　　　　　　FAX　212-727-8404
　　• New and used guitars, amps, effects, repairs. CREDIT CARDS •

UNIVERSAL MUSICAL INSTRUMENT CO.　　　　　　212-254-6917
　732 Broadway, (8th-Waverly Pl.) NYC, NY 10003
　Hours: 10-4:30 Mon-Fri • 10-4 Sat
　　• All types of instruments and accessories including finger cymbals, castanets and sheet music. •

VILLAGE FLUTE & SAX SHOP　　　　　　　　　212-243-1276
　35 Carmine St., (off Bleecker & 6th Ave.) NYC, NY 10014
　Hours: call for hours
　　• See Rick; some relics and parts make great props. RENTALS CREDIT CARDS •

NOTES

M-N

NOTES

ATAC

N-IM

NEON

See also **SIGNS & LETTERS**

ARTKRAFT STRAUSS SIGN CORP.   212-265-5155
   830 Twelfth Ave., (57th St.) NYC, NY 10019
   Hours: 9:00-5:00 Mon-Fri   FAX   212-265-9436
   • Custom signs: metal, wood, neon & computerized. •

LET THERE BE NEON, INC.   212-226-4883
   38 White St., (Church-Broadway) NYC, NY 10013
   Hours: 8:30-5:30 Mon-Fri   FAX   212-431-6731
   • Custom and stock neon; speak to Rudi or Jeff. RENTALS •

MANHATTAN NEON SIGN, CORP.   212-714-0430
   335 West 38th St., (8th-9th Ave.) NYC, NY 10018
   Hours: 8-4 Mon-Fri or by appt.   FAX   212-947-3906
   • Custom and stock neon. Contact Pat or Marilyn Tomasso. RENTALS •

MERCURY LIGHTING AND SIGNS UNLIMITED   212-473-6366
   104 East 7th St., NYC, NY 10009
   Hours: 9-5 Mon-Fri by appt.   FAX   212-979-8322
   • Neon signs and lighting fixtures; custom and rental. •

MIDTOWN NEON SIGN CORP.   212-736-3838
   550 West 30th St., (10-11th Ave.) NYC, NY 10001
   Hours: by appt.
   • Stock and custom neon, name brand and generic. RENTALS •

SUPER NEON LIGHTS CO.   718-236-5667
   7813 16th Ave., (78th St.) Brooklyn, NY 11214
   Hours: 8-4:45 Mon-Fri
   • Neon signs; good work; good prices. •

NETS

SINCO NET COMPANY   203-267-2545
   PO Box 361, Sinco Pl., East Hampton, CT 06424   800-243-6753
   Hours: 9-5 Mon-Fri
   • Cargo, safe-fall, boarding, aviary nets & rope ladders. Custom and some stock. Insured.
   MC/VISA •

STERLING NET   201-783-9800
   18 Label St., Montclair, NJ 07042
   Hours: 9-5 Mon-Fri
   • Theatrical, decorative, agricultural, fishing, & cargo nets. Bulk and custom. •

NEWSPAPERS

BAUMWELL GRAPHICS INC.
212-868-3340
450 West 31st St., (9-10th Ave.) NYC, NY 10001
Hours: 8:30-6 Mon-Fri   FAX   212-689-3386
• Custom replicas of current and back-dated newspapers, magazines, etc. Custom transfers. Reasonably priced. Contact Clyde Baumwell. •

DEPENDABLE DELIVERY INC.
212-586-5552
360 West 52nd St., (8-9th Ave.) NYC, NY 10019
Hours: 8am-1pm Mon-Fri
• Back-dated NYC newspapers, previous 6 months only; all current issues of U.S. and foreign newspapers. •

ECLECTIC PRESS
212-645-8880
620 West 26th St. 4th Fl., (11-12th Ave.) NYC, NY 10001
Hours: 9-5 Mon-Fri or by appt.   FAX   212-243-6508
• Creation and reproduction of custom newspapers and other printed props; also current and back dated papers and magazines, in-stock generic product labels. •
(See display ad in this section.)

THE HAND PROP ROOM, INC.
213-931-1534
5700 Venice Blvd., Los Angeles, CA 90019
Hours: 7-7 Mon-Fri   FAX   213-931-2145
• Full printing and graphics service; newspapers, license plates, IDs, "Greeked" product labels, and credit cards. •

EARL HAYS PRESS
818-765-0700
10707 Sherman Way, Sun Valley, CA 91352
Hours: 8-5 Mon-Fri   FAX   818-765-5245
• Period repro newspapers, books, diplomas etc.; also license plates, "Greeked" product labels, etc. •

HISTORIC NEWSPAPER ARCHIVES
908-381-2332
800-221-3221
1582 Hart St., Rahway, NJ 07065
Hours: 9-5 Mon-Fri or leave message
• Back-dated newspapers, 1880-1989, from major US cities; catalog available. Original papers available for gift items. •

HOTALING NEWS AGENCY
212-840-1868
142 West 42nd St., (B'way-6th Ave.) NYC, NY 10036
Hours: 7:30am-9pm Mon-Fri • 7:30am-8pm Sat & Sun   FAX   212-944-8857
• In business since 1905! Large selection current foreign and out-of-town newspapers and magazines. Will ship. MC/VISA •

VICTOR KAMKIN, INC.
212-673-0776
925 Broadway, (21st St.) NYC, NY 10010
Hours: 9:30-5:30 Mon-Fri (Thurs till 6) • 10-5 Sat
• Current Russian newspapers, periodicals, books, and gifts. Also related subject books in English. •

KLEAR COPY RUBBER STAMPS
212-243-0357
55 Seventh Ave. S., (Bleecker-Morton St.) NYC, NY 10014
Hours: 1:30-6:30 Mon, Wed, Fri • 12:30-6:30 Tues, Thurs, Sat   FAX   212-645-5335
• Newspaper headlines; stock and custom rubber stamps; while-u-wait. •

N–M

M-N

CARMEN D. VALENTINO RARE BOOKS   215-739-6056
   2956 Richmond St., (Ann-Indiana) Philadelphia, PA 19134
   Hours: By appt. only or leave message on machine
      • Specializes in American printed matter, mostly pre-1920, newspapers, periodicals, calendar art, etc. •

YOMIURI PRESS / YOMIURI SHIMBUN   212-765-1111
   666 6th Ave., (52nd-53rd St.) NYC, NY 10103
   Hours: 9:30-5:30 Mon-Fri
      • Current Japanese newspapers. •

NOTIONS: GENERAL & TAILORS

AGH TRIM SOURCE   212-643-7300
   229 West 36th St., (7th Ave.) NYC, NY 10018   800-PRO-TRIM
   Hours: 9-5 Mon-Fri   FAX   212-268-3385
      • Zippers, thread, trim, seam binding, elastic, horsehair, hook & loop fasteners, boning. No credit cards. •

AMERICAN NOTION CO., INC.   212-563-0480
   336 West 37th St., (8-9th Ave.) NYC, NY 10018
   Hours: 9-5 Mon-Fri   FAX   212-563-0584
      • Notions, horsehair, zippers, elastic. •

BAER FABRICS
515 East Market, Louisville, KY 40202   (costumes) 800-769-7778
Hours: 9-9 Mon • 9-5 Tue-Sat   (fashion) 800-769-7776
     FAX   502-582-2331
• Every kind of wholesale tailors' supply; prompt shipment. CREDIT CARDS •

CLOTILDE INC.   800-772-2891
2 Sew Smart Way B8031, Stevens Point, WI 54481-8031
Hours: 8:30-5 Mon-Fri   FAX   715-341-3082
• Comprehensive selection of unusual sewing and craft supplies; free catalog available.
MC/VISA •

DESIGN CRAFT FABRIC CORP.   708-527-2580
7227 Oak Park, Niles, IL 60648   800-755-1010
Hours: 9-5 Mon-Fri
• Foam-backed fabrics, 60" wide loop weave fabric. Wholesale. •

40TH ST. TRIMMINGS, INC.   212-354-4729
252 West 40th St., (7-8th Ave.) NYC, NY 10018
Hours: 9-5:45 Mon-Fri • 10-5 Sat
• Notions, trimmings, novelties; wholesale and retail. CREDIT CARDS •

FRIEDMAN & DISTILLATOR / OWL MILLS   212-226-6400
53 Leonard St., (Church-W.B'way) NYC, NY 10013
Hours: 9-5 Mon-Fri   FAX   212-219-1402
• Ribbons, braids, cords, french belting, millinery supplies; speak to Toni. No credit cards. •

GIZMO NOTION CORP..   212-477-2773
160 First Ave., (9-10th St.) NYC, NY 10009
Hours: 10-5 every day
• Patterns, buttons thread, zippers, etc.; including machines. Contact Rosa or Hossein. No
credit cards. •

GREENBERG & HAMMER INC.   212-246-2835
24 West 57th St., (5-6th Ave.) NYC, NY 10019   800-955-5135
Hours: 9-6 Mon-Fri • 10-5 Sat (closed Sat: July, Aug)   FAX   212-765-8475
• Enormous selection of sewing notions, sewing tools and wardrobe kit supplies. Phone and
mail orders; see Dottie or Frank. CREDIT CARDS •

HARLOU   212-564-0265
347 West 36th St., (8-9th Ave.) NYC, NY 10018
Hours: 8-5 Mon-Fri
• Tubular pipings and trimmings. •

HAROLD TRIMMING CO.   212-695-4098
237 West 35th St., 8th Fl., (7-8th Ave.) NYC, NY 10018
Hours: 8:30-5 Mon-Fri
• Elastic, zippers, buttons, etc.; see Harold. •

HERSH – 6TH AVE. BUTTON   212-391-6615
1000 Sixth Ave., (37th St.) NYC, NY 10018
Hours: 9:30-5:30 Mon-Fri • 11-4 Sat
• Notions and tailors' supplies. CREDIT CARDS •

HOWARD NOTION & TRIMMING CO.   212-674-4550
149 Essex St., (Houston-Delancey) NYC, NY 10002   212-674-1321
Hours: 9-6 Mon-Thurs • 9-5 Fri   FAX   212-228-4960
• General notions wholesaler. •

KREINIK MFG. CO., INC. 800-537-2166
9199 Reisterstown Rd., Suite 209B, Owing Mills, MD 21117
Hours: 8:30-5 Mon-Fri
• Needles, metallic and silk threads, etc. Catalog available. •

LEVITT INDUSTRIAL TEXTILE INC. 516-933-7553
PO Box 7150, 15 William St., Hicksville, NY 11801 800-548-0097
Hours: 9-5 Mon-Fri
• VELCRO® brand hook & loop fasteners in tape, "coins" and cloth for immediate delivery; speak to Ken Kantner. •

J.M. LYNNE 516-582-4300
59 Gilpin Ave., Hauppauge, NY 11788 800-645-5044
Hours: 8:30-8 Mon-Fri FAX 516-582-4112
• VELCRO® brand hook & loop fasteners; by the roll; also VELCRO® brand fabrics. •

NEWARK DRESSMAKER SUPPLY CO. 215-837-7500
PO Box 20730, Lehigh Valley, PA 18002
Hours: 8-4 Mon-Fri • or leave message FAX 215-837-9115
• Large supply of general notions and some unusual items; catalog available; fast delivery. CREDIT CARDS. •

OSHMAN'S 212-226-7448
85 Eldridge St., (Hester-Grand St.) NYC, NY 10002
Hours: 9-4 Sun-Fri
• Tailors' trimmings. •

M–N

"I found it in the N.Y. Theatrical Sourcebook." **299**

PRIMROSE TRIMMING CO.　　　　　　　　　　　　516-486-7388
　798 Princeton Rd., Franklin Sq., NY 11010
　Hours: by appt.
　• All tailors' notions. •

PRYM DRITZ CORP.　　　　　　　　　　　　　　803-576-5050
　PO Box 5028, Spartanburg, SC 29304　　　　　800-845-4948
　Hours: 8-5 Mon-Fri
　• Manufacturer of sewing notions; catalog. •

RICHARD THE THREAD / ROY COOPER　　　　213-852-4997
　8320 Melrose Ave., Los Angeles, CA 90069　800-473-4997
　Hours: 9-5 Mon-Fri
　• Specializes in hard-to-find items; silk dress shields; catalog, mail and phone orders. UPS
　C.O.D.s. •

SERVICE TRIMMINGS　　　　　　　　　　　　212-921-1680
　256 West 38th St., (7-8th Ave.) NYC, NY 10018　800-508-7353
　Hours: 8:30-5 Mon-Fri
　• Labels, ribbons, zippers. Retail and wholesale. •

SEWING CENTER INC. (BURLINGTON FABRICS)　212-354-9275
　202 West 40th St., (7-8th Ave.) NYC, NY 10018
　Hours: 9-6 Mon-Fri • 10-5 Sat
　• Notions, patterns, trimmings. CREDIT CARDS. •

SISKA, INC.　　　　　　　　　　　　　　　　201-794-1124
　8 Rosol Lane Ext., Saddle Brook, NJ 07662
　Hours: 8-5 Mon-Fri　　　　　　　　　FAX　201-794-8147
　• Eyelets, grommets, washers, rivets in stock. Accepts orders of any size. Large selection. •

STEINLAUF & STOLLER INC.　　　　　　　　212-869-0321
　239 West 39th St., (7-8th Ave.) NYC, NY 10018　800-637-1637
　Hours: 8-5:30 Mon-Fri
　• One of the most complete suppliers of sewing notions, sewing tools, cleaning supplies,
　wardrobe kit supplies. MC/VISA •
　(See display ad in this section.)

SUCCESS BINDING CORP.　　　　　　　　　212-226-6161
　Brooklyn Navy Yard Bldg. 275, Brooklyn, NY 11205　718-260-8660
　Hours: 8-4:30 Mon-Fri • sometimes 8-2 Sat
　• Bias, straight, spaghetti, cord-edge, picot edge, folded, etc. Check about minimum orders. •

TALON ZIPPERS　　　　　　　　　　　　　212-564-6300
　1350 Broadway #212, (36th St.) NYC, NY 10018
　Hours: 9-5 Mon-Fri
　• Zippers, cut to length. •

M-N

NOTIONS: BONES, BONING, HOOPWIRE

BAER FABRICS
(costumes) 800-769-7778
(fashion) 800-769-7776
FAX 502-582-2331
515 East Market, Louisville, KY 40202
Hours: 9-9 Mon • 9-5 Tues- Sat
• Rigilene, feather boning, metal hooping, stays, spiralflex stays; prompt shipment. CREDIT CARDS •

CORSET ACCESSORIES
718-339-9099
FAX 718-339-8207
2370 Coney Island Ave., (Aves. T&U) Brooklyn, NY 11223
Hours: 8:30-4:30 Mon-Fri
• Boning, hook and snap tape, bust pads. •

FINEBRAND
213-588-3228
FAX 213-588-4835
3720 S. Santa Fe Ave., Vernon, CA 90058
Hours: 6:00-3:00 Mon-Fri
• Flat and spiral boning. $25.00 minimum. •

GREENBERG & HAMMER, INC.
212-246-2835
800-955-5135
FAX 212-765-8475
24 West 57th St., (5-6th Ave.) NYC, NY 10019
Hours: 9-6 Mon-Fri • 10-5 Sat (closed Sat: July, Aug)
• Enormous selection of sewing notions including feather boning, corset boning, spring steel, etc.; phone and mail orders; see Dottie or Frank. CREDIT CARDS •

L. LAUFER & CO., INC.
212-242-2345
115 West 27th St. 12th Fl., (6-7th Ave.) NYC, NY 10001
Hours: 9-4 Mon-Fri • call first
• Corset supplies, Scotch-mate hook & loop fasteners. No credit cards. •

NATHAN'S BONING CO.
212-244-4781
302 West 37th St., 4th Fl., (8-9th Ave.) NYC, NY 10018
Hours: 8:30-5:30 Mon-Thurs • 8:30-5 Fri
• Feather and spring steel boning, tutu wire in buckram. •

PATRIARCHE & BELL, INC.
201-824-8297
212-242-4400
94 Parkhurst St., Newark, NJ 07114
Hours: 8:30-4:30 Mon-Fri
• Hoop steel. •

STEINLAUF & STOLLER INC.
212-869-0321
800-637-1637
239 West 39th St., (7-8th Ave.) NYC, NY 10018
Hours: 8-5:30 Mon-Fri
• One of the most complete suppliers of sewing notions including feather boning, corset boning and wiggle bones. MC/VISA •
(See display ad under NOTIONS: GENERAL & TAILORS.)

NOTIONS: BUTTONS, BUCKLES, GROMMETS, SNAPS

ALBEST STAMPING CORP.
718-388-6000
1 Kent Ave., (N.13-N.14th St.) Brooklyn, NY 11211
Hours: 8-5 Mon-Fri
• Wholesale metal buckles, hardware for leatherwork; minimum order $150. •

ARLENE NOVELTY CORP.　　　　　　　　　　　　　　　　212-921-5711
　　263 West 38th St., (7-8th Ave.) NYC, NY 10018
　　Hours: 9-5 Mon-Fri
　　• Plastic covered buttons. No credit cards. •

BOND BUTTON CO.　　　　　　　　　　　　　　　　　　718-851-0936
　　1632 58th St., Brooklyn, NY 11204
　　Hours: 8-4 Mon-Fri
　　• Buttons, buckles, ornaments. Leave message on machine and someone will return your
　　call. •

BURGESS MFG. CORP., MAXANT MIRACLE DIVISION　　　　404-932-1111
　　3600 Windsor Park Dr. Swanee, GA 30174
　　Hours: 8:30-5 Mon-Fri
　　• Coverable buttons, belt hooks, belting. Catalog available. MC/VISA. •

C & C METAL PRODUCTS　　　　　　　　　　　　　　　212-819-9700
　　39 West 37th St., (5-6th Ave.) NYC, NY 10018　　　　　201-569-7300
　　Hours: 8-5 Mon-Fri
　　• Wholesale only; metal buttons, buckles, nailheads, rhinestones; large catalog available to
　　volume purchasers. •

CORSET ACCESSORIES　　　　　　　　　　　　　　　　718-339-9099
　　2370 Coney Island Ave., (Aves. T-U) Brooklyn, NY 11223
　　Hours: 8:30-4:30 Mon-Fri　　　　　　　　　　　FAX　718-339-8207
　　• Boning, hook and snap tape, bust pads. •

DIANE BUTTON CO.　　　　　　　　　　　　　　　　　212-921-8383
　　247 West 37th St., (7-8th Ave.) NYC, NY 10018
　　Hours: 8:30-5 Mon-Fri
　　• Wood, metal, plastic, casein buttons. Wholesale. •

DUPLEX NOVELTY　　　　　　　　　　　　　　　　　　212-564-1352
　　575 Eighth Ave., (38-39th St.) NYC, NY 10018
　　Hours: 8:15-5 Mon-Fri
　　• Wooden buttons, buckles, beads; wholesale; catalog. •

DYNA-LINE　　　　　　　　　　　　　　　　　　　　201-569-7300
　　456 Nordhoff Pl., Englewood, NJ 07631
　　Hours: 9-5 Mon-Fri　　　　　　　　　　　　　FAX　201-569-4112
　　• Metal buttons, studs and grommets; place order by phone one week ahead; $100 minimum
　　order. •

EISEN BROTHERS INC.　　　　　　　　　　　　　　　　212-398-0263
　　239 West 39th St., 3rd Fl., (7-8th Ave.) NYC, NY 10018
　　Hours: 9-5 Mon-Fri　　　　　　　　　　　　　FAX　212-575-2153
　　• Studs. •

FASTEX, DIV. OF ILLINOIS TOOL WORKS　　　　　　　　708-299-2222
　　195 Algonquin Rd., Des Plaines, IL 60016
　　Hours: 9-6:15 Mon-Fri
　　• Grommets, rivets, fasteners of all kinds in plastic; wholesale large orders; catalog. This
　　main office will refer you on to your local retailer. •

FRIEDMAN & DISTILLATOR / OWL MILLS　　　　　　　212-226-6400
　　53 Leonard St., (Church-W.B'way) NYC, NY 10013
　　Hours: 9-5 Mon-Fri　　　　　　　　　　　　　FAX　212-219-1402
　　• Hook & eye tape, snap tape; millinery supplies; speak to Toni. No credit cards. •

GORDON BUTTON CO. INC.   212-921-1684
222 West 38th St., (7-8th Ave.) NYC, NY 10018
Hours: 9-5 Mon-Fri
• Buckles, buttons. Retail and wholesale. •

GREENBERG AND HAMMER INC.   212-246-2835
24 West 57th St., (5-6th Ave.) NYC, NY 10019   800-955-5135
Hours: 9-6 Mon-Fri • 10-5 Sat (closed Sat: July, Aug)   FAX   212-765-8475
• Enormous selection of sewing notions including grommets, grommet kits, snaps, snap tape, buttons, etc.; phone and mail orders; see Dottie or Frank. CREDIT CARDS •

GUARDIAN RIVET & FASTENER   516-585-4400
70 Air Park Dr., Ronkonkoma, NY 11779
Hours: 8:30-5 Mon-Fri
• Wholesale rivets. •

HANOY & LIBERTY   212-564-3860
1328 Broadway, #1046 (34th St.) NYC, NY 10001
Hours: 9-5 Mon-Fri
• Manufacturer of button molds; fabrication in metal, buckles. •

JOSEPH M. HART & SONS   516-567-7722
365 Central Ave., Bohemia, NY 11716
Hours: 9-5 Mon-Fri   FAX   516-567-7809
• Studs, boot hooks, grommets. •

METROPOLITAN-KELLER CO.   212-391-0990
270 West 38th St., (7-8th Ave.) NYC, NY 10018
Hours: 8:30-4:30 Mon-Thurs • 8:30-3 Fri   FAX   212-391-1395
• Buttons, belts. •

M & J TRIMMINGS   212-391-9072
1008 Sixth Ave., (37-38th St.) NYC, NY 10018
Hours: 9-6 Mon-Fri • 10-5 Sat
• Pricey; buttons, buckles, frogs, general trimmings. CREDIT CARDS •

PETITE BUTTONS   212-840-7711
78 West 36th St., (5-6th Ave.) NYC, NY 10018
Hours: 7-4 Mon-Fri
• All types of covered buttons. •

RICHARD THE THREAD / ROY COOPER   213-852-4997
8320 Melrose Ave., Los Angeles, CA 90069   800-473-4997
Hours: 9-5 Mon-Fri
• Whopper Poppers, #4 and #6 hooks and bars, zig-zag wire; specializes in hard-to-find items; catalog, mail and phone orders. UPS C.O.D.s. •

SHER PLASTICS   212-760-9660
462 7th Ave., 12th floor, (35th St.) NYC, NY 10018
Hours: 8:30-5:30 Mon-Fri   FAX   212-629-5271
• Studs, buttons, gold-coin studs. •

SIFF BROTHERS   212-730-1045
251 West 39th St., (7-8th Ave.) NYC, NY 10018
Hours: 8-5:30 Mon-Fri by appt.   FAX   212-730-0762
• Buttons, collar studs. Wholesale. •

M-N

SISKA, INC.   201-794-1124
    8 Rosol Lane Ext Saddle Brook, NJ 07662
    Hours: 8-5 Mon-Fri   FAX   201-794-8147
    • Large selection of grommets, eyelets, rivets. Accepts orders of any size; samples on
    request. Will ship anywhere. •

STEINLAUF & STOLLER, INC.   212-869-0321
    239 West 39th St., (7-8th Ave.) NYC, NY 10018   800-637-1637
    Hours: 8-5:30 Mon-Fri
    • One of the most complete suppliers of sewing notions including eyelets, grommets, eyelet
    and grommet kits, snaps, snap tape and buttons, hook & eyes, metal goods. MC/VISA •
    (See display ad under NOTIONS: GENERAL & TAILORS.)

STIMPSON CO., INC.   516-472-2000
    900 Sylvan Ave., Bayport, NY 11705
    Hours: 8:30-4:45 Mon-Fri   FAX   516-472-2425
    • Grommets, snaps, rivets. •

SURE-SNAP CORP.   212-921-5515
    505 8th Ave., 4th floor, (35-36th St.) NYC, NY 10018
    Hours: 8:30-5 Mon-Fri
    • Buckles, snaps, rivets, grommets, eyelets; snap tape made-to-order; machines and dies. •

TENDER BUTTONS   212-758-7004
    143 East 62nd St., (Lexington-3rd Ave.) NYC, NY 10021
    Hours: 11-6 Mon-Fri •11-5:15 Sat (closed Sat: July, Aug)   FAX   212-319-8474
    • Beautiful antique and modern buttons, buckles; antique cufflinks. •

M-N

NOTIONS: ELASTIC

AMERICAN CORD & WEBBING CO., INC.   401-762-5500
    88 Century Dr., Woonsocket, RI 02895
    Hours: 8-5 Mon-Fri   FAX   401-762-5514
    • Elastic cord; also webbing tape, binding; $150 minimum. •

PRYM DRITZ CORP.   617-999-6431
    PO Box C-903, 90 Hatch St., New Bedford, MA 02741   800-845-4948
    Hours: 8-5 Mon-Fri
    • Stay elastic; $20 minimum order. •

FALCON SAFETY PRODUCTS INC.   908-707-4900
    PO Box 1299, 25 Chub Way,   Somerville, NJ 08876
    Hours: 8:30-4:30 Mon-Fri   FAX   908-707-8855
    • All sizes elastic cord. •

GREENBERG & HAMMER INC.   212-246-2835
    24 West 57th St., (5-6th Ave.) NYC, NY 10019   800-955-5135
    Hours: 9-6 Mon-Fri •10-5 Sat (closed Sat: July, Aug)   FAX   212-765-8475
    • Enormous selections of sewing notions including elastic in a variety of widths and colors;
    phone and mail orders; see Dottie or Frank. CREDIT CARDS •

STEINLAUF & STOLLER, INC.
239 West 39th St., (7-8th Ave.) NYC, NY 10018
Hours: 8-5:30 Mon-Fri

212-869-0321
800-637-1637

• One of the most complete suppliers of sewing notions including elastic in a variety of widths: flat, cord, horsehair, non-roll, etc. MC/VISA •
(See display ad under NOTIONS: GENERAL & TAILORS.)

NOTIONS: NEEDLES & PINS

COLONIAL NEEDLE CO.
11 East 31st St., (Madison-5th Ave.) NYC, NY 10016
Hours: 9-5 Mon-Fri

212-684-0226

FAX   212-889-7064

• Hand sewing, glover's lacing needles; wholesale. MC/VISA •

COOPER HARDWARE & COMPONENTS
158 Pinebridge Road, Beacon Falls, CT 06403
Hours: 8-4:30 Mon-Fri

203-888-4528

FAX   203-888-9484

• Formerly Union Pins. They sell Pins! •

DIAMOND NEEDLE
159 West 25th St., (6-7th Ave.) NYC, NY 10001
Hours: 8:30-5 Mon-Fri

212-929-2277
800-221-5818
FAX   212-242-8882

• Industrial or domestic: shears and machine feet. CREDIT CARDS •

GREENBERG & HAMMER INC.
24 West 57th St., (5-6th Ave.) NYC, NY 10019
Hours: 9-6 Mon-Fri • 10-5 Sat (closed Sat: July, Aug)

212-246-2835
800-955-5135
FAX   212-765-8475

• Enormous selections of sewing notions including large assortment of hand-sewing, specialty and machine needles and all kinds of pins; phone and mail orders; see Dottie or Frank. CREDIT CARDS •

STEINLAUF & STOLLER, INC.
239 West 39th St., (7-8th Ave.) NYC, NY 10018
Hours: 8-5:30 Mon-Fri

212-869-0321
800-637-1637

• One of the most complete suppliers of sewing notions including needles sold in single packages or in bulk and all kinds of pins - straight, safety, T's, hat, quilters, etc. MC/VISA. •
(See display ad under NOTIONS: GENERAL & TAILORS.)

NOTIONS: THREAD

ATWATER, INC.
PO Box 247, 627 West Main St., Plymouth, PA 18651
Hours: 8:30-5 Mon-Fri

717-779-9568

FAX   717-779-2331

• Nylon fuzzy thread. •

CRITERION THREAD CO.
55 West 17th St., (5-6th Ave.) NYC, NY 10011
Hours: 8-4:30 Mon-Fri

212-645-9600

FAX   212-645-9711

• Formaery Ideal Thread Co. Silk, cotton, synthetic, sewing and embroidery threads; also notions. •

M-N

GREENBERG & HAMMER INC.   212-246-2835
   24 West 57th St., (5-6th Ave.) NYC, NY 10019   800-955-5135
   Hours: 9-6 Mon-Fri • 10-5 Sat (closed Sat: July, Aug)   FAX   212-765-8475
    • Enormous selections of sewing notions including spools, tubes and cones of threads of all
kinds; phone and mail orders; see Dottie or Frank. CREDIT CARDS •

LA LAME, INC.   718-482-0500
   250 West 39th St., 4th Fl., (7-8th Ave.) NYC, NY 10018   212-921-9770
   Hours: 9-5 Mon-Fri
    • Lumi thread - metallic for Merrow machines. No credit cards. •

PARAMOUNT THREAD   718-482-0500
   29-02 Borden Ave., (29-30th St.) L.I.C., NY 11101   718-937-7700
   Hours: 8:30-5 Mon-Fri
    • Manufacturer of nylon thread, industrial threads. •

SEBRO THREAD CORP.   516-872-6125
   258 Maple Ave., Rockville Center, NY 11570   718-525-1004
   Hours: 8:30-4:30 Mon-Fri
    • Stretch thread; wholesale only. •

SOLTEX THREAD CO. INC.   212-243-2000
   30 West 24th St., (5th-6th Ave.) NYC, NY 10011
   Hours: 9-5:30 Mon-Thurs • 9-3 Fri   FAX   212-243-1112
    • Cotton and synthetic thread for industrial use, embroidery supplies for machine
embroidery. •

STEINLAUF & STOLLER, INC.   212-869-0321
   239 West 39th St., (7-8th Ave.) NYC, NY 10018   800-637-1637
   Hours: 8-5:30 Mon-Fri
    • One of the most complete suppliers of sewing notions including cotton, poly, poly blend,
nylon and silk thread. MC/VISA. •
   (See display ad under NOTIONS: GENERAL & TAILORS.)

NOTES

OCCULT PARAPHERNALIA

ENCHANTMENTS, INC.   212-228-4394
        341 East 9th St., (1st-2nd Ave.) NYC, NY 10003
        Hours: 12-9 Mon-Sat • 1-8 Sun
         • Books, herbs, oils, incense, crystal balls, robes, jewelry and occult paraphernalia. Mail order catalog $3.00. •

WARLOCK SHOP / MAGICKAL CHILDE, INC.   212-242-7182
        35 West 19th St., (5th-6th Ave.) NYC, NY 10011
        Hours: 11-8 Mon-Sat • 12-6 Sun
         • Human skulls, weapons, incense, crystal balls, occult paraphernalia; odd assortment. CREDIT CARDS •

SAMUEL WEISER, INC.   212-777-6363
        132 East 24th St., (Park Ave. S.-Lexington Ave.) NYC, NY 10010
        Hours: 9-6 Mon-Wed • Thurs-Fri 10-7 • Sat 9:30-5:30 • Sun 12-5
         • Many kinds of Tarot cards, crystal balls, large selection of related books. Occult paraphernalia and incense. •

PACKING MATERIALS

See also **TAPE, ADHESIVE**
See also **TWINES & CORDAGE**
See also **PAPER, CARDBOARD & FOAMCORE PRODUCTS**

ABBOT & ABBOT BOX CORP.   718-392-2600
        37-11 10th St., (37-38th Ave.) L.I.C., NY 11101
        Hours: 8-4:30 Mon-Fri   FAX   718-392-8439
         • Wooden boxes/crates to order; fast service, will deliver; see Joe. •

ACME FOAM CORP.   718-622-5600
        900 Dean St., (Classon-Grand) Brooklyn, NY 11238
        Hours: 9-5 Mon-Fri
         • Excelsior wood shavings, foam rubber, ethafoam and polystyrene. Catalog. $35 minimum on phone orders. •

ARCHIVART   201-804-8986
        7 Caesar Pl., Moonachie, NJ 07074
        Hours: 9-4:45 Mon-Fri   FAX   201-935-5964
         • Acid-free tissue,boxes,rolling tubes; ship large quantities. MC/VISA •

ATLAS MATERIALS   718-875-1162
        193 Coffey St., (Van Brunt-Ferris) Brooklyn, NY 11231   718-875-1163
        Hours: 8-4 Mon-Fri
         • Excelsior in 15 colors. Shreaded paper and packing materials. AB Foam. See Mr. Levine. •

BETTER-PAK CONTAINER CO.   212-675-7330
        675 Dell Rd., Carlstadt, NJ 07072
        Hours: 5-3 Mon-Fri
         • Corrugated boxes. •

O-P

DURA-FOAM PRODUCTS
718-894-2488
63-02 59th Ave., Maspeth, NY 11378
Hours: 8-4:30 Mon-Fri   FAX   718-894-2493
• Large selection of flexible and rigid urethane foam, foam rubber, beads, and wrapping materials. •
(See display ad under FOAM SHEETING & SHAPES.)

ERIC FRANK PAPER CORP.
718-383-1815
254 Johnson Ave., (Bushwick-Montrose) Brooklyn, NY 11206
Hours: 9-5 Mon-Fri
• Paper, paper towels, paper bags, twine, shopping bags, and garbage bags. •

FALCON SUPPLY CO.
908-396-8200
55 Randolph, Avanel, NJ 07001   800-365-8273
Hours: 9-5 Mon-Fri
• Tapes, staples and staplers, packing lists. •

GREATER ATLANTIC PAPER PACKING CORP.
718-858-3636
281-289 Butler St., (Nevins-3rd Ave.) Brooklyn, NY 11217
Hours: 9-5 Mon-Fri
• Gaffers, duct, many types of pressure sensitive tapes. Catalog. $200 min. •

ROBERT KARP CONTAINER CORP.
212-586-4474
618 West 52nd St., (11-12th Ave.) NYC, NY 10019
Hours: 8-4:30 Mon-Fri
• Boxes, twine, tape, tissue, kraft paper, jiffy bags, bubble-pak; large or small orders. •

KEYSTONE PAPER
212-662-9500
243 W. 124 St., (7-8th Ave.) NYC, NY 10027
Hours: 8-5 Mon-Fri   FAX   212-662-9505
• Complete line of packing materials. •

GEORGE MILLAR & CO., DIV. OF MARGUARDT & CO., INC.
212-645-7200
161 Sixth Ave. 2nd Fl., (Spring St.) NYC, NY 10013
Hours: 9-5 Mon-Fri
• General packaging. •

MOVERS SUPPLY HOUSE, INC.
212-671-1200
1476 East 222nd St., (Baychester) Bronx, NY 10469
Hours: 8-5 Mon-Fri
• Packing blankets, loading straps, hampers, j-bars; good prices; will ship COD. CREDIT CARDS •

NATIONAL VAN EQUIPMENT CO., INC.
718-326-1900
8000 Cooper Ave., Glendale, NY 11385
Hours: 9-5 Mon-Fri   FAX   718-894-8315
• Formerly Canvas Specialty Co. Packing blankets, webbing, burlap, canvas, cheesecloth, muslin. MC/VISA •

SNOW CRAFT CO., INC.
516-739-1399
200 Fulton Ave., Garden City Park, NY 11040
Hours: 9-5 Mon-Fri
• Plastic foam, will cut to size; other foam and packing materials. delivery is extra. $150 minimum. •

O-P

TECHNICAL LIBRARY SERVICES, INC./TALAS 212-736-7744
213 West 35th St. 9th Fl., (7-8th Ave.) NYC, NY 10001
Hours: 9-4:30 Mon-Fri (closed for lunch 11:30-1)
• Acid-free tissue for costume packing. •

VIKING-CRITERION CORP. 718-392-7400
55-30 46th St., (55th Ave.) Maspeth, NY 11378
Hours: 9-5 Mon-Fri
• Bubble wrap. Brochure available. •

WOLF PAPER & TWINE CO. 212-675-4870
680 Sixth Ave., (21-22nd St.) NYC, NY 10010
Hours: 9-4:30 Mon-Fri
• Boxes, corrugated paper, padded envelopes; will take small orders. •

PAINTS & DYES: BRONZING POWDERS & LEAFING SUPPLIES

CRESCENT BRONZE POWDER CO., INC. 312-539-2441
3400 N. Avondale Ave., Chicago, IL 60618
1841 S. Flower St., Los Angeles, CA 90015 213-748-5285
Hours: 8-4 Mon-Fri
• A full spectrum of bronzing powders and liquids, glitters, tinsels, diamond dust, pearlescent and fluorescent paint, metallic paints, aerosol paint; color cards and price lists available. 1 lb. min. •

M. EPSTEIN'S SONS, INC. 212-265-3960
809 Ninth Ave., (53-54th St.) NYC, NY 10019
Hours: 8-5:15 Mon-Fri • 8:30-3 Sat (closed Sat in summer) FAX 212-765-8841
• Bronzing powders, theatrical paint supplies. •
(See display ad under PAINTS & DYES: SCENIC.)

GOTHIC LTD./LONG ISLAND PAINT 516-676-6600
PO Box 189, 1 Continental Hill, Glen Cove, NY 11542
Hours: 7:30-5 Mon-Fri
• Bronzing powders; also aniline dye, powdered pigments, animal glue, scenic brushes; contact Wendy Stern. Catalog. •
(See display ad under PAINTS & DYES: SCENIC.)

LEE'S ART SHOP 212-247-0110
220 West 57th St., (7th-B'way) NYC, NY 10019
Hours: 9:30-7 Mon-Fri • 9:30-6:30 Sat • 12-5:30 Sun FAX 212-247-0507
• Leafing supplies; drafting, framing, drawing, and painting supplies. No phone orders. CREDIT CARDS •

NEW YORK CENTRAL ART SUPPLY, INC. 212-473-7705
62 Third Ave., (11th St.) NYC, NY 10003
Hours: 8:30-6:15 Mon-Sat FAX 212-475-2513
• Bronzing powders; gold, silver and metal leafs, dry pigments, sizing, agate burnishers, patinas, and glitter. Accepts phone orders. •

OBRON ATLANTIC CORP./ GOLD LEAF & METALLIC POWDERS 212-267-4900
74 Trinity Pl., Rm. 2000, (Cedar-Rector) NYC, NY 10006
Hours: 9-5 Mon-Fri
• Genuine and composition gold, silver, aluminum leaf; bronzing powder, glitter; call ahead to check stock. •

O-P

PEARL PAINT CO., INC.   212-431-7932
    308 Canal St., (B'way-Church) NYC, NY 10013   (mail order) 800-221-6845
    Hours: 9-5:30 Mon-Sat • Thurs 9-7 • Sun 11-4:45   FAX   212-431-6798

    2411 Hempstead Turnpike, East Meadow, NY 11554   516-731-3700
    Hours: 9:30-5:45 Mon-Sat • Wed, Fri till 8:45 • Sun 12-4:45   FAX   516-731-3721
    • Dutch metal, silver, copper and gold leaf; bronzing powders and liquids at very good prices;
catalog. Phone orders over $50.00. CREDIT CARDS •

SEPP LEAF PRODUCTS, INC.   212-683-2840
    381 Park Ave. S., Rm. 1301, (27th St.) NYC, NY 10016
    Hours: 9-5 Mon-Fri
    • German and Italian gold leaf, imitation leaf in rolls and sheets; list of products available. •

UNITED STATES BRONZE POWDERS   908-782-5454
    PO Box 31, Rt. 202, Flemington, NJ 08822
    Hours: 9-5 Mon-Fri
    • Wholesale; minimum order $100. •

WOLF PAINTS, S. WOLF DIV. OF JANOVIC PLAZA   212-245-3241
    771 Ninth Ave., (51-52nd St.) NYC, NY 10019
    Hours: 7:30-6:15 Mon-Fri • 8-4:45 Sat.   FAX   212-974-0591
    • Bronzing powders, dyes, brushes; house and theatrical paints. CREDIT CARDS •

PAINTS & DYES: FABRIC

See also **ARTISTS MATERIALS**
For Fiebings & Magix, see **LEATHERCRAFTERS & FURRIERS TOOLS & SUPPLIES**

ALJO. MFG. CO., INC.   212-226-2878
    81-83 Franklin St. 4th Fl., (B'way-Church) NYC, NY 10013   212-966-4046
    Hours: 9-6 Mon-Fri • 10:30-4:30 Sat   FAX   212-274-9616
    • Direct, disperse, fiber-reactive, acid, basic and vat dyes; neon pigment dyes. No credit
cards. •
    (See display ad in this section.)

BACHMEIER COLORS DIV., SPECTRA COLORS CORP.   201-997-0606
    25 Rizzolo Rd., Kearny, NJ 07032   800-527-8588
    Hours: 8-5 Mon-Fri   FAX   201-977-0504
    • Direct, disperse, acid dyes; 24 hours to pickup. No credit cards. •

BARBIZON   212-586-1620
    426 West 55th St., (9-10th St.) NYC, NY 10019
    Hours: 8:30-5:30 Mon-Fri • 9-1 Sat   FAX   212-247-8818

    3 Draper St., Woburn, MA 01801   617-935-3920
    Hours: 8:30-5:30 Mon-Fri • 9-2 Sat   FAX   617-935-9273

    6437G General Green Way, Alexandria, VA 22312   703-750-3900
    Hours: 8:30-5:30 Mon-Fri • 9-1 Sat   FAX   703-750-1448

O-P

"I found it in the N.Y. Theatrical Sourcebook."

BARBIZON (cont.)
2401 Mercer Ave., W. Palm Beach, FL 33401   407-833-2020
Hours: 8:30-5:30 Mon-Fri • 9-1 Sat   FAX   407-833-3582

101 Krog St., Atlanta, GA 30307,   404-681-5124
Hours: 8-5 Mon-Fri • 9-1 Sat   FAX   404-681-5315
• Distributor for Rosco (incl. paints): also lighting and electrical supplies. •

COLORCRAFT / CREATEX COLORS   203-653-5505
14 Airport Park Rd., East Grandby, CT 06026   (orders) 800-243-2712
Hours: 8:30-5 Mon-Fri
• Manufacturer of Createx, a heat-set fabric paint; non-toxic water based dyes; catalog.
MC/VISA •

CROWN ART PRODUCTS   201-777-6010
90 Dayton Ave., Passaic, NJ 07055
Hours: 9-4:30 Mon-Fri   FAX   201-777-3088
• Fabric paint, silkscreening supplies; catalog available; also classes, workshops and seminars. CREDIT CARDS •

W. CUSHING & CO.   207-967-3711
PO Box 351, Kennebunkport, ME 04046   800-626-7847
Hours: 9-4 Mon-Fri
• Manufacturer of dyes and disperse agents; also rug-hooking supplies. MC/VISA •

DHARMA TRADING CO.   (store) 415-456-1211
PO Box 150916, San Rafael, CA 94915   (mail order) 800-542-5227
Hours: 8-5 Mon-Fri • for mail order.   FAX   416-456-8747
• Textile art supplies; dyes, fabrics, tools, books; catalog; mail and phone orders. CREDIT CARDS •

DIXON TICONDEROGA   800-824-9430
2600 Maitland Center Pkwy. Rm.200, Maitland, FL 32751
Hours: 8:30-5 Mon-Fri
• Accolite colors, Prang textile paints. Wholesale. •

EMPIRE DYESTUFFS CORP.   212-925-8737
206 Spring St., (6th Ave.) NYC, NY 10012
Hours: 9-4 Mon-Fri
• Disperse Dyes. •

FINE ART MATERIALS, INC.   212-343-9277
148 Mercer, (Prince-Houston) NYC, NY 10012   800-237-0061
Hours: 9:30-6 Mon-Fri • 11-6 Sat   FAX   212-614-9784
• Tinfix in quarts, stretchers for silk; art materials; catalog. Mail and phone orders accepted.
CREDIT CARDS •

INKO   510-235-8330
530 MacDonald Ave., Richmond, CA 94801
Hours: 9-4:30 Mon-Fri   FAX   510-235-1038
• Cotton and silk dyes, silkscreening equipment and manuals; catalog available. MC/VISA •

IVY IMPORTS   301-595-0550
12213 Distribution Way, Beltsville, MD 20705
Hours: 10-5 Mon-Fri   FAX   301-595-7868
• Fabric paints, dyes, resists and all associated products; books and instructional materials.
CREDIT CARDS •

O-P

0–P

NEW YORK CENTRAL ART SUPPLY, INC.   212-473-7705
    62 Third Ave., (11th St.) NYC, NY 10003
    Hours: 8:30-6:15 Mon-Sat   FAX   212-475-2513
    • Silk dyes, Procion dyes for natural fabrics, glitter, puffy, slick and spatter fabric paints, batik supplies. Accepts phone orders. •

PRO CHEMICAL & DYE, INC.   508-676-3838
    PO Box 14, Somerset, MA 02726
    Hours: 24 hour phone service.   FAX   508-676-3980
    • Cold water dyes, wide range of colors. MC/VISA •

RIT DYE/CPC SPECIALTY PRODUCTS, INC.   317-231-8044
    P.O. Box 21070, 1437 W. Morris Rd., Indianapolis, IN 46221
    Hours: 8-4 Mon-Fri   FAX   317-636-2120
    • Quantity packing for the industry. Minimum 20 doz. boxes. Info. & color card on request. No credit cards. •

RIVOLI MERCHANDISE CO.   212-966-5035
    50 Howard St., (Mercer St.) NYC, NY 10013
    Hours: 9-6 Sun-Fri
    • Rit and Tintex by the dozen. •
    (See display ad under PARTY GOODS.)

RUPERT, GIBBON, & SPIDER, INC.   800-442-0455
    P.O. Box 425, Healdsburg, CA 95448   707-433-9577
    Hours: 8-5 Mon-Fri   FAX   707-433-4906
    • Imported silk for costumes (white and natural), economical bulk amounts; novelty paints, metallics, fluorescents, sparkles. Catalog. Will C.O.D. MC/VISA •

STROBLITE CO., INC.
    430 West 14th St. #507, (9-10th Ave.) NYC, NY 10014
    Hours: 9-4:30 Mon-Fri
    • Ultraviolet fabric paints, feather dip; flier. •
    212-929-3778

TEXTILE RESOURCES
    5866 Naples Plaza, Long Beach, CA 90803
    Hours: 10-5 Mon-Sat
    • Textile art supplies; dyes, fabrics, tools, resists, chemicals; catalog; workshops. MC/VISA •
    310-434-1522

TRICON COLORS, INC.
    16 Leliarts Lane, Elmwood Park, NJ 07407
    Hours: 8:30-5 Mon-Fri
    • Dyes; soluble in water, alcohol, oil; small minimum orders; flier. No credit cards. •
    201-794-3800

PAINTS & DYES: GLASS & SLIDE, SPECIALIZED, MISC.

See also **CASTING & MODELING SUPPLIES**
See also **FLORAL SUPPLIES**
See also **LEATHERCRAFTERS & FURRIERS TOOLS & SUPPLIES**

AMERICAN AUTO BODY SUPPLIES
    27-10 Astoria Blvd., (31st St.) Astoria, NY 11102
    Hours: 8-5 Mon-Fri • 8-12:30 Sat.
    • Auto lacquer, urethane and enamel. •
    718-274-2322
    FAX 718-274-1989

BARBIZON
    426 West 55th St., (9-10th Ave.) NYC, NY 10019
    Hours: 8:30-5:30 Mon-Fri • 9-1 Sat
    212-586-1620
    FAX 212-247-8818

    3 Draper St., Woburn, MA 01801
    Hours: 8:30-5:30 Mon-Fri • 9-2 Sat
    617-935-3920
    FAX 617-935-9273

    6437G General Green Way, Alexandria, VA 22312
    Hours: 8:30-5:30 Mon-Fri • 9-1 Sat
    703-750-3900
    FAX 703-750-1448

    2401 Mercer Ave., W. Palm Beach, FL 33401
    Hours: 8:30-5:30 Mon-Fri • 9-1 Sat
    407-833-2020
    FAX 407-833-3582

    101 Krog St., Atlanta, GA 30307
    Hours: 8-5 Mon-Fri • 9-1 Sat
    404-681-5124
    FAX 404-681-5315
    • Distributor for Rosco (incl. glass paints); also lighting and electrical supplies. •

JURGEN INDUSTRIES, INC.
    1202 Chestnut, #2, Everett, WA 98201
    Hours: 9-4 Mon-Fri
    • Glass stain color designed for simulated "Tiffany" glass. Also have synthetic non-toxic product for stain glass production. Catalog. •
    800-735-7248
    FAX 206-258-9454

MEARL CORP.
    41 East 42nd St. #708, (Madison Ave.) NYC, NY 10017
    Hours: 9-5 Mon-Fri
    • Pearlizer pigment for make-up and paint. Brochure. •
    212-573-8500

O-P

MUTUAL SPRAY EQUIPMENT CORP.   212-677-5600
   6 East Second St., (Bowery-2nd Ave.) NYC, NY 10003
   Hours: 8:30-4:30 Mon-Fri
   • Spray paint equipment. RENTALS MC/VISA •

OLD-FASHIONED MILK PAINT CO.   508-448-6336
   PO Box 222, Groton, MA 01450
   Hours: 9-5 Mon-Fri • 10-3 Sat
   • Dry powder milk base paint; natural earth colors. Catalog. •

PEARL PAINT CO., INC.   212-431-7932
   308 Canal St., (B'way-Church St.) NYC, NY 10013   (mail order) 800-221-6845
   Hours: 9-5:30 Mon-Sat • Thurs 9-7 • Sun 11-4:45   FAX 212-431-6798

   411 Hempstead Turnpike, East Meadow, NY 11554   516-731-3700
   Hours: 9:30-5:45 Mon-Sat • Wed, Fri till 8:45 • Sun 12-4:45   FAX 516-731-3721
   • Stained glass paints; also great selection of art supplies at very good prices; catalog. Phone
   orders over $50.00. •

PLAID ENTERPRISES   404-923-8200
   1649 International Blvd., Norcross, GA 30091
   Hours: 8-5 Mon-Fri   FAX 404-381-6705
   • Pre-mixed paints, stencils, patterns, brushes, glass stains and paints, specialty products. No
   credit cards. Wholesale only. •

ROSCO LABORATORIES, INC.   914-937-1300
   36 Bush Ave., Port Chester, NY 10573   800-ROSCONY
   Hours: 9-5 Mon-Fri
   • Transparent lacquer colors for glass projection slides. Colorine Lamp Dip. Test kits available. •

S & G AUTO BODY SUPPLIES   718-388-5151
   172 Graham Ave., (Montrose) Brooklyn, NY 11206   718-384-8196
   Hours: 8-4:30 Mon-Fri • 8-3 Sat.
   • Good selection of metalflake and candy apple lacquer paints. CREDIT CARDS •

SCHWARTZ CHEMICAL CO., INC.   718-784-7592
   50-01 Second St., (26-27th Ave.) L.I.C., NY 11101
   Hours: 8:30-5 Mon-Fri
   • Dyes, lacquer paints and adhesives; brochure. Phone ahead. •

SHANNON LUMINOUS MATERIALS, INC.   714-550-9931
   304A North Townsend St., Santa Ana, CA 92703
   Hours: 8-5 Mon-Fri
   • Blacklight reactive chalks, paints, crayons, etc. Catalog. $25 minimum. •

SPECIALTY COATING & CHEMICAL, INC.   213-875-0055
   7360 Varna Ave., N. Hollywood, CA 91605
   Hours: 7-3:30 Mon-Fri   FAX 818-764-8669
   • Pigments for making translucent paints, also tints, dyes and polyurethane. MC/VISA •

STENCIL WORLD   401-847-0870
   PO Box 1112, Newport, RI 02840
   Hours: 10-5 Mon-Fri
   • World's largest mail order catalog of stencils, patterns, illustration books, tools, paints,
   brushes; retail. Catalog $3.50 •

STROBLITE CO., INC. 212-929-3778
　430 West 14th St. #507, (9-10th Ave.) NYC, NY 10014
　Hours: 9-4:30 Mon-Fri
　• Fluorescent and luminous colors; blacklight lamps, temperas, lacquers, feather dip, acrylic
　and more. Catalog. •

UNITED MINERAL & CHEMICAL CORP. 201-507-3314
　1100 Valley Brook Ave., Lyndhurst, NJ 07071
　Hours: 9-5:15 Mon-Fri FAX 201-507-1606
　• UV phosphorous colors. A line of pigments that are white in natural light but can change to
　a vibrant spectrum mural in black light. Expensive. •

PAINTS & DYES: HOUSEHOLD

M. EPSTEIN'S SONS, INC. 212-265-3960
　809 Ninth Ave., (53-54th St.) NYC, NY 10019
　Hours: 8-5:15 Mon-Fri • 8:30-3 Sat (closed Sat in summer) FAX 212-765-8841
　• Rollers, brushes, household and theatrical paints, roller patterns, etc. CREDIT CARDS •
　(See display ad under PAINTS & DYES: SCENIC.)

JANOVIC PLAZA 212-627-1100
　161 Sixth Ave., (Spring St.) NYC, NY 10014
　Hours: 7:30-6:30 Mon-Fri • 9-6 Sat • 11-5 Sun FAX 212-691-1504

　215 Seventh Ave., (22-23rd St.) NYC, NY 10011 212-645-5454
　Hours: 7:30-6:30 Mon-Fri • 9-6 Sat • 11-5 Sun

　1150 Third Ave., (67th St.) NYC, NY 10021 212-772-1400
　Hours: 7:30-6:30 Mon-Fri • 8 -5:45 Sat • 11-5 Sun

　159 West 72nd St., (B'way-Columbus) NYC, NY 10023 212-595-2500
　Hours: 7:30-6:15 Mon-Fri (Thurs till 7:45) • 9-4:45 Sat • 11-4:45 Sun
　• Household paints and paint supplies; tile, home decorating center; catalog of paint products.
　(Paint dept. opens at 7:30, other departments 9:30). Very good prices. •

PEARL PAINT CO. 212-431-7932
　308 Canal St., (B'way-Church St.) NYC, NY 10013 (mail order) 800-221-6845
　Hours: 9-5:30 Mon-Sat• 9-7 Thurs •11-4:45 Sun FAX 212-431-6798

　411 Hempstead Turnpike, East Meadow, NY 11554 516-731-3700
　Hours: 9:30-5:45 Mon-Sat • Wed, Fri till 8:45 • Sun 12-4:45 FAX 516-731-3721
　• Large selection of household paints; fluorescent and wrinkle spray paint; also art supplies;
　catalog. Very good prices. Phone orders over $50.00. •

PINTCHIK PAINTS 718-783-3333
　478 Bergen St., Brooklyn (Flatbush), NY 11217
　Hours: 8-6:50 Mon-Fri • 8:30-5:30 Sat • 10-4:50 Sun
　• This is the "Mothership," the largest store. •

　278 Third Ave., (22nd St.) NYC, NY 10010 212-982-6600
　Hours: 8:30-6:50 Mon-Fri • 9-6 Sat • 11-5 Sun

　2475 Broadway, (92nd St.) NYC, NY 10025 212-769-1444
　Hours: 8:30-6:50 Mon-Fri • 10-6 Sat • 11-5 Sun
　• Household and theatrical paints and wallcoverings. •

O-P

"I found it in the N.Y. Theatrical Sourcebook." **315**

WOLF PAINTS, S. WOLF DIV. OF JANOVIC PLAZA   212-245-3241
    771 Ninth Ave., (51-52nd St.) NYC, NY 10019
    Hours: 7:30-6:15 Mon-Fri • 8-4:45 Sat   FAX   212-974-0591
    • Household and theatrical paints; roller patterns. •

PAINTS & DYES: SCENIC

ALCONE CO., INC.   718-361-8373
    5-49 49th Ave., (5th St.-Vernon) L.I.C., NY 11101
    Hours: 9:30-4 Mon-Fri   FAX   718-729-8296
    • Scenic paints and supplies. Theatrical supply house; catalog, $5. (Subway #7 to
L.I.C.,Vernon/Jackson stop.) •

ALJO MFG. CO., INC.   212-966-4046
    81-83 Franklin St. 4th Fl., (B'way-Church St.) NYC, NY 10013   212-226-2878
    Hours: 9-6 Mon-Fri • 10:30-4:30 Sat   FAX   212-274-9616
    • ALJO scenic aniline dyes and Lockwood transparent wood dyes and stains. No credit cards. •
    (See display ad under PAINTS & DYES: FABRIC)

DAY-GLO CORP   800-289-3294
    4515 St. Clair Ave., Cleveland, OH 44103
    Hours: 8:30-5 Mon-Fri   FAX   213-391-7751
    • Carries Day-glo fluorescent colors in dry pigment and dispersible bases- water and oil. •

O-P

O-P

M. EPSTEIN'S SONS, INC.
212-265-3960
809 Ninth Ave., (53-54th St.) NYC, NY 10019
Hours: 8-5:15 Mon-Fri/ 8:30-3 Sat (closed Sat in summer)
• A major supplier of scenic supplies, paints, dyes, brushes and expendables to the television, film, and theatrical businesses of NYC. Computer matching of color. CREDIT CARDS •
(See display ad in this section.)

GOTHIC LTD.
516-676-6600
PO Box 189, 1 Continental Hill, Glen Cove, NY 11542
Hours: 7:30-5 Mon-Fri
• Casein, fresco, video ultimate paint, bronzing powders; also aniline dye, flexible and animal glue, flame proofing, scenic brushes; contact Wendy Stern. Catalog. •
(See display ad in this section.)

A. HAUSSMANN INTERNATIONAL CORP.
415-431-1336
132 Ninth St., San Francisco, CA 94103
Hours: 8-4 Mon-Fri
• Full line of high quality scenic paints, dyes and brushes; also casting materials and weave fillers. Catalog. No minimum. •

MANN BROTHERS
213-936-5168
757 North La Brea Ave., Los Angeles, CA 90038
Hours: 7-5 Mon-Fri • 8-3 Sat   FAX   213-936-1980
• Scenic paint supplier. Carry Mearl pearlescent products in manageable quantities. Catalog. MC/VISA •

MUTUAL HARDWARE CORP.
718-361-2480
5-45 49th Ave., (Vernon) L.I.C., NY 11101
Hours: 8:30-5 Mon-Fri   FAX   718-729-8296
• Scenic supplies and Flo-paint; catalog available. •

ROSCO LABORATORIES, INC.
914-937-1300
36 Bush Ave., Port Chester, NY 10573   800-ROSCONY
Hours: 9-5 Mon-Fri   FAX   914-937-5984
• Wide variety of scenic paints to meet diverse needs. Flame proofing. Brochures. Shipping available. •

SCULPTURAL ARTS COATING, INC.
910-299-5755
PO Box 13113, Greensboro, NC 27415   800-743-0379
Hours: FAX   910-299-1359

ARTIST'S CHOICE saturated paints are deep, pure colors for use in theatre, television, film and exhibit work that won't spoil. They are concentrated; extendible with water. Opaque results in 1:1...1:5, translucent results in 1:10...1:20. The paint has excellent hiding ability, one coat coverage, that dries fast, in less than one hour.

Sculptural Arts
Coating, Inc.

• Distributor of Artist's Choice paints. A new non-toxic water base scenic paint with 25 colors. Very extendible. Also **Sculpt or Coat** and Plastic Varnish. Product brochure. •

SILVER AND SONS HARDWARE
212-247-6969
711 Eighth Ave., (44-45th St.) NYC, NY 10036   212-247-6977
Hours: 9-5:30 Mon-Fri • 10-2 Sat
• Spray paint, fluorescent paints in many colors, primers and deck paint. Deliveries, UPS, COD. •

O-P

SYMPHONY ART, INC. 800-654-6279
130 Beckwith Ave., Patterson, NJ 07502 201-278-7200
Hours: 8:30-5 Mon-Fri FAX 201-278-6789
• Scenic brushes. Catalog available. MC/VISA •

TECHNICAL ILLUSIONS, INC. 708-879-6919
20 N. Island, Batavia, IL 60510
Hours: 8-5 Mon-Sat FAX 708-879-9212
• High quality theatrical paints and supplies: scenic paint, latex, duplicated Iddings, clear sealer, water base materials. MC/VISA •

TRICON COLORS, INC. 201-794-3800
16 Leliarts Lane, Elmwood Park, NJ 07407
Hours: 8:30-5 Mon-Fri
• Colors and dyes soluble in water, alcohol, oil; anilines. No credit cards. •

WOLF PAINTS, S. WOLF DIV. OF JANOVIC PLAZA 212-245-3241
771 Ninth Ave, (51-52nd St.) NYC, NY 10019
Hours: 7:30-6:15 Mon-Fri • 8-4:45 Sat FAX 212-974-0591
• Theatrical paint and dyes, clear latex, brushes; delivery. •

PAPER, CARDBOARD & FOAMCORE PRODUCTS

See also **ARTISTS MATERIALS**
See also **PACKING MATERIALS**

GILSHIRE CORP. SCENERY STUDIO PRODUCTS DIVISION. 718-786-1381
11-20 46th Rd., (11th St.) L.I.C., NY 11101
Hours: 8:30-4:30 Mon-Fri FAX 718-937-0227
• Wax, Kraft and Grey Bogus scenery papers. •

HEXACOMB CORP. 203-288-7722
458 Sacket Point Rd., North Haven, CT 06473 800-331-7420
Hours: 8:15-5 Mon-Fri
• Air-Lite panels, white or Kraft finish, 1/2" thick. •

INTERNATIONAL PAPER COMPANY 704-872-8974
PO Box 1839, Highway 90, Statesville, NC 28677 800-438-1701
Hours: 8-5 Mon-Fri
• Manufacturer of Gatorfoam; available in 4'x8' sheets; 5 thicknesses from 3/16 to 1 1/2"; wholesale only. •

LENOBLE LUMBER CO., INC. 212-246-0150
525 West 52nd St., (10-11th Ave.) NYC, NY 10019
Hours: 8-5 Mon-Fri (closed for lunch 12-1)
• Sonotube, Gatorboard; also masonite, Formica, plywood, etc. •

MODERN MILTEX CORP. 718-525-6000
130-25 180th St., (Farmers Blvd.-Springfield) Springfield Gardens, NY 11434
Hours: 7:30-5 Mon-Fri FAX 718-276-4595
• Fabricators and distributors of Styrofoam Brand plastic foam and every other type of rigid plastic foam. Catalog. $100 minimum. •

O-P

PARTY BAZAAR   212-695-6820
    390 Fifth Ave., (36th St.) NYC, NY 10018   FAX   212-643-9462
    Hours: 8-6:30 Mon-Wed • 8-8 Thurs • 8-7 Fri • 9:30-6 Sat • 12-5 Sun
    • Colored corrugated cardboard in two widths; party supplies. •

ROSEBRAND TEXTILES INC.   212-594-7424
    517 West 35th St., (10-11th Ave.) NYC, NY 10001   800-223-1624
    Hours: 8:30-5 Mon-Fri   FAX   212-629-4826
    • Full line of shop papers: Bogus, semi-wax, Kraft and clear vinyl. Now available: Grid Kraft.
    Excellent for cartooning, layout & welding application. •
    (See display ad under TAPE & ADHESIVE)

THE SET SHOP   212-979-9790
    37 East 18th St., (B'way-Park Ave. S.) NYC, NY 10003
    Hours: 8:30-6 Mon-Fri • 10-4 Sat   FAX   212-979-9852
    • 50 colors of 9' or 12' wide seamless; foamcore, gatorfoam. •

SONOCO PRODUCTS CO. (TUBES & CORES)   201-263-1400
    PO Box 582, 227 Changebridge Rd., Montville, NJ 07045   800-331-7340
    Hours: 8:30-5 Mon-Fri
    • Sonotube, spiral tubes and cores. Will ship. •

THEATRICAL SERVICES & SUPPLIES, INC.   516-588-9550
    1610 9th Ave., Bohemia, NY 11716
    Hours: 8-4:30 Mon-Fri   FAX   516-588-9553
    • Honeycomb air-Lite panels, kraft finishes, 1/2"-1" thick. Catalog available. Shipping. Also
    theatrical supplies. MC/VISA •

VIKING-CRITERION CORP.   718-392-7400
    55-30 46th St., (55th Ave.) Maspeth, NY 11378
    Hours: 9-5 Mon-Fri
    • Kraft paper. Adhesives and glues, packing materials. Brochures. •

O-P

PARTY GOODS

See also **MAGIC SUPPLIES & NOVELTIES**

ARENSON OFFICE FURNISHINGS   212-838-8880
    315 E. 62nd St., (1-2nd Ave.) NYC, NY 10021
    Hours: 9-5 Mon-Fri • or by appt.
    • Folding chairs & tables, coat racks etc. in depth variety and inventory. Contact Richard
    Slavin. •
    (See display ad under FURNITURE RENTAL AND PURCHASE: OFFICE.)

BROADWAY FAMOUS PARTY RENTALS   718-783-2700
    868 Kent Ave., (Myrtle-Park Ave.) Brooklyn, NY 11205   212-269-2666
    Hours: 9-5 Mon-Fri
    • Party rental items: A-Z. Many patterns and colors of table linens; phone orders for delivery.
    Brochures available. •

CENTRAL PROPERTIES OF 49TH STREET
514 West 49th St., (10th Ave.) NYC, NY 10019
Hours: 8-5 Mon-Fri

212-265-7767

FAX   212-582-3746

Fine china, crystal and tableware from such respected names
as Lenox, Mikasa, Spode, Fitz and Floyd and many more!
Theme decor and accessories for complete restaurant and
banquet settings. Large quantities available.

* Quality pieces. *
(See display ad under PROP RENTAL HOUSES)

PAPER HOUSE
678 Broadway, (3rd-Bond St.) NYC, NY 10012
Hours: 10-8:30 Mon-Thurs • 10-10:30 Fri • 10-11 Sat • 10-8 Sun

212-388-0082

1020 Third Ave., (60-61St) NYC, NY 10021
Hours: 9:30-8:30 Mon-Fri • 9-8:30 Sat • 10:30-8 Sun

212-223-3774

269 Amsterdam Ave., (72-73rd Street) NYC, NY 10023
Hours: 8:30-10 Mon-Wed • 8:30-10:30 Thurs, Fri • 9-11 Sat • 10-10 Sun

212-724-8085

1370 Third Ave., (78th Street) NYC, NY 10021
Hours: 9:30-8:30 Mon-Fri • 9-8:30 Sat • 10:30-7 Sun

212-879-2937

180 East 86th St., (Lexington-3rd) NYC, NY 10028
Hours: 9-8:30 Mon-Sat • 10:30-8 Sun
* Giftwrap, cards, paper plates, napkins, streamers, party favors, etc. CREDIT CARDS *

212-410-7950

PARTY BAZAAR
390 Fifth Ave., (36th St.) NYC, NY 10018
Hours: 8-6:30 Mon-Wed •8-8 Thurs • 8-7 Fri • 9:30-6 Sat • 12-5 Sun
* Great selection party favors, giftwrap, streamers, glitter, cards, paper plates etc. *

212-695-6820
FAX   212-643-9462

PARTY TIME, DIV. ACADEMY CHAIR RENTAL CO.
82-33 Queens Blvd., Elmhurst, NY 11373
Hours: 9-5 Mon-Fri • 9-2 Sat
* Everything for party rentals; dance floors to napkins; frankfurter and ice cream wagons. *

718-457-1122
718-688-8838

PROPS FOR TODAY
121 West 19th St. Reception: 3rd Fl., (6-7th Ave.) NYC, NY 10011
Hours: 8:30-5 Mon-Fri
* Full service party and restaurant rental facility from the traditional to the unique. Phone
orders accepted. *
(See display ad under PROP RENTAL HOUSES.)

212-206-0330

FAX   212-924-0450

RIVOLI MERCHANDISE
20 Howard St., (Mercer) NYC, NY 10013
Hours: 9-6 Mon-Fri
* Party supplies: wholesale, also seasonal merchandise, stationary, school supplies & props. *
(See display ad in this section.)

212-966-5035

RUBENSTEIN'S & SON MERCHANDISE, INC.
874 Broadway, (18th St.) NYC, NY 10003
Hours: 9-6 Mon-Fri • 9-2:30 Sat (closed Sat: July-Aug)
* Great party supplies; wholesale and retail; cheap. MC/VISA *

212-254-0162

O-P

All Seasonal Merchandise

Rivoli
Merchandise Co.
54 Howard St.
near Canal St. & Broadway
212-966-5035
Hours, 9AM - 6 PM
Monday thru Friday

Wholesale
Dyes - Tintex & Rit

Valentines Day
St. Patrick's
Easter
Halloween
Thanksgiving
X-Mas
New Years
Toys
Novelties
Props
Notions
Party Goods

Our Two Buildings in Soho Available for Productions
Established for 68 years
30 - 50% off retail prices

WE SHIP THE SAME DAY...ANYWHERE IN THE WORLD

SERVICE PARTY-RENTAL CO.   212-288-7384
    333 Star St., (Cypress Ave.) Brooklyn, NY 11237
    Hours: 8-5 Mon-Fri
      • Chairs, tables, bars, coat racks, silverware, china, linens, etc. for party rentals. MC/VISA •

PERSONAL PROTECTION EQUIPMENT

ACTS/ARTS, CRAFTS & THEATRE SAFETY   212-777-0062
    181 Thompson St. #23, NYC, NY 10012-2586
    Hours: by appt.

ACTS is a non-profit corporation dedicated to providing safety
services to the arts. ACTS answers inquiries about products used in
theater, refers callers to doctors and clinics, publishes a newsletter,
and provides speakers and consultants for lectures, OSHA training,
and surveys of theaters and shops.

ACTS
ARTS, CRAFTS, AND THEATER SAFETY

    • Contact Monona Rossol •   •

ANCHOR TOOL & SUPPLY CO.   201-887-8888
    PO Box 265, Chatham, NJ 07928
    Hours: 1-5 Tues-Fri • 10-1 Sat (call first)
      • Non-asbestos cloth, high temperature gloves, aluminized aprons. Catalog available. Will ship.
    MC/VISA •

"I found it in the N.Y. Theatrical Sourcebook."

CARBORUNDUM CO. FIBERS DIVISION   716-278-2000
P.O. Box 808, Niagara Falls, NY 14302
Hours: 8-4:30 Mon-Fri
• Non-Asbestos yarn, rope, boards, heat shields, drapes. Catalogs available. Will ship •

DIRECT SAFETY CO.   800-528-7405
7815 S. 46th St., Phoenix, AZ 85044
Hours: 6-6 Mon-Fri   FAX   800-760-2975
• Bulk or individual safety gear. Rubber gloves, barrier skin creams, face masks and filters. Catalog available. Will ship. MC/VISA •

EASTCO INDUSTRIAL SAFETY CORP.   516-427-1802
130 West 10th St., (New York Ave.) Huntington Station, NY 11746
Hours: 8:30-5 Mon-Fri
• 3M, Willson, Glendale safety equipment in stock; can order any other brand; call for minimum order. MC/VISA •

EASTERN SAFETY EQUIPMENT CO., INC.   718-894-7900
59-20 56th Avenue, (59th St.) Maspeth, NY 11378
Hours: 8:30-4:30 Mon-Fri
• NIOSH approved respirators for organic vapors, paint spray and dust. Catalog available. •

ECO DESIGN CO. THE NATURAL CHOICE   505-438-3448
1365 Rufina Circle, Santa Fe, NM 87501
Hours: 8-6 Mon-Fri • 10-3 Sat   FAX   505-438-0199
• Carry environmentally friendly hand cleaners. Catalog available. MC/VISA •

FIBRE-METAL PRODUCTS CO.   215-459-5300
Rt. 1 Brinton Lake Rd., Concordville, PA 19331   800-523-7048
Hours: 8-4:30 Mon-Fri
• Safety equipment, hard hats. Catalog. Will ship. •

HARRIS HARDWARE   212-243-0468
15 West 18th St., (5-6th Ave.) NYC, NY 10011
Hours: 8:30-5 Mon-Fri • 10-4 Sun
• NIOSH approved respirators for organic vapors, paint spray and dust. •

SIMON SUPPLIES   516-694-3131
21 North Mall, Plainville, NY 11803   (outside NY only) 800-543-3686
Hours: 9-5 Mon-Fri   FAX   516-694-3135
• Formerly Industrial Utilities; 3M respirators and safety equipment; minimum 1 box; all factory supplies; phone orders, catalog. MC/VISA •

LAB SAFETY SUPPLY CO   800-356-0783
PO Box 1368, Janesville, WI 53547
Hours: 6-9 Mon-Fri   FAX   800-543-9910
• Safety equipment and supplies, catalog available. CREDIT CARDS •

MINE SAFETY APPLIANCES CO.   412-273-5000
PO Box 426, Pittsburgh, PA 15230   800-672-2222
Hours: 8:30-5 Mon-Fri

1100 Globe Ave., Mountainside, NJ 07092   908-232-3490
Hours: 8-5 Mon-Fri
• NIOSH approved respirators. Will ship any size order, open account billing; respirators, gloves, disposable clothing, goggles, etc. Catolog. MC/VISA •

O-P

NEWARK SAFETY EQUIPMENT CO.　　201-344-1051
664 Ferry St., (Foundry) Newark, NJ 07105
Hours: 8-5 Mon-Fri • 9-1 Sat (except summer)　　FAX　201-344-6572
• 3M and Pulmosan safety equipment, hard hats, steel-toed shoes, disposable clothing, etc. Will ship small orders; COD. Fast service. MC/VISA •

NORTON SAFETY PRODUCTS　　401-943-4400
2000 Plainfield Pike, Cranston, RI 02921
Hours: 8-4:30 Mon-Fri　　FAX　401-942-9360
• NIOSH approved respirators, sizes for men and women; catalog available. •

O.K. UNIFORM CO.　　212-966-1984
507 Broadway, (Spring-Broome) NYC, NY 10012　　800-966-4733
Hours: 9:30-5:30 Mon-Thurs • 9:30-call Fri • 11:30-4:30 Sun　　FAX　212-226-6668
• Sales only. Disposable paper suits and all types of work clothes, protective clothing and accessories. •
(See display ad under CLOTHING RENTAL & PURCHASE; UNIFORMS.)

H.G. PASTERNACK, INC.　　212-691-9555
151 West 19th St., (7th Ave.) NYC, NY 10011　　800-433-3330
Hours: 9-5:30 Mon-Fri　　FAX　212-924-0024
• Authorized distributor of 3M respirators and masks. $25 minimum for phone orders, brochures available. •

SARA GLOVE CO.　　203-574-4090
PO Box 1940, Waterbury, CT 06722　　(outside NY) 800-243-3571
Hours: 8:30-4:30 Mon-Fri　　FAX　800-243-3570
• Many types and sizes of latex and neoprene gloves. Catalog, shipping. MC/VISA •

SCOTT AVIATION (DIV. OF FIGI, INC.)　　716-683-5100
225 Erie St., Lancaster, NY 14086
Hours: 8-4:30 Mon-Fri
• NIOSH approved respirators. •

W.H. SILVER'S HARDWARE　　212-247-4406
832 Eighth Ave., (50-51st St.) NYC, NY 10019　　212-247-4425
Hours: 8-5:30 Mon-Fri only　　FAX　212-246-2041
• Silicone cloth, gloves, and protective masks. First-aid kits and fire extinguishers. •

SOUTHERN MANUFACTURING, INC.　　704-372-2880
PO Box 32427, Charlotte, NC 28232
Hours: 8-5 Mon-Fri　　FAX　704-377-2790
• Non-asbestos mineral fiber textiles; also fiberglass fabrics. Catalog available. •

3-M COMPANY　　(product information) 612-737-6501
3M Center, St. Paul, MN 55144
Hours: 7:45-4:30 Mon-Fri
• NIOSH approved respirators. Best line of paper masks available. Non-toxic adhesives. Catalog available. •

WILLSON SAFETY PRODUCTS, VIVISION WGM SAFETY　　215-376-6161
PO Box 622, (Second & Washington St.) Reading, PA 19603　　800-345-4112
Hours: 8-5 Mon-Fri
• NIOSH approved respirators. Catalog available. •

O-P

PET SUPPLIES

See also **TROPICAL FISH**

AMERICAN KENNELS   212-838-8460
   789 Lexington Ave., (61st St.) NYC, NY 10021
   Hours: 10-7 Mon-Sat • 12-6 Sun
      • Basic neighborhood pet supply store. •

ANIMAL WORLD   212-685-0027
   219 East 26th St., (2-3rd Ave.) NYC, NY 10010
   Hours: 10-7 Mon-Fri • 10-6 Sat
      • Pet toys, food, accessories; good dog bowls. •

BIRD JUNGLE   212-242-1757
   401 Bleeker St., (11th St.) NYC, NY 10014
   Hours: 12:30-6:30 Mon-Sat • 11-5:30 Sun
      • Good selection of large birdcages and birds; will order. CREDIT CARDS •

FISH & PET TOWN   212-752-9508
   241 East 59th St., (2-3rd Ave.) NYC, NY 10022
   Hours: 11-7 Mon-Sat • 12:30-6 Sun
      • Large selection fish, dog, and cat supplies. •

JBJ DISCOUNT PET SHOP   212-982-5310
   151 East Houston St., (1-2nd Ave.) NYC, NY 10002
   Hours: 10-6 Mon-Sat
      • Good selection small animals, rabbits, mice, etc. •

JUST CATS   212-888-2287
   244 East 60th St., (2-3rd Ave.) NYC, NY 10022
   Hours: 10-6 Mon-Sat
      • A feline boutique with cat motif items, food bowls, placemats, litter box houses. •

OMAHA VACCINE CO.   800-367-4444
   PO Box 7228, 3030 L St., Omaha, NE 68107
   Hours: 7-9 Mon-Fri • 8-5 Sat • 11-5 Sun
      • Veterinary and animal care supplies; good source for oversized medical equipment. CREDIT
   CARDS •

PETLAND DISCOUNTS   212-694-1821
   132 Nassau St., (Ann-Beekman St.) NYC, NY 10038
   Hours: 9-7 Mon-Fri • 10-6 Sat • 11-5 Sun

   7 East 14th St., (5th Ave.) NYC, NY 10003   212-675-4102
   Hours: 10-8 Mon-Fri • 10-7 Sat • 11-6 Sun

   304 East 86th St., (2nd Ave) NYC, NY 10028   212-472-1655
   Hours: 10-9 Mon-Fri • 10-6 Sat • 11-6 Sun

   2675 Broadway, (102nd St.) NYC, NY 10025   212-222-8851
   Hours: 10-9 Mon-Fri • 10-7 Sat • 11-6 Sun
      • Good selection of pet supplies; birds, fish, small animals. CREDIT CARDS •

O-P

PEWTER ITEMS

See also **ANTIQUES: ALL HEADINGS**

LOVELIA ENTERPRISES INC.   212-490-0930
356 41st St., (Tudor City Place) NYC, NY 10017
Hours: by appt.
• Antique pewter; also large selection of reproduction Gobelin and wool Aubusson tapestries; prefers short-term rentals. •

MACY'S   212-736-5151
151 West 34th St., (Broadway) NYC, NY 10001
Hours: 10-8:30 Mon, Thur, Fri. • 10-7:30 Tues, Wed, Sat • 11-6 Sun
• Pewter in Colonial Shop, 8th floor. CREDIT CARDS •

HYMAN E. PISTON ANTIQUES   212-753-8322
1050 Second Ave., (55-56th St.) NYC, NY 10022
Hours: 10-4 Mon-Fri • 10-2 Sat (call first on Sat.)
• Antique copper, brass and pewter items. •

QUEENS ART WINDSOR   718-625-7097
Brooklyn Navy Yard, (Bldg 120) Brooklyn, NY 11205
Hours: 8-4:30 Mon-Fri
• Quality pewter items: tankards, cups, pitchers, candlesticks, coffee servers, trays, serving pieces; bright or dull finish. Catalog available. •

WILTON ARMETALE   717-653-5594
P.O. Box 600, (Plumb & Square Sts.) Mount Joy, PA 17552
Hours: 9:30-5:30 Mon-Sat
• Wholesale pewter dinnerware, goblets, pitchers, mugs, candleholders; mail order only; catalog; quick delivery, call for retail outlets. •

PHOTOGRAPHIC EQUIPMENT: USED AND ANTIQUE

See also **PROP RENTAL HOUSES**

ACE PROPS   212-206-1475
1 West 19th St. Ground Floor, (5th Ave.) NYC, NY 10011   212-580-9551
Hours: 8-5 Mon-Fri • 9-4 Sat • or by appt.   FAX   212-929-9082
• Rental of consumer and professional cameras -1930's contemporary-still, film, and video. CREDIT CARDS •
(See display ad under PROP RENTAL HOUSES)

BARGAIN SPOT   212-674-1188
64 Third Ave., (11th St.) NYC, NY 10032   212-674-1189
Hours: 9-4:45 Tues-Sat
• New and used camera equipment, rental or purchase; also musical instruments, binoculars, etc. CREDIT CARDS •

E. BUK, ANTIQUES & ART
212-226-6891
151 Spring St., 2nd floor, (W. Broadway-Wooster) NYC, NY 10012
Hours: Every day by appt.
(toll call) 700-SCIENCE

ANTIQUE AND HISTORICAL studio and field photographers' equipment; cameras, enlargers, tripods, glasses, accessories, retouching and darkroom equipment, still and moving image devices, projectors, wood and brass era, large and small format; binoculars, telescopes. Entire studio and darkroom setups.

• Complete period settings and custom work. RENTALS •
(See display ad under PROP RENTAL HOUSES)

CAMERA WORKS
203-389-2688
12 Fountain St., (Whaley Ave.) New Haven, CT 06515
Hours: 9-6 Tues-Fri • 9-5 Sat
• Modern and antique cameras, very knowledgeable. Speak to Paul MacBeth. MC/VISA. •

WALL ST. CAMERA EXCHANGE, INC.
212-344-0011
82 Wall St., (Pearl-Walter) NYC, NY 10005
Hours: 9-6 Mon-Thurs • 9-2:30 Fri • 10-3 Sun
• New and used cameras, camera equipment, repairs; calculators, computers, watches. •

PHOTOGRAPHIC EQUIPMENT

See also **PROP RENTAL HOUSES**

ACE PROPS
212-206-1475
1 West 19th St. Ground fl., (5th Ave.) NYC, NY 10011
212-580-9551
Hours: 8-5 Mon-Fri • 9-4 Sat or by appt.   FAX   212-929-9082
• Rental of consumer and professional cameras- 1930's to contemporary- still, film and video. CREDIT CARDS •
(See display ad under PROP RENTAL HOUSES.)

B & H FOTO & ELECTRONICS CORP.
212-206-1010
119 West 17th St., (6-7th Ave.) NYC, NY 10011
212-807-7474
Hours: 9-6 Mon-Tue • Wed-Thurs 9-7:30 • 9-1 Fri • 9:45-4:45 Sun
• Good prices on film, photographic equipment and accessories. MC/VISA •

BARGAIN SPOT
212-674-1188
64 Third Ave., (11th St.) NYC, NY 10032
Hours: 8:30-5 Mon-Sat
• A pawn shop with a good selection of new and used camera equipment; rental or purchase; also musical instruments, binoculars, etc. CREDIT CARDS •

BI-RITE PHOTO ELECTRIC, INC.
212-685-2130
15 East 30th St., (5th- Madison Ave.) NYC, NY 10016
800-223-1970
Hours: 9-6 Mon-Thurs • 9-1 Fri • 10:30-3:30 Sun   FAX   212-679-2986
• Very low prices on cameras and electronic equipment. MC/VISA •

CAMERA WORKS
203-389-2688
12 Fountain St., (Whaley Ave.) New Haven, CT 06515
Hours: 9-6 Tue-Fri • 9-5 Sat
• Modern and antique cameras, very knowledgeable. Speak to Paul MacBeth. MC/VISA •

EXECUTIVE PHOTO & SUPPLY CORP. 212-947-5290
120 West 31st St., (6-7th Ave.) NYC, NY 10001 800-223-7323
Hours: 9-6 Mon-Thurs • 9-2 Fri • 9:30-5 Sun FAX 212-239-7157
• Stock all leading brands of cameras and equipment. CREDIT CARDS •

47TH ST. PHOTO, INC. 212-398-1410
115 West 45th St., (6th-B'way) NYC, NY 10036
Hours: 9:30-7 Mon-Thurs • 9:30-2 Fri • 10-5 Sun
• Cameras and photo equipment, computers, typewriters, etc; watch for frequent sales. •

67 West 47th St., (5-6th Ave.) NYC, NY 10036 212-260-4410
Hours: 9-6:30 Mon-Thurs • 9-2 Fri • 10-5 Sun
• Cameras and photo equipment; darkroom store. •

KEN HANSEN PHOTOGRAPHIC CO. 212-777-5900
920 Broadway 2nd Fl., (21st St.) NYC, NY 10010
Hours: 9:30-5:00 Mon-Fri FAX 212-473-0690
• Stock many leading brands of cameras and equipment for the professional. RENTALS CREDIT CARDS •

NATIONAL ARTISTS MATERIALS CO., INC. 212-675-0100
4 West 20th St., (5-6th Ave.) NYC, NY 10011
Hours: 8:30-6 Mon-Fri •10-4 Sat FAX 212-691-0474
• Seamless paper, mat board, transparent slide, negative and photo pages, light stands, clamps, filters, gels. RENTALS •

OLDEN CAMERA 212-725-1234
1265 Broadway, (32nd St.) NYC, NY 10001
Hours: 9-7 Mon-Fri • 9-6 Sat •10-5 Sun FAX 212-725-1325
• Photographic equipment and darkroom supplies; knowledgeable staff; rentals available. CREDIT CARDS •

TWENTIETH CENTURY PLASTICS 714-441-4500
205 South Puente St., La Brea, CA 92621 800-767-0777
Hours: 6-5 Mon-Fri FAX 714-441-4550
• Photo albums and storage boxes; plastic sleeves for slides and photos; quick mail order service. CREDIT CARDS •

WALL ST. CAMERA EXCHANGE, INC. 212-344-0011
82 Wall St., (Pearl-Walter) NYC, NY 10005
Hours: 9-6 Mon-Thurs • 9-2:30 Fri • 10-3 Sun
• New and used cameras, camera equipment, repairs; calculators, computers, watches. •

WILLOUGHBY-PEERLESS CAMERA STORE 212-564-1600
136 West 32nd St., (6-7th Ave.) NYC, NY 10001
Hours: 9-7 Mon-Fri • (Thurs till 8) • 9-6:30 Sat • 10:30-5:30 Sun
• Excellent selection camera equipment and accessories; while-you-wait print processing. MC/VISA •

O–P

PHOTOGRAPHIC EQUIPMENT REPAIR

PHOTO TECH REPAIR SERVICE 212-673-8400
110 East 13th St., (3rd-4th St.) NYC, NY 10003
Hours: 8:30-4:45 Mon-Fri FAX 212-673-8451
• Photo equipment repair. Polaroid repair. CREDIT CARDS •

PROFESSIONAL CAMERA REPAIR SERVICE, INC. 212-382-0550
37 West 47th St. Rm. 902, (5-6th Ave.) NYC, NY 10036
Hours: 8:30-5 Mon-Fri FAX 212-382-2537
• Repair of cameras and accessories. •

PANORAMA CAMERA 212-563-1651
110 West 30th St., (6th-7th Ave.) NYC, NY 10001
Hours: 9-6 Mon-Fri FAX 212-643-8796
• Camera repairs. MC/VISA •

WALL ST. CAMERA EXCHANGE, INC. 212-344-0011
82 Wall St., (Pearl-Water) NYC, NY 10005
Hours: 9-6 Mon-Thurs • 9-2:30 Fri • 10-3 Sun
• Repair of camera equipment; sale of new and used cameras. •

PHOTOGRAPHIC SERVICES

For photographic process backdrops, see **BACKDROPS**
For photostats, see **PRINTING & COPYING**

O-P

AUTHENTICOLOR 212-867-7905
227 East 45th St., (2-3rd Ave) NYC, NY 10022 800-977-4687
Hours: 8:30-6:30 Mon-Fri FAX 212-687-6980 OR 212-370-1028
• One of the few labs that do real sepia prints. Can match tones and work in large format. •

BAUMWELL GRAPHICS, INC. 212-868-3340
450 West 31st St., (9-10th Ave.) NYC, NY 10001
Hours: 8:30-6 Mon-Fri FAX 212-689-3386
• Custom color rubdown transfers, enlargements, black and white prints, mounting and laminating. Contact Clyde Baumwell. •

BOX ONE PHOTOGRAPHIC SERVICE / PICTURE YOURSELF 212-239-0283
112 West 31st St. 3rd Fl., (6-7th Ave) NYC, NY 10001
Hours: 9-6 Mon-Fri
• Inexpensive photo work, head shots. CREDIT CARDS •

CHROMA COPY 212-399-2420
423 West 55th St., (9-10th Ave.) NYC, NY 10019
Hours: 10-4 Mon-Fri FAX 212-582-4107

122 Fulton St., (Nassau St.) NYC, NY 10038 212-619-8282
Hours: 9-5 Mon-Fri FAX 212-962-6135
• Color prints, translucencies, transparencies from artwork or transparencies. Photo murals
up to 50" x 144"; checks only, no cash. •

COLOR WHEEL, INC. 212-697-2434
227 East 45th St., (2-3rd Ave.) NYC, NY 10017
Hours: 9-5 Mon-Fri FAX 212-953-2174
• Quality custom printing. •

CROWN PHOTO 212-382-0233
432 West 45th St., (9-10th Ave) NYC, NY 10036
Hours: 8:30-5:45 Mon-Fri FAX 212-956-4512
• Photo blow-ups; speak to Arthur. MC/VISA •

THE DARKROOM, INC. 212-687-8920
222 East 46th St. #203, (2-3rd Ave.) NYC, NY 10017
Hours: 8:30-6 Mon-Fri FAX 212-687-1319
• Will print photos in sepia tone; B&W, color prints, slides. MC/VISA •

DUGGAL COLOR PROJECTS, INC. 212-242-7000
9 West 20th St., (5-6th Ave.) NYC, NY 10011 800-382-2000
Hours: 24 Hours Mon-Thurs • Fri 'till Midnight • 9-6 Sat-Sun FAX 212-633-1266
• Fast service on slides; photo murals, cibachromes, studio rental. CREDIT CARDS •

FOUR COLORS PHOTO LAB 908-241-3311
136 Market St., Kenilworth, NJ 07033 212-889-3399
Hours: 9-5 Mon-Fri
• Contact prints, transparencies, C-prints, B&W, retouching. AMEX •

GIANT PHOTO, INC. 212-477-1792
200 Park Ave. South #501, (17th St.) NYC, NY 10003
Hours: 9-5 Mon-Fri FAX 212-977-7319
• Very large blow-ups; photostats, dry-mounting. Rush service at higher price. Reliable, helpful service. •

H-Y PHOTO SERVICE 212-986-0390
10 East 39th St., 2nd Floor, (5th Ave.) NYC, NY 10016
Hours: 9-6 Mon-Fri FAX 212-753-9072
• Photo blow-ups, will mount work. •

JELLYBEAN PHOTOGRAPHICS 212-679-4888
99 Madison Ave., 14th Fl., (29-30th St.) NYC, NY 10016
Hours: 9-5:30 Mon-Fri FAX 212-545-0986
• Complete photo lab; reasonable prices. •

NEW YORK FILM WORKS 212-475-5700
928 Broadway, (21-22nd St.) NYC, NY 10010
Hours: 8-9 Mon-Fri • 9-5 Sat
• Color photo enlargements; good work. •

PHOTO IMAGING 212-489-1190
321 West 44th St., #604, (8-9th Ave.) NYC, NY 10036
Hours: 8:30-5:30 Mon-Fri FAX 212-586-1310
• Formerly Studio West Ltd. Full service lab; B&W and color slides and prints; mounting; Duratrans up to 50" x 10'; excellent quality work. •

S M P GRAPHIC SERVICE CENTER, INC. / STAT SHOP   212-929-2010
    26 East 22nd St., (B'way-Park Ave.) NYC, NY 10010
    Hours: 8am-midnight Mon-Thurs • 8-10 Fri • 11-6 Sat, Sun   FAX   212-979-2934

    142 West 26th St., (6th-7th Ave.) NYC, NY 10001   212-929-2010
    Hours: 9-6 Mon-Fri
    • Dry mounting, blow-ups to 4'x 8', many other services. CREDIT CARDS •

SUPERIOR FOTOTECH, INC.   212-246-5110
    432 West 45th St., (9-10th Ave.) NYC, NY 10036
    Hours: 9-5:30 Mon-Fri   FAX   212-956-4512
    • Good prices on large format photo blow-ups. •

THRU THE LENS FOTO CO.   212-734-0245
    1296 First Ave., (69-70th St.) NYC, NY 10021
    Hours: 10-6 Mon-Fri • 10:30-2:30 Sat   FAX   212-472-5132
    • Arthur Laszlo, owner, quick Kodak processing. MC/VISA •

JACK WARD COLOR / SLIDE SHOP, INC.   212-725-5200
    220 East 23rd St. 4th Fl., (2-3rd Ave.) NYC, NY 10010
    Hours: 8am-9pm Mon-Fri   FAX   212-779-8977
    • Color lab; high contrast copy, reverse image negative slides; slides from artwork. MC/VISA •

PIPE & TUBING

See also **ELECTRICAL & ELECTRONIC SUPPLIES**
See also **MEDICAL & SCIENTIFIC EQUIPMENT & SUPPLIES: LAB & SCIENTIFIC**
See also **PLASTICS; SHEETS, TUBES, RODS, SHAPES**
See also **PLUMBING SUPPLIES & FIXTURES**
For sonotube, see **PAPER, CARDBOARD & FOAMCORE PRODUCTS**

CANAL RUBBER SUPPLY CO.   212-226-7339
    329 Canal St., (Greene St.) NYC, NY 10013
    Hours: 9-5 Mon-Fri • 9-4:30 Sat   FAX   212-219-3754
    • Latex and rubber tubing, ventilation and vacuum hoses, dental dams, also air and water. No credit cards. •

FLEISCHER TUBE DISTRIBUTING CORP.   516-968-8822
    71 Saxon Ave., Bayshore, NY 11706
    Hours: 9-5 Mon-Fri • 9-2 Sat   FAX   212-968-5032
    • Any kind of metal tube, including thin wall; will deliver. •

PENWELL BELTING CO., INC.   718-539-1339
    131-15 Sanford Ave., Flushing, NY 11355
    Hours: 8-4:30 Mon-Fri   FAX   718-539-1448
    • Latex and rubber tubing, related rubber products. •

PVC SUPPLY CO.   212-741-0900
    304 Spring St., (Hudson-Greenwich St.) NYC, NY 10013
    Hours: 8-4:30 Mon-Fri   FAX   212-633-6408
    • Complete stock of PVC and CPVC. •

SILVER & SONS HARDWARE   212-247-6969
    711 Eighth Ave., (44-45th St.) NYC, NY 10036   212-247-6977
    Hours: 9-5:30 Mon-Fri • 10-2 Sat
    • All sizes and lengths of pipe; cut to order. CREDIT CARDS •

O-P

W. H. SILVER'S HARDWARE   212-247-4406
   832 Eighth Ave., (50-51st St.) NYC, NY 10019   212-247-4425
   Hours: 8-5:30 Mon-Fri   FAX   212-246-2041
   • Galvanized, black, brass, aluminum, PVC by the length or cut to size. •

PLASTIC ITEMS

AIN PLASTICS, INC.   212-473-2100
   300 Park Ave. South, (22-23rd St.) NYC, NY 10010   212-823-4200
   Hours: 9-5:30 Mon-Fri • 10-4 Sat
   • Plastic items, sheets, rods, tubes, film. •

INDUSTRIAL PLASTICS   212-226-2010
   309 Canal St., (B'way-Mercer St.) NYC, NY 10013
   Hours: 9-5 Mon-Fri • 9-4 Sat
   • Plastic items, shapes, sheets, film, rods, tubes; fiberglass statuary and supplies. •

OUTWATER PLASTICS   201-340-1040
   PO Drawer 403, Wood Ridge, NJ 07075   800-631-8375
   Hours: 9-5 Mon-Fri
   • Decorative trim, tubing, frames, boxes in plastic. Good catalogs. $25 min. MC/VISA •

PLASTIC WORKS   212-362-1000
   2107 Broadway, (74th St.) NYC, NY 10023
   Hours: 10-7 Mon-Wed • 10-8 Thurs •10-6 Fri,Sat • 10-5:30 Sun
   • Ready-made acrylic and other plastic household goods; bath accessories, picture frames.
   CREDIT CARDS •

PLEXABILITY LTD.   212-679-7826
   200 Lexington Ave. 5th Fl., (32-33rd St.) NYC, NY 10016
   Hours: 9:45-5 Mon-Fri
   • Lucite furnishings and props; sales, custom work available. RENTALS CREDIT CARDS •

PLEXI-CRAFT QUALITY PRODUCTS CORP.   212-924-3244
   514 West 24th St., (10-11th Ave.) NYC, NY 10011
   Hours: 9:30-5 Mon-Fri • 11-4 Sat
   • Lucite furniture and accessories; catalog. •

ROTOCAST DISPLAY PRODUCTS   305-693-4680
   3645 N.W. 67th St., Miami, FL 33147   800-327-5062
   Hours: 8-5 Mon-Fri

   4700 Mitchell St., Las Vegas, NV 89030   800-423-8539
   Hours: 8-4 Mon-Fri
   • Polyethylene urns and planters in many shapes, sizes, colors; polyethylene rocks, pedestals, globes, bird baths, garden benches; catalog. •

THE SET SHOP   212-979-9790
   37 East 18th St., (B'way-Park Ave. S.) NYC, NY 10003
   Hours: 8:30-6 Mon-Fri • 10-4 Sat   FAX   212-979-9852
   • Ten types of ice cubes and shards, large selection of acrylic sheets. Custom fabrication available. CREDIT CARDS •

STARBUCK STUDIO   212-807-7299
    162 West 21st St., (6-7th Ave.) NYC, NY 10011
    Hours: 10-5:30 Mon-fri
      • Rents acrylic ice cubes; also does custom acrylic work; call first. •

PLASTIC FABRICATION

See also **VACUUMFORMING & VACUUMFORMED PANELS**

ACCURATE PLASTICS   914-476-0700
    18 Morris Place, Yonkers, NY 10705
    Hours: 8-5:30 Mon-Fri
      • Plexiglass fabrication. •

AIN PLASTICS, INC.   212-473-2100
    300 Park Ave. South, (22-23rd St.) NYC, NY 10010   (warehouse) 212-823-4200
    Hours: 9-5:30 Mon-Fri • 10-4 Sat
      • Fabrication and manufacturing of sheets, rods, tubes, film; stops cutting half-hour before
    closing. CREDIT CARDS •

IMT SERVICES   914-691-3665
    5 Pine Terr., Highland, NY 12528
    Hours: 9-6 Mon-Fri   FAX   914-691-3684
      • Modelmaking, sculpture, flexibles, fake food for ECU, casting: miniature to oversize.
    Electro-mechanical effects. ATAC member •

JUST PLASTICS, INC.   212-569-8500
    250 Dykman St., (B'way) NYC, NY 10034
    Hours: 8-5 Mon-Fri
      • Quality custom work; contact Lois. •

PLATI-VUE CORP.   718-463-2300
    41-30 Murray St., (Barclay-41st Ave.) Flushing, NY 11355
    Hours: 8-4:30 Mon-Fri
      • Profile shapes, boxes, museum cases, wrapped cylinders; vacuumforming, drape-forming;
    speak to Gary Fischer. •

PLEXABILITY LTD.   212-679-7826
    200 Lexington Ave. 5th Fl., (32-33rd St.) NYC, NY 10016
    Hours: 9:45-5 Mon-Fri
      • Lucite furnishings and props; sales, rentals, or custom work available. CREDIT CARDS •

S. POMPONIO   212-925-9453
    315 Church St., (Lispenard-Walker St.) NYC, NY 10013
    Hours: 9-5:30 Mon-Fri
      • Will cut plastic or any other material. Makes stencils and molds. •

PREMIER PLASTICS CORP.   718-274-7400
    240-30 Brooklyn-Queens Expressway West, Woodside, NY 11377
    Hours: 9-4:30 Mon-Fri
      • Plastics. See Frank or Delores; very helpful on special orders. •

STARBUCK STUDIO   212-807-7299
    162 West 21st St., (6-7th Ave.) NYC, NY 10011
    Hours: 10-5:30 Mon-Fri • call first
      • Custom acrylic work; specializes in model making; call first; also rents acrylic ice cubes. •

O-P

PLASTICS: SHEETS, TUBES, RODS, SHAPES

AAA GLASS CO., INC.   212-463-8000
    152 West 36th St., (6-7th Ave.) NYC, NY 10001
    Hours: 8-5 Mon-Fri
    • Plexiglass sheets, cut to size while you wait. •
    (See display ad under GLASS & MIRRORS.)

ACCURATE PLASTICS   914-476-0700
    18 Morris Place, Yonkers, NY 10705
    Hours: 8-5:30 Mon-Fri
    • Plexi sheets, tubes, rods. •

AIN PLASTICS, INC.   212-473-2100
    300 Park Ave. South, (22-23rd St.) NYC, NY 10010   (warehouse) 212-823-4200
    Hours: 9-5 Mon-Fri • 10-4 Sat
    • Plexi sheets, rods, tubes, shapes; rather pricey; stops cutting half-hour before closing.
    CREDIT CARDS •

ALMAC PLASTICS, INC.   516-938-7300
    385 W. Johns St., Hicksville, NY 11801
    Hours: 8:30-4:30 Mon-Fri
    • Latex tubing, Teflon, nylon, plexi, Lexan, acetate. •

APEX PLASTIC INDUSTRIES, INC.   516-231-8888
    155 Marcus Blvd., Box 11008, Hauppauge, NY 11788-0701   (outside NY)800-APEX-INC
    Hours: 8-5 Mon-Fri   FAX 516-231-8890
    • Very large selection of vinyl, plastic and mylar sheetings and films: prisms, marble, cracked
    ice; vinyl ribbon; full rolls 40" to 60" and wider. Will ship. See Michael Rosenthal for samples
    and information on other products. •

BLOOMFIELD PLASTIC CO.   201-743-6900
    28 Montgomery, (Exit 148 off Pkwy.) Bloomfield, NJ 07003
    Hours: 8-5 Mon-Fri
    • All types of plastics: colors, mirrors, cloth; catalog; fabricators. •

CADILLAC PLASTIC & CHEMICAL CO.   800-862-4589
    1801 U.S.1, Linden, NJ 07036
    Hours: 8:30-4:30 Mon-Fri
    • Plexiglass, nylon, Lexan, Teflon. Some custom work. •

CAMCO SUPPLIES   718-786-1791
    80 21st St., Brooklyn, NY 11232
    Hours: 7-5 Mon-Fri (pick-ups 7:15-3:30)
    • Formerly Styro Sales. Brochure available. Sheet plastic foam, Insta-foam, other foams;
    good stock, reasonable prices. No minimum. •

CANAL PLASTIC CENTER   212-925-1032
    345 Canal St., (Wooster-Greene St.) NYC, NY 10013   212-925-1164
    Hours: 10-5 Mon-Sat   FAX 212-431-5901
    • Wholesale and retail Lexan, plexi, acetate, vinyl, rods, tubes, mirror. No credit cards. •

CRAIG TECHNOLOGY   215-622-3900
    P.O.Box 38, 1050 E. Ashland Ave., Folcroft, PA 19032
    Hours: 9-5 Mon-Fri
    • Formerly Clifton Plastics. Precision plastic balls in PVC, phenolic, polyethylene, nylon. •

O-P

COMMERCIAL PLASTICS　　　　　　　　　　　718-849-8100
　　98-31 Jamaica Ave., (101st St.) Richmond Hill, NY 11418
　　Hours: 8:30-4 Mon-Fri
　　• Plexi, Lexan, nylon, Teflon, mylar, acetate, Comstik cements. •

E & T PLASTICS MFG. CO., INC.　　　　　　　718-729-6226
　　45-45 37th St., (Queens Blvd.) L.I.C., NY 11101
　　Hours: 9-5 Mon-Fri
　　• Plexi, acrylic, acetate, Lexan, Teflon, mylar, polystyrene, vacuumforming. •

FRANKLIN FIBRE-LAMITEX CORP.　　　　　　302-652-3621
　　PO Box 1768, 903 13th St., Wilmington, DE 19899
　　Hours: 8:30-5 Mon-Fri
　　• Nylon stocks, coils, sheets, tubes; acetate, Lexan, Teflon, mylar. $50 min. Catalog. •

HUNT-BEINFANG PRODUCTIONS　　　　　　800-873-4868
　　P.O. Box 5819, Statesville, NC 28687　　　　704-873-9511
　　Hours: 8-7:30 Mon-Fri　　　　　　　　FAX　704-872-1766
　　• Foam board in colors. Also Exacto tools. Free catalog. •

INDUSTRIAL PLASTICS　　　　　　　　　　212-226-2010
　　309 Canal St., (B'way-Mercer) NYC, NY 10013
　　Hours: 9-5:30 Mon-Fri • 9-4 Sat
　　• Plexiglass, fiberglass supplies, Lexan, mylar, acetate, component foams and resins. Plastic
　　tubes, shapes of all kinds and materials; findings •

JIFFY FOAM, INC.　　　　　　　　　　　401-846-7870
　　221 Third St., P.O. Box 3609, Newport, RI 02840
　　Hours: 8-5 Mon-Fri　　　　　　　　　FAX　401-847-9966
　　• Sells Balsa-Foam: a plastic product that carves like butter and paints like wood. Comes in
　　variety of sizes. •

PLASTI-CRAFT PRODUCT CORP.　　　　　　914-358-3490
　　164 West Nyack Rd., Nyack, NY 10994
　　Hours: 8-5 Mon-Fri　　　　　　　　　FAX　212-358-3007
　　• Plastic sheets, rods, and tubes; adhesives; laminates. •

PREMIER PLASTICS CORP.　　　　　　　　718-274-7400
　　24-30 Brooklyn-Queens Expressway West, Woodside, NY 11377
　　Hours: 9-4:30 Mon-Fri
　　• See Frank or Delores: very helpful on special orders. •

SCULPTURAL ARTS COATING INC.　　　　　910-299-5755
　　P.O. Box 13113, Greensboro, NC 27415　　　800-743-0379
　　Hours: 9-5 Mon-Fri　　　　　　　　　FAX　910-299-1359
　　• Distributor of Sculpt or Coat, a non-toxic, plastic cream coating for polystyrene and foam
　　rubber, and sculpting compound for scenery, costumes and props. •

SPECIALTY RESOURCES CO.　　　　　　　310-514-1581
　　1156 West 7th St., Suite B, San Pedro, CA 90731-2930
　　Hours: 8:30-5 Mon-Fri　　　　　　　　FAX　310-514-2997
　　• Astonishing collection of science fiction construction materials and props used in the film
　　industry, 8' diameter acrylic domes, cargo pods, chemical chambers, and other industrial com-
　　ponents. Call for color catalog. •

O-P

UNNATURAL RESOURCES, INC.
14 Forest Ave., Caldwell, NJ 07006
Hours: 9-6 Mon-Fri by appt.

201-228-5384
800-992-5540
FAX   201-891-8662

• Thermoplastics in mesh, solid, perforated sheets, skin-like and textured fabrics, even a putty material you can mold, in white and colors. Safe, non-toxic, fast setting, recyclable and biodegradable. Excellent substitute for Celastic. Also coatings for foam. Speak to Loretta. •
(See display ad under CASTING AND MODELING SUPPLIES.)

PLATING & METAL FINISHES

ANACOAT ANODIZING
10-01 45th Ave., Long Island City, NY 11101
Hours: 7-6:30 Mon-Fri • Factory 7-5:30 Mon-Thurs
• Anodizing. No credit cards. Catalog. •

718-361-1740

FAX   718-392-1842

BLACK OX METAL FINISHING
1-01 27th Ave., (1-2nd St.) L.I.C., NY 11102
Hours: 8:30-5 Mon-Fri
• Black oxide finishes; $45 minimum order. •

718-274-2104

C & C PLATING
51 West 21st St., (5th-6th Ave.) NYC, NY 10010
Hours: 8:30-5 Mon-Fri
• Metal plating and finishing. Good variety of finishes. $50 minimum. •

212-929-1296

FAX   212-645-0917

COLUMBIA HOME DECOR
493 3rd Ave., (33-34 St.) NYC, NY 10016
Hours: 9:30-6 Mon-Fri • (Thurs till 8) • 10-6 Sat • 11-5 Sun
• Formerly Columbia Lighting and Silversmith. Brass and silver plating. •

212-725-5250

ARTHUR FRISCH CO., INC.
1816 Boston Rd., (175th St.) Bronx, NY 10460
Hours: 9-4:30 Mon-Fri
• Vacuum plating on plastic, glass, metal, other surfaces. •

212-589-4100

J.C. GORHAM
625 Harris, Providence, RI 02909
Hours: 8-5 Mon-Fri
• Metal plating on plastics. More durable than vacuum metallizing. •

401-274-2610

FAX   401-274-1313

HYGRADE POLISHING & PLATING CO.
22-07 41st Ave., (22nd St.) L.I.C., NY 11101
Hours: 7-4 Mon-Thurs • 7-1 Fri • 7-12 Sat • (closed for lunch 12-12:30)
• Chrome, copper, brass, gold, black nickel and antique plating. Rush work done, reliable. •

718-392-4082

REGAL PLATING CO., INC.
85 South St., Providence, RI 02903
Hours: 8-3:30 Mon-Fri
• Decorative plating of costume jewelry. •

401-421-2704

RETINNING AND COPPER REPAIRS, INC.
525 West 26th St., (10-11th Ave.) NYC, NY 10001
Hours: 9-5 Mon-Fri
• Retinning and polishing, sheetmetal work and some repairs; see James Gibbons. •

212-244-4896

O-P

"I found it in the N.Y. Theatrical Sourcebook."

T & M Plating   212-243-9228
153 W. 27th St., (6-7th Ave.) NYC, NY 10001
Hours: 8:30-5 Mon-Fri   FAX   212-243-9405
• Metal plating & polishing. Fast service, $50 minimum. •

PLUMBING SUPPLIES & FIXTURES

A.F. Supply   212-243-5400
22 West 21st St., 5th FL., (5-6th Ave.) NYC, NY 10010
Hours: 8-5 Mon-Fri   FAX   212-243-2403
• Large showroom of bath fixtures, shower, enclosures, faucets, sinks, etc. RENTALS
MC/VISA •

Davis & Warshow, Inc.   212-977-3169
701 10th Ave., (47-48th St.) NYC, NY 10036   (plumbing supply) 212-247-7710
Hours: 8-4:30 Mon-Fri • 8-11:30 Sat (showroom closed for lunch, 1-2) FAX   212-593-0446

150 East 58th St., 4th Floor, (3rd-Lexington) NYC, NY 10022
                                                (main showroom)212-688-5990
Hours: 9-5 Mon-Fri • 12-4 Sat
• Kohler, American Standard, Kallista, and European imported bath and kitchen fixtures.
RENTALS CREDIT CARDS •

Deco ware, Inc.   718-871-1212
944 McDonald Ave., (Ave. F-18th Ave) Brooklyn, NY 11230
Hours: 9-6 Mon-Wed • 9-7 Thurs • 9-2 Fri • 10-6 Sun   FAX   718-972-3277
• Large selection of decorative hardware and plumbing fixtures. Delivery service available •

East Side Plumbing Specialties   212-772-1112
231 East 77th St., (2-3rd Ave.) NYC, NY 10021
Hours: 8-5 Mon-Fri • 8-1 Sat   FAX   212-628-5663
• Replacement parts for fixtures, obsolete parts duplicated. CREDIT CARDS •

Eigen Supply Co., Inc.   212-255-1200
236 West 17th St., (7-8th Ave.) NYC, NY 10011 (showroom)

1751 First Ave., (90-91st St.) NYC, NY 10128   212-255-1200

317 Atlantic Ave., (Smith-Hoyt) Brooklyn, NY 11201   212-255-1200
Hours: 7:30-4:30 Mon-Fri   FAX   212-691-9882
• Large basic plumbing supply house with showroom, wholesale and retail. MC/VISA •

Greenwich Village Plumbers Supply   212-254-9450
35 Bond St., (Bowery-Lafayette St.) NYC, NY 10012
Hours: 7-4:30 Mon-Fri   FAX   212-353-3801
• Basic plumbing supplies, wholesale and retail. CREDIT CARDS •

P.E. Guerin   212-243-5270
23 Jane St., (Greenwich Ave.-8th Ave.) NYC, NY 10014
Hours: 9-4:30 Mon-Fri by appt.   FAX   212-727-2290
• Wonderful hardware and bathroom fixtures, primarily custom with a 6-8 week delivery; catalog; expensive. •

0-P

ISABELLA   718-278-7272
24-24 Steinway St., (Astoria Blvd.) Astoria, NY 11103
Hours: 9:30-7 Mon,Tue,Th,Fri • 9:30-6 Wed • 9:30-5 Sat (closed Sat: July, Aug)
       FAX   718-545-4324
• Kitchen and bathroom sinks, faucets, vanities, some kitchen cabinets; period pieces.
RENTALS MC/VISA •

LEESAM KITCHEN & BATH   212-243-6482
124 Seventh Ave., (17-18th St.) NYC, NY 10011
Hours: 9:30-6 Mon-Fri • (Thurs till 8) • 12-5 Sat   FAX   212-243-9538
• Sinks, toilets, bathtubs, shower doors, vanities, faucets, cabinets. RENTALS MC/VISA •

METROPOLITAN LUMBER & HARDWARE   212-966-3466
175 Spring St., (W. B'way-Thompson St.) NYC, NY 10012
Hours: 8-6 Mon-Fri • 8-6 Sat • 9-4 Sun

617 Eleventh Ave., (46th St.) NYC, NY 10036   212-246-9090
Hours: 7-6:30 Mon-Fri • 8-6 Sat • 10-4 Sun

108-56 Roosevelt Ave., (108-111th St) Corona, NY 11368   718-898-2100
Hours: 8-7 Mon-Fri • 8-6 Sat • 9-4:30 Sun
• Some retail plumbing supplies. CREDIT CARDS •

NEW YORK REPLACEMENTS PARTS   212-534-0818
1456 Lexington Ave., (94th St.) NYC, NY 10128
Hours: 7:30-4:30 Mon-Fri • (Thurs till 7) • 8-12 Sat   FAX   212-410-5783
• Repro faucet and plumbing parts: bring in sample for repro. CREDIT CARDS •

ROY ELECTRIC CO., INC. /ANTIQUE PLUMBING FIXTURE CO.   718-434-7002
1054 Coney Island Ave., (Foster) Brooklyn, NY 11230   800-366-3347
Hours: 10-5 Mon-Sat   FAX   718-421-4678
• Stock and custom plumbing fixtures; bathroom fixtures, accessories and hard-to-find parts;
Claw tubs, pedestal sinks, antique faucets and shower fixtures; needs some notice. Plumbing
catalog $6. RENTALS CREDIT CARDS •

W.H. SILVER'S HARDWARE   212-247-4406
832 Eighth Ave., (50-51st St.) NYC, NY 10019   212-247-4425
Hours: 8-5:30 Mon-Fri   FAX   212-246-2041
• Fittings, specialties, Apollo valves, rigging for fire and rain effects. •

SIMON'S HARDWARE   212-532-9220
421 Third Ave., (29-30th St.) NYC, NY 10016
Hours: 8-5:30 Mon-Fri • (Thurs till 7) • 10-5 Sat   FAX   212-725-3609
• Bathroom fixtures, accessories, decorative hardware, faucets; get there early in the morn-
ing for better service. Catalog. Expensive. MC/VISA •

SMOLKA CO., INC.   212-686-2300
231 East 33rd St., (2-3rd Ave.) NYC, NY 10016
Hours: 10-6 Mon-Fri • (Thurs till 7) •10-5 Sat   FAX   212-779-0652
• Bathroom fixtures and accessories; expensive. RENTALS MC/VISA •

SOLCO INDUSTRIES   212-243-7575
209 West 18th St., (7-8th Ave.) NYC, NY 10011
Hours: 7-4:30 Mon-Fri   FAX   212-924-0217
• Wholesale/retail plumbing supplies. CREDIT CARDS •

O-P

GEORGE TAYLOR SPECIALTIES   212-226-5369
100 Hudson, (Franklin) NYC, NY 10013
Hours: 7:30-6 Mon-Thurs • 7:30-4 Fri   FAX   212-274-9487
• Porcelain knobs and reproduction faucets; obsolete parts replaced, repaired and/or reproduced. Full machine shop. RENTALS CREDIT CARDS •

SHERLE WAGNER INTERNATIONAL, INC.   212-758-3300
60 East 57th St., (Park Ave.) NYC, NY 10022
Hours: 9:30-5 Mon-Fri   212-207-8010
• Stylish bathroom fixtures and hardware; wall surfaces, tiles and custom tiles. Expensive. RENTALS •

POLICE EQUIPMENT

See also **CLOTHING RENTAL & PURCHASE: UNIFORMS**

ACE PROPS   212-206-1475
1 West 19th St. Ground Fl., (5th Ave.) NYC, NY 10011   212-580-9551
Hours: 9-7 Mon-Fri • 9:30-2 Sat • or by appt.   FAX   212-929-9082
• Rental of non-working replicas of famous firearms - Uzis, 357 Magnums, etc. No license required. CREDIT CARDS •
(See display ad under FIREARMS & ARMOR.)

BEST EMBLEM & INSIGNIA CO.   718-392-7171
37-11 35th Ave., L.I.C., NY 11101   800-237-8362
Hours: 8:30-5 Mon-Fri
• Bobby badges, custom metalwork. •

F & J POLICE EQUIPMENT   718-665-4535
378 East 161st St., (Melrose) Bronx, NY 10451
Hours: 9-6 Mon-Fri • 9-5 Sat   FAX   718-292-8455
• Uniforms, guns, shoes, and bulletproof vests, everything. CREDIT CARDS •

ROBERT S. FRIELICH, INC.   212-254-3045
211 East 21st St., (2-3rd Ave.) NYC, NY 10010   212-777-4477
Hours: 8-6 Mon-Fri • 10-4 Sat   FAX   212-228-3951
• Police equipment and accessories; handcuffs, billy clubs, flashlights, badges, and holsters. CREDIT CARDS •

REEF INDUSTRIES   713-484-6892
PO Box 750245 Houston, TX 77275   800-231-2417
Hours: 7-7 Mon-Fri
• Yellow barricade ribbon; "Crime Scene," "Do Not Cross," etc.; brochure available. MC/VISA •

B. SCHLESINGER & SONS, INC.   212-206-8022
249 West 18th St., (7-8th Ave.) NYC, NY 10011
Hours: 9-6 Mon-Fri • 10-4 Sat (closed major holidays)
• Handcuffs, nightsticks, police and security guard uniforms, and accessories. No rentals. Phone orders OK. CREDIT CARDS •

O-P

SMITH & WARREN CO.
127 Oakley Ave., White Plains, NY 10601
Hours: 8-4:30 Mon-Fri
Badges only. •
914-948-4619
FAX 914-948-1627

SOME'S UNIFORMS
65 Rt. 17, Paramus, NJ 07652
Hours: 9-6 Mon-Fri (Thurs till 8 • Sat till 5)
• Police uniforms, nightsticks, handcuffs, and holsters. Also firefighters uniforms and equipment. Catalog. Phone orders. CREDIT CARDS •
201-843-1199
212-564-6274
FAX 201-842-3014

POSTERS & PRINTS

See also **MEMORABILIA: THEATRE & FILM**

ACANTHUS BOOKS
54 W. 21st. St., Room 908, (5-6th Ave.) NYC, NY 10010
Hours: by appt.
• Architectural and design prints; rare and out-of-print books. •
212-463-0750
FAX 212-463-0752

ARGOSY BOOK STORES, INC.
116 East 59th St., (Park-Lexington Ave.) NYC, NY 10022
Hours: 9-6 Mon-Fri • 10-5 Sat (Oct-April)
• Prints, maps, out-of-print books. •
212-753-4455

BENNER MEDICAL PROPS
601 West 26th St. (11-12th Ave.) NYC, NY 10001
Hours: 9-4:30 Mon-Fri
• Large selection of new & antique medical equipment, examining room furnishings, utensils, research, medical staff uniforms & accessories; also medical consulting & coordinating services. •
212-727-9815
FAX 212-727-9824

MARGO FEIDEN GALLERIES
699 Madison Ave., (62-63rd St.) NYC, NY 10021
Hours: 10-6 every day.
• Art and drama prints, lithographs, Hirshfield drawings. CREDIT CARDS •
212-677-5330

DAN GREENBLATT GALLERY
979 Third Ave., 7th Fl., (58-59th St.) NYC, NY 10022
Hours: 9-5 Mon-Fri
• Frames and unframed prints and posters. RENTALS •
212-421-5970

PHYLLIS LUCAS GALLERY
981 Second Ave., (52nd St.) NYC, NY 10022
Hours: 9-5:30 Tues-Sat
• Rental of framed and unframed prints; specializes in 30's, circus, travel and movie posters. •
212-755-1516

NEW YORK GRAPHIC SOCIETY
35 River Rd., Cos Cob, CT 06807
Hours: 9-6 Mon-Fri
• Large catalog of fine art posters; phone orders taken; will ship UPS. CREDIT CARDS •
203-661-2400

O-P

"I found it in the N.Y. Theatrical Sourcebook."

NOSTALGIA DECORATING CO.   717-472-3764
PO Box 1312, Kingston, PA 18704
Hours: 9-5 Mon-Fri (call first)
• Repro prints, ads and magazine covers. $50 minimum wholesale, any quantity retail.
Brochure. No movie posters. •

OLD PRINT SHOP   212-683-3950
150 Lexington Ave., (29-30th St.) NYC, NY 10016
Hours: 9-5 Mon-Fri • 9-4 Sat (closed Sat in summer)
• 18th and 19th century European prints and maps; 19th and 20th century Americana prints.
No rentals. •

PACE EDITIONS   212-219-8000
72 Spring St., 8th Fl., (Crosby) NYC, NY 10012
Hours: 9:30-5:30 Mon-Fri
• Contemporary fine art posters. •

PAGEANT BOOK & PRINT SHOP   212-674-5296
114 W. Houston (Sullivan-Thompson) NYC, NY 10012
Hours: call for new hours

ALL TYPES OF PRINTS AND MAPS.
NOTICE NEW ADDRESS

> # PAGEANT
> ## BOOK and PRINT SHOP

• All types of prints & maps. Book rental and purchase; see Shirley Solomon. •

PERSONALITY POSTERS   212-529-7262
37 West 8th St., (5-6th Ave.) NYC, NY 10011
Hours: 10-9 every day
• Call first for in-stock personality posters. CREDIT CARDS. •

O-P

J. POCKER & SON, INC.   212-838-5488
135 East 63rd St. (Lexington-3rd) NYC, NY 10021
Hours: 9-5:30 Mon-Fri • 10-5:30 Sat   FAX 212-752-2172
• Good stock posters and prints. Custom orders shipped within two weeks; framing service
available; rental of framed prints. CREDIT CARDS •

POSTER AMERICA   212-206-0499
138 West 18th St., (6-7th Ave.) NYC, NY 10011
Hours: 11-6 Tues-Sat
• Original American and European posters 1890-1950; original movie posters; silent-1960.
RENTALS •

POSTER MAT   212-228-4027
37 West 8th St., (5-6th Ave.) NYC, NY 10011
Hours: 10-9 Mon-Sat • 11-7 Sun
• Rock & Roll posters, movie posters, novelties and t-shirts. CREDIT CARDS •

POSTER ORIGINALS LTD. ART POSTERS   212-620-0522
330 Hudson St., (Van Dam - Charleton) NYC, NY 10013
Hours: 9-5 Mon-Sat   FAX 212-627-3324
• Contemporary American art posters. CREDIT CARDS •

PRINT FINDERS   914-725-2332
> 15 Roosevelt Place, Scarsdale, NY 10583
> Hours: Leave message, will get back to you
> • Mail and phone order print finding service. Access to over 50,000 prints and posters; very helpful. CREDIT CARDS •

R.O. GALLERY   718-937-0901
> 47-15 36th St., (47th Ave.) L.I.C., NY 11101
> Hours: By Appt.   FAX   718-937-1206
> • Paintings, prints and posters. 3,000 images on hand. All manner of subjects. Will ship. RENTALS CREDIT CARDS •

STAR MAGIC   212-228-7770
> 745 Broadway, (8th-Waverly) NYC, NY 10003
> Hours: 10-10 Mon-Sat • 11-9 Sun
>
> 275 Amsterdam Ave. (73rd St.) NYC, NY 10023   212-769-2020
> Hours: 10-10 Mon-Sat • 11-9 Sun
>
> 1256 Lexington Ave. (84-85th St) NYC, NY 10028   212-988-0300
> Hours 10-9 Mon-Sat • 11-7:30 Sun
> • Space related posters, books, star maps and finders. CREDIT CARDS •

CARMEN D. VALENTINO RARE BOOKS   215-739-6056
> 2956 Richmond St., (Ann-Indiana) Philadelphia, PA 19134
> Hours: By appt. only, leave message on machine.
> • Specializes in American printed matter, mostly pre-1920. Prints, calendar art, periodicals, newspapers, antiquarian books, etc. •

PHILIP WILLIAMS   212-226-7830
> 60 Grand St., (W. B'way) NYC, NY 10013
> Hours: 11-7 Tues-Sun   FAX   212-226-0712
> • Over 30,000 posters 1880-1990, rental or purchase. MC/VISA •

O-P

POTTERY & GREENWARE

BRASSCRAFTERS   800-645-1101
> 4791 N.W. 157th Ave. Miami, FL 33014
> Hours: 9-5 Mon-Fri   FAX   305-685-7667
> • Unique selection of pottery, vases & urns. Color catalog available. •

CERAMIC SUPPLY OF NJ   201-340-3005
      800-723-7262
> 7 Route 46 West, Lodi, NJ 07644
> Hours: 9-5 Mon-Fri • 9-1 Sat
> • Ceramic materials & supplies, potter's plaster & casting plaster. •

CERAMIC SUPPLY OF NY & NJ,, INC.   212-475-7236
      800-723-7264
> 534 La Guardia Place, (Bleeker-3rd) NYC, NY 10012
> Hours: 9-6 Mon-Fri
> • Ceramic materials and supplies, potter's plaster and casting plaster. •

CLAY CRAFT CO.   212-242-2903
      (lot) 212-268-0530
> 807 Sixth Ave., 2nd Fl., (27-28th St.) NYC, NY 10001
> Hours: 9-5 Mon-Fri • 10-5 Sat
> • Wholesale terra cotta and glazed pottery, vases, planters. RENTALS MC/VISA •

✓THE CLAY POT
162 Seventh Ave., (Garfield-1st) Brooklyn, NY 11215
Hours: 10:30-7:30 Mon-Fri • 10:30-6:30 Sat • 11:30-6:30 Sun
• A "pottery gallery" featuring a number of quality potters; glass, jewelry and wooden crafts.
RENTALS CREDIT CARDS •

718-788-6564
800-989-3579
FAX 718-965-1138

EARTHWORKS & ARTISANS
2182 Broadway, 2nd Floor, (77th St.) NYC, NY 10024
Hours: 1-7 Mon-Fri • 12-6 Sat,Sun
• Nice pottery pieces: bowls, vases, mugs, and tea sets; also gives pottery classes. CREDIT CARDS •

212-873-5220

LINDA'S CERAMICS
401 Broadway, Bayonne, NJ 07002
Hours: 12-10pm Mon-Fri
• Greenware; see Linda. •

201-436-3161
(home) 201-858-2197

✓MAD MONK
500 Sixth Ave., (12-13th) NYC, NY 10011
Hours: 11-7 Tues-Sat
• Basic pottery: mugs, tea sets, bowls, platters, & gift items. •

212-242-6678

✓MUD, SWEAT & TEARS
654 Tenth Ave., (46th St.) NYC, NY 10036
Hours: 11-8 Mon-Fri • 11-7 Sat, Sun.
• Nice gift selection and classes. CREDIT CARDS •   *East*   *570-6868*

212-974-9121

PEROSI CERAMIC STUDIO
166 Morningstar Rd., Staten Island, NY 10303
Hours: 9:30-3 Mon-Thurs • 7:30-10:30 Mon & Tues eve.
• Greenware, ceramic supplies, classes, glazes, kilns, molds. Call for directions. •

718-981-9686

SOUTHERN FLORALS
705 East Market St., Louisville, KY 40202
Hours: 9-5 Mon-Fri
• Plaster composition urns, corbels, brackets and garden figures at reasonable prices; finishing available. Some stock. Shipping. See Garwood Linton for catalog and ordering information. Showrooms around the country. •

502-587-7455
FAX 502-584-0412

SUPERMUD POTTERY / THE CLAY HAND
212 West 105th St., (B'way-Amsterdam) NYC, NY 10025
Hours: 12-6 Every day
Pottery, and classes available. CREDIT CARDS •

212-865-9190

Lectarps -
pottr Bird~

Re Ameriny CRAFTman.
Re Greenger House.
YWCA.

Gobets~

P-O

PRINTING & COPYING

See also **GRAPHICS & TYPESETTING**

380 SERVICES 212-255-6652
380 Bleeker St., (Perry-Charles) NYC, NY 10014
Hours: 8-7:30 Mon-Fri • 10-6 Sat FAX 212-627-5191
• B&W, color copies, typesetting and binding. Excellent service. CREDIT CARDS. •

57TH ST. COPY CENTER 212-581-8046
151 West 57th St., (6-7th Ave.) NYC, NY 10019
Hours: 8:30-5 Mon-Thurs • 8:30-2 Fri • call for Sun hours
• Full service photocopying, color copies from slides. No credit cards. •

ALLIED REPRODUCTIONS 212-943-9067
11 Stone St., 5th Fl., (B'way-Broad) NYC, NY 10004
Hours: 9-5 Mon-Fri FAX 212-943-9069
• Offset printing, good service, inexpensive. •

ASSOCIATED MUSIC COPY SERVICE 212-265-2400
333 West 52nd St., 7th Fl., (8-9th Ave.) NYC, NY 10019
Hours: 9-5:30 Mon-Fri
• Photocopying to 24", width on newsprint if you supply paper. Also many other papers in stock; see Judy. No credit cards. •

ATLANTIC BLUE PRINT CO., INC. 212-755-3388
575 Madison Ave., (57th St.) NYC, NY 10022
Hours: 8:30-5 Mon-Fri (machines stop at 4:30) FAX 212-751-5598
• Blueprinting, offset, and photocopies, including (color xerox); pickup and delivery if you have a charge account. •

THE BLUE PRINT CO. 212-686-2436
295 Madison Ave., (41st St.) NYC, NY 10017
 FAX 212-532-8397
2 East 16th St., (5th Ave.) NYC, NY 10011 212-627-2111
Hours: 8:45-5:15 Mon-Fri FAX 212-727-2396
• Blue prints, B&W and color copying, photo stats, etc. MC/VISA •

BORO BLUE PRINT CO., INC. 718-625-3227
52 Court St., (Joralemon-Livingston) Brooklyn, NY 11201
Hours: 8:30-5 Mon-Fri
• Blueprints, photocopy, photostats, offset and microfilm. •

CHROMA COPY 212-399-2420
423 West 55th St., (9-10th Ave.) NYC, NY 10019
Hours: 10-4 Mon-Fri FAX 212-582-4107

122 Fulton St. 4th Fl. (Nassau) NYC, NY 10038 212-619-8282
Hours 9-5 Mon-Fri FAX 212-962-6135
• Xerochrome: fantastic quality color copies on bond paper. Checks only, no cash. •

CIRCLE BLUE PRINT CO. 212-265-3674
225 West 57th St., 2nd floor, (B'way) NYC, NY 10019
Hours: 9-5 Mon-Fri
• Blueline, blackline, sepia; large size photocopies and reductions. •

O-P

CORINNE OFFSET
212-777-8083 737
Broadway, (8th-Waverly) NYC, NY 10003
Hours: 8-6 Mon-Fri • 11-5 Sat
FAX 212-674-8104
• Very dependable and reasonable. Specializes in resumes, J. cards (cassette covers).
MC/VISA •

A. ESTEBAN & CO.
212-989-7000
8-10 West 19th St., 6th Fl., (5-6th Ave.) NYC, NY 10011
Hours: 9-5:30 Mon-Fri
FAX 212-989-6087
• Blueprints, sepias, and giant photocopies to 24". Pickup and delivery service available with
account. •

EVER READY BLUE PRINT
212-228-3131
200 Park Ave. South, 13th Fl., (17th St.) NYC, NY 10003
Hours: 8-5:30 Mon-Fri • 10-5 Sat • 12-4 Sun
FAX 212-505-8083
• The slow elevator takes you to THE best and quickest service in town. Blueprints, sepias,
mylar prints; color copies, photostats; giant photocopies to 36" wide (variable
enlargement/reduction) on bond, vellum and mylar film. Plotting service. Flier. MC/VISA •

HART MULTI-COPY, INC.
212-695-8822
323 West 39th St., (8-9th Ave.) NYC, NY 10018
Hours: 8:30-5:30 Mon-Fri
FAX 212-695-9293
• Photocopying, offset printing and typesetting. •

INDEPENDENT PRINTING CO.
212-689-5100
171 Madison Ave., Room #905, (33-34 St.) NYC, NY 10016
Hours: 8:30-5:00 Mon-Fri
FAX 212-867-1440
• Blueprinting on a variety of stocks. Rush service may be available. •

KINKO'S, THE COPY CENTER
212-924-0802
24 East 12th St., (University-5th) NYC, NY 10003
FAX 212-675-0732

2872 Broadway (111-112th St.) NYC, NY 10025
212-675-0732
Hours: 24 Hours every day
FAX 212-316-3795
• Part of the huge national chain. Full service. B&W and color copies, FAX service and busi-
ness cards. CREDIT CARDS. •

MILLNER BROTHERS
212-966-1810
20 Vandam St., (6th-Varick) NYC, NY 10013
Hours: 9-5 Mon-Fri
FAX 212-627-9892
• Offset printing. •

NATIONAL REPROGRAPHICS, INC.
212-366-7000
253 West 35th St. (7-8th Ave.) NYC, NY 10001
246 West 54th St. (7th-8th Ave.) NYC, NY 10019
44 West 18th St. (5-6th Ave.) NYC, NY 10011
666 Third Ave. (42-43rd St.) NYC, NY 10017
Hours: 9-4:30 Mon-Fri
• Blueprinting, photostats, photocopies - color, B&W and color acetate. •

PARK HEIGHTS STATIONERS COPY CENTER
718-398-0202
164 Park Pl., (Flatbush-7th Ave.) Brooklyn, NY 11217
Hours: 9-7:30 Mon-Fri • 10-7:30 Sat • 11:30-6 Sun
FAX 718-622-3860
• Copy service; color & B&W. Commercial stationer. Stationery supplies. •

PARK SLOPE TYPING & COPY CENTER
718-783-0268
123 Seventh Ave., (President-Carroll) Brooklyn, NY 11215
Hours: 8:30-7 Mon-Fri • 10-6 Sat • 11:30-5 Sun
FAX 718-622-8373
• Typing, word processing, color and B&W copies, printing and small blueprinting jobs. •

O-P

"I found it in the N.Y. Theatrical Sourcebook." **345**

POST DIRECT MAIL   212-685-5622
   171 Madison Ave., (33rd St.) NYC, NY 11016
   Hours: 9-5:30 Mon-Fri
   • Photo transfers and logo printing on caps and T-shirts. •

PRO PRINT COPY CENTER   212-807-1900
   134 Fifth Ave., (18th St.) NYC, NY 10011   FAX   212-627-4391
   Hours: 8:30-8 Mon-Fri • 10-5 Sat,Sun

   236 Park Ave. South (19th St) NYC, NY 10003   212-677-7691
   Hours: 8:30-6 Mon-Fri • 10-5 Sat   FAX   212-979-5528

   460 Park Ave. South (31st) NYC, NY 10016   212-532-1220
   Hours: 8:30-6 Mon-Fri • 10-5 Sat   FAX   212-532-7341

   51 West 43rd St. (5-6th Ave.) NYC, NY 10036   212-302-0446
   Hours: 8:30-6 Mon-Fri   FAX   212-768-3548

   18 West 45th St., (5th-6th Ave.) NYC, NY 10036   212-354-0400
   Hours: 8:30-6 Mon-Fri   FAX   212-768-3550

   48 West 48th St., (5th-6th Ave.) NYC, NY 10036   212-391-0003
   Hours: 8:30-6 Mon-Fri   FAX   212-391-8579

   1285 Sixth Ave., concourse level, (51st St.) NYC, NY 10019   212-245-1212
   Hours: 8-5:30 Mon-Fri   FAX   212-489-8783

   118 East 41st St., (Lexington & Park Ave.) NYC, NY 10017   212-972-5300
   Hours: 8:30-6 Mon-Fri   FAX   212-687-7467
   • Printing, photocopying, stats, veloxes, color photocopies, typesetting, binding and
   layout/design. •

QUIK COPY   212-807-0465
   15 East 13th St., (5th-University Pl.) NYC, NY 10003
   Hours: 8am-11pm Mon-Fri • 10-7 Sat • 12-7 Sun   FAX   212-463-0232
   • B&W and Color copying, Kodak Ektaprint. CREDIT CARDS. •

ROYAL OFFSET CO, INC.   212-255-3753
   37 West 20th St., Room 702, (5th-6th Ave.) NYC, NY 10011
   Hours: 9-5 Mon-Fri   FAX   212-206-7065
   • Commercial printing specializing in the entertainment industry. Programs, table cards,
   resumes, catalogs and brochures; up to 4 colors. Contact Ivan Prefer. •

SPEED GRAPHICS   212-486-0209
   150 East 58th St., (Lexington-3rd Ave.) NYC, NY 10155
   Hours: 8-6 Mon-Fri   FAX   212-752-8845
   • Transfers, bubble, duplicating chromes, photo CD's. See Chuck for photo stats, very good,
   prompt service. •

STUDIO 305, INC.   212-724-8758
   313 B Amsterdam Ave., (74th-75th St.) NYC, NY 10023
   Hours: 9-6:30 Mon-Fri • 10-5:30 Sat   FAX   212-595-5846
   • Photocopies, color and B&W photostats, offset. •

O-P

THE VILLAGE COPIER   212-966-0606
   91 Worth St., (B'way-Church) NYC, NY 10013
   Hours: 8:30-6 Mon-Fri   FAX   212-966-0041

   20 East 13th St. (University-5th) NYC, NY 10003   212-727-2239
   Hours: 24 hours every day   FAX   212-255-9157

   25 West 43rd St. Lobby (5-6th Ave.) NYC, NY 10036   212-869-9665
   Hours: 8-11 Mon-Fri • 9:30-4:30 Sat   FAX   212-764-7144
   • Copies, Canon color laser copies, FAX service and resumes. CREDIT CARDS •

PROMOTIONAL MATERIALS

ABAT PRINTED NOVELTIES   212-695-4651
   130 West 29th St., (6-7th Ave.) NYC, NY 10001
   Hours: 9-5 Mon-Fri
   • Advertising buttons, mugs, sashes, banners, badges, etc. Quick custom service; will do
   small quantities. •

PACKAGE PUBLICITY SERVICE   212-255-2872
   27 West 24th St.,#402, (5-6th Ave.) NYC, NY 10010
   Hours: 10-5 Mon-Fri
   • Press kits for hundreds of shows; show posters, logos, buttons and other promotional
   items. •

POST DIRECT MAIL   212-685-5622
   171 Madison Ave., (33rd St.) NYC, NY 10016
   Hours: 9-5:30 Mon-Fri
   • Photo transfers and logo printing on caps and t-shirts. •

THE QUEENSBORO SHIRT CO.   718-782-0200
   80 North 5th St., Williamsburg/ Brooklyn, NY 11211   800-847-4478
   Hours: 9-5 Mon-Fri
   • Quantity purchase of cotton polo and sweat shirts; many sizes and several colors. Will
   embroider your logo. Catalog. •

PROP & SCENIC CRAFTSPEOPLE

A **BOLD LISTING** indicates the person or company is a member of ATAC, Association of Theatrical Artists and
Craftspeople, a professional trade association for craftspeople working in the entertainment, performance and presentational media industries. See display ad in this section.

ACME STIMULI DESIGN & PRODUCTION   212-465-1071
   548 W. 28th Street, NYC, NY 10001
   Hours: by appt.
   • Prop construction, mold making and sculpture. Set design & construction. Contact Marc
   Rubin. •

DANIEL J. ARONSON   212-567-3250
   12 Dongan Pl. #405 ,   NYC, NY 10040
   Hours: by appt.
   • Art Direction; Inside/Outside Props; Design and Construction of Sets and Props;
   Commercials, Film and Video Production, Industrials, Stills, Theatre. •

ART LAB   212-228-0880
  150 First Avenue, (9-10th St.) NYC, NY 10009
  Hours: by appt.
  • Art services for film & print, custom backdrops, scenic painting, prop construction, art
  research; Betsy Rosenwald •

ATMOSPHERICS   201-659-8537
  113 Willow Avenue,   Hoboken, NJ 07030
  Hours: by appt.   **FAX** 201-659-8087
  • Custom murals, floorcloths & drops. Rental drops for photographic shoots. Speak to Gillian
  Bradshaw-Smith. •

ROBERT W. BAKER   212-740-4915
  801 West 181st St. #69, (Ft. Washington) NYC, NY 10033
  Hours: by appt.
  • Sculpting, casting and prop construction. •

ALICE BALDWIN   502-893-5887
  807 Chamberry Dr., Louisville, KY 40206
  Hours: by appt.
  • Prop craft work, foam carving, mask making, and scenic painting for ballet and opera. •

BILL BALLOU SERVICES   914-626-2118
  2985 Lucas Turnpike, Accord, NY 12404
  Hours: by appt.   **FAX** 914-626-2127
  • Construction and production management, rigging, stage machinery, drafting, consulting.
  "Have tools will travel." •

O-P

Association of
Theatrical Artists and Craftspeople, Inc.

"A professional trade association for
the craftspeople working in the professional fields of
entertainment, performance, and presentational
media industries. A.T.A.C. authors THE NEW YORK
THEATRICAL SOURCEBOOK, publishes the ATAC
QUARTERLY, sponsors craft-related seminars and
workshops for members."

For membership information, call or write to:
Association of Theatrical Artist & Craftspeople, Inc.
604 Riverside Dr. #6E, New York, NY 10031
212-234-9001

BEAUX ARTS STUDIOS
914-666-7388
14 Dogwood Rd.,   Mt. Kisco, NY 10549
Hours: by appt.
• Custom painted finishes, murals and display backdrops. Commercial or residential. Contact Elizabeth or Timothy. •

JOANNE BECKERICH
201-963-8575
400 Madison St., (4th St.) Hoboken, NJ 07030
Hours: by appt.
• Displays, exhibits, showrooms, trade shows, graphics. •

ANDREW BENEPE STUDIO
212-226-8570
43 Bridge St., Brooklyn, NY 11121
Hours: by appt.
• Monster and animal costumes, sculpture, special effect rigging, costume crafts, props and puppets. •

BIRDS IN WOOD STUDIO
203-634-1953
525 Broad St., Meriden, CT 06450
Hours: 9-5 Mon-Fri
• Contact Brian McGray. Wooden bird carvings, also custom taxidermy services and teaches taxidermy. •

CHRIS BOBIN
212-255-5225
20 West 20th St. c/o Fabric Effects, (5th-6th Avenue) NYC, NY 10011
Hours: By appt.   212-475-7268
• Sewn solutions for props, costumes and illustrations; miniature and oversize--quilting, applique and embroidery. •

OLIVIA BOOTH
212-279-3054
484 West 43rd St. #5F, (9-10th) NYC, NY 10036
Hours: by appt.
• Prop and costume crafts, sculpture, millinery, fabric and costume painting for stage, film, TV. •

SHARON BRAUNSTEIN
404-872-3762
393 Fifth St. #2, Atlanta , GA 30308
Hours: by appt.
• Sculptor, upholsterer, shopper, craftsperson, propmaster for TV, film, video and photography. •

DONNA BRUEGER
212-410-7683
21 East 108th St., (Madison-5th Ave.) NYC, NY 10029
Hours: by appt.
• Decorative painting, gold leaf, decorative plaster restoration. •

ELLEN CALDWELL
718-392-3884
49-13 Vernon Blvd., L.I.C., NY 11101
Hours: by appt.
• Set decoration, art decoration, producing, prop construction, graphic design, shopping; inventive solutions for specialty props and graphics. •

SAYZIE CARR
212-529-3669
96 East 7th St. Rm. 5, (1st St.-Ave. A) NYC, NY 10009
Hours: by appt.
• Custom design & fabrication of promotional items, display, backdrops & furnishing; on the spot draping. •

0-P

NADINE CHARLSEN
212-307-0035
344 W. 49th St. #5D, (8-9th Ave.) NYC, NY 10019
Hours: by appt.
• Research and design of sets, lights, props. Macintosh computer graphics. Equity S.M. •

CLOCKWORK APPLE INC.
212-431-8996
57 Laight St., #1 (Hudson-Greenwich) NYC, NY 10013
Hours: 9-6 Mon-Fri   FAX   212-226-4906
• Specialized model makers. Contact Christo Holloway •

EILEEN CONNER
212-246-6346
PO Box 154, Radio City Station, NYC, NY 10101
Hours: by appt.
• Scenic painting and faux finishes, fabric painting, prop and costume crafts. •

SUZANNE COUTURE MODELMAKING
212-714-9310
524 West 34th St., (10-11th Ave.) NYC, NY 10001
Hours: by appt.   FAX   212-714-0759
• Custom masks, display and promotional props; oversized, sculpted, and cast. Brochure available. •

MARGARET CUSACK
718-237-0145
124 Hoyt St., (Dean) Brooklyn, NY 11217
Hours: by appt.
• Fabric illustrations and props, soft sculpture, hand-stitched samplers. •

BETSY DAVIS BACKDROPS
212-645-4197
397 West 12th St. 2nd Fl., (Washington-West) NYC, NY 10014
Hours: by appt.
• Custom-made backdrops and props. Backdrop rental. •

DECOR COUTURE DESIGN
212-727-0123
25-37 37th St. 3rd Floor,   Astoria, NY 11103   212-627-3495
Hours: 10-5 Mon-Fri by appt.
• Design and fabrication of custom soft goods for theatre, film, video, display, residential. •

SAL DENARO
718-875-1711
174 Degraw St., (Hicks-Henry) Brooklyn, NY 11231
Hours: by appt.
• Character design puppets, props, stop-motion models, soft sculpture. •

DGL
212-679-0857
Moving, call for new address.
• Set props, carpentry, furniture construction & repair, stripping, staining, painting & refinishing, upholstery, custom work only; contact Laura DeGregorio. •

OLIVIA EATON
718-875-4592
PO Box 40-0161,   Brooklyn, NY 11240
Hours: by appt.
• Sculpture, metal fabrication, costume construction, knitting and sewing. •

STEPHEN EDELSTEIN
212-666-9198
771 West End Ave. #4C, (97th St.) NYC, NY 10025
Hours: by appt.
• Scenic/lighting designer, tech director; scenery, prop construction, knitting and sewing. •

O-P

DAVID ELLERTSON　　　　　　　　　　　　　　201-729-5005
　　23 Hillside Rd.,　　Sparta, NJ 07871
　　Hours:　by appt.
　　• Scenic designer, woodworking, furniture, models, fiberglass, foams, weaponry. •

MARJORIE FEDYSZYN　　　　　　　　　　　　　612-377-9742
　　515 S. Cedar Lake Rd.,　　Minneapolis, MN 55405
　　Hours:　by appt.
　　• Prop shopping, styling, model making, set decoration, scene painting. •

JAMES FENG　　　　　　　　　　　　　　　　718-499-1601
　　221 Eighth Ave., (2nd St.) Brooklyn, NY 11215
　　Hours:　by appt.
　　• Scenery and art direction, models; designed, built and painted. •

ELIZABETH K. FISHER　　　　　　　　　　　　803-559-9849
　　6569 Foxfire Road, Wadmalaw Island, SC 29487
　　Hours:　by appt.
　　• Scenic artist for film and theatre, sculpting, and prop fabrication. •

DAVID T. FLETCHER　　　　　　　　　　　　　203-787-4284
　　c/o Long Wharf Theatre, 222 Sargeant Dr.,　　New Haven, CT 06511
　　Hours:　by appt.
　　• Props manager; road work. Outside props. •

DAN FOLKUS/VISUAL SYNTAX DESIGNS　　　　　609-858-9736
　　465 Haddon Ave.,　　Collingswood, NJ 08108
　　Hours:　by appt.
　　• Murals, sculpture, props, puppets (especially cast urethane rubber), exhibit design. •

CHRISTINE FYE　　　　　　　　　　　　　　212-627-1663
　　147 W. 22nd St., Apt. 3S, (6-7th Ave.) NYC, NY 10011
　　Hours:　8-4 Mon-Fri
　　• Sculpting in plasticine and clay, portraiture, decorative animals, figurine restoration, scenic artist. •

MATTHEW GILMORE　　　　　　　　　　　　212-673-3445
　　150 East 18th St. #5-O, (3rd Ave.) NYC, NY 10003
　　Hours:　by appt.
　　• Props; windows and display; decorating for special events; visual merchandising. •

GIRARD DESIGNS/ JANET GIRARD　　　　　　　718-782-6430
　　300 Morgan Ave., (Metropolitan-Grand) Brooklyn, NY 11211
　　Hours:　by appt.　　　　　　　　　　FAX　718-782-3805
　　• Custom draperies, window treatments, upholstery, fabric tension structures; quilting, soft sculpture, leather sculpture, fabric painting. •

PAMELA B. GOLDMAN　　　　　　　　　　　212-459-4217
　　PO Box 636, New Rochelle, NY 10802　　　　914-636-7624
　　Hours:　by appt.
　　• Specialty costumes, special effects painting and backdrops. Shopping, props, costume collection rental. Available for print, theatre, TV, film. Member Local 829. •

ELIZABETH GOODALL　　　　　　　　　　　212-645-9480
　　78 Bedford St. NYC, NY 10014
　　Hours:　by appt.
　　• Prop and model making, sculpting, scenic painting, faux finishing, illustration. •

O-P

LOUISE GRAFTON 609-921-1919
151 Hartly Ave., Princeton, NJ 08540
Hours: by appt.
• Prop building and problem solving; upholstery, sculpture, circus and clown props, jewelry. •

HAND TO MOUTH INDUSTRIES 212-580-1291
225 West 80th St. #4B, (Broadway) NYC, NY 10024
Hours: by appt.
• Sculptor/Designer; display and promotional props, prototypes and novelties. •

TOM HOGAN 718-387-7028
133 Middleton St., (March-Harrison) Brooklyn, NY 11206
Hours: by appt.
• Sculpture, toy prototypes in wax and classical figure, model making. •

LOUISE HUNNICUTT 212-925-1785
65 Roebling St., Brooklyn, NY 10012
Hours: by appt. • 24-hour phone service FAX 212-219-0331
• Experienced scenic artist; specializing in detail painting, hand lettering and photo realism. •

IMT SERVICES 914-691-3665
5 Pine Terrace, Highland, NY 12528 718-472-9511
Hours: 9-6 Mon-Fri FAX 914-691-3684
• Model making, sculpture, casting, plastics and metalwork; see Mark McAniff. •

MARTIN IZQUIERDO STUDIO 212-807-9757
118 West 22nd St. 9th Floor, (6-7th Ave.) NYC, NY 10011
Hours: 9-6 Mon-Fri • weekends by appt. FAX 212-366-5249
• Custom props; sculpture & casting, silkscreening, fabric painting, upholstery & drapes for
theatre, film, commercials, display and video; full service shop. No rentals. •
(See display ad under COSTUME RENTAL & CONSTRUCTION.)

JERMANN PAINTING STUDIO 914-359-7535
2 Union Ave., Sparkill, NY 10976
Hours: by appt.
• Experienced scenic painter; faux finishes, murals. Contact David Jermann. •

ROBERT W. JONES 212-569-8532
97 Arden St. #3C, NYC, NY 10040
Hours: by appt.
• Props for theatre and commercials; masks, Celastic fabricator. •

WARREN JORGENSON 914-699-5054
21 E. Lincoln Ave., Mount Vernon, NY 10552
Hours: by appt. FAX 914-699-5054
• Set design, furniture and hand props; foams, resins, sculpting. •

CINDY PICKERING KAMINSKI 212-679-6507
10 Park Ave. #24S, NYC, NY 10016
Hours: by appt.
• Prop coordinator, scenic design, art direction, film, video, industrial, theatre. •

JANET KNECHTEL 44-71-354-0762
7 Asteys Row, London, England N12DA
Hours: by appt. FAX 44-71-354-9827
• Puppets, masks, costume props •

O-P

THE *GATE HOUSE* STUDIO

•914-359-8853   **FAX•914-398-2821**

CUSTOM:

MASKS
COSTUMES
MODELS
PROPS
PUPPETS
SCULPTURE

| Theater - Film |
| Print - Display |

For more information
or to register call
Ms. Laura Lopez

ALSO AVAILABLE THROUGH
THE STUDIO
Faux & Fantasy Finishes - Sponging -
Stenciling - Murals - Trompe l'oile -
Gilding
Neon - Stained Glass - Cabinetry -
Carpentry

This studio serves as a Network for Artists, Artisans, and Craftspeople in Westchester, Rockland, Putnam, and Dutchess counties as well as parts of New Jersey and Connecticut. Available 24 hours a day 7 days a week, for free-lance and collaborative work at reasonable rates.

VALERIE KUEHN   216-889-2979
   425 Greenville Rd. N.E., Bristolville, OH 44402
   Hours: By appt.
   • Properties artist, scenic sculptor, mold making, fiberglass casting and fabrication. •

BETH KUSHNICK   212-502-1147
   Hours: by appt.   516-324-5985
   • Art direction, set decoration, member IATSE Local 52 •

CATHY LAZAR COSTUMES & SOFT PROPS   212-473-0363
   Hours: by appt.
   • Specialty costumes and soft props for TV, film, print, performance, promotion. •

DANIELLE LEON/FAULTLESS FAUX   718-956-7868
   PO Box 1285, (Murray Hill Sta.) NYC, NY 10156   516-725-2729
   Hours: 9-5 Mon-Fri
   • Prop shopper, set decoration for outside/inside and location work, speciality. Historical
   props for theatre, film, video and print work. Specializing in Faux Finishes and reproduction
   furniture. •

LISA J. LINDEN   212-627-3495
   25-37 37th St., (28th -25th Ave.) Astoria, NY 11103
   Hours: 10-6 Mon-Fri by appt.
   • Shopping, upholstery, fabric painting, faux finishing and design assistance. •

ELLEN LEO
718-728-6441
30-03 41st St. #4, Astoria, NY 11103
Hours: by appt.
• Props, models, sculpture, and mold making, welding. •

LAURA LOPEZ/GATE HOUSE
914-359-8853
P.O. Box 495, Piermont, NY 10968
Hours: by appt.
FAX 914-398-2821
• Network of suburban craftspeople; specialty costumes, masks and fabric works. •
(See display ad in this section.)

DANIEL MACK RUSTIC FURNISHINGS
914-986-7293
14 Welling Ave., Warwick, NY 10990
Hours: by appt.
• Custom rustic/twig furniture •

VICTORIA MARIN
718-783-4081
200 Greene Ave., (St. James-Grand) Brooklyn, NY 11238
Hours: by appt.
• Scenic design and painting for theatre, video and film; hand-painted slides for projections, also trompe l'oeil and faux finishes. •

JENNIE MARINO/MOONBOOTS PROD.
914-358-0199
6 Washington St., Nyack, NY 10960
Hours: by appt.
• Props, puppets, make-up, masks and fantasy costumes. Design and decoration for social, corporate and civic; performing variety artist. •

DEBORAH ALIX MARTIN
718-499-4649
580 Tenth St., (7-8th Ave.) Brooklyn, NY 11215
Hours: by appt.
• Prop/scenic construction, all materials; upholstery and soft goods. •

SUANNE MARTIN
718-782-4529
248 North 6th St, Brooklyn, NY 11211
Hours: by appt.
• Sculpting for toy prototypes, masks and life casting; experienced in a variety of mold making techniques and materials. •

KAREN McDUFFEE
718-643-1655
72A Fourth Ave., (Bergen) Brooklyn, NY 11217
Hours: by appt.
• Soft goods sewn to your specifications, pillows, cushions, draperies, quilts, bedcoverings, tablecloths; some dyeing and distressing. •

MCL DESIGNS, INC.
212-587-1511
47 Ann St., NYC, NY 10010
Hours: by appt.
• Customized costumes, full-figure puppets, hand puppets, props. Contact Susan McClain-Moore. •

MARIA McNAMARA
612-224-7267
122 W. Isabel St., St. Paul, MN 55107
Hours: by appt.
• Puppets, props, and craft work. •

O-P

MARY MEYERS 718-956-1466
24-13 33rd St., (24th) L.I.C., NY 11102
Hours: by appt.
• Prop and costume crafts, scenic painting and decorative finishes, costume display work. •

NICK MILLER 212-663-0037
825 West End Ave. #15D, NYC, NY 10025
Hours: by appt.
• Construction coordinator for feature films. Member Local 52. •

NANCY MOORE-BESS 212-691-2821
5 E. 17th St. 6th Floor, (5th Ave.) NYC, NY 10003
Hours: by appt.
• Custom basketry. •

STACY MORSE 718-783-4375
42 Berkeley Place, (5-6th Ave.) Brooklyn, NY 11217 802-257-5660
Hours: by appt.
• Scenic painting, oversized props, 2D and 3D portraiture; for TV, film and theatre. •

ZOE MORSETTE 718-784-8894
11-14 46th Ave. #2I, (11th St.) L.I.C, NY 11101
Hours: by appt.
• Theatrical and display props, specialty costumes, full-head masks, millinery, sculpture, soft goods. •

MULDER / MARTIN, INC. 212-727-0471
604 Riverside Dr. NYC, NY 10031
Hours: 9-5 Mon-Fri FAX 212-234-0885
• Full body character costumes, costume props and puppets for theatre, film, television and promotional events. •
(See display ad under COSTUME CRAFTSPEOPLE & MILLLINERY.)

RONALD NAVERSON 618-453-5741
Southern Illinois University, c/o Dept. of Theatre Carbondale, IL 62901-6608
Hours: by appt FAX 618-453-7714
• Scenic, properties and lighting design. •

ANDREW NESS 718-786-0070
25-34 Crescent St., Astoria, NY 11102
Hours: by appt.
• Specialty props and model making for television, film and theatre; also SAG puppeteer. •

WILLIAM NIEMIER 212-260-7973
195 Chrystie St. #900, NYC, NY 10002
Hours: by appt.
• Models, props, showroom display, plexiglass, castings, sculpted foam; large and small. •

FREDERICK NIHDA 718-834-1276
374 Union St. (Smith-Hoyt) Brooklyn, NY 11231
Hours: 10-6 Mon-Fri by appt.
• Body puppets, masks, jewelry, armor, mechanisms and hand props; available for freelance work or staff position. •

NINO NOVELLINO/ COSTUME ARMOUR, INC. 914-534-9120
PO Box 85, 2 Mill St., Cornwall, NY 12518
Hours: 9-4 Mon-Fri FAX 914-534-8602
• Sculpture, props, armor. •
(See display ad under PROP SHOPS.)

O-P

REID PALEY   718-384-3714
  94 Bedford Ave. #3L, Brooklyn, NY 11211
  Hours: by appt.
  • Set & props for film. Construction, rigging and wiring of scenery and props for all media;
  flexible. •

DENNIS PAVER/ECCENTRICITIES   212-924-9411
  41 Union Square West #1027, (Broadway-17th St.) NYC, NY 10003
  Hours: 10-6 Mon-Fri
  • Costume design, construction, illustration; costumes, props for theatre, display •

KARL PEHME, SCULPTOR   718-875-8151
  175 Johnson St., Brooklyn, NY 11545   After Hours 516-676-2982
  Hours: 9-5 Mon-Fri   FAX 718-855-8228
  • Theatrical props and three dimensional displays. Forty years of experience in the
  industry. •

ENRIQUE PLESTED   212-799-2950
  126 Riverside Drive #6A, (85th St.) NYC, NY 10024
  Hours: by appt.
  • Sculpting, portraiture, model building. •

JULIE PRINCE   212-486-9249
  141 East 56th St. #9G, (Lexington-3rd) NYC, NY 10022
  Hours: by appt.
  • Props, life-casting, masks, sculptures. •

KATHERINE RADCLIFFE   212-691-4697
  7 Jane St., NYC, NY 10014
  Hours: 11-7 Mon-Fri by appt.
  • Hand marbled paper and fabric to create faux marble finishes; malachite, lapis, tortoise,
  etc.; applied to set pieces, floors and props. •

JOHN A. RALBOYSKY   718-836-2577
  307 72nd St. #1D, (4th Ave.) Brooklyn, NY 11209
  Hours: by appt.
  • U.S.A local 829; scenic artist, sculpture, appliqued and painted finishes, mold making, prop
  craftsman. •

JUDY RHEE   212-529-4435
  173 Ave. A #9, (11th St.) NYC, NY 10009   Pager 917-874-7138
  Hours: by appt.
  • Art Direction, Set Decoration •

LESLIE E. ROLLINS   203-429-5216
  986 Mansfield City Road, Storrs, CT 06268
  Hours: by appt.   FAX 203-487-4919
  • Set Decorator for feature films. Also skilled in prop fabrication for films and theatre.
  Member IATSE locals #44 & 52. •

BILL RYBAK   212-674-5673
  149 Ave. A #5FN, NYC, NY 10009
  Hours: by appt.
  • Props and miniature sets for display and film; sculpting, carpentry, cabinetmaking. Work in
  clay, plaster, latex, plastics and wood. •

O-P

CATHERINE SCHMITT
201-573-9150
7 Ethridge Pl., Park Ridge, NJ 07656
Hours: by appt.
• Sculpture and soft sculpture, custom props and costumes, display figures. •

LINDA SCHULTZ
212-222-0477
125 West 96th St. #6J, (Columbus-Amsterdam) NYC, NY 10025
Hours: by appt.
• Costumer, stylist, wardrobe cutter, draper, soft goods (props). •

LISA SHAFTEL
206-706-0868
333 N. 79th St., Seattle, WA 98103
Hours: by appt.
• Scenic/lighting design, scene painting, puppets, animal figures, masks, property crafts, soft goods. •

NINA SHEFTY
212-982-0454
28 East 10th St., (University-Broadway) NYC, NY 10003
Hours: by appt.
• Set decorator, still life stylist specializing in propping, sets, soft goods. •

JAMES P. SHERMAN
212-874-3086
34 West 65th St. #4C, (Lincoln Sq.-CPW) NYC, NY 10023
Hours: by appt.
• Art director, set decorator for film, TV, and theatre; prop crafts. •

SPECIAL EFFECTS WORKSHOPS
212-245-3624
410 West 47th St. NYC, NY 10036
Hours: 9-5 Mon-Fri

Special Effects Workshops is a complete make-up effects and film animation studio. We also specialize in mechanical & animatronic puppets, 35 mm stop-motion animation, front & rear screen projection, silicone & resin mold making, foam latex prosthetics, breakaway props, models & miniatures, specialty costumes and masks.

SPECIAL EFFECTS WORKSHOPS

• Contact Carl Paoline or Scott Sliger. •

STANLEY ALLEN SHERMAN/MASK ARTS CO.
212-243-4039
203 West 14th St. #5F, (7th Ave.) NYC, NY 10011
Hours: by appt.
• Handcrafted molded leather masks and simple leather masks for theatre, opera, dance, commedia, parties, etc. Specialty in molding leather. Also sword and metal repair, upholstery. •

DAVID SMITH
213-850-7065
360 N. Sycamore Ave.,   Los Angeles, CA 90036
Hours: by appt.
• Set decorator, prop shopper, designer's asst; member U.S.A local 829. •

STUDIO E 15
718-797-4561
79 Washington St., (York & Front) Brooklyn, NY 11201
Hours: 9-6 Mon-Fri
FAX 718-797-4562
• Custom lifecast figures for museums and display. •

RICHARD TAUTKUS
212-691-8253
21-07 41st Ave., (21-22nd St.) L.I.C, NY 11101
718-729-1010
Hours: by appt.
• Special and unusual props and costumes; masks, millinery. •

O-P

JORGE LUIS TORO   718-626-7403
  2575 36th St. #2L, (Astoria Blvd.-28th Ave.) Astoria, NY 11103
  Hours: by appt.
  • Prop construction and prop shopping. •

KATHY URMSON   718-522-0368
  252 Carlton Ave., (DeKalb-Willoughby) Brooklyn, NY 11205
  Hours: by appt.
  • Trompe l'oeil, faux finishes, glazing, stenciling and other decorative painted finishes. •

JESSIE WALKER   212-675-7320
  142 W. 26th St. #2, (6-7th Ave.) NYC, NY 10001
  Hours: by appt.   FAX 212-695-3058
  • Scenic artist for theatre, film and display; murals, faux and fantasy finishes, model making,
  sculpture, design •

JIM WALLACE   914-726-3457
  229 Goodridge Road, Westtown, NY 10998
  Hours: 9-6 Mon-Fri   FAX 914-726-4236
  • SPFX model and prop maker. •

PROP RENTAL HOUSES

ACE PROPS   212-206-1475
  1 West 19th St., Ground Fl., (5th Ave.) NYC, NY 10011   212-580-9551
  Hours: 8-5 Mon-Fri • 9-4 Sat • or by appt.   FAX 212-929-9082

Wide variety of hard to get props - electronic gear, video cameras,
microphones, lighting and projection equipment, prop guns,
photographic equipment and good technical support.

                  • A full service prop rental house. CREDIT CARDS. •
                  (See display ad in this section.)

ART & INDUSTRIAL DESIGN SHOP   212-477-0116
  399 Lafayette, NYC, NY 10003
  Hours: 12-7 Mon-Sat.

Specializing in 20th Century Decorative Art, Art Furniture,
American Deco, Italian Glass, Italian Furniture, Art, Antiques,
Paintings & Sculpture. Industrial Design.

                  • 11,000 Sq. foot showroom of 20th Century designer & Art Deco furniture for all settings,
                  clocks, lighting fixtures, art & collectibles. RENTALS CREDIT CARDS •
                  (See display ad under ANTIQUES; VICTORIAN & 20TH CENTURY.)

O-P

ARENSON OFFICE FURNISHINGS, INC.
212-838-8880
315 East 62nd St., (1st-2nd Ave.) NYC, NY 10021
Hours: 9-5 Mon-Fri • or by appt.
FAX 212-758-5001

A complete selection-from budget to up-scale. Contemporary, hi-tech, transitional, and traditional furniture for commercials, print, features, industrials and T.V. Including: desks, desk top accessories, partitions, folding chairs and tables, chairs from clerical to CEO, filing cabinets, credenzas, coat racks, book cases, reception furniture, computer furniture, board rooms, conference rooms, etc. We also have complete production office set-ups.

ARENSON *office* FURNISHINGS

* Long and short term rentals- same day delivery! *
(See display ad in this section.)

BENNER MEDICAL PROPS
212-727-9815
601 West 26th St. (11-12th Ave.) NYC, NY 10001
Hours: 9-4:30 Mon-Fri
FAX 212-727-9824
 * Large selection of new & antique medical equipment, examining room furnishings, utensils, research, medical staff uniforms & accessories; also medical consulting & coordinating services. *

E. BUK, ANTIQUES & ART
212-226-6891
151 Spring St., 2nd Fl., (W. B'way-Wooster) NYC, NY 10012
Hours: 10-7 every day or by appt.
(toll call) 700-science

ANTIQUE AND HISTORICAL; technical, mechanical, scientific, medical, nautical props and settings. Tools, machines, devices, boxes, tabletop accessories, lab equipment and glassware, brass, furniture, surfaces, cameras, radios, televisions, telescopes, sextants, globes, telephones, scales, microscopes, clocks, typewriters, meters, phonographs, microphones, high-wheeled bicycles, lamps, sewing machines, astronomy. Tools for all trades. 25 years collection of hard-to find specialties.

E.BUK
Antiques and Art

* Rentals, complete period settings and custom work. *
(See display ad in this section and under ANTIQUES.)

CENTRAL PROPERTIES OF 49TH ST.
212-265-7767
514 West 49th St., (10th Ave.) NYC, NY 10019
Hours: 8-5 Mon-Fri
FAX 212-582-3746

ALL the RENTAL NEEDS for today's Art Directors, Set Designers, Stylists and Photographers. ALL UNDER ONE ROOF!
Among the largest sources in Manhattan for furniture, accessories, and reproductions from every period . . . with an inventory that's complete!
Furniture refinishing, Custom Upholstering, Transport, and much much more!

CENTRAL PROPERTIES

* Large selection of furniture and accessories in very fine condition. Well suited for commercials and television, as well as other media. *
(See display ad in this section.)

CINEMA WORLD PRODUCTS, INC.
718-389-9800
220 DuPont St., (Provost) L.I.C., NY 11222
Hours: 9-7 Mon-Fri by appt.
FAX 718-389-9897
 * Complete medical equipment rental and consultation. Contact Mark Oppenheimer or Maurice Keshner. No credit cards. *
(See display ad under MEDICAL & SCIENTIFIC EQUIPMENT & SUPPLIES: HOSPITAL & SICK-ROOM)

0-P

"I found it in the N.Y. Theatrical Sourcebook."

OFFICE FURNITURE
FOR
PROP RENTAL
AND SALES

**A COMPLETE SELECTION OF CONTEMPORARY • HI-TECH
TRANSITIONAL • TRADITIONAL FURNITURE FOR COMMERCIALS
PRINT • FEATURES • INDUSTRIALS • TV
FROM BUDGET TO UPSCALE**

**Desks
Desk Top Accessories
Partitions
Folding Chairs and Tables
Chairs: From Clerical To CEO
Filing Cabinets
Credenzas
Coat Racks
Book Cases
Reception Furniture
Computer Furniture
Board Rooms
Conference Rooms
Any Office Set.
PRODUCTION OFFICE SET-UPS.**

212-838-8880
FAX 212-758-5001

*Contact Richard Slavin
"King of Props"*

315 East 62nd. St. New York, NY 10021

O-P

ARENSON*office*FURNISHINGS

"I found it in the N.Y. Theatrical Sourcebook."

SCIENTIFIC INSTRUMENTS.
MEDICAL, MECHANICAL, INDUSTRIAL AND ELECTRICAL DEVICES.

A fine and extensive collection of period and historical objects, including cameras, radios, televisions, telescopes, sextants, scales, microscopes, globes, furniture, desk accessories, lab apparatus, clocks, typewriters, telephones, tools, machines, microphones, meters, etc.

MANY RARE AND HARD TO FIND OBJECTS.
COMPLETE PERIOD SETTINGS AND CUSTOM WORK.

 E. BUK, Antiques and Art
151 Spring St., N.Y.C. 10012 (212) 226-6891
Appointment Advisable

0-P

THE HIGHEST QUALITY

Antique country & formal furniture, paintings, lamps, china, pewter, copper, linens, baskets and kitchen, garden & desktop accessories.

KUTTNER PROP RENTALS

56 West 22 St., N.Y., N.Y 10010 **212-242-7969** Fax **212-242-1293**

Eclectic/Encore Properties, Inc.

O-P

"I found it in the N.Y. Theatrical Sourcebook."

0-P

O-P

"I found it in the N.Y. Theatrical Sourcebook."

EARLY HALLOWEEN
212-691-2933
212-243-1499
130 West 25th St., 11th Fl., (6-7th Ave.) NYC, NY 10001
Hours: By appt. only.

Vintage luggage, linens, draperies, sporting goods, memorabilia.

• Also vintage clothing, hats, shoes & accessories. •

ECLECTIC / ENCORE PROPERTIES, INC.
212-645-8880
620 West 26th St., 4th Fl., (11-12th Ave.) NYC, NY 10001
Hours: 9-5 Mon-Fri • or by appt.   FAX   212-243-6508
• An large and interesting collection. Many antiques and "character" items. A full service prop rental company. Call Jim Gill. •
(See display ad in this section)

ECLECTIC PRESS
212-645-8880
620 West 26th St., 4th Fl., (11-12th Ave.) NYC, NY 10001
Hours: 9-5 Mon-Fri or by appt.   FAX   212-243-6508
• Extensive collections of antique and period paper goods and ephemera, signage, advertising, travel related items, brochures and military ephemera. Custom reproduction of any paper items. •
(See display ad under NEWSPAPERS)

FOREMOST FURNITURE
212-884-6347
8 West 30th St., (5th Ave.-B'way) NYC, NY 10001
Hours: 9-5 Mon-Fri   FAX   212-213-0260
• Huge selection of original & period furniture, furnishings art & oddities; 75,000 sq. ft. warehouse of history & memorabilia for rent. Call Regina of Barry. •

O-P

KATONAH IMAGE INC.
914-232-0961
10 Woodsbridge Road, Katonah, NY 10536
Hours: 9-5 Mon-Sat   FAX   914-232-3944
• Antiques, memorabilia, and collectables for rent or sale. MC/VISA •

KUTTNER PROP RENTALS, INC.
212-242-7969
56 West 22nd St., 5th Fl., (5-6th Ave.) NYC, NY 10010
Hours: 10-5:30 Mon-Fri   FAX   212-242-1293

Extensive selection of antique furniture, paintings, prints, lamps, vases, desk top accessories; frames, clocks, china, silver, pewter, copper and brass items, wicker & garden furniture, baskets, folk art, luggage, linens, quilts, Christmas decorations, flatware & bread boards. Superb collection of antique kitchenware.

• American & English furniture, paintings, accessories, china, glassware, silver, linens & kitchenware. A nice collection of detail items. Great for tabletop and print work. Rental only. •
(See display ad in this section.)

NEWEL ART GALLERY
212-758-1970
425 East 53rd St., (Sutton Pl. S.- 1st Ave.) NYC, NY 10022
Hours: 9-5 Mon-Fri
• Extraordinary selection antique furniture, art, lamps & architectural pieces; all periods. Expensive. RENTALS •

NICCOLINI ANTIQUES–PROPS RENTALS
19 West 21st St., (5-6th Ave.) NYC, NY 10010
Hours: 10-5 Mon-Fri • or by appt.
• Complete selection of furniture, mainly American wood, antiques and accessories. Rental only. •

212-243-2010
212-254-2900
FAX 212-366-6779

OFF STAGE DESIGN
63 Central Ave., Ossening, NY 10562
Hours: by appt.

914-762-4658

Furniture, Decorative Arts, Luggage, Medical, Softgoods, a little of everything. Ephemera a specialty. Will assist in locating items.

• Contact Denise Grillo or Denny Clark. •

ONE–STOP PROPPING
531 West 26th St., (10-11 th Ave.) NYC, NY 10001
Hours: 8-6 Mon-Fri
• For film: custom prop kit rental, location catering supplies and production supplies. •

212-465-8654

FAX 212-947-0856

PAPER PROPS PROVIDER COMPANY
140 3rd St., (3rd Ave.-Bond) Brooklyn, NY 11231
Hours: 8-5 Mon-Fri

718-384-6322

FAX 718-596-6322

Providing large lots of generalized paper props used in movies and television advertising. Specializing in paper props for office, bank, commercial, residential settings. Other customized paper props such as books, journals, newspapers, boxes, etc. Warehouse also available for settings.

• Contact Jim DeMarco •

THE PROP COMPANY, KAPLAN & ASSOC.
111 West 19th St., 8th Fl., (6-7th Ave.) NYC, NY 10011
Hours: 9-5 Mon-Fri

212-691-7767

FAX 212-727-3055

Contemporary, antique and ethnic furniture and table top accessories to include: china, glassware, silver, linens, baskets, textiles, vases, frames, surfaces, memorabilia, lighting, paintings, prints, and a great selection of antique kitchenware. Many one of a kind items.

• Contemporary tabletop, decorative accessories, antiques, ephemera and furniture . A very nice collection of linens. See Maxine Kaplan. RENTALS •
(See display ad in this section.)

PROPOSITION RENTALS, INC.
118 West 22nd St., 10th Fl., (6-7th Ave.) NYC, NY 10011
Hours: 9:30-5 Mon-Fri or by appt.
• Good selection of tabletop props & linens, all in good condition. •

212-929-9999
212-929-0025

O-P

PROPS FOR TODAY
212-206-0330
121 West 19th St. Reception: 3rd Fl., (6-7th Ave.) NYC, NY 10011
Hours: 8:30-5 Mon-Fri   FAX   212-924-0450

Come to us first and we'll work with your budget!
- EXPANDED! Furniture and accessories from Country/Antique
to Modern/High Tech.
- A unique collection of period advertising items, photographs,
playbills, valentines, menus, police equipment, telephones, eyeglasses, lab equipment, vintage radios, wristwatches, and more!
- Designer home furnishings are our specialty.

NOW ON 3 FLOORS! ONE STOP PROPPING!

- Full service prop rental house. Good selection of contemporary and antique furniture. And a vast selection of china and glassware. Helpful service. Phone orders accepted. •
(See display ad in this section.)

PROPTRONICS
800-362-8118
1175 McCabe, Elk Grove Village, IL   708-952-1851
Hours: 8-4 Mon-Fri   FAX   708-952-8098
- Realistic & durable simulated electronic equipment; many items available. Good prices, sales only; brochure & price list available. •

RENT-A-THING
914-628-9298
Rt. 6, Baldwin, NY 10505   800-287-9298
Hours: 24 hrs., leave message, will return call.
- Props, costumes, and antique cars and boats for rent. Also many interesting sites for location filming. Will help locate items. •

LEONARD SCHILLER ANTIQUE AUTOS
718-788-3400
811 Union St., (6-7th Ave.) Brooklyn, NY 11215
Hours: 24 Hour phone

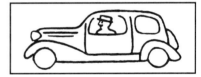

Providing any motor vehicle with the owner as driver - antique,
classic or contemporary. E.G. 1926 Taxi, 1938 Milk Truck, 1942
Fire Truck, 1947 Seltzer Truck, 1950 Pickup, 1953 Jaguar Roadster,
1958 Motor Scooter and a 1965 Good Humor Truck.

- Old bicycles & automotive related props. •

SECONDHAND ROSE
212-431-7673
270 Lafayette St., (Prince St.) NYC, NY 10012   212-431-ROSE
Hours: 10-6 Mon-Fri • 12-6 Sat
- Furniture and accessories, primarily 20th Century antiques. Many unusual & character pieces. Period wallpaper and linoleums; 1850's-1940's. Contact Suzanne Lipschutz. •

S & S SOUND CITY
212-575-0210
58 West 45th St., (5-6th Ave.) NYC, NY 10036
Hours: 9-7 Mon-Fri • 9-6 Sat   FAX   212-221-7907
- Complete selection of consumer electronics; stereos, TV's, telephones, home office equipment, etc. Will rent anything in store! Speak to Mel Tillman. •

STATE SUPPLY EQUIPMENT & PROPS, INC.
212-645-1430
210 Eleventh Ave., (24-25th St.) NYC, NY 10001
Hours: 8:30-5 Mon-Fri   FAX   212-675-3131
- Good source for many items; including coolers, canvas folding chairs, lockers, sterno, lamp oil, props etc. Large stock. •

PROP & MODEL SHOPS

For display props, see also **DISPLAY HOUSES & MATERIALS**

ACME STIMULI- DESIGN & PRODUCTION　　　　　　212-465-1071
548 West 28th St., (10-11th Ave.) NYC, NY 10001
Hours: by appt.
• Prop construction, mold making and sculpture. Also design service and construction. Contact Mark Rubin.

ARTS & CRAFTERS, INC.　　　　　　　　　　　718-875-8151
175 Johnson St., (Flatbush-Prince) Brooklyn, NY 11201
Hours: 9-5:30 Mon-Fri
• Sculpture, 3-D effect props in any material to your specifications. •

BARGSTEN STUDIOS　　　　　　　　　　　　201-420-8680
111 First St., Jersey City, NJ 07302
Hours: 9-5 Mon-Fri
• SPFX shop, props; also involved in film production and scenery. Design service available. •

BAUMWELL GRAPHICS　　　　　　　　　　　212-868-3340
450 West 31st St. (9-10th Ave.) NYC, NY 10001
Hours: 8:30-6 Mon-Fri
• Contact Clyde Baumwell. •

THOMAS BRAMLETT & ASSOCIATES, INC.　　　　908-850-0301
430 Sandshore Rd., Hackettstown, NJ 07840
Hours: 9-6 Mon-Fri • 9-1 Sat　　　　　FAX　908-850-6318
• Scenery, props & special effects. Ask for Tom. •

BROOKLYN MODEL WORKS　　　　　　　　718-834-1944
60 Washington Ave., (Park- Flushing) Brooklyn, NY 11205
Hours: 9-5 Mon-Fri　　　　　　　　　FAX　718-596-8934

• SPECIAL EFFECTS FOR FILM AND VIDEO •

Mechanical effects, electronic effects, custom props, miniatures, logo formats, vacuumforming, casting and reproductions.

• Experienced and reliable. •

CIMMELLI, INC.　　　　　　　　　　　　914-735-2090
16 Walter St., Pearl River, NY 10965
Hours: 8:30-5:30 Mon-Fri • Sat by appt.　　　FAX　914-735-1643
• Masks, sculpture, puppets, props, models, rigs, and special effects. Custom sculpture for any application. •

O-P

COSTUME ARMOUR, INC.   914-534-9120
PO Box 85, 2 Mill St., Cornwall, NY 12518
Hours: 9-4 Mon-Fri   FAX   914-534-8602

Sculpture, armor, custom props, vaccumforming, masks, display, artificial food. CREDITS INCLUDE: *Siegried & Roy - Vegas '90, Beauty & the Beast, Sunset Boulevard, Phantom of the Opera, Miss Saigon, Secret Garden, Cats, Meet Me in St. Louis, Chess, Into the Woods, Gypsy, Grand Hotel, Jerome Robbins, Lock Up,* The Met, NYC Opera, ABT, and NYC Ballet.

• Beautiful custom work. Sculpting by Nino Novellino is some of the best around. Many services. Rentals available . •
(See display ad in this section.)

ALEXSANDER DANEL SCULPTURE STUDIO   516-728-3761
2 Skyes Neck Ct., East Quogue, NY 11942
Hours: 8-6 Mon-Sun
• Custom work only. Casting and sculpting actual scale, oversized and miniature in bronze, fiberglass, plaster, vacuumforming; period duplication is their specialty. Will send photocopies of prior commissions on request. •

DECOUR COUTURE DESIGN   212-727-0123
25-37 37th St., (28-25th Ave.) Astoria, NY 10003   212-627-3495
Hours: 10-5 Mon-Fri by appt.
• Design & fabrication of custom soft goods. Costume crafts & props, decorative finishes and leafing. Contact Lisa Linden & Corey Mansueto. •

DGL ASSOCIATES   212-679-0857
103 Lexington Ave. (Franklin-Classon) Brooklyn, NY 11238
Hours: 10-6 Mon-Fri
• Set props, carpentry, furniture construction and repair, stripping, staining, painting and refinishing, upholstery, custom work only; contact Laura DeGregorio. •

JAMES DONAHHUE SETS & PROPS   718-388-9175
143 Roebling St., (Metropolitan-Hope) Brooklyn, NY 11211
Hours: 9-5 Mon-Fri   FAX   718-388-9175
• Display and promotional props; also miniature sets and models. •

ECLECTIC PRESS   212-645-8880
620 West 26th St.,4th Fl., (11-12th Ave.) NYC, NY 10001
Hours: 9-5 Mon-Fri • or by appt.   FAX   212-243-6508
• Custom printed props in any quantity; graphics design, mechanical reproduction; in-stock generic household product & food labels, generic newspaper covers, ID's, credit cards and documents of all kinds. •
(see display ad under NEWSPAPERS.)

GEPPETTO SOFT SCULPTURE & DISPLAY   718-398-9792
107 Lexington Ave., (Franklin-Classon) Brooklyn, NY 11238
Hours: 10-6 Mon-Fri
• Custom construction of soft sculpture props and costumes, foam rubber masks, foam props, and 3-D illustrations. Contact Scott. Brochure available. •
(See display ad in this section.)

THE HOUSE, WORLD FAMOUS ARTISTS   212-691-7050
163 West 22nd St. (6-7th Ave.) NYC, NY 10011
Hours: by appt.
• Props, display, custom furniture, art gallery; large scale paper mache & foam sculpture. Custom painted furniture. Contact Geoffrey Hoffman or Eric Brown. •

0-P

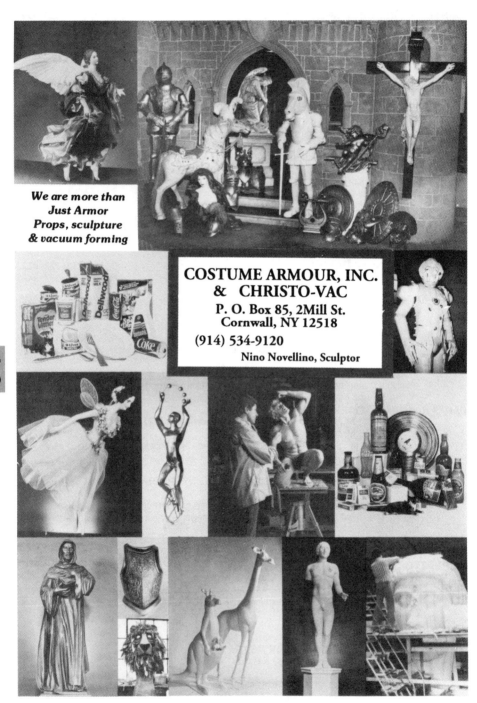

*We are more than
Just Armor
Props, sculpture
& vacuum forming*

**COSTUME ARMOUR, INC.
& CHRISTO-VAC**

P. O. Box 85, 2Mill St.
Cornwall, NY 12518

(914) 534-9120

Nino Novellino, Sculptor

O-P

"I found it in the N.Y. Theatrical Sourcebook."

𝒢EPPETT𝒪
SOFT SCULPTURE, INC.
107 Lexington Avenue • Brooklyn, NY 11238

custom display/props, costumes, puppets, masks... for
video/television, film, entertainment, 3-D illustration,
advertising, trade show exhibits, photography, etc.

Tel: (718) 398-9792   Fax: (718)622-2991

O-P

IMT SERVICES
914-691-3665

5 Pine Terrace, Highland, NY 12528
Hours: 9-6 Mon-Fri

FAX 914-691-3684

Custom fabricates three dimensional representations of ideas
and objects; in plastic, wood, rubber and metal...

I make things!

• Modelmaking, sculpture, flexibles, fake food for ECU, casting miniature to oversize. Electro-
mechanical effects. ATAC member. •

MARTIN IZQUIERDO STUDIOS
212-807-9757

118 West 22nd St. 9th Fl., (6-7th Ave.) NYC, NY 10011
Hours: 9-6 Mon-Fri • weekends by appt.

FAX 212-366-5249

PROPS, CUSTOM DISPLAY, UPHOLSTERY, DRAPERY, SCULPTURE
AND CASTING, MOLD MAKING, SOFT SCULPTURE, FABRIC
PAINTING, DYEING, AGING, SILKSCREENING, COSTUME CRAFTS.

COMPLETE PROP SHOP AND DYE LAB,
FACILITIES AVAILABLE FOR RENTAL.

• Full service custom work for theater, film, commercials, display and video. No rentals. •
(See display ad under COSTUME RENTAL & CONSTRUCTION.)

LIGHT IN FORM
212-226-7627

13-17 Laight St., #12, (Varick-6th Ave.) NYC, NY 10013
Hours: 9-5 Mon-Fri

FAX 212-219-1461

• Specializing in sculpting exquisite miniature figures and characters for prototypes. See
Cynthia Woodie. •

OFFSTAGE DESIGN
914-762-4658

63 Central Ave., Ossening, NY 10562
Hours: by appt.

Custom & Stage Furniture ... Your design or Ours.
Set Pieces, Upholstery, Shopping & Crafts.
Ephemera a specialty: all types of period products reproduced.

• Contact Denise Grillo or Denny Clark. •

PARALLEL DISPLAY, INC.
212-724-8784

585 West End Ave., (88th St.) NYC, NY 10024
Hours: By appt.

FAX 212-724-2656

• Props, built work; also breakaway glass sheets, mirror balls and flex mirror. •

RAVENSWOOD THEATER SCENIC STUDIOS
718-956-4276
212-543-9870

42-16 West St., (Jackson Ave.) L.I.C., NY 11101
Hours: 8:30-5:30 Mon-Fri • Sat by appt.

• Property and scenery construction for theater, exhibits, television, film and video. •

SCENIC SPECIALTIES, INC.
718-788-5379

232 7th St., (3-4th Ave.) Brooklyn, NY 11215
Hours: 8:30-5 Mon-Fri • by appt.

FAX   718-768-9173

We specialize in custom props and set pieces for stage and film. Construction of stage furniture, designing and fabricating breakaways, and creating special effects for the stage are some of the other services we offer. Through our services and scenery rental, we can help with your production needs.

• Custom props, stage furniture, aluminum fabrication, breakaways, special effects, scenery rental. See Lou Miller. •
(See display ad under ADHESIVES & GLUES.)

S.R. SEITZER & ASSOCIATES
914-365-1390

Bell-Ans Park, 103 Greenbush Rd. S., Orangeburg, NY 10962
Hours: 8:30-5 Mon-Fri or by appt.

FAX   914-365-1074

• Formerly Seitzer & Miller Assoc. Custom props including carpentry, metalwork, soft goods, upholstery, and craft work. Speak to Scott. •

SPECIAL EFFECTS WORKSHOPS
212-245-3624

410 West 47th St. (9-10th Ave.) NYC, NY 10036
Hours: 9-5 Mon-Fri

Special Effects Workshops is a complete make-up effects and film animation studio. We also specialize in mechanical and animatronic puppets, 35 mm stop-motion animation, front & rear screen projection, silicone & resin mold making, foam latex prosthetics, breakaway props, models & miniatures, specialty costumes and masks.

SPECIAL EFFECTS WORKSHOPS

• Contact Carle Paolino or Scott Sliger. ATAC member. •

EOIN SPROTT STUDIO, LTD.
718-784-1407

c/o Kaufman-Astoria Studio, 37-11 35th Ave., (37-38th St.) Astoria, NY 11101
Hours: 8-5:30 Mon-Fri

FAX   718-784-1629

Custom props, model making, miniatures, sculptures/molds and animation rigs.

EOIN
SPROTT
STUDIO
LTD.

• Very fine work. Contact Eoin or Susan. ATAC member. •

STIEGELBAUER ASSOC., INC.
718-624-0835

Bldg. 20 Bklyn Navy Yard, (Cumberland-Flushing) Brooklyn, NY 11205
Hours: 7-2:30 Mon-Fri

FAX   718-624-0844

• Mechanical props and special effects for TV, theater and industrials, also set construction; contact Mike. RENTAL •

STUDIO E 15
718-797-4561

79 Washington St., (York-Front St.) Brooklyn, NY 11201
Hours: 9-6 Mon-Fri

FAX   718-797-4562

• Custom lifecast figures for museums and display. •

O-P

TRENGROVE STUDIOS, INC.

60 West 22nd St., (5-6th Ave.) NYC, NY 10010
Hours: 9-5 Mon-Fri

212-255-2857
800-366-2857
FAX 212-633-8982

Handcrafted ice and water effects in acrylic and glass. For sale and rent. Custom props, acrylic embedments. Chemicals for smoke, steam, ice and water effects. Super realistic food replicas cast from life. Our free brochure describes these and many other creativity enhancing products.

• Brochure and product sheet available. Great custom work in glass and acrylic. Stock purchase of fake ice. MC/VISA •

PUPPETRY

3-DESIGN STUDIOS

212-627-1010

147 West 24th St., 3rd floor, (6-7th Ave.) NYC, NY 10011
Hours: By appt.
• Puppets for television and film, special effects, toy design, and illustration. •

PAM ARCIERO

203-429-0786
212-580-7257

7 Bebbington Rd., Ashford, CT 06278
Hours: By appt.
• Professional puppeteer; designs and builds puppets. •

ANDREW BENEPE STUDIO

212- 226-8570

43 Bridge St. , Brooklyn, NY 11121
Hours: By appt.
• Puppetry and props. Monster and animal costumes, sculpture, special effects and rigging. •

ARLEY BERRYHILL

718-204-4913

21-05 33rd St, #5B, (21st Ave.) Astoria, NY 11105
Hours: By appt.
• Puppets, masks, costume crafts, foam sculpture, millinery and mold making. •

CHERYL BLALOCK

212-769-3168

308 West 78th St., (WEA-Riverside Dr.) NYC, NY 10024
Hours: By appt.
• Professional puppeteer including character voices for hand and rod puppets. •

RANDY CARFAGNO

212-947-0302

347 West 39th St., #7E, (8th-9th Ave.) NYC, NY 10018
Hours: By appt.
• Professional puppeteer for TV, film, and stage. Puppet mascot building---all types. Masks, sculpting, latex shoes, mold making, foam and wood carving. •

EDWARD G. CHRISTIE

212-666-8978

760 West End Ave., #10B, (97th St.) NYC, NY 10025
Hours: By appt.
• Puppet design and construction (no costumes), puppeteer for TV, stage and screen. •

O-P

"I found it in the N.Y. Theatrical Sourcebook."

CIMMELLI, INC.
914-735-2090
16 Walter St., Pearl River, NY 10965
Hours: 8:30-5:30 Mon-Fri • Sat by appt.   FAX   914-735-1643
• Masks, sculpture, puppets, props, models, rigs and special effects. Custom sculpture for any application. •

COSTUMES AND CREATURES
612-333-2223
420 N. 5th St., #350, Minneapolis, MN 55401
Hours: 8-6 Mon-Thurs
• A division of VEE Corp., producer of Sesame St. Live tours. Specializing in full body character and animal costumes; period garments, accessories and soft props. Custom design and construction. Contact Janet Delvoye. •

SAL DENARO/MOTION BY DESIGN
718-965-9557
225 Prospect Ave., (1st St.) Brooklyn, NY 11215
Hours: By appt.
• Puppet creator/designer and toy model sculptor; stop motion models, foam, latex and mold making. •

ISABELLE DUFOUR
201-216-5738
253 10th St., #4A, (Park-Willow) Hoboken, NJ 07030
Hours: 9-7 Mon-Fri
• Puppet design and construction. Woodcarving, fiberglass, Celastic and foam sculpture. •

HENRI EWASKIO
718-727-0899
3 Vine St., Staten Island, NY 10301
Hours: By appt.
• Puppets, milliner, display miniatures, masks, costume props and construction. •

FLEXITOON LTD.
212-877-2757
46 West 73rd St., #3A, (CPW-Columbus Ave.) NYC, NY 10023
Hours: By appt.
• Creators of flexible cartoon puppets. Speak to Craig Marin. •

O-P

PRESTON FOERDER
201-217-1482
610 Madison St. #2, Hoboken, NJ 07030
Hours: By appt.
• Professional puppeteer for stage, film and TV. •

GEPPETTO SOFT SCULPTURE AND DISPLAY
718-398-9792
107 Lexington Ave., (Franklin-Classon) Brooklyn, NY 11238
Hours: 10-6 Mon-Fri
• Custom construction of soft sculpture puppets and character costumes, oversized foam props, and window displays. Contact Scott. Brochure available. •
(See display ad under PROP SHOPS.)

JANE GOOTNICK
212-724-2056
204 West 88th St., (Broadway) NYC, NY 10024
Hours: by appt.
• Puppets and special effects (Radio-cable) creatures.

LYNN HIPPEN
212-861-9510
314 East 83rd St. #1E, (1st-2nd Ave.) NYC, NY 10028
Hours: by appt.
• Professional puppeteer; designs & builds portrait puppets in all sizes; celastic & puppet costumes. •

HUDSON VAGABOND PUPPETS   914-359-1144
P.O. Box 131, Blauvelt, NY 10913
Hours: by appt.
• Performs musicals with life-size puppets. Will build large scale puppets. Lois Bohovesky,
Director. •

LAURA LOPEZ/GATE HOUSE   914-359-8853
P.O. Box 495, Piermont, NY 10968
Hours: by appt.   FAX   914-398-2821
• Network of suburban craftspeople; specialty costumes, masks and fabric works. •
(See display ad under PROP & SCENIC CRAFTPEOPLE.)

MARIA MCNAMARA   612-224-7267
122 West Isabel St., St. Paul, MN 55107
Hours: by appt.
• Puppets, props, and craft work. •

MCL DESIGNS, INC.   212-587-1511
47 Ann St., NYC, NY 10010
Hours: by appt.
• Customized costumes, full-figure puppets, hand puppets, props. Contact Susan McClain-
Moore. •

MULDER / MARTIN, INC.   212-234-0889
604 Riverside Dr.,#6E, (137th St.) NYC, NY 10031
Hours: 9-5 Mon-Fri   FAX   212-234-0885
• Full body and hand puppets for theater, film, television, trade shows and special events. •
(See display ad under COSTUME CRAFTSPEOPLE, MASKS & MILLINERY.)

NATIONAL THEATER OF PUPPET ARTS   516-487-3684
58 Rose Ave., Great Neck, NY 11021
Hours: by appt.
• Performer oriented school for professionals, educators and others. Available for commercials. •

ANDREW NESS   718-786-0070
25-34 Crescent St., Astoria, NY 11102
Hours: by appt.
• Specialty props and model making for television, film and theatre; also SAG puppeteer. •

PANDEMONIUM PUPPET CO./ BART ROCCOBERTON, DIRECTOR   203-423-5882
58 Spring St., Williamantic, CT 06226
Hours: by appt.
• Performs custom designed or packaged shows; video, commercials, live; workshops and res-
idencies. •

PHILADELPHIA MARIONETTE THEATER & MUSEUM, PLAYHOUSE IN THE PARK
Belmont Mansion Dr., Philadelphia, PA 19131   215-879-1213
Hours: call first
• Performs and builds full marionette shows. Puppet collection from around the world.
Contact Catherine Brownholtz. •

POKO PUPPETS, INC.   718-972-5723
2 East 2nd St., (McDonald) Brooklyn, NY 11218
Hours: by appt.
• Puppets/props: custom designed and created, performed for commercials, industrials and
live shows. Larry Engler, Artistic Director. •

THE PUPPET PEOPLE   212-924-8389
    Hours: by appt.
        • Custom or package shows; commercials, industrials; body puppet, marionette construction.
    Ask for Mr. Williams. •

THE PUPPET WORKS, INC.   718-965-3391
    338 Sixth Ave., (4th St.) Brooklyn, NY 11215
    Hours: 9-4 every day
        • Creates shows for touring schools, industrials, film, TV and workshops. Primarily mari-
    onettes; theater on site. Nicholas Coppola, Director. •

ELLEN RIXFORD STUDIO   212-865-6586
    308 West 97th #71, (WEA-Riverside Dr.) NYC, NY 10025
    Hours: 9-6 Mon-Fri
        • Unusual puppets with interesting mechanisms and costumes: sculptural illustration and soft
    sculpture for publishing, advertising theatre. •

MARTIN P. ROBINSON   212-226-9205
    519 Broadway, #3F, (Spring-Broome) NYC, NY 10012
    Hours: By appt.
        • Professional puppeteer, puppet designer and builder. •

ROBERT ROGERS CO.   (Outside CT.) 800-457-0785
    20-4 East Pembroke Road, Danbury, CT 06811   (In CT.) 203-791-1907
    Hours: 8-5 Mon-Fri
        • Stock and custom character display figures and puppets from 18" to life size. See Robert
    Rogers for brochures and pricing. •

SUE SCHMIDT   212-932-3577
    69 West 105th St., (Columbus- Manhattan) NYC, NY 10025
    Hours: By appt.   FAX 212-724-2800
        • Puppet and puppet mechanics; textile painting, masks and modelmaking. •

JODY SCHOFFNER   818-992-6574
    24118 Philiprimm, Woodland Hills, CA 91367
    Hours: By appt.
        • Puppet maker; draper for stage or specialty costumes. •

DANNY SEGRIN   212-227-5986
    56 Warren St., (Church- W. B'way) NYC, NY 10007
    Hours: By appt.
        • Professional puppeteer; puppet maker; puppets for film, TV and commercials. •

LISA SHAFTEL   206-706-0868
    333 N. 79th St., Seattle, WA 98115   206-361-0733
    Hours: By appt.
        • Puppets, animal figures and masks. Prop crafts, soft goods, scenic/lighting design and
    scene painting. •

ROD YOUNG   212-929-1568
    93 Perry St. , (Hudson-Bleeker) NYC, NY 10014
    Hours: By appt.
        • One-man show performing puppeteer; marionettes, rod, shadow and hand puppets. •

STEVE YOUNG   914-757-4273
    414 West Kerley Corner Rd. Tivoli, NY 12583
    Hours: By appt.
        • Professional puppeteer (15 years experience) for film, rodeo, industrials; major credits. •

O-P

"I found it in the N.Y. Theatrical Sourcebook."

O–P

"I found it in the N.Y. Theatrical Sourcebook."

QUILTS

AMERICA HURRAH ANTIQUES 212-535-1930
766 Madison Avenue, (66th St.) NYC, NY 10021
Hours: 11-6 Tues-Sat FAX 212-249-9718
• Noted for quilts, Americana, American Indian. RENTALS •

CHRIS BOBIN 212-255-5225
20 West 20th St. c/o Fabric Effects, (5-6th Ave.) NYC, NY 10011 212-475-7268
Hours: By appt.
• Custom, non-traditional quilts and wall-hangings including patchwork, applique and embroidery. •

LAURA FISHER/ ANTIQUE QUILTS & AMERICANA 212-838-2596
1050 2nd Ave., Gallery #84, NYC, NY 10022
Hours: 11-6 Mon-Sat
• Quilts, American textiles, hooked rugs. RENTALS •

THE GAZEBO 212-832-7077
127 East 57th St., (Park-Lexington) NYC, NY 10022 FAX 212-754-0571
Hours: 10-7 Mon-Sat • 12-6 Sun
• Quilts, wicker furniture, rag rugs, pillows and country home furnishings: Expensive.
RENTALS CREDIT CARDS •

KELTER-MALCE 212-675-7380
74 Jane St., (Greenwich & Washington) NYC, NY 10014
Hours: 11-7 Mon-Sat
• Quilts, American country and primitive antiques. RENTALS CREDIT CARDS •

JUDITH & JAMES MILNE, INC. 212-427-0107
506 East 74th St., 2nd Fl., (York) NYC, NY 10021
Hours: 9:30-5:30 Mon-Fri • or by appt. FAX 212-427-0107
• Beautiful quilts; sales & rental; specializing in American country antiques. •
(See display ad under ANTIQUES: VICTORIAN & 20TH CENTURY)

LUCY ANNA 212-645-9463
502 Hudson St., (Christopher) NYC, NY 10014
Hours: 12-7 Tue-Sat • 12-5 Sun
• Nice selection of quilts and chenille bed spreads. Antique cribs and children's furniture. Hand
made cloth dolls and folk art. •

SUSAN PARRISH 212-645-5020
390 Bleecker St., (Perry-11th St.) NYC, NY 10014
12-6 Tues-Sat • or by appt.
• Large selection of quilts, navajo and southwestern rugs; folk art. RENTALS CREDIT
CARDS •

ELLEN RIXFORD STUDIO 212-865-5686
308 West 97th St., #71, (WEA-Riverside) NYC, NY 10025
Hours: 9-6 Mon-Fri • or by appt.
• Picture quilts and architectural wall hangings for collectors, decorators, illustration and
advertising. •

THOS. K. WOODARD AMERICAN ART & ANTIQUES 212-988-2906
799 Madison Avenue, (67-68th St.) NYC, NY 10021
Hours: 12-6 Tue-Sat • or by appt. FAX 212-734-9665
• Extensive collection; also quilt tops, pieces, and fragments. CREDIT CARDS •

RATTAN, REED, RAFFIA, WILLOW

BAMBOO & RATTAN WORKS, INC.   908-370-0220
4470 Oberlin Ave. S., Lakewood, NJ 08701
Hours: 8:30-4:30 Mon-Fri
• Wholesale rattan, matting, bamboo and caning. •

CHARLES DEMAREST, INC.   201-492-1414
P.O. Box 238, Bloomfield, NJ 07430
Hours: 9-5 Mon-Fri
• Wholesale only. Bamboo poles, decorative matting. •

FRANK'S CANE AND RUSH SUPPLY   714-847-0707
7252 Heil Ave., (Gothard St.) Huntington Beach, CA 92647
Hours: 8-5 Mon-Fri
• Retail and wholesale caning and basketry supplies; huge stock, catalog and will ship
UPS/CODs fast. •

INTER-MARES TRADING CO., INC.   516-957-3467
P.O.Box 617, 1064 Rt.109, Lindenhurst, NJ 11757
Hours: 9-5 Mon-Fri
• Distributors of rattan, reed, willow, cane; full rolls, bales, eases, and reels; also natural
grass skirts. Some brochures. Will ship. •

PEERLESS RATTAN & REED MFG. CO.   513-323-7353
624 S. Burnett Rd., Springfield, OH 45505
Hours: 9-4 Mon-Fri
• Rattan, reed and cane. Catalog. •

H.H. PERKINS, INC.   203-389-9501
10 S. Bradley Rd., Woodbridge, CT 06525
Hours: 9-5 Mon-Fri • 9-12 Sat
• Basketry and seat weaving supplies; catalog, will ship UPS/COD. •

RAINBOW TRADING CO., INC.   718-784-3700
5-05 48th Ave., (5th St.-Vernon) L.I.C., NY 11101
Hours: 9-5 Mon-Fri
• Manufacture of rattan, reed and chair caning. •

VETERAN'S CANING SHOP   212-868-3244
550 West 35th St., (10-11th Ave.) NYC, NY 10001
Hours: 8- 4:30 Mon-Thurs • 8-4 Fri • 9-12 Sat (in Winter season)
• Repairs and refinishes cane furniture. Fast and friendly service. Also sells supplies. •

YORKVILLE CANING, INC.   212-432-6464
3104 60th St., (31st-32nd Ave.-2 blks N. of Northern Blvd.) Woodside, NY 11377
        718-274-6464
Hours: 7:30-4 Mon-Fri   FAX 718-274-8525
• Repair of cane, wicker, rush, splint and wood furniture. No stripping. N.J. drop off
available. •

Q-R

RECORDS, TAPES & CDS

See also **AUDIO & VIDEO EQUIPMENT**

COLONY RECORDS 212-265-2050
1619 Broadway, (49th St.) NYC, NY 10019
Hours: 9:30-Midnight Sun-Thurs/ 10am-2am Fri&Sat   FAX 212-956-6009
• Large selection of records, CDs and tapes, sheet music: will ship anywhere. CREDIT CARDS •

FINYL VINYL 212-533-8007
89 Second Ave., (5-6th) NYC, NY 10003
Hours: 12-8 Mon-Sat • 1-6 Sun
• Buy and sell records from the 30's through the 70's: rock, blues, soul, etc. CREDIT CARDS •

FOOTLIGHT RECORDS 212-533-1572
113 East 12th St., (3-4th) NYC, NY 10003
Hours: 11-7 Mon-Fri • 10-6 Sat • 12-5 Sun
• Out-of-print, Broadway, film soundtracks, jazz, country, rock. Bought and sold. CREDIT CARDS •

SAM GOODY 212-246-8480
666 Third Ave., (43 St.) NYC, NY 10017
Hours: 9-8 Mon-Fri • 10-8 Sat
• Records, CDs and tapes, current top 40s. CREDIT CARDS •

HMV, INC. 212-348-0800
1280 Lexington Ave., (86th) NYC, NY 10028
Hours: 10-10 Sun-Thurs • 10-11 Fri-Sat

2081 Broadway, (72nd St) NYC, NY 10023 212-721-5900
Hours: 9-Midnight Mon-Sat • 10-11 Sun
• Enormous selection of cassettes, CDs. CREDIT CARDS •

HOUSE OF OLDIES 212-243-0500
35 Carmine St., (6th - Bleecker) NYC, NY 10014
Hours: 11-7 Mon-Sat   FAX 212-989-1697
• Large selection of rock 'n roll, 45's, 78's, 33's and beyond. Catalog available. CREDIT CARDS •

J&R MUSIC WORLD 212-732-8600
23 Park Row, (Beekman-Ann) NYC, NY 10038
Hours: 9-6:30 Mon-Sat • 11-6 Sun   FAX 212-406-4443
• Popular CDs and tapes: good selection, well priced; also stereo equipment, TV, VCR. CREDIT CARDS •

33 Park Row, (Beekman-Ann) NYC, NY 10038 212-349-8400
Hours: 9-6:30 Mon-Sat   (jazz) 212-238-9070
• Classical and jazz records, CDs and tapes; video; good selection and prices. CREDIT CARDS •

MIDNIGHT RECORDS 212-675-2768
263 West 23 St., (7-8th Ave) NYC, NY 10011
Hours: 12-8 Tue-Sat
• Specialists in rare rock 'n roll, 50's through 90's. Buy and sell. CREDIT CARDS •

Q-R

TOWER RECORDS   212-505-1500
  692 Broadway, (4th) NYC, NY 10012
  1961 Broadway, (66th) NYC, NY 10023   212-799-2500
  Hours: 9am-midnight everyday
  • Excellent selection; extensive classical, jazz, soundtrack, original casts, electronic, foreign,
  popular, 45's, tape and video; budget annex at 4th St. store. CREDIT CARDS •

RELIGIOUS GOODS

See also **CLOTHING RENTAL & PURCHASE: ECCLESIASTICAL**

AMERICAN BIBLE SOCIETY   212-408-1200
  1865 Broadway, (61st St.) NYC, NY 10023
  Hours: 9-5 Mon-Fri   FAX   212-408-1512
  • King James Bibles. •

BARCLAY CHURCH SUPPLY, INC.   212-267-9432
  28 Warren St., 2nd Fl., (B'way-Church St.) NYC, NY 10007
  Hours: 10-5 Mon-Fri • 10-3 Sat (call first)
  • Crosses, rosaries and church supplies. Shipping. RENTALS •

BENDIX CARVING INC.   516-775-2512
  51 Covert Ave., Floral Park, NY 11001
  Hours: 10-5 Mon-Fri   FAX   516-775-2538
  • Carved wooden crucifixes, creches, statuary, etc. Shipping. RENTALS •

CALVARY BOOK STORE   212-315-0230
  139 West 57th St., (6th-7th Ave.) NYC, NY 10019
  Hours: 3-9 Mon • 12-7 Wed • 12:30-4 Sun
  • Good selection of Bibles. •

HOLY LAND ART CO. INC.   212-962-2130
  160 Chambers St., (Greenwich St.) NYC, NY 10007   800-962-4659
  Hours: 9-4:30 Mon-Thurs • 9-4 Fri   FAX   212-962-5740

Call toll-free for information and business hours
Largest Supplier to Entertainment Industry. Stock includes:
vestments, wood carvings, statues, rosaries, crosses, chalices,
candles (all sizes and battery-operated), candlesticks, clerical
clothing and altar furniture.Credits include: *Godfather I & III, The
Cosby Show, The Equalizer, The Exorcist, My One & Only* and
many more.

Holy Land Art Company, Inc.

  • Full line of church goods and religious items. Shipping. RENTALS CREDIT CARDS •

ISRAELI GIFTS   212-391-4928
  575 7th Ave., (40th-41st St.) NYC, NY 10018
  Hours: 9:30-6 Mon-Fri
  • Jewish religious goods in Midtown; pricey. CREDIT CARD •

PARACLETE BOOK CENTER   212-535-4050
  146 East 74th St., (Lex-3rd Ave.) NYC, NY 10021
  Hours: 10-6 Tue-Fri • 10-5 Sat
  • Religious bookstore. •

WEISZBURG   212-674-1770
> 45 Essex St., (Grand-Hester) NYC, NY 10002
> Hours: 9:30-5 Sun-Thurs • 9:30-3 Fri
> • Consertive Jewish religious items. RENTALS •

RESTORATION & CONSERVATION

GLASS RESTORATIONS   212-517-3287
> 308 East 78th St., (1-2nd Ave.) NYC, NY 10021
> Hours: 9:30-5 Mon-Fri
> • Cuts, grinds and repairs chipped or scratched glass; also repairs broken glass and polishes; speak to Gus. •

MARGO FEIDEN GALLERIES   212-677-5330
> 699 Madison Ave., (62-63rd St.) NYC, NY 10021
> Hours: 10-6 every day
> • Restoration of paper, drawings, watercolors and paintings. •

HAKIM RUG GALLERY   212-750-0606
> 208 East 51st St., (2nd-3rd Ave) NYC, NY 10022
> Hours: 9:30-5:30 Mon-Fri • Sun by appt.   FAX   212-826-6395
> • Restoration & hand-cleaning: appraisals of carpets, tapestries, Aubossons & kilims: speak to Mr. Hakim. •

DAVID IMMERMAN   914-632-6463
> 40 Calton Lane, New Rochelle, NY 10804
> Hours: By appt.
> • Restoration of oil paintings, re-stretching and portrait painting. •

A. LAUB GLASS   212-734-4270
> 1873 2nd Ave., (96-97th St.) NYC, NY 10029
> Hours: 8-5 Mon-Fri • 9-4 Sat
> • Stained and leaded glass repair and restoration. •

SARAH LOWENGARD   212-860-2386
> P.O. Box 6611, 1080 Park Ave., (88th St.) NYC, NY 10128
> Hours: By appt.
> • Textile conservator specializing in archaeological textiles and 18th-20th century embroidery and costumes. •

JULIUS LOWY FRAME & RESTORING CO., INC.   212-586-2050
> 28 West End Ave., (60-61st St) NYC, NY 10023
> Hours: 9-5:30 Mon-Fri (call first)   FAX   212-489-1948
>
> 223 East 80th St., (2-3rd Ave.) NYC, NY 10021   212-861-8585
> Hours: 8:30-5 Mon-Fri • 10-4 Sat   FAX   212-988-0443
> • Restoration of oil on canvas, art work on paper, gold leaf and antique frames. •

PHILLIS MAGINSEN   ext. 252 212-534-1672
> c/o Museum of the City of NY
> 1220 5th Ave., (103rd St.) NYC, NY 10029
> Hours: 9-5 Mon- Fri
> • Consultation about fashion and textiles; conservation. •

Q-R

POOR RICHARD'S RESTORATION ATELIER　　　　　　　201-783-5333
101 Walnut St., (N. Willow) Montclair, NJ 07042
Hours: By appt.
• Antique restoration, conservation and repair of wood, metals, ceramics, paper, clocks, crystal, photographs, mirror resilvering, gold and silver leafing. •

RAMBUSCH　　　　　　　212-675-0400
40 West 13th St., (5th-6th Ave.) NYC, NY 10011
Hours: By appt.　　　　　FAX　212-620-4687
• Painting and mural restoration. •

TRADITIONAL LINES LTD.　　　　　　　212-627-3555
143 West 21st St., (6th-7th Ave.) NYC, NY 10011
Hours: 9-5 Mon-Fri　　　　　FAX　212-645-8158
• Historical restoration; interiors. Will also fabricate paneling, fireplaces, molding and hardware. •

REWEAVERS

THE FRENCH-AMERICAN RE-WEAVERS CO.　　　　　　　212-765-4670
119 West 57th St., Rm.1406, (6th-7th Ave.) NYC, NY 10019
Hours: 10:30-5:30 Mon-Fri • 11-2 Sat (call first)
• Reweaving of damaged clothing and costumes. •

ALICE ZOTTA　　　　　　　212-840-7657
2 West 45th St., (5th Ave.) NYC, NY 10036
Hours: 9:30-5 Mon-Fri • 10-2 Sat
• Reweaving; personal service. •

RIDING EQUIPMENT

CLAREMONT RIDING ACADEMY　　　　　　　212-724-5100
175 West 89th St., (Columbus-Amsterdam) NYC, NY 10024
Hours: 6:30 am-10 pm Mon-Fri • 8-5 Sat & Sun　　　FAX　212-799-3568
• Horse and riding equipment; hay. RENTALS •

COUNTRY SUPPLY　　　　　　　800-637-6721
1305 E. Mary St., Ottuma, IA 52501　　　　　515-682-8161
Hours: 9-5 Mon-Fri • orders 24 Hours a day
• Horse tack and equipment, various diameters of cotton rope, whips; catalog available; prompt service. •

E.A. HUTCHISON　　　　　　　212-242-5689
23 King St., (6th-7th Ave.) NYC, NY 10014 (showroom)
31 W. 11th St.,Suite 8c, NYC, NY 10011 (mail)
Hours: by appt.
• Specializing in equestrian antiques: English and Western. Jewelry, crops, blankets, saddles; formal and vintage riding clothes. RENTALS •

H. KAUFMAN & SONS SADDLERY CO., INC. 212-684-6060
419 Park Ave., (29th St.) NYC, NY 10016
Hours: 9:30-6 Mon-Sat • 11-5 Sun
• Riding equipment and western apparel; riding crops, whips, harnesses, saddle bags. Catalog. CREDIT CARDS •

HORSE COUNTRY 203-245-1668
150 Boston Post Road, (I-95-Exit 59) Madison, CT 06443
Hours: 10-5:30 Tue-Fri • 10-5 Sat
• Horse riding equipment, see Pat or Geoffry. Mail order; sorry, no catalog. •

MILLER HARNESS CO., INC. 212-673-1400
117 East 24th St., (Park- Lexington Ave.) NYC, NY 10010
Hours: 9-5:30 Mon-Sat
• Riding equipment. •

NATIONAL MOUNTED TRAINING GROUP 914-359-3854
P.O. Box J, Main St., Sparkill, NY 10976
Hours: 9-5 Mon-Sat
• Saddles, bridles, halters, horse equipment and tack; mounted police uniforms and boots; catalog. CREDIT CARDS •

ROCKS & MINERALS

See also **MARBLE**
For artificial rocks, see **DISPLAY HOUSES & MATERIALS**

AMERICAN MUSEUM OF NATURAL HISTORY–MINERALOGY DEPT. 212-769-5390
79th St and Central Park West, NYC, NY 10024
Hours: 9-5 Mon-Fri • best by appt.
• Consultation and some rentals; contact Dr. Harlow. Museum is open 10-4:30. •

ASTRO GALLERY 212-889-9000
185 Madison Ave., (34th St) NYC, NY 10016
Hours: 10-6 Mon-Sat • Thurs til 8 • 11-6 Sun FAX 212-689-4016
• Rocks, gems, polished stones, and crystals. RENTALS CREDIT CARDS •

CIMMELLI, INC. 914-735-2090
16 Walter Street, Pearl River, NY 10965
Hours: 8:30-5:30 Mon-Fri • Sat by appt. FAX 914-735-1643
• Crystals and minerals; cutting and polishing equipment. •

NORTH SHORE MASONRY 516-482-6200
96 Cutter Mill Road, Great Neck, NY 11021
Hours: 7-4 Mon-Fri • 7-1 Sat FAX 516-482-5039
• Sand, granite, marble and lava/feather rock. •

Q-R

STAR MAGIC   212-228-7770
   745 Broadway, (8th St- Waverly) NYC, NY 10003
   Hours: 10-10 Mon-Sat • 11-9 Sun

   275 Amsterdam Ave., (73rd) NYC, NY 10023   212-769-2020
   Hours: 10-10 Mon-Sat • 11-9 Sun

   1256 Lexington Ave., (84th-85th) NYC, NY 10028   212-988-0300
   Hours: 10-9 Mon-Sat • 11-7:30 Sun
      • Crystals and gem stones. Space related books, posters, toys, star maps and finders. •

RUBBER STAMPS

See also **STATIONERY & OFFICE SUPPLIES**

ADEQUATE RUBBER STAMP CO., INC.   212-840-1588
   141 West 41st St., 2nd Fl., (6th Ave.-Broadway) NYC, NY 10036
   Hours: 8:30-4:45 Mon-Fri
      • Better than adequate. Custom stamps, silkscreening and engraved signs. •

CENTURY RUBBER STAMP CO., INC.   212-962-6165
   121 Fulton St., (Nassau-Williams) NYC, NY 10038
   Hours: 7:30-4 Mon-Fri
      • Rubber stamps, reasonable prices; next day service. •

KLEAR COPY DESIGN RUBBER STAMPS   212-243-0357
   55 7th Ave. South, (Bleeker-Morton) NYC, NY 10014
   Hours: 1:30-6:30 Mon, Wed, Fri • 12:30-6:30 Tue, Thurs, Sat   **FAX** 212-645-5335
      • Stock and custom rubber stamps while-u-wait; newspaper headlines. •

RUBBER STAMPS, INC.   212-675-1180
   30 West 24th St., 4th Fl., (5th-6th Ave.) NYC, NY 10011
   Hours: 7:30-4 Mon-Fri   **FAX** 212-675-3849
      • Some stock, mostly custom work. MC/VISA •

Q–R

SCALES

E. Buk, Antiques & Art
212-226-6891
151 Spring St., 2nd Fl., (W. B'way-Wooster) NYC, NY 10012 (toll call) 700-SCIENCE
Hours: Every day by appt.

ANTIQUE AND PERIOD scales: floor, hanging, tabletop, tiny to
large, very fine to primitive; iron, brass, mahogany, glass, oak;
American, European; 18th to mid-20th century; apothecary,
medical, assay, laboratory, jewelers, food scales, letter scales,
candy scales, and weight sets.

• Complete period settings and custom work. RENTALS •
(See display ads under ANTIQUES and under PROP RENTAL HOUSES)

Detecto Industrial Scales
201-944-3888
240 Grand Ave., Leonia, NJ 07605
Hours: 9-4:30 Mon-Fri
FAX 201-944-3808
• Scales for every weighing need. RENTALS •

Sussman Brothers Cash Register Corp.
718-226-0290
2010 Coney Island Ave., (Quentin Rd.) Brooklyn, NY 11223
Hours: 8-5 Mon-Fri • 8-1 Sat
FAX 718-998-8012
• Scales, antique and new cash registers. RENTALS •

SCENIC SHOPS

See also **BACKDROPS**

Acadia Scenic Inc.
201-653-8889
130 Bay St., P.O. Box 197, Jersey City, NJ 07303
Hours: 7:30-5 Mon-Fri
FAX 201-653-4717
• Non-union full service shop. See David Lawson. •

Adirondack Scenic
518-747-3335
40 Hudson Falls Rd., South Glens Falls, NY 12803
Hours: 8-6 Mon-Fri
FAX 518-747-6738
• Set, prop, soft goods, lighting equipment rental and sales. •

Atlantic Studios Inc.
201-481-9242
661 North 4th St., Newark, NJ 07107
Hours: 8-5 Mon-Fri
FAX 201-481-9159
• Custom fabrication of scenery, backdrops and fiberglass pieces. Exhibit installations. Ask for
John. •
(See display ad in this section.)

Atlas Scenic Studios Ltd
203-334-2130
46 Brookfield Ave., (Exit 30, CT Tpk.) Bridgeport, CT 06610
Hours: 8-4 Mon-Fri
FAX 203-222-3077
• Full service union shop. Fabrication, rigging. RENTALS •

S-T

BERHNARD-LINK THEATRICAL   212-629-3522
  320 West 37th St., (8-9th Ave.) NYC, NY 10018
  Hours: 10-5 Mon-Fri   FAX 212-629-3525
  • Non-union; consultation, design, fabrication, installation of scenery, lighting, sound, a/v for industrials, fashion shows and theatre. RENTALS •

BESTEK STAGING & LIGHTING   516-225-0707
  218 W. Hoffman Ave., Lindenhurst, NY 11757   (sales • rentals) 516-225-0106
  Hours: 9-5 Mon-Fri   FAX 516-225-0787
  • Non-union shop; platforms,scenery. Equipment for sale and rent. MC/VISA •

CBS TELEVISION SCENIC SHOPS   212-975-2751
  524 West 57th St., (10th-11th Ave.) NYC, NY 10019
  Hours: 9:30-5:30 Mon-Fri   FAX 212-975-7530
  • Full service scenic facility; all phases of scenic construction and painting. •
  (See display ad in this section.)

CENTER LINE STUDIOS, INC.   914-534-7143
  P.O. Box 2 Mill St., Cornwall, NY 12518
  Hours: 8-4:30 Mon-Fri   FAX 914-534-4560

IATSE shop providing scenery for Theater, Ballet, Opera, Dance and Film. Specialty in steel and aluminum fabrication, and the best triple swivel casters in the business. Projects include Broadway shows, regional opera, and international performing arts. Innovative ideas for today's and tomorrow's entertainment projects.

    • Ask for Roger Gray or Paul King. •

DGL ASSOCIATES   212-679-0857
  Moving, call for new business.
  Hours: 10-6 Mon-Fri
Custom fabrication of scenery and props for
Theatre, Industrials, and Commercials.
A full service non union shop.

    • Contact Laura DeGregorio. •

ECTS SCENIC TECHNOLOGY   914-534-3558
  Box 335 Shore Rd., Cornwall-on-Hudson, NY 12520
  Hours: 8-5 Mon-Fri   FAX 914-534-3752
  • Great mechanized effects, set construction and painting, rigging and equipment. Contact Kevin Gailey. RENTALS •
  (See display ad in this section.)

FELLER PRECISION INC.   914-359-9431
  377 Western Hwy., Tappen, NY 10983
  Hours: 9-5 Mon-Fri   FAX 914-359-9530
  • Standard and custom automation, mechanical devices and structures. •

S-T

CUSTOM FABRICATION
FOR

•THEATRE   •TRADE SHOWS
•TELEVISION   •FASHION SHOWS
•FILM   •SPECIAL EVENTS

TEL:212-594-8649   TEL: 210-481-9242
FAX: 212-594-8290   FAX 201-481-9159
547 WEST 27TH STREET   661 NORTH 4TH STREET
NEW YORK, NY 10001   NEWARK, NJ 07107

RED DOT...

QUALITY SCENERY & PROPS

☞THEATRE   ☞DISPLAY

☞VIDEO   ☞PHOTOGRAPHY

☞FILM   ☞INDUSTRIALS

David Bruné   RED DOT SCENIC, INC.   *Tel: 212-675-9041*
Tom Carroll   *601 West 26th Street* *Fax: 212-675-5608*
                 New York, NY 10001

S–T

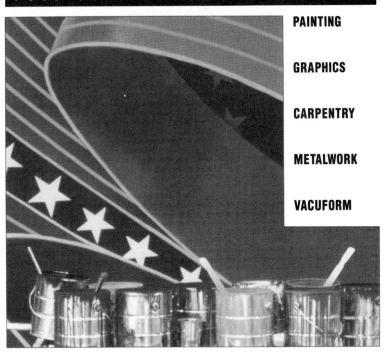

S-T

"I found it in the N.Y. Theatrical Sourcebook."

Design

Standing

Automated Rigging

Scenic Construction

Turntables & Lifts

Ovations

Mechanization

Rental Equipment

Control Systems

Guaranteed!

Consultation Services

Scenic Technologies

From scenic painting to complex mechanical effects, we provide the most comprehensive, single source and cost-effective solutions for any production. We have a reputation for providing the highest quality and widest range of theatrical production services; from scenery construction to engineering. Our Stage Command Systems™ is the world leader in scenic motion control, dazzling audiences night after night in such spectacular productions as *The Phantom of the Opera, Miss Saigon, The Who's Tommy and Les Miserables.* Whatever your project, Scenic Technologies can bring your vision to life. So call us–and be prepared to take a bow!

S–T

SCENIC TECHNOLOGY
Box 335, Shore Rd.
Cornwall-on-Hudson, NY 12520

Tel: 914 534 6700
Fax: 914 534 3752

Broadway Shows
Industrial Shows
Touring Shows
Exhibits
Fashion Shows
Commercials
Film & Television
Special Events
Theatre Renovations
Theme Park Attractions

4170 West Harmon Ave., Ste. 6
Las Vegas, Nevada 89103

Tel: 702 876 8413
Fax: 702 876 2795

FOREPLAY STUDIOS 212-226-0188
33 Greene St., (Grand) NYC, NY 10013
Hours: 8:30-5:30 Mon-Fri • 24hr. calling service. **FAX** 212-226-0387
• Local 52 Union scene shop. Scenery for motion pictures; also print work. Contact Merle Eckert. Some rentals of doors, windows and hardware. •

HUDSON SCENIC STUDIO 718-589-7600
1311 Ryawa Ave., (Lighting Pl.) Bronx, NY 10474
Hours: 8:00-5:30 Mon-Fri **FAX** 718-617-9142
• Union scene shop. Primarily custom work. Speak to Neil Mazzella. •

LINCOLN SCENIC STUDIOS INC. 212-244-2700
560 West 34th St., (10th-11th Ave.) NYC, NY 10001
Hours: 8-5 Mon-Fri **FAX** 212-643-0467

Scenery, design, and construction for
Television, Film and Theatre.
Transportation, Storage and Crews available.

• Full service union scenic shop. •

LYNX PRODUCTIONS 718-784-1414
10-41 47th Ave., L.I.C., NY 11101
Hours: by appt.
• Consultation, construction & design for all media; prop shopping, set dressing, scenic painting. Contact David Raphel or Elizabeth English. •

MULTI FAB, INC. 203-348-9539
520 Canal St., Stamford, CT 06902
Hours: 7:30-4 Mon-Fri • 8:30-3 Sat
• Contact Randy Thomas. •

NETWORK SCENERY RENTAL, INC. 212-244-2700
560 West 34th St., (10th-11th Ave.) NYC, NY 10001
Hours: 8-5 Mon-Fri **FAX** 212-643-0467

WHY BUY WHEN YOU CAN RENT FOR A MERE FRACTION OF THE COST?
The finest quality STOCK SETS, complete with FLOOR PLANS, to RENT and CUSTOMIZED to suit individual set design needs.
TRANSPORT AND CREWS AVAILABLE.

• Part of Lincoln Scenic. Rental only. Call for catalog. •

RAINTREE DESIGNS, LTD. 516-242-7246
44C Jefryn Blvd. West, Deer Park, NY 11729
Hours: 8:30-5:30 Mon-Fri • Sat by appt. **FAX** 516-242-7249
• Scenery, display props, gardenscapes, wholesale to the trade. •

RED DOT SCENIC 212-675-9041
601 West 26th St., (11-12th Ave.) NYC, NY 10001
Hours: 9:30-5:30 Mon-Sat **FAX** 212-675-5608
• Scene shop providing construction and painting. Also prop construction and rental. Contact Tom or David. RENTALS •
(See display ad in this section.)

"I found it in the N.Y. Theatrical Sourcebook."

ROMEO SCENERY STUDIO   914-454-1955
224 Noxon St., (Market St.) Poughkeepsie, NY 12601
Hours: 8-4:30 Mon-Fri   FAX   914-454-2105
• Non-union shop; theatrical, film, industrial work and scenic painting. Delivery service available. RENTALS •

SET II   212-777-2811
37 East 18th St., (B'way-Park Ave. S.) NYC, NY 10003
Hours: 8:30-5 Mon-Fri   FAX   212-979-9852
• Full service shop; photography, video, film, theatre. •

SHOWMAN FABRICATORS, INC.   718-935-9899
29 Imlay St., (Hamilton Ave- Bowne St.) Brooklyn, NY 11231
Hours: 8-5:30 Mon-Fri   FAX   718-855-9823

• Full range scenery shop providing quality service to the
Theatre/Television, Corporate Promotions, Restaurant/Night
Club industries.
• Platform and flat rental.
• Storage space available.
• Specialists in Gusmer Technology spray foam.
• Specialists in Computer Routing.

• Contact Robert Usdin or Michael Cioffi. •

SHOWTECH, INC.   203-854-9336
P.O. Box 210, 20 Belle Ave., (Chestnut-S. Main) So. Norwalk, CT 06854
Hours: 8-5:30 Mon-Fri   FAX   203-854-9485
• Theatrical contractors and consultants; scenery, drops, rigging, props, mechanization. •

STIEGELBAUER ASSOC.   718-624-0835
Bldg 20, Brooklyn Navy Yard, (Cumberland-Flushing) Brooklyn, NY 11205
Hours: 7-2:30 Mon-Fri   FAX   718-624-0844
• Union: TV, theatrical, industrial set construction, also props and special effects; Contact Mike. RENTALS •

THE THEATRE AND EXHIBIT MACHINE   201-345-5564
55 First Ave., Paterson, NJ 07514
Hours: 9-5 Mon-Fri   FAX   201-354-1476

CUSTOM SCENERY FOR ALL INDUSTRIES: Steel and Aluminum
Metalworking, Drapery and Upholstery, Scenic Painting, Carpentry,
Electrical and Mechanical Engineering. RENTALS: 727 & 747
Airplane interiors & DC-10 Cockpit, Backdrops, Platforms,
Columns, Snow Machines, Soft Goods, Track, Doors, Windows,
and more. Free instant pricing on drawings, and storyboards.
Telephone information....

• Scenery construction for theatre, television, industrials and special events. Contact Pat Moeser. •

UNITED THEATRICAL SERVICES INC.   718-589-1121
1311 Ryawa Ave., (Lighting Pl.) Bronx, NY 10474
Hours: 8-6 Mon-Sat   FAX   718-784-2919
• Union scene shop providing construction, painting, and rental of automation equipment including turntables for entertainment and exhibit industries. •

VARIETY SCENIC STUDIOS   718-392-4747
25-19 Borden Ave., (25-27th) L.I.C., NY 11101
Hours: 7-5 Mon-Fri (Office)   FAX   718-784-2919
• Full service union shop. •

S-T

"I found it in the N.Y. Theatrical Sourcebook."

SCISSORS

GINGHER, INC.　　　　　　　　　　　　　　　　　　910-292-6237
　　PO Box 8865, Greensboro, NC 27419　　　　　　800-446-4437
　　Hours: 8:30-5 Mon-Fri　　　　　　　　　　FAX　910-292-6250
　　• Manufacturers of fine scissors and shears; discount to costumers, price list available. •

HOFFRITZ　　　　　　　　　　　　　　　　　　　212-924-7300
　　515 West 24th St. (Main office), (10th-11th Ave.) NYC, NY 10011
　　Hours: 9-5 Mon-Fri

　　Penn Station Terminal, (34th St.-7th-8th Ave.) NYC, NY 10001　212-736-2443
　　Hours: 8-6 Mon-Fri • 9-6 Sat

　　Grand Central Terminal, NYC, NY 10017　　　　　　212-682-7808
　　Hours: 8-7 Mon-Fri • 9-6 Sat

　　331 Madison Ave., (43rd St.) NYC, NY 10017　　　212-697-7344
　　Hours: 8-6 Mon-Fri • 9-6 Sat

　　203 West 57th St., (7th-B'way) NYC, NY 10019　　212-757-3431
　　Hours: 9-6 Mon-Fri • 10-6 Sat
　　• Scissors, Swiss army knives, cutlery, bar supplies; catalog. CREDIT CARDS •

HENRY WESTPFAL & CO.　　　　　　　　　　　　　212-563-5990
　　105 West 30th St., (6th-7th Ave.) NYC, NY 10001
　　Hours: 9-6 Mon-Fri
　　• Scissors, cutlery, and blades sharpened. Also Swiss Army knives. •

WOODLINE/JAPAN WOODWORKER　　　　　　　　　510-521-1810
　　1731 Clement Ave., Almeda, CA 94501　　　　　　800-537-7820
　　Hours: 9-5 Mon-Sat
　　• Importer of Japanese tools, shears, scissors, punches, stencil knives; catalog available.
　　CREDIT CARDS •

SEASHELLS

CAPT. HOOK MARINE ANTIQUES & SHELLS　　　　212-344-2262
　　South Street Seaport, (Fulton St.) NYC, NY 10038
　　Hours: 10-7 Mon-Sat • 11-6 Sun (extended summer hours)
　　• Seashells, marine novelties and some antiques. Phone orders. CREDIT CARDS •

CREST HILLS INDUSTRIES/ ROTH & STEINER　　　212-947-1960
　　519 8th Ave., (35th-36th St.) NYC, NY 10018
　　Hours: 8:30-4 Mon-Fri
　　• Seashells & large selection of light fixtures made from seashells. Wholesale. •

MAXILLA AND MANDIBLE LTD.　　　　　　　　　　212-724-6173
　　451 Columbus Ave., (81st-82nd Street) NYC, NY 10024
　　Hours: 11-7 Mon-Sat • 1-5 Sun　　　　　　　FAX　212-721-1073
　　• Seashells, human and animal skulls, bones, fossils, skins, horns; rental and purchase; cata-
　　log $7.95. Phone orders. CREDIT CARDS •

S-T

SEWING MACHINES & DRESS FORMS

AMERICAN TRADING / D.B.A. SPACESAVER HDWE.   212-691-3666
132 West 23rd St., (6th-7th Ave.) NYC, NY 10011
Hours: 8-8 Mon-Sat   FAX   212-989-7468
• Industrial & domestic machines. Sales and repairs. RENTALS •

BAER FABRICS   800-769-7778
515 East Market, Louisville, KY 40202
Hours: 9-9 Mon • 9-5 Tue-Sat   FAX   502-582-2331
• Most industrial sewing machines sales and service; many types of adjustable dress forms.
Shipping. CREDIT CARDS •

IRVING BERKOWITZ   212-242-2050
33 West 26th St., (B'way-6th) NYC, NY 10010
Hours: 8:30-4:30 Mon-Fri
• Merrow machines, supplies. •

CUTTERS EXCHANGE (DIVISION OF SINGER SEWING)   800-251-2142
4500 Singer Road, Murfreesboro, TN 37133   (tech service center) 615-893-6493
Hours: 8-4:30 Mon-Fri   FAX   615-895-3210
• Complete factory supply for industrial machines and stock attachments. Technical service
center will assist with machine technical problems and applications. $5.95 Catalog. CREDIT
CARDS •

DIAMOND NEEDLE   212-929-2277
159 West 25th St., (6th-7th Ave.) NYC, NY 10001   800-221-5818
Hours: 9-5 Mon-Fri   FAX   212-242-8882
• Industrial and domestic machines, machine feet. CREDIT CARDS •

FOX SEWING MACHINE INC.   212-594-2438
307 West 38th St., (8th-9th Ave.) NYC, NY 10018
Hours: 8-5 Mon-Fri
• Sewing machine sales, rental, repair, new and used dress and coat forms; steam irons, cutting machines, factory supplies. •

GARMENT CENTER SEWING MACHINE INC.   212-279-8774
555 Eighth Ave., (37th-38th St.) NYC, NY 10018
Hours: 8-5 Mon-Fri   FAX   212-564-1436
• Used machines and dress forms, factory supplies. CREDIT CARDS •

GIZMO NOTION CORP   212-477-2773
160 First Ave., (9th-10th St.) NYC, NY 10009
Hours: 10-7 every day
• New & rebuilt sewing machines. Also parts & supplies. Contact Rosa or Hossein. No credit
cards. RENTALS •

HECHT SEWING MACHINE & MOTOR CO. INC.   212-563-5950
304 West 38th Street, (8th-9th Ave.) NYC, NY 10018
Hours: 8-5 Mon-Fri
• Machine sales, service; lamps, oil, and belting. RENTALS •

S. HOFFMAN SEWING CENTER   718-851-1776
55 Thirteenth Ave., (55th-56th St.) Brooklyn, NY 11219   800-246-2086
Hours: 10-7 Mon-Thurs • 10-4 Fri • 10-6 Sun
• Most types; industrial, Merrow; sales and repairs. CREDIT CARDS •

S-T

MERROW SALES CORP.
PO Box 1026, 160 Converse Rd., Marion, MA 02738
Hours: 7:30-4 Mon-Fri
• Merrow machines; service, parts, needles. •

800-431-6677

FAX   516-748-3813

PARK EAST SEWING CENTER
1358 Third Ave., (77th Street) NYC, NY 10021
Hours: 9-6 Mon-Fri • Thurs til 7
• Sales, service, parts, supplies; domestic and industrial. CREDIT CARDS •

212-737-1220
212-737-9189

PARK SLOPE SEWING CENTER
297 Seventh Ave., (7th-8th St.) Brooklyn, NY 11215
Hours: 10-7 Mon-Fri • 10-6 Sat • 12-5 Sun
• Elna sales and service; also fabric, notions and sewing classes. •

718-832-2556

SUPERIOR MODEL FORMS CO.
306 West 38th St., (8th-9th Ave.) NYC, NY 10018
Hours: 8:30-4 Mon-Fri
• Dress forms. •

212-947-3633

FAX   212-947-3752

T & R DISTRIBUTING
P.O. Box 105, 311 N. Wheeler, Grand Island, NE 68802
Hours: 8:30-5:30 Mon-Fri
• Sells Thompson mini-walking foot sewing machines (portable) for heavy jobs and leathers; attachments and parts. Brochure available. CREDIT CARDS •

308-382-8137

FAX   308-382-4587

WOLF FORMS CO., INC.
PO Box 510, 17 Van Nostrand Ave., Englewood, NJ 07631
Hours: 7:30-3:30 Mon-Fri (closed for lunch 12-12:30)
• The very best custom dress forms, full body forms, and the small "student scale" forms . No stock. Large or small orders. •

212-255-4508
201-567-6556

SHELVING & LOCKERS

AAAA METROPOLITAN CO.
165 West 23rd St., (6th-7th Ave.) NYC, NY 10011
Hours: 8-5 Mon-Fri • 9-3 Sat
• Steel shelving, new and used; lockers and office furniture. •

212-741-3385

ABLE STEEL EQUIPMENT CORP.
50-02 23rd St., (50th) L.I.C., NY 11101
Hours: 8-4 Mon-Fri
• New and used lockers, steel shelving. RENTALS •

718-361-9240

ALLRACKS INDUSTRY INC.
489 Ninth Ave., (37th-38th St.) NYC, NY 10018
Hours: 8:30-4:30 Mon-Fri
• Shelving, garment racks. •

212-244-1069

B & Z STEEL
78 Greene St., (Spring-Broome) NYC, NY 10012
Hours: 8:30-4 Mon-Fri
• Steel shelving. •

212-966-5855

S-T

"I found it in the N.Y. Theatrical Sourcebook."

EVANS–FRIEDLAND STEEL PRODUCTIONS   212-532-1011
155 East 29th St., (3rd Ave.) NYC, NY 10016
Hours: 9-5 Mon-Fri
  • Steel shelves, lockers, cabinets, office furniture, parts bins, flammable liquids cabinets, etc;
catalog •

GREAT AMERICAN STEEL EQUIPMENT CORP.   718-417-8900
52-01 Flushing Ave., Maspeth, NY 11378
Hours: 8-5 Mon-Fri   FAX 718-417-4848
  • New and used lockers; steel shelving, store gondolas, toilet partitions. Speak to Paul or
Herb. RENTALS •

M. LEVIN INC.   212-674-3579
269 Broadway, (Houston) NYC, NY 10002
Hours: 9-5 Mon-Fri
  • Store fixtures, display cases, gondolas. •

SHIPPING

See also **MOVING, TRANSPORT, & STORAGE.**

DHL WORLDWIDE COURIER EXPRESS   800-225-5345
2 World Trade Center, NYC, NY 10048
Hours: 8-5:30 Mon-Fri
  • Overnight domestic and worldwide delivery; 3-day Service worldwide also available. •

EMERY WORLDWIDE   800-443-6379
184-54 149th Ave., (184th St.) Springfield Garden, NY 11413
Hours: 5:30-midnight Mon-Fri
  • Fast service by air. •

FEDERAL EXPRESS   800-238-5365
560 West 42nd St., (10th-11th Ave.) NYC, NY 10036
Hours: 9-9 Mon-Fri • 9-6 Sat (call for latest pickup in your area)
  • Overnight and 2 day delivery nationwide; international service; door to door service or will
accept packages and hold for pickup at offices. Over 30 locations in NYC; free catalog; 150 lb.
limit, maximum size; 130" girth or 108" long. CREDIT CARDS •

GREYHOUND PACKAGE SERVICE   212-971-6331
Port Authority Bus Terminal, (9th Ave. & 41st St.) NYC, NY 10036
Hours: 6:30am-6:30pm Mon-Fri
  • Inexpensive shipping by bus; check for size limitations. •

PREFERRED AIR FREIGHT, INC.   201-624-2520
Hanger 15, Newark Airport, Newark, NJ 07114   718-527-6002
Hours: 24 hours every day
  • Worldwide shipping; highly recommended. •

RADIX GROUP INTERNATIONAL/FRIEDMAN& SLATER   718-917-4800
Cargo Plaza, Bldg. 75, JFK Int'l Airport, N. Hanger Rd., Jamaica, NY 11430
Hours: 8:30-5 Mon-Fri
  • International service. •

S-T

"I found it in the N.Y. Theatrical Sourcebook."   **399**

SKY COURIER   212-279-4687
    1270 Broadway, Rm. 708, (32nd-33rd St.) NYC, NY 10001   800-336-3344
    Hours: 24 Hours
      • Domestic and international service; no size or weight limitation; reliable; call for pickup. •

UNITED PARCEL SERVICE   212-695-7500
    601 West 43rd St., (11th Ave.) NYC, NY 10036   914-592-1700
    Hours: 8am-9:30pm Mon-Fri • pickups; 7:30am-8 pm Mon-Fri
      • Overnight, 2-day, or guaranteed 5 day service. •

SHOE ALTERATION, REPAIR & DRESSINGS

ANANI BROTHERS   212-869-5335
    34 West 46th St., (5th-6th Ave.) NYC, NY 10036
    Hours: 9-6 Mon-Fri
      • Shoe alteration, repair; also orthopedic shoes. •

COWBOY BOOT HOSPITAL   212-941-9532
    4 Prince St., (Bowery-Elizabeth) NYC, NY 10012
    Hours: 9-6 Mon-Fri • 11-3 Sat
      • Fabulous custom and one-of-a-kind cowboy boots to your design or theirs. Great vintage
    designs a la Roy Rogers. Fast shoe repair. Very friendly and helpful. See Jim Babchak, boot-
    maker. •

DRAGO SHOE REPAIR   212-475-1296
    125 Rivington St., (Essex) NYC, NY 10002
    Hours: 8-6 Mon-Fri • 9-5 Sat

    195 Sixth Ave., (Charlton St.) NYC, NY 10002   212-924-7199
    Hours: 7:30-5:30 Mon-Fri • 9-4 Sat

    Eighth Ave. & 42nd St., (Port Authority) NYC, NY 10036   212-947-8946
    Hours: 7-6 Mon-Fri

    230 Park Ave., (45th St) NYC, NY 10017   212-599-9204
    Hours: 7-5:15 Mon-Fri

    644 Lexington Ave., (54th-55th St.) NYC, NY 10022   212-308-8171
    Hours: 7:30-6 Mon-Fri • 9-4:45 Sat

    308 West 57th St., (8th Ave.) NYC, NY 10019   212-757-5514
    Hours: 8-6 Mon-Fri • 8:30-6 Sat

    2214 Broadway, (79th St.) NYC, NY 10024   212-799-0559
    Hours: 8-6 Mon-Sat

    2348 Broadway, (86th St.) NYC, NY 10024   212-799-1940
    Hours: 8-5:45 Mon-Fri • 8:30 -5:30 Sat
      • Shoe repairs and alterations; supplies. •

HOLLYWOOD SHOE SERVICE   212-239-8625
    78 West 36th St., (6th Ave.) NYC, NY 10018
    Hours: 7:30-5:45 Mon-Fri
      • Shoe repair and dressings. •

S-T

KAUFMAN   212-777-1700
346 Lafayette St., (Houston-Bleeker St.) NYC, NY 10012
Hours: 6:30-2 Mon-Fri   FAX 212-777-1747
• Shoe making & repair supplies; crepe soles, dance rubber, sole materials, leather, barge, Magix, elastic & lacings. MC/VISA •

PETE KTENAS   212-247-2130
1650 Broadway, 2nd Fl., (entrance on 51st St.) NYC, NY 10019
Hours: 9:30-5:45 Mon-Fri • 9:30-4:30 Sat
• This is Pete's who puts rubber on all dance shoes and even work boots; also taps and heel braces; now on premises of Capezio Dance Theatre Shop. •

PECK & GOODIE SKATE & SHOE SPECIALISTS   212-246-6123
919 Eighth Ave., (54th-55th St.) NYC, NY 10019
Hours: 10-6 Mon-Fri • 12-5 Sat   FAX 212-807-6115

1414 Second Ave., (73rd-74th St.) 10021   212-249-2176
Hours: 11-7 Mon-Fri • 10-6 Sat • 12-6 Sun
• Repairs and prep of all types of theatrical shoes: taps, dance rubbers, heel braces. Sale and repair of ice and roller skates and roller blades. Best selection of skates for professional athletes and beginners. •

PERFECT 10 SHOE REPAIR   212-974-9499
855 Ninth Ave., (55th-56th St.) NYC, NY 10019
Hours: 7-7 Mon-Sat.
• Quality shoe repair, all types of leather work, free pick-up and delivery; speak to Alexandro Lopez. •

SHOES & BOOTS

A & R ENTERPRISES   212-567-7289
P.O. Box 47, Ft. George Station, NY 10040
Hours: 9:30-6 Mon-Sat
• Imported dance shoes for jazz, ballroom and ballet. •

AMBASSADOR SPAT CO.   215-739-3134
2400 Jasper St., Philadelphia, PA 19125
Hours: 8-3 Mon-Fri
• Spats in many styles. •

J.C. BANKS THEATRICAL & CUSTOM FOOTWEAR   212-529-1125
890 Broadway, 5th Fl., (19th St.) NYC, NY 10003
Hours: 9-5 Mon-Fri
• Excellent work, especially on one-of-a-kind items; see Jacob Citerer. •

BLOOM SHOE STORE   212-995-0046
738 Broadway, (Astor Pl.) NYC, NY 10003
Hours: 10:30-8 Mon-Sat • 12-6:45 Sun
• Men's and women's leather shoes, sandals, cowboy boots and the traditional. CREDIT CARDS •

S-T

CAPEZIO DANCE-THEATRE SHOP
212-245-2130
1650 Broadway, 2nd Fl., (Entrance on 51st) NYC, NY 10019
Hours: 9:30-6:30 Mon-Fri (Thurs till 7) • 9:30-6 Sat   FAX   212-757-7635
• Can accommodate stock and special order shoes. Very helpful and knowledgeable. Ask for David. •
(See display ad under CLOTHING RENTAL & PURCHASE; DANCEWEAR.)

CATSKILL MOUNTAIN MOCCASINS
914-679-7302
21 Tinker St., P. O. Box 294, Woodstock, NY 12498
Hours: 9-9 every day   FAX   914-679-7094
• Custom footwear made of leather or exotic skins, ankle to knee high, any period or design. Will travel for fittings. CREDIT CARDS •

CHURCH'S ENGLISH SHOES LTD.
212-755-4313
428 Madison Ave., (48th-49th St.) NYC, NY 10017
Hours: 8:30-6:30 Mon-Fri • 9-6 Sat.
• High-quality men's dress and sport shoes, classic styles. Phone and mail orders. CREDIT CARDS •

COWBOY BOOT HOSPITAL
212-941-9532
4 Prince St., (Bowery-Elizabeth) NYC, NY 10012
Hours: 9-6 Mon-Fri • 11-3 Sat
• Fabulous custom and one-of-a-kind cowboy boots to your design or theirs. Great vintage designs a la Roy Rogers. Fast shoe repair. Very friendly and helpful. See Jim Babchak, boot-maker. •

PASQUALE DIFABRIZIO
213-655-5248
8216 West Third St., Los Angeles, CA 90048
Hours: 8-5 Mon-Fri • 8-12 Sat   FAX   213-655-1321
• Custom boots & shoes, also belts & bags. No credit cards. •

DORNAN UNIFORMS
212-247-0937
653 Eleventh. Ave., 2nd Fl., (47-48th St.) NYC, NY 10036   800-223-0363
Hours: 8:30-4 Mon-Fri (Thurs till 6)   FAX   212-956-7672
• Footwear for uniformed personnel. No rentals. Phone orders and shipping. CREDIT CARDS •

FAYVA SHOE STORES
212-228-8025
387 First Ave., (22nd-23rd St.) NYC, NY 10010
Hours: 9:30-7 Mon-Sat • 11-5 Sun

18-20 East 14th St., (5th.-Univ. Pl.) NYC, NY 10003   212-691-5997
Hours: 10-7 Mon-Sat • 12-5 Sun

2230 Broadway, (79th-80th St.) NYC, NY 10024   212-877-5535
Hours: 10-7 Mon-Sat • 12-5 Sun

1954 Third Ave., (107th-108th St.) NYC, NY 10029   212-410-5526
Hours: 10-7 Mon-Sat • 12-5 Sun
• Inexpensive shoes; will refund for returned items. CREDIT CARDS •

B. E. FLESH
406-685-3420
208 Broadway, Pony, MT 59747
Hours: 10-7 Tue- Fri • 10-5 Sat
• Leather accessories for theatrical purposes; repairs and alterations; specializes in applica-tion of taps; also makes boot and shoe to lasts. •

S-T

FOOT SAVER BLDG. CORP   212-736-9081
  38 West 34th St., (5th-6th Ave.) NYC, NY 10001
  Hours: 9:30-7 Mon-Fri • 9:30-6 Tues, Wed. Sat • 9:30-8 Thurs
  • Shoes up to size 12, all widths and half sizes. Phone orders and shipping available. CREDIT
  CARDS •

PETER FOX SHOES   212-874-6399
  378 Amsterdam Ave., (78th St.) NYC, NY 10024
  105 Thompson St., (Spring-Prince St.) NYC, NY 10012   212-431-6359
  Hours: 11-7 Mon-Sat • 12-5:30 Sun

  806 Madison, (76th-68th St.) NYC, NY 10021   212-744-8340
  Hours: 10-6 Mon-Sat (till 7 Thurs) • 12-5 Sun
  • Superb Italian made high top lace-up boots with Louis heel, satin covered. CREDIT
  CARDS. •

FREED OF LONDON LTD.   212-489-1055
  922 Seventh Ave., (58th Street) NYC, NY 10019
  Hours: 10-6 Mon-Sat   FAX   212-262-0041
  • Specializes in dance shoes, also makes custom period shoes. •

GIORDANO'S   212-688-7195
  1118 First Ave., (61st-62nd St.) NYC, NY 10021
  Hours: 11-7 Mon-Fri • 11-6 Sat
  • Small size women's shoes; 4-6M & 5 1/2-6 1/2AA. •

GREAT NORTHERN BOOT CO.   406-862-9129
  185 Reservoir Rd., Whitefish, Mt. 59937
  Hours: by appt. (June-Aug)
  • Shoes & boots. •

THE GREAT WESTERN BOOT CO.   317-848-1020
  96th & Keystone Ave., Indianapolis, IN 46240
  Hours: 10-9 Mon-Sat • 11-6 Sun
  • Western wear; discount prices. •

HARRY'S   212-874-2035
  2299 Broadway, (corner of 83rd St.) NYC, NY 10024
  Hours: 10-6: 45 Mon-Sat • 12-5:30 Sun   FAX   212-874-7616
  • Large selection of men's & women's contemporary footwear. Some lace-up boots. CREDIT
  CARDS •

S-T

JOEL ASSOCIATES – ON STAGE   201-377-6466
  PO Box 434, Madison, NJ 07940
  Hours: by appt.
  • Gamba shoes, custom period and dance shoes; good prices; will come to you for fittings.
  Contact Mirth Lovingham. •

KAUFMAN'S ARMY AND NAVY   212-757-5670
  319 West 42nd St., (8th-9th Ave.) NYC, NY 10036
  Hours: 10-6 Mon-Sat • Thurs till 7
  • Good selection of military and work boots. Also rentals and sales of military uniforms, equip-
  ment and related props. •
  (See display ad under CLOTHING RENTAL & PURCHASE; UNIFORMS.)

KULYK THEATRICAL FOOTWEAR   212-674-0414
  80 East 7th St., (1st-2nd Ave.) NYC, NY 10003
  Hours: by appt.
  • Custom made boots. •

LEE'S MARDI GRAS ENTERPRISES INC.   212-645-1888
400 West 14th St., 3rd Fl., (9th Ave.) NYC, NY 10003
Hours: 11:30-6:30 Mon-Sat
• Ladies shoes for men; complete line of ladies apparel for men; also wigs and make-up. CREDIT CARDS •

FREDERICK LONGTIN/HANDMADE SHOES   902-532-2233
Box 141, Granville Ferry, Nova Scotia, CAN BOS 1KO
Hours: 10-6 Mon-Fri • or by appt.
• Custom boots, shoes, sandals, dance footwear for theatre; contact Fred. Federal Express next day shipping. •

LORD JOHN BOOTERY   212-719-1552
428 Third Ave., (29th-30th St.) NYC, NY 10016
Hours: 10-7 Mon-Fri • 10-6 Sat

213 E. 59th St., (2nd-3rd Ave.) NYC, NY 10022   212-759-9241
Hours: 9-7 Mon-Sat • 12-6 Sun
• Cowboy boots, men's dress boots (high), men's & women's boots and dress shoes. CREDIT CARDS •

McCREEDY & SCHREIBER BOOTS & SHOES   212-719-1552
37 West 46th St., (5th-6th Ave.) NYC, NY 10036
Hours: 9-7 Mon-Sat

213 East 59th St., (2nd-3rd Ave.) NYC, NY 10022
Hours: 9-7 Mon-Sat • 12-6 Sun
• High quality men's shoes and boots; good ankle lace-ups for period shoes; 19th-20th century. Mail and phone orders accepted. CREDIT CARDS •

LIZ McGARRITY   212-533-2386
230 East 12th St., #9J, (2nd-3rd Ave.) NYC, NY 10003
Hours: 9-6 Mon-Sat
• Custom made shoes for people or puppets. All periods & styles. •

MONTANA LEATHERWORKS LTD.   212-431-4015
47 Greene St., (Grand-Broome) NYC, NY 10003
Hours: 10-6 Mon-Fri (Sept-May)

Theatrical footwear and leather accessories. Period boots and shoes for Theatre, Dance, Opera and Film. Custom work from your designs and measurements.

• Contact Sharlot Battin. Winter location in NYC, summers in Montana. •

O.K. UNIFORM CO.   212-966-1984
507 Broadway, (Spring-Broome St.) NYC, NY 10012   212-966-4733
Hours: 9:30-5:30 Mon-Thurs • 9:30-call Fri • 11:30-4:30 Sun   **FAX** 212-226-6668
• Sales only. Selection of men's and women's white nurses shoes and sturdy black work shoes. •
(See display ad under CLOTHING RENTAL & PURCHASE; UNIFORMS.)

ODDS COSTUME RENTAL   212-268-6227
231 West 29th St., Rm 304, (7th-8th Ave.) NYC, NY 10001
Hours: 9:30-5 Mon-Fri • Sat by appt.
• Men's and women's, vintage through modern. Also construction, cowboy and novelty boots.
Rental only. •
(See display ad under COSTUME RENTAL & CONSTRUCTION.)

REPETTO   212-582-3900
30 Lincoln Plaza, (62nd-63rd on Broadway) NYC, NY 10023
Hours: 12-6 Mon-Thur • 11-7 Fri & Sat • (Office 9-6 Mon-Fri)   FAX   212-582-5545
• Complete line of dance shoes, theatrical footwear, and dancewear for children and adults.
Phone orders taken. CREDIT CARDS •

JOHN SHRADER, BOOTMAKER   415-459-6576
1508 San Anselmo Ave., San Anselmo, CA 94960
Hours: 8-6 Mon-Sat
• Specializing in custom-made theatrical boots (especially "bucket boots") and period
footwear; flyer available. No credit cards. •

TALL SIZE SHOES   212-736-2060
3 West 35th St., (5th-6th Ave.) NYC, NY 10001
Hours: 9:30-6 Mon-Sat • Thurs till 7
• Women's large sizes. Mail and phone orders ok. Personal checks. CREDIT CARDS •

SIGNS & LETTERS

See also **FLAGS & BANNERS**
See also **NEON**
See also **SILKSCREENING**

ABE SIGN CO. INC.   212-594-6171
44 East 29th St., (Madison-Park Ave. So.) NYC, NY 10016
Hours: 9-5 Mon-Fri   FAX   212-779-9299
• Manufacturer of interior and exterior signage: banners, vinyl, silkscreening. CREDIT
CARDS •

ACTIVE SIGNS   212-564-9696
122 West 29th St., (6th-7th Ave.) NYC, NY 10001
Hours: 9-5:30 Mon-Fri
• All types: handpainted and vinyl letters, logos; speak to Frank Soldo; rush service, works
with film industry. •

ADMIRAL ENGRAVING & ETCHING, LTD.   212-924-3400
555 West 25th St., (10th-11th Ave.) NYC, NY 10001
Hours: 9-5 Mon-Fri   FAX   212-924-3589
• Etching, engraving, plaques, photo metal, vinyl letters. •

ALPHA ENGRAVING CO.   212-247-5266
254 West 51 St., (8th Ave.-B'way) NYC, NY 10019
Hours: 9-5:30 Mon-Fri
• Metal and plastic engraved signs, also name tags. •

S-T

S-T

We specialize in rush orders –
especially for the motion picture &
commercial industries.

1000's of signs in stock to choose from.
Letters sold prespaced, ready to apply or as a
finished sign. Our state-of-the-art
equipment makes any design easy to create.

Removable vinyl lettering & graphics are
computer cut for precision & sizing.
Engraving & silkscreening also available.

- magnetic removable signs
- door & window signs & lettering
- lettering for vans & trucks

- decals, nameplates, banners
- paper, acrylic & aluminum signs
- over 300 typefaces to choose from
- more than 200 colors (opaque,
  translucent, fluorescent, metallic,
  reflective, mirror or frosted)

Call for a free phone estimate:
(212) 243-8521
Outside NY 1-800-394-3433

Or, stop in to our shop:
54 West 21st St. (5th-6th) 2nd Fl.,
New York, NY 10010.
FAX: (212) 243-6457.

Specialty Signs. Especially Fast.
Specializing in the Motion Picture Industry.

"I found it in the N.Y. Theatrical Sourcebook."

ANCIENT ART   212-662-2571
   336 West 95th St., (Riverside) NYC, NY 10025
   Hours: by appt.
   • Gold leaf lettering and sign painting. •

ARTKRAFT STRAUSS SIGN CORP   212-265-5155
   830 Twelfth Ave., (57th St.) NYC, NY 10019
   Hours: 9-5 Mon-Fri   FAX   212-265-9436
   • Custom signs; metal, wood, neon, computerized. They do many of the large displays in Time
   Square. Will do the small job too. •

BIG APPLE SIGN CORP.   212-575-0706
   247 West 35th St., (7th-8th Ave.) NYC, NY 10001
   Hours: 8:30-6 Mon-Fri • 10-5 Sat   FAX   212-629-4954
   • Full service sign company; 24 hour service available. Banners, vinyl, engraving. CREDIT
   CARDS •

BRUSHFIRE STUDIO   908-220-1472
   155 Joyce Kilmer Ave., New Brunswick, NJ 08901
   Hours: by appt.
   • Union-made signs, banners and murals, lettering, airbrush and pictorials; contact Mike
   Alewitz. •

BULLETIN BOARDS & DIRECTORY PRODUCTS, INC.   914-248-8008
   2986 Navajo St., Yorktown Heights, NY 10598
   Hours: 8-5 Mon-Fri   FAX   914-248-5150
   • Mfg. of directory boards; also engraved nameplates, vinyl letters, chalkboards, etc. 84 page
   catalog available; contact Jerry Martin. •

NICK CHEFFO SIGNS   718-769-0034
   2317 East 21st St., (Gravesend Neck Rd.-Ave. W) Brooklyn, NY 11229
   Hours: 9-5 Mon-Fri
   • Wood and metal signs, wooden letters. •

DE–SIGN LETTERS   212-673-6211
   15 East 18th St., (5th-B'way) NYC, NY 10003
   Hours: 9-4 Mon-Fri
   • Custom cut letters, logos, and designs as per customer order. •

ELECTRA DISPLAYS   516-585-5659
   90 Remington Blvd., Ronkonkoma, NY 11779   212-420-1188
   Hours: 9-5 Mon-Fri
   • Electric signs and letters; mirror balls, projecting kaleidoscopes. •

EMPTYBIRDCAGE DESIGN STUDIO   516-321-7521
   PO Box 424, Babylon, NY 11702
   Hours: by appt.
   • Graphic and editorial design, signage, computer typesetting and illustration. Contact Annette
   or T.J. •

EYE CATCHERS   310-834-7171
   24424 Main St., Suite 607, Carson, CA 90745
   Hours: 8-5 Mon-Fri Mon-Fri   FAX   310-834-7005
   • Sells Solaray (the sparkly discs used on outdoor ads), holograph and sparkle vinyl. Catalog
   and samples. See John Turton. •

S–T

S-T

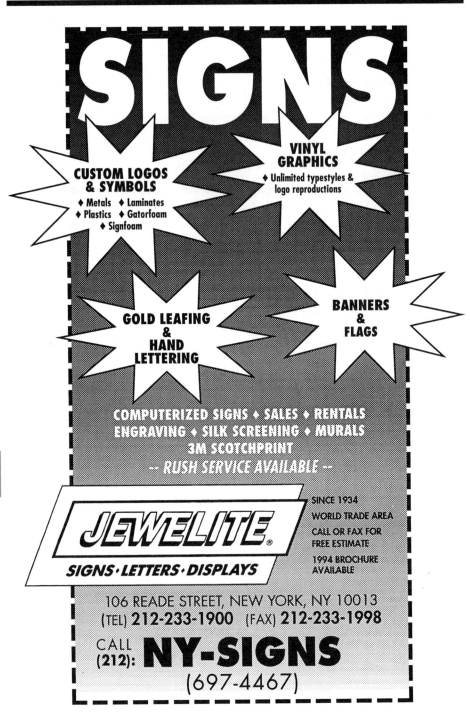

SIGNS

VINYL GRAPHICS
♦ Unlimited typestyles & logo reproductions

CUSTOM LOGOS & SYMBOLS
♦ Metals   ♦ Laminates
♦ Plastics   ♦ Gatorfoam
♦ Signfoam

GOLD LEAFING & HAND LETTERING

BANNERS & FLAGS

**COMPUTERIZED SIGNS ♦ SALES ♦ RENTALS
ENGRAVING ♦ SILK SCREENING ♦ MURALS
3M SCOTCHPRINT
-- RUSH SERVICE AVAILABLE --**

JEWELITE®

SIGNS · LETTERS · DISPLAYS

SINCE 1934
WORLD TRADE AREA
CALL OR FAX FOR
FREE ESTIMATE
1994 BROCHURE
AVAILABLE

106 READE STREET, NEW YORK, NY 10013
(TEL) **212-233-1900**   (FAX) **212-233-1998**

CALL
(212): **NY-SIGNS**
(697-4467)

"I found it in the N.Y. Theatrical Sourcebook."

JEWELITE SIGNS & LETTERS, INC.
106 Reade St., (Hudson-Greenwich St.) NYC, NY 10013
Hours: 24 hours every day

212-NY-SIGNS
212-233-1900
FAX 212-233-1998

- Plastic, wood, brass, showcards, dimensional letters, computerized signs (rental available).
- Banners, vinyl graphics, hand lettering, gold leafing, silkscreening, engraving.
- Custom logos.
- 24 hours - 7 days a week.
- *"WE'LL DO ANYTHING, ANYTIME!"*

• Contact Bobby or Dana Bank. Reliable. •
(See display ad in this section.)

LET THERE BE NEON, INC.
38 White St., (Church-B'way) NYC, NY 10013
Hours: 9:30-5:30 Mon-Fri by appt.
• Custom and stock neon; speak to Rudi. RENTALS •

212-226-4883

FAX 212-431-6731

LETTER CRAFT INC.
280 Midland Ave., Bldg. M, Saddlebrook, NJ 07662
Hours: 8-5 Mon-Fri
• Stock letters in plastic. Also does custom work. •

212-582-7799
201-794-3630

MAIL ORDER PLASTICS INC.
56 Lispenard St., (B'way-Church) NYC, NY 10013
Hours: 9-5 Mon-Fri • 9-4 Sat
• Plastic letters in stock. •

212-226-7308

BERNARD MAISNER CALLIGRAPHY AND HAND-LETTERING STUDIOS
41 Bleeker St., (Lafayette) NYC, NY 10001
Hours: 9-6 Mon-Fri
• Creative hand-lettering and calligraphy, also professional hand model for live writing for TV and film. •
(See display ad in this section.)

212-477-6776

MANHATTAN NEON SIGN CORP.
335 West 38th St., (8th-9th Ave.) NYC, NY 10018
Hours: 8-4 Mon-Fri • by appt.

212-714-0430

FAX 212-947-3906

- Metal - Plexiglas illuminated displays.
- Moving - Message display sales / rentals.
- We design, fabricate and install.
- Rush orders are welcome.
QUALITY AND SERVICE ARE #1.

• Custom & stock neon. Contact Pat or Marilyn Tomasso. RENTALS •

MERCURY NEON SIGNS / FRIEDMAN SIGNS
157 Second Ave., 2nd Fl., (9th-10th St.) NYC, NY 10003
Hours: 8:30-5 Mon-Fri • or by appt.
• Neon signs and lighting fixtures; custom and rental. •

212-473-6366

FAX 212-979-8322

MIDTOWN NEON SIGN CORP.
550 West 30th St., (10th-11th Ave.) NYC, NY 10001
Hours: by appt.
• Stock and custom neon, name brand and generic. RENTALS •

212-736-3838

S-T

SCOTT SIGN SYSTEM   800-237-9447
  PO Box 1047, Tallevast, FL. 34270
  Hours: 8-6 Mon-Fri
   • Plexiglas, plastic foam, gypsum letters in many styles and thicknesses, custom repro of
  logos, graphics, and ABC's. Catalog. CREDIT CARDS •

SIGNCAST   212-966-4286
  480 Canal St., (Hudson) NYC, NY 10013
  Hours: 9-5 Mon-Fri
   • Custom signs and graphics. •

SPECIALTY SIGNS CO. INC.   212-243-8521
  54 West 21st St., 2nd Fl., (5th-6th Ave.) NYC, NY 10010   800-394-3433
  Hours: 8:30-5 Mon-Fri   FAX   212-243-6457
   • Stock signs and custom work; name tags; rush orders. •
  (See display ad in this section.)

SUPER NEON LIGHTS CO.   718-236-5667
  7813 16th Ave., (78th St.) Brooklyn, NY 11214
  Hours: 8-4:45 Mon-Fri
   • Neon signs; good work; good prices. •

SWEETBRYAR CALLIGRAPHICS   212-233-6682
  124 East Broadway, (Pike-Essex) NYC, NY 10002
  Hours: 10-7 Mon-Sat • or by appt.   FAX   212-233-6682
   • Calligraphy, sign painting, air brush, hand lettering on many types of surfaces. Will do location work. •

SILKSCREENING

See also **SIGNS & LETTERS**
For supplies, see **ARTISTS MATERIALS**

AMBASSADOR ARTS   212-243-4290
  601 West 26th St., 8th Fl., (11th-12th) NYC, NY 10001
  Hours: 9-5 Mon-Fri
   • Does large screening art and signs on plexi, wood, etc. •

ARTISAN / SILKSCREEN   212-807-9660
  122 West 26th St., (6th-7th Ave.) NYC, NY 10001
  Hours: 9-5 Mon-Thurs • 9-3 Fri
   • Custom silkscreening, your t-shirts, jackets, etc. or theirs; also posters, signs, etc; catalog available. •

FABRIC EFFECTS   212-255-5225
  20 West 20th St., 5th Fl., (5th-6th Ave.) NYC, NY 10011
  Hours: 9-5 Mon-Fri • or by appt.   FAX   212-255-3077

Specializing in silkscreening, dyeing and hand painting.
Custom orders and small production.
Extensive experience in Theatre, Film, and Fashion.

   • Dyeing, silkscreening, hand painting - all kinds of fabric coloring - done by three of NY's top
  textile artisans. •
  (See display ad under COSTUME CRAFTSPEOPLE & MILLINERY.)

MARTIN IZQUIERDO STUDIO
118 West 22nd St. 9th Fl., (6th-7th Ave.) NYC, NY 10011
Hours: 9-6 Mon-Fri • weekends by appt.

212-807-9757

FAX   212-366-5249

CUSTOM SILKSCREENING AND HAND PAINTED
DESIGNS ON T-SHIRTS, YARDAGE, PLEXI, WOOD, ETC.
RUSH SERVICE AVAILABLE.

• Custom work; full service costume and prop shop. •
(See display ad under COSTUME RENTAL & CONSTRUCTION.)

JANUS SCREEN GRAPHICS STUDIO
580 Eighth Ave., (38th-39th St.) NYC, NY 10018
Hours: 9-5 Mon-Fri
• High quality custom silkscreening for all needs. •

212-869-0386

FAX   212-819-1938

JEWELITE SIGNS & LETTERS INC.
106 Reade St., (Hudson-Greenwich St.) NYC, NY 10013
Hours: 24 hours every day
• Silkscreening, custom signs and letters. Contact Bobby or Dana Bank. •
(See display ad under SIGNS & LETTERS.)

212-NY-SIGNS
212-233-1900
FAX   212-233-1998

PROFESSIONAL PROMOTION SERVICES
270 West 38th St., Rm. 2001, (7th-8 Ave.) NYC, NY 10013
Hours: 8-6 Mon-Fri
• Computer silkscreening and embroidery on all kinds of varsity jackets, baseball caps, and other premium items. Specializes in B'way show and crew jackets. •

212-239-7211

FAX   212-239-7318

STANDARD SCREEN SUPPLY CO.
480 Canal, (Hudson St.) NYC, NY 10013
Hours: 8-4:30 Mon-Fri

212-925-6800

FAX   212-334-8349

• Silkscreen inks, emulsions, supplies
• Custom made screens
• Fabric inks
• Water and solvent based systems
• Professional consultations

• Wholesale/retail sales; catalog available. Very helpful. •

S-T

SILVER ITEMS

See also **ANTIQUES: ALL HEADINGS**

CENTRAL PROPERTIES OF 49TH STREET
212-265-7767
514 West 49th St., (10th Ave.) NYC, NY 10019
Hours: 8-5 Mon-Fri

FAX 212-582-3746

Beautiful selection from the most respected names.
Silverware, decorative candelabra and tea sets,
chafing dishes and tabletop accessories.

CENTRAL PROPERTIES

• Large selection of table top and decorative items. •
(See display ad under PROP RENTAL HOUSES.)

COLUMBIA HOME DECOR
212-725-5250
493 3rd Ave., (33rd-34th St.) NYC, NY 10016
Hours: 9:30-6 Mon-Fri • Thrus til 8 • 10-6 Sat • 11-5 Sun
• Silversmiths. Brass and silver plating. See Matthew. •

ECLECTIC/ENCORE PROPERTIES
212-645-8880
620 West 26th St., 4th Fl., (11th-12th Ave.) NYC, NY 10001
Hours: 9-5 Mon-Fri • or by appt.   FAX   212-243-6508
• 18th, 19th & 20th Century furniture, accessories, and art. Vast collection of period & character furniture 1920's-1970's. Call Regina or Barry. •
(See display ad under PROP RENTAL HOUSES)

MICHAEL C. FINA CO.
212-869-5050
3 West 47th St., (5th-6th Ave.) NYC, NY 10036
Hours: 9:30-6 Mon-Fri • (Thurs till 7) • 10:30-6 Sat
• Silver, silverware, china, jewelry; good prices; E Mail, catalog. CREDIT CARDS •

FORTUNOFF
212-758-6660
681 Fifth Ave., (53rd-54th St.) NYC, NY 10022
Hours: 10-6 Mon-Sat • (Thurs till 8)
• Reasonably priced silver items. Some antiques. Phone orders. CREDIT CARDS •

GRAND STERLING CO. INC
212-674-6450
345 Grand St., (Essex-Ludlow) NYC, NY 10002
Hours: 10:30-6 Sun-Thurs • Closed Fri & Sat   FAX   212-979-0578
• Wide selection of sterling items of all kinds. CREDIT CARDS •

JEAN'S SILVERSMITHS
212-575-0723
16 West 45th St., (5th Ave.) NYC, NY 10036
Hours: 9:30-4:45 Mon-Thrus • 9:30-3:45   FAX   212-921-0991
• Large selection of tea sets, candelabras, etc; expensive. Go early in the day. RENTALS
CREDIT CARDS •

MIRMO
718-837-5824
1644 60th St., (16th-17th Ave.) Brooklyn, NY 11204
Hours: 9-9 Mon-Thurs • 9-4 Fri • Sun by appt.   FAX   718-236-7371
• Sterling silver table top items, vases, tea sets, trophies, silverware, etc. RENTALS •

PROPS FOR TODAY   212-206-0330
121 West 19th St. Reception 3rd Fl., (6th-7th Ave.) NYC, NY 10011
Hours: 8:30-5 Mon-Fri   FAX   212-924-0450
• Full service prop rental house. Large selection of serving pieces and flatware from all periods. •
(See display ad under PROP RENTAL HOUSES.)

REGENCY SERVICE CART   718-855-8304
337-361 Carroll St., (Hoyt-Bond) Brooklyn, NY 11231
Hours: 7-5 Mon-Fri
• Silver plated domes and desert carts, room service carts: catalog. Ask for Jack Abbate. •

SERVICE PARTY-RENTAL CO.   212-288-7384
152 E. 74th St., (Lex-3rd Ave.) NYC, NY 10021
Hours: 9-5 Mon-Fri   FAX   212-288-7042
• Silverware, candelabras, chafing dishes, coffee pots, etc. RENTALS CREDIT CARDS •

SMOKING SUPPLIES

ARNOLD TOBACCO SHOP   212-697-1477
323 Madison Ave., (42-43 St.) NYC, NY 10017
Hours: 8:30-5:30 Mon-Fri • 9:30-5 Sat
• Pipes, tobacco, cigars, lighters, pipe repairs. CREDIT CARDS •

BARCLAY-REX PIPE SHOP   212-692-9680
70 East 42nd St., (Park Ave.) NYC, NY 10165
Hours: 8-6:30 Mon-Fri • 10-5:30 Sat

7 Maiden Lane, (Broadway) NYC, NY 10038   212-962-3355
Hours: 8-6 Mon-Fri
• Pipes, cigars, tobacco, humidors, repairs. CREDIT CARDS •

CONNOISSEUR PIPE SHOP   212-247-6054
1285 Sixth Ave. Concourse level, (51st St.) NYC, NY 10019
Hours: 8-6 Mon-Fri
• Briar, Meerschaum, custom pipes and repairs, pouches, accessories. CREDIT CARDS •

DE LA CONCHA   212-757-3167
1390 Sixth Ave., (56th-57th St.) NYC, NY 10019
Hours: 8:30-8:30 Mon-Fri • 10-8 Sat
• Cigars, cigarettes, pipes, tobacco; imported and domestic. •

OLIVERIO DIAZ   212-475-7080
866 Broadway, (17th-18th St.) NYC, NY 10003
Hours: 8:30-5:30 Mon-Fri • 8:30-2 Sat
• Cigars, cigarettes, tobacco. •

ALFRED DUNHILL OF LONDON   212-753-9292
450 Park Ave., (57th St.) NYC, NY 10022
Hours: 9:30-6 Mon-Sat (Thurs till 8)
• Pipes, cigars, tobacco, humidors; expensive. CREDIT CARDS •

J R TOBACCO CORP.   212-983-4160
11 East 45th St., (5th-6th Ave.) NYC, NY 10017
Hours: 7:45-5:50 Mon-Fri • 9-3:50 Sat
• Large selection of cigars, pipe tobacco, lighters, etc. •

S-T

MANTIQUES, LTD.   212-759-1805
    1050 Second Ave., (55th-56th St) NYC, NY 10021
    Hours: 11-5:30 Mon-Sat
    • Fine antiques, smoking accessories, desk dressing & canes. RENTALS •

PIPEWORKS AT WILKE   212-956-4820
    16 West 55th St., (5th-6th Ave.) NYC, NY 10019
    Hours: 9:30-5:45 Mon-Fri • 9:30-4:45 Sat
    • Handmade briar, American pipes and repairs, tobacco. •

NAT SHERMAN   212-764-5000
    500 5th Ave., (42nd St.) NYC, NY 10022
    Hours: 9-6:15 Mon-Sat • (Thurs till 7:15)
    • Large selection cigars, cigarettes, tobacco. RENTALS CREDIT CARDS •

SOUND EQUIPMENT RENTAL & PURCHASE

For consumer & household equipment, see **AUDIO & VIDEO EQUIPMENT**

ACE PROPS   212-580-9551
    1 West 19th St., NYC, NY 10011
    Hours: 8-5 Mon-Fri • 9-4 Sat • or by appt.
    • Working & non-working electronic equipment for rent. Specializing in contemporary and period consumer and professional AV equipment. CREDIT CARDS •
    (See display ad in this section)

CLEAR-COM INTERCOM SYSTEMS   510-527-6666
    945 Camelia St., Berkley, CA 94710
    Hours: 7-5 Mon-Fri   FAX 510-527-6699
    • Manufacturer of portable intercoms, wall mounted intercom systems. •

CP COMMUNICATIONS INC.   212-496-9111
    4 Executive Plaza, Yonkers, NY 10701   800-762-4254
    Hours: 9-5 Mon-Fri
    • Communication and RF related equipment rentals and sales. Intercom systems, wireless mics and headsets, walkie-talkies, cellular telephones. Contact Gailyn Fisher. •

ERSKINE-SHAPIRO THEATRE TECHNOLOGY INC.   212-929-5380
    37 West 20th St., (6th Ave.) NYC, NY 10011
    Hours: 10-6 Mon-Fri   FAX 212-691-7163

Rental of pro sound equipment. Specialists in wireless microphones and large or small intercom systems. Sound system design and running crews available.

    • Contact Lou Shapiro or Peter Erskine. CREDIT CARDS •

MASQUE SOUND & RECORDING CORP.   201-939-8666
  100 Redneck Ave., Moonachie, NJ 07074
  Hours: 9:30-5 Mon-Fri   FAX 201-939-4704

A full service company providing rentals,
sales, installation and consulting.
We can also provide custom fabrication.

MASQUE SOUND
& Recording Corporation

• Contact Bob Bender, Tom Corce, or Dennis Short. •

PRO MIX INC.   914-668-8886
  40 Hartford Ave., Mount Vernon, NY 10550
  Hours: 9-5 Mon-Fri   FAX 914-668-6844
  • Rental and sales of all kinds of sound equipment. •

SEE FACTOR INDUSTRY INC.   718-784-4200
  37-11 30th St., L.I.C., NY 11101
  Hours: 9-7 Mon-Fri   FAX 718-784-0617
  • Sound and lighting rental company. Complete production services and personnel available
  for any event. •

SOUND ASSOCIATES INC.   212-757-5679
  424 West 45th St., (9th-10th) NYC, NY 10036
  Hours: 10-5:30 Mon-Fri   FAX 212-265-1250
  • Full sound shop; mail and phone orders. RENTALS •

S-T

SPECIAL EFFECTS

See also **BREAKAWAYS**
See also **MAGIC SUPPLIES & NOVELTIES**
See also **LIGHTING & PROJECTION EQUIPMENT**
See also **FOG MACHINES & JUICE**

H. Aoki Studio Inc.
212-564-4285
424 West 33rd St., (9th-10th Ave.) NYC, NY 10001
Hours: 9-6 Mon-Fri   FAX 212-563-2411
• SPFX, props, models, miniatures, special construction. All types of rigging and motion control. Speak to Heather Cox. •

APA Studios
212-929-9436
230 West 10th St., (Bleecker-Hudson) NYC, NY 10014 212-675-4894
Hours: 10-6 Mon-Fri   FAX 212-727-7508
• Special effects for film and tape; motion and computer control. High speed photography. Custom casting and reproductions. •

Associates & Ferren
516-537-7800
Wainscott NW Rd., Wainscott, NY 11975
Hours: 8:30-6 Mon-Fri   FAX 516-537-7895
• Atmospherics, pyrotechnics, lasers, computerized motion control, projection and video effects, for stage and screen. •

Bargsten Studios
201-420-8680
111 First St., Jersey City, NJ 07302
Hours: 9-5 Mon-Fri
• SPFX shop, and props for film, TV and theatre. Scenery design service available. •

Brooklyn Model Works
718-834-1944
60 Washington Ave., (Park-Flushing) Brooklyn, NY 11205
Hours: 9-5 Mon-Fri   FAX 718-596-8934

• SPECIAL EFFECTS FOR FILM AND VIDEO •
Mechanical effects, electronic effects, custom props, miniatures, logo formats, vacuumforming, casting and reproductions.

• Experienced and reliable. •

Fred Buchholz/Acme Special Effects
212-874-7700
202 West 88th St., (B'way-Amsterdam) NYC, NY 10024
Hours: by appt.
• Special effects, props, rigging and pyrotechnics for film, theatre, video; props incorporating light. •

"I found it in the N.Y. Theatrical Sourcebook."

CIMMELLI, INC.   914-735-2090
16 Walter St., Pearl River, NY 10965
Hours: 8:30-5:30 Mon-Fri • Sat by appt.   FAX   914-735-1643

Special effects, props, models, miniatures, and special construction. Electro-mechanical, hydraulic, and pneumatic rigs. Rentals of turntables and linear motion rigs. Large, full-service shop.

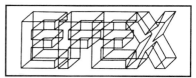

• Fast service; will pickup and deliver. •

CLOCKWORK APPLE INC.   212-431-8996
57 Laight St. #1, (Hudson-Greenwich) NYC, NY 10013
Hours: 9-6 Mon-Fri   FAX   212-226-4906
• Specialized model makers; miniatures, prototypes, liquid and mechanical effects for photography, film and advertising. Contact Christo Holloway. •

DANCING WATERS   212-988-3258
150 E. 77th St., #6D, (Lexington Ave.) NYC, NY 10021
Hours: 10-6 Mon-Fri   FAX   212-582-6819
• Rental of large musically choreographed theatrical fountains for stage and TV; custom designed water effects. •

DOM DEFILIPPO STUDIO INC.   212-986-5444
215 East 37th St., (2-3rd Ave.) NYC, NY 10016   212-867-4220
Hours: 9-6 Mon-Fri
• Effects and special props for film and tape. RENTALS •

EFEX RENTALS INC.   718-937-2417
43-17 37th St., (43rd Ave.) L.I.C., NY 11101
Hours: 8:30-5:30 Mon-Fri   FAX   718-937-3920

Creators of mechanical and visual special effects, including rain, wind, fog, snow, lightning, bullet hits, explosions, fire, stunt rigging and breakaways. Equipment and supplies for rental or purchase. Licensed and experienced crews available. Call for catalog and price list.

• Major distributors of many different types of fog machines, smoke cookies, fog juice; also turntables and rigging. •

ELECTROKINETICS   212-473-1125
380 Lafayette, Rm #304, NYC, NY 10003
Hours: 9-6 Mon-Fri   FAX   212-473-3717
• Custom motion control equipment, some small scale machining, electronics. •

FIREWORKS BY GRUCCI   516-286-0088
1 Grucci Lane, Brookhaven, NY 11719
Hours: 9-6 Mon-Fri   FAX   516-286-9036
• The legendary family company of fireworks entertainment in the country. •

GIZMO INC.   201-242-1504
622 Rt. 10, Unit #24, Whippany, NJ 07981
Hours: by appt.   FAX   201-884-2621
• Reliable, inexpensive tabletop effects, motion control systems; see Ed Hansen. RENTALS •

S-T

IMT Services
914-691-3665
5 Pine Terr., Highland, NY 12528
Hours: 9-6 Mon-Fri   FAX 914-691-3684
• Modelmaking, sculpture, flexibles, fake food for ECU, casting miniature to oversize. Electro-mechanical effects. ATAC member. See Mark. RENTALS •

Jauchem & Meeh Inc.
718-875-0140
43 Bridge St., (Plymouth-Water) Brooklyn, NY 11201
Hours: 9-5 Mon-Fri or by appt.   FAX 718-596-8329
• Full service special effects shop; design, construction, rental, sales of equipment and supplies. Speak to Greg Meeh. •
(See display ad in this section.)

K-F/X Inc.-Steve Kirshoff
914-937-9345
52 Cottage St., Port Chester, NY 10573
Hours: by appt.   FAX 914-937-4247
• Pyrotechnics, atmospherics, rigging and equipment, electro-mechanical. RENTALS •

Peter Kunz Co. Inc.
914-687-0400
55 Creek Rd., Highfalls, NY 12440
Hours: 8:30-5:30 Mon-Fri   FAX 914-687-0579
• Pyrotechnics, atmospherics, electro-mechanical effects. Model making. RENTALS •

Luna Tech Inc.
205-725-4224
148 Moon Dr., Owens Cross Rd., AL 35763
Hours: 9-6 Mon-Fri   FAX 205-725-4811
• Atmospheric, pyrotechnic devices; Pyropak brand. •

Michael Maniatis
212-620-0398
48 West 22nd St., (5th-6th Ave.) NYC, NY 10010
Hours: 9-5 Mon-Fri   FAX 212-620-4281
• Special props, custom casting and reproduction, vacuumforming, remote control, electrical/mechanical effects. •

Deed Rossiter
914-353-6333
1040 RT 9W, Upper Grandview, NY 10960
Hours: by appt.   FAX 914-353-1933
• Mechanical/electrical rigging, pyrotechnics, models and props for film and tape. •

Scenic Specialties Inc.
718-788-5379
232 7th St., (3rd-4th Ave.) Brooklyn, NY 11215
Hours: 8:30-5 Mon-Fri by appt.   FAX 718-768-9173
• Custom effects designed and built; breakaway furniture, custom props, aluminum fabrication. See Lou. •
(See display ad under ADHESIVES & GLUE.)

SFX Design
614-459-3222
6099 Godown Rd, Columbus, OH 43235
Hours: 7:30-4:30 Mon-Fri   FAX 614-459-3222
• Formerly Theatre Magic. Pyrotechnics and miniature pneumatics, blood effects, atmospherics; custom projects. •

Sound Sculpture Inc.
416-462-0242
50 Carroll St., Rm 305, Toronto, Ontario M4M 3G3   800-462-0242
Hours: 9-5 Mon-Fri   FAX 416-462-0894
• Custom electronics and digital radio control for film, dance, sculpture and theatre; contact Jim Smith. •

BREAKAWAYS,
LIGHTNING, WIND, FOG, RAIN, SNOW,
EXPLOSIONS, FIRE, SIMULATED FIRE, TORCHES,
STARDROPS, COSTUME ELECTRIFICATION, BLOOD,
PISTOLS, RIFLES, SWORDS, RETRACTABLE KNIVES...

ANGLES IN AMERICA, AN INSPECTOR CALLS,
TOMMY, SHOWBOAT, CITY OF ANGLES, SPOLETO,
PHANTON OF THE OPERA, GRAPES OF WRATH,
MISS SAIGON, LES MISERABLES, BOLSHOI BALLET,
I.B.M., COCA-COLA, MADONNA, LAURIE ANDERSON...

JAUCHEM & MEEH, INC.
43 BRIDGE STREET, BROOKLYN, NY 11201
718 875-0140/FAX 718 596-8329

SPECIAL EFFECTS - SALES, RENTAL, DESIGN

SPECIAL F/X INC.   908-469-0519
 PO Box 293, South Bound Brook, NJ 08880
 Hours: 10-5 Mon-Fri   908-469-1294
  • Consultant for special effects users and publishers of Special F/X News Journal. Sell special
 effects books, electronic devices and aerotechnics products. Mail order only. •

SPECIAL EFFECTS WORKSHOPS   212-245-3624
 410 West 47th St., NYC, NY 10036
 Hours: 9-5 Mon-Fri

Special Effects Workshops is a complete make up effects and film animation studio. We specialize in mechanical & animatronic puppets, 35mm stop-motion animation, front & rear screen projection, silicone & resin mold making, foam latex prosthetics, breakaway props, models & miniatures. Also, specialty costumes and masks.

SPECIAL EFFECTS WORKSHOPS

  • Contact Carle Paolino & Scott Sliger. ATAC member. •

EOIN SPROTT STUDIO LTD. c/o Kaufman-Astoria Studio   718-784-1407
 37-11 35th Ave., (37th-38th St.) Astoria, NY 11101
 Hours: 8-5:30 Mon-Fri   FAX 718-784-1629

Custom props, model making, miniatures, sculpture, molds, mechanical animation rigs.

EOIN
 SPROTT
  STUDIO
   LTD.

  • Very fine work. Contact Eoin or Susan. ATAC member. •

S-T

TRENGOVE STUDIOS, INC.
60 West 22nd St., (5th-6th Ave.) NYC, NY 10010
Hours: 9-5 Mon-Fri

212-255-2857
800-366-2857
FAX 212-633-8982

Handcrafted ice and water effects in acrylic and glass.
For sale and rent. Custom props, acrylic embedments.
Chemicals for smoke, steam, ice and water effects. Super
realistic food replicas cast from life. Our free brochure describes
these and many other creativity-enhancing products.

• Brochure and product sheet available. Breakaways, fog, plastics fabrication. Wonderful
water and ice effects. •

TRI-ESS SCIENCES INC.
1020 West Chestnut St., Burbank, CA 91506
Hours: 8:30-5 Mon-Fri • 8-12 Sat

213-245-7685
800-274-6910
FAX 818-848-3521

• Catalog includes special effects, special effects make-up, anatomical models, books and fir-
ing boxes. •

WELLINGTON ENTERPRISES
PO Box 315, 55 Railroad Ave. Bldg. 5, Garnerville, NY 10923
Hours: 7-5:30 Mon-Thurs.

914-429-3377
FAX 914-429-3765

• Custom magicians illusions, levitations, productions and transformation; contact Bill
Schmelk. •

MARK YURKIW AND COMPANY
180 Varick St., 14th Fl., (Charleston) NYC, NY 10014
Hours: 9-6 Mon-Fri

212-229-0741
212-229-0734

Three dimensional art and sculpture laboratory for problem
solving and special effects. Models, miniatures, exhibits,
electro/mechanical rigging, 4,000 sq. ft. high tech. workshop.
Machining and vacuumforming. Work done for feature film,
television, commercials, print advertising. Portfolio and reel on
request.

MARK YURKIW AND CO.

MY!

MODELMAKERS/SPECIAL EFFECTS

• Model making and special effects studio. Reliable and very helpful. •

ZELLER INTERNATIONAL LTD.
Main St. Box Z, Downsville, NY 13755 (factory)
Hours: 9-5 Mon-Fri

800-722-USFX
212-627-7676
FAX 607-363-2071

• Casting materials, flameproofing, fog, make-up supplies, breakaways. Atmospherics. Mail
order and rentals available. RENTALS •

SPONGES

NATIONAL SPONGE CORP.
   275 Morgan, Brooklyn, NY 11211
   Hours: 8:30-5 Mon-Fri • 8-12 Sat
   • Natural and synthetic sponges. $200 minimum. •
   718-388-5700
   800-426-5948
   FAX 718-388-5800

J. RACENSTEIN CO.
   224 West 30th St., (7th-8th Ave.) NYC, NY 10001
   Hours: 8:30-4:30 Mon-Fri
   • Natural Mediterranean sponges and synthetics. •
   212-967-0790

SCULPTURE HOUSE INC.
   30 East 30th St., (Park-Madison Ave.) NYC, NY 10016
   Hours: 10-4 Mon-Fri
   • Natural sponges. •
   212-679-7474

SHELL SPONGE & CHAMOIS CO.
   261 East 134 th St., (Lincoln-3rd Ave.) Bronx, NY 10454
   Hours: 9-5 Mon-Fri
   • Natural and synthetic sponges, janitorial supplies. No minimum. •
   718-402-6200

SPORTING GOODS

See also **FENCING EQUIPMENT**
See also **RIDING EQUIPMENT**

ABC-AMERICAN BATON CO.
   PO Box 266, 300 S. Wright Rd., Janesville, WI 53545
   Hours: 8-5 Mon-Fri • (closed for lunch 12-1)
   • All types of batons, accessories, and cases. Catalog. Shipping. MC/VISA •
   608-754-2238
   FAX 608-754-1986

BLATT BOWLING & BILLARD CORP.
   809 Broadway, (11th-12th St.) NYC, NY 10003
   Hours: 9-6 Mon-Fri • 10-4 Sat
   • All types bowling and billiard supplies, tables. RENTALS MC/VISA •
   212-674-8855

BRIGADE QUARTERMASTERS, LTD.
   1025 Cobb International Blvd., Kennesaw, GA 30144
   Hours: 10-6 Mon-Sat (store) • 8:30-8 Mon-Fri • 10-4 Sat(phone orders)
   • Survival, camping, climbing, hunting and expedition gear. Clothing in military (combat) styles. No rentals. Catalog. CREDIT CARDS •
   404-428-1234
   800-241-3125
   FAX 800-892-2999

GERRY COSBY & CO., INC.
   3 Penn Plaza, (Madison Square Garden) NYC, NY 10001
   Hours: 9:30-6:30 Mon-Fri • 9:30-6 Sat • 12-5 Sun (open till game time - Knicks & Rangers night games.)
   • Athletic outfitters for official sport uniforms. Will rent sports equipment for photographic use. Clothing: sales only. Phone orders. See Patty or Herb. CREDIT CARDS •
   212-563-6464
   FAX 212-967-0676

COUGAR SPORTS INC.
   917 Saw Mill River Rd., Ardsley, NY 10502
   Hours: 10-6 Mon-Sat • (Thurs till 8)
   • Archery equipment, arrows made to size; also scuba diving gear. Will ship. CREDIT CARDS •
   914-693-8877

S-T

CRAN BARRY   617-631-8510
130 Condor St., East Boston, MA 02128   800-992-2021
Hours: 9-5 Mon-Fri   FAX   671-567-9953
• Cheerleading clothes and pom-poms; field hockey and lacrosse equipment. Will ship.
MC/VISA •

CUTLER OWENS INTERNATIONAL   212-688-4222
45 East 51st St., (Park-Madison Ave.) NYC, NY 10022
Hours: 9-6 Mon-Fri • 10-5 Sat
• Rentals and sales of exercise equipment at the "Gym Source". CREDIT CARDS •

DART MART INC.   212-366-6981
160 West 26th St., (6th-7th Ave.) NYC, NY 10001
Hours: 10-6:30 Mon-Fri • 11-5 Sat
• Incredible selection of darts and boards. CREDIT CARDS •

EASTERN MOUNTAIN SPORTS   212-505-9860
611 Broadway, (Houston) NYC, NY 10012
Hours: 10-9 Mon-Fri • 10-6 Sat • 12-6 Sun

20 West 61st St. (Broadway-Columbus) NYC, NY 10023   212-397-4860
Hours: 10-9 Mon-Fri • 10-6 Sat • 12-6 Sun
• Sleeping bags, tents, clothing, outdoor gear; Equipment rental and sales. CREDIT CARDS •

EMPIRE SPORTING GOODS MFG.   800-221-3455
443 Broadway, (Grand-Howard) NYC, NY 10013   212-966-0880
Hours: 9-4 Mon-Fri • or by appt.   FAX   212-941-7113
• Manufacturer of athletic uniforms, team jackets, emblems and lettering. Mainly wholesale;
will service the industry by appt: Call Richard Chwang. Catalog available. MC/VISA •

EVERLAST SPORTING GOODS MFG.   718-993-0100
750 East 132nd St., (Willow Ave.) Bronx, NY 10454
Hours: 9-5 Mon-Fri
• Mostly boxing equipment, also aerobic and exercise equipment. Catalog. •

FITNESS AND RECREATION   516-273-2092
50 Cain St., Brentwood, NY 11717   516-424-8350
Hours: 8-5 Mon-Fri • leave message   FAX   516-273-2150
• Seating systems, recreational props, boxing rings, etc. Bleachers and risers. Playground
equipment and trampolines. RENTALS •

FRANK'S SPORT SHOP   718-299-9628
430 East Tremont Ave., (Park) Bronx, NY 10457
Hours: 9-8 Mon-Fri • 9-7 Sat   FAX   718-583-1652
• Full line of sporting goods; including professional wear for baseball and football; career uniforms; embroidery and silkscreen lettering. Catalog available. CREDIT CARDS •

S-T

HERMAN'S WORLD OF SPORTING GOODS　　　212-233-0733
　　　39 West 34th St., (5th-6th Ave.) NYC, NY 10001
　　　Hours: 9-7 Mon-Fri (till 8 Thurs) • 9:30-6:30 Sat • 11 -5 Sun

　　　135 West 42nd St., (6th-Broadway) NYC, NY 10036　　　212-730-7400
　　　Hours: 9:30-7 Mon-Fri • 9:30-6 Sat • 12-5 Sun

　　　1185 Sixth Ave., (47th St.) NYC, NY 10036　　　212-944-6689
　　　Hours: 9-7 Mon-Fri • 9-6 Sat • 12-5 Sun

　　　860 Broadway, (17th St.) NYC, NY 10003
　　　Hours: 9-7 Mon-Sat • 11-6 Sun

　　　845 Third Ave., (51st St.) NYC, NY 10022　　　212-688-4603
　　　Hours: 9-7 Mon-Fri • 9:30-6 Sat • 12-7 Sun
　　　• Large selection of sporting goods. CREDIT CARDS •

ISLAND WINDSURFING　　　212-744-2000
　　　1623 York Ave., (85th-86th St.) NYC, NY 10028
　　　Hours: 9:30-7 Mon-Fri • (Thurs till 8) • 10-6:30 Sat
　　　• Windsurfing, snowboarding equipment, rollerblades. RENTALS CREDIT CARDS •

J. C. P. CONSTRUCTION CORP.　　　516-582-5450
　　　200 Oval Dr., Central Islip, NY 11722
　　　Hours: 9-5 Mon-Fri　　　FAX　516-582-5875
　　　• Bowling equipment: used and refurbished shoes, balls; parts and supplies. For sale or
　　　rental. Contact Rich Heinz. •

LEVY'S SPORTS CENTER　　　201-861-7100
　　　Bergenline Ave. and 62nd St., West New York, NJ 07093
　　　Hours: 9-6 Mon-Thurs • Fri 9-8 • 9-6 Sat　　　FAX　201-861 -8836
　　　• Complete athletic equipment and clothing. Also custom pads and matting. Will ship. CREDIT
　　　CARDS •

V. LORIA & SONS INC.　　　212-925-0300
　　　178 Bowery, (Delancey St.) NYC, NY 10012
　　　Hours: 10:30-6 Mon-Fri • 10:30-4 Sat
　　　• Billiard tables and equipment, also bowling equipment; new, used, antique. RENTALS CRED-
　　　IT CARDS •

MODELL'S　　　212-964-4007
　　　200 Broadway, (John-Fulton St.) NYC, NY 10038
　　　Hours: 8:30-6:30 Mon-Fri • 9-4:45 Sat

　　　280 Broadway, (Chambers St.) NYC, NY 10007　　　212-267-2882
　　　Hours: 8:30-6:45 Mon-Fri • 8:30-5 Sat • 11:30-5:15 Sun

　　　109 East 42nd St., (Park-Lexington Ave.) NYC, NY 10017　　　212-661-5966
　　　Hours: 8:30-6:30 Mon-Fri • 9-6 Sat

　　　243 West 42nd St., (7th-8th Ave.) NYC, NY 10036　　　212-575-8111
　　　Hours: 9-7 Mon-Sat (Fri till 8:30) • 11:30-5:15 Sun

　　　A & S Plaza, 901 Sixth Ave., (33rd St.) NYC, NY 10001　　　212-594-1830
　　　Hours: 10-8:30 Mon, Thurs, Fri • 10-6:30 Tues, Wed, Sat • 11-5:30 Sun
　　　• Discount sporting goods and camping equipment. CREDIT CARDS •

S-T

ORVIS   212-697-☓
    355 Madison Ave., (Entrance on 45th St.) NYC, NY 10017
    Hours: 9-6 Mon-Fri • 10-5 Sat
        • Fly fishing supplies, gentlemen's outdoor equipment and clothing, catalog. CREDIT CARI

PARAGON SPORTING GOODS CO   212-255-☓
    867 Broadway, (18th St.) NYC, NY 10003
    Hours: 10-8 Mon-Sat • 11-6:30 Sun
        • Very large store; excellent selection of sporting goods, camping, hiking and climbing gea
    CREDIT CARDS •

PECK & GOODIE SKATE & SHOE SPECIALISTS   212-246-☓
    919 Eighth Ave., (54th-55th St.) NYC, NY 10019
    Hours: 8-6:30 Mon-Sat • 12-5 Sun.   FAX   212-807-☓

    1414 Second Ave., (73rd-74th St.) NYC, NY 10021   212-249-☓
    Hours: 11-7 Mon-Fri • 10-6 Sat • 12-6 Sun
        • Also prep and repair all types of theatrical shoes; taps, dance rubbers heel braces. •

SAFARI ARCHERY   718-441-☓
    86-15 Lefferts Blvd., Richmond Hill, NY 11418
    Hours: 1-11 Mon-Fri • 1-8 Sat-Sun
        • Archery equipment. •

SCANDINAVIAN SKI SHOP   212-757-☓
    40 West 57th St., (5th-6th Ave.) NYC, NY 10019
    Hours: 9-6:45 Mon-Fri • 9-6 Sat
        • Rental and sales of ski equipment. CREDIT CARDS •

SOCCER SPORT SUPPLY CO.   212-427-☓
    1745 First Ave., (90th-91st St.) NYC, NY 10128
    Hours: 9:30-6 Mon-Fri • 9-6 Sat
        • Good selection of anything related to soccer. CREDIT CARDS •

SPIEGELS   212-227-☓
    105 Nassau St., (Ann St.) NYC, NY 10038
    Hours: 9-6:30 Mon-Fri • 10-6 Sat
        • Sporting goods, team equipment and uniforms. •

TENT & TRAILS   212-227-☓
    21 Park Place, (Church-B'way) NYC, NY 10007
    Hours: 9:30-6 Mon-Wed • 9:30 -7 Thurs-Fri • 9:30-6 Sat • 12-6 Sun
        • Large selection camping and climbing equipment, backpacks, sleeping bags, clothing, ac
    sories, camping foods. Knowledgeable staff. RENTALS CREDIT CARDS •

WEISS & MAHONEY   212-675-☓
    142 Fifth Ave., (Corner of 19th St.) NYC, NY 10011   212-675-☓
    Hours: 9-7 Mon-Fri   FAX   212-633-☓
        • Inexpensive camping attire and equipment; military clothes, shoes, medals, work clothe:
    rentals. CREDIT CARDS •

S–T

SPRINGS, SPRING STEEL & WIRE

See also **FLORAL SUPPLIES**
See also **MILLINERY SUPPLIES**
See also **NOTIONS: BONES, BONING, HOOPWIRE.**

ABC SPRING CO   212-675-1629
    115 West 27th St., 6th Fl., (6th-7th Ave.) NYC, NY 10001
    Hours: 10-4:30 Mon-Fri
    • Stock and custom made springs, spring steel. •

FORD PIANO SUPPLY CO.   212-569-9200
    4898 Broadway, (204th-207th St.) NYC, NY 10034
    Hours: 8-5:30 Mon-Fri • call for Sat hours   FAX   212-567-5408
    • Piano wire. Rental and sales of pianos. CREDIT CARDS •

LEE SPRING CO.   718-236-2222
    1462 62nd St., (15th Ave.) Brooklyn, NY 11219
    Hours: 8-5 Mon-Fri
    • Stock and custom order springs. •

MAGNET WIRE INC.   517-667-9315
    161 Rodeo Dr., Edgewood, NY 11717
    Hours: 9-5 Mon-Fri   FAX   516-254-2099
    • Carries piano wire, tungsten wire, as well as good selection of other wire. MC/VISA •

MODERN INTERNATIONAL WIRE   718-728-1475
    PO Box 6072, 35-11 Ninth St., (35th Ave.) L.I.C., NY 11106
    Hours: 9-5 Mon-Fri
    • All types of wire. $100 minimum. •

NEW ERA HARDWARE & SUPPLY   212-265-4183
    832 Ninth Ave., (54th-55th St.) NYC, NY 10019
    Hours: 7:30-4:30 Mon-Fri • 8-3 Sat
    • Piano wire, rigging, casters, trucks, handling equipment, tools. •

PARAMOUNT WIRE CO. INC.   718-232-8866
    1523 63rd St., (15th-16th Aves.) Brooklyn, NY 11219
    Hours: 9-4:30 Mon-Fri
    • Millinery, piano, ribbon wire, cotton and rayon covered wire, paper stakes. $100 min. •

S-T

STATIONERY & OFFICE SUPPLIES

For office equipment, see **COMPUTERS & BUSINESS MACHINES**
For office furniture, see **FURNITURE RENTAL & PURCHASE: OFFICE**

ARROW STATIONERS INC.   212-719-4125
    1 West 47th St., (5th Ave.) NYC, NY 10036
    Hours: 8-5:30 Mon-Fri
    • Office supplies, pens, rubber stamps. MC/VISA •

FLYNN STATIONERS   212-758-2080
55 East 59th St., (Madison-Park) NYC, NY 10022
Hours: 8:30-5:30 Mon-Fri   FAX   212-751-8824
• Large general store of stationery supplies with printing service, also fountain pens. CREDIT CARDS •

FOUNTAIN PEN HOSPITAL/FPH OFFICE SUPPLIES   212-964-0580
10 Warren St., (B'way-Church) NYC, NY 10007
Hours: 7:30-5:45 Mon-Fri   FAX   212-227-5916
• Sells and repairs vintage fountain pens. CREDIT CARDS •

GOLDEN TYPEWRITER & STATIONERY CORP.   212-749-3100
2512 Broadway, (94th) NYC, NY 10025
Hours: 9:30-6:45 Mon-Sat
• Stationery, office supplies, artist supplies. CREDIT CARDS •

GROLAN STATIONERS INC.   212-247-2676
1800 Broadway, (58th St.) NYC, NY 10019   212-247-1684
Hours: 8:45-5:45 Mon-Fri
• Stationery, office supplies, including legal forms. CREDIT CARDS •

HUDSON ENVELOPE CORP.   212-473-6666
111 Third Ave., (13th-14th St.) NYC, NY 10003
Hours: 8:30-7 Mon-Fri • 10-6 Sat   FAX   212-473-7300
• All sizes of envelopes, also makes rubber stamps. •

IL PAPIRO   212-288-9330
1021 Lexington, (73th-74th St.) NYC, NY 10021
Hours: 10-6 Mon-Sat • 12-5 Sun   FAX   212-570-1587
• Marbled papers and Italian stationery items; expensive. CREDIT CARDS •

JAM ENVELOPE & PAPER CO.   212-255-4593
611 Sixth Ave., (17th-18th St) NYC, NY 10011
Hours: 8:30-7 Mon-Fri • 10-6 Sat
• All sizes and colors of envelopes, paper; pens, rubber stamps; low prices. •

JULIUS BLUMBERG INC.   212-431-5000
62 White St., (B'way-Church) NYC, NY 10013   800-221-2972
Hours: 8:45-5:45 Mon-Fri   FAX   212-431-5111
• Main store; all legal forms on file; purchase by the sheet or pad. Speak to Bob Blumberg for large orders. CREDIT CARDS •

KATE'S PAPERIE   212-633-0570
8 West 13th St., (5th-6th Ave.) NYC, NY 10011
Hours: 10-7 Mon-Fri • 10-6 Sat   FAX   212-366-6532

561 Broadway, (Spring- Prince St.) NYC, NY 10012   212-941-9816
Hours: 10:30-7 Mon-Fri • 10-6 Sat
• Wonderful stock of unusual papers, many hand made, cards, gift wraps, photo albums, frames and lamps with paper shades. CREDIT CARDS •

KROLL STATIONERS   212-750-5300
145 East 54th St., (Lexington-3rd Ave.) NYC, NY 10022
Hours: 8:30-6 Mon-Fri   FAX   212-838-9878
• Excellent stock of stationery supplies. CREDIT CARDS •

S-T

MENASH INC.   212-695-8888
  462 Seventh Ave., (35th-36th St.) NYC, NY 10018
  Hours: 8:30-5:30 Mon-Fri
  • Artists, drafting, graphics, office supplies; stationery. •

NORTHERN STATIONERY COMPANY   718-424-3900
  64-05 Roosevelt Ave., Woodside, NY 11377
  Hours: 9-6 Mon-Fri
  • Carries supplies for older typewriters and adding machines as well as column ledgers,
  mechanical pencils, mimeograph supplies, etc. No credit cards. See Mr. Feldblum. •

RIVOLI MERCHANDISE CO.   212-966-5035
  50 Howard St., (Mercer) NYC, NY 10013
  Hours: 9-6 Mon-Fri
  • Commercial stationery and school supplies-wholesale; also seasonal merchandise and
  props. •
  (See display ad under PARTY GOODS)

STAPLES   212-944-6791
  1075 Sixth Ave., (40th-41st St) NYC, NY 10036   800-333-3330
  Hours: 7-7 Mon-Fri • 9-6 Sat   FAX 212-944-2754
  • Discount office supplies, furniture, desk accessories. Very well stocked; catalog. CREDIT
  CARDS •

STATE OFFICE SUPPLY & PRINTING CO. INC.   212-243-8025
  150 Fifth Ave., (20th St.) NYC, NY 10011
  Hours: 9-5:30 Mon-Fri • 12-5 Sat
  • Good selection of general office supplies and desk accessories,(some fancy). CREDIT
  CARDS •

STEVDAN STATIONERS   212-243-4222
  474-A Sixth Ave., (11th-12th Ave.) NYC, NY 10011
  Hours: 9-6:20 Mon-Fri • 10-5 Sat   FAX 212-727-9424
  • Stationery, rubber stamps. Small leather goods; desk calenders. CREDIT CARDS •

TUNNEL STATIONERY   212-431-6330
  301 Canal St., (B'way) NYC, NY 10013
  Hours: 8-5 Mon-Fri • 10-5 Sat   FAX 212-226-0154
  • Good selection of discount priced stationery. CREDIT CARDS •

TUNNEL II STATIONERY   212-431-6663
  414 Broadway, (Canal St.) NYC, NY 10013
  Hours: 9-6 Mon-Fri   FAX 212-226-0514
  • Discount priced stationery. CREDIT CARDS •

S-T

STATUARY

See also **CASTING, CUSTOM**
See also **DISPLAY HOUSES**
See also **PROP & SCENIC CRAFTSPEOPLE**

CO-GNO-SCEN-TI LTD.   718-277-4525
  242 Chestnut St., (Atlantic-Fulton) Brooklyn, NY 11208
  Hours: 8-4:30 Mon-Fri
  • Fiberglass pedestals, columns, jars, urns, animals, Statue of Liberty; catalog ; see Libby. •

ELIZABETH STREET, INC.   212-941-4800
210 Elizabeth St., (Spring-Prince) NYC, NY 10012
Hours: 9-6 Mon-Fri • 12-5 Sat   FAX   212-274-0057
• Garden statuary and furniture, architectural elements. RENTALS •

ERCOLE INC.   212-941-6098
116 Franklin St., (at W. B'way) NYC, NY 10013
Hours: 9-5 every day   FAX   212-941-6720
• Plaster busts, angels, cherubs, architectural details; faux finishes and fresco work. Catalog
available in some cases. Will ship. •

F.A.S.T. CORP.   608-269-7110
P.O. Box 258, Sparta, WI 54656
Hours: 8-5 Mon-Fri   FAX   608-269-7514
• Manufactures of all types and sizes of fiberglass animals, statuary and fountains. Catalog.
RENTALS •

FLORENTINE CRAFTSMEN INC.   212-532-3926
46-24 28th St., (Skillman-47th Ave.) L.I.C., NY 11101   718-937-7632
Hours: 8-4:30 Mon-Fri   718-937-9858
• Outdoor statuary, fountains, garden furniture; expensive; $5 catalog. RENTALS CREDIT
CARDS •

INDUSTRIAL PLASTICS   212-226-2010
309 Canal St., (B'way-Mercer) NYC, NY 10013
Hours: 9-5 Mon-Fri • 9-4 Sat
• Fiberglass statuary, urns, fountains, animals. RENTALS •

KENNETH LYNCH & SONS   203-762-8363
84 Danbury Rd., Wilton, CT 06897
Hours: 8-5 Mon-Fri   FAX   203-762-2994
• Statuary in metal and stone. Catalog. •

MODERN ARTIFICIAL FLOWERS & DISPLAYS LTD.   212-265-0414
517 West 46th St., (10th-11th Ave.) NYC, NY 10036
Hours: 8:30-5 Mon-Fri   FAX   212-265-6841
• Fiberglass statuary, urns, columns, garden items for purchase. RENTALS •

NIEDERMAIER   212-675-1106
435 Hudson, (Morton St.) NYC, NY 10014
Hours: 9-5 Mon-Fri
• Chic display items; pottery, columns, sculpture, some oversized items. •

PLASTER GALLERY   718-769-8500
2827 Coney Island Ave., (Ave Z) Brooklyn, NY 11235
Hours: 11-6 Every day   FAX   718-891-2879
• Stock and custom figurines, busts, etc. in plaster; also columns and pedestals. •

SCULPTURE HOUSE CASTING   212-645-9430
155 West 26th St., (6th-7th Ave.) NYC, NY 10001
Hours: 8-6 Mon-Fri • 10-4 Sat
• Plaster and metal statuary including busts. Casting materials. •

ZAFERO BY LESLIE JOHN KOESER ASSOCIATES   215-763-7054
1530 Parrish St., Philadelphia, PA 19130
Hours: 9-5 Mon-Fri
• Stock or custom fiberglass columns, urns, statuary. Catalog. •

S-T

STERNO

A. SARGENTI CO. INC.   212-989-5555
   453 West 17th St., (9th-10th Ave.) NYC, NY 10011
   Hours: 9-5 Mon-Fri
   • Sterno by the case. •

W.H. SILVER'S HARDWARE   212-247-4406
   832 Eighth Ave., (50th-51st St.) NYC, NY 10019   212-247-4425
   Hours: 8-5:30 Mon-Fri   FAX   212-246-2041
   • Sterno by the can or case. •

NOTES

S-T

S-T

"I found it in the N.Y. Theatrical Sourcebook."

TAPE, ADHESIVE

See also **PACKING MATERIALS**

DUO-FAST CORP.   201-768-3322
  20 Corporate Dr., (off Blaisdell Rd.) Orangeburg, NY 10962
  Hours: 8- 5 Mon-Fri (phone orders) • 8:30-4 Mon-Fri (repairs) (close half an hour early on Fri
  during summer)
    • High and low tack tapes, hot melt glues and applicators. Catalog. No minimum. •

EUROPORT   717-581-9388
  425 Longmeadow Rd., Lancaster, PA 17601
  Hours: 8:30-5 Mon-Fri   FAX   717-295-7833
    • Great selection; color catalog available. $75.00 Minimum •

GREAT ATLANTIC PAPER PACKAGING CORP.   718-858-3636
  281-289 Butler St., (Nevins-3rd Ave.) Brooklyn, NY 11217
  Hours: 9-5 Mon-Fri
    • Gaffers, duct, many types of pressure sensitive tapes. Catalog. $200 minimum. •

H.G. PASTERNACK   212-691-9555
  151 West 19th St., (7th Ave.) NYC, NY 10011   800-433-3330
  Hours: 9-5:30 Mon-Fri   FAX   212-924-0024
    • Authorized distributor of 3M tapes. Brochure. $25 minimum on phone orders. •

ROSE BRAND TEXTILE FABRICS   212-494-7424
  517 West 35th St., (10th-11th Ave.) NYC, NY 10001   800-223-1624
  Hours: 8:30-5 Mon-Fri   FAX   212-629-4826

3M232 Painter's Masking. Spike tape in vinyl, cloth & paper
(13+ colors). Now available: custom widths, printed, decorative
and specialty tapes. Adhesives: Phlexglu, Sculpt or Coat.
Call Tom Cololuris for quantity discounts, packaging
needs and special projects. All items in stock.

THEATRICAL SUPPLIES, FABRICS & FABRICATION
ROSE ✶ BRAND
517 WEST 35th STREET, NEW YORK, NY 10001

    • Large selection of tapes including gaffers, spike tape in 10 colors, duct tape in 5 colors, lumi-
    nous glow tape and masking tape. Case lot discounts available. Catalog. •
    (See display ad under CURTAINS & DRAPERIES and in this section)

THE SET SHOP   212-979-9790
  37 East 18th St., (B'way-Park Ave. S.) NYC, NY 10003
  Hours: 8:30-6 Mon-Fri • 10-4 Sat   FAX   212-979-9852
    • Four types and strengths of spray adhesives and 50 different kinds of tapes. •

SILVER & SONS HARDWARE   212-247-6969
  711 Eighth Ave., (44th-45th St.) NYC, NY 10036   212-247-6978
  Hours: 9-5:30 Mon-Fri • 10-3 Sat
    • Wide variety of spike, gaffers, glow, electrical, carpet and masking tapes. CREDIT CARDS •

W.H. SILVER'S HARDWARE   212-247-4406
  832 Eighth Ave., (50th-51st St.) NYC, NY 10019   212-247-4425
  Hours: 8-5:30 Mon-Fri   FAX   212-246-2041
    • Largest selection of tapes and glues in one place; phone orders. •

STICK-A SEAL TAPE/UNIMICA PLASTICS & PACKAGING   212-966-4330
  75 Varick St., (Canal St.) NYC, NY 10013
  Hours: 9-4:30 Mon-Fri • call first
    • Full line of common type gaffers, electrical, duct tapes, etc. $50 minimum. •

S-T

TAXIDERMISTS & TAXIDERMY SUPPLIES

BIRDS IN WOOD STUDIO   203-634-1953
   525 Broad St., Meriden, CT 06450
   Hours: 9-5 Mon-Fri
   • Custom taxidermy from wolves to raccoons. Rentals and sales of mounted animals and birds. Also teaches taxidermy. Contact Brian McGray. •

HEMINGWAY AFRICAN GALLERY   212-838-3650
   1050 Second Ave. #95, (55th-56th St.) NYC, NY 10022   212-752-5867
   Hours: 10:30-6 Mon-Sat • 12-5 Sun   FAX 212-838-3650
   • Rental of skins, zebra and animal trophy mounts. •

JONAS BROTHERS TAXIDERMY SUPPLIES   303-466-3377
   2260 Industrial Lane, Bloomfield, CO 80220
   Hours: 8-5 Mon-Fri • 8-12 Sat
   • Animal forms, taxidermy supplies. Catalog. No minimum. •

E. J. MORAN   201-933-0284
   539 Jefferson St., Carlsdadt, NJ 07072
   Hours: 9-5 Mon-Fri
   • Custom taxidermy. Some rental on stock. Talk to Josh. •

S-T

SCHOEPFER STUDIO   212-736-6939
138 W. 31st St., (6th-7th Ave.) NYC, NY 10001   212-736-6934
Hours: 9:30-3 Mon-Fri
• Rental or purchase of stuffed animals. •

G. SCHOEPFER, INC.   203-250-7794
460 Cook-Hill Rd., Cheshire, CT 06410
Hours: 9-4 Mon-Fri
• New address for the glass eye collection from Schopfer on 31st St. Glass eyes for dolls, decoys and animals; catalog. $25 minimum. •

WESTCHESTER TAXIDERMY QUALITY MOUNTS   914-245-1728
Rt. 6 at Church St., Carmel, NY 10512   914-225-3607
Hours: by appt.
• Rental and purchase; over 700 animals and birds; taxidermy supplies; very nice. •

TELEPHONES

ACE PROPS   212-206-1475
1 West 19th St., Ground Fl., (5th Ave.) NYC, NY 10011   212-580-9551
Hours: 8-5 Mon-Fri • 9-4 Sat • or by appt.   **FAX**   212-929-9082
• Rental of telephones, fax machines, answering machines and many kinds of hard to get props. CREDIT CARDS •
(See display ad under PROP RENTAL HOUSES.)

E. BUK, ANTIQUES & ART   212-226-6891
151 Spring St., 2nd Fl., (W. B'way-Wooster) NYC, NY 10012
Hours: by appt.
• Antique and vintage telephones, headphones, microphones, switchboards and related technical equipment. •
(See display ads under PROP RENTAL HOUSES and under ANTIQUES.)

CEI, INC. (CUSTOM ELECTRONICS INDUSTRIES)   319-382-5659
PO Box 51, Rt. 4 Box 17, Decorah, IA 52101
Hours: 9-5 Mon-Fri (Central Time)   **FAX**   319-382-0041
• Tele-Q telephone ringing system works with any phone. For brochure and information contact Bruce Larson. •

CHICAGO OLD TELEPHONE   (cust. serv.) 919-774-6625
PO Box 189, Lemon Springs, NC 28355   (orders) 800-843-1320
Hours: 8-5 Mon-Fri   **FAX**   919-774-7666
• Working antique telephones; brochure, publications on history and styles of telephones. •

THE FONE BOOTH   212-751-8310
829 3rd Ave., (50th-51st St.) NYC, NY 10022
Hours: 10-6 Mon-Sat   **FAX**   212-319-3663
• Good selection of telephones, old and new; some foreign phones and adapter jacks; repairs and rewiring. See Calvin. Also answering machines, fax machines, cellular phones. RENTALS CREDIT CARDS •

S–T

47TH ST. PHOTO INC.   212-398-1410
   67 West 47th St., (5th-6th Ave.) NYC, NY 10036
   Hours: 9-6:30 Mon-Thurs • 9-2 Fri • 10-5 Sun

   115 West 45th St., (6th Ave.-Broadway) NYC, NY 10036   212-921-1287
   Hours: 9:30-7 Mon-Thur • 9:30-2 Fri • 10-5 Sun
   • Cameras and photo equipment, computers, typewriters, telephones, etc; watch for frequent
   sales. •

J & R MUSIC WORLD   212-513-1858
   15 Park Row, (Beekman-Ann) NYC, NY 10038   212-238-9070
   Hours: 9-6:30 Mon-Sat • 11-6 Sun
   • Telephones and answering machines. CREDIT CARDS •

PHONE BOUTIQUE   212-319-9650
   828 Lexington Ave., (63rd-64th St.) NYC, NY 10011
   Hours: 10-6:30 Mon-Sat   FAX   212-319-5277
   • Telephones, including cordless, cellular; answering machines, beepers; repairs and installations. RENTALS CREDIT CARDS •

PHONECO   608-582-4124
   PO Box 70, 207 E. Mill Rd., Galesvile, WI 54630
   Hours: 9-5 Mon-Fri • (will take calls till 9)   FAX   608-582-4593
   • Antique and repro telephones; ship UPS/COD; see Ron. RENTALS CREDIT CARDS •

STATE SUPPLY EQUIPMENT & PROPS INC.   212-645-1430
   210 Eleventh Ave., (24th-25th Street) NYC, NY 10001
   Hours: 8:30-5 Mon-Fri   FAX   212-675-3131
   • Period and contemporary phone equipment, including switchboards. Large selection.
   RENTALS •

S & S SOUND CITY   212-575-0210
   58 West 45th St., (5th-6th Ave.) NYC, NY 10036   212-221-7907
   Hours: 9-7 Mon-Fri • 9-6 Sat
   • Telephones, cellular phones, fax machines. Will rent anything in the store: Speak to Mel
   Tillman. CREDIT CARDS •

WAVES   212-989-9284
   21 East 13th St., (5th Ave- Univ. Pl.) NYC, NY 10003
   Hours: 12-6 Tues-Fri • 12-5 Sat   FAX   201-461-7121
   • Vintage telephones, radios, 78's Victrolas. RENTALS •

TELESCOPES & BINOCULARS

BARGAIN SPOT   212-674-1188
   64 Third Ave., (11th St.) NYC, NY 10003   212-674-1189
   Hours: 9-4:45 Mon-Sat
   • A good pawn shop. Telescopes, binoculars, cameras, musical instruments; rental or purchase. CREDIT CARDS •

E. Buk, Antiques & Art
212-226-6891
151 Spring St., 2nd Fl., (W. B'way-Wooster) NYC, NY 10012 (toll call) 700-SCIENCE
Hours: by appt.

ANTIQUE AND PERIOD telescopes, large and small, astronomical, terrestrial, brass and mahogany; microscopes, binoculars, cameras, transits, theodolites, sextants and assorted optical equipment; star maps; 18th-early 20th century.

• Antique telescopes and binoculars, all styles, large and small. RENTALS •
(See display ads under ANTIQUES and under PROP RENTAL HOUSES.)

Clairmont-Nichols, Inc.
212-758-2346
1016 First Ave., (56th) NYC, NY 10022
Hours: 9-6 Mon-Fri • (Thurs till 7) • 9-5 Sat   FAX   212-750-3583
• Sales and repairs; good quality telescopes, binoculars. RENTALS CREDIT CARDS •

Rensay, Inc.
212-688-0195
48 East 58th St., (Madison-Park Ave.) NYC, NY 10022
Hours: 8:30-5:30 Mon-Fri
• Sales, repairs of telescopes, binoculars and magnifiers. RENTALS CREDIT CARDS •

Star Magic
212-228-7770
745 Broadway, (8th-Waverly) NYC, NY 10003
Hours: 10-10 Mon-Sat • 11-9 Sun

275 Amsterdam Ave., (73rd St.) NYC, NY 10023   212-769-2020
Hours: 10-10 Mon-Sat • 11-9 Sun

1256 Lexington Ave., (84th-85th St.) NYC, NY 10028   212-988-0300
Hours: 10-9 Mon-Sat • 11-7:30 Sun
• Telescopes, star maps and finders, space related books and posters. CREDIT CARDS •

Tower Optical
203-866-4535
PO Box 251, South Norwalk, CT 06856
Hours: 8-5 Mon-Fri   FAX   203-866-2467
• Maintains and owns all coin operated binoculars in the NYC area. RENTALS •

THEATRICAL HARDWARE & RIGGING EQUIPMENT

See also **THEATRICAL SUPPLY HOUSES**

Automatic Devices Co.
215-797-6000
2121 South 12th St., Allentown, PA 18103
Hours: 8-5 Mon-Fri
• Manufactures curtain tracks and motors, stage hardware; call for local dealer. •

Bestek Lighting & Staging
516-225-0707
218 W. Hoffman Ave., Lindenhurst, NY 11757   (Sales/rentals) 516-225-0106
Hours: 9-5 Mon-Fri   FAX   516-225-0787
• Dealers for major suppliers; installation and rentals available; confetti cannons, platforms, etc. MC/VISA •

EVERYTHING IMAGINABLE!

HARDWARE VENDORS SINCE 1936

Distributors of Special Effects, Prop, Grip, Gaffer Construction Equipment & Supplies, with prices that are not theatrical.

Hinges, Fastenings, Pneumatics, Hydraulics, Controls, Electrical, Electronics, Welding, Ladders & Scaffolding, Power & Hand Tools, Blocks Tackle & Rigging, Safety Equipment, Tape, Adhesives, Janitorial, Pipe, Plumbing, Hampers & Trucks etc.

FEATURING MURALO CHROMA KEY & VOGUE DEEP COLOR QUALITY PAINTS

DON'T SPEND YOUR TIME IN LINE --

DAILY DELIVERY TO STUDIO OR LOCATION OR QUICK PICK-UP AT OUR COUNTER

HARD TO FIND ITEMS A SPECIALTY

INDUSTRIAL SUPPLY COMPANY OF LONG ISLAND

Call: 718-784-1291
Fax: 718-482-9353
47-30 Vernon Blvd.
L.I.C., New York 11101

"I found it in the N.Y. Theatrical Sourcebook."

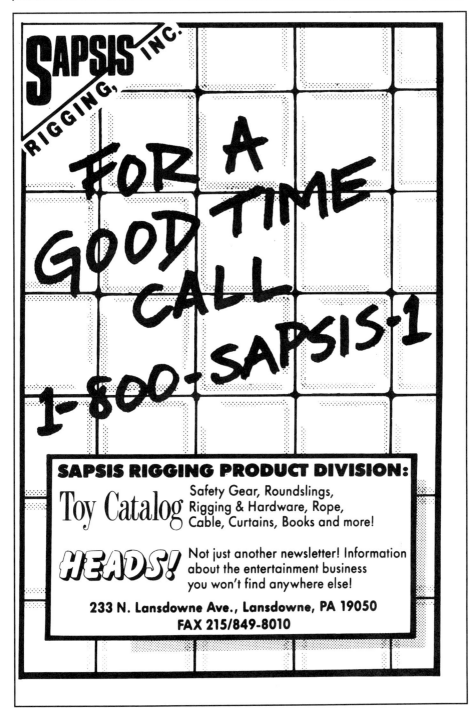

J.R. CLANCY, INC.   315-451-3440
  7041 Interstate Island Rd., Syracuse, NY 13209
  Hours: 7:30-5 Mon-Fri
    • Rigging equipment, stage and rigging hardware, winches; price list available. •

COLSON CASTERS   516-354-1540
  137 Meacham Ave., (Hempstead Tpk.) Elmont, NY 11003
  Hours: 9-5 Mon-Fri
    • Specializes in casters; catalog available. •

COMMERCIAL DRAPES CO., INC.   718-649-8080
  9209 Flatlands Ave., (E. 92-93rd St) Brooklyn, NY 11236
  Hours: 8-4:30 Mon-Fri   FAX   718-272-2295
    • Sales and installation of curtain tracks and hardware. •

J. COWHEY & SONS, INC. MARINE EQUIP.   718-625-5587
  440 Van Brunt St., (Beard-Van Dyke) Brooklyn, NY 11231
  Hours: 8-4:30 Mon-Fri   FAX   718-625-5772
    • Rigging equipment, rope, wire, blocks, fittings; good prices. Phone orders. Catalog. •

ECTS SCENIC TECHNOLOGY   914-534-3558
  PO Box 335, Shore Rd., Cornwall-on Hudson, NY 12520
  Hours: 8-5 Mon-Fri   FAX   914-534-3752
    • Mechanized effects: rigging and equipment rentals; turntables, scissor lifts, traveller track.
  See Kevin Bailey •
  (See display ad under SCENIC SHOPS)

HOBOKEN BOLT & SCREW   201-792-0450
  612 Adams St., Hoboken, NJ 07030
  Hours: 9-5 Mon-Fri   FAX   201-792-0492
    • Stock and custom rigging and cable. Catalog of extensive line of cable and fittings
  available. •

INDUSTRIAL SUPPLY COMPANY OF LONG ISLAND   718-784-1291
  47-30 Vernon Blvd., (47th-48th Ave.) L.I.C., NY 11101
  Hours: 7-5:30 Mon-Fri • FAX#, 24 hours every day   FAX   718-482-9353
    • Distributor of hardware and construction supplies. Also ladders. Call for 1700 page catalog-
  $4.95, refundable. •
  (See display ad in this section.)

KEE KLAMPS   716-896-4949
  PO Box 207, Buffalo, NY 14225
  Hours: 8:30-4:45 Mon-Fri
    • Manufacturers of Kee Klamps, use with 1/2" to 2" pipe. •

MAGNET WIRE INC.   516-667-9315
  161 Rodeo Dr., Edgewood, NY 11717
  Hours: 9-5 Mon-Fri   FAX   516-254-2099
    • Carries tungsten wire, piano wire, as well as a large selection of other wire. CREDIT
  CARDS •

MUTUAL HARDWARE CORP.   718-361-2480
  5-45 49th Ave., (Vernon) L.I.C., NY 11101
  Hours: 8:30-5 Mon-Fri   FAX   718-729-8296
    • Complete stage hardware, rigging supplies, casters, catalog. Contact John or Mike. •

S–T

NEW ERA HARDWARE & SUPPLY 212-265-4183
832 Ninth Ave., (54-55th St) NYC, NY 10019
Hours: 7:30-4:30 Mon-Fri • 8-3 Sat
• Rigging supplies, casters, handtrucks and handling equipment, piano wire, tools. •

NOVELTY SCENIC 516-671-5940
40 Sea Cliff Ave., Glen Cove, NY 11542
Hours: 8-4:30 Mon-Fri
• Curtains, tracks, rigging, motors, custom curtains and drops. Contact Howard Kessler. •

FREDERICH PFEIFER 212-964-5230
53 Warren St., (W B'way-Church) NYC, NY 10007
Hours: 9-4:45 Mon-Fri
• Theatrical hardware, great selection of casters, dollies. •

POOK DIEMONT & OHL, INC. 212-402-2677
701 East 132nd St., (Cypress-Willow) Bronx, NY 10454-3404
Hours: 8-6 Mon-Fri FAX 212-402-2859
• Rigging contractors and consultants; speak to Barbara. Knowledgeable and helpful. •

REYNOLDS DRAPERY SERVICE INC. 315-845-8632
7440 Main St., Newport, NY 13416
Hours: 8-4 Mon-Fri FAX 315-845-8645
• Curtain tracks, rigging; drapery mfg. and maintenance. •

SAPSIS RIGGING, INC. 215-849-6660
233 North Lansdowne Ave., Lansdowne, PA 19050
Hours: 8-5 Mon-Fri • 24-hour emergency service. FAX 215-849-8010
• Theatrical rigging; counterweight, hemp-winch systems; fire curtains, draperies, turntables, etc. Catalog. •
(See display ad in this section.)

SEGAL BROTHERS 718-383-2995
205 Nassau, (Russell) Brooklyn, NY 11222
Hours: 8-5 Mon-Fri
• Large selection of industrial hardware, tools, motors. •

SILVER & SONS HARDWARE 212-247-6969
711 Eighth Ave., (44th-45th St) NYC, NY 10036 212-247-6978
Hours: 9-5:30 Mon-Fri • 10-3 Sat
• Cable, piping, hanging equipment, rope, tools, etc. CREDIT CARDS •

W.H. SILVER'S HARDWARE 212-247-4406
832 Eighth Ave., (50th-51st St) NYC, NY 10019 212-247-4425
Hours: 8-5:30 Mon-Fri FAX 212-246-2041
• Great selection of theatrical hardware, aircraft and steel cable, casters, rope, rigging equipment, tools, tape. CREDIT CARDS •
(See display ad in this section)

SIMMONS FASTENER COMPANY 518-463-4234
PO Box 1985, 1750 Broadway, Albany, NY 12204
Hours: 8-5 Mon-Fri
• Case hardware, roto-locks, screw buttons. Catalog. •

S-T

I. WEISS & SONS, INC.
718-706-8139

2-07 Borden Ave., (Vernon-Jackson) L.I.C., NY 11101
Hours: 8-5 Mon-Fri

FAX   718-482-9410

Full line of stage & TV studio curtain tracks.
Pipe, rope, cable & full line of rigging hardware.
Delivery & installation available.

STAGE DRAPERIES & RIGGING. SINCE 1900. WE DO IT ALL.

• 90 years in the theatrical business supplying drapery track and rigging. •
(See display ad under CURTAINS & DRAPERIES, THEATRICAL.)

THEATRICAL SUPPLY HOUSES

ALCONE CO., INC.
718-361-8373

5-49 49th Ave., (5th St.-Vernon) L.I.C., NY 11101
Hours: 9:30-4 Mon-Fri

FAX   718-729-8296

• Celastic, hardware, rigging equipment, paint, etc. Catalog, $5. Convenient to subway (#7 train to L.I.C. Vernon/Jackson stop). •

BARBIZON
212-586-1620

426 West 55th St., (9th-10th) NYC, NY 10019
Hours: 8:30-5:30 Mon-Fri • 9-1 Sat

FAX   212-247-8818

3 Draper St, Woburn, MA 01801
Hours: 8:30-5:30 Mon-Fri • 9-2 Sat

617-935-3920
FAX   617-935-9273

6437 General Green Way, Alexandria, VA 22312
Hours: 8:30-5:30 Mon-Fri • 9-1 Sat

703-750-3900
FAX   703-750-1448

2401 Mercer Ave., W. Palm Beach, FL 33401
Hours: 8:30-5:30 Mon-Fri • 9-1 Sat

407-833-2020
FAX   407-833-3582

101 Krog St., Atlanta, GA 30307
Hours: 8-5 Mon-Fri • 9-1 Sat

404-681-5124
FAX   404-681-5315

• Full line of replacement lamps, lighting and dimming equipment, fog machines and theatrical related products. •

BESTEK LIGHTING & STAGING
516-225-0707

218 W. Hoffman Ave., Lindenhurst, NY 11575
Hours: 9-5 Mon-Fri

(sales/rentals) 516-225-0106
FAX   516-225-0787

• Full line of lighting and rigging equipment, hardware and supplies. RENTALS •

S-T

"I found it in the N.Y. Theatrical Sourcebook."

BMI SUPPLY

28 Logan Ave., Glens Falls, NY 12801

	518-793-6706
	800-836-0524
FAX	518-793-6181

60 Airview Dr., Greenville, SC 29607

	803-288-8983
FAX	803-281-0841

Hours: 8-5 Mon-Fri

• Hardware, rigging, lighting, draperies. Catalogs. MC/VISA •

Full line of:
- Hardware and Rigging
- Lighting and Dimming Equipment
- Lamps, Paint and Specialties
- Theatrical Draperies, Scrims and Drops

JUST A PHONE CALL AWAY

LIMELIGHT PRODUCTIONS, INC.

Route 102, Lee, MA 01238

	413-243-4950
	800-243-4950
FAX	413-243-4993

Hours: 9-5 Mon-Fri • or by appt.

• Authorized service for Rosco foggers, Beyer Headsets and Strong Followspots •

Lighting, control and special effects
equipment for sales and rental.
Custom soft goods fabricated in our plant.

NORCOSTCO, INC.

373 Rt. 46 West, Fairfield, NJ 07004

	201-575-3503
	212-690-5567
FAX	201-575-2563

Hours: 9:30-6 Mon-Fri • 10-5 Sat

• Theatrical supply house; rentals including costumes; catalog. •

THE PRODUCTION ADVANTAGE

17 Pine Haven Shore, Shelburne, VT 05482

	800-424-9991
	802-985-3956
FAX	802-985-1028

Hours:

Good selection of lamps, Rosco products, stage fabrics, and accessory supplies. Price list available, contact John.

ROSE BRAND TEXTILE FABRICS

517 West 35th St., (10th-11th Ave.) NYC, NY 100001

	212-594-7424
	800-223-1624
FAX	212-629-4826

Hours: 8:30-5 Mon-Fri

Specializing in scenic and production textiles, custom fabrication of cycs, drops, drapes, legs, borders, etc. Full line of scenic art supplies, shop papers, brushes, tape, fire retardants and load-out supplies. Scenic paints in stock: Rosco, Gothic, Vinyl Flo. New: Grid Kraft scenic paper, Foamcoat, Inherently Flame Retardant Sharkstooth Scrim, Imported Square Gauze, metallic fabrics, tutu nets. Call for technical assistance, catalog and/or samples. Quantity discounts. Fast service.

THEATRICAL SUPPLIES, FABRICS & FABRICATION

ROSE BRAND

517 WEST 35th STREET, NEW YORK, NY 10001

• Wide selection flame retardant fabrics, by the yard or bolt. Also carry scenic paint and accessories. Catalog available. •

(See display ad under CURTAINS & DRAPERIES: THEATRICAL)

THEATRICAL SERVICES & SUPPLIES INC.

170 Oval Dr., Central Islip, NY 11722

516-348-0262

Hours: 8-4:30 Mon-Fri

• Theatrical supplies; air-lite panels; shipping. CREDIT CARDS •

S-T

DIANN 8.00 → (2day-)

TOBINS LAKE STUDIOS, INC. 810-229-0221 ~~313~~-229-6666
810
7030 Old U.S. Hwy. 23, Brighton, MI 48116
Hours: 9-5 Mon-Fri
• Theatrical supply house, including rental of backdrops and fog machines, paint, hardware, vacuumformed architectural detail and ornaments. Catalog. •

VADAR CORP. 305-978-8442
1300 West McNab Rd., Fort Lauderdale, FL 33309 800-221-9511
Hours: 9-5 Mon-Fri FAX 305-978-8446
• Scenic supplies and lighting equipment, stage hardware, fabric and draperies, tapes, fire retardant specialties; catalog. •

THRIFT SHOPS

BARTER SHOP 203-846-1242
140 Main St., (I-95, Exit 15 to Exit 2) Norwalk, CT 06851
Hours: 11-6 every day
LARGEST SHOP OF ITS KIND
Period to recent, furniture, accessories, kitchen, farm & primitive collectibles, pictures, & frames. EXCELLENT for theatre, movie, TV & commercial decorators. SAVE TIME: One stop can get many items needed.. ONLY 45 minutes from NYC.

BARTER SHOP
THE ELITE JUNK SHOP

• Three buildings, over 50,000 items; antiques, collectibles and used furniture. Checks accepted. MC/VISA •

CANCER CARE THRIFT SHOP 212-879-9868
1480 Third Ave., (84th St.) NYC, NY 10028
Hours: 11-6 Mon-Fri • Thurs til 7 • 10-4:30 Sat
• Mostly clothing, some jewelry, linens, picture frames, knick-knacks. CREDIT CARDS •

EVERYBODY'S THRIFT SHOP 212-355-9263
261 Park Ave. South, (20th-21st St.) NYC, NY 10010
Hours: 10-4:45 Mon-Fri • 10-3:45 Sat
• Shoes, clothing, linens, bric-a-brac. No credit cards. •

GOODWILL INDUSTRIES OF GREATER NY 212-679-0786
402 Third Ave., (29th St.) NYC, NY 10016
Hours: 11-7 Mon-Fri • 10-6 Sat
• Limited selection, mostly clothing, furniture, housewares. CREDIT CARDS. •

IRVINGTON HOUSE THRIFT SHOP 212-879-4555
1534 Second Ave., (80th St.) NYC, NY 10021
Hours: 10-6 Mon-Sat • Wed-Thurs til 8 • 12-5 Sun
• Good selection; furniture, clothing, dishes, knick-knacks; sometimes pricey. MC/VISA •

MEMORIAL SLOAN-KETTERING THRIFT SHOP 212-535-1250
1440 Third Ave., (82nd St.) NYC, NY 10028
Hours: 10-4:30 Mon-Sat
• Limited selection; furniture, clothing, books, knick-knacks. CREDIT CARDS. •

S–T

POP'S USED CLOTHING   718-782-2020
    511-513 Kent Ave., (Division) Brooklyn, NY 11211
    Hours: 8-4 Mon-Fri • 9-3 Sat (closed Sat in July)
     • Used men's clothing; work clothes, pants, coveralls, jackets, overcoats, jeans; low prices. No
    credit cards. •

REPEAT PERFORMANCE THRIFT SHOP   212-684-5344
    220 East 23rd St., (2nd-3rd Ave.) NYC, NY 10010
    Hours: 10-5:30 Mon-Fri •11-6:30 Thurs • 10-5 Sat
     • Clothing, furniture, carpets, silver items, jewelry, knick-knacks. CREDIT CARDS. •

RICHMAN AND ASSOCIATES   201-772-9027
    509 Westminster, Lodi, NJ 07644
    Hours: 9-5 Wed-Sat
     • Used furniture and estate sale items. Some antiques. Eager to work with film & theatre.
    Worth the trip. Sales only. •
    (See display ad under FURNITURE RENTAL & PURCHASE: GENERAL)

SALVATION ARMY STORE   212-757-2311
    536 West 46th St., (10th-11th Ave.) NYC, NY 10036
    Hours: 9-4:45 Mon-Sat
     • Main store. Lots of furniture, large clothing dept. •

    112 Fourth Ave., (12th St.) NYC, NY 10003   212-673-2741
    Hours: 10-5:45 Mon, Tues, Wed, Sat • 10-7:45 Thurs, Fri

    208 Eighth Ave., (20th-21st St.) NYC, NY 10011   212-929-5214
    Hours: 10-7:45 Mon-Fri • 10-5:45 Sat

    268 West 96th St., (Broadway-West End Ave.) NYC, NY 10025   212-663-2258
    Hours: 10-5:45 Mon-Sat

    26 East 125th St., (5th-Madison Ave.) NYC, NY 10035   212-289-9617
    Hour: 10-6 Mon-Sat

    34-02 Steinway St., (34th Ave.) L.I.C. 11101   718-472-2414
    Hours: 10-7:30 Mon-Fri • 10-5:30 Sat
     • Main store; large selection, good prices. CREDIT CARDS •

    11 Downing St., (near Gates & Classon Ave.) Brooklyn, NY 11238   718-857-1671
    148-15 Archer Ave., (149th St.) Brooklyn, NY 11435   718-523-4648
    572-76 Fifth Ave., (16th-Prospect) Brooklyn, NY 11215   718-499-6557
    176 Bedford Ave., (N. 7th St.) Brooklyn, NY 11211   718-388-9249
    3522 Nostrand Ave., (V-W Ave.) Brooklyn, NY 11229   718-648-8930
    117-15 Myrtle Ave., (Richmond Hill Triangle) Brooklyn, NY 11418 718-846-4670
    182-25 Jamaica Ave., (182nd Pl.) Brooklyn, NY 11423   718-523-5084
    815 Seneca Ave., (2 blocks off Myrtle) Brooklyn, NY 11385   718-381-6687
    268 Knickerbocker Ave., (Willoughby Ave.) Brooklyn, NY 11237   718-821-7477
    220-01 Linden Blvd., (220th St.) Brooklyn, NY 11411   718-525-1219
    239 Flatbush Ave., (Bergen-7th Ave.) Brooklyn, NY 11217   718-857-7967
    963 Coney Island Ave., (Ditmas Ave.) Brooklyn, NY 11230   718-856-5280
    6822 Third Ave., (67th-68th St.) Brooklyn, NY 11220   718-745-1202
    829 Broadway, (Lewis-Ellroy St.) Brooklyn, NY 11206   718-384-4840
    981 Manhattan Ave., (Java-Huron St.) Brooklyn, NY 11222   718-383-5005
    282 Broadway, (Marcy Ave.) Brooklyn, NY 11211   718-387-9286
    436 Atlantic Ave., (Bonds-Nevins St.) Brooklyn, NY 11217   718-834-1562

    74 Pennington St., Newark, NJ   201-589-8904
    1059 Springfield Ave, Irvington, NJ   201-375-0454

S-T

SALVATION ARMY STORES (cont.)
    520 Main St., E. Orange, NJ   201-673-4070
    526 Broadway, Newark, NJ   201-483-9219
    1155 Elizabeth Ave., Elizabeth, NJ   908-965-0137
    326 Park Ave., Plainfield, NJ   908-756-9509
    • These additional locations vary in stock and hours. •

SPENCE-CHAPIN THRIFT SHOP   212-737-8448
    1430 Third Ave., (81st-82nd St.) NYC, NY 10028
    Hours: 11-7 Mon-Fri • 11-8 Thurs • 10-5 Sat
    • Mostly clothing, some books, magazines, furniture, bric-a-brac. •

STUYVESANT SQUARE THRIFT SHOP   212-831-1830
    1704 Second Ave., (88th-89th St.) NYC, NY 10028
    Hours: 11-6:30 Mon-Sat • 11-5 Sun
    • Two floors of clothing at great prices and well organized. Some jewelry, furniture, knick-knacks, etc. The place to go for "no budget" projects. CREDIT CARDS •

TILE, BRICKS & COBBLESTONES

BELLA TILE CO., INC.   212-475-2909
    178 First Ave., (10th-11th St.) NYC, NY 10009 212-674-2176
    Hours: 8:30-4:30 Mon-Fri • 8-3 Sat
    • American Olean dealer, fast service, samples available. •

BERGEN BLUESTONE CO. INC.   201-261-1903
    404 Rt. 17N, Paramus, NJ 07652   800-955-7625
    Hours: 7:30-4:30 Mon-Fri • 8-1 Sat   FAX 201-261-8856
    • Natural stone suppliers and contractors. Carries marble, granite, limestone, slate, sandstone, quarzite, landscaping stones, boulders, petrified wood. •

BERGEN TILE CORP.   718-789-9000
    215 Flatbush Ave., (Dean-Bergen) Brooklyn, NY 11217
    Hours: 8:30-5:45 Mon-Sat (Mon, Thurs till 8) • 10-5 Sun
    • Ceramic and vinyl tiles, linoleum. CREDIT CARDS •

COLOR TILE, INC.   212-979-8788
    903-907 Broadway, (20th St.) NYC, NY 10010
    Hours: 10-7 Mon-Fri • (Mon & Thurs till 8) • 10-6 Sat • 11-5 Sun
    • Part of the national chain. Ceramic tile, floor tile, linoleum, carpet. CREDIT CARDS •

COUNTRY FLOORS   212-627-8300
    15 East 16th St., (Univ. Pl.-5th Ave.) NYC, NY 10003
    Hours: 9-6 Mon-Fri • (Thurs till 8) • 9-5 Sat
    • Handpainted tiles, large selection of terra cotta tiles. CREDIT CARDS •

HASTINGS TILE & IL BAGNO COLLECTION   212-674-9700
    230 Park Ave. S., (19th St) NYC, NY 10010
    Hours: 9:30-5:30 Mon-Fri • (Thurs till 7:30) • 10-5:30 Sat
    • Huge selection of ceramic tile; samples available, quick service CREDIT CARDS •

IDEAL TILE   212-759-2339
    405 East 51st St., (1st Ave.) NYC, NY 10022
    Hours: 9-5:30 Mon-Fri • 10-5 Sat
    • Italian ceramic tile importers. •

S-T

ITALIAN TILE IMPORT CORP.   201-796-0722
   410 Market St., Elmwood Park, NY 07407   212-736-0383
   Hours: 9-5 Mon-Fri • (Thurs till 8) • 10-4 Sat
    • Ceramic tile by the square foot; reasonably priced, good quality. •

MANHATTAN BUILDERS SUPPLY CORP   212-924-5847
   154 Leroy St., (Washington-West) NYC, NY 10014
   Hours: 7-4 Mon-Fri
    • Brick, cinderblocks, glass block, sand, cement, gravel, plaster. •

NEW YORK BUILDERS SUPPLY CORP   212-564-5050
   545 W. 28th St., (10th-11th Ave.) NYC, NY 10011
   Hours: 7-3:30 Mon-Fri
    • Bricks, cinderblocks, sand, plaster. •

QUARRY TILE MARBLE & GRANITE   212-679-2559
   128 East 32nd St., (Lexington Ave.) NYC, NY 10016
   Hours: 9-5:30 Mon-Fri • 10-3:30 Sat
    • Ceramic tile, marble, granite, excellent selection, samples available. CREDIT CARDS •

VEDOVATO BROS.   212-534-2854
   246 East 116th St., (2nd Ave.) NYC, NY 10029
   Hours: 8-4 Mon-Fri
    • Good selection of ceramic tiles, including mosaics. •

SHERLE WAGNER INTERNATIONAL INC.   212-758-3300
   60 East 57th St., (Park) NYC, NY 10022
   Hours 9:30-5:00 Mon-Fri   FAX   212-207-8010
    • Bathroom fixture and hardware. Wall surfaces, tiles and custom tiles. RENTALS •

TOOLS & HARDWARE

For jeweler's tools, see **JEWELER'S TOOLS & SUPPLIES**
For leather craft tools, see **LEATHERCRAFTER'S & FURRIERS TOOLS & SUPPLIES**
For sculptors tools, see **CASTING & MODELING SUPPLIES**
For upholstery tools, see **UPHOLSTERY TOOLS & SUPPLIES**
For machine tools and parts, see **MACHINISTS AND MACHINIST TOOLS**

ABBEY RENT-ALL   718-428-0400
   203-16 Northern Blvd., Bayside, NY 11361
   Hours: 8-5:30 Mon-Sat   FAX   718-428-0404

   301 S. Broadway, (Rt. 107) Hicksville, NY 11801   516-681-1323
   Hours: 8-5 Mon-Sat
    • Power tool rental. CREDIT CARDS •

B & N HARDWARE   212-242-1136
   12 West 19th St., (5th-6th) NYC, NY 10011
   Hours: 8-5 Mon-Fri • 9-2 Sat
    • Good selection of hardware, tools, paint. Ask for Dave. CREDIT CARDS •

BARRY SUPPLY CO.   212-242-5200
   36 West 17th St., (5th-6th Ave) NYC, NY 10011
   Hours: 10:30-4:30 Mon-Fri   FAX   212-675-7094
    • Replacement parts for all windows and patio doors. •

S-T

BEST HARDWARE & MILL SUPPLY, INC.   516 354-0529
   1513 Jericho Turnpike, New Hyde Park, NY 11040
   Hours: 8-5:30 Mon-Fri • 8-5 Sat   FAX   516-354-1908
     • Cobalt drill bits, milling supplies, tools, case-hardened bolts, hardware. CREDIT CARDS •

BROWN & SILVER, INC.   718-589-7200
   813 Westchester Ave., (158th St.) Bronx, NY 10455
   Hours: 8-5 Mon-Fri   FAX   718-842-5815
     • General hardware. •

E. BUK, ANTIQUES & ART   212-226-6891
   151 Spring St., 2nd Fl., (W.B'way-Wooster) NYC, NY 10012
   Hours: by appt.

ANTIQUE tools, hardware and equipment for all trades:
blacksmithing, tinsmith's bookbinding, printing, machinist's
and machine tools, motors, leatherworking, upholstery,
cabinetmaking, woodworking, drafting, watch and clockmaking.
Electricals and tool boxes. Large selection.

     • Rentals, complete period settings and custom work. •
   (See display ads under PROP RENTAL HOUSES)

C K & L SURPLUS   212-966-1745
   307 Canal St., (B'way-Mercer) NYC, NY 10013
   Hours: 8:30-6 Mon-Sat • 9:30-5:30 Sun
     • Inexpensive, home-quality hand tools. Always crowded. Classic Canal Street. MC/VISA •

CANAL HARDWARE   212-226-0825
   305 Canal St., (B'way-Mercer) NYC, NY 10013
   Hours: 8-6 Mon-Sat • 10-5:30 Sun
     • Hardware, tools. Good prices. CREDIT CARDS •

CARTER, MILCHMAN & FRANK   718-361-2300
   28-10 37th Ave., (29th St.) NYC, NY 11101
   Hours: 8-5 Mon-Fri   FAX   718-937-5671
     • Large power tools, repair parts for tools. MC/VISA •

ALBERT CONSTANTINE & SONS   718-792-1600
   2050 Eastchester Rd., (Seminole-McDonald) Bronx, NY 10461
   Hours: 8-5 Mon-Fri • (Thurs till 8) • 8-3 Sat • (May-August: 8-1 Sat)
     • Fine woodworking tools; hardwoods, veneers. Good products, good service; catalog. •

RUDOLPH BASS   212-226-4000
   175 Lafayette St., (Broome) NYC, NY 10013
   Hours: 8:30-5 Mon-Fri • 9-1 Sat   FAX   212-226-4005
     • Specialty is large power tools, including parts and maintenance. CREDIT CARDS •

CORCORAN MFG. CO., INC.   800-362-6776
   1140 E. Howell, Anaheim, CA 92803   714-634-8854
   Hours: 7-4:30 Mon-Fri   FAX   714-634-9066
     • Carry Foam-Pro foam painting tools. Catalog. •

CUTAWL CO./DIV. OF BLACKSTONE   201-792-8622
   16 Story Hill Rd., Bethel, CT 06801
   Hours: 8-4:30 Mon-Fri   FAX   201-790-9832
     • Cutawls, catalog available. •

S–T

Decorators Wholesale Hardware Co./Legs, Legs, Legs/M. Wolchonk & Son, Inc.
16 East 30th St., (5th-Madison Aves.) NYC, NY 10016   212-696-1650
Hours: 9-6 Mon - Fri • 9-4:30 Sat   FAX   212-696-1664
• Large assortment of hardware and bathroom accessories; also metal and wood furniture legs; wholesale and retail. CREDIT CARDS •

Direct Fastening Service Corp.
212-533-4260
132 West Houston St., (MacDougal-Sullivan) NYC, NY 10012
Hours: 8-4:30 Mon-Fri   FAX   212-979-5444
• Mostly heavy equipment; Skil, Milwaukee power tools; also drywall screws. •

Duo-Fast Corp
201-768-3322
20 Corporate Dr., (off Blaisdell Rd.) Orangeburg, NY 10962
Hours: 8-5 Mon-Fri (phone orders) • 8:30-4 Mon-Fri (repairs) (close at 3:30 on Fri during summer)
• Staplers, nailers, tackers (air and electric); tapes and adhesives; hot melt glue guns. Phone orders, catalog. No minimum. •

Eastern Chain Works, Inc.
212-242-2500
144 West 18th St., (6th-7th) NYC, NY 10011
Hours: 8-4 Mon-Fri   FAX   212-242-2506
• Chain; all types, all metals •

Electric Appliance Rental & Sales Co./AC/DC Appliance/AAA Appliance Rentals & Sales Co.
212-686-8884
40 West 29th St., (B'way-6th Ave.) NYC, NY 10001
Hours: 8:30-5:30 Mon-Fri
• Electric power tool rental and sales. •

Enkay Trading Co., Inc.
718-272-5570
660 Atkins Ave., (Stanley-Wortman) Brooklyn, NY 11208
Hours: 8-4 Mon-Fri
• Polishing equipment, drill bits, files, rotary files; imported and domestic tools; minimum order $200. •

Force Machinery Co.
908-688-8270
2271 US Hwy. 22, Union, NJ 07083
Hours: 7:30-8 Mon-Fri • 8:30-5 Sat
• Excellent for shop equipment; all types of hand and power tools. CREDIT CARDS •

Forrest Manufacturing Co., Inc.
800-473-7111
461 River Rd., Clifton , NJ 07014   201-473-5236
Hours: 9-5 Mon-Fri   FAX   201-471-3333
• The finest circular saw blades on the market. Expensive, but worth it. Duraline A.T. or Woodworker 1 for acrylic cuts. Also sell dado sets. Very nice people. CREDIT CARDS •

The Garrett Wade Co., Inc.
212-807-1155
161 Sixth Ave., Mezz., (Spring St.) NYC, NY 10013   800-221-2942
Hours: 9-5:30 Mon-Fri • 10-3 Sat   FAX   212-255-8552
• Fine woodworking tools from all countries; small selection of solid brass furniture hardware; Also a few antique tools for the collector. Catalog. CREDIT CARDS •

Glaziers Hardware Products
718-361-0556
25-07 36th Ave., (Crescent) L.I.C., NY 11106
Hours: 8-4:30 Mon-Fri   FAX   718-361-0762
• Moldings, accessories, tools for the mirror, glass, storefront and picture framing industry. Carries suction grips for handling glass. MC/VISA •

S-T

GRAINGER, DIV. OF W.W. GRAINGER, INC.   212-629-5660
   527 West 34th St., (10th-11th Ave) NYC, NY 10001
   150 Varick St., (Spring St.) NYC, NY 10013   212-463-9566
   Hours: 8-5 Mon-Fri
    • Wide selection of hand and power tools, tool boxes, chests. Large catalog. Wholesale only.
MC/VISA •

H.T. SALES   212-265-0747
   718 Tenth Ave., (49th-50th St.) NYC, NY 10019   (billing) FAX 212-262-0150
   Hours: 7:30-4:30 Mon-Fri • 9-1 Sat   (orders) FAX 212-262-5082
    • Rental and sales of hand and power tools. CREDIT CARDS •

HALMOR HARDWARE & SUPPLY CO., INC.   212-675-0277
   48 West 22nd St., (5th-6th Ave.) NYC, NY 10010
   Hours: 8:30-5:30 Mon-Fri
    • SpecializeS in service to theatre, photography and design industry in Chelsea. Will special
order wheels, handtrucks, precision tools, specialty hardware, etc. MC/VISA •

INDUSTRIAL SUPPLY COMPANY OF LONG ISLAND   718-784-1291
   47-30 Vernon Blvd., (47th-48th Ave.) L.I.C., NY 11101
   Hours: 7-5:30 Mon-Fri • fax #, 24 hours every day   FAX 718-482-9353

Distributor of theatrical, special effects and construction supplies, power and hand tools, plumbing, electrical, rigging, welding, fastenings, hinges, paint, tape, ladders, scaffolding, adhesives, pneumatics, hydraulics, safety, handling equipment and more. Hard-to-find items a specialty. Daily delivery to studio or location. Since 1936.

"EVERYTHING
ISCO
FOR INDUSTRY"

    • Call for 1700 page catalog-$4.95, refundable. •
(See display ad under THEATRICAL HARDWARE & RIGGING EQUIPMENT.)

LUBANKO TOOL CO.   718-786-1980
   38-25 Greenpoint Ave., Sunnyside, NY 11101
   Hours: 9-5 Mon-Fri
    • Good selection of portable power tools. •

McKILLIGAN SUPPLY   607-798-9335
   435 Main St., Johnson City, NY 13790
   Hours: 8-5 Mon-Fri   FAX 607-729-4820
    • Suppliers of foundry equipment, heavy equipment, tools, bench tools, hardwoods to schools;
catalog. MC/VISA •

McMASTER-CARR SUPPLY CO.   908-329-3200
   PO Box 440, Monmouth Junction Rd., New Brunswick, NJ 08903-0440
   Hours: 7-4 Mon-Fri   FAX 908-329-3772
    • Top quality tools, hardware, supplies, components. Huge catalog. CREDIT CARDS •

MICROFLAME, INC.   612-935-3777
   14873 DeVeau, Minnetonka, MN 55345
   Hours: 8-5 Mon-Fri
    • Miniature butane torches. •

MIDTOWN HARDWARE   212-682-7858
   238 East 45th St., (2nd-3rd Ave) NYC, NY 10017
   Hours: 9-6 Mon-Fri • 9-5 Sat
    • Good selection of hardware, paint and houseware items. CREDIT CARDS •

S-T

    "I found it in the N.Y. Theatrical Sourcebook."

MUTUAL HARDWARE CORP. 718-361-2480
5-45 49th Ave., (Vernon) L.I.C., NY 11101
Hours: 8:30-5 Mon-Fri   FAX   718-729-8296
• Cutawls, Dremels, routers, drills, saws, sanders, hand tools, hardware. Catalog available. •

NEW ERA HARDWARE & SUPPLY 212-265-4183
832 Ninth Ave., (54th-55th) NYC, NY 10019
Hours: 7:30-4:30 Mon-Fri • 8-3 Sat
• Large selection of power tools; hardware, rigging supplies, casters, piano wire, tools, handtrucks. Friendly help. •

NEW HIPPODROME HARDWARE 212-840-2791
23 West 45th St., (5th-6th Ave.) NYC, NY 10036
Hours: 8-5:45 Mon-Fri • 9-2:45 Sat   FAX   212-302-3306
• Dremel accessories, hardware, Black & Decker, Stanley, Makita tools. CREDIT CARDS •

DAVE SANDERS & CO. 212-334-9898
111 Bowery, (Grand-Hewter) NYC, NY 10002
Hours: 8-4:30 Mon-Fri   FAX   212-966-4185
• One of NYC's largest selections of power tools; hardware. •

SEGAL BROTHERS 718-383-2995
205 Nassau Ave., (Russell) Brooklyn, NY 11222
Hours: 9-5 Mon-Fri
• Large selection of tools, Crosby clamps, motors. CREDIT CARDS •

SEVEN CORNERS ACE HARDWARE 800-328-0457
216 West 7th St., St. Paul, MN 55102
Hours: 7-5:30 Mon-Fri   FAX   612-224-8263
• Very good prices on power and hand tools; catalog. CREDIT CARDS •

SID'S HARDWARE 718-875-2259
345 Jay St., (Murtle-Willoughby) Brooklyn, NY 11201
Hours: 8-6:15 Mon-Fri • 8-5:45 Sat   FAX   718-852-3369
• Huge selection of general and household hardware, power tools, and household supplies. Delivery. CREDIT CARDS •

SILVER & SONS HARDWARE 212-247-6969
711 Eighth Ave. (44th-45th St.) NYC, NY 10036   212-247-6978
Hours: 9-5:30 Mon-Fri • 10-2 Sat
• Authorized distributor of most major brands of tools and theatrical maintenance equipment. CREDIT CARDS •

W.H. SILVER'S HARDWARE
212-247-4406
832 Eighth Ave., (50th-51st St.) NYC, NY 10019   212-247-4425
Hours: 8-5:30 Mon-Fri   FAX   212-246-2041
• Great selection of hardware, cable, locks, rope, tools, tape, prop maintenance kit supplies. •

SKIL CORP. 212-226-7630
75 Varick St., (Canal St.) NYC, NY 10013
Hours: 8-5 Mon-Fri   FAX   212-226-6893
• Tool sales and service. CREDIT CARDS •

SPROTZER TOOL & HARDWARE 718-349-2580
36 Eagle St., (Franklin-West St.) Brooklyn, NY 11222
Hours: 8-5 Mon-Fri
• Wholesale supplier of hand tools and cutting tools. Phone orders accepted. •

S-T

TRAVERS TOOL CO.
PO Box 1550, 128-15 26th Ave., Flushing, NY 11354
Hours: 8:30-4:30 Mon-Fri
718-886-7200
• Drill bits, chuck keys, clamps, sanding belts, etc. CREDIT CARDS •

UNIVERSAL TOOL
60 Willow Park Center, Farmingdale, NY 11735
Hours: 8:30-6 Mon-Fri • 9-5 Sat • 10-3 Sun
516-420-1420
• Formerly Tool Warehouse. Good discounts on hand tools and power tools. CREDIT CARDS •

WEINSTOCK BROTHERS, INC.
504 West 16th St., (10th-11th Ave.) NYC, NY 10011
Hours: 7-3 Mon-Fri
212-366-4626
• Nuts, bolts, washers, twine; rigging equipment for large scale industrial builders. •

HAROLD C. WOLFF, INC. HARDWARE
127 Fulton St., 3rd Fl., (Williams-Nassau) NYC, NY 10038
Hours: 8-4 Mon-Fri
212-227-2128
FAX 212-385-0794
• Power and hand tools, casters. •

WOOD WORKERS STORE
21801 Industrial Blvd., Rogers, MN 55374
Hours: 7-10 PM Mon-Fri • 8-4:30 Sat
800-279-4441
FAX 612-428-8668
• Especially good selection of hardware, some for knockdowns, caning supplies, veneers and veneering. Wooden parts, Catalog. CREDIT CARDS •

WOODCRAFT
210 Wood Country Industrial Park, Parkersburg, WV 26102
(orders) 800-225-1153
(customer service) 800-535-4482
Hours: 8:30-5 Mon-Fri
• Excellent selection of quality tools, some hardware. Catalog. CREDIT CARDS •

WOODLINE / JAPAN WOODWORKER
1731 Clement Ave., Almeda, CA 98501
Hours: 9-5 Mon-Sat
510-521-1810
800-537-7820
• Importer of Japanese tools, shears, scissors, punches, stencil knives; catalog available. CREDIT CARDS •

WOODWORKERS SUPPLY OF N.C., N.M., WYO
11108 N. Glenn Rd., Casper, WY 82601
Hours: 8-5 Mon-Fri • 9-1 Sat
800-645-9292
• Tools, power tools and hardware. Catalog. CREDIT CARDS •

TOYS & GAMES

See also **ARCADE & AMUSEMENT DEVICES**
See also **DOLLS & DOLLHOUSES**

BIG CITY KITES
1201 Lexington Ave., (81st-82nd St) NYC, NY 10028
11-6:30 Mon-Fri • (Thurs till 7:30) •10-6 Sat
212-472-2623
FAX 212-274-2998
• Kites, all types and sizes; also darts and dart boards. CREDIT CARDS •

"I found it in the N.Y. Theatrical Sourcebook."

CHESS SHOP   FAX   212-475-9580
  230 Thompson St., (Bleeker-3rd St) NYC, NY 10012
  Hours: 12-12 every day
  • Chess sets, books, boards; can also play here. CREDIT CARDS •

CLASSIC TOYS   212-941-9129
  218 Sullivan St., (Bleeker-3rd St.) NYC, NY 10012
  Hours: 12-6:30 Tue-Sun
  • Old and new miniature figures and die-cast vehicles, good selection of 50's and 60's toys, stuffed animals, some games and play sets. RENTALS •

THE COMPLEAT STRATEGIST   212-685-3880
  11 East 33rd Street (Madison-5th Ave.) NYC, NY 10016
  Hours: 10:30-6 Mon-Sat • (Thurs till 9)

  320 West 57th St., (8th-9th Ave.) NYC, NY 10019   212-582-1272
  Hours: 11-8 Mon-Sat • 12-5 Sun
  • Games, miniatures figures, soldiers, tanks, military model kits. Books on period uniforms. •

CREATIVE TOYMAKERS   203-773-3522
  934 State St., New Haven, CT 06511
  Hours: 10-6 Mon-Fri • 11:30-4 Sun.
  • Dolls and doll furniture; also general toys. •

DARROW'S FUN ANTIQUES   212-838-0730
  309 East 61st St., (1st-2nd Ave.) NYC, NY 10021
  Hours: 11-7 Mon-Fri • 11-4 Sat & Sun
  • Large selection antique and not-so-antique toys and games. RENTALS •

THE ENCHANTED FOREST
  85 Mercer St., (Spring-Broome) NYC, NY 10012   212-925-6677
  Hours: 11-7 Mon-Sat • 12-6 Sun
  • Unique collection of toys and stuffed animals. Expensive. CREDIT CARDS •

FAO SCHWARZ   212-644-9400
  767 Fifth Ave., (58th St.) NYC, NY 10153
  Hours: 10-6 Mon-Sat • (Thurs till 8) • 12-6 Sun
  • Large selection stuffed toys, dolls, dollhouses, games, trains, playground equipment. CREDIT CARDS •

RITA FORD, INC.   212-535-6717
  19 East 65th St., (Madison-5th St.) NYC, NY 10021
  Hours: 9-5 Mon-Sat
  • All kinds of music boxes, antique and reproduction; repairs. RENTALS MC/VISA •

MARION & CO.   212-727-8900
  147 West 26th St., (6th-7th Ave.) NYC, NY 10001
  Hours: 8-5:30 Mon-Fri
  • Manufacturer of playing cards, dice and casino equipment. RENTALS CREDIT CARDS •

PALO IMPORTS   203-792-2411
  184 Greenwood Ave., Bethel, CT 06801
  Hours: 9:30-6 Mon-Sat • Thurs till 8
  • Doll house supplies. Retail toy store; novelties. •

S-T

PENNY WHISTLE TOYS   212-925-2088
132 Spring St., (Wooster-Greene) NYC, NY 10012
Hours: 11-7 every day

448 Columbus Ave., (81st-82nd St.) NYC, NY 10024   212-873-9090
Hours: 10-6 Mon • 9-7 Tues-Sat (Thurs till 8) • 11-6 Sun

1283 Madison Ave., (91st-92nd St.) NYC, NY 10128   212-369-3868
Hours: 9-6 Mon-Wed • 9-7 Thurs, Fri • 10-6 Sat • 11-5 Sun
• Interesting selection of quality toys,(some European), games, books, and tapes. CREDIT
CARDS •

PROPS FOR TODAY   212-206-0330
121 West 19th Street Reception: 3rd Fl., (6th-7th Ave) NYC, NY 10011
Hours: 8:30-5 Mon-Fri   FAX   212-924-0450
• Full service prop rental house. Contemporary and antique dolls, toys and games, trophies
and school supplies. •
(See display ad under PROP RENTAL HOUSES.)

RIVOLI MERCHANDISE COMPANY   212-955-5035
54 Howard St., (Mercer) NYC, NY 10013
Hours: 9-6 Mon-Fri
• Toys-wholesale also seasonal merchandise, stationary, school supplies & props. •
(See display ad under PARTY GOODS.)

B. SHACKMAN & CO., INC.   212-989-5162
85 Fifth Ave., (16th St) NYC, NY 10003
Hours: 9-5 Mon-Fri • 10-5 Sat
• Antique repro toys, dolls, dollhouses and dollhouse furniture, paper dolls & Victorian paper
toys; wholesale (catalog) and retail. •

STAR MAGIC   212-228-7770
745 Broadway, (8th-Waverly) NYC, NY 10003
Hours: 10-10 Mon-Sat • 11-9 Sun

275 Amsterdam Ave., (73rd St.) NYC, NY 10023   212-769-2020
Hours: 10-10 Mon-Sat • 11-9 Sun

1256 Lexington Ave., (84th-85th St.) NYC, NY 10028   212-988-0300
Hours: 10-9 Mon-Sat • 11-7:30 Sun
• Space-related toys, posters, books, star maps and finders; crystals. CREDIT CARDS •

TOY PARK   212-427-6611
112 East 86th St., (Park-Lexington Ave.) NYC, NY 10028
Hours: 10-7 Mon-Sat • 12-6 Sun
• Large selection toys, games, models, dolls, stuffed animals. CREDIT CARDS •

TOYS `R' US   212-594-8697
1293 Broadway, (33th-34th St.) NYC, NY 10001
Hours: 9-9 Mon, Fri • 9-8 Tues, Wed • 9-9:30 Thurs • 9-8 Sat • 11-7 Sun
• Giant toy retailer with good selection and prices, even in this smaller urban store. CREDIT
CARDS •

UNIVERSAL BINGO SUPPLIES   201-345-5653
69 Grove St., Patterson , NJ 07503
Hours: 9-4 Mon-Fri   FAX   201-345-7234
• Formerly Universal Games. Casino, bingo, carnival game equipment. See Walter. RENTALS •

S-T

"I found it in the N.Y. Theatrical Sourcebook."

TRIMMINGS: GENERAL

ADDIS RIBBON, INC.   201-659-1719
317 St. Paul Ave. Building #3, Jersey City, NJ 07306
Hours: 8-4:30 Mon-Fri   FAX   201-659-9160
• Laces, satins, grosgrains, vinyls and novelty ribbons of all kinds. Dress & display, straight edge & wired, sizes 1-100. Full rolls only. Call for specific samples and wholesale price list. •

ALFRED MFG. CORP.   201-332-9100
350 Warren, (near Holland Tun.) Jersey City, NJ 07302
Hours: 9-4:30 Mon-Fri • call first   FAX   201-332-1201
• Manufacturer of rayon, cotton, chainette, cord; mostly wholesale. •

ANTAN   203-661-4769
12 West Putnam Ave., (Greenwich Ave.) Greenwich, CT 06830
Hours: 10-5 Mon-Sat   FAX   203-661-0657
• French trims and tassels, lamps, shades and antiques. Good prices. •

ARTISTIC RIBBON & NOVELTY CO.   212-255-4224
22 West 21st St., (5th-6th Ave.) NYC, NY 10010
Hours: 9-5 Mon-Fri   FAX   212-645-6589
• Satin, grosgrain, velvet, poly ribbon; washable, flame retardant. No credit cards. •

S. AXELROD CO., INC.   212-594-3022
7 West 30th St., (5th Ave.-B'way) NYC, NY 10001
Hours: 9-5 Mon-Fri
• Decorative trims, rhinestones, metal findings, and moving eyes for dolls. •

BAER FABRICS   (fashion) 800-769-7776
515 East Market, Louisville, KY 40202   (costumes) 800-769-7778
Hours: 9-9 Mon • 9-5 Tue-Sat   FAX   502-582-2331
• Distributor of full line of "Conso" trims and supplies; prompt shipment. CREDIT CARDS •

BEER-STERN CO.   212-279-4380
50 West 34th St., (5th Ave.-B'way) NYC, NY 10001
Hours: 9-5 Mon-Fri • by appt. only   FAX   516-673-5581
• By the piece only; jacquard, fancy braid, fringe, novelty trimmings. •

BRIMAR, INC.   708-272-9585
P.O. Box 2621, 1706 Marcee Lane, Northbrook, IL 60065
Hours: 9-5 Mon-Fri   FAX   708-272-1097
• Importers of tassels, braids, fringes, cordings, etc. Very helpful. Will sell wholesale to designers and decorators. Supplies some items to M&J. Call for free catalog & prices. •

C & C METAL PRODUCTS   212-819-9700
39 West 37th St., (5th-6th Ave.) NYC, NY 10018
Hours: 8-9:30 and 4-5 Mon-Fri for salesman • or by appt.   FAX   212-819-9777
• Rhinestones, jewels, settings, metal buttons, buckles, nailheads; large catalog available. •

C.M. OFFRAY & SON, INC.   908-879-4700
PO Box 601, Rt. 24, Chester, NJ 07930
Hours: 8:30-4:30 Mon-Fri   FAX   908-879-8588
• Wholesale ribbons; satin, grosgrain, velvet, etc.; woven-edge, craft, and floral ribbons. Catalog •

S-T

DAYTONA TRIMMINGS CO.   212-354-1713
    251 West 39th St., (7th-8th Ave.) NYC, NY 10018
    Hours: 8-6 Mon-Fri   FAX   212-391-0716
    • Ric-rac, laces, scarves, emblems, shoulder pads; wholesale. No credit cards. •

DUPLEX NOVELTY   212-564-1352
    575 Eighth Ave., (38th St.) NYC, NY 10018
    Hours: 9-5 Mon-Fri
    • Wooden beads, buttons, buckles; wholesale; catalog •

ELLIS IMPORT CO., INC.   212-947-6666
    44 West 37th St., (5th-6th Ave.) NYC, NY 10018
    Hours: 8:30-5 Mon-Fri   FAX   212-594-9367
    • Rhinestones, jewels, spangles, pearls, beads, chains, novelties. •

ELVEE PEARL CO.   212-947-3930
    21 West 38th St., (5th-6th Ave.) NYC, NY 10018
    Hours: 9-5 Mon-Fri   FAX   212-575-0931
    • Simulated pearls and beads; wholesale; minimum: 1 gross, 1 doz. strings; catalog. •

FRED FRANKEL & SONS, INC.   212-840-0810
    19 West 38th St., (5th-6th Ave.) NYC, NY 10018
    Hours: 8:45-4:30 Mon-Fri
    • Rhinestone, pearl, beaded, sequined trims and motifs; catalog. •

FRIEDMAN & DISTILLATOR/OWL MILLS   212-226-6400
    53 Leonard St., (Church-W.B'way) NYC, NY 10013
    Hours: 9-5 Mon-Fri   FAX   212-219-1402
    • Trimmings, braids, ribbons and fabrics; catalog; speak to Toni. No credit cards. •

GAMPEL SUPPLY CORP.   212-398-9222
    39 West 37th St., (5th-6th Ave) NYC, NY 10018   212-398-9223
    Hours: 8:30-4 Mon-Fri
    • Rattail, soutache, decorative and beaded cord. •

GELBERG BRAID CO., INC.   212-730-1121
    243 West 39th St., (7th-8th Ave.) NYC, NY 10018
    Hours: 8:30-5 Mon-Fri
    • Manufacturer of dress trimmings, braids, tassels, cords, braided buttons; see Irwin. •

ELLIOT GREENE & CO., INC.   212-391-9075
    37 West 37th St., (5th-6th Ave.) NYC, NY 10018
    Hours: 9-4 Mon-Fri   FAX   212-391-9079
    • Rhinestones, spangles, jewels, pearls, beaded trims. •

GREY OWL INDIAN CRAFTS   718-341-4000
    132-05 Merrick Blvd., (Bel Knapp) Jamaica, NY 11434
    Hours: 9-5 Mon-Fri
    • Indian beads, feathers, kits; catalog. CREDIT CARDS •

HARMAN IMPORTING CORP.   212-947-1440
    16 West 37th St., (5th-6th Ave.) NYC, NY 10018
    Hours: 9-4 Mon-Fri
    • Jewels, findings. No credit cards. •

HYMAN HENDLER & SONS   212-840-8393
   67 West 38th St., (5th-6th Ave.) NYC, NY 10018
   Hours: 9-5:30 Mon-Fri • 10-3 Sat
   • Quality ribbons; grosgrain, satin, all types; some drapery, upholstery, antique trims.
Beautiful stuff. •

JAY NOTIONS & NOVELTIES, INC.   212-921-0440
   22 West 38th St., (5th-6th Ave.) NYC, NY 10018
   Hours: 8-5 Sun-Fri   FAX   212-575-2620
   • Wholesale ribbon, braid, trim. •

K. TRIMMING COMPANY   212-431-8929
   519 Broadway, (Spring St.) NYC, NY 10012
   Hours: 9:30-5:30 Sun-Fri
   • Buttons, notions, trims, and laces, rhinestones and trims, Velcro. •

KAHANER CO., INC.   212-840-3030
   228 West 38th St., (7th-8th Ave.) NYC, NY 10018
   Hours: 8:30-4:30 Mon-Fri
   • Trims, especially rhinestone, sequin and beaded; catalog. •

LA LAME, INC.   212-921-9770
   250 West 39th St., 4th Fl., (7th-8th Ave.) NYC, NY 10018
   Hours: 9-5 Mon-Fri
   • Selection of metallic laces, braids, and cords is excellent. No credit cards. •

M & J TRIMMINGS   212-391-9072
   1014 Sixth Ave.(Upholstery)
   1008 Sixth Ave.(Fashion), (37th-38th Street) NYC, NY 10018
   Hours: 9-6 Mon-Fri • 10-5 Sat
   • Upholstery and drapery trimmings, tassels, tie-backs, etc. Pricey, but excellent quality and
good selection. At fashion annex: sequins, beads, braids, cords, ribbons, tassles. Wide selection. CREDIT CARDS •

MARGOLA IMPORT CORP.   212-695-1115
   48 West 37th St., (5th-6th Ave.) NYC, NY 10018
   Hours: 9-6 Mon-Fri   FAX   212-594-0071
   • Rhinestones, beads, rosemontees, pearls, beaded and embroidered trims. MC/VISA •

MAY ART   203-661-3732
   P.O. Box 478, Riverside, CT 06878
   Hours: 9-5 Mon-Fri   FAX   203-661-3222
   • Sells beautiful imported French organdy silk ribbons, and flowers. Wholesale. Minimum
order $100. •

MAYER IMPORT CO., INC.   212-391-3830
   25 West 37th St., (5th-6th Ave.) NYC, NY 10018
   Hours: 8:30-4:30 Mon-Fri   FAX   212-768-9183
   • Jewels, pearls, cameos, trade beads, faceted plastic domes, etc.; catalog. •

METROPOLITAN IMPEX, INC.   212-564-0398
   966 Sixth Ave., (35th-36th St.) NYC, NY 10018   212-502-5243
   Hours: 9-6:30 Mon-Sat   FAX   212-564-0460
   • Good selection of general trimmings; feathers, laces, beads, etc. CREDIT CARDS •

S-T

NOVELTY POM POM CO.
264 West 40th St., 4th Fl., (7th-8th Ave.) NYC, NY 10018
Hours: 9-4:30 Mon-Fri
• Manufacturers of pompoms, tassels, braids, fringe, piping, cords, frogs, passementeries; wholesale or retail. •

212-391-9174
212-391-9175

OBEROI MARKETING, INC.
977 Sixth Ave., (36th St.) NYC, NY 10018
Hours: 9-6 Mon-Fri
• Indian imports, beaded fringe, emblems, buttons, appliques, and trims. •

212-967-8540

ORNAMENTAL RESOURCES
P.O.Box 3010, 1427 Miner St., Idaho Springs, Co 80452
Hours: 9-5 Mon-Fri   FAX
• Beads, findings, trims. Fabulous finds. One time $25 subscription gets you a huge ring binder; updated for at least one year. Worth the price. CREDIT CARDS •

303-567-4987
303-567-4988
303-567-4245

PENN BRAID & TRIMMING CO.
141 West 36th St., (B'way-7th Ave.) NYC, NY 10001
Hours: 9-5 Mon-Fri
• Metallic trims, edging braid, fringe, soutache, embroidered motifs, hood cords. •

212-736-4606

PENN & FLETCHER
242 West 30th St., 2nd Fl., (7th-8th Ave.) NYC, NY 10001
Hours: 9-5 Mon-Fri   FAX
• Fine quality trims and lace; also beading and embroidery services. MC/VISA •

212-239-6868
212-239-6914

PIRATES TREASURE COVE
6212 Kracker Ave. E., Gibsonton, FL 33534
Hours: 9-5 Mon-Sat   FAX
• Sequins, jewels, trims, fabrics; good prices, will ship anywhere, fast service; catalog. MC/VISA •

813-677-1137
813-671-2915

QUALITY BRAID
60-01 31st Ave., Woodside, NY 11377
Hours: 9-5 Mon-Fri   FAX
• Formerly Ruben Bead Importing of Manhattan. Manufacturer of sequin fabrics, stretch and non-stretch, 45", all colors. All trims. •

718-204-0002
718-204-0999

ROTH IMPORT CO.
13 West 38th St., (5th-6th Ave.) NYC, NY 10018
Hours: 9-5 Mon-Fri • 9-5:30 Sat
• Sequin and beaded applique, sequins and rhinestones by the yard, metallic braids and cords, beaded fringe; wholesaler, large orders only. •

212-840-1945

ROYALE DRAPERIES, INC.
289 Grand St., (Eldridge) NYC, NY 10002
Hours: 9-5:30 Mon-Thurs • Fri only til 5 • 10-5 Sun   FAX
• Good variety trims, braids; cable cord, remnants; inexpensive. CREDIT CARDS •

212-431-0170
212-431-3882

SEQUINS INTERNATIONAL, INC.
49 West 38th St., 9th Fl., (5th-6th Ave.) NYC, NY 10018
Hours: 9-5 Mon-Fri   FAX
• Sequin cloth and sequin trims. •

212-221-3121
212-869-4319

S–T

SHELLCRAFT, DIV. CRESTHILL INDUSTRIES 212-947-1960
519 Eighth Ave., 11th Fl., (35th-36th St.) NYC, NY 10018
Hours: 9-5 Mon-Fri FAX 212-564-2392
• Beads, sequins. •

SHERU 212-730-0766
49 West 38th St., (5th-6th Ave.) NYC, NY 10018
Hours: 9-6 Mon-Fri • 9:30-5 Sat FAX 212-840-2368
• Beads, shells, findings, sequins, jewelry, craft supplies; wholesale and retail. Go early in the day. Gets crazy around lunch time. Surly service. CREDIT CARDS •

MARTIN SCHORR CO., DIV. OF WILLIAM GINSBERG CO. 212-719-4870
242 West 38th St., (7th-8th Ave.) NYC, NY 10018 212-244-4539
Hours: 9-5 Mon-Fri FAX 212-921-2014
• Washable ribbons, velvet, grosgrain, satin, jacquard; braids. •

SIDNEY COE, INC. 908-495-9285
State Highway 36, Airport Plaza, Hazlet, NJ 07730
Hours: 9-5 Mon-Thurs • 9-4 Fri
• Beads, jewels, motifs, sew-on mirrors. CREDIT CARDS •

SO-GOOD 212-398-0236
28 West 38th St., (5th-6th Ave.) NYC, NY 10018
Hours: 9-5 Mon-Fri FAX 212-768-1325
• Ribbons, braid, piping. •

S-T

TINSEL TRADING   212-730-1030
  47 West 38th St., (5th-6th Ave.) NYC, NY 10018
  Hours: 10-5 Mon-Fri • 10-3 some Saturdays (call first)
   • Metallic /bullion trims and tassels; antique trims; see Marsha. A beautiful collection.
  CREDIT CARDS •

TOHO SHOJI,, INC.   212-868-7465
  990 Sixth Ave., (36th-37th St.) NYC, NY 10018   212-868-7466
  Hours: 9-6 Mon-Fri • 10-5 Sat   FAX   212-868-7464
   • Large selection of beads, buttons, chains, jewelry components and findings, in a well lighted
  new shop. Wholesale and retail. CREDIT CARDS •

UNNATURAL RESOURCES, INC.   201-228-5384
  14 Forest Ave., Caldwell, NJ 07006   (orders) 800-992-5540
  Hours: 9-6 Mon-Fri • or by appt.   FAX   201-226-8106
   • Distributors of metallic beaded mesh(MBM): acetate beads fastened to a polyester mesh
  and coated with a variety of metallic (and non-metallic) finishes. Speak to Loretta. •
  (See display ad under CASTING & MODELING SUPPLIES.)

VABAN   212-889-3088
  225 5th Ave., (26th-27th St.) NYC, NY 10010
  Hours: 9:30-4:30 Mon-Fri   FAX   212-683-6761
   • Supplier of European wired ribbons. No credit cards. Wholesale only. Min. $100. Catalog. •

WORLD BEADS AND TRIMMINGS,, INC.   212-944-5709
  25 West 38th St., (5th-6th Ave.) NYC, NY 10018
  Hours: 8:30-6:30 Mon-Fri
   • Asian imported beads, acrylic stones and findings. •

YORK NOVELTY IMPORTS INC   212-594-7050
  10 West 37th St., (5th-6th Ave.) NYC, NY 10018   800-223-6676
  Hours: 9-5 Mon-Fri   FAX   212-768-8823
   • Beads, jewels, pearls, spangles, rhinestones, trims, chain, novelties. •

TRIMMINGS: CUSTOM

S-T

LENDING TRIMMING CO., INC.   212-563-5140
  179 Christopher St., (West Side Hwy.) NYC, NY 10014
  Hours: 9-5 Mon-Fri   FAX   212-714-1338
   • Chainette made to order; Jerry Wolf is sales rep. •

STANDARD TRIMMING CORP. (A DIVISION OF SCALAMANDRE)   212-980-3888
  950 Third Ave., (57th St.) NYC, NY 10022
  Hours: 9-5 Mon-Fri   FAX   212-688-7531
   • Custom trims and tassels; some stock of overruns occasionally. Allow plenty of time: can
  make elaborate wood mold fringe. Expensive. •

TRIMMINGS: FEATHERS & FLOWERS

AA FEATHER COMPANY   212-695-9470
16 West 36th St., (5-6 Ave.) NYC, NY 10018   212-695-9471
Hours: 9-5:30 Mon-Thurs • 9-4 Fri
• Natural and dyed feathers. •

AMERICAN PLUME & FANCY FEATHER CO., INC.   718-729-1552
26-32 Skillman Avenue, (27th Street) L.I.C., NY 11101
Hours: 7-4 Mon-Thurs • 7-3 Fri   FAX   718-784-3392
• Formerly American Feather Company. Natural and dyed feathers, boas, dyed turkey, etc;
referrals for smaller orders available. •

ASSOCIATED FABRICS CORPORATION   212-689-7186
104 East 25th St., (Lexington-Park Ave.) NYC, NY 10010
Hours: 8:30-4:30 Mon-Fri (closed 12-1)   FAX   212-260-3531
• Nice ostrich plumes over 18", ask for Bruce. MC/VISA •

CINDERELLA FLOWER & FEATHER CORPORATION   212-840-0644
60 West 38th St., (5-6th Ave.) NYC, NY 10018
Hours: 9-5:15 Mon-Fri • 9-4:15 Sat
• Good selection of fancy feathers, boas, flowers, fruit. CREDIT CARDS •

DERSH FEATHER & TRADING CORP.   212-714-2806
62 West 36th St., (5th-6th Avenue) NYC, NY 10018
Hours: 9-5 Mon-Thurs • 9-2 Fri
• Good selection of feathers; recommended. •

DULKEN & DERRICK, INC.   212-929-3614
12 West 21st St., 6th Floor, (5th-6th Avenue) NYC, NY 10010
Hours: 9-4 Mon-Fri
• Silk and fancy flowers; will custom-make. •

ESKAY NOVELTY   212-391-4110
34 West 38th St., (5th-6th Avenue) NYC, NY 10018   800-237-2202
Hours: 8-4 Mon-Thurs • 8-Noon Fri   FAX   212-921-7926
• Excellent selection of all types of feathers. Phone orders accepted until 8pm Mon-Thurs. •
(See display ad this section)

GREY OWL INDIAN CRAFTS   718-341-4000
132-05 Merrick Blvd., (Bel Knap) Jamaica, NY 11434
Hours: 9-5 Mon-Fri
• Feathers for American Indian headdresses; also beads, kits. CREDIT CARDS •

LISTOKIN & SONS FABRICS, INC.   212-226-6111
87 Hester St., (Orchard-Allen) NYC, NY 10002
Hours: 9:30-5:30 Sun-Thurs • 9-2 Fri
• Bridal fabric, boas, white cotton net. CREDIT CARDS •

MANGROVE FEATHER CO., INC.   212-431-5806
468 Greenwich Street, (Canal-Watts) NYC, NY 10013
Hours: 9-5 Mon-Thurs • 9-2 Fri   FAX   212-941-8272
• Raw and dyed feathers, ostrich boa, marabou, chandelle, etc. •

MANNY'S MILLINERY SUPPLY CO.   212-840-2235
26 West 38th St., (5th-6th Ave.) NYC, NY 10018
Hours: 9:30-5:30 Mon-Fri • 9-4 Sat   FAX   212-944-0178
• Small selection of feathers and fruit; good selection of millinery supplies. 2 ply Buckram. •

S-T

PAUL'S VEIL & NET CORP.
    42 West 38th St., (5th-6th Ave.) NYC, NY 10018
    Hours: 8:30-4 Mon-Fri • 8:30-2 Sat
    • Bridal laces, flowers. •
212-391-3822
212-391-3823
FAX 212-575-5141

ROTH IMPORT CO.
    13 West 38th St, (5th-6th Avenue) NYC, NY 10018
    Hours: 9-5 Mon-Fri • 9-5:30 Sat
    • Pure silk flowers, feathers, and good selection of trimmings; wholesaler, large orders only. •
212-840-1945

M SCHWARTZ & SONS, INC.
    45 Hoffman Avenue, Hauppauge, NY 11788
    Hours: 8:30-5 Mon-Fri
    • Wholesale natural and dyed feathers and novelties. •
516-234-7722

S.A. FEATHERS
    58-52 Enterprise Parkway, Ft. Myers, FL 33905
    Hours: 9-4 Mon-Fri
    • Natural and custom-dyed feathers by the pound, boas, and band plumes. •
800-226-8698
813-693-6363

TRIMMINGS LACE & LACE MOTIFS

AMERICAN FABRICS CO.
    29 West 36th St., (5th-6th Ave.) NYC, NY 10018
    Hours: 9-5 Mon-Fri
    • Lace, schiffle embroidery, embroidered collars, table linens, flame retardant lace. •
212-868-0100

ASTOR LACE & TRIMMINGS
    132 West 36th St., (B'way-7th Ave.) NYC, NY 10018
    Hours: 9-4:30 Mon-Fri
    • Laces, schiffle embroideries, novelties, trims. •
212-736-0475

40TH ST. TRIMMINGS., INC.
    252 West 40th St., (7th-8th Ave.) NYC, NY 10018
    Hours: 9-5:45 Mon-Fri • 10-5 Sat
    • Notions, trimmings, novelties; wholesale and retail. CREDIT CARDS •
212-354-4729

LEW NOVIK, INC.
    381 Sunrise Highway, Lynebrook, NY 11563
    Hours: 9-5 Sun-Fri
    • Lace motifs and yardage; nets, maline, tulle, marquisette; wholesale only; must order from sample books. CREDIT CARDS •
516-599-8678
FAX 516-599-8696

PAUL'S VEIL & NET CORP.
    42 West 38th St., (5th-6th Ave.) NYC, NY 10018
    Hours: 8:30-4Mon-Fri • 8:30-2 Sat
    • Flowers, bridal laces, lace gloves, etc. •
212-391-3822
212-391-3823
FAX 212-575-5141

PENN & FLETCHER
    242 West 30th St., 2nd Fl., (7th-8th Ave.) NYC, NY 10001
    Hours: 9-5 Mon-Fri
    • High quality laces and trims; also beading and embroidery services. MC/VISA •
212-239-6868
FAX 212-239-6914

"I found it in the N.Y. Theatrical Sourcebook."

TRIMMINGS: UPHOLSTERY & DRAPERY

See also **TRIMMINGS: GENERAL**

BAER FABRICS (commercial) 800-769-7779
515 East Market, Louisville, KY 40202 502-583-5521
Hours: 9-5:30 Mon-Sat FAX 502-582-2331
• Distributor of full line of "Conso" trims and supplies; prompt shipment. CREDIT CARDS •

BRUNSCHWIG & FILS, INC. 212-838-7878
979 Third Ave., (58th-59th St.) NYC, NY 10022
Hours: 9-5 Mon-Fri
• Account required. Decorator house, to the trade only; traditional American and European trims, fabric, wallpaper; expensive. Limited stock. •

CLARENCE HOUSE 212-752-2890
211 East 58th St. (2nd-3rd. Ave.) NYC, NY 10022
Hours: 9-5 Mon-Fri
• Expensive but unique European tassels & trims. Some stock but allow plenty of time; account required; to the trade. •

CONSO PRODUCTS 212-686-7676
261 5th Ave., Suite 1011, NYC, NY 10016
Hours: 9-5 Mon-Fri FAX 212-686-9890
• Wholesale drapery and upholstery trims and supplies. •

GLADSTONE FABRICS 914-783-1900
PO Box 566, Orchard Hill Rd., Harriman, NY 10926 800-724-0168
Hours: 9-6 Mon-Fri • Sat by appt. FAX 914-783-2963

FAMOUS SELECTION OF THEATRICAL FABRICS:
Spandex, milliskin, nude souffle, sequin cloth, metallic lame' and lace, novelty nets and tulle, buckram and fake furs. Also unique antique ribbons, braids, trims, beaded and feathered applique's as well as the fundamental cottons, linens, woolens and silks.

• Fast shipping & swatching service. CREDIT CARDS •
(See display ad under FABRICS: GENERAL)

GREENTEX UPHOLSTERY SUPPLIES 212-206-8585
236 West 26th St., (7th-8th Ave.) NYC, NY 10001
Hours: 8-4 Mon-Thurs • 8-1:45 Fri
• Upholstery supply house; simple selection, in good quantities. •

KRAVET FABRICS 212-421-6363
979 Third Ave., 3rd Fl., (58th-59th St.) NYC, NY 10022
Hours: 9-5 Mon-Fri
• To the trade, account required. Mostly to order, some stock, fringe, braid, gimp, tassels. •

M & J TRIMMINGS 212-391-9072
1014 Sixth Ave., (37th-38th St.) NYC, NY 10018
Hours: 9-6 Mon-Fri • 10-5 Sat
• Upholstery and drapery trimmings, tassels, tie-backs, etc. at this annex. Pricey, but excellent quality and good selection. CREDIT CARDS •

STANDARD TRIMMING CORP. (A DIVISION OF SCALAMANDRE)   212-950-3888
950 Third Ave., (57th St.) NYC, NY 10022
Hours: 9-5 Mon-Fri   FAX   212-688-7531
• Custom trims and tassels; allow plenty of time! Can make elaborate woodmold fringe, some stock of overruns occasionally. Expensive. stock of very old and elaborate trims; see Ed Goodman. •

I. WEISS & SONS, INC.   212-246-8444
2-07 Borden Ave., (Vernon-Jackson) L.I.C., NY 11101   718-706-8139
Hours: 8:30-5 Mon-Fri   FAX   718-482-9410
• Custom manufacturer of stage curtains. Trims to match. Custom appliques, tassels, rope, fringe, etc. Also scenic fabrics and flameproofing. •
(See display ad under CURTAINS & DRAPERIES, THEATRICAL.)

TROPHIES & ENGRAVERS

A-1 HOUSE OF TROPHIES   212-966-4742
431 Canal St., (Varick St.) NYC, NY 10013
Hours: 8-5:30 Mon-Thurs • 8-4 Fri • 8:30-1 Sat
• Large selection of trophies, plaques; good prices; catalog. •

ADMIRAL ENGRAVING & ETCHING LTD.   212-924-3400
555 West 25th St., (10th-11th Ave.) NYC, NY 10001
Hours: 9-5 Mon-Fri   FAX   212-924-3489
• Awards, trophies, certificates, ribbons, silver cups; printing and engraving. •

ALPHA ENGRAVING CO.   212-247-5266
254 West 51 St., (8th Ave.-B'way) NYC, NY 10019
Hours: 9-5:30 Mon-Fri
• Engraves trophies, awards; metal and plastic engraved signs; name tags. •

BASKIN ENGRAVERS   212-869-5048
15 West 47th St., (5th-6th Ave.) NYC, NY 10036
Hours: 9:30-6 Mon-Fri • 11-5 Sat
• Engraving while you wait, jewelry, crests, nameplates; silverware, pewter, etc. Beautiful work. •

KRAUS & SONS, INC.   212-620-0408
158 West 27th St., (6th-7th Ave.) NYC, NY 10001
Hours: 9-5 Mon-Fri
• Custom trophies and ribbons, also flags and banners. No credit cards. •

V. LORIA & SONS, INC.   212-925-0300
178 Bowery, (Delancey St.) NYC, NY 10012
Hours: 10:30-6 Mon-Fri • 10:30-4 Sat
• All types of trophies, plaques, engraving, ribbons, etc. CREDIT CARDS •

MURRAY RACKOFF   212-924-4111
59 West 19th St., (5th-6th Ave.) NYC, NY 10011
Hours: 8:30-5 Mon-Fri   FAX   212-924-1317
• Large selection of trophies; engraving. Free catalog. CREDIT CARDS •

TRUART STRYPPMAN ENGRAVING 201-867-7445
705 27th St., (Summit Ave.) Union City, NJ 07087
Hours: 9-5 Mon-Fri FAX 201-867-7974
• Dimensionally precise figurative brass engraving. No credit cards. •

TROPICAL FISH

See also **PET SUPPLIES**

AQUARIUS AQUARIUMS 212-586-9093
214 Riverside Dr., Suite 612, (93-94th St.) NYC, NY 10025 (pager)917-556-7058
Hours: by appt. FAX 212-397-0295
• Acrylic & glass, salt & fresh water aquarium design & installation. •

AQUARIUM DESIGN 212-308-5224
979 Third Ave., (58th-59th St.) NYC, NY 10022 914-352-1640
Hours: by appt. (24 hour emergency service)
• Design, manufacture, install, and maintain aquarium systems. •

BROADWAY AQUARIUM & PET SHOP 212-724-0536
652 Amsterdam Ave., (91st-92nd St.) NYC, NY 10025
Hours: 10-7 Mon-Fri • 10-5 Sat
• Basic neighborhood pet supply store. CREDIT CARDS •

CRYSTAL AQUARIUM 212-534-9003
1659 Third Ave., (93rd St.) NYC, NY 10128
Hours: 10-7 Mon-Fri • 9-7 Sat • 12-5 Sun • (closed Sun; July, Aug)
• Aquariums and fish specialists; also birds, reptiles, small animals. CREDIT CARDS •

FISH TOWN USA 212-889-3296
513 Third Ave., (34th St.) NYC, NY 10016
Hours: 12-9 Mon-Fri • 10:30-7 Sat •10:30-6 Sun
• A very good collection of rare and exotic fish, aquariums and books. CREDIT CARDS •

PETLAND DISCOUNTS 212-964-1821
132 Nassau St., (Ann-Beekman) NYC, NY 10038
Hours: 9-7 Mon-Fri • 10-6 Sun • 11-5 Sun

7 East 14th St., (5th Ave.) NYC, NY 10003 212-675-4102
Hours: 10-8 Mon-Fri • 10-7 Sat • 11-5 Sun

2675 Broadway, (102nd St.) NYC, NY 10025 212-222-8851
Hours: 10-9 Mon-Fri • 10-7 Sat • 11-6 Sun

304 East 86th St., (2nd Ave.) NYC, NY 10028 212-472-1655
Hours: 10-9 Mon-Fri • 10-7 Sat •11-6 Sun
• Good selection of pet supplies; birds, fish, small animals. CREDIT CARDS •

S-T

TWINES & CORDAGE

See also **PACKING MATERIALS**

AMALGAMATED CORDAGE   516-484-5470
    34 Harbor Park Dr., Port Washington, NY 11050
    Hours: 8-5 Mon-Fri   FAX   516-484-5672
     • Wholesale cotton jute, sisal twine and cord. •

AMERICAN CORD & WEBBING CO., INC.   401-762-5500
    88 Century Dr., Woonsocket, RI 02895
    Hours: 8-5 Mon-Fri   FAX   401-762-5514
     • Wholesale cotton, jute, webbing, tape, binding, elastic cord and webbing. •

HARTFORD CORDAGE & TWINE CO.   203-231-9787
    PO Box 330510, Elmswood, CT 06133   800-235-6610
    Hours: 9-5 Mon-Fri
     • Wholesale hemp, black trick line, sash cord, aircraft cable. •

NORMAN LIBRETT, INC.   914-636-1500
    64 Main St., New Rochelle, NY 10801
    Hours: 8-5 Mon-Fri
     • Wholesale rope and cordage. •

SEABOARD TWINE & CORDAGE CO., INC.   212-732-6658
    7 Caesar Pl., Moonachie, NJ 07074
    Hours: 8:30-4 Mon-Fri   FAX   201-935-5964
     • Twines of all description; natural and synthetic fibres. MC/VISA •

WILLIAM USDAN & SONS   201-472-5544
    9 Peekay≥, Clifton, NJ 07014
    Hours: 8-4:30 Mon-Fri   FAX   201-472-6388
     • Poly cordage. •

NOTES

S-T

"I found it in the N.Y. Theatrical Sourcebook."

UMBRELLAS & CANES

DORNAN UNIFORMS 212-247-0937
653 Eleventh Ave. 2nd Fl., (47-48th St) NYC, NY 10036 800-223-0363
Hours: 8:30-4 Mon-Fri (Thurs till 6) FAX 212-956-7672
• Doorman umbrellas. Phone orders, shipping. No rentals. CREDIT CARDS •

MAN-TIQUES, LTD. 212-759-1805
1050 2nd Ave., (55-56th St.) NYC, NY 10021
Hours: 11-5:30 Mon-Sat
• Fine antiques, canes & accessories for men. Also smoking accessories & desk dressing.
RENTALS •

STANLEY NOVAKS CO. 212-947-8466
115 West 30th St. (5-6th Ave.) NYC, NY 10001
Hours: 9:30-4 Mon-Fri
• Large selection of canes, good quality. RENTALS •

PEERLESS UMBRELLA 201-485-4900
600 7th St., Harrison, NJ 07029
Hours: 9-5 Mon-Fri
• Made to order; see Ed Moskowitz. •

UNCLE SAM UMBRELLA SHOP 212-247-7163
161 West 57th St., (6-7th) Ave. NYC, NY 10019 212-582-1976
Hours: 9:30-6 Mon-Fri • 10-5 Sat
• Wide selection, every type imaginable. Custom umbrellas, walking sticks. CREDIT CARDS •

ZIP JACK CUSTOM UMBRELLA 914-592-2000
141 South Central Ave., Elmsford, NYC, NY 10523
Hours: 9-4 Mon-Sat FAX 914-692-3023
• Custom work including huge market umbrellas and bases. •

UPHOLSTERERS

See also **PROP & SCENIC CRAFTSPEOPLE**

DECOR COUTURE DESIGN 212-727-0123
25-37 37th St., 3rd Fl. Astoria, NY 11103 212-627-3495
Hours: 10-5 Mon-Fri by appt.
• Design & fabrication of custom soft goods for theatre, film, video, display, residential. •

MARTIN IZQUIERDO STUDIO 212-807-9757
118 West 22nd St. 9th Fl., (6-7th) NYC, NY 10011
Hours: 9-6 Mon-Fri weekends by appt. FAX 212-366-5249

CUSTOM UPHOLSTERY, SLIPCOVERS, DRAPES, ETC. FOR
THEATRE, FILM, COMMERCIALS, DISPLAYS AND VIDEOS.
RUSH SERVICE AVAILABLE.

• Full service costume & prop shop. •
(See display ad under COSTUME RENTAL & CONSTRUCTION.)

MAGLIO & SONS   212-244-4644
   548 West 28th St., (10-11th Ave.) NYC, NY 10001
   Hours: 7-4 Mon-Fri
   • Custom upholstery and slipcovers, rush work. See Bruce. •

PRETTY DECORATING   212-674-1310
   29 Avenue A, (2nd) NYC, NY 10009
   Hours: 9-5 Sun-Thurs • 9-1:45 Fri
   • Fast service, upholstery, slipcovers, draperies; reasonable rates. •

ROY RUDIN DECORATORS INC.   212-265-4716
   545 8th Ave. 7th Fl., (37-38th) NYC, NY 10036   212-967-2611
   Hours: 9-5 Mon-Fri
   • Formerly Harold Rudin Decorators. Experienced theatrical & film upholstery & soft goods.
   Quick service, reasonable prices. •

TWENTIETH CENTURY DRAPERIES INC.   212-925-7707
   70 Wooster St., (Spring-Broome) NYC, NY 10012
   Hours: 9:30-4:30 Mon-Fri
   • Upholstery & slipcovers for film, TV, theatre. Fast. •

UPHOLSTERY TOOLS & SUPPLIES

See also **DOWN, BATTING & FIBREFILL**
See also **FABRICS; DRAPERY, SLIPCOVER & UPHOLSTERY**
See also **FOAM SHEETING & SHAPES**
See also **TRIMMINGS; UPHOLSTERY & DRAPERY**
For caning supplies, see **RATTAN REED, RAFFIA, & WILLOW**

AMERICAN CORD & WEBBING CO., INC.   401-762-5500
   88 Century Dr., Woonsocket, RI 02895
   Hours: 8-5 Mon-Fri   FAX   401-762-5514
   • Webbing, binding, cotton, jute, elastic webbing; wholesale. •

BAER FABRICS   502-583-5521
   515 East Market, Louisville, KY 40202   (Commercial) 800-769-7779
   Hours: 9-5:00 Mon-Sat (till 9 Mon.)   FAX   502-582-2331
   • Full selection of upholstery tools and supplies. Supplier of full line to the upholstery trade;
   prompt shipment. CREDIT CARDS •

BZI DISTRIBUTORS   212-966-6690
   105 Eldridge St., (Grand-Broome) NYC, NY 10002
   Hours: 9-5:30 Sun-Fri   FAX   212-219-3666
   • Major upholstery supply house; trimmings, foam rubber, $25. minimum on CREDIT CARDS •

GREENTEX UPHOLSTERY SUPPLIES   212-206-8585
   236 West 26th St., (7-8th) NYC, NY 10001
   Hours: 8-4 Mon-Thurs/8-2 Fri
   • Upholstery needles, tacks, staples, snap tape, hook & loop tape, trims, webbing. •

NATIONAL WEBBING PRODUCTS   516-741-9660
   77 Second Ave., Garden City Park, NY 11040
   Hours: 9-4:30 Mon-Fri
   • Nylon, cotton, elastic and polypropylene webbings. Some minimums. •

U-Z

C.S. OSBORNE TOOLS
201-483-3232
125 Jersey St., Harrison, NJ 07029
Hours: 8:30-5 Mon-Fri
• Tools for upholstery; specialty pins, curved & round point needles. Catalog available. •

VACUUMFORMING & VACUUMFORMED PANELS

BROOKLYN MODEL WORKS
718-834-1944
60 Washington Ave., (Park-Flushing) Brooklyn, NY 11205
Hours: 9-5 Mon-Fri   FAX   718-596-8934
• Special props, casting and reproduction, vacuumforming, mechanization. •

CBS TELEVISION PLASTIC DESIGNS
212-975-2751
524 West 57th St., (10-11th Ave.) NYC, NY 10019
Hours: 9-5 Mon-Fri   FAX   212-975-7530
• Full scenic staff available for custom molds. Panels made to order, good selection stock molds (Catalog); speak to Gary Katz. •
(See display ad in this section.)

CHRISTO VAC/COSTUME ARMOUR, INC.
914-534-9120
PO Box 85, 2 Mill St., Cornwall, NY 12518
Hours: 9-4 Mon-Fri   FAX   914-534-8602

Sculpture, armour, custom props, vacuumforming, masks, display, and artificial food. *Beauty and the Beast, Sunset Boulevard, Phantom of the Opera, Miss Saigon, Secret Garden,* Siegfried & Roy - Vegas '90, *Cats, Meet Me in St. Louis, Chess, Into the Woods, Gypsy, Grand Hotel, Jerome Robbins, Lock Up,* The Met, NYC Opera, ABT, and NYC Ballet.

COSTUME ARMOUR, INC. & CHRISTO-VAC

• Custom work and stock molds. Painted/unpainted. 4' x 12' max. Kydex, Tenamatte, metalized vinyl, etc. •
(See display ad under PROP SHOPS.)

E & T PLASTIC MFG. CO., INC.
718-729-6226
45-45 37th St., (Queens Blvd.) L.I.C., NY 11101
Hours: 9-5 Mon-Fri
• Vacuumforming, plexi, acrylic, acetate, lexan, teflon. Also drape forming. •

ELECTRA DISPLAYS
516-585-5659
90 Remington Blvd., Ronkonkoma, NY 11779   212-420-1188
Hours: 9-5 Mon-Fri
• Vacuumformed panels; signs, brick, etc. •

HONATECH, INC.
914-965-7677
185 Riverdale Ave., Yonkers, NY 10705
Hours: 8-5 Mon-Fri
• Small scale plastic fabrication machines; vacuumform, injection mold, blow mold, etc. •

PROVOST DISPLAYS
212-719-2803
505 Eighth Ave. #1110 (35th St.) NYC, NY 10001
Hours: 9-5 Mon-Fri   FAX   212-869-1463
• Manufacturers of GIANTFOAME™; flame and weather proof vacuumformed plastic decorative panels up to 4' x 12'. Custom molds made to order; catalog of stock designs available. •
(See display ad in this section.)

U-N

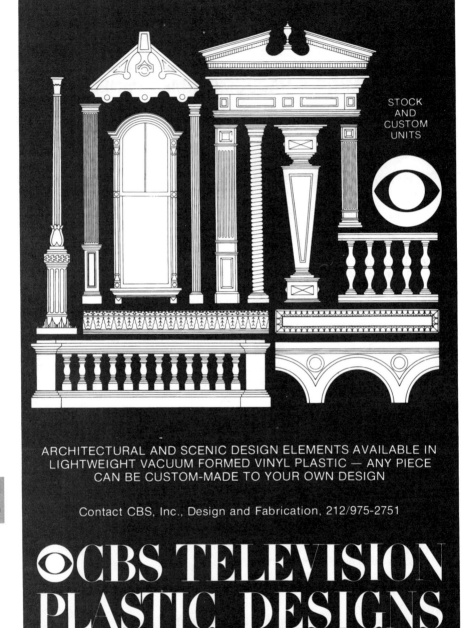

STOCK
AND
CUSTOM
UNITS

ARCHITECTURAL AND SCENIC DESIGN ELEMENTS AVAILABLE IN
LIGHTWEIGHT VACUUM FORMED VINYL PLASTIC — ANY PIECE
CAN BE CUSTOM-MADE TO YOUR OWN DESIGN

Contact CBS, Inc., Design and Fabrication, 212/975-2751

⊙CBS TELEVISION
PLASTIC DESIGNS

U-Z

    "I found it in the N.Y. Theatrical Sourcebook."

718-779-5071   FAX • 718-779-5085
SLIK-PAK, INC.
101-23 44th Ave. Corona, N.Y. 11368

VACUUM FORMING AND PRESSURE FORMING.
Working with Designers & Craftspeople since 1957.

SEVEN FORMING MACHINES ON PREMISES.
Allowing us to do many different kinds of jobs.

PROTOTYPES, SPECIALITY PROPS, MODELS and MOLDS.
We do it all; reproduction, over-sized, and miniatures.

SPECIALISTS IN FINE DETAILING and HIGH ACCURACY.
Huge inventory of plastics in different thicknesses and colors.

SET II   212-777-2811
37 East 18th St. (B'way-Park Ave. S.) NYC, NY 10003
Hours: 8:30-5 Mon-Fri   FAX   212-979-9852
• Glass brick, stock brick, shingles, cobblestones & more. •

SLIK-PAC, INC.   718-779-5071
101-23 44th Ave., (102nd-National St.) Corona, NY 11368
Hours: 8-6 Mon-Sat • Sun by appt.   FAX   718-779-5085
• Vacuumformed and fabricated plastics; costumes, props, molds, scale models, etc..One piece
minimum. Will do sub-contracts, call Victor. •
(See display ad in this section.)

TOBINS LAKE STUDIOS, INC.   313-229-6666
7030 Old U.S. Hwy. 23, Brighton, MI 48116
Hours: 9-5 Mon-Fri
• Vacuumformed armor and helmets, columns, mantels, windows, ornamental detail, pay
phones. Catalog. •

M.B. WINSTON   718-388-1500
300 Winston St. (Kingsland-Debevoise) Brooklyn, NY 11222
Hours: 8-5 Mon-Fri
• Vacuumforming; small to 10' panels; also fiberglassing. Close to Astoria Studios. •

U-N

VARIETY STORES

CANAL SELF SERVICE STORES, INC.   212-966-3069
395 Broadway, (Walker) NYC, NY 10013
Hours: 8-5:30 Mon-Fri • 10-5 Sat & Sun
• A bit of everything; housewares, household supplies, hardware, etc., like an old fashioned general store. •

WOOLWORTH'S   212-563-3523
120 West 34th St., (6-7th Ave.) NYC, NY 10001   (evenings) 914-855-3966
Hours: 10-7:45 Mon, Thurs, Fri • 10-5:45 Tues, Wed, Sat, Sun
• Toys, pets, sewing supplies and all the other things you'd expect from one of the biggest Woolworths in the U.S. •

VENDING MACHINES

ANTIQUE SODA MACHINES & AMUSEMENTS   914-232-9433
18 Woodsbridge Road, Katonah N.Y. 10536
Hours: 9-6 Mon-Fri
• Antique soda machines from the 1930's - 1950's. Also pinball machines, juke boxes, amusements, etc. Contact Ron Jack. •

W. CHORNEY ANTIQUES   203-387-0707
827 Whalley Ave., (Westville Section), New Haven, CT 06515
Hours: 11:30-5 Tues-Sat • call for Sun hours
• Period cigarette, gumball, vending, soda machines and jukeboxes. Will research; see Wayne. RENTALS CREDIT CARDS •

JUKEBOX CLASSICS & VINTAGE SLOT MACHINES,, INC.   718-833-8455
6742 Fifth Ave., 67-68th St. Brooklyn, NY 11220
Hours: by appt.   FAX 718-833-0560
• Jukeboxes and coin operated antiques. Will help locate unusual items. RENTALS CREDIT CARDS •

LORELL GAMES   516-931-4486
37 Jefry Lane, Hicksville, NY 11801
Hours: 9-5 Mon-Fri   FAX 516-931-4487
• New, used and antique games, slot machines & jukeboxes. Service. RENTALS •

NOVEL AMUSEMENT CO., DIV. A-PARAMOUNT VENDING   212-279-1095
587 Tenth Ave., (42-43rd St.) NYC, NY 10036
Hours: 9-6 Mon-Fri
• Vending machines, juke boxes, video games of all kinds. RENTALS •

U-Z

WALL COVERINGS

See also **CORK**
See also **VACUUMFORMING & VACUUMFORMED PANELS**

LAURA ASHLEY, INC.   212-735-5022
    714 Madison Ave. (63-64th St.) NYC, NY 10021   (interior design) 212-735-5010
    Hours: 10-6 Mon-Sat (Thurs. till 8) • 12-6 Sun
    • Fabrics and wallcoverings in coordinating patterns. •

BENTLEY BROTHERS   502-581-0705
    2709 S. Park Rd., Louisville, KY 40219   800-824-4777
    Hours: 10-6 Mon-Fri
    • Anaglypta and Lincrusta wall papers; wall, ceiling and border patterns. Main distributor-no retail sales-call for a local retailer. •

BRADBURY & BRADBURY WALLPAPER   707-746-1900
    PO Box 155, Benicia, CA 94510
    Hours: 9-5 Mon-Fri
    • Manufacturer of handprinted wallpapers of 19th century designs. Catalog $10. •

BRUNSCHWIG & FILS, INC.   212-838-7878
    979 Third Ave., (58-59th St.) NYC, NY 10022
    Hours: 9-5 Mon-Fri
    • To the trade, account required. Traditional American and European styles. Expensive. •

CLARENCE HOUSE   212-752-2890
    211 East 58th St., (2-3rd Ave.) NYC, NY 10022
    Hours: 9-5 Mon-Fri
    • Wallpaper to the trade, account required. Repros of traditional and historical patterns; custom coloring. Expensive. •

DECORATORS WALK   212-319-7100
    979 Third Ave., 18th Fl. (58-59th St.) NYC, NY 10022
    Hours: 9-5 Mon-Fri
    • To the trade; account required. A good selection of contemporary and traditional patterns. Flocked paper. Some very interesting "character" selections. Also fabrics and furnishings. •

DONGHIA TEXTILES   212-925-2777
    979 Third Ave. (58-59th St) NYC, NY 10022   212-935-3713
    Hours: 9-5 Mon-Fri
    • Contemporary patterns, floral and paisley wallcoverings and fabrics; custom furniture. To the trade, account required. Expensive. •

M. EPSTEIN'S SONS, INC.   212-265-3960
    809 Ninth Ave., (53-54th St.) NYC, NY 10019
    Hours: 8:-5:15 Mon-Fri • 8:30-3 Sat • (closed Sat in summer)   FAX 212-765-8841

We have same day service for
Anaglypta and period wallcoverings.

M. EPSTEIN'S SON, INC.

    • Stock & special orders available. CREDIT CARDS •
    (See display ad under PAINTS & DYES; SCENIC.)

U-Z

"I found it in the N.Y. Theatrical Sourcebook."   **471**

JANOVIC PLAZA
212-627-1100
161 Sixth Ave., (Spring) NYC, NY 10014
Hours: 7:30-6:30 Mon-Fri • 9-6 Sat • 11-5 Sun

215 Seventh Ave. (22-23rd St.) NYC, NY 10011   212-645-5454
Hours 7:30-6:30 Mon-Fri • 9-6 Sat • 11-5 Sun   FAX   212-691-1504

1150 Third Ave. (67-68th St.) NYC, NY 10021   212-772-1400
Hours: 7:30-6:30 Mon-Fri • 8-5:45 Sat • 11-5 Sun

159 West 72nd St. NYC, NY 10023   212-595-2500
Hours: 7:30-6:15 Mon-Fri (Tues till 7:45) • 9-4:45 Sat • 11-4:45 Sun
• Home decorating center; wallpaper including Anaglypta wallpapers, paint and supplies.
(Wallpaper dept. opens at 9:30) CREDIT CARDS •

KIRK-BRUMMEL   212-477-8590
979 Third Ave., (58-59th St.) NYC, NY 10022
Hours: 9-5 Mon-Fri
• To the trade; account required; stylish wallcoverings. •

SECONDHAND ROSE   212-431-7673
270 Lafayette St., (Prince) NYC, NY 10012   212-431-ROSE
Hours: 10-6 Mon-Fri • 12-6 Sat
• Period wallpaper, linoleum and fabrics. Very good selection. Contact Suzanne Lipschutz. •

F. SCHUMACHER & CO (SHOWROOM)   212-415-3900
939 Third Ave., (56th Street) NYC, NY 10022
Hours: 9-5 Mon-Fri   FAX   212-415-3907
• Large collection Victorian wallpapers and matching fabrics; to the trade, account required. •

SHEILA'S WALL STYLES   212-966-1663
274 Grand St., (Eldridge-Allen) NYC, NY 10002
Hours: 9-5 Sun-Thurs
• Fabulous selection of wallpapers; thousands of rolls in stock. •

WOLF PAINTS, S. WOLF DIV. OF JANOVIC PLAZA   212-245-3241
771 Ninth Ave., (51-52nd St) NYC, NY 10019
Hours: 7:30-5:15 Mon-Fri • 8-4:45 Sat   FAX   212-974-0591
• Large selection of wallpapers including Anaglypta wallpapers, blinds, fabrics; also paints and
supplies. CREDIT CARDS •

WOLF-GORDON WALLCOVERING, INC.   212-319-6800
979 Third Ave., Rm. 1518, (58-59th St.) NYC, NY 10022
Hours: 9-5 Mon-Fri
• Wallcoverings: vinyl, cork. To the trade, account required. •

WEAVING, KNITTING & NEEDLECRAFT SUPPLIES

For handmade items, see **HANDICRAFTS**

FIBRE YARN CO., INC., DIV. OF FARBER BRAID CO., INC.   212-719-5820
48 West 38th St., (5-6th Ave.) NYC, NY 10018
Hours: 9-5 Mon-Fri
• Wholesale. Many types of yarn, including silk; embroidery thread, some metallic braids and
trims; speak to Fredor Glen. •

GLIMAKRA LOOMS & YARNS　　　　　　　　　　　　800-289-9276
　　1338 Ross St. , Petaluma, CA 94954　　　　　　707-762-3362
　　Hours: 8:30-5 Mon-Fri
　　• Wide selection wool, linen, cotton, hemp yarns. Catalog. •

JOAN'S NEEDLECRAFT STUDIO　　　　　　　　　　212-532-7129
　　240 East 29th St., (2nd-3rd Ave.) NYC, NY 10016
　　Hours: 11-7 Tues-Fri • 11-6 Sat
　　• Large stock of yarns and supplies for embroidery and needlepoint. Patternbooks, framing
　　service and expert advice. CREDIT CARDS for purchases over $25. •

SCHOOL PRODUCTS　　　　　　　　　　　　　　　212-679-3516
　　1201 Broadway, 3rd Fl., (28th-29th St.) NYC, NY 10001
　　Hours: 9-5 Mon-Fri • 10-3 Sat • (except during summer)　　**FAX 212-679-3519**
　　• Wide selection of yarn for hand or machine knitting and weaving. Also pattern books, weav-
　　ing looms and Brother knitting machines. MC/VISA •

STITCHES EAST　　　　　　　　　　　　　　　　212-421-0112
　　55 East 52nd St., (Madison-Park) NYC, NY 10022
　　Hours: 10-6 Mon-Sat
　　• Yarn, custom and published patterns. •

STRAW INTO GOLD　　　　　　　　　　　　　　　510-548-5247
　　3006 San Pablo Ave., (Ashby) Berkeley, CA 94702
　　Hours: 12-5:30-Tues-Fri • 10-5:30 Sat
　　• Natural fibers and hair, spinning supplies, yarn. Catalog. •

SUNRAY YARNS RETAIL　　　　　　　　　　　　212-465-9655
　　349 Grand St. , (Essex-Ludlow St.) NYC, NY 10002
　　Hours: 10-5 Sun-Thurs
　　• Yarn for knitting, crocheting, and needle point. Pattern books and framing service. •

WALLIS MAYERS NEEDLEWORK　　　　　　　　　212-861-5318
　　30 East 68th St., (Madison-Park) NYC, NY 10021
　　Hours: 11:30-6:30 Tues-Fri • 11:30-5:30 Sat
　　• Yarn, supplies, patterns, needlepoint. •

JOHN WILDE & BRO., INC.　　　　　　　　　　　215-482-8800
　　PO Box 4662, 3737 Main St.,   Philadelphia, PA 19127
　　Hours: 8:30-4:30 Mon-Fri
　　• Wool yarns and carded wools; mail order only. Catalog. •

ERICA WILSON NEEDLE WORKS　　　　　　　　　212-832-7290
　　717 Madison Ave., 2nd Fl., (63-64th St.) NYC, NY 10021
　　Hours: 10-6 Mon-Sat • (till 7 Thurs)
　　• Appleton yarns, all needlecraft supplies, books, kits, and best of all, advice. Will finish pil-
　　lows. •

THE YARN CENTER　　　　　　　　　　　　　　　212-719-5648
　　1011 Sixth Ave., (37-38th St.) NYC, NY 10018
　　Hours: 10-6 Mon-Fri • (Thurs till 7) •10-5 Sat
　　• Wide selection of yarns, including tapestry yarns, knitting needles and supplies. •

YARN COMPANY　　　　　　　　　　　　　　　　212-787-7878
　　2274 Broadway, (82nd Street) NYC, NY 10024
　　Hours: 11-6 Mon-Sat • 12-5 Sun
　　• Yarn, designer patterns, workshops. CREDIT CARDS •

U-Z

THE YARN CONNECTION 212-685-5099
218 Madison Ave., (36-37th St.) NYC, NY 10016
Hours: 10-6 Mon-Fri • 10-5 Sat
• Nice selection of yarns for hand knitting, embroidery and needlepoint. Knitting needles, patterns and books. Very helpful staff. MC/VISA •

WELDERS & SPOT WELDERS

ABC SPRING CO 212-675-1629
115 West 27th St., 6th Fl., (6-7th St.) NYC, NY 10001
Hours: 10-4:30 Mon-Fri
• Spring steel wire, rod; custom fabrication. •

BOURNONVILLE IRONWORKS 212-246-7558
622 West 130th St., (B'way) NYC, NY 10027
Hours: 8-4:30 Mon-Fri
• Spot welders, any size item, also cutting; sometimes while you wait. •

KERN/ROCKENFIELD, INC. 718-486-7878
345 Devoe St., (Morgan) Brooklyn, NY 11211
Hours: 8-5 Mon-Fri FAX 718-486-5138
• Custom metalwork; welding, bending, shaping in aluminum, steel, brass, and other metals. Very helpful; willing to try anything! •

WIRE FRAME SHOP 212-586-4239
622 West 47th St., (11-12th Ave.) NYC, NY 10036
Hours: by appt.
• Iron and spot welding; wire frames for headpieces and costumes; small custom work a specialty. •

WELDING SUPPLIES

AMERICAN COMPRESSED GASSES 718-392-9800
3452 Laurel Hill Blvd., Maspeth, NY 11378
 FAX 718-937-1218
• Full range of supplies, gasses (including helium), torches, rods, etc. •

INDUSTRIAL SUPPLY COMPANY OF LONG ISLAND 718-784-1291
47-30 Vernon Blvd., (47-48 Ave.) L.I.C., NY 11101
Hours: 7-5:30 Mon-Fri • Fax #, 24 hours every day FAX 718-482-9353
• Welding supplies, hardware, tools, rigging supplies, handling equipment, etc. Call for 1700 page catalog $4.95, refundable. •
(See display ad under THEATRICAL HARDWARE & RIGGING EQUIPMENT.)

MCKINNEY WELDING SUPPLY 212-246-4305
535 West 52nd St., (10-11th Ave.) NYC, NY 10019
Hours: 7-4:30 Mon-Fri FAX 212-582-3105
• Industrial, medical and specialty gasses; welding and cutting equipment. No credit cards. •

T.W. SMITH WELDING SUPPLY 718-388-7417
885 Meeker Ave., (Bridgewater-Varick) Brooklyn, NY 11222
Hours: 7:30-4:30 Mon-Fri • 8-12 Sat • (closed holiday weekends)
• Soldering and welding supplies; propane tanks and regulators; will buy back empties. •

WINE RACKS & ACCESSORIES, WINEMAKING & BREWING SUPPLIES

KEDCO WINE STORAGE SYSTEMS   516-454-7800
564 Smith St., (Rt. 110 & Pinelawn-Wellwood) Farmingdale, NY 11735   800-654-9988
Hours: 9-5 Mon-Fri   FAX   516-454-4876
• Complete line of wine storage systems; coolers, racks, equipment for wine and liquor retailing; wine accessories and gifts; also brewing and winemaking supplies. Catalog available. CREDIT CARDS •

MILAN HOME BREWING LAB   212-226-4780
57 Spring St., (Lafayette-Mulberry) NYC, NY 10012
Hours: 9-6 Mon-Fri • 9-5 Sat   FAX   212-431-6985
• Good selection wine bottles, jugs, corks, vats, barrels, caps and cappers, etc; brochure. CREDIT CARDS •

WINE & BEER CONNECTION   203-467-8388
259 Commerce St., (Hemingway) East Haven, CT 06512
Hours: 8-6 Mon-Fri • 8-1 Sat.   FAX   203-468-2596
• Beer and cordial supplies; barrels, vats; catalog. CREDIT CARDS •

WILLIAMS BREWING   800-759-6025
PO Box 2195, San Leandro, CA 94577   415-895-2739
Hours: 8-5 Mon-Fri • 10-5 Sat   FAX   800-283-2745
• Beer-making supplies only. Big catalog. $20 minimum on CREDIT CARDS •

SOMMER CORK CO.   800-242-0808
6342 W. Irving Park Rd≤≤, Chicago, Il 60634   312-283-5340
Hours: 9-4:30 Mon-Fri   FAX   312-283-4822
• Cork stopperS and bulletin board cork. •

WINE ENTHUSIAST   (showroom) 800-356-8466
PO Box 39, 404 Irvington St., Pleasantville, NY 10570   (orders) 800-822-8846
Hours: 9-5:30 Mon-Fri • 10-5 Sat (showroom) • 24-hour phone orders
• Catalog of wine racks, cellars, and accessories. CREDIT CARDS •

U-N

NOTES

(handwritten notes)

NOTES

U-Z

"I found it in the N.Y. Theatrical Sourcebook."

Appendixes

DESIGN RESOURCES

AMERICAN HERITAGE PUBLISHING CO. LIBRARY　　　　　　212-206-5500
　　60 Fifth Ave., (12-13th St.) NYC, NY 10011
　　Hours: 9-5 Mon-Fri (by appt.)　　　　　　　　　FAX　212-620-2332
　　• Art and history, primarily American; 3000 pictures; B&W and color. •

AMERICAN MUSEUM OF NATURAL HISTORY LIBRARY　　　212-769-5000
　　79th & Central Park West, NYC, NY 10024
　　Hours: 11-4 Tues-Fri year round
　　• Photographic collection: 500,000 black and white; 60,000 slides. •

ANTHOLOGY FILM ARCHIVES LIBRARY　　　　　　　　212-505-5181
　　32-34 Second Ave. (2nd St.) NYC, NY 10003
　　Hours: 10-6 Mon-Fri
　　• Films, stills, posters, books; also shows independent films. •

BETTMANN ARCHIVES/BETTMANN NEWS PHOTOS
UPI & REUTER PHOTO LIBRARY　　　　　　　　　212-777-6200
　　902 Broadway (20th-21st St.) NYC, NY 10010
　　Hours: 24 hours by appt.　　　　　　　　　FAX　212-533-4034
　　• Collections of movie, theatre, jazz, science and NY Daily Mirror; $75 minimum research fee.
　　News Photo collection, UPI Historical News Images, Fine Arts arrangement with Christies
　　Images in London. •

THE BROOKLYN MUSEUM:
ART REFERENCE LIBRARY AND WILBOUR LIBRARY OF EGYPTOLOGY
　　　　　　　　　　　　　　　　　　(ext 308) 718-638-5000
　　200 Eastern Parkway (Washington Ave.) Brooklyn, NY 11238
　　Hours: 1:30-4:30 Wed-Thur by appt.　　　　　　FAX　718-638-3731
　　• Art and ethology relating to American painting and sculpture, Asian art, decorative arts, cos-
　　tumes and textiles. Fashion sketches: 1900-1950, leading American designers in museum
　　archives. Wilbour library has great references on ancient Egypt. •

COLUMBIA UNIVERSITY:
AVERY ARCHITECTURAL & FINE ARTS LIBRARY
　　Avery Hall, Columbia University (B'way & 116th St.) NYC, NY 10027　212-854-8403
　　Hours: 9-11 Mon-Thurs • 9-9 Fri • 10-7 Sat • 12-10 Sun　　FAX　212-854-8904
　　• Architecture, archeology, city planning, housing, painting, sculpture, decorative arts, graphic
　　arts. Columbia ID required or contact Library information office at 212-854-2271. •

CONDE NAST PUBLICATION INC. LIBRARY　　　　　　212-880-8343
　　350 Madison Ave. (44-45th St.) NYC, NY 10017
　　Hours: 1-4 Mon-Fri by appt.　　　　　　　　　FAX　212-880-8289
　　• Fashions, houses and gardens, including artwork for Conde Nast magazines. •

COOPER HEWITT MUSEUM OF DESIGN LIBRARY　　　　212-860-6883
　　2 East 91st St. (5th Ave.) NYC, NY 10128
　　Hours: 9:30-5 Mon-Fri (by appt. only)
　　• Decorative arts and design books on textiles, wallpaper, early natural history, architecture
　　and interiors. The picture collection of 1,500,000 items filed by category (available 1996). ID
　　required. •

APP

COSTUME SOCIETY OF AMERICA   410-275-2329
55 Edgewater Dr., PO Box 73, Earleville, MD 21919
Hours: 9:00-4:30 Mon-Fri   FAX   410-275-8936
• Referral service for the identification and conservation of costumes; various publications,
newsletter and journal; annual membership fee. Contact Kay Boyer by letter for information. •

CULVER PICTURES   212-645-1672
150 West 22nd St. #300 (6th-7th Ave.) NYC, NY 10011
Hours: 9-5 Mon-Fri by appt.   FAX   212-627-9112
• 9,000,000 choice old photos, engravings, prints, movie stills, trade cards, sheet music covers, old greeting cards, tintypes and glass plate negatives. Leased for reproduction. •

DOVER PUBLICATIONS INC.   212-255-3755
180 Varick St. 9th Fl. (Charlton) NYC, NY 10014
Hours: 9-4:30 Mon-Fri

31 E. 2nd St. Mineola, NY 11501   516-294-7000
Hours: 9-3 Mon-Fri
• Mail order catalogs with a thorough collection of paperback books on fine arts and crafts
with many facsimile reproductions and excellent pictorial archives. •

FASHION INSTITUTE OF TECHNOLOGY, DESIGN LABORATORY   212-760-7708
7th Ave. at 27th St., NYC, NY 10001
Hours: by appt.
• Extensive collection of costumes and textile swatches. Research fee, letter of reference
required. •

FASHION INSTITUTE OF TECHNOLOGY, LIBRARY   212-760-7590
7th Ave. at 27th St., NYC, NY 10001
Hours: by appt.
• Fashion, textile and interior design books and magazines; also original sketches by designers, historical and contemporary. •

FPG INTERNATIONAL LIBRARY   212-777-4210
32 Union Square East, 6th Fl., NYC, NY 10003
Hours: 8-8 Mon-Fri   FAX   212-995-9652
• 6 million color transparencies and B&W photos, CD ROM; contemporary and historical collection; large format scenic transparencies. Agents in 30 key cities worldwide; charge for
reproduction. Not for individual use, company authorization required. •

FRICK ART REFERENCE LIBRARY   212-288-8700
10 East 71st St. (5th Ave.) NYC, NY 10021
Hours: 10-5 Mon-Fri • 9:30-1 Sat (closed Sat: June, July/closed in Aug)
• Paintings, drawings, sculpture and illuminated MSS of Western Europe and the US from the
4th century AD to 1860. Over 400,000 classified study photographs. ID required. •

HUNTINGTON FREE LIBRARY AND READING ROOM   718-829-7770
9 Westchester Sq. (Westchester Ave.-E. Tremont Ave.) Bronx, NY 10461
Hours: 1:30-4:30 Mon-Fri
• American Indian Collection. Non-circulating collection contains current newspapers, journals
and reference books as well as photographs and other materials on local Bronx history. Easily
accessible via IRT #6. •

THE METROPOLITAN MUSEUM OF ART COSTUME INSTITUTE   (ext 3908) 212-879-5500
1000 Fifth Ave. (82nd St.) NYC, NY 10028
Hours: by appt.
• Excellent collection of costumes from 17th-20th centuries emphasizing haute couture and
regional clothing. Richard Martin, curator •

THE METROPOLITAN MUSEUM OF ART:
IRENE LEWISOHN COSTUME REFERENCE LIBRARY
(ext 3018) 212-879-5500
1000 Fifth Ave. (82nd St.) NYC, NY 10028
Hours: by appt.
• Fashion sketches (originals), photographs, books, patterns, prints (fashion plates) from late 16th through second half of 20th century. Speak to Robert Kaufman. •

THE METROPOLITAN MUSEUM OF ART:
PHOTOGRAPH AND SLIDE LIBRARY
(ext 3261) 212-879-5500
1000 Fifth Ave. (82nd St.) NYC, NY 10028
Hours: 10-4:30 Tues-Fri
Extensive color and B&W slide and photograph collection covering history of art; call for further information. •

NATIONAL MUSEUM OF THE AMERICAN INDIAN LIBRARY
718-829-7770
9 Westchester Sq. (Westchester Ave.-E. Tremont Ave.) Bronx, NY 10461
Hours: 10-4:30 Mon-Fri • 10-4:30 1st & 3rd Sat of the month
• Over 40,000 volumes on the archeology, ethology and history of native people of the Americas. For a small fee the staff will photocopy while you wait . Easily accessible via the IRT #6. •

MUSEUM OF THE CITY OF NEW YORK
212-534-1672
Fifth Ave. at 103rd St., NYC, NY 10029
Hours: 10-5 Wed-Sat • 1-5 Sun
• Extensive collection of 18th-20th century costumes and accessories, collection either made or purchased by New Yorkers. •

THE MUSEUM OF MODERN ART LIBRARY
212-708-9433
11 West 53rd St., (5th Ave.) NYC, NY 10019
Hours: 11-5 Mon-Fri (by appt.)
• Painting, sculpture, graphic arts, drawing, architecture, design, photography, film of modern period, 1880's to present. •

NEW YORK CITY ARCHIVES MUNICIPAL DEPT.
212-788-8250
31 Chambers St., (Centre St.) NYC, NY 10007
Hours: 9-4:30 Mon-Fri   FAX   212-788-8580
• History of the five boroughs. Pictures of NYC from the turn-of-the-century to present; also court dockets. Photocopy service available. Good for pictures of specific neighborhoods. •

NEW YORK PUBLIC LIBRARY:
MID MANHATTAN LIBRARY, ART DEPARTMENT
212-340-0871
455 Fifth Ave. (40th St.) NYC, NY 10016
Hours: 9-9 Mon, Wed • 11-7 Tues, Thurs • 10-6 Fri, Sat
• Books on visual and graphic arts, costume, textile design. •

NEW YORK PUBLIC LIBRARY FOR THE PERFORMING ARTS AT LINCOLN CENTER
40 Lincoln Center Plaza (1st Fl), (65th St.) NYC, NY 10023   212-870-1630
Hours: call for hours
• The most thorough selection of music books and scores, records, drama, dance reference and circulating collections; also non-book materials including videotape archives and specialized research collections, clippings, sketches, etc.; photocopying service. •

NEW YORK PUBLIC LIBRARY PICTURE COLLECTION
MID-MANHATTAN LIBRARY 3RD FL.
212-340-0877
455 Fifth Ave., (40th St.) NYC, NY 10016
Hours: Mon, Wed, Sat 1-5 • Tues, Thurs 12-7 • Fri 10-5
• 2 1/4 million clippings from books and magazines covering pictorial subjects of all areas and periods; free consultation. Have coin photocopy machines •

APP

NEW YORK PUBLIC LIBRARY SCHOMBURG CENTER FOR RESEARCH IN BLACK CULTURE
135th St. & Malcolm X Blvd., NYC, NY 10025   212-491-2200
Hours: 12-8 Mon-Wed • 10-6 Thur-Sat
• Rare books, records, tapes, artifacts, photographic and film archives and picture file. •

THE NEW YORK TIMES PICTURES   212-556-1243
229 West 43rd St., (7th-8th Ave.) NYC, NY 10036
Hours: 9-5 Mon-Fri   FAX   212-556-3535
• Over 4 million photos from date of 1st publication: requests for specific photos must be
phoned in with date information, fees vary. If research is required add $100 fee. •

REFERENCE PICTURES   212-254-0088
900 Broadway, (20th St.) NYC, NY 10003
Hours: 9-5 Mon-Fri   FAX   212-353-9152
• Picture library of over 11 million pictures; historic through 90's including famous people.
Rental only; $25 per category, up to ten pictures per category. •

SCHOOL OF VISUAL ARTS LIBRARY   (ext 2660) 212-679-7350
380 Second Ave., (22nd St.) NYC, NY 10010
Hours: 9-9 Mon-Thurs • 9-7 Fri • 10:30-5:30 Sat
• Fine arts, art history, photography, film, graphic design: 30,000 pictures, 30,000 slides.
Metro referral card required for non-students. •

SLIDE PRESENTATIONS , PUBLISHERS   212-677-2200
175 Fifth Ave., (23rd St.) NYC, NY 10010
Hours: Leave message
• Slide presentations with text on the history of architecture, interiors, furniture and costume
in Western Civilization; contact Beverly Grossman. •

SOCIETY FOR CREATIVE ANACHRONISM   408-263-9305
c/o King's Taste Productions, 1039 E. Confederate Ave. S.E., Atlanta, GA 30316
Hours: by appt.
• Contact group for artisans specializing in medieval costumes, weaponry, furniture, related
props. Publications •

THEATRE PROJECTS   203-431-3949
871 Ethan Allen Hwy., Ridgefield, CT 06877
Hours: 9-5 Mon-Fri   FAX   203-431-4790
• Advice on planning, design and technology for all types of new and restored cultural facilities. •

ORGANIZATIONS, UNIONS, & SUPPORT SERVICES

ACTORS' EQUITY ASSOCIATION   212-869-8530
   165 West 46th St., (7th Ave.) NYC, NY 10036
   Hours: 9:30-5:30 Mon-Fri (membership 10-4:30)
   • Union for actors and stage managers in legitimate theatre. •

ADVERTISING PHOTOGRAPHERS OF AMERICA (APA)   212-807-0399
   27 West 20th St. #601, (5th-6th Ave.) NYC, NY 10011
   Hours: 9-5 Mon-Fri
   • APA is a professional trade association serving advertising photographers and companies
   and individuals supplying the photography community. In addition to the New York organization, there are chapters in Chicago, Los Angeles, Atlanta, Honolulu, Coconut Grove, FL,
   Portland, ME, and Warren, MI. Newsletter, business forms, information hotline, member discounts. •

ALLIANCE FOR THE ARTS   212-947-6340
   330 West 42nd St. #1701, (8th-9th Ave.) NYC, NY 10036
   Hours: 9:30-5:30 Mon-Fri
   • Publishes Space Search, a guide to performing, rehearsal, exhibition and audio visual spaces
   in the five boroughs. •

ALLIANCE OF RESIDENT THEATRES / ART/NEW YORK   212-989-5257
   131 Varick St. Rm. 904, (Spring St.) NYC, NY 10013   212-989-4880
   Hours: 10-6 Mon-Fri
   • ART/New York serves over 80 of New York City's not-for-profit professional theatres.
   Through discussion groups, consultations and publications, the Alliance provides its members
   with services, skills and information to help them survive and flourish. ART/New York also
   functions as an information center for other artists, related professionals, students, the press,
   funding sources and the general public. Publishes 'Theatre Times' and a list of Off-Off
   Broadway Theatres. Kate C. Bush, Executive Director. •

AMERICAN CRAFT COUNCIL / AMERICAN CRAFT MUSEUM   212-956-3535
   40 West 53rd St., (5th-6th Ave.) NYC, NY 10019
   Hours: 10-8 Tues • 10-5 Wed-Sun • closed Mon
   • National not-for-profit organization devoted exclusively to the support and encouragement of
   American crafts through a variety of educational programs that stimulate public interest in
   modern handcrafted objects of high quality design and workmanship. Resources include a
   museum, reference library, gift shop, slides, films, and publications for sale. •

ASSOCIATION OF THEATRICAL ARTISTS AND CRAFTSPEOPLE (ATAC)   212-234-9001
   604 Riverside Dr. #6E, (137th-138th St.) NYC, NY 10003 (mailing address)
   Hours: by appt./leave message
   • A not-for-profit professional trade association for craftspeople working in the production
   fields of entertainment, performance, and presentational media industries. ATAC edits THE
   NEW YORK THEATRICAL SOURCEBOOK, publishes the ATAC Quarterly, sponsors craft-related
   seminars and workshops and makes group health insurance available to members. See Display
   adds under PROP AND SCENIC CRAFTSPEOPLE, COSTUME CRAFTS PEOPLE, MASKS, and
   MILLINERY. •

APP

BUSINESS COMMITTEE FOR THE ARTS, INC.   212-664-0600
   1775 Broadway Rm.510, (57th-58th St.) NYC, NY 10019
   Hours: 9-5 Mon-Fri
   • National not-for-profit organization of business leaders committed to supporting the arts. •

CENTRAL OPERA SERVICE　　　　　　　　　　202-347-2800
　c/o OPERA America, 777 14th St. NW, Suite 520　Washington, D.C., 20005
　Hours: 9-5 Mon-Fri
　• Maintains a library of books and periodicals, and the most comprehensive operatic and musical theatre archives in the United States. COS draws on this unique resource to supply information to its members. Research areas include: repertory, performances, musical materials, translations, captions and projections, scenery, costumes, props (rental, sale or exchange opportunities), company statistics, annual opera and musical theatre statistics for the United States. •

COMPU-TAB SERVICES INC.　　　　　　　　　914-273-1220
　160 North State Rd., Briarcliff Manor, NY 10510
　Hours: 9-5 Mon-Fri
　• Provides ongoing accounting services to not-for-profit organizations and small businesses at a reduced fee. •

DANCE NOTATION BUREAU　　　　　　　　　212-807-7899
　31 West 21st St., 3rd Fl., (5th-6th Ave.) NYC, NY 10010
　Hours: 9-5 Mon-Fri • call first
　• A non-profit service organization for dance. Referral of certified dance notators, notation teachers, and dance reconstructors. Library (for members) and dance studio. •

DANCE THEATRE WORKSHOP　　　　　　　　212-691-6500
　219 West 19th St., (7th-8th Ave.) NYC, NY 10011
　Hours: 10-6 Mon-Fri • 1-8 Sat • 11:30-6 Sun
　• Publishes the Poor Dancer's Almanac, a survival manual for choreographers, dancers and management personnel. •

DIRECTOR'S GUILD OF AMERICA　　　　　　212-581-0370
　110 West 57th St., (6th-7th Ave.) NYC, NY 10019
　Hours: 9-6 Mon-Fri
　• National union representing film and television directors and assistant directors. •

FILM VIDEO ARTS　　　　　　　　　　　212-673-9361
　817 Broadway 2nd Fl., (12th St.) NYC, NY 10003
　Hours: 10-6 Mon-Fri
　• Film rental to non-profit groups or artists at very reasonable rates. •

FOUNDATION CENTER　　　　　　　　　212-620-4230
　79 Fifth Ave. 8th Fl., (15-16th St.) NYC, NY 10003
　Hours: 10-5 Mon-Fri (Wed till 8)
　• Clearinghouse for private funding information for non-profit groups and individuals. Reference library available. •

GRAPHIC ARTISTS GUILD　　　　　　　　212-463-7730
　11 West 20th St., 8th Fl., (5th Ave.) NYC, NY 10011
　Hours: 9-5 Mon-Fri
　• Member service organization for graphic and commercial artists. Offers pricing scale and ethical guidelines. Dues are based on annual income. •

IATSE LOCAL 1　　　　　　　　　　　212-333-2500
　320 West 46th St., (8-9th Ave.) NYC, NY 10036
　Hours: 7:30-6 Mon-Fri
　• Union representing stagehands for TV, theatre and the Javits Center. Local 1's jurisdiction is Manhattan, Staten Island and the Bronx. •

IATSE Local 52
326 West 48th St., (8-9th Ave.) NYC, NY 10019
Hours: 7:30-5:30 Mon-Fri
• Film local for New York City. •

212-399-0980

FAX 212-315-1073

IATSE Local 764
151 West 46th St., 8th floor, (6-7th Ave.) NYC, NY 10036
Hours: 9-5 Mon-Fri
• Theatrical Wardrobe Attendants Union covering film, television and Broadway. •

212-221-1717

IATSE Local 798
31 West 21st St., (5-6th Ave.) NYC, NY 10010
Hours: 8:30-6 Mon-Fri
• Union representing hair and make-up artists for TV and film. •

212-627-0660

International Alliance of Theatrical Stage Employees (IATSE)
1515 Broadway #601, (44-45th St.) NYC, NY 10036
Hours: 9-5 Mon-Fri
National office for union representing stagehands and motion picture operators. •

212-730-1770

League of American Theatres and Producers
226 West 47th St., 5th Fl., (B'way-8th Ave.) NYC, NY 10036
Hours: 9:30-5:30 Mon-Fri
• An association of Broadway and regional promoters, producers and theatre owners.
Research and statistics on the professional theatre and a data bank of technical specs on road houses. •

212-764-1122

League of Off Broadway Producers and Theatre Owners
c/o Geo. Elmer Circle in the Square Theatre
1633 Broadway, (50th St.) NYC, NY 10019
Hours: 10-5 Mon-Fri
• The association for Off Broadway producers and theatre owners. •

212-307-2700

Management Services
155 6th Ave., 14th floor, (3rd St.) NYC, NY 10013
Hours: 9:30-5:00 Mon-Fri
• Formerly The Cultural Council Foundation. Fiscal management for non-profit arts groups and city agencies. •

212-366-6900

Materials for the Arts Warehouse
410 West 16th St., (9th-10th Ave.) NYC, NY 10011
Hours: 9-5 Mon-Fri • call for appt.
• Free goods and materials to legitimate NYC non-profit qualifying artists and organizations. 10,000 sq. ft. warehouse of books, construction equipment, furniture, etc. Joint project of the NYC Dept. of Cultural Affairs and Sanitation's recycling program. •

212-255-5924

National Association of Display Industries (NADI)
133 West 25th St., (6th-7th Ave.) NYC, NY 10001
Hours: 9-5 Mon-Fri
• A trade association comprised of visual merchandising materials, store fixtures, mannequins and other decorative materials. N.A.D.I. sponsors two major trade shows in NYC each year, in June and December. Admission to the showrooms is free; call for exact dates and registration information. •

212-989-7331

APP

YOUR TICKET TO THE PERFORMING ARTS!

UNITED STATES INSTITUTE FOR THEATRE TECHNOLOGY, INC. IS THE AMERICAN ASSOCIATION FOR DESIGN AND PRODUCTION PROFESSIONALS

JOIN TODAY AND SEE WHAT WE HAVE TO OFFER YOU!

★ Annual Conference & Stage Expo ★
Las Vegas - March 20-23, 1995

Special Interest Commissions

Publications

TD&T - *Theatre Design & Technology, Sightlines, Cutters' Research Journal and many more!*

Professional Recognition & Awards
Grants & Scholarships

For more information, contact
USITT
10 West 19th Street, Suite 5A
New York, NY 10011-4206
212-924-9088

"I found it in the N.Y. Theatrical Sourcebook."

NATIONAL ENDOWMENT FOR THE ARTS　　　　　　　　　202-682-5400
1100 Pennsylvania Ave., NW, Washington, D.C., 20506
Hours: 9-5:30 Mon-Fri
 • An independent federal agency which receives annual appropriations from Congress from which it awards matching grants to non-profit, tax exempt arts organizations of outstanding quality and fellowships to artists of exceptional talent. •

NEW YORK CITY DEPARTMENT OF CULTURAL AFFAIRS　　　212-841-4100
2 Columbus Circle, (B'way-8th Ave.) NYC, NY 10019
Hours: 9-5 Mon-Fri
 • Support of cultural institutions and activities through a variety of programs; materials for the arts, an arts apprenticeship program, a city gallery for group art shows, and a public works project providing personnel assistance for cultural institutions. •

NEW YORK CITY OFFICE OF FILM, THEATER, & BROADCASTING　212-489-6710
254 West 54th St. 13th Fl.,   NYC, NY 10019
Hours: 9-5 Mon-Fri
 • Mayor's office of theatre and film. •

PAINTERS FORUM　　　　　　　　　　　　　　　　　212-427-9782
PO Box 6801, NYC, NY 10128
Hours: by appt.　　　　　　　　　　　　　FAX　212-427-9782 *51
 • Produces and develops educational videos on scenic painting; newsletter. •

PERFORMING ARTS RESOURCES INC.　　　　　　　　　212-966-8658
270 Lafayette St. #809, NYC, NY 10012
Hours: by appt.
 • Provides job referrals for production personnel, craftspeople, administrators, managers, consultation services, information resources including technical specifications on over 500 theatres around the world, and The Dance Floor Anthology. Holds workshops and seminars. Call for free schedules and further information. Speak to Donna Brady. ATAC member. •

PUPPETEERS OF AMERICA INC.　　　　　　　　　　　818-797-5748
5 Cricklewood Path, Pasadena, CA 91107
Hours: 9-5 Mon-Fri
 • National non-profit corporation for professionals and amateurs. Sponsors festivals, workshops and seminars. Maintains publications, advisory and educational services and an endowment fund. Their audio-visual library is a resource center with archives of recorded history; selections available for borrowing by members. Contact Gayle Schulter. •

PUPPETRY GUILD OF GREATER NEW YORK　　　　　　212-929-1568
PO Box 117, NYC, NY 10116
Hours: by appt.
 • Independent non-profit corporation chartered by Puppeteers of America. Serves as a public awareness and support organization for amateurs, professionals and educators in the New York area. Contact Rod Young. •

SOCIETY OF STAGE DIRECTORS AND CHOREOGRAPHERS (SSDC)　212-391-1070
1501 Broadway, 31st Fl., NYC, NY 10036
Hours: 10-6 Mon-Fri　　　　　　　　　　　FAX　212-302-6195
 • Union representing stage directors and choreographers. Holds semiannual meetings, publishes a monthly newsletter, SSDC Notes and through the SDC Foundation, gives awards, holds staged readings and roundtable discussions, and publishes a biannual journal. •

APP

Stage Managers' Association (SMA)
212-691-5633
PO Box 2234, Times Sq. Station, NYC, NY 10108-2020
Hours: Leave message
• An association for professional union and non-union stage managers. Information and skill seminars given. Newsletter published with list of job openings. Projects include "Operation Observation", in which stage managers observe their peers working backstage; also publishes THE STAGE MANAGERS DIRECTORY. •

Support Services Alliance Inc.
518-295-7966
PO Box 130, Schoharie, NY 12157
(NY) 800-322-3920
Hours: 8:30-5 Mon-Thurs • 8:30-4:30 Fri
• Organization serving self-employed, small business and not-for-profit groups. Offers group health insurance, disability and life insurance, rental cars, credit union, discount prescription and vitamin service, travel agency, One-Write bookkeeping system, Harvard medical newsletter and educational loans. Low membership fee; bimonthly newsletter. •

Theatre Communications Group (TCG)
212-697-5230
355 Lexington Ave. 4th Fl., (40th-41st St.) NYC, NY 10017
Hours: 10-6 Mon-Fri
• National organization for not-for-profit professional theatres. Provides nearly 30 centralized programs and services for theatre institutions and individuals. Publishes American Theatre Magazine, several books and a directory of member theatres. •

Theatre Development Fund (TDF)
212-221-0885
1501 Broadway, 21st floor, (43rd-44th St.) NYC, NY 10036
Hours: 10-6 Mon-Fri
• An audience development organization supporting theatre, music and dance. Administers the Costume Collection, TKTS booths, and "Theatre Access Project" for disabled individuals. Discount tickets available by mail for qualifying individuals and groups (send stamped, self-addressed envelope for information and application.) •

United Scenic Artists (USA) Local 829
212-581-0300
16 West 61st St., 11th floor, (B'way) NYC, NY 10023
Hours: 9-5 Mon-Fri
• Union representing scenic artists, set, costume and lighting designers, craftspeople, mural artists, diorama, model and display makers. •

United States Institute For Theatre Technology (USITT)
212-924-9088
10 West 19th St. #5A, (5-6th Ave.) NYC, NY 10011
Hours: 10-6 Mon-Fri
FAX 212-924-9343
• "The American Association of Design and Production Professionals in the Performing Arts." Provides an active forum for the development and exchange of practical and theoretical information through its quarterly journal, regular newsletters, annual national conference, and frequent regional meetings. •
(See display ad in this section.)

University of Connecticut Puppet Arts Program
203-486-1632
802 Bolton Rd. U-127, Storrs, CT 06269
Hours: by appt.
• Formal training in puppetry; BFA, MA, MFA. •

Volunteer Lawyers for the Arts
212-319-2787
1 East 53rd St., 6th floor, (5th Ave.) NYC, NY 10022
Hours: 9:30-5 Mon-Fri • by appt.
• Provides free legal assistance and information to individual artists and not-for-profit arts. •

APP

HEALTH & SAFETY SERVICES

ARTS, CRAFTS AND THEATER SAFETY (ACTS)
181 Thompson St., #23, NYC, NY 10012

212-777-0062

ACTS is a non-profit corporation dedicated to providing safety services to the arts. ACTS answers inquiries about products used in
the theatre; refers callers to doctors and clinics; publishes a
newsletter, and provides speakers and consultants for lectures,
OSHA training, and surveys of theatre and shops.

ACTS
ARTS, CRAFTS, AND THEATER SAFETY

• Contact Monona Rossol. •

CENTER FOR SAFETY IN THE ARTS
5 Beekman St., #820, (Park Row-Nassau St.) NYC, NY 10038

212-227-6220

Hours: 9-5 Mon-Fri
• A national clearinghouse for research and education on hazards in the visual and performing
arts. It sponsors: Art Hazards Information Center, which answers written and telephone
inquiries on art hazards and distributes a number of publications including Art Hazards News;
lectures, workshops, seminars, and consultations on art hazards. Other publications include,
Stage Fright, A Guide To Health And Safety In The Theatre. Speak to Angela Babin or Dr.
Michael McCann. Very helpful. •

CHEMICAL WASTE DISPOSAL CO.
42-14 19th Ave., (42nd) Astoria, NY 11105

718-274-3339

Hours: 8-4 Mon-Fri
• Chemical waste disposal; see Diane Levy or Ralph Duca. •

DEPT. H.H.S., REGION 1
JFK Building, #1875, Boston, MA 02203

617-565-1439

Hours: 8:30-4:30 Mon-Fri   FAX   617-565-1162
• Very helpful with NIOSH information. Speak to Edward Kaiser, regional consultant for occu-
pational safety and health. •

POISON CONTROL CENTER OF NYC
455 First Ave., (26th-27th St.) NYC, NY 10016

212-764-7667
212-447-2205

Hours: 24 Hours every day/phone service
• Very helpful with poison control information. Covers Metropolitan NYC region. This and the
Rocky Mountain Center are the two most comprehensive poison control centers in the U.S. •

RADIAC RESEARCH
261 Kent Ave., (Grand) Brooklyn, NY 11211

718-963-2233

Hours: 7:30-5 Mon-Fri
• Waste chemical disposal and radioactive disposal pickup. •

ROCKY MOUNTAIN POISON CONTROL CENTER
645 Bannock St., Denver, CO 80204

303-629-1123

Hours: 24 Hours every day/phone service
• Regional poison control information center. This and the NYC center are the two most comprehensive poison control centers in the U.S. •

U.S. DEPARTMENT OF LABOR–
OCCUPATIONAL SAFETY AND HEALTH ASSOC. (OSHA)
90 Church St., #1407, (Vesey-Barclay St.) NYC, NY 10007

212-264-9840

Hours: 8-4:30 Mon-Fri
• OSHA information and regulations. •

APP

BROADWAY THEATRES

AMBASSADOR THEATRE
215 West 49th St., (B'way-8th Ave.) NYC, NY 10019
(b.o.) 212-239-6200

BROOKS ATKINSON THEATRE
256 West 47th St., (B'way-8th Ave.) NYC, NY 10036
(backstage) 212-974-9424
(b.o.) 212-719-4099

ETHEL BARRYMORE THEATRE
243 West 47th St., (B'way-8th Ave.) NYC, NY 10036
(backstage) 212-974-9534
(b.o.) 212-944-3847

VIVIAN BEAUMONT THEATRE
150 West 65th St., (Lincoln Center) NYC, NY 10023
(admin. office) 212-362-7600
(b.o.) 212-239-6200

MARTIN BECK THEATRE
302 West 45th St., (8th-9th Ave.) NYC, NY 10036
(backstage) 212-245-9770
(b.o.) 212-246-6363

BELASCO THEATRE
111 West 44th St., (B'way-6th Ave.) NYC, NY 10036
(backstage) 212-730-9344
(b.o.) 212-239-6200

BOOTH THEATRE
222 West 45th St., (B'way-8th Ave.) NYC, NY 10036
(b.o.) 212-239-6200

BROADHURST THEATRE
235 West 44th St., (B'way-8th Ave.) NYC, NY 10036
(backstage) 212-730-9035
(b.o.) 212-239-6200

BROADWAY THEATRE
1681 Broadway, (53rd St.) NYC, NY 10019
(backstage) 212-664-9587
(b.o.) 212-239-6200

CIRCLE IN THE SQUARE THEATRE
1633 Broadway, (50th St.) NYC, NY 10019
(b.o.) 212-239-6200

CITY CENTER
131 West 55th St., (6th-7th Ave.) NYC, NY 10019
(backstage) 212-974-9833
(b.o.) 212-581-7907

CORT THEATRE
138 West 48th St., (6th-7th Ave.) NYC, NY 10036
(backstage) 212-997-9776
(b.o.) 212-239-6200

EDISON THEATRE
240 West 47th St., (B'way-8th Ave.) NYC, NY 10036
(backstage) 212-997-9473
(b.o.) 212-302-2302

GERSHWIN THEATRE (URIS)
222 West 51st St., (B'way-8th Ave.) NYC, NY 10019
(backstage) 212-664-8473
(admin. office) 212-586-6510
(b.o.) 212-246-0102

JOHN GOLDEN THEATRE
252 West 45th St., (B'way-8th Ave.) NYC, NY 10036
(backstage) 212-764-0199
(b.o.) 212-239-6200

HELEN HAYES THEATRE
240 West 44th St., (B'way-8th Ave.) NYC, NY 10036
(backstage) 212-730-9197
(admin. office) 212-944-9450
(b.o.) 212-246-0102

IMPERIAL THEATRE
249 West 45th St., (B'way-8th Ave.) NYC, NY 10036
(backstage) 212-245-9374
(b.o.) 212-239-6200

WALTER KERR THEATRE
219 West 48th St., (B'way-8th Ave.) NYC, NY 10036
(backstage) 212-664-9154

LONGACRE THEATRE 220 West 48th St., (B'way-8th Ave.) NYC, NY 10036	(backstage) 212-974-9462 (b.o.) 212-239-6200
LUNT/FONTANNE THEATRE 205 West 46th St., (B'way-8th Ave.) NYC, NY 10036	(backstage) 212-997-8816 (b.o.) 212-575-9200
LYCEUM THEATRE 149 West 45th St., (B'way-6th Ave.) NYC, NY 10036	(backstage) 212-997-9472 (b.o.) 212-239-6200
MAJESTIC THEATRE 247 West 44th St., (B'way-8th Ave.) NYC, NY 10036	(backstage) 212-764-1750 (b.o.) 212-239-6200
MARQUIS THEATRE 1535 Broadway, (45th-46th St.) NYC, NY 10036	(backstage) 212-764-0182 (b.o.) 212-382-0101
MINSKOFF THEATRE 200 West 45th St., (B'way-8th Ave.) NYC, NY 10036	(backstage) 212-840-9797 (b.o.) 212-869-0550
MUSIC BOX THEATRE 239 West 45th St., (B'way-8th Ave.) NYC, NY 10036	(backstage) 212-245-9850 (b.o.) 212-239-6200
NEDERLANDER THEATRE 208 West 41st St., (B'way-8th Ave.) NYC, NY 10036	(backstage) 212-221-9770 (b.o.) 212-921-8000
NEW APOLLO THEATRE 234 West 43rd St., (7th-8th Ave.) NYC, NY 10036	(backstage) 212-997-9059 (b.o.) 212-730-0307
NEW YORK STATE THEATRE 62nd & Columbus Ave., (Lincoln Center) NYC, NY 10023	(backstage) 212-877-4700 (b.o.) 212-870-5570
MITZI E. NEWHOUSE 150 West 65th St., (Lincoln Center) NYC, NY 10023	(admin. office) 212-362-7600 (b.o.) 212-239-6200
EUGENE O'NEILL 230 West 49th St., (B'way-6th Ave.) NYC, NY 10019	(backstage) 212-245-9442 (b.o.) 212-246-0220
PALACE THEATRE 1564 Broadway, (46th-47th St.) NYC, NY 10036	(backstage) 212-221-9057 (b.o.) 212-730-8200
PLYMOUTH THEATRE 236 West 45th St., (B'way-8th Ave.) NYC, NY 10036	(backstage) 212-391-8878 (b.o.) 212-944-3880
RADIO CITY MUSIC HALL 1260 Sixth Ave., (50th St.) NYC, NY 10020	(b.o.) 212-632-4000
RICHARD RODGERS THEATRE 226 West 46th St., (B'way-8th Ave.) NYC, NY 10036	(backstage) 212-997-9416 (b.o.) 212-221-1211
ROYALE THEATRE 242 West 45th St., (B'way-8th Ave.) NYC, NY 10036	(backstage) 212-391-8879 (b.o.) 212-239-6200
ST. JAMES THEATRE 246 West 44th St., (B'way-8th Ave.) NYC, NY 10036	(backstage) 212-730-9506 (b.o.) 212-398-0280
SHUBERT THEATRE 225 West 44th St., (B'way-8th Ave.) NYC, NY 10036	(backstage) 212-764-0184 (b.o.) 212-239-6200

APP

"I found it in the N.Y. Theatrical Sourcebook."

NEIL SIMON THEATRE (ALVIN)
   250 West 52nd St., (B'way-8th Ave.) NYC, NY 10019

(backstage) 212-974-9445
(b.o.) 212-757-8646

VIRGINIA THEATRE
   245 West 52nd St., (B'way-8th Ave.) NYC, NY 10019

(backstage) 212-974-9853
(b.o.) 212-977-9370

WINTER GARDEN THEATRE
   1634 Broadway, (50th-51st St.) NYC, NY 10019

(backstage) 212-664-9608
(b.o.) 212-239-6200

OFF BROADWAY THEATRES

ACTORS PLAYHOUSE
   100 Seventh Ave. S., (Bleecker-Grove St.) NYC, NY 10014

(b.o.) 212-691-6226

(admin. office) 212-741-1215

AMERICAN PLACE THEATRE
   111 West 46th St., (6th-7th Ave.) NYC, NY 10036

(b.o.) 212-840-3074
(admin. office) 212-840-2960

JUDITH ANDERSON THEATRE
   422 West 42nd St., (9th-10th Ave.) NYC, NY 10036

(bookings) 212-921-9341

ASTOR PLACE THEATRE
   434 Lafayette, (Astor Pl.-W. 4th St.) NYC, NY 10003

212-254-4370

BEACON THEATRE
   2124 Broadway, (74th St.) NYC, NY 10023

(b.o.) 212-496-7070

SAMUEL BECKETT THEATRE
   410 West 42nd St., (9th-10th Ave.) NYC, NY 10036

(b.o.) 212-594-2826

SUSAN BLOCH THEATRE
   307 West 26th St., (8th Ave.) NYC, NY 10011

(b.o.) 212-420-1883
(bookings) 212-420-1360

CHERRY LANE THEATRE
   38 Commerce, (7th Ave.-Houston St.) NYC, NY 10014

(b.o.) 212-989-2020

CIRCLE-IN-THE-SQUARE, DOWNTOWN
   159 Bleecker St., (Thompson-Sullivan St.) NYC, NY 10012

(b.o.) 212-254-6330
(reh'l studio) 212-475-9899
(backstage) 212-475-9899

CIRCLE REPERTORY COMPANY
   99 Seventh Ave. S., (W. 4th St.) NYC, NY 10014

(b.o.) 212-924-7100
(backstage) 212-924-9354

CITY CENTER
   131 West 55th St., (6th-7th Ave.) NYC, NY 10019

(b.o.) 212-581-7907
(admin. office) 212-247-0430

EQUITY LIBRARY THEATRE
   310 Riverside Dr., (at 103rd St.) NYC, NY 10025

(prod. office) 212-663-2880

DOUGLAS FAIRBANKS THEATRE
   432 West 42nd St., ((9th-10th Ave.) NYC, NY 10036

(b.o.) 212-239-4321
(backstage) 212-239-4323

"I found it in the N.Y. Theatrical Sourcebook."

FORTY SEVENTH STREET THEATRE (PUERTO RICAN TRAVELING THEATRE)
304 West 47th St., (8th-9th Ave.) NYC, NY 10036   (b.o.) 212-265-0794

THE HECKSCHER THEATRE PF MUSEO DEL BARRIO   (b.o.) 212-831-7949
1230 Fifth Ave., (104th St.) NYC, NY 10025   FAX   212-831-7927

LAMB'S THEATRE   (b.o.) 212-997-1780
130 West 44th St., (B'way-6th Ave.) NYC, NY 10036   (admin. office) 212-997-0210
(backstage) 212-840-3142

LUCILLE LORTEL THEATRE   (b.o.) 212-924-8782
121 Christopher St., (Bleecker-Hudson St.) NYC, NY 10014
(admin. office) 212-924-2817

MANHATTAN THEATRE CLUB   (admin. office) 212-645-5590
453 West 16th St., (9th-10th Ave.) NYC, NY 10011   (b.o.) 212-581-7907

MINETTA LANE THEATRE   (b.o.) 212-420-8000
18 Minetta Lane, (6th-MacDougal St.) NYC, NY 10012

MUSICAL THEATRE/WORKS   (office) 212-677-0400
440 Lafayette (astor-East 4th St.) NYC, NY 10003   (bookings) 212-982-5100

NEGRO ENSEMBLE CO.   (admin. office) 212-575-5860
155 West 46th St., (6-7th Ave.) NYC, NY 10036

NEW YORK SHAKESPEARE FESTIVAL / PUBLIC THEATRE   (b.o.) 212-598-7150
425 Lafayette St., (Astor Pl.-W. 4th St.) NYC, NY 10003
(admin. office) 212-598-7100
Delecorte Theatre (81st-Central Park) NYC, NY   (b.o.) 212-861-7277

ORPHEUM THEATRE   (b.o.) 212-477-2477
126 Second Ave., (7-8th St.) NYC, NY 10003

PLAYERS THEATRE   (b.o.) 212-254-5076
115 MacDougal St., (W. 3rd St.) NYC, NY 10012   (admin. office) 212-254-8138
(backstage) 212-674-9281

PLAYHOUSE 91   (b.o.) 212-831-2000
316 East 91st St., (1st-2nd Ave.) NYC, NY 10128   (admin. office) 212-831-2001

PLAYWRIGHTS HORIZONS   (b.o.) 212-279-4200
416 West 42nd St., (9-10th Ave.) NYC, NY 10036   (admin. office) 212-564-1235

PROMENADE THEATRE   (b.o.) 212-580-1313
2162 Broadway, (76th St.) NYC, NY 10024   (admin. office) 212-924-2817

PROVINCETOWN PLAYHOUSE   (b.o.) 212-477-5048
133 MacDougal St., (W. 3rd-4th St.) NYC, NY 10013   (backstage) 212-777-9351

RIDICULOUS THEATRICAL CO.   212-691-2271
1 Sheridan Square, (W. 4th St.-7th Ave. S.) NYC, NY 10014
(admin. office) 212-989-6524

ROUNDABOUT THEATRE   (b.o.) 212-420-1883
100 East 17th St., (Park Ave. S.) NYC, NY 10003   (admin. office) 212-420-1360

APP

"I found it in the N.Y. Theatrical Sourcebook."   **491**

ST. CLEMENT'S CHURCH / MUSIC THEATRE GROUP   (b.o.) 212-265-4375
    423 West 46th St., (9th-10th Ave.) NYC, NY 10036 (church)
        (admin. office) 212-924-3108

SECOND STAGE   (b.o.) 212-873-6103
    2162 Broadway, (76-77th St.) NYC, NY 10024   (admin. office) 212-787-8302

SULLIVAN STREET PLAYHOUSE   (b.o.) 212-674-3838
    181 Sullivan St., (Bleecker-W. Houston St.) NYC, NY 10012
        (admin. office) 212-674-4573
        (backstage) 212-473-9374

THEATRE OFF PARK   (admin. office) 212-627-2556
    224 Waverly Pl., (Perry-11th St.) NYC, NY 10014

VILLAGE GATE   212-475-5120
    160 Bleecker St., (Thompson St.) NYC, NY 10012

THEATRE ROW STUDIOS   (b.o.) 212-594-2370
    412 West 42nd St., (9-10th Ave.) NYC, NY 10036   (admin. office) 212-695-5429

TOP-OF THE GATE   212-982-9292
    160 Bleecker St., (Thompson St.) NYC, NY 10012

WESTSIDE ARTS THEATRE   (admin. office) 212-315-2302
    407 West 43rd St., (9-10th Ave.) NYC, NY 10036   (backstage) 212-315-2244

WPA THEATRE   (b.o.) 212-206-0523
    519 West 23rd St., (10-11th Ave.) NYC, NY 10011   (admin. office) 212-691-2274

OFF-OFF BROADWAY THEATRES

ACTING STUDIO INC.   212-228-2700
    29 East 19th St. 4th Fl., (B'way-Park Ave.) NYC, NY 10003

ACTOR'S OUTLET   212-807-1590
    120 West 28th St., (6-7th Ave.) NYC, NY 10001

RICHARD ALLEN CENTER THEATRE   212-281-2220
    550 West 155th St., (B'way-Amsterdam Ave.) NYC, NY 10032

AMAS REPERTORY THEATRE   212-369-8000
    1 East 104th St. Rm. 359, (5th Ave.) NYC, NY 10029

AMERICAN THEATRE OF ACTORS   212-581-3044
    314 West 54th St., (8-9th Ave.) NYC, NY 10019

THE ANNEX (WOMEN'S INTERART THEATRE)   212-246-1050
    552 West 53rd St., (10-11th Ave.) NYC, NY 10019

BOWERY LANE THEATRE / JEAN COCTEAU REP.   212-677-0060
    330 Bowery, (2nd Ave.) NYC, NY 10012

CITY STAGE CO. (CSC REP.)   212-677-4210
    136 East 13th St., (3rd-4th Ave.) NYC, NY 10003

"I found it in the N.Y. Theatrical Sourcebook."

ENSEMBLE STUDIO THEATRE
549 West 52nd St., (10th-11th Ave.) NYC, NY 10019
(b.o.) 212-247-3405
(admin. office) 212-247-4982

NEW YORK THEATRE WORKSHOP
79 East 4th St., (Bowery-2nd Ave.) NYC, NY 10003
(backstage) 212-995-8367
(b.o. 212-505-1892)

HAFT THEATRE (FASHION INST. TECH.)
Katie Murphy Amphitheatre
227 West 27th St., (7th-8th Ave.) NYC, NY 10001
212-760-7644
212-760-7644

HARTLEY HOUSE THEATRE / ON STAGE PRODUCTIONS
413 West 46th St., (9th-10th Ave.) NYC, NY 10036
212-666-1716

HENRY STREET SETTLEMENT, LOUIS ABRONS ART CENTER
466 Grand St., (Pitt-Willet) NYC, NY 10002
212-598-0400

THE NAT HOME THEATRE
440 West 42nd St., (9th-10th Ave.) NYC, NY 10036
(b.o.) 212-736-7185
(admin. office) 212-736-7128

JOHN HOUSEMAN THEATRE CENTER
450 West 42nd St., (9th-10th Ave.) NYC, NY 10036
(b.o.) 212-967-9077
(admin. office) 212-967-7079

INTAR
420 West 42nd St., (9th-10th Ave.) NYC, NY 10036
212-695-6134

JRT (JEWISH REPERTORY THEATRE)
316 East 91st St., (1st-2nd Ave.) NYC, NY 10128
212-831-2000

KAUFMAN THEATRE
534 West 42nd St., (10th-11th Ave.) NYC, NY 10036
212-563-1684

LA MAMA ETC.
74A East 4th St., (2nd-3rd Ave.) NYC, NY 10003
212-475-7710

NEW DRAMATISTS
424 West 44th St., (9th-10th Ave.) NYC, NY 10036
212-757-6960

NEW FEDERAL THEATRE
466 Grand St., (Pitt-Willet) NYC, NY 10002
212-598-0400

OHIO THEATRE
66 Wooster St., (Greene St.) NYC, NY 10012
212-966-4844

OPEN EYE: NEW STAGINGS
270 West 89th St., (B'way-West End Ave.) NYC, NY 10024
(b.o.) 212-769-4143
(admin. office) 212-769-4141

THE PERFORMING GARAGE
33 Wooster St., (Grand-Broome St.) NYC, NY 10013
(b.o.) 212-966-3651
(admin. office) 212-966-9796

PERRY STREET THEATRE
31 Perry St., (7th Ave.-W.4th St.) NYC, NY 10014
(b.o.) 212-691-2509
(admin. office) 212-255-7190

PUERTO RICAN TRAVELING THEATRE
276 West 43rd St., (8th Ave.) NYC, NY 10036 (offices)
(admin. office) 212-354-1293
(b.o.) 212-265-0794

RAPP ARTS CENTER
220 East 4th St., (Aves. A & B) NYC, NY 10019
(admin. office) 212-529-5921
(b.o.) 212-529-6160

APP

"I found it in the N.Y. Theatrical Sourcebook."

RIVERSIDE SHAKESPEARE CO. 212-369-2273
316 East 91st St., (1st-2nd Ave.) NYC, NY 10128

ROYAL COURT REP. 212-956-3500
300 West 55th St., (8th-9th Ave.) NYC, NY 10019

SOHO REPERTORY THEATRE (admin. office) 212-977-5955
46 Walker, (Church-B'way) NYC, NY 10013

SOUTH STREET THEATRE 212-564-0660
424 West 42nd St., (9th-10th Ave.) NYC, NY 10036

THEATRE EAST 212-838-0177
211 East 60th St., (2nd-3rd Ave.) NYC, NY 10022

THEATRE EIGHTY ST. MARKS 212-254-7400
80 St. Marks Pl., (1st Ave.) NYC, NY 10003

THEATRE FOR THE NEW CITY 212-254-1109
155 First Ave., (9th-10th St.) NYC, NY 10003

THEATRE 22 212-243-2805
54 West 22nd St., (5th-6th Ave.) NYC, NY 10011

UBU REPERTORY THEATRE 212-679-7540
15 West 28th St., (B'way-5th Ave.) NYC, NY 10001

VINEYARD THEATRE 212-353-3366
108 East 15th St., (Park Ave. S.-Irving Pl.) NYC, NY 10003

VORTEX THEATRE 212-206-1764
164 Eleventh Ave., (22nd-23rd St.) NYC, NY 10011

WESTBETH THEATRE CENTER (b.o.) 212-741-0391
151 Bank St., (Washington) NYC, NY 10014   (admin. office) 212-691-2272

WOMEN'S INTERART THEATRE 212-246-1050
549 West 52nd St., (10-11th Ave.) NYC, NY 10019

WRITERS' THEATRE 212-869-9770
145 West 46th St. 3rd Fl., (6-7th Ave.) NYC, NY 10036

DANCE, CONCERT & OPERA HOUSES

ALICE TULLY HALL (b.o.) 212-875-5050
1941 Broadway (Lincoln Center) NYC, NY 10023   (admin. office) 212-875-5000

AVERY FISHER HALL (b.o.) 212-875-5050
132 West 65th St., (Lincoln Center) NYC, NY 10023   (admin. office) 212-580-8700

BROOKLYN ACADEMY OF MUSIC, OPERA HOUSE (admin. office) 718-636-4111
30 Lafayette Ave. (Ashland-St. Felix) Brooklyn, NY 11217
(theatre mgr.) 718-636-4144
(backstage) 718-636-4150
(prod. office) 718-636-4146

"I found it in the N.Y. Theatrical Sourcebook."

CARNEGIE HALL | (b.o.) 212-247-7800
57th St. at 7th Ave. NYC, NY 10019 | (admin. office) 212-903-9601

DANCE THEATRE WORKSHOP | (b.o.) 212-924-0077
219 West 19th St. (7th-8th Ave.) NYC, NY 10011 | (admin. office) 212-691-6500

THE GOLDEN FLEECE LTD. CHAMBER THEATRE | (office) 212-691-6105
204 West 20th St. (7th-8th Ave.) NYC, NY 10011

THE JOYCE THEATRE | (b.o.) 212-242-0800
175 Eighth Ave. (19th St.) NYC, NY 10011 | (admin. office) 212-691-9740

THE JUILLIARD SCHOOL | 212-799-5000
Broadway at 66th St. (Lincoln Center) NYC, NY 10023

THE MARYMOUNT MANHATTAN THEATRE | 212-517-0475
221 East 71st St. (2nd-3rd Ave.) NYC, NY 10021

THE METROPOLITAN OPERA | (b.o.) 212-362-6000
Broadway at 65th St. (Lincoln Center) NYC, NY 10023 | (admin. office) 212-799-3100

NEW YORK STATE THEATRE | (b.o.) 212-870-5570
62nd & Columbus Ave. (Lincoln Center) NYC, NY 10023

(admin. office) 212-870-5500

RIVERSIDE CHURCH | 212-864-2929
120th St. at Claremont Ave.,   NYC, NY 10017

ST. MARK'S CHURCH IN THE BOWERY | 212-533-4650
131 East 10th St. (2nd-3rd Ave.) NYC, NY 10003

SYMPHONY SPACE | (b.o.) 212-864-5400
2537 Broadway (95th St.) NYC, NY 10025 | (admin. office) 212-864-1414

TOWN HALL | (b.o.) 212-840-2824
123 West 43rd St. (B'way-6th Ave.) NYC, NY 10036

(admin. office) 212-997-1003

SOUND STAGES

BOKEN STAGES | 212-581-5507
513 W.54th St.,(10th-11th) NY, NY 10019

III SOUND STAGE | 212-924-0438
111 Leroy St., (Greenwich-Hudson) NY, NY 10014
• Formerly Boken II •

CBS BROADCAST CENTER | 212-975-4321
524 West 57th St., (10-11th) NY, NY 10019 | 212-975-2627
Hours:9-6 Mon-Fri • (facilities open 24 hrs.)

CINE STUDIO | 212-581-1916
241 West 54th St., (Broadway-8th) NY, NY 10019

APP

CINEMA WORLD STUDIOS   718-389-9800
   220 DuPont St., (Provost) Long Island City, NY 11222
   Hours:9-7 Mon-Fri • by appt   FAX   718-389-9897

DEFILIPPO STUDIO, INC.   212-986-5444
   215 East 37th St., (2-3rd St.) NY, NY 10016

EMPIRE STAGE OF NEW YORK   718-392-4747
   50-20 25th St., (50-51st Ave.) Long Island City, NY 11101

EUE/SCREEN GEMS LTD.   212-867-4030
   222 East 44th St., (2-3rd Ave.) NY, NY 10017

FARKAS FILM   212-679-8212
   385 Third Ave., (27-28th) NY, NY 10016

HORVATH & ASSOCIATES   212-741-0300
   95 Charles St., (Bleecker-Hudson) NY, NY 10014

HORVATH STUDIOS   212-463-0061
   335 West 12th St., (Washington-Greenwich) NY, NY 10014

KAUFMAN–ASTORIA STUDIOS   718-392-5600
   34-12 36th St. (34-35th Ave.) Astoria, NY 11106   FAX   718-706-773

MOTHERS SOUND STAGE   212-529-5097
   210 East Fifth St., (2-3rd Ave) NY, NY 10003

NATIONAL VIDEO CENTER   212-279-2000
   460 West 42nd St., (9-10th Ave.) NY, NY 10036

3–G STAGE CORPORATION   212-956-6447
   236 West 61st St., (Amsterdam-WEA) NY, NY 10023   Stage I 212-247-3130
                                                       Stage II 212-397-9569

TIME SQUARE STUDIOS   212-704-9700
   1481 Broadway, (42nd St.) NY, NY 10036
   Hours: 9-6 Mon-Fri

VERITAS   212-581-2050
   527 West 45th St., (10-11th St.) NY, NY 10036

SILVERCUP STUDIOS   718-784-3390
   42-25 21st., (Bridge Plaza S.-43rd) Long Island City, NY 11101   212-349-8600

APP

Product Index

IND

IND

"I found it in the N.Y. Theatrical Sourcebook."

IND

IND

IND

IND

IND

"I found it in the N.Y. Theatrical Sourcebook."

IND

IND

IND

"I found it in the N.Y. Theatrical Sourcebook."

IND

nickelodeons, 22
nightsticks, 339
non-asbestos textiles, 322, 324
non-asbestos items, 323
NOTIONS:
notions for sewing w/ man made furs, 165, 247
novelties, 269
novelty nets & tulles, 168
nuts, 65
nuts and bolts, 450
nylon, 334
nylon fabric, 157, 158
nylon fishline, 179
nylon fuzzy thread, 305
nylon thread, 306
nylon webbing, 466

- O -

offset printing, 344, 345
offset printing, newspaper, 215
organs, 293
organza fabric, 153, 156
Oriental decor, 133
original cast recordings, 384
ornament, fiberglass, 67
ornaments, clothing, 302
orthopedic equipment, 276
OSHA training, 322
ostrich plumes, 459
outdoor fabric, 158
overcoats, 443
overlock machines, 397
oversized items, 133
oversized props, 269

- P -

packing blankets, 290, 308, 308
padded envelopes, 309
PAINTS & DYES:
paint, auto, 313
paint, blacklight, 314
paint, caesin, 318
paint, deck, 318

paint, flexible, 67
paint, flourescent, 315, 318
paint, flourescent fabric, 312
paint, fresco, 318
paint, glitter, 312
paint, heat set fabric, 311
paint, lacquer, 314
paint, luminous, 315
paint, metalflake, 314
paint , metallic, 309
paint, metallic fabric, 312
paint, milk, 314
paint, pearlescent, 309
paint, puffy, 312
paint, stained glass, 314
paint, ultraviolet fabric, 313
painting, fabric, 107, 110, 112, 113, 119, 126, 138
painting restoration, 385
painting, scenic, 390, 394, 395
paintings, 11, 14, 19, 20, 26,150
paisleys, 162
panel lights, 141
paneling, 264
PAPER, CARDBOARD & FOAMCORE PRODUCTS
paper, art, 33
paper bags, 308
paper, corrugated, 309
paper, grey bogus, 319
paper, Grid Kraft, 320
paper, hand marbled, 112
paper, handmade, 31, 148, 149, 426
paper, kraft, 319, 320
paper, marbled, 426
paper masks, 324
paper money, foreign, 100
paper sculptures, 133
paper, shredded, 307
paper towels, 308
paper, waxed, 319
paperdolls, 452
papergoods, 279, 321
papergoods, restaurant, 239
papermaking supplies, 30, 31, 54
parade floats, 131
parts bins, 399
party favors, 321
party rentals, 321, 322
party supplies, 65, 321
party ware, 74
Pasche, 30
passementeries, 456
pastries, Greek, 147
patch panels, 142
patio door replacement parts, 445
patterns, 300

IND

IND

scissor lifts, 438
sclera cover shells, 134
sconces, 23,256, 257, 258
Scotch-mate, 301
Scotchgarding, 166
Scotfoam, 136, 189
screening rooms, 255
screens, oriental, 196
screens, shoji, 199
screw buttons, 439
screws, miniature, 226
scrim, 161, 167, 168
scripts, 55, 281
scuba gear, 274, 421
Sculpey, 226
Sculpt-or-Coat, 71, 72
sculpture bases, 71
sculpture, leather, 126
SEA SHELLS **396**
    see also: 256, 274, 279
seam binding, 297
seamless paper, 33, 328
seating systems, 422
security equipment, 140
security systems, 36, 139, 235
semi-wax paper, 320
sepia prints, 329, 330, 344, 345
sequin trims, 454, 455, 456
sequined fabrics, 153, 159
sequins, 455, 456
servo systems, 286
set decoration, 349, 351, 353, 356, 357
sewing classes, 398
SEWING MACHINES & DRESS FORMS **397-398**
sewing machine belts, 397
sewing machine feet, 305, 397
sewing machine lamps, 397
sewing machine needles, 305
sewing machine oil, 397
sewing machine repair, 397
sewing machines, leather, 398
sex toys, 144
sextants, 274
sharkstooth scrim, 167
shears, 305, 396
sheers, 162
sheet metal, 283
sheetmetal work, 336
sheet music, 383
sheet music, vintage, 281
SHELVING & LOCKERS **398-399**
shelves, glass, 211
ship models, 274
SHIPPING **399-400**
shipping cases, fibre, 173
shirring, 143
shirting fabrics, 153
shirts - collarless, 94

shirts, custom, 94
shirts, Hawaiian, 149
SHOE ALTERATION, REPAIR & DRESSINGS
                                                            400-401
SHOES & BOOTS **401-405**
    see also: 12, 233
shoe lasts, custom, 402
shoe rubber, 248
shoes, antique, 80
shoes, children's, 84
shoes, custom, 85, 401, 403, 404
shoes, dance, 85, 401, 403, 405
shoes, drag, 404
shoes, Gamba, 403
shoes, latex, 106
shoes, nurses, 404
shoes, oriental, 148
shoes, orthopedic, 400
shoes, Victorian, 79
shoes, vintage, 81, 83
shoji screens, 148
shopping bags, 308
shopping carts, 241
shoulder pads, 454
shower curtains, 259, 260
shower doors, 338
shower enclosures, 337
shrink wrapping, 193
shutters, 24
sign painter's supplies, 31, 32
sign painting, 216, 405, 407
SIGNS & LETTERS **405-410**
    see also: 244, 295
signs, engraved, 388
signs, tin, 258
silicone, 2, 70, 70, 71, 73
silicone cloth, 324
silk thread, 299, 305, 306
silk yarn, 472
SILKSCREENING **410-411**
    see also: 107, 134, 138, 180, 352
silkscreening supplies, 31, 33, 311, 411
SILVER ITEMS **412-413**
    see also: 7, 11, 13, 19, 76
silver leaf, 309
silver loving cups, 462
silverware, 74, 75, 412
Singer Sewing Machines, 397
sinks, 20, 24, 337, 338
sinks, marble, 273
sinks, pedestal, 338
sisal twine, 464
sizing, hat, 285
skates, 424
skeletons, 278
ski equipment, 424
Skil powertools, 447, 449
Skin-Flex, 67

IND

IND

IND

"I found it in the N.Y. Theatrical Sourcebook."

IND

IND

IND

ADVERTISING INFORMATION

The NEW YORK THEATRICAL SOURCEBOOK is widely used and respected by professionals in film, television, theatre, photography, display and special events. No other directory contains the in-depth coverage of the "theatrical crafts" sources in the New York area.

Advertising in the SOURCEBOOK:
- -- Reaches thousands of designers, stylists, craft and production people in all media
- -- Provides your company with the visiblity it needs to remain competitive
- -- Gives potential customers complete & accurate information about your products and services.

ADVERTISING RATES:

Inside Covers: $1,200.00 (subject to availability)
Full Page: $ 500.00
Half Page: $ 325.00
Logo Ad: $ 150.00
Bold Listing: $ 50.00

FOR MORE INFORMATION about being listed in, and advertising in, the SOURCEBOOK please contact:

Kevin S. Kuney, Advertising Manager
Sourcebook Press, Inc.
163 Amsterdam Avenue #131
New York, NY 10023

Voice: 212-496-1310
Fax: 212-496-7549

FREE CATALOG SERVICE

To obtain more information about some of the advertisers in the SOURCEBOOK, including their catalogs, product brochures and other information simply fill out the following card, put a stamp on it and drop it in the mail.

1 ACE PROPS
  Brochure describing services.
2 ADM TRONICS UNLIMITED INC.
  Brochure and SAMple of Pros-Aide.
3 AMERICAN HARLEQUIN CORP..
  Descriptive catalog of studio, stage, & exhibit floor coverings.
4 ARENSON OFFICE FURNISHINGS
  Brochure describing extensive line of furniture from budget to up-scale.
5 BMI SUPPLY
  Catalog of scenic and lighting products.
6 BONOMO'S GRACE LTD.
  Brochure and product information describing line of flame retardent compounds & services.
7 BULBTRONICS
  Product brochure and price list.
8 CBS TELEVISION PLASTIC DESIGN
  Catalog of vacuumformed scenery.
9 CEMENTEX CO. INC.
  Catalog of mold-making and casting supplies.
10 COLLECTOR'S ARMOURY, INC.
  24 page color catalog.
11 COSTUME ARMOUR INC.
  Catalog of vacuumformed armor.
12 THE COTTON COLLECTION
  Brochure & measurement chart for Spring-weave cotton dancewear.
13 DRAMA BOOK SHOP
  Catalog of theatre books.
14 EFEX RENTALS INC.
  Brochure with price list.
15 ESKAY NOVELTY INC.
  Comprehinsive feather catalog.
16 FABULOUS-FURS
  Color brochure and newsletter.
17 GEPPETTO SOFT SCUPLTURE & DISPLAY
  Brochure with description and examples of sculpted foam characters and masks.

18 GERRIETS INTERNATIONAL INC.
  Product handbook, price list and RP screen sample.
19 GLADSTONE FABRICS
  Catalog of theatrical and general fabrics.
20 JAUCHEM & MEEH
  Descriptive brochure of products & design services.
21 JEWELITE SIGNS & LETTERS
  Brochure describing stock and custom signs.
22 OLIPHANT BACKDROPS
  Catalog of stock painted backdrops.
23 ON STAGE
  Illustrated catalog of dance clothes & accessories.
24 PROPS FOR TODAY INC.
  Catalog and video tape describing full-service prop rental house.
25 PROPTRONICS COMPANY
  Color catalog of simulated electronics products. Color brochure of fake books. (price list and order form)
26 PUTNAM ROLLING LADDER CO. INC.
  28 page catalog, price sheet and brochure.
27 ROSE BRAND TEXTILE FABRICS
  Catalog and color media swatchbook.
28 SAPSIS RIGGING
  Brochure & price list for theatrical rigging systems.
29 SCULPTURAL ARTS COATING, INC.
  Product brochures.
30 SLD LIGHTING
  Catalog of lighting fixtures and supplies.
21 SMOOTH-ON INC.
  Catalog of adhesives, molding & casting compounds.
32 TRENGOVE STUDIOS INC.
  Illustrated and descriptive brochure of custom & stock products.
33 UNNATURAL RESOURCES INC.
  Descriptive brochures on available products and their application with current price list.

From:_____

_____

_____

Sourcebook Press Inc.
163 Amsterdam Avenue #131
New York, NY 10023

.... fold here & tape closed ....

THE NEW YORK THEATRICAL
SOURCEBOOK

**THEATRE • FILM • TELEVISION • DANCE • DISPLAY
PHOTOGRAPHY • PROMOTIONAL INDUSTRIES**

CATALOG & INFORMATION CARD

Circle the number corresponding to the company information you would

1 2 3 4 5 6 7 8 9 10 11 12 13
14 15 16 17 18 19 20 21 22 23 24
25 26 27 28 29 30 31 32 33 34 35
36 37 38 39 40 41 42 43 44 45 46
ALL (Send me one of each)

In order to make the SOURCEBOOK more useful to you, please take a moment to answer the following questions.

What is your occupation? _____

In which industry(ies) are you involved? (check as many as apply)
__Theatre __Film __Television __Photo __Display __Spec. Events

How are you employed? __Freelance __Company __Other

What is your annual
budget for materials? __$1-5,000 __$5-10,000 __$10,000 and up

What is your annual
budget for services? __$1-5,000 __$5-10,000 $10,000 and up

Where did you get this copy of the Sourcebook? _____

How often, per year, do you refer to the Sourcebook? _____

How many people use this copy of the Sourcebook? _____

What other buyer's guides do you use?_____

What trade publications/newsletters do you read?_____

Do you find the Sourcebook easy to use? ___Yes ___No

What categories in the Sourcebook do you find most useful? _____

_____

Which categories do you find missing? _____

_____

What would make the Sourcebook more useful to you? _____

_____

Does the expanded information contained in ads or enhanced listings
__Influence your choices __Make no difference __Are distracting

Please note any comments or suggestions for future editions: _____

_____